EMERGING ECONOMIES AND MULTINATIONAL ENTERPRISES

ADVANCES IN INTERNATIONAL MANAGEMENT

Series Editors: (To Volumes 22) Joseph L. C. Cheng and Michael A. Hitt
(Volumes 23–28) Timothy M. Devinney, Torben Pedersen and Laszlo Tihanyi

Recent Volumes:

Volume 16: Edited by M. A. Hitt and J. L. C. Cheng

Volume 17: Edited by Thomas Roehl and Allan Bird

Volume 18: Edited by D. L. Shapiro, M. A. Von Glinow and J. L. C. Cheng

Volume 19: Edited by M. Javidan, R. M. Steers and M. A. Hitt

Volume 20: Edited by José Antonio Rosa and Madhu Viswanathan

Volume 21: Edited by John J. Lawler and Gregory S. Hundley

Volume 22: Edited by Joseph L. C. Cheng, Elizabeth Maitland and Stephen Nicholas

Volume 23: Edited by Timothy M. Devinney, Torben Pedersen and Laszlo Tihanyi

Volume 24: Edited by Christian Geisler Asmussen, Torben Pedersen, Timothy M. Devinney and Laszlo Tihanyi

Volume 25: Edited by Laszlo Tihanyi, Timothy M. Devinney and Torben Pedersen

Volume 26: Edited by Timothy M. Devinney, Torben Pedersen and Laszlo Tihanyi

Volume 27: Edited by Torben Pedersen, Markus Venzin, Timothy M. Devinney and Laszlo Tihanyi

ADVANCES IN INTERNATIONAL MANAGEMENT
VOLUME 28

EMERGING ECONOMIES AND MULTINATIONAL ENTERPRISES

EDITED BY

LASZLO TIHANYI
Texas A&M University, USA

ELITSA R. BANALIEVA
Northeastern University, USA

TIMOTHY M. DEVINNEY
University of Leeds, UK

TORBEN PEDERSEN
Bocconi University, Italy

Emerald

United Kingdom – North America – Japan
India – Malaysia – China

Emerald Group Publishing Limited
Howard House, Wagon Lane, Bingley BD16 1WA, UK

First edition 2015

British Library Cataloguing in Publication Data
A catalogue record for this book is available from the British Library

ISBN: 978-1-78441-740-6
ISSN: 1571-5027 (Series)

This volume is dedicated to our colleague Alan M. Rugman (1945–2014). He will be remembered as one of the true innovators and drivers of the field of international business and a mentor and role model for many of the authors included in this and many other volumes of Advances in International Management.

ACKNOWLEDGMENTS

Prior to publishing this volume, the editors hosted a two-day conference (September 27–28, 2014) on the topic of Emerging Markets and Multinational Enterprises at Northeastern University in Boston, Massachusetts. The conference was co-sponsored by the Center for Emerging Markets at Northeastern University, the Center for International Business Studies at Texas A&M University, and Emerald Group Publishing.

The conference gave the opportunity to the authors to present, refine, and integrate their ideas. The editors would like to thank all the conference participants – authors, discussants, guest speakers, and attendants – for their valuable time and contributions, which greatly enhanced the quality of the volume. We extend our special thanks to Dean Hugh Courtney, Dean of the D'Amore-McKim School of Business for hosting the conference; Ravi Ramamurti, Sheila Puffer, and Dan McCarthy for their time and stimulating contributions as guest speakers; and Joseph A. Clougherty, Denise Dunlap, Wenxin Guo, Kiattichai Kalasin, Grigorios Livanis, Tatiana S. Manolova, Valentina Marano, and Jay Mulki, for their invigorating feedback as discussants of the presented papers.

Elitsa R. Banalieva and Laszlo Tihanyi extend their gratitude to Ravi Ramamurti, Director of the Center for Emerging Markets at Northeastern University, and Julian Gaspar, Executive Director of the Center for International Business Studies at Texas A&M University, for their support for the conference and volume and to Anne Benware and Tianyuan Bai for their administrative help with the conference. Elitsa R. Banalieva also gratefully acknowledges the support from the Gary Gregg Fellowship. She would like to dedicate this volume to her late dissertation advisor, Professor Alan Rugman, whose kindness and intellectual rigor inspired much of her own research.

CONTENTS

LIST OF CONTRIBUTORS *xiii*

EDITORS' BIOGRAPHIES *xvii*

EDITORS' INTRODUCTION *xix*

PART I

INTRODUCTION TO PART I: PWC STRATEGY& EMINENT SCHOLAR IN INTERNATIONAL MANAGEMENT 2014
Timothy M. Devinney 3

FROM INTERNATIONAL BUSINESS TO INTRANATIONAL BUSINESS
Pankaj Ghemawat 5

THE VALUE OF BREADTH AND THE IMPORTANCE OF DIFFERENCES
David J. Collis 29

SEMIGLOBALIZATION: A RELEVANT REALITY
Africa Ariño 35

PART II

INTRODUCTION TO PART II: EMERGING ECONOMIES AND MULTINATIONAL ENTERPRISES
Elitsa R. Banalieva, Laszlo Tihanyi, Timothy M. Devinney and Torben Pedersen 45

THE CO-EVOLUTION OF PRO-MARKET REFORMS AND EMERGING MARKET MULTINATIONALS
Alvaro Cuervo-Cazurra 71

A RESOURCE ENVIRONMENT VIEW OF COMPETITIVE ADVANTAGE
Heechun Kim and Robert E. Hoskisson 95

THE EFFECTIVENESS OF THE STATE IN CHINESE OUTWARD FOREIGN DIRECT INVESTMENT: THE "GO GLOBAL" POLICY AND STATE-OWNED ENTERPRISES
Wenxin Guo and Joseph A. Clougherty 141

HOW EXTERNAL AND INTERNAL SOURCES OF KNOWLEDGE IMPACT NOVEL AND IMITATIVE INNOVATION IN EMERGING MARKETS: EVIDENCE FROM COLOMBIA
Sandra Corredor, Clemente Forero and Deepak Somaya 161

MANAGING INNOVATION IN EMERGING ECONOMIES: ORGANIZATIONAL ARRANGEMENTS AND RESOURCES OF FOREIGN MNES IN THE CHINESE PHARMACEUTICAL INDUSTRY
Vittoria Giada Scalera, Alessandra Perri and Ram Mudambi 201

DETERMINANTS OF BOARD ROLES IN IJVS IN CHINA: CONTROL AND COLLABORATION
Xuanli Xie, Jeffrey J. Reuer and Elko Klijn 235

SOURCES OF COMPETITIVENESS AND MULTINATIONALITY: EMERGING MARKET FIRMS IN THE ELECTRONICS INDUSTRY
Sumon Kumar Bhaumik, Nigel Driffield and Ying Zhou 267

CORRUPTION AND FOREIGN DIRECT INVESTMENT: A STUDY OF GUATEMALA
José Godinez and Mauricio Garita 297

AN INTEGRATED MODEL OF UPGRADING AND CATCHUP BY EMERGING ECONOMY FIRMS
Murali D. R. Chari 327

FRAMING INTERNATIONAL OPERATIONS MANAGEMENT: CONTRIBUTIONS FROM EMERGING COUNTRY MULTINATIONALS
Afonso Fleury, Yongjiang Shi, Maria Tereza Leme Fleury, Silas Ferreira Jr., Jose Henrique Cordeiro and Xingkun Liang 351

BUSINESS GROUP EFFECTS ON THE INNOVATION-INTERNATIONALIZATION RELATIONSHIP: EVIDENCE FROM THE INDIAN PHARMACEUTICAL SECTOR
Saptarshi Purkayastha, Tatiana S. Manolova and Linda F. Edelman 379

WHAT DO WE KNOW ABOUT STATE-OWNED EMERGING-ECONOMY FIRMS, AND HOW? EVALUATING LITERATURE ABOUT INWARD AND OUTWARD MULTINATIONAL ACTIVITIES
Xavier Martin and Cha Li 403

WHY DO THE TURKISH FIRMS INVEST IN MAINLAND EUROPE?
Sathyajit R. Gubbi and Sinan A. Sular 441

FOREIGN ENTRY MODE CHOICES OF EMERGING MARKET MULTINATIONALS: THE ROLE OF INSTITUTIONAL VOIDS IN SHAPING STRATEGIC COGNITION
Michael Hilb 471

IS SPRINGBOARD FDI STRATEGY EFFECTIVE? EVIDENCE FROM TURKISH ACQUISITIONS
Victor Z. Chen and Sedat Aybar 503

AUTHORS' BIOGRAPHIES 529

LIST OF CONTRIBUTORS

Africa Ariño	IESE Business School, Barcelona, Spain
Sedat Aybar	Istanbul Aydin University, Istanbul, Turkey
Elitsa R. Banalieva	Northeastern University, Boston, MA, USA
Sumon Kumar Bhaumik	University of Sheffield, Sheffield, UK
Murali D. R. Chari	Rensselaer Polytechnic Institute, Troy, NY, USA
Victor Z. Chen	University of North Carolina at Charlotte, Charlotte, NC, USA
Joseph A. Clougherty	University of Illinois at Urbana-Champaign, Champaign, IL, USA
David J. Collis	Harvard Business School, Boston, MA, USA
Jose Henrique Cordeiro	University of São Paulo, São Paulo, Brazil
Sandra Corredor	University of Illinois at Urbana-Champaign, Champaign, IL, USA
Alvaro Cuervo-Cazurra	Northeastern University, Boston, MA, USA
Timothy M. Devinney	University of Leeds, Leeds, UK
Nigel Driffield	Warwick Business School, Coventry, UK
Linda F. Edelman	Bentley University, Waltham, MA, USA
Silas Ferreira Jr.	University of São Paulo, São Paulo, Brazil
Afonso Fleury	University of São Paulo, São Paulo, Brazil

Maria Tereza Leme Fleury	Fundação Getulio Vargas, São Paulo, Brazil
Clemente Forero	Universidad de Los Andes, Bogotá, Colombia
Mauricio Garita	Universidad del Valle at Guatemala, Guatemala
Pankaj Ghemawat	New York University, New York, NY, USA; IESE Business School, Barcelona, Spain
José Godinez	Merrimack College, North Andover, MA, USA
Sathyajit R. Gubbi	University of Groningen, Groningen, The Netherlands
Wenxin Guo	Georgia Institute of Technology, Atlanta, GA, USA
Michael Hilb	University of Fribourg, Fribourg, Switzerland; University of St. Gallen, St. Gallen, Switzerland
Robert E. Hoskisson	Rice University, Houston, TX, USA
Heechun Kim	Georgia State University, Atlanta, GA, USA
Elko Klijn	Centre for International Business, University of Leeds, Leeds, United Kingdom
Cha Li	Tilburg University, Tilburg, The Netherlands
Xingkun Liang	University of Cambridge, Cambridge, UK
Tatiana S. Manolova	Bentley University, Waltham, MA, USA
Xavier Martin	Tilburg University, Tilburg, The Netherlands
Ram Mudambi	Temple University, Philadelphia, PA, USA
Torben Pedersen	Bocconi University, Milan, Italy

Alessandra Perri	Ca' Foscari University of Venice, Venice, Italy
Saptarshi Purkayastha	Indian Institute of Management Calcutta, Kolkata, India
Jeffrey J. Reuer	Leeds School of Business, University of Colorado, Boulder, CO, USA
Vittoria Giada Scalera	DIG-Politecnico di Milano, Milan, Italy
Yongjiang Shi	University of Cambridge, Cambridge, UK
Deepak Somaya	University of Illinois at Urbana-Champaign, Champaign, IL, USA
Sinan A. Sular	University of Groningen, Groningen, The Netherlands
Laszlo Tihanyi	Texas A&M University, College Station, TX, USA
Xuanli Xie	Peking University, Beijing, China
Ying Zhou	University of Birmingham, Birmingham, UK

EDITORS' BIOGRAPHIES

Elitsa R. Banalieva is an Associate Professor of International Business and Gary Gregg Faculty Fellow at the D'Amore-McKim School of Business at Northeastern University. She received her Ph.D. in Business Economics and Public Policy from the Kelley School of Business at Indiana University, Bloomington. Her research focuses on the geographic scope and institutional contexts that enable or constrain the strategies of family and non-family firms, especially from emerging markets in general and transition economies in particular. She has published in journals such as *Journal of International Business Studies*, *Strategic Management Journal*, *Management International Review*, *Global Strategy Journal*, and *Journal of World Business*, among others.

Timothy M. Devinney is a Professor of International Business and University Leadership Chair at the University of Leeds. He has published 10 books and more than 90 articles in leading journals. In 2008, he was the first recipient in management of an Alexander von Humboldt Research Award and was Rockefeller Foundation Bellagio Fellow. He is a Fellow of the Academy of International Business, an International Fellow under the auspices of the AIM Initiative in the United Kingdom and a Fellow of ANZAM (Australia New Zealand Academy of Management). He served as Chair of the International Management Division of the Academy of Management. He is Co-Editor of *Academy of Management Perspectives* and the head of the International Business & Management Network of SSRN. He is on the editorial board of more than 10 of the leading international journals.

Torben Pedersen is professor at Bocconi University in International Business. His research interests are in the interface between strategy and international management and he has published over 100 articles and books in this area. His research has appeared in prominent journals such as *Academy of Management Journal*, *Strategic Management Journal*, *Journal of Management*, *Journal of International Business Studies*, and *Organization Science*. In addition, he has published more than 25 teaching cases. He is currently Co-Editor of *Global Strategy Journal* and on the editorial boards of numerous journals. He is a Fellow of the Academy of International

Business and has previously served as Vice-President for both AIB and EIBA.

Laszlo Tihanyi is Professor of Management and the Robyn L. '89 and Alan B. Roberts '78 Chair in Business in the Mays Business School at Texas A&M University. His main research areas are internationalization, corporate governance in multinational firms, and organizational adaptation in emerging economies. His papers have been published in the *Academy of Management Journal*, *Academy of Management Review*, *Strategic Management Journal*, *Organization Science*, *Journal of International Business Studies*, and others. He presently serves as an Associate Editor for the *Academy of Management Journal*.

EDITORS' INTRODUCTION

We are pleased to present our sixth volume as co-editors of the *Advances in International Management* series. We took over the series in 2009 with the goal of publishing collections of cohesive papers that focus on influential theories and areas of research in international business and management. We wanted to provide a forum for scholars of the field to discuss novel ideas and present thought-provoking findings on a variety of topics. By acknowledging that authors have many outlets to publish their work, we wanted to enhance the reputation of this series by collecting exceptional theoretical analyses and empirical studies from leading and emerging experts of the field. Our previous volumes focused on topics ranging from the general state of research in International Management over location aspects, institutional theory, meta-analysis in IM research to the structure of multinational companies. We hope that the series has developed its niche as an essential outlet for groundbreaking ideas and has been complemented other publication formats in the field, such as journals, books, and conference proceedings.

The main section of this volume focuses on Emerging Economies and Multinational Enterprises. We invited Elitsa R. Banalieva of Northeastern University, an expert on emerging economies, as a special co-editor of this volume. The chapters in the volume cover the opportunities and challenges of multinational enterprises that consider emerging economies as their destinations or their homes. The chapters have been written by a diverse group of international scholars who have been studying emerging economies and the implications of local institutional conditions for multinational and other firms.

OVERVIEW OF VOLUME 28

Part I of this volume is dedicated to our annual feature from a leading scholar. The 2014 Recipient of the PWC Strategy& Eminent Scholar in International Management Award was Professor Pankaj Ghemawat of

IESE and New York University. Professor Ghemawat was honored by this Award by the International Management Division of the Academy of Management at its annual conference in Philadelphia. His acceptance speech reveals why he received the award. It is a mixture of sophisticated evidential inquiry as to the need to think differently about the nature of global industry structure and the meaning and drivers of globalization. The speech is followed by the commentaries by two colleagues: David J. Collis from Harvard Business School and Africa Ariño from IESE.

Part II of this volume includes 15 chapters on *Emerging Economies and Multinational Enterprises*, the theme of this year's volume. We started out the process by posting a Call for Papers on professional e-mail lists. We organized a conference at Northeastern University in September 2014, which was attended by about 30 prospective authors, discussants, and other conference participants. The main part of the editorial process was the reviews and revisions of completed chapters. The majority of accepted chapters went through two or three rounds of revisions before their final acceptance. We felt fortunate to receive high-quality submissions and to have the opportunity to work with an outstanding group of researchers who worked diligently on the drafts of their chapters. We hope the readers of this volume will find several thought-provoking theoretical ideas, discussions, reviews, and reports of empirical research in the 16 chapters that will provide the foundation for future research projects and doctoral dissertations on emerging economies.

Laszlo Tihanyi
Torben Pedersen
Timothy M. Devinney
Series Editors

PART I

INTRODUCTION TO PART I

PWC STRATEGY& EMINENT SCHOLAR IN INTERNATIONAL MANAGEMENT 2014

Timothy M. Devinney

The PWC Strategy& Eminent Scholar in International Management is an annual award given by the International Management Division of the Academy of Management. The award was previously known as the Booz & Co/Strategy+Business Eminent Scholar award and this year it has been renamed as PWC Strategy & representing the new ownership structure of Booz & Co.

The 2014 awardee was Professor Pankaj Ghemawat, Global Professor of Management and Strategy, Director of Centre for Global Education and Management at the New York University, and the Anselmo Rubiralta Professor of Global Strategy at IESE. Professor Ghemawat was recognized for his contribution to the field of international business and management based upon his long-standing and well-respected work dissecting the nature of global industry structure and the nature of global economy. Professor Ghemawat is not just recognized for being a scholar but also a scholar with

Emerging Economies and Multinational Enterprises
Advances in International Management, Volume 28, 3–4

ISSN: 1571-5027/doi:10.1108/S1571-502720150000028001

an impact on practice, having been named as the youngest "guru" in *The Economist's* guide to the greatest management thinkers of all time.

Professor Ghemawat attended Harvard University where he graduated in 1979 with a degree in Applied Mathematics. He then continued his studies at Harvard where he received his PhD in Business Economics in 1982. He spent most of his career at Harvard Business School before moving onto IESE and most recently NYU. He has published more than 70 journal articles and has authored seven books. It is for the latter that he is perhaps most recognized both by academics and management practitioners. These books include *Commitment*, *Games Businesses Play*, *Strategy and the Business Landscape*, *Redefining Global Strategy*, and *World 3.0*. *World 3.0* won the Thinkers50 book award for 2010–2011.

Professor Ghemawat is a fellow of both the Academy of International Business and the Strategic Management Society and has won numerous other academic awards, including the McKinsey Award for the best article published in Harvard Business Review and Educator of the Year from the Business Policy & Strategy Division of the Academy of Management.

Following Professor Ghemawat's paper, we have two cogent commentaries. Professor David Collis of Harvard Business School provides an outline of Professor Ghemawat's contribution to both strategy and international business from the broader perspective of a colleague who has known him since they both first took positions at Harvard Business School as junior scholars. Professor Africa Ariño of IESE provides an overview of his contribution by concentrating on one of Professor Ghemawat's key conceptualizations, the concept of "semiglobalization" as a counter to competing beliefs about the progress of global markets, particularly the popular view espoused by Thomas Friedman in *The World Is Flat*. As she notes in her commentary, the hallmark of Professor Ghemawat's take on globalization is one that is rigorous in terms of the application of economics, convincing in terms of the evidential base he uses to justify his position, and practical in its meaning for business and policy practitioners. As both of these scholars note, Professor Ghemawat's immense contribution is in arguing, in both the academic and management forums, for a more balanced and sophisticated view of globalization so as to avoid the pitfalls of believing "globaloney."

FROM INTERNATIONAL BUSINESS TO INTRANATIONAL BUSINESS

Pankaj Ghemawat

ABSTRACT

This chapter argues that international business has much to contribute to intranational business in helping develop a theory of the business enterprise in space. It makes its arguments by articulating four propositions about international business that appear to carry over directly to intranational business. According to the first three propositions, business activities of multiple types are dampened by borders and those that do cross them typically diminish with geographic as well as other types of distance. The fourth proposition supplements these general discussions of the landscape of business with a focus on a specific business application: it works through the case of business strategy by discussing how insights from the international domain can be applied to the intranational domain in that field of business.

Keywords: business strategy; CAGE framework; globalization; international business; law of distance; semiglobalization

Emerging Economies and Multinational Enterprises
Advances in International Management, Volume 28, 5–28

ISSN: 1571-5027/doi:10.1108/S1571-502720150000028002

> The modern theory of multinational enterprise has the potential to become a general theory of the enterprise in space, and as such, to encompass theories of the multiregional and multiplant firm. The theory of the uninational single plant firm under perfect competition – a theory which used to be known quite simply as "the theory of the firm" – turns out to be a quite trivial, special case. (Casson, 1987, p. 1)

Mark Casson's observation that for purposes of theory-building, one might treat international business as the general case and intranational business as the special case, is striking because it conflicts with academic conventions that assume exactly the opposite. It also seems to be materializing: nearly three decades on, we have moved past Casson's articulation of the *potential* for developing a general theory of the enterprise in space out of research on international business toward its *realization*. Or so this essay argues by specifying four propositions about international integration/business that seem directly and usefully translatable to intranational business at various levels.

The first proposition points out that borders seem to be associated with drop-offs in cross-border economic interactions. The second and third propositions discuss, respectively, the dampening effects of geographic distance and of other kinds of differences – cultural, administrative/political, and economic – on economic interactions. The fourth proposition focuses on the implications of the first three for a specific field of business, strategy (with applications to other fields discussed *en passant*).

I begin by citing evidence for each proposition's validity at the international level before presenting evidence in slightly more detail about its intranational applicability. Given the ground to be covered, the treatment is meant to be illustrative rather than comprehensive. It deliberately ranges across different levels of intranational analysis and draws to a significant extent on areas in which I have done basic empirical work myself.

P1. MOST MARKETS ARE FAR FROM COMPLETELY INTEGRATED ~~INTERNATIONALLY~~ INTRANATIONALLY

Most markets are still far from completely integrated, internationally or intranationally. I summarized some of the evidence in support of incomplete international integration – what I called semiglobalization – in my

2003 article in the *Journal of International Businesss Studies* (Ghemawat 2003). Subsequently, I have assembled systematic data on 11 different kinds of international interactions (involving trade, capital, information, and people flows) and updated it in biennial releases, with Steven A. Altman, of the DHL Global Connectedness Index (most recently, in Ghemawat & Altman, 2014). In addition to presenting global and regional data, this index ranks 140 countries in terms of the depth and breadth of their global connections – which would make no sense if average globalization levels were zero or complete. It turns out that while there are large variations in connectedness across countries, even the top-ranked country, the Netherlands, has significant room to improve its levels of international connectedness.

There is no comparably comprehensive summary of data on actual levels of intranational integration. But most of the studies that have sought to address this issue point in the same broad direction, that is, toward significant residual intranational market fragmentation. Consider some striking findings about the limited intranational integration of product, labor, capital, and knowledge markets.

(Product) Trade

The best way to make the point about intranational fragmentation of product markets is with trade flows, which have been extensively studied by "gravity modelers" – in some cases at the intranational as well as the international level. A widely cited paper (Poncet, 2005) estimated that trade within China's provinces in 1997 was 31 times more intense than between them, equivalent to a 53% interprovincial tariff. Subsequent studies reported lower, though still significant, Chinese provincial border effects. Xing and Li (2011), using data from 2004 to 2005 report that their preferred model yielded border effect estimates between 4 and 6. Turning to another large emerging economy, Brazilian states have been estimated to trade 12 times more with themselves, on average, than with other Brazilian states, after controlling for economic size and distance. While this intrastate-to-interstate multiplier is much smaller than its interstate-to-foreign equivalent, 42, it also suggests a significant degree of intranational fragmentation (Daumal & Zignago, 2010).

Border effects in large advanced economies tend to be smaller than in large emerging economies, implying higher levels of internal market integration. Aggregating results across 40 models of U.S. interstate trade from four papers, U.S. states' border effects range from 2 to 16 and average 6 (Coughlin & Novy, 2013; Hillberry & Hummels, 2003; Millimet & Osang, 2007; Wolf, 2000). Combes, Lafourcade, and Mayer (2005) find a similar internal border effect of 6 for non-contiguous *départements* in continental France (and 3 for contiguous ones). Available estimates for Spain's non-contiguous *comunidades autónomas*, however, are significantly higher: one paper (Requena & Llano, 2010) reports an average of 17 for all tradables and 30 for manufactures while another (Gil-Pareja, Llorca-Vivero, Martínez-Serrano, & Oliver-Alonso, 2005) reports a range from 9 for Madrid (central both geographically and to transport links) to 60 for the Balearic Islands (an archipelago in the western Mediterranean).

The preceding material on border effects provided evidence of intranational product market fragmentation based on quantity measures. However, economists often prefer price-based indicators of integration as being more closely connected to the underlying economic theory of market integration (often summarized as "the law of one price"). Unfortunately, data constraints limit the availability of such measures, especially when intranational as well as international coverage is required. One study that does combine both is that of Landry (2011), which was inspired by *The Economist*'s tongue-in-cheek *Big Mac Index* of currency under/overvaluation (www.economist.com/content/big-mac-index). Landry found that Big Mac prices varied more in McDonald's restaurants within New York City than internationally across the 15 countries in his study.

Labor

Turning to input rather than output markets, intranational labor market fragmentation *is* most comprehensively illustrated with price rather than quantity data, on the dispersion of wages across states or regions.[1] Thus, in 2013, the standard deviation of average state-level wages in the United States was about $7,450 or one-sixth of the U.S. average wages (implying a coefficient of variation of 0.16). Or to make the same point in another way, wages in Massachusetts, the richest, were 47% higher, on average, than in Mississippi, which was the poorest. Significant differences persist after controls for variations in skills and occupational mix.

That said, the United States, with its generally high labor mobility, is not the large country that exhibits the most such variation. In China, for example, the inter-provincial coefficient of wage variation is 0.24: wages in Beijing, the richest, are over twice as high as in Guangxi, the poorest province. Of course, both intra-U.S. and intra-China variation are much lower than the international coefficient of variation which, based on per capita income rather than wages, comes to about 1.84 (on a mean worldwide income about one-fifth that for the United States as a whole). But even the intranational variation does seem quantitatively significant.

To this assessed quantitative significance, one can add the qualitative weight of dimensions of intranational labor market variation that are not picked up by calculations of wage dispersion. Thus, while wages in California – also in the top decile of U.S. states – come close to matching those in Massachusetts, there are other important differences between the two. Specifically, Almeida and Kogut (1999) compared high-technology industrial districts in the two states and found that employees moved between companies in Silicon Valley 10 times faster than along Massachusetts' Route 128. This difference, apparently due to California's prohibition of post-employment covenants not to compete or functional substitutes (vs. Massachusetts' willingness to enforce them subject to the rule of reason), is cited as a key driver of Silicon Valley's greater success despite Route 128's head start (Gilson, 1999; Schwartzman & Bodoff, 1971).

Other Inputs

Capital and knowledge are generally more footloose as inputs than labor but still continue to display significant intranational market fragmentation. The best data on intranational capital fragmentation are, once again, for the United States which, again, is likely to be relatively integrated rather than fragmented internally in this respect when compared to other large countries. Looking at a form of capital investment that involves relatively little commitment, Coval and Moskowitz found that "The average [mutual] fund manager generates an additional return of 2.67 percent per year from her local investments (defined as holdings within 100 kilometers of the fund headquarters) relative to her nonlocal holdings" (2001, p. 812). And Hong, Kubik, and Stein (2005) report that U.S. fund managers are also more likely to buy or sell as stock when other managers in the same city are doing so, implying a word-of-mouth effect operating over a fairly small geographic area. The pattern of "home-state bias" also shows up in private equity (PE) investments by public pension funds, where Hochberg and Rauh (2013) found overweighting of home-state investments equal to 9.8% of all PE investments and 16.5% of the holdings of the average limited partner. And location-specificity seems to loom much larger for forms of investment that involve significant commitment and engagement with management, for example, the traditional "15-minute rule" about how proximate a venture capitalist should be to a portfolio company.

Finally, strong intranational localization effects even seem to apply to knowledge flows. Thus, Alcácer and Gittelman (2006) compared the percentage of patent citations (by examiner vs. inventor) for different geographic subunits within the United States: cities, counties, metropolitan areas, and states. They found that 10% of U.S. citations come from patent examiners in the same cities as the corresponding inventors, 20% from the same counties, 26% from the same metropolitan areas, and 30% from the same states. Again, the degree of localization is less than that observed at national versus international boundaries – Alcacer and Gittelman also calculate that 66% of examiners' citations to patents filed by U.S.-based inventors are localized to the United States and 34% occur outside the United States – but still registers as significant.

Based on this and other evidence, the limits to intranational integration (or the extent of intranational fragmentation) need to be taken seriously. In recognition of this point, it is useful to generalize semiglobalization to what I will call *semi-integration*: a coinage meant to cover intermediate levels of international *and* intranational market integration. Semi-integration implies that no matter at which level you draw borders, cross-border interactions tend to be more limited than one would expect in a world without home bias. Propositions 2 onward move beyond the registration of home bias to look at patterns evident in the cross-border interactions that do take place.

P2. GEOGRAPHIC DISTANCE DAMPENS ~~INTERNATIONAL~~ INTRANATIONAL BUSINESS

Proposition 2 focuses on how interactions are attenuated with geographic distance. In international research, geographic distance turns out to have a significantly negative effect on all of the 11 types of interactions to which Ghemawat and De la Mata (2015) have fitted gravity models, although the estimated coefficients – the exponents on geographic distance – do vary greatly by type of interaction. The lowest is for patent citations, –0.27, and the highest, –1.92 – for printed publications exports. (Printed copies are generally exported only very close by: over longer distances, dissemination occurs through local printing or electronically.) In the former case, a 10-fold increase in distance decreases interactions by less than one-half; in the latter case, by about 99%.

Again, while we lack comprehensive data at the intranational level, it seems fair to say that studies that look for the effects of geographic distance generally find them to be significant.

(Product) Trade

The gravity modeling literature that was used to identify internal (state/province) border effects on merchandise trade in the previous section also indicates that trade diminishes significantly with geographic distance, even after controlling for border effects. Based on the average effect reported across 23 models from three papers, if one pair of locations in the United States is twice as distant as another, the more distant pair will trade only 57% as much as the more proximate one (Coughlin & Novy, 2013; Hillberry & Hummels, 2003; Millimet & Osang, 2007). Significant distance effects on merchandise trade are also reported in other countries, for example, Brazil (Daumal & Zignago, 2010), China (Xing & Li, 2011), and Spain (Requena & Llano, 2010).

Hillberry and Hummels (2008) examined distance effects at an even more granular level by analyzing product shipments within the United States using a five-digit zip code. They found trade within zip codes (which have a 4 mile radius, on average) to be three times greater than across zip code boundaries. Their research also points to the need for care in distinguishing border effects from distance effects, since it finds U.S. state borders to be insignificant when using their fine-grained distance measures.

Capital

Starting again with stock market investments by professional fund managers, Coval and Moskowitz found that "the average U.S. fund manager invests in companies that are between 160 to 184 kilometers, or 9 to 11 percent, closer to her than the average firm she could have held" (1999, p. 2047). Distance effects on stock market investments also show up in a much smaller country such as Finland, where Grinblatt and Keloharju (2001) found them to be significant and to diminish with investor savvy and for firms based in the capital, Helsinki.

Turning to venture capital investment, Sorenson and Stuart reported that U.S. VC firms "invest in companies 10 miles from their offices at twice the rate of ones situated 100 miles away" (2001, p. 1581). They also found distance effects to help explain syndication patterns among VC investors: firms are more likely to invest in distant targets when they have previously invested together with a syndicate member located close to the target firm. Sorenson and Stuart note such patterns of cooperation between VC firms on the East and West coasts of the United States as a potential explanation for an increase in investment probability at the distance between the coasts.

Acquisitions of one operating company by another imply coordination requirements far surpassing those between VC firms and their portfolio companies, and evidence from the U.S. chemical industry, unsurprisingly, identifies large distance effects in this context as well. Acquisitions that involve operational integration seem to be even more distance sensitive. Chakrabarti and Mitchell (2013) found that U.S. chemical firms were 80% less likely to acquire other chemical firms located within 40 miles of their own headquarters but outside their own zip codes than targets within their own zip codes, and then 90.2% and 96.8% less likely, respectively, to acquire firms 200 and 2,500 miles away. The negative effects of distance on acquisition behavior among firms in their sample persisted even as firms grew and gained experience as acquirers.

Information

Based on domestic data, phone calls also seem to be subject to significant distance effects, although there is a nonlinearity at around the 10-km mark, with intensity of connections peaking around then (as a substitute for face-to-face interaction) but being dampened by further increases in geographic distance (Krings, Calabrese, Ratti, & Blondel, 2009). Similarly, Takhteyev et al.'s work (Takhteyev, Gruzd, & Wellman, 2012) on the incidence of ties on Twitter highlights a strong distance-dependence and fails to find any particular salience for the often-asserted international ties between five leading global cities: New York, London, Los Angeles, Tokyo, and Sao Paulo. Fig. 1 indicates that the overall pattern of extreme distance-dependence is affected noticeably only by a spike in the New York–Los Angeles distance (a domestic link); New York–London is just a blip, if that, in the overall pattern, and the other pairings highlighted have no discernible effect at all. Even "global cities" seem locally/nationally embedded,

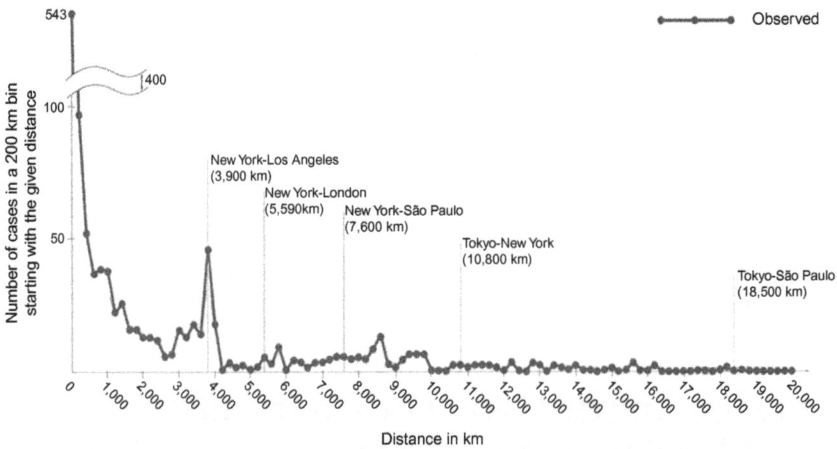

Fig. 1. The Distance-Dependence of Ties on Twitter. *Source*: Takhteyev et al. (2012). Reprinted with permission from Elsevier.

contrary to assertions that they connect more with their counterparts abroad than with their national hinterlands.[2]

Overall, 39% of all Twitter ties turn out to be local as in within the same (roughly metropolitan) regional cluster, 36% fall outside the regional cluster but within the same country, and 25% are international. Note that domestic (local and other intranational) ties are three times as numerous as international ties in this case: a significant degree of home bias that reflects discontinuities at national borders as well as the dampening effects of geographic distance. Looking across a broad range of indicators, the domestic-to-international multiple is often 5, 10, or even 20 (Twitter has a relatively high intensity of globalization compared to most other types of interactions I have measured).

People

The earliest forerunners of modern gravity models were models of intranational people flows. Desart (1846) studied passenger traffic on Belgium's railway network, and Ravenstein (1889) analyzed migration within the United Kingdom (both as cited in Odlyzko, 2014). Recent studies continue to identify large negative effects of distance on both short-term and long-term people flows. De la Mata and Llano (2010) report strongly negative distance effects on tourism trade within Spain. An example of a study of how distance shapes internal migration within the United States is that by Schwartz (1973), which related the distance elasticity to movers' age and education levels. My own rough analysis of U.S. migration flows indicates that state population and interstate distance alone explain more than 70% of the variation among U.S. interstate migrant stocks.[3]

This section has presented evidence that the subset of interactions that do cross intranational borders diminish with geographic distance. The next section will introduce the CAGE Distance Framework to incorporate effects of other (non-geographic) types of distance (Ghemawat, 2001).

P3. IN ADDITION TO GEOGRAPHIC DISTANCE, CULTURAL, ADMINISTRATIVE, AND (OFTEN) ECONOMIC DISTANCES ALSO DAMPEN ~~INTERNATIONAL~~ INTRANATIONAL BUSINESS

Ghemawat's CAGE framework is based on a synthesis of a broad range of research for thinking about international differences, with the CAGE acronym meant to evoke the *C*ultural, *A*dministrative, *G*eographic, and *E*conomic dimensions of differences across countries (see Table 1). The underlying representation is of countries as nodes in a network rather than as a heap of structurally equivalent objects, with an emphasis on analyzing variations in the links between the nodes (bilateral analysis) as well as just the nodes themselves (unilateral analysis).

At the international level, augmented gravity models that incorporate cultural, administrative, and economic explanatory variables alongside their geographic counterparts underline the importance of thinking in terms of CAGE distances. Thus, Ghemawat and De la Mata (2015) analyzed 11 different types of international interactions using an augmented gravity model that incorporates the distance variables highlighted in bold in Table 1. Shifting from the basic gravity specification, with geographic distance as the only distance variable, to the augmented specification significantly increases the explanatory power of the model in all cases.

While the CAGE framework was developed from international research, one can think of some of the nodes within the basic network representation as being states or cities within the same country. (Note that with the exception of some of the administrative differences listed in the table, most can arise at the intranational level as well as internationally.) And we do have

Table 1. The CAGE Framework for Thinking about International Differences.

	Cultural Differences	Administrative Differences	Geographic Differences	Economic Differences
Bilateral measures	– **Different languages** – Different ethnicities/ lack of connective ethnic or social networks – Different religions – Differences in national work systems – Different values, norms, and dispositions	– **Lack of colonial ties** – **Lack of shared regional trading bloc** – Lack of common currency – Different legal system – Political hostility	– **Physical distance** – **Lack of land border** – Differences in climates (and disease environments)	– **Differences in incomes** – Differences in availability of: Natural resources Financial resources Human resources Intermediate inputs Infrastructure Information or knowledge – Differences in industry structure
Unilateral measures	– Traditionalism – Insularity – Spiritualism – Inscrutability	– Nonmarket/closed economy (home bias vs. foreign bias) – Nonmembership in international organizations – Weak legal institutions/ corruption – Lack of government checks and balances – Societal conflict – Political/expropriation risk	– Landlockedness – Geographic size – Geographic remoteness	– Economic size – Low per capita income – Low level of monetization – Limited infrastructure, other specialized factors

Reprinted with permission from "Distance Still Matters: The Hard Reality of Global Expansion" by Pankaj Ghemawat. Harvard Business Review, September 2001.

scattered evidence of the importance of the effects of non-geographic types of distance.

Consider, for instance, the map prepared by the U.S. Department of Commerce on the export emphases of major U.S. metropolitan areas. The title of Fig. 2 – also due to the Commerce Department – explicitly highlights the influence of cultural and geographic proximity as opposed to distance. Especially in a large country, different positions within it may have major implications for a city's international as well as domestic (largely local/regional) interactions.

Grinblatt and Keloharju (2001) also highlighted cultural factors in their analysis of the geographic patterns of stock market investment in Finland, alongside the geographic distance effects mentioned above. A common language (in this case either Finnish or Swedish) between an investor and a firm's financial reporting was positively associated with investment, as was commonality between the investor and the firm's cultural origin (assessed based on its CEO's name and native language).

U.S. interstate migration patterns can be related to all four legs of the CAGE framework by augmenting the gravity model mentioned in the discussion of geographic distance effects in the previous section. Adding differences in state mean wages (an economic factor) and voting patterns in the last presidential election (one that spans the political and cultural realms) increases the model's explanatory power and both variables are significant.

Trading relationships among *comunidades autónomas*, within Spain also exhibit multi-dimensional distance effects (for a more detailed analysis, see Ghemawat, Llano, & Requena, 2010). Consider trade between Catalonia and its two leading domestic trading partners, Valencia and Aragon. Culturally, the Valencian and Catalan languages are similar and are both considered as co-official (together with Castellano, i.e., "Spanish") for their respective regions. Administratively, the three regions fell under the Crown of Aragon for centuries – which probably created some additional linkages – before being integrated under the Crown of Spain. Geographically, both Valencia and Aragon share common land borders with Catalonia. And economically, Valencia, in particular, is one of Spain's larger regions, so it is natural, in a sense, that it be one of Catalonia's largest regional trading partners.

From this perspective, what is more surprising is how significant Aragon is as a trading partner since the Aragonese economy is only one-third as large as Valencia's. The greater intensity of Catalonia's trade with Aragon seems to rest, for the most part, on geographical factors. Although Aragon

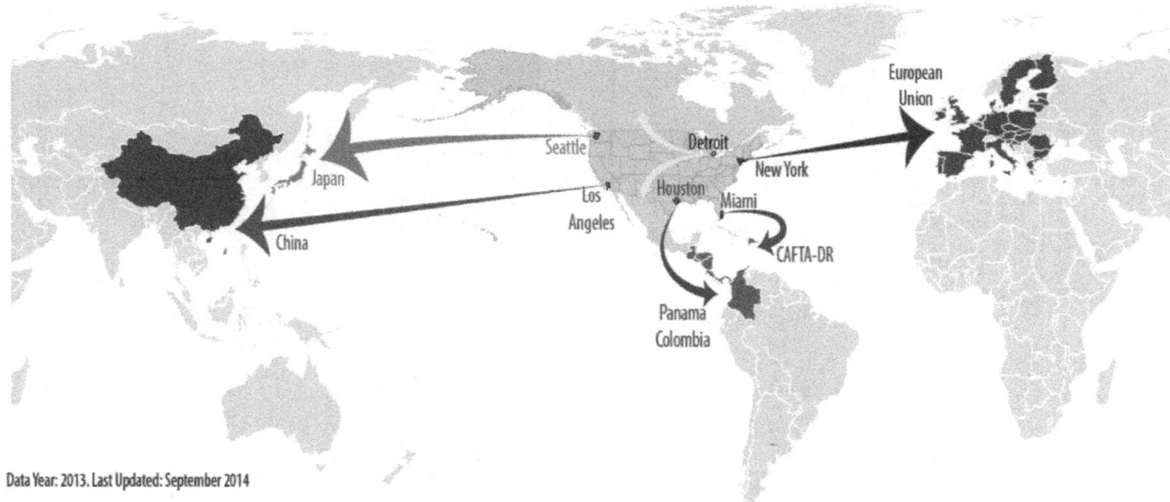

Fig. 2. Metro Area Trade Relationships often Reflect Geographic and Cultural Ties. *Source*: U.S. Department of Commerce – International Trade Administration (2013).

and Valencia are both adjacent to Catalonia, Zaragoza, Aragon's capital and principal city, is only about one-third as far from Barcelona as is the city of Valencia. Based on the effects of physical distance alone, this should offset the difference in Aragonese and Valencian GDPs. Trade with Aragon also gets boosted more by Zaragoza's role as a transport hub within Spain and the apparent inferiority of transport infrastructure connecting Valencia and Catalonia – a perennial political issue. In addition, Aragon is landlocked which, coupled with difficulties crossing the Pyrenees, means that Catalonia serves as its trading intermediary with the rest of the world in a way that Valencia, which is on the sea, simply doesn't require. Catalan-Aragonese trade should also be boosted relative to Catalan-Valencian trade by the fact that Aragon is among Spain's richest regions (as is Catalonia), with a per capita GDP nearly 20% higher than Valencia's. And finally, there is the undeniable if idiosyncratic effect of the major foreign investment in Aragon, Opel's auto plant, which is tied to supply and demand chains in Catalonia that generate significant intraregional trade flows.

The example of Catalonia-Aragon/Valencia suggests that the CAGE distances highlighted by the framework may be correlated. This reduces the ability to separate out their influences, but matters less from the standpoint of predictive power.

P4. THE DIMENSIONS OF DISTANCE SUGGEST AN EXPANDED SET OF STRATEGIES FOR DEALING WITH ~~INTERNATIONAL~~ INTRANATIONAL DIFFERENCES

The discussion has focused, so far, on using international research to understand the business landscape within countries instead of treating countries as point masses, that is, as perfectly integrated internally. Such understanding can help make differences visible so it is clearly of broad importance. But to go deeper, this section will focus very specifically on strategy – on making choices about how to compete in the business landscape, not just accurately discerning it. The CAGE framework can, in addition to helping identify differences, spark creativity in thinking about how to address them.

To start with a very brief recap of international strategy, discussions of it have long focused on the tension flagged by Fayerweather (1969) between pressures for unification within companies and for fragmentation due to national differences: Prahalad and Doz (1987) elaborated this into the trade-off between global integration and national responsiveness – or what might be referred to as *aggregation* (to overcome cross-country differences, e.g., through regionalization) versus *adaptation* (to adjust to cross-country differences, e.g., through variation). A useful direction in which to expand this basic strategy set is suggested by the economic theory of multinational enterprises (MNEs), which distinguishes between *horizontal* MNEs that exploit the similarities across countries despite cross-country differences (e.g., Coca-Cola), and *vertical* MNEs that exploit differences along selected dimensions (e.g., oil companies). This distinction suggests the generalization in Figs. 3(a) and (b) adding *arbitrage* to exploit differences to the strategies of adaptation and aggregation. Note that adding arbitrage/verticalization to exploit differences fits well with the recent surge in interest in the globalization of production as well as the globalization of markets: the latter is easy to assimilate into horizontal models, but the former is mostly a vertical phenomenon.

What are the intranational implications of this construct of international strategy? Consider, in turn, the three strategies of adaptation, aggregation, and arbitrage. The discussion of these AAA strategies will rely more heavily on case vignettes than the previous section, since there is less systematic empirical evidence on firms' responses to intranational differences than on the differences themselves.

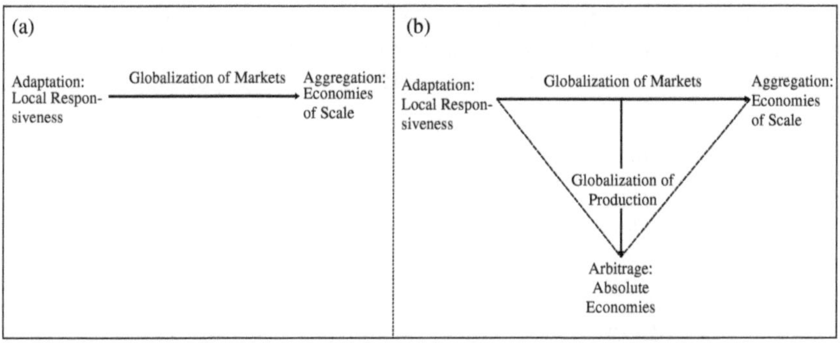

Fig. 3. (a) The Horizontal Dimension: Adaptation versus Aggregation. (b) The Vertical and Horizontal Dimensions: The AAA Triangle. *Source*: Reprinted with permission from "Redefining Global Strategy: Crossing Borders in a World Where Differences Still Matter" by Pankaj Ghemawat. Harvard Business Press Books, 2007. Copyright 2007 by Harvard Business Publishing; all rights reserved.

Adaptation

Even when intranational strategy has acknowledged the need for adaptation, it is often narrowed to the choice of how much variety to offer and thereby demoted to a problem in marketing rather than strategy. International strategy, by virtue of the larger differences it has had to grapple with, not only highlights possibilities for variation that go well beyond product variety but also suggests a range of complementary actions to limit the implied costs of complexity.

Consider the partial list of levers and sublevers for adaptation, derived primarily from international research and case studies, in Table 2. All seem applicable to at least some extent in the intranational context as well. To see this, start with the lever of variation in the first column of the table. The variation in products within a country can obviously be substantial. One of the keys to KFC's success in China (it has more than twice as many restaurants there as McDonalds) was learning quickly to adjust to different tastes in different parts of the country. Before they did so, the same recipe would provoke Shanghai customers to complain that the food is too spicy while those in Sichuan said it was too bland (Bell & Shelman, 2011). Insight into regional differences within China was also cited as a reason why Starbucks took on separate partners in different parts of the country (Wang, 2012).

Requirements for restaurants to cater to different tastes are unsurprising, but similar differences also show up in less obvious industries. Car buyers in China's northeastern Shandong province, for example, care more about external styling while those in southeastern Fujian focus more on price, even though both have similar levels of GDP per capita (data on

Table 2. Levers and Sublevers for Adaptation.

Variation	Focus: Reduce Need for Variation	Externalization: Reduce Burden of Variation	Design: Reduce Cost of Variation	Innovation: Improve Effectiveness of Variation
Products	Products	Strategic alliances	Flexibility	Transfer
Policies	Geographies	Franchising	Partitioning	Localization
Positioning	Verticals	User adaptation	Platforms	Recombination
Metrics	Segments	Networking	Modularity	Transformation
...	...	...	...	...

Source: Reprinted with permission from "Redefining Global Strategy: Crossing Borders in a World Where Differences Still Matter" by Pankaj Ghemawat. Harvard Business Press Books, 2007.

consumer preferences from Wang, Liao, & Hein, 2012). And such intranational differences seem important not only in big emerging markets but also in big established ones. One major branded clothing maker found that tailoring its products more closely to differences among and even within U.S. metropolitan areas could as much as double sales while reducing inventory and markdowns (Rigby & Vishwanath, 2006). Duncan MacNaughton, Wal-Mart's chief merchandising and marketing officer dubbed 2013 "the year of localization," when he announced plans to boost promotion of regional food brands within the United States (Schroeder, 2013).

So variation is important at the intranational level. But the trouble with relying on it as the sole lever for adapting to differences is, as Fayerweather originally pointed out in the international context, that it increases fragmentation, complexity, and associated costs. The other columns in Table 2 list complementary levers that can help improve the cost-benefit tradeoffs associated with variation. Focus – the idea of concentrating on particular products, geographies, etc. as a way of reducing the need for variation – is the one complementary lever that has been discussed relatively extensively in intranational strategy; for example, the focus variants on Porter's (1980, Chapter 2) generic strategies of cost leadership and differentiation. Some of the subcategories under the other levers have attracted intranational attention as well, but that has mostly occurred outside the strategy field (e.g., the marketing-oriented work by Prahalad and Ramaswamy (2004) on co-creation of value with customers, which mixes elements of externalization and innovation, or work in technology and operations management by Baldwin and Clark (1997), among others, on modularity and other design approaches). So international perspectives can help extend the list of intranational adaptation levers and sublevers as well as raising consciousness about the importance of intranational adaptation in the first place – both of which are likely to lead to more creative responses to intranational differences.

Aggregation

Aggregation is a second way of dealing with differences: by grouping subunits as to minimize within-group differences and maximize the potential for group-level economies. While there are many bases for aggregation, it seems useful to strive for concreteness by focusing on one in some detail. So the discussion in this subsection will focus on aggregation by geographic regions – the G component of the CAGE framework.

The attractions of aggregating by geographic region have been emphasized in the international context by Rugman and Verbeke (2004). What should be mentioned here is that some of the insights from the international context can be applied to the intranational context. Schwartzman and Bodoff's (1971) early work on U.S. manufacturing estimated that 24% of value added was accounted for by industries in which competition was geographically localized or regionalized and casual empiricism suggests that while such fragmentation has probably decreased since then, it remains significant – and looms even larger in the (larger) service sector.

My work for an oil company in the United States gives an illustration of how distinguishing among geographic regions can shift thinking about intranational strategy. Looking at the U.S. market for gasoline, in particular, revealed a highly regionalized structure, with five regions linked by the (relatively limited) flows depicted in Fig. 4. Subsequent work focused on adapting techniques and insights encountered in the international context to the intranational context, starting with basic linear programming models and then overlaying strategic considerations (the West Coast region, for instance, is particularly highly concentrated). Similar experiences were encountered with cement in Brazil and beer in China, to cite just two other examples.

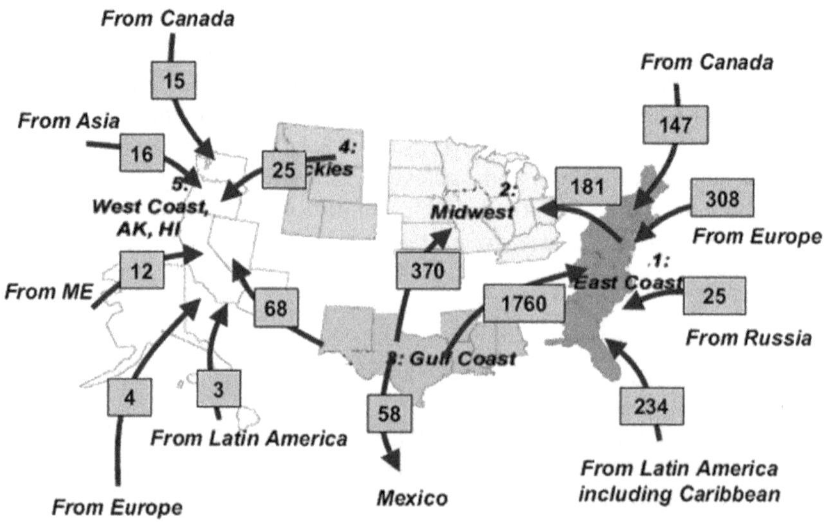

Fig. 4. Major Gasoline Flows in the United States (Thousand Barrels per Day, 2003).

It is worth adding that the international context does not just call attention to the importance of geographic regions, there are many other possible bases of aggregation: by business unit, global customer, function, language, income levels. Again, many of these have, in principles, counterparts at intranational levels.

Arbitrage

Arbitrage involves exploiting selected dimensions of differences across locations instead of simply treating differences as constraints to be adjusted to (adaptation) or overcome (aggregation). As we know from the international context, any CAGE difference can underpin arbitrage opportunities. Country-of-origin advantages, whether "real" or perceived, sustain opportunities for cultural arbitrage (e.g., Italian ham, French wine and liqueur, U.S. fast food, and Jamaican reggae music). Differences in tax rates, health, safety and environmental regulations, enforcement regimes, etc. open up a vast array of administrative arbitrage opportunities. Geographic arbitrage, the oldest reason for trade, continues to be important as well, particularly in the primary sectors (agriculture, fishing, forestry, and mining). And economic arbitrage is a catch-all category that captures differences in costs of labor and capital, as well as other, more industry-specific inputs such as knowledge, the availability of complementary products, and technologies or infrastructure, etc.

Once again, it is easy to imagine these forms of arbitrage in operation at the intranational level, and to cite specific examples. Many of the most valuable denominations of origin (e.g., Parma ham, Cognac brandy) pertain not to countries but to states or localities that are culturally privileged *within* their home countries as well as around the world, which generates opportunities for intranational as well as international cultural arbitrage. A powerful example of intranational administrative arbitrage is provided by the legal incorporation of more than half of all U.S. publicly traded companies in Delaware. Geographic arbitrage, the oldest reason for trade, continues to be a major driver of intranational as well as international commodity flows. And intranational economic arbitrage is illustrated by fashion retailer Zara's reliance on relatively low wages in Galicia, where its Spanish production is concentrated, to defend its position against competitors that engage (more heavily) in international arbitrage by purchasing from the Far East. Intranational economic arbitrage may also be motivated by considerations of upgrading as well as lowering costs: the clustering of the most successful firms in many industries in a few locations hints at intranational and international knowledge arbitrage possibilities between those locations and others (e.g., knowledge-seeking firms headed to Silicon Valley).

To wrap up this section, it seems that this richer palette of competitive strategies – in both the intranational *and* international contexts – has tended to be overlooked by strategists because they have tended to shy away from differences, relegating them to functional specialists or sidestepping them by presuming, for instance, that once geographic boundaries have been drawn appropriately, further fragmentation within those boundaries can be ignored. (Similar sidesteps have been suggested for other dimensions of difference, e.g., the advice to deal with differences across buyers through segmentation, with the presumption that the market segments that result can be treated as internally homogenous.) But in a world marked by digitization and the long tail, big/real-time/geographically tagged data, the diffusion of (open source) software and analytics and the development of 3D printing and advanced robotics – not to mention the big shift in demand in many sectors to emerging economies that look much more like each other than they do like advanced economies – less "averaging" and more attention to differences and to variation seems likely to be required.

CONCLUSIONS

This chapter has argued that international business has much to contribute to intranational business. It has done so by articulating four propositions and providing supporting evidence for each of them. According to the first three propositions, business activities of multiple types are dampened by borders and those that do cross them typically diminish with geographic as well as other types of distance. The fourth proposition, using strategy as an example, illustrated how insights from international business can be applied to intranational business.

The focus on strategy is, as noted earlier, meant to serve just as an example. Research on international business would seem to have the potential to supply valuable insights across most – if not all – business functions. The relation to marketing and its emphasis on segmentation has already been mentioned. While intranational differences tend to receive less attention in finance, the evidence cited above on financial fragmentation within economies has clear implications for firms and investors. In human resources, one can think of the potential for linkages between intranational and international diversity and mobility programs. In the technology arena, tools that boost a firm's ability to deal with international differences could also enhance its capacity to cater to intranational diversity. And so on. Clearly, the scope for further work on these topics is large.

NOTES

1. The estimates that follow were calculated using Bureau of Labor Statistics data for the United States (April, 2014), the Chinese Statistical Yearbook (2014) data for China, and the International Monetary Fund (October, 2014) data for per capita GDP around the world. The data series used for China was "Average Wage of Employed Persons in Urban Units by Sector."

2. See Sassen (1991). Similarly, Richard Florida – in one of his few attempts to consider the connections among the "peaks" (cities) that interest him – talks about increasing peak-to-peak connectivity, see Florida (2005).

3. Based on U.S. Census data covering the current homes and birthplaces of U.S. residents surveyed between 2011 and 2013.

ACKNOWLEDGMENTS

I am grateful to Steven Altman for his help in researching and writing up some of the examples in this article and to IESE Business School and Stern School of Business, NYU, for financial support.

REFERENCES

Alcácer, J., & Gittelman, M. (2006). Patent citations as a measure of knowledge flows: The influence of examiner citations. *Review of Economics and Statistics*, *88*(4), 774–779.

Almeida, P., & Kogut, B. (1999). Localization of knowledge and the mobility of engineers in regional networks. *Management Science*, *45*(7), 905–918.

Baldwin, C. Y., & Clark, K. B. (1997). Managing in an age of modularity. *Harvard Business Review*, *75*(5), 84–93.

Bell, D., & Shelman, M. L. (2011). KFC's radical approach to China. *Harvard Business Review*, *89*(11), 137–142. Retrieved from https://hbr.org/2011/11/kfcs-radical-approach-to-china

Casson, M. (1987). *The firm and the market: Studies on multinational enterprise and the scope of the firm*. Cambridge, MA: MIT Press.

Chakrabarti, A., & Mitchell, W. (2013). The persistent effect of geographic distance in acquisition target selection. *Organization Science*, *24*(6), 1805–1826.

China Statistical Yearbook 2014. (2014). China Statistics Press.

Combes, P.-P., Lafourcade, M., & Mayer, T. (2005). The trade-creating effects of business and social networks: Evidence from France. *Journal of International Economics*, *66*(1), 1–29.

Coughlin, C. C., & Novy, D. (2013). Is the international border effect larger than the domestic border effect? Evidence from U.S. trade. *CESifo Economic Studies*, *59*(2), 249–276.

Coval, J. D., & Moskowitz, T. J. (1999). Home bias at home: Local equity preference in domestic portfolios. *The Journal of Finance*, *54*(6), 2045–2073.

Coval, J. D., & Moskowitz, T. J. (2001). The geography of investment: Informed trading and asset prices. *Journal of Political Economy*, *109*(4), 811–841.

Daumal, M., & Zignago, S. (2010). Measure and determinants of border effects of Brazilian states. *Papers in Regional Science*, *89*(4), 735–758.

De la Mata, T., & Llano, C. (2010). Modelo gravitatorio y turismo: Una aplicación a los flujos monetarios interregionales del sector Turismo en España (Gravity model and tourism: An application to the interregional monetary flows of the Spanish tourist sector). *Revista de Estudios Regionales*, *89*, 211–243.

Desart, H. G. (1846). *Bruxelles vers gand, par alost, en communication avec les stations diverses de la capitale.* Meémoire á l'appui du projet et considérations geéneérales sur l'influence qu'exerce la longueur du parcours, á l'égard des mouvements de voyageurs. Bruxelles: E. Devroye et Cie, imprimeur du roi.

Fayerweather, J. (1969). *International business management: A conceptual framework*. New York, NY: McGraw-Hill.

Florida, R. (2005). The world is spiky. *Atlantic*, 296(3), 48–51.

Ghemawat, P. (2001). Distance still matters: The hard reality of global expansion. *Harvard Business Review*, *79*(8), 137–147.

Ghemawat, P. (2003). Semiglobalization and international business strategy. *Journal of International Business Studies*, *34*(2), 138–152.

Ghemawat, P. (2007). *Redefining global strategy: Crossing borders in a world where differences still matter*. Boston, MA: Harvard Business School Press.

Ghemawat, P., & Altman, S. A. (2014). *DHL Global Connectedness Index 2014*. Retrieved from http://www.dhl.com/en/about_us/logistics_insights/studies_research/global_connectedness_index/global_connectedness_index.html

Ghemawat, P., & De la Mata, T. (2015). *Globalization and gravity*. Unpublished working paper.

Ghemawat, P., Llano, C., & Requena, F. (2010). Competitiveness and interregional as well as international trade: The case of Catalonia. *International Journal of Industrial Organization*, *28*(4), 415–422.

Gil-Pareja, S., Llorca-Vivero, R., Martínez-Serrano, J. A., & Oliver-Alonso, J. (2005). The border effect in Spain. *World Economy*, *28*(11), 1617–1631.

Gilson, R. J. (1999). The legal infrastructure of high technology industrial districts: Silicon valley, route 128, and covenants not to compete. *New York University Law Review*, *74*(3), 575–629.

Grinblatt, M., & Keloharju, M. (2001). How distance, language, and culture influence stockholdings and trades. *The Journal of Finance*, *56*(3), 1053–1073.

Hillberry, R., & Hummels, D. (2003). Intranational home bias: Some explanations. *Review of Economics and Statistics*, *85*(4), 1089–1092.

Hillberry, R., & Hummels, D. (2008). Trade responses to geographic frictions: A decomposition using micro-data. *European Economic Review*, *52*(3), 527–550.

Hochberg, Y. V., & Rauh, J. D. (2013). Local overweighting and underperformance: Evidence from limited partner private equity investments. *Review of Financial Studies*, *26*(2), 403–451.

Hong, H., Kubik, J. D., & Stein, J. C. (2005). Thy neighbor's portfolio: Word-of-mouth effects in the holdings and trades of money managers. *The Journal of Finance*, *60*(6), 2801–2824.

International Monetary Fund (IMF). Retrieved from http://www.imf.org/external/index.htm. Accessed in October, 2014.

Krings, G., Calabrese, F., Ratti, C., & Blondel, V. D. (2009). Urban gravity: A model for inter-city telecommunication flows. *Journal of Statistical Mechanics: Theory and Experiment*. Retrieved from http://iopscience.iop.org/1742-5468/2009/07/L07003

Landry, A. (2011). *Borders and Big Macs*. Federal Reserve Bank of Dallas, Globalization and Monetary Policy Institute Working Paper No. 95. Retrieved from http://www.dallasfed.org/assets/documents/institute/wpapers/2011/0095.pdf

Millimet, D. L., & Osang, T. (2007). Do state borders matter for U.S. intranational trade? The role of history and internal migration (Est-ce que les frontières des états ont de l'importance pour le commerce américain intranational? Le rôle de l'histoire et de la migration interne). *Canadian Journal of Economics/Revue canadienne d'économique*, *40*(1), 93–126.

Odlyzko, A. (2014). The forgotten discovery of gravity models and the inefficiency of early railway networks. Preprint. School of Mathematics. University of Minnesota. Retrieved from http://www.dtc.umn.edu/~odlyzko/doc/mania09.pdf

Poncet, S. (2005). A fragmented China: Measure and determinants of Chinese domestic market disintegration. *Review of International Economics*, *13*(3), 409–430.

Porter, M. E. (1980). *Competitive strategy*. New York, NY: Free Press.

Prahalad, C. K., & Doz, Y. L. (1987). *The multinational mission: Balancing local demands and global vision*. New York, NY: Free Press.

Prahalad, C. K., & Ramaswamy, V. (2004). *The future of competition: Co-creating unique value with customers*. Boston, MA: Harvard Business School Publishing.

Ravenstein, E. G. (1889). The laws of migration. *Journal of the Royal Statistical Society*, *52*(2), 241–305.

Requena, F., & Llano, C. (2010). The border effects in Spain: An industry-level analysis. *Empirica*, *37*(4), 455–476.

Rigby, D. K., & Vishwanath, V. (2006). Localization: The revolution in consumer markets. *Harvard Business Review*, *84*(4), 82–92. Retrieved from https://hbr.org/2006/04/localization-the-revolution-in-consumer-markets#

Rugman, A. M., & Verbeke, A. (2004). A perspective on regional and global strategies of multinational enterprises. *Journal of International Business Studies*, *35*(1), 3–18.

Sassen, S. (1991). *The global city: New York, London, Tokyo*. Princeton, NJ: Princeton University Press.

Schroeder, E. (2013). Wal-Mart adopting local strategy. Retrieved from http://www.foodbusinessnews.net/articles/news_home/Food-Service-Retail/2013/06/Wal-Mart_adopting_local_strate.aspx?ID=%7BB77C8CD6-4047-4EE2-83CE-AC44C30D3E8C%7D&cck=1

Schwartz, A. (1973). Interpreting the effect of distance on migration. *Journal of Political Economy*, *81*(5), 1153–1169.

Schwartzman, D., & Bodoff, J. (1971). Concentration in regional and local industries. *Southern Economic Journal*, *37*(3), 343–348.

Sorenson, O., & Stuart, T. E. (2001). Syndication networks and the spatial distribution of venture capital investments. *American Journal of Sociology*, *106*(6), 1546–1588.

Takhteyev, Y., Gruzd, A., & Wellman, B. (2012). Geography of twitter networks. *Social Networks*, *34*(1), 73–81.

U.S. Bureau of Labor Statistics. Retrieved from http://www.bls.gov/. Accessed in April, 2014.

U.S. Department of Commerce; International Trade Administration. (2013, September). *Exports from U.S. metropolitan areas total $1.4 trillion in 2013*. Retrieved from http://www.trade.gov/mas/ian/build/groups/public/@tg_ian/documents/webcontent/tg_ian_004073.pdf

Wang, A., Liao, W., & Hein, A.-P. (2012). *Bigger, better, broader: A perspective on China's auto market in 2020*. McKinsey China. Retrieved from http://www.mckinseychina.com/bigger-better-broader-a-perspective-on-chinas-auto-market-in-2020/

Wang, H. H. (2012). Five things starbucks did to get China right. www.forbes.com. Retrieved from http://www.forbes.com/sites/helenwang/2012/08/10/five-things-starbucks-did-to-get-china-right/

Wolf, H. C. (2000). Intranational home bias in trade. *Review of Economics and Statistics*, *82*(4), 555–563.

Xing, W., & Li, S. (2011). Home bias, border effect and internal market integration in China: Evidence from inter-provincial value-added tax statistics. *Review of Development Economics*, *15*(3), 491–503.

THE VALUE OF BREADTH AND THE IMPORTANCE OF DIFFERENCES

David J. Collis

ABSTRACT

Pankaj Ghemawat is honored not only for the breadth of his contribution to International Management as a scholar but also as an educator and passionate advocate of his ideas to practitioners. His work extends from industrial organization applications within the traditional strategy field all the way to international business insights into global strategy. The methodologies he employs straddle theoretical models, field-based cases, and even the creation of original databases. This suggests that in the hands of a true intellectual, there is value to an eclectic approach in academia. This is particularly true since the key insight of Pankaj's work is that differences among countries remain central to global strategy and that it is those differences that can be arbitraged into competitive advantage.

Keywords: Globalization; geographic scope; global strategy; multinationals; adaptation; international

Emerging Economies and Multinational Enterprises
Advances in International Management, Volume 28, 29–33

ISSN: 1571-5027/doi:10.1108/S1571-502720150000028003

Pankaj Ghemawat is currently the Global Professor of Management and Strategy and Director of Centre for Global Education and Management at the Stern School NYU, and the Anselmo Rubiralta Professor of Global Strategy at IESE. These extensive titles at two eminent institutions not only acknowledge his status within academia, but also graphically capture the scope of Pankaj's work for which he is being recognized as the "PWC Strategy&" Eminent Scholar.

As his titles suggest, as a research scholar Pankaj has had enormous impact on both the traditional competitive strategy field and in the arena for which this honor is awarded – global strategy. But again, as his titles denote, his impact goes far beyond academic research. He has made contributions to both the practice of management and to teaching. His numerous cases and books provide valuable advice and pedagogical material for practitioners and educators everywhere. Indeed, this is the second award Pankaj has received from the Academy of Management – previously, he was recognized by the Business Policy and Strategy Division as the Irwin Outstanding Educator in 2008. In fact, half his prolific output has been directed toward disseminating ideas that improve the practice and teaching of management, rather than just advancing knowledge of the field.

His titles also highlight the global scope of his work. With positions at both North American and European institutions, and a family connection to India, Pankaj is the archetypal cosmopolitan citizen. He then draws on this personal experience when making his astute observations about differences around the world.

Lastly, Pankaj is not just an ivory tower academic. He actually applies his ideas when consulting with companies and influencing policy makers around the world. In this regard, his advisory role with Tata Consulting Services, which has seen the company grow from its early days to employing over 250,000 people, has perhaps been the most fulfilling.

Pankaj's three-decade career can actually be divided into two parts. To demonstrate this, I borrow a technique that Pankaj has used to great effect in his own work by examining empirical data (Table 1). This identifies his incredible productivity. How many of us could sustain a pace that produces one quarter of a book, two published articles, and one and a half cases every year for 30 years? But more interesting is the division of Pankaj's output between the core strategy field and global strategy. Until he received tenure at the Harvard Business School in 1991 (as the youngest ever professor to receive tenure), Pankaj's work was more or less exclusively related to the industrial organization field with a book on "Commitment" and articles on sustainable competitive advantage, the experience curve, and exit among

Table 1. Ghemawat Published Output.

		Pretenure (1991)	Posttenure (1991)
Global	Books	0	4
	Articles	3	30
	Cases	1	23
Strategy	Books	1	2
	Articles	12	23
	Cases	9	12

others. He had a couple of articles for Mike Porter and Mike Spence – two of his thesis advisors – on global issues but was awarded tenure for research in competitive strategy.

What this means is that Pankaj is being honored as an eminent scholar for work that he has done since tenure. How many other scholars are able to perhaps make their greatest contributions for research *after* they receive tenure? And note that his output of traditional strategy work hardly slows while he shifts fields.

So what are Pankaj's specific contributions to International Management? I identify two major themes that run through Pankaj's work which have generated insights for us all.

First, to borrow from Michael Douglas in the movie "Wall Street," Pankaj has driven home the point that "Differences are Good." Indeed, without important differences among countries there would not even be a distinct field of international management! In his very public takedown of "globaloney" and in debate with Tom Friedman over how flat the world has become, Pankaj effectively demonstrated that we live in a world of "Semiglobalisation" (Ghemawat, 2003a). Indeed, from examination of a number of data sources covering product, capital, labor, and intellectual markets, he made the "10% presumption" – that the world is only about 10% of the way to complete integration (Ghemawat, 2007).

But Pankaj was not content to just note the presence of important differences around the world, he actually developed an approach to represent, and even quantify, those differences. His CAGE framework has become the standard way to identify and measure the "distance" between countries (Ghemawat, 2001), and can be used to assess both where firms should compete around the world and where to locate their various activities.

Finally, Pankaj built on the presence of substantive differences among countries to remind us of the value of arbitrage as a source of global competitive advantage. In one of his most cited articles, he revived the driver for the existence of vertical MNEs as one of the three ways multinationals could create value (Ghemawat, 2003b). In his AAA global strategy framework, Pankaj then argued that rather than seeking to respond to differences (Adapt) or overcome those differences (Aggregate), firms could actually exploit differences (Arbitrage) to create value (Ghemawat, 2013).

The second theme that underpins Pankaj's work is its grounding in empirical evidence and data. Pankaj is not just an ivory tower theorist, rather he bases his reasoning on data, much of which he carefully constructs himself. Whether it is his fieldwork developing cases or his ability to identify and then find just the right set of information, he is the master of marshaling the facts to develop and support theoretical insights.

He even goes beyond finding existing data sources to create his own data. This is then made available to others and often captured in graphical representations that make it both accessible and a powerful communication tool. Data like the CAGE comparator, rooted maps, and the Global Connectedness Index are now available to both academics and practitioners for use in their own research or strategic decision-making.

Pankaj's work has obviously had a profound impact on the strategy field in general, and on international management in particular (Table 2). With over 10,000 citations on Google Scholar, more than two and a half million Harvard Business School cases and nearly half a million Harvard Business Review articles sold, Pankaj's work has clearly been noticed by, and found to be useful by scholars, practitioners, and educators around the world. Interestingly, his impact has been as important in his original strategy domain with pieces on commitment and sustainable competitive advantage,

Table 2. Ghemawat Professional Impact.

• Google Scholar citation (count)	10,537
– Commitment 1,426; distance still matters 1,024; sustainable competitive advantage 648; business groups 396; exit 395	
• Harvard Business School cases (sold)	2,528,268
– Walmart 804k, Zara 222k, Barnes & Noble 205k, creating competitive advantage 185k, Coors 163k	
• Harvard Business Review articles (sold)	403,164
– Sustainable advantage 129k, distance still matters 102k, managing differences 46k	
• Google Hits (for Pankaj Ghemawat Global)	69,300
– Redefining global strategy, why the world is not flat, distance still matters, CAGE framework	
• Co-authors	50
– Spence, Porter, Caves ... Levinthal, Nalebuff, Ricart ... Khanna, Siegel ...	

as it has in international strategy with articles on distance, differences, and global strategy.

Perhaps a better measure of his impact is the list of Pankaj's co-authors (including, I am pleased to say, myself). Not only is that list long – 50 others have seen value to collaborating with Pankaj – but it includes three different sets of colleagues. First were his "elders and betters," including Nobel Prize winner Mike Spence, Mike Porter, and Dick Caves his thesis advisors. Second, were peers, like Barry Nalebuff and Dan Levinthal, acknowledged leaders in their own field's. Third, are students and those who have built on his contributions, like Tarun Khanna and Jordan Siegel. That one person can work with three such celebrated groups demonstrates the extent to which Pankaj is a role model within academia.

On a more personal level it should be noted that Pankaj graduated from Harvard with a full set of degrees, up to and including a PhD, six years after arriving at that institution at the tender age of 16! In fact, when he started his career as a new assistant professor at the Harvard Business School, the first class he taught featured only two students younger than himself! In spite of his years in the profession and his widespread recognition, no one yet appears to be able to pronounce his name. I have heard him referred to as Pancash, Punkuj, Pancadge, Pancarsh ... none of which appears to faze him, reflecting personal humility in the face of outstanding success.

Lastly, it would be remiss not to recognize the contribution that Pankaj himself would acknowledge his wife and daughter have made to his productivity and insight – Anirhadda and Ananya.

REFERENCES

Ghemawat, P. (2001). Distance still matters. *Harvard Business Review*, *79*(8), 137–147.

Ghemawat, P. (2003a). Semiglobalization and international business strategy. *Journal of International Business Studies*, *34*(2), 138–152.

Ghemawat, P. (2003b). The forgotten strategy. *Harvard Business Review*, *81*(11), 76–84.

Ghemawat, P. (2007). Why the world isn't flat. *Foreign Policy*, *159*, 54–60.

Ghemawat, P. (2013). *Redefining global strategy: Crossing borders in a world where differences still matter*. Boston, MA: Harvard Business Press.

The CAGE Comparator. (2010). *Online analytical tool*. DHL Global Connectedness Index 2012 (with Steven Altman). Retrieved from www.ghemawat.com/cage

SEMIGLOBALIZATION: A RELEVANT REALITY

Africa Ariño

ABSTRACT

This essay is a commentary on Ghemawat's work on the reality of semi-globalization and its relevance to the International Business (IB) field and to the world of practice. It recognizes Ghemawat's contributions to the IB field – at par with his earlier contributions to the competitive strategy area and highlights Ghemawat's emphasis on well-grounded empirical research. This approach serves well to establish the case that markets are semi-integrated, and the world is semiglobal. Through his work, Ghemawat has brought back to center stage a central premise of the IB field: that locations and distance across locations matter.

Keywords: Semiglobalization; location; distance

> At the core of my work lies the reality that, while globalization is indeed a powerful force, the extent of international integration varies widely across countries and companies and generally remains more limited than is commonly supposed. (Ghemawat, 2012)

Emerging Economies and Multinational Enterprises
Advances in International Management, Volume 28, 35–42

ISSN: 1571-5027/doi:10.1108/S1571-502720150000028004

INTRODUCTION

I have chosen Pankaj Ghemawat's words above to open this commentary about his work on international business (IB) as I believe they synthesize both his overarching contribution to the field and his approach to research. On the one hand, at a time when the IB field struggled to define its own identity (e.g., Buckley, 2002), Ghemawat's work showed that the extent of international integration is highly heterogenous. This brought back to stage a central premise of the field: that location, and distance across locations matter. On the other hand, Ghemawat's approach to research has been pivotal. An emphasis on understanding reality through well-grounded empirical evidence serves well the case that we live in a semiglobal world, one in which country differences are relevant. Additionally, the fact that the quote comes from an article in *The McKinsey Quarterly* serves as an indicator of the relevance of his work to the world of practice. What the words above hide – and I want to highlight, even if the reader already knows – is that Pankaj's work in IB builds on his earlier, equally notable contributions to the competitive strategy domain.

This essay is organized in three sections. First, I will give an idea of the type of empirical evidence that Pankaj uses to base his claim that semiglobalization is a reality. Second, I will comment on the relevance of his work on semiglobalization to the IB field and to managers and policymakers. Finally, I will share some ideas about how Pankaj's work is pertinent to the further advancement of corporate international strategy, and I will close with some concluding remarks.

SEMIGLOBALIZATION: A REALITY

Semiglobalization refers to the "condition of incomplete cross-border integration" (Ghemawat, 2003, p. 139) in which "neither the barriers nor the links among markets in different countries can be neglected" (Ghemawat, 2003, p. 139). This condition covers a broad continuum, the extremes of which are total integration and complete isolation. Friedman (2005) is a clear proponent of total cross-border integration and the full globalization hypothesis. The *Ghemawat vs. Friedman* debates are well-known (Friedman, 2007; Ghemawat, 2007a). It is the amount and nature of the empirical evidence Ghemawat provides that lends support to the semiglobalization case. The esteemed, late Alan Rugman (Rugman, 2012;

Rugman & Verbeke, 2004) also provides evidence that – even if at a different level of analysis – is consistent with the semiglobalization thesis.

While I will not enter into the *Ghemawat vs. Friedman* debate, I want to bring in here the type of data that grounds the claim that semiglobalization is a reality. Ghemawat (2003) offers a synthetic review of the evidence from both product and factor markets. First, in terms of product markets, he examines (1) trade flows, (2) foreign direct investment, and (3) price integration. Second, in terms of factor markets, he analyzes (1) capital, (2) labor, and (3) knowledge. Across all measures, the data indicate that market integration in recent decades is higher than ever before, but is still far from being a perfect integration. The interested reader may find details in the original article.

Ghemawat's emphasis on examining data to separate the facts about globalization from the myths extends to other aspects believed to accompany the phenomenon of increasing market integration. In particular, he inspects whether empirical evidence supports the "widespread belief that increases in the cross-border integration of markets are associated with increases in global concentration" (Ghemawat & Ghadar, 2006, p. 595) – a belief that is shared by both supporters and opponents of globalization.

Once again, by turning to empirical evidence at both the company and the country/geographic levels he sheds light on the myth that concentration goes hand-in-hand with globalization. Pankaj and his co-author examine a number of concentration-related indicators at both the company and the country levels. The evidence provided suggests that globalization has not been accompanied by company concentration nor country hegemony.

Whether the evidence is comprehensive or not might be discussed. What cannot be discussed is that Pankaj provides data that support his claims.

THE RELEVANCE OF SEMIGLOBALIZATION

Ghemawat's contributions about the reality of semiglobalization are of relevance to the IB field as well as to managers and policymakers. First, if semiglobalization were not real, there would be a substantial question mark around the need for IB as an academic field. Periodically, IB researchers undergo a debate on the identity of the field, and on the big questions that define its boundaries (e.g., Buckley, 2002; Buckley & Ghauri, 2004; Peng, 2004). This debate at times reflects doubts about the future of the field relative to germane areas, with some researchers showing greater optimism than others (e.g., Shenkar, 2004). If the world were flat, the international dimension would be irrelevant. As an academic field, IB, and more specifically international strategy, would be void of meaning, and its scope an empty space (Ghemawat, 2003).

Ghemawat's evidence that semiglobalization is a certain fact provides solid ground for IB optimists. His work comes as a needed reminder that location – a reality at the basis of the IB field – matters, and it matters beyond setting the context in which activities take place (Ghemawat, 2003). Understanding which value-creating activities should be undertaken in which geographic locations is necessary to understand what determines success or failure in international competition (Rumelt, Schendel, & Teece, 1994, p. 420). Location-specificity is one potential source of market imperfections that the international dimension adds (Ghemawat, 2003). To the extent that the assets and resources that support activities are location-specific (Williamson, 1985), their redeployment to other locations results in a value loss. Not only products but also certain production factors are subject to location-specificity, although to different extents (Ghemawat, 2003); thus, location matters because of the potential resource base companies may access in each particular location (Ariño, 2011).

Related and obvious, location determines distance between home and host countries. Distance across countries includes not only the geographical dimension, but economic, cultural, and administrative dimensions as well – the famous CAGE model (Ghemawat, 2001, 2007b). The idea of cross-country distance as applied to IB can be traced back to Beckerman's (1956) concept of psychic distance. Johanson and Vahlme (1977) were pioneers in relating home/host country psychic distance – "the sum of factors preventing the flow of information from and to the market" (Johanson & Vahlme, 1977, p. 24) – to the pattern and pace of firm internationalization. They present examples of the factors that prevent those information flows differences such as those in language, education, business practices, culture, and institutional development. Subsequently, Kogut and Singh (1988) focused on home/host country differences in culture and language, and developed an index based on Hofstede's (1980) cultural dimensions. From then on, research practice focused on cultural distance – or more precisely, on the Kogut-Singh (1988) index of cultural distance [see Tihanyi, Griffith, and Russell (2005) for a meta-analytical review]. Gradually, cultural distance was treated as equivalent to psychic distance, and other dimensions of country distance were lost in this process (Shenkar, 2001; Tung & Verbeke, 2010). Ghemawat's (2001, 2007b) work came as a timely call to reconsider cross-country distance in a multidimensional way.

Second, Ghemawat's work proves impactful for managers and policymakers as well. On the one hand, his work may assist managers think systematically about their global strategy. Ghemawat (2007b) offers a framework to help managers respond to cross-country differences in ways that add value by adjusting to, overcoming, or exploiting differences – or what he calls the AAA strategies: "a*daptation,* a*ggregation,* a*rbitrage.*" Consideration of cross-country differences may prove very valuable for competing on a global basis. On the contrary, ignoring differences across the CAGE dimensions may have tremendous consequences for companies operating in multiple countries, as some of the cases he studied in depth suggest (Ghemawat, 2007b). Also, Pankaj gives food for thought to both managers and policymakers in his latest book (Ghemawat, 2011) where he synthesizes the empirical evidence collected tenaciously, and his thinking about semiglobalization.

Beyond offering tools to guide strategic thinking, Ghemawat provides valuable data to inform strategy- and policy-making processes. I am referring to the *DHL Global Connectedness Index* (Ghemawat & Altman, 2014) that he has developed along with his research team at IESE Business School and the NYU Stern Business School. The index ranks 140 countries in terms of their global connectedness. Beyond the ranking per se, the wealth of information offered is of most value: analysis of 12 types of trade, capital, information, and people flows (or cumulative stocks) since 2005 results in examination of the depth of each country's international interactions, their geographic distribution, and their directionality. Insightful comments at both the regional and the country levels accompany the information. This wealth of information has the potential to impact academic work as much as that of managers and policymakers.

WHAT'S NEXT?

Ghemawat (2003) claims the need to develop the corporate international strategy area further. Bringing location-specificity to the forefront, Ghemawat's work is highly relevant to this endeavor. However, whether the country is the relevant unit to consider location and distance between locations is being questioned (Tung & Verbeke, 2010).

On the one hand, Ghemawat's work is pertinent to corporate international strategy. To the extent that markets vary in the degree to which they are integrated and semiglobalization is a reality, location of key activities is a critical issue to study simultaneously diversification across locations and diversification across industries. However, location decisions cannot be decoupled from other elements that contribute to the value-adding function of the global enterprise, as the concept of *strategic assembly* illustrates (Koza, Tallman, & Ataay, 2011).

"Strategic assembly is the process of constructing a business firm in a calculated and forward-looking manner with the intention of gaining and maintaining competitive advantage under the dynamic environmental and competitive conditions facing that firm" (Koza et al., 2011, p. 28). It reflects a global strategic perspective on the firm's activities that "requires strategic purpose in considering any asset, in any location, for inclusion and integration through any means of governance" (Koza et al., 2011, p. 28).

The strategic assembly process involves making decisions around four elements: (1) location of the firm's activities; (2) ownership of the assets needed to carry out the activities; (3) design of the organizational structure to coordinate the various activities; and (4) development of corporate capabilities needed to undertake the activities in a value-enhancing manner. All of these elements are intertwined, and strategic assembly seeks consistency among them (Ariño, 2011). Some of the location-specific assets needed to carry out the desired activities in a particular location are not freely available in many cases (Hennart, 2009). Integration of the activities via full ownership may not be feasible. Instead, links to other firms – in the form of joint ventures or other types of intermediate forms – may be necessary. Coordinating activities that cross country boundaries requires an organizational structure that takes into account similarities and differences across countries. Exposure to a diversity of national contexts entails the opportunity to develop a number of corporate-level capabilities – for example, a learning capability that allows benefiting from exposure to a diversity of contexts, partners, and industry structures; multidexterity to manage a range of organizational forms across various geographic settings and businesses; or the ability to orchestrate all of the elements that integrate the strategic assembly process (Ariño, 2011).

On the other hand, the adequacy of the country as the relevant unit to consider location and distance is challenged increasingly (e.g., Tung & Verbeke, 2010). While some advocate for larger units such as the region, and a focus on inter-regional distance (e.g., Rugman & Verbeke, 2004), others emphasize the importance of within-country differences (e.g., Tung & Verbeke, 2010). Most likely, whether the region, the country, or within-country geographic units are the right unit to consider depends largely on the research question being asked. What Ghemawat's work and the data he provides make clear is that "the world" is unlikely to be the right unit to consider, as the world is anything but flat.

CONCLUSION

Ghemawat is a great example of how to ground the prevalence and scale of a phenomenon such as semiglobalization in empirical evidence. By doing so, he brings back location and distance to the forefront, providing a solid ground that justifies the existence of IB as an academic field. In addition, he develops frameworks that are useful tools to guide strategic thinking of both managers and policymakers. Furthermore, his work may contribute to the advancement of research on corporate international strategy, and not only to competitive international strategy – the area in which his work is positioned. In closing, I want to appreciate the opportunity to have reflected on the work and contributions of Pankaj, whom I esteem both as a scholar and as a colleague.

REFERENCES

Ariño, A. (2011). Building the global enterprise: Strategic assembly. *Global Strategy Journal*, *1*, 47–49.

Beckerman, W. (1956). Distance and the pattern of intra-European trade. *The Review of Economics and Statistics*, *38*, 31–40.

Buckley, P. J. (2002). Is the international business agenda running out of steam? *Journal of International Business Studies*, *12*(summer special issue), 5–16.

Buckley, P. J., & Ghauri, P. N. (2004). Globalization, economic geography and the strategy of multinational enterprises. *Journal of International Business Studies*, *35*, 81–98.

Friedman, T. L. (2005). *The world is flat: A brief history of the globalized world in the twenty-first century*. London: Allen Lane.

Friedman, T. L. (2007). Is the world flat? *Foreign Policy*, *160*, 4.

Ghemawat, P. (2001). Distance still matters: The hard reality of global expansion'. *Harvard Business Review*, *79*(9), 137–147.

Ghemawat, P. (2003). Semiglobalization and international business strategy. *Journal of International Business Studies*, *34*, 138–152.

Ghemawat, P. (2007a). Why the world isn't flat. *Foreign Policy*, *159*, 54–60.

Ghemawat, P. (2007b). *Redefining global strategy: Crossing borders in a world where differences still matter*. Boston, MA: Harvard Business Review Press.

Ghemawat, P. (2011). *World 3.0: Global prosperity and how to achieve it*. Boston, MA: Harvard Business Review Press.

Ghemawat, P. (2012). Developing global leaders. *The McKinsey Quarterly*, *3*, 100–109.

Ghemawat, P., & Altman, S. A. (2014). *DHL global connectedness index 2014: Analyzing global flows and their power to increase prosperity*. Retrieved from http://www.dhl.com/content/dam/Campaigns/gci2014/downloads/dhl_gci_2014_study_low.pdf

Ghemawat, P., & Ghadar, F. (2006). Global integration ≠ global concentration. *Industrial and Corporate Change*, *15*, 595–623.

Hennart, J. F. (2009). Down with MNE centric theories! Market entry and expansion as the bundling of MNE and local assets. *Journal of International Business Studies*, *40*, 1432–1454.

Hofstede, G. (1980). *Culture's consequences: International differences in work-related values*. Beverly Hills, CA: Sage.

Johanson, J., & Vahlme, J. E. (1977). The internationalization process of the firm: A model of knowledge development and increasing foreign market commitments. *Journal of International Business*, *8*(1), 23–32.

Kogut, B., & Singh, H. (1988). The effect of national culture on the choice of entry mode. *Journal of International Business Studies*, *19*(3), 411–432.

Koza, M. P., Tallman, S., & Ataay, A. (2011). The strategic assembly of global firms: A microstructural analysis of local learning and global adaptation. *Global Strategy Journal*, *1*, 27–46.

Peng, M. W. (2004). Identifying the big question in international business research. *Journal of International Business Studies*, *35*, 99–108.

Rugman, A. M. (2012). *The end of globalization: Why global strategy is a myth*. Sydney: Random House Business.

Rugman, A. M., & Verbeke, A. (2004). A perspective on regional and global strategies of multinational enterprises. *Journal of International Business Studies*, *35*, 3–18.

Rumelt, R. P., Schendel, D. E., & Teece, D. J. (1994). *Fundamental issues in strategy: A research agenda*. Boston, MA: Harvard Business School Press.

Shenkar, O. (2001). Cultural distance revisited: Towards a more rigorous conceptualization and measurement of cultural differences. *Journal of International Business Studies*, *32*, 519–535.

Shenkar, O. (2004). One more time: International business in a global economy. *Journal of International Business Studies*, *35*, 161–171.

Tihanyi, L., Griffith, D. A., & Russell, C. J. (2005). The effect of cultural distance on entry mode choice, international diversification, and MNE performance: A meta-analysis. *Journal of International Business Studies*, *36*, 270–283.

Tung, R. L., & Verbeke, A. (2010). Beyond Hofstede and GLOBE: Improving the quality of cross-cultural research. *Journal of International Business Studies*, *41*, 1259–1274.

Williamson, O. E. (1985). *The economic institutions of capitalism*. New York, NY: Free Press.

PART II

INTRODUCTION TO PART II

EMERGING ECONOMIES AND MULTINATIONAL ENTERPRISES

Elitsa R. Banalieva, Laszlo Tihanyi, Timothy M. Devinney and Torben Pedersen

ABSTRACT

Do multinational enterprises evolve differently in emerging and developed economies? Although one camp argues that emerging economy multinationals are different from their developed country counterparts owing to the underdeveloped institutions in their home countries, another camp counters that they are the same and the existing international business theories can fully explain their strategies. A third camp suggests a more nuanced perspective by finding value in both approaches. In this introductory chapter, we review this debate and offer new perspectives on how to extend existing theories by accounting for four specific aspects of the home country institutional environments of emerging economies: breadth,

Emerging Economies and Multinational Enterprises
Advances in International Management, Volume 28, 45–69

ISSN: 1571-5027/doi:10.1108/S1571-502720150000028006

depth, timing, and duration of exposure to institutional development. We then discuss how the chapters in this volume extend these ideas.

Keywords: Emerging market multinationals; home country institutions; firm-specific advantages

In 2015, like in recent years, hardly a day goes by without emerging economies appearing in the news or academic research. In terms of news coverage, stories about emerging economies include *geo-political conflicts* (the Ukraine-Russia crisis or the Arab Spring); *economic success stories* (Nigeria hosting the World Economic Forum in 2014, China overtaking the United States as the largest economy in the world measured by purchasing power,[1] or the latest entry of former communist states such as Bulgaria, Romania, and Croatia into the European Union); *financial aspects* (the BRICS – Brazil, Russia, India, China, and South Africa – forming a New Development Bank that aims to re-balance the concentrated power of the International Monetary Fund (IMF) and the World Bank as the world's largest lenders for economic development, the recent downgrading of Greece, South Korea, and Taiwan from advanced to emerging economies,[2] or the rise of Chinese-based Alibaba as the largest initial public offering in U.S. history[3]); and *socio-cultural events* (Brazil's hosting of the FIFA World Cup in 2014, Russia's hosting of the Winter Olympics in 2014, or India's first launch of a Mars-bound exploration rocket[4]). Projections are that by 2025, emerging economies will constitute approximately 45% of the Fortune 500 Global rankings – a significant increase from the 5% they represented in 2000 (McKinsey, 2013).

In terms of academic research, although there were 99 published papers on emerging economies between 2001 and 2005 in the top international business and strategy journals, the number has increased to 161 for 2006–2010 (Xu & Meyer, 2013). This trend has continued strong, with more journals publishing special issues that cover various aspects of emerging economies, including the 2011 special issue on emerging economy firm competitiveness in the *Journal of International Management*,[5] the 2012 focus on global strategy and emerging economies in the *Global Strategy Journal*,[6] the 2013 special issue on country of origin effects in emerging economies in the *Asia Pacific Journal of Management*,[7] the 2014 special issues on institutional voids and state-owned enterprises (SOEs) in emerging economies in the *Journal of International Business Studies,*[8,9] and the 2015 special issue on emerging economy multinationals from Latin America in the *Journal of World Business.*[10] Recent influential books have also increased our understanding of emerging economies and their home-grown and foreign multinationals (e.g., Ciravegna, Fitzgerald, & Kundu, 2014; Cuervo-Cazurra & Ramamurti, 2014; Hansen, Larsen, Pedersen, Petersen, & Wad, 2010; Nolke, 2014; Ramamurti & Singh, 2009; Sauvant, 2008; Tihanyi, Devinney, & Pedersen, 2012; Williamson, Ramamurti, Fleury, & Fleury, 2013).

WHAT IS AN EMERGING ECONOMY?

A common theme across the news and academic research is the abundance of definitions used to differentiate emerging economies from their advanced country counterparts. Hoskisson, Eden, Lau, and Wright (2000, p. 249) provided one of the first specific definitions of emerging economies in the management literature: "low-income, rapid growth countries using economic liberalization as their primary engine of growth." Hoskisson, Wright, Filatotchev, and Peng (2013) further differentiated among four types of emerging economies based on their levels of institutional development and infrastructure/factor market development: traditional emerging economies (low-low on both types of development), mid-range emerging economies (high infrastructure/factor market development-low institutional development), mid-range emerging economies (high institutional development-low infrastructure/factor market development), and newly developed economies (high-high on both types of development). Others have followed the IMF's breakdown of countries into advanced and developing economies (e.g., Cuervo-Cazurra, 2012). The IMF's category of developing countries includes less developed or low-income countries with underdeveloped industrial infrastructure, and emerging economies or "high growth countries that are not advanced economies" (Cuervo-Cazurra, 2012, p. 153). The World Bank provides yet another categorization by using GDP per capita to designate countries into low-income, middle-income, and high-income, with the developing countries clustering around the low- and middle-income categories (World Bank, 2014). Additionally, some research has used the Morgan Stanley Capital International (MSCI) Emerging Markets Index to define emerging economies (e.g., Erb,

Harvey, & Viskanta, 2000; Gelos & Wei, 2005). MSCI defines countries as emerging based on economic development, size, liquidity, and market accessibility criteria (MSCI Market Classification Framework, 2014; MSCI Index of Emerging Markets (2014)).

Despite these nuanced definitions, most scholars agree on a few common elements that make up emerging economies – that is, rapid economic growth from pro-market reforms and institutional voids that increase the risk and uncertainty of doing business there (Cuervo-Cazurra, 2012; Hoskisson et al., 2000; Hoskisson, Johnson, Tihanyi, & White, 2005; Xu & Meyer, 2013).

THE DEBATE ON THE UNIQUENESS OF EMERGING ECONOMY MULTINATIONALS

The renewed interest in emerging economies and their companies has generated a debate in the literature regarding how unique the multinationals from emerging economies (i.e., home-grown multinationals) really are. Some scholars have argued that emerging economy companies are different from their advanced country counterparts due to the underdeveloped institutions in emerging economies and, hence, merit the development of their own theories (e.g., Guillen & Garcia-Canal, 2009; Luo & Tung, 2007). Conversely, other scholars have noted that the emerging economy multinational is just another type of a multinational enterprise and the existing general theories are fully capable of explaining its strategies (e.g., Dunning, Kim, & Park, 2008; Rugman, 2010; for a fuller overview of the debate, see Cuervo-Cazurra, 2012).

A third camp takes a more nuanced perspective. It finds value in both approaches and suggests that while brand-new theories are not necessarily warranted, extending current theories can be helpful to clarify the differences between emerging economy firms and their advanced country counterparts (e.g., Banalieva, Eddleston, & Zellweger, 2014; Cuervo-Cazurra, 2012; Cuervo-Cazurra & Genc, 2011; Liang, Ren, & Sun, 2015; Ramamurti, 2009, 2012). This third camp suggests that emerging economy multinationals are exposed to significant institutional voids in their domestic markets which usually increase the uncertainty and risk of doing business there. Thus, different dimensions of the domestic institutional environment create sufficient differentiation from advanced economy firms that can help further explain the successes and failures of multinational firms from emerging economies.

We next synthesize the different approaches to characterizing the home country's institutional environment that existing research has taken. We then make recommendations on how to extend existing theories that can help further clarify the debate on the uniqueness of multinationals from emerging economies.

CLARIFYING THE DEBATE: RECENT THEORETICAL EXTENSIONS ON EMERGING ECONOMY MULTINATIONALS

Recent research has clarified the debate by increasing our understanding of how the type (developed or emerging) and location (home or host country) of the institutional contexts can alter the predictions of existing theories when transferred to the context of emerging economy multinationals (Peng, Wang, & Jiang, 2008).

Some of this research has suggested that it is useful to extend existing theories about the ownership advantages of multinational firms with contextual factors such as the global context for internationalization (affecting the ease of internationalization), the stage of evolution of the multinational firm (affecting the degree of internationalization), the industry of the multinational (affecting the motives of internationalization), and the country of origin effects (affecting the liability of foreignness during internationalization; e.g., Ramamurti, 2012). This research has highlighted that emerging economy firms have an ownership advantage (e.g., political connections with the government, state financial support, etc.), which differs from the typical ownership advantage of advanced economy firms (e.g., sophisticated technology, marketing, etc.).

Other research has suggested that emerging economy multinationals are exposed to different dimensions of institutional environments in their home and host countries. Obligating, pressuring, and supporting institutional dimensions can affect the firms' competitive advantage vis-a-vis their advanced country counterparts operating in the same market (Cuervo-Cazurra & Genc, 2011). Obligating environments mandate companies to adapt, pressuring environments force companies to invest resources to develop capabilities for survival, and supporting environments enable the multinational firms' operations so that the multinationals do not have to invest resources to overcome deficiencies in the host environments. More recent research has further suggested that the home country's institutional environment includes administrative and market-based dimensions that can extend the predictions of agency theory, especially in the context of SOEs from emerging economies (Liang et al., 2015). While the administrative institutions align the interests of the manager (as the agent) and the state (as the principal) by relying on political connections, market-based institutions rely on ownership arrangements that can increase the agency costs between the state, the SOEs, and the foreign subsidiary managers. Thus, emerging economy SOEs adjust their international strategies depending on which of these dimensions prevails.

COMPLEMENTARY THEORETICAL PERSPECTIVES ON EMERGING ECONOMY MULTINATIONALS

We next build on this prior research and suggest four complementary perspectives of the institutional environment that can further extend existing theories on emerging economy multinationals: breadth, depth, timing, and duration of exposure to the process of institutional development in the home country. In so doing, we address recent calls in the literature that existing theories can also be extended by considering further topics from the perspective of the home country of the emerging economy firm and clarifying how they modify existing theoretical explanations (Cuervo-Cazurra, 2012). We use the term institutional development broadly to refer to the institutional progress emerging economies make toward reaching developed country status.

Our proposed four aspects of institutional development aim to make two core contributions to theory. First, we suggest that the institutional development of emerging economies can be analyzed from a static or dynamic perspective. The static perspective captures the policy achievements of the local government in a given year and offers a contemporaneous view on institutional development. It is reflected in the breadth and depth of the institutional development in a given year. The dynamic perspective captures the policy processes that unfold over time and offers a historical view on institutional development. It is reflected in the timing and duration of exposure to the institutional development over time. Second, we further review how the chapters in this volume extend our understanding of these dimensions of institutional development. Table 1

Table 1. Complementary Theoretical Perspectives on Emerging Economy Multinationals.

Dimension of Institutional Development in Home Country	STATIC (A Contemporaneous Perspective in a Given Year)		DYNAMIC (A Historical Perspective over Time)	
	Breadth	Depth	Timing	Duration of exposure
Definition	The spectrum of pro-market reforms (broad vs. narrow) that the emerging economy government takes to develop the country in a given year	The degree of active government ownership (extensive vs. limited) of an emerging economy in a given year	The rate of change (fast vs. slow) in the institutional development of the emerging economy over time	The length of time (short vs. long) to which the emerging economy firm has been exposed to the government development policies over time
Key theories dimension relates to	Institutional economics, entrepreneurship theories	Agency theory, varieties of capitalism, institutional economics	Institutional economics, economic complementarities	Imprinting, institutional economics, evolutionary economics
Key assumption of each dimension	A wider range of reforms raise profit-maximizing incentives and reduce reliance on informal economy	Single-agency (principal-agent) conflicts	Radial reforms can lead to a theoretical First Best outcome of optimal welfare	Firms are imprinted by the historical conditions at founding, which persist over time
Modification of key assumption	The Washington Consensus has increased social inequality in emerging economies: can consider social benefits from reforms too for a more sustainable development	Varieties of capitalism create additional heterogeneity and conflicting goals among principals and agents in SOEs, even more so in SOE multinationals: can consider SOE heterogeneities	First Best outcome may be difficult to achieve in practice: can consider Second Best outcomes too	Emerging economy firms are imprinted by the past but they learn to function under reforms too: can consider limits of distant imprinting and opportunities from recent imprinting
Existing theoretical extensions	• The Washington Consensus (scope of pro-market reforms) • Minimum threshold of the Washington Consensus to raise firm performance	• Degree of state ownership (full, majority, or minority) • Locus of state power (central vs. local) • Dual agency conflict in SOEs: Principal: citizens, Agent 1:	• Average speed of reforms in reform portfolio (rapid or gradual), effect on family versus non-family firms • Synchronization of reform speeds in reform portfolio	• Manager entered workforce during communism versus reforms (individual-level) • Company founded before versus after start of reforms (firm-level) • Time with reform (country-level)

Table 1. *(Continued)*

Dimension of Institutional Development in Home Country	STATIC (A Contemporaneous Perspective in a Given Year)		DYNAMIC (A Historical Perspective over Time)	
	Breadth	Depth	Timing	Duration of exposure
	• Effect of Washington Consensus policies on the behavior of different types of emerging economy firms (private vs. SOE, business group-affiliated vs. nonaffiliated, local vs. foreign, multinational vs. non-multinational)	politicians, Agent 2: SOE managers hired by politicians • Triple agency conflict in SOE MNEs: Principal: citizens, Agent 1: politicians, Agent 2: SOE headquarter managers, Agent 3: SOE subsidiary managers	(horse-race), effect firms with different resource endowments (excess vs. insufficient)	
Complementary theoretical extensions for future research	• The Beijing Consensus (Scope of sociomarket reforms) • Chinese MNEs entering other emerging economies that have followed a Washington Consensus style of reforms: opportunities and challenges	• Interaction between degree of state ownership and locus of state power (four cases: central-majority, central-minority, local-majority, local-minority) • Quadruple agency conflict in SOE MNEs: triple agency conflict in SOEs + Agent 1a: central govt; Agent 1b: local govt	• Velocity of reforms at home and effect on emerging market multinationals • Sequencing of economic, social, political, and legal reforms at home and effect on emerging market multinationals	• Duration of firm's exposure to communism/reforms • The co-evolution between firm's communist/reform imprints and country's institutions

synthesizes our complementary perspectives on emerging economy multinationals, which we describe next.

Breadth of Institutional Development

The breadth of institutional development of the home country of an emerging economy multinational refers to the spectrum of pro-market reforms (broad vs. narrow) that the local government implements to develop the country in a given year. The more the institutions improve toward market economy (reverse toward central planning), the greater (smaller) the breadth of institutional development.

Pro-market reforms are government policies of economic development that aim to accomplish three key goals: achieve macroeconomic stability, increase the scope of the private sector in the economy, and open up the market to new foreign and domestic competition (Williamson & Haggard, 1994). They are referred to as the Washington Consensus as they are supported by institutions located in Washington D.C.: the IMF and the World Bank. Existing firm-level research on the effect of Washington Consensus policies on the behavior of emerging economy firms has focused on firm performance, persistence of superior profits, internationalization, and entrepreneurship. Extending the institutional, economic geography, and knowledge-based theories, studies have found that firms benefit from greater (e.g., Banalieva et al., 2014; Cuervo-Cazurra & Dau, 2009; Dau, 2012a; Kim, Kim, & Hoskisson, 2010; Park, Li, & Tse, 2006) and synchronized (Banalieva, 2014; Gates, Milgrom, & Roberts, 1996) Washington-style pro-market reforms due to increased profit-maximizing incentives for managers. Washington-style policies may also decrease the persistence of superior profits for emerging economy firms as they struggle to maintain competitive positions after increased competition (Chari & David, 2012). While reforms may initially hurt performance for emerging economy firms, they can ultimately improve their performance as local governments implement complementary reforms (Chari & Banalieva, 2014). Additionally, Washington-style policies at home encourage firms in emerging economies to internationalize more in response to declining local institutional imperfections (Dau, 2012b). Other recent studies have also analyzed how specific components of the Washington-style pro-market reforms affect formal and informal entrepreneurship across both developed and emerging economies (Dau & Cuervo-Cazurra, 2014). Economic liberalization increased both types of entrepreneurship, but governance reforms had a differential impact: they increased formal and decreased informal entrepreneurship. While radical pro-market reforms increase opportunity recognition for entrepreneurs operating in the informal economy, bureaucracy first increases and then decreases it (Webb, Bruton, Tihanyi, & Ireland, 2013). Webb, Tihanyi, Ireland, and Sirmon (2009) further extended this theory by distinguishing between the formal, informal, and degenerate economy and how each contribute to entrepreneurship (opportunity recognition and exploitation) in emerging economies.

In addition to these Washington-style policies for economic development, other studies have begun analyzing an alternative, narrower scope of policies – the Beijing Consensus (e.g., Halper, 2010; Huang, 2010; McKinnon, 2010; Ramo, 2004). The Beijing Consensus is similar to the Washington Consensus in its aspiration for economic development, but it differs from it in terms of the means to achieve it. These means can be summarized in three key policies, significantly fewer than Williamson's 10 prescribed policies for the Washington Consensus (Ramo, 2004; Williamson, 2010).

First, the Beijing Consensus aims to grow the market by innovation and experimentation to discover which policies work and which do not work. Unlike the Washington Consensus, the Beijing Consensus aims to accomplish this goal without the need to start from fundamentals. Ramo (2004, p. 20) offers the following analogy as an example: "It is better, in this worldview, to wire some of the country with fiber-optics instead of patiently waiting to wire everything with copper first." Thus, the Beijing Consensus aims to achieve improvements faster than the problems these improvements could create (Ramo, 2004). Second, the Beijing Consensus aims to grow the market gradually and sustainably; that is, by crossing the river holding onto one stone at a time (McKinnon, 2010). The focus is on raising people out of poverty and into the middle class, while enhancing their quality of life. The Beijing Consensus considers stable development to be a prerequisite for the sustainable and equitable growth of the country. As Ramo (2004, p. 29) notes: "what is most notable about the Beijing Consensus is not its departure from Washington Consensus values, but rather that it begins its analysis of the problem from a whole different place: the individual." Third, The Beijing Consensus aims to grow the market through self-determination and the use of leverage to hedge against external influences of the advanced economies. The policymakers' underlying belief here is that all nations are created equal regardless of size and should be treated with equal respect. As Ramo (2004, p. 38) clarifies, the Beijing Consensus emphasizes that "every nation can be a power in its own right. Perhaps not powerful enough for domination, but at least strong enough for self-determination."

While some scholars suggest that the Beijing Consensus may be better for economic development (Ramo, 2004), others note the Washington Consensus fits China's growth strategies better (Huang, 2010). Future research can compare whether either the Washington or Beijing Consensus has a stronger effect on the competitive advantage, entrepreneurship, innovation, or internationalization strategies of home-grown emerging economy multinationals or foreign multinationals entering the emerging economy. It is possible that advanced economy multinationals that have benefited from efficiency-based Washington-style reforms at home may find it challenging to operate under the socio-market-based Beijing-style policies when entering emerging economies like China. Such policies may require stronger embeddedness with local government and business networks, as well as cultural traditions that foreign companies may be slower to capitalize on. An example is the failure of U.S.-based eBay in China after Chinese-based Alibaba drove the foreign competitor out of the Chinese market. While eBay focused on functionality and efficiency in China, Alibaba created an all Chinese consumer-to-consumer (C2C) e-commerce experience – Taobao – that was made by Chinese for the Chinese and introduced to the Chinese market. Contrary to eBay's globally standardized site EachNet, Alibaba's CEO Jack Ma customized Taobao to fit Chinese consumer tastes: no initial fee policy, colorful and dynamic website resembling a traditional Chinese teahouse, employees selecting names from popular kung fu characters, direct communication between buyers and sellers, and a popular payment platform through Alipay (for further details, see Xin, Nie, & Pucik, 2012). Alibaba also established a strong business group network that became a key element of its competitive advantage in China: in addition to Alipay and Taobao, Alibaba launched an online advertizing exchange (Alimama), partnered with Yahoo! China to take ownership of their Chinese operations, and invested in an online business software platform (Alisoft). Additionally, Alibaba established strong connections with local governments that became another core element of its competitive advantage in China. Since Alibaba enhanced the local economy and society through job creation and positive online consumer experiences, the local government, in return, created policies to protect the e-commerce giant (Greeven et al., 2010). Mr. Liang Lu, Taobao's Senior Director for Wireless Businesses, notes "we are very dependent on the government and have to be cautious and nurture a good relationship with it" (Greeven et al., 2010).

Depth of Institutional Development

The depth of institutional development of the home country of an emerging economy multinational refers to the degree of active government ownership (extensive vs. limited) of an emerging economy in a given year. The more the state releases control of the economy and relegates it to the private sector, the deeper the institutional development toward an advanced country status in the emerging economy, and vice versa. As such, the depth of institutional development involves some combination of old (centrally planned) and new (market-based) features of the institutional environment (Aoki, Jackson, & Miyajima, 2007), which result in varieties of state capitalism across emerging economies (Hall & Soskice, 2001; Li, Cui, & Lu, 2014; Musacchio & Lazzarini, 2014).

State capitalism has been on the rise. While there were only 11 SOEs among the top 100 firms in the Fortune 500 Global in 2005, the number increased to 25 in 2010 (Musacchio & Lazzarini, 2014). Although there were no SOEs among the top 10 Fortune 500 Global firms in 2005, there were four SOEs in 2010 (Musacchio & Lazzarini, 2014). Existing firm-level research on the varieties of state capitalism has adopted agency theory and institutional economics perspectives. Specifically, studies have analyzed the degree of government ownership (full, majority, or minority) of SOEs from emerging economies (Musacchio & Lazzarini, 2014), the locus of government power (central vs. local government) in these SOEs (Li et al., 2014), and the possible agency conflicts that arise among various principals and agents in both internationalizing and non-internationalizing SOEs (Cuervo-Cazurra, Inkpen, Musacchio, & Ramaswamy, 2014).

With respect to the degree of government ownership, Musacchio and Lazzarini (2014) differentiate between the old (1970s–1980s) and new (post-1990s) models of state capitalism. Under the old model of a typical centrally planned economy, the state was viewed as a Leviathan with full and active ownership of nationalized firms, which for the most part prohibited other investors from owning a stake in the firms. Thus, the state was conceived as a "grabbing hand" that reduced economic efficiency (Shleifer & Vishny, 1998). Conversely, the new model of modern state capitalism differentiates between various degrees of government ownership in private firms, while allowing for other types of investors too. The government can hold a majority stake in private firms (Leviathan as a majority owner). For instance, although the state is the majority shareholder of Agricultural Bank of China, private investors are allowed to hold shares too (Musacchio & Lazzarini, 2014). Other types of firms with the government as a majority owner can also include partially privatized companies such as public SOEs that have improved governance and greater management autonomy. The government can also hold a minority stake in private firms through sovereign wealth funds, pension funds, or the government itself (Leviathan as a minority owner). For instance, companies that receive loans and some equity funds from state-owned or development banks can fit this category (Musacchio & Lazzarini, 2014). Musacchio and Lazzarini (2014) find that Leviathan as a minority investor includes 20–30% of the SOEs, with the rest being majority-owned by the government. Thus, this new model of state capitalism conceives of the government as a "helping hand" that can help reduce market failure through the use of industrial policy (Musacchio & Lazzarini, 2014). Accordingly, research suggests that "even if the new forms of state ownership we study are a second best solution from the point of view of economic efficiency, they are a solution that is often politically acceptable" (Musacchio & Lazzarini, 2014, p. 18).

With respect to the locus of government power, Li et al. (2014) differentiate between SOEs that are owned by the central (i.e., federal, national) government versus SOEs that are owned by the local (i.e., provincial) government in emerging economies. The authors suggest that this is an important type of heterogeneity among SOEs because it leads to the SOEs behaving according to different logics in the market place. Centrally owned SOEs have been typically consolidated into national champions that must achieve a government mandate of a specific industrial policy that focuses on welfare rather than profit maximization. Conversely, locally owned SOEs have received greater management autonomy to set their own business priorities that focus on profit rather than welfare maximization (Li et al., 2014). As such, locally owned SOEs are more nimble in acquiring market information about their consumers and adapting to the changing institutions at home than their centrally owned counterparts. Because of their lower dependence on government resources, locally owned SOEs more likely enter foreign markets gradually through business groups (rather than undiversified), through a joint ownership (rather than sole), or through greenfield investments (rather than acquisition) than their nationally owned SOEs (Li et al., 2014).

With respect to agency conflicts, the simple principal-agent problem occurring in private firms is complicated in the context of these different types of state capitalism. Specifically, research has differentiated between agency conflicts in purely domestic SOEs versus in SOE multinationals (Cuervo-Cazurra et al., 2014). On one hand, there is a dual agency conflict in purely domestic SOEs. The key principals of SOEs are the citizens of the country on whose behalf the government owns the companies. However, there are two key agents: the politicians who are "hired" by the citizens to manage the SOE and the managers of the SOE who are "hired" by the politicians to manage the SOE. On the other hand, there is a triple agency conflict in SOE multinationals. The agency conflicts in domestic SOEs are further complicated by the presence of a third agency problem, which emerges between the SOE managers at headquarters at home and the SOE managers in the foreign subsidiary.

Future studies can examine the interaction between the degree of government ownership and the locus of government power and their effects on the behavior of emerging economy multinationals. Four theoretical cases can be outlined from such an interaction: (1) central-majority; (2) central-minority; (3) local-majority; and (4) local-minority. The agency conflicts are likely to be worsened under cases (1) and (3) that involve the government as a majority owner because the citizens are unable to employ monitoring mechanisms to oversee how well their agents (the government) implement policies of national welfare and development. It is also theoretically interesting to analyze possible triple agency conflicts (or quadruple in the case of SOE multinationals) if the locus of government power is further explored. Does the local government act as an agent on behalf of the central government as the principal? If so, such agency conflicts between the different branches of government further complicate and modify the baseline agency conflicts identified in current research.

Timing of Institutional Development

The timing of institutional development of the home country of an emerging economy multinational refers to the rate of change (fast vs. slow) in the institutional environment over time. The rate of change is movement in the scope of reforms over time, capturing the speed with which institutions develop (i.e., the speed of reforms) (Heybey & Murrell, 1999). The faster (slower) the speed of reforms in an emerging economy, the faster (slower) the emerging economy approaches an advanced country status.

As emerging economies implement a number of reforms, the reforms can be perceived as a portfolio (e.g., Banalieva, 2014; Banalieva et al., 2014; Braga de Macedo & Martins, 2008; Gates et al., 1996; Heybey & Murrell, 1999). Studies have analyzed the average speed of reforms (e.g., Banalieva et al., 2014; Heybey & Murrell, 1999) and synchronization of reforms in the portfolio (e.g., Banalieva, 2014; Braga de Macedo & Martins, 2008; Gates et al., 1996). The average speed of reforms captures the average rate of change (rapid or gradual) across the reforms. Economists have debated what average speed of reforms is best for countries' welfare. Research has found that Chinese family firms outperform non-family firms under gradual reforms and Chinese non-family firms perform better under faster reforms (Banalieva et al., 2014), providing a nuanced perspective on the debate. As the average speed does not differentiate among the timing of the different reforms (simultaneous or sequenced), the synchronization of reform speeds provides an alternative perspective by also capturing the degree of coordination across the reform speeds. It thus adopts a horse-race view on the reform portfolio. Economists have debated if a horse-race of "radial" reforms ("proportional reductions in all distortions at the same time" Braga de Macedo & Martins, 2008, p. 142) is an achievable First Best outcome. Research has found that Eastern European incumbent firms with excess high-discretion slack obtain greater performance gains from faster reform synchronization; they have sufficient resources to adapt as the returns from one reform are augmented with the concurrent implementation of other reforms (Banalieva, 2014; Braga de Macedo & Martins, 2008; Gates et al., 1996).

Future research can explore how the timing of institutional development affects the internationalization, governance, or innovation strategies of emerging economy firms. Different timing components – for example, velocity of reforms that captures the direction (forward or backward) of institutional change or sequencing of reforms that captures the order of reforms – can be also considered. How does the velocity of reform affect firms' competitive advantage and capability development? The sequencing of different types of reforms beyond the economic reforms traditionally analyzed in the literature – for example, social, political, or legal reforms – and how it affects the internationalization strategies of home-grown multinationals and foreign multinationals entering the emerging economies can also be explored. Do firms benefit if political reforms are implemented before economic reforms in an effort to avoid the potential loss of political good will to complete initiated reforms? Should legal reforms be implemented before or after stabilizing the economy and what effect does this have on the strategies of emerging market multinationals, both home-grown and foreign entrants?

Duration of Exposure to Institutional Development

The duration of exposure to institutional development of the home country of an emerging economy multinational refers to the length of time (short vs. long) to which the emerging economy firm has been exposed to the country development policies over time. A firm's duration of exposure to a country's institutional development policies is not necessarily of the same length as a country's exposure to the policies as analyzed in some prior country-level research (e.g., Khoury & Peng, 2011). For instance, the firm may have been founded after the start of the specific reforms, in which case the firm's duration of exposure to those reforms would be shorter than the country's exposure to the reforms.

Broadly, the ideologies of economic development range from communism in transition economies (where the government controls all production/distribution) (Tihanyi & Hegarty, 2007) to capitalism in advanced economies (whereby the private sector manages production/distribution and the government simply facilitates commerce, Williamson & Haggard, 1994). During short periods of susceptibility such as, for example, the time of company founding, firms adopt key features of their institutional environment that tend to persist over time; that is, the organizations become imprinted by the institutional ideology under which they were founded and which persists after founding (Marquis & Tilcsik, 2013; Shinkle & Kriauciunas, 2012; Stinchcombe, 1965). Thus, the longer an emerging economy firm has operated under either economic development ideology after founding, the longer the firm's duration of exposure to the respective types of policies.

Existing institutional imprinting research has focused on comparing the behavior of managers and firms before versus after the start of pro-market reforms in transition economies. At the individual-level, some studies have analyzed how such a communist versus reform imprinting affects the subordinate influence ethics of managers (e.g., Danis, Liu, & Vacek, 2011). Others have also compared the probability of becoming an entrepreneur between Eastern and Western German people, finding that older East Germans are less likely to be self-employed than their West German counterparts (Wyrwich, 2013). At the firm-level, the founding communist institutional imprint significantly increased two types of competitive aspirations of transition economy firms – that is, customer satisfaction and quality improvements (Shinkle & Kriauciunas, 2012). The current promarket institutional imprint significantly increased all four types of competitive aspirations the authors studied – export and domestic growth, customer satisfaction, and quality improvements (Shinkle & Kriauciunas, 2012). The interaction between current and founding institutional imprints reflected a significant decrease in the firms' competitive aspirations in terms of export growth, customer satisfaction, and quality improvement (Shinkle & Kriauciunas, 2012). Additionally, firms founded in China's state socialist period (1955–1992) have been found to be more likely to adopt social insurance provisions (i.e., medical, unemployment, and retirement insurance) than their counterparts in China's market socialist period (1993 onward) (Han, Zheng, & Xu, 2014).

Future research can also analyze the duration of exposure emerging economy firms, especially those from transition economies with prolonged histories of communism, have to these founding imprints. Communist imprints likely have an expiration date, but current research is yet to analyze this more deeply (Marquis & Tilcsik, 2013). How long does it take for a communist (or reform) imprint to subside over time? Can it be completely eradicated or does it remain as an indelible part of the organizational memory? Can communist and reform imprints reinforce or cancel each other out? Do the different durations of exposure of emerging economy firms to various institutional ideologies affect the development of these ideologies and vice versa? Evolutionary economics has suggested that firms and environments coevolve; however, does longer communist exposure, affect policymakers' choices for certain types of government policies, and vice versa? More research is needed for a better understanding of how institutions and companies' imprints coevolve in emerging economies.

PERSPECTIVES ON EMERGING ECONOMIES AND MULTINATIONAL ENTERPRISES: THE CHAPTERS IN THIS VOLUME

We outlined four goals for the 2015 Volume of the *Advances in International Management* in our Call for Papers. Specifically, we wanted to

- conceptualize the co-evolution of and dynamic interaction between emerging markets and foreign and home-grown multinational firms,
- examine the rise of home-grown multinational firms in emerging economies and the challenges they face when they enter developed markets, and

- provide an overview of successful strategies that foreign multinationals have adopted in emerging economies,
- publish a collection of papers with original ideas and theoretical advances that will provide the foundation for future doctoral dissertations and other research projects on emerging economies.

The chapters published on the following pages of this volume offer interesting theoretical insights and new empirical evidence on the challenges multinational enterprises face in emerging economies and on the rise of emerging economy multinationals.

The first chapter by Cuervo-Cazurra examines the co-evolutionary process between pro-market reforms in home countries and the transformation of domestic firms into emerging economy multinationals. Using institutional economics and evolutionary economics perspectives, the author theorizes how different mechanisms, such as learning, spillovers, and lobbying, enhance promarket reforms and how firm, industry, and country characteristics, in turn, shape the co-evolutionary process. In so doing, the author provides fresh insights into the dynamic dimension of co-evolutionary processes between institutions and firms. Adding to this co-evolutionary perspective, Kim and Hoskisson's chapter contributes to the understanding of the environmental origins of competitive advantage in emerging economies. They propose *a resource environment view* to explain the "paradox of environmental embeddedness," the notion of differential effects of similar strategic factor markets and institutional conditions on firms that attempt to create and sustain their competitive advantage. Their work offers insights on how firms cope with the paradox of environmental embeddedness by using internal and external resource-oriented strategies.

Guo and Clougherty analyze in their chapter the implications of "Go Global" policies of China for the local state-owned and private firms. The authors provide valuable insights about the international behavior and strategies of two different firm populations, state-owned and private, and outline several policy implications that the Chinese government may consider to employ in order to facilitate outward foreign direct investment and economic growth. Accordingly, the authors provide valuable perspectives on the depth of economic development in emerging markets.

Corredor, Forero, and Somaya study how external and internal sources of knowledge influence the novelty of innovation outcomes in an emerging economy. Using data from the Colombian Innovation Survey, they demonstrate that both external and internal knowledge sources are valuable for innovation in an emerging economy context. However, they find that different types of innovation require different sources of knowledge. Although new-to-world innovation may come from the ideas of clients and interdisciplinary groups, less novel types of innovation are associated with non-scientific secondary knowledge. Thus, the authors reveal the importance of a wider breadth of institutional development for the innovation strategies of emerging market firms.

Adding to the breadth dimension of institutional development, Scalera, Perri, and Mudambi study how knowledge-intensive foreign direct investments shape local innovative arrangements in emerging economies. Their empirical study of the Chinese pharmaceutical industry shows that the industry includes several leading foreign multinational players that bring tremendous learning opportunities for local firms. However, they find that local firms are unable to realize these opportunities in the short term due to those local firms' insufficient absorptive capacity.

The following chapter by Xi, Reuer, and Klijn provides useful insights into the depth of institutional development and accompanying agency conflicts in emerging markets. The chapter is about the governance of international joint ventures in China. They argue that boards in joint ventures fulfill both control and collaboration roles depending on certain organizational attributes and environmental contexts. On the one hand, investments in knowledge-based assets and in joint ventures between culturally similar partners lead to boards' engagement in collaboration rather than in control. On the other hand, investments in specific assets or in acquisitive joint ventures are associated with greater control by the board.

Bhaumik, Driffield, and Zhou, in their chapter, investigate the sources of competitiveness and multinationality among Chinese and foreign multinational enterprises and Chinese domestic firms. They show that both types of multinational enterprises have significant advantages over their domestic counterparts. However, the sources of their productivity growth are different: scale economies for Chinese and technological progress for foreign multinationals. Thus, the authors shed more light to the importance of a wider breadth of institutional development for the competitive advantage of Chinese and foreign multinationals and Chinese domestic firms.

The lack of breadth of institutional development, which leads to large institutional voids and corruption, is also the focus of Godinez and Garita's chapter. They present the result of a qualitative study about corruption experienced by foreign multinational firms in an emerging market. After providing a review of the literature on corruption, the authors report interview evidence from 32 multinational firms operating in Guatemala.

They argue that the corruption levels in the firms' home countries relative to the level of corruption in the host country of Guatemala motivate foreign managers differently to accept or refuse the use of corruption in their dealings with local firms and government officers.

The next chapter by Chari introduces an integrated model of upgrading and catch-up by firms from rapidly growing emerging markets like India. He argues that upgrading takes place through four mechanisms, including spillovers from multinational enterprises, business and technology linkages, acquisitions, and internal R&D. His model takes the timing of institutional development as a context against which he analyzes several relevant firm and environmental factors that influence the four upgrading mechanisms. The chapter by Fleury, Shi, Fleury, Ferreira, Cordeiro, and Liang adopts a Comparative Historical Analysis perspective on multinationals' strategies: the authors investigate the international operations networks of emerging country multinationals during different historical time-frames. Their framework integrates prior research in international business and international operations management for SOEs and non-SOEs, thereby extending our knowledge on the depth and timing of institutional development in emerging markets. The authors use this framework to provide a comparative analysis of four leading emerging economy multinational firms from Brazil and China using field interviews.

Purkayastha, Manolova, and Edelman's chapter is about the internationalization of the Indian pharmaceutical industry in the more recent years after the start of market liberalization. Taking the breadth and depth of institutional development as a context, the authors investigate the relationship between innovation and internationalization with special attention to business group membership, a feature of the institutional environment of India and other emerging economies. Martin and Li, in their chapter, provide bibliographic analysis of the literature on the internationalization of emerging economy SOEs. Their comprehensive analysis covers important trends, a wide range of theories on the subject, and dominant methodologies. The authors make several helpful recommendations for researchers studying the strategies of SOEs from emerging markets, including precision in the use of key concepts, research on the foreign direct investments of emerging economy state-owned firms in less developed and other emerging economies, focusing on the collaboration among local and foreign state-owned and private firms, and studying the behavior of SOEs from different institutional contexts. Thus, Martin and Li contribute to our understanding of the breadth and depth of institutional development among emerging economies and the need to distinguish purely emerging from less-developed and advanced economies.

Another chapter that takes a finer-grained perspective on the breadth and depth of institutional development of countries is Gubbi and Sular's chapter. The subject of their chapter is the outward foreign direct investment of Turkish firms in the developed markets of the European Union. The authors find that Turkish firms often favor greenfield investments over other modes of entry and use the developed markets of the Union as springboards for their future internationalization as well as to obtain tax benefits. Furthermore, they are attracted by the quality of local infrastructure and education and central location of the developed market within the European Union, such as the Netherlands.

The next chapter by Hilb focuses on the foreign entry decision process by emerging market multinational firms. He examines the roles of organizational identity, organizational routines, and strategic frames in deciding the modes of foreign market entry. The chapter aims to extend the literature on strategic cognition by conceptualizing how institutional voids in emerging economies motivate the selection of certain modes of entry into foreign markets. The volume is concluded by a chapter that examines the effectiveness of springboard foreign direct investment by emerging economy firms. Chen and Aybar, in their study of domestic acquisitions by over 700 Turkish firms, investigate almost 200 acquisitions by firms that employ a springboard foreign direct investment strategy, which is a means by emerging economy multinational firms to increase their competitive advantage at home through the new knowledge and business partnerships they obtain in foreign markets.

NOTES

1. *Source*: http://www.newsweek.com/chinas-economy-overtakes-us-worlds-largest-276104 (October 26, 2014).
2. *Sources*: http://online.wsj.com/articles/msci-removes-korea-taiwan-from-developed-market-consideration-1402435763; http://www.msci.com/products/indexes/country_and_regional/em (October 26, 2014).
3. *Source*: http://money.cnn.com/2014/09/18/investing/alibaba-ipo-price-68-dollars-jack-ma/ (October 26, 2014).
4. *Source*: http://in.reuters.com/article/2014/06/30/india-space-pslv-modi-idINKBN0F50G520140630 (October 26, 2014).
5. *Source*: http://www.fox.temple.edu/cms/wp-content/uploads/2013/01/JIM-CallforPapers.pdf (October 26, 2014).

6. *Source*: http://onlinelibrary.wiley.com/doi/10.1002/gsj.v2.1/issuetoc (October 26, 2014).

7. *Source*: http://www.hampp-ejournals.de/hampp-verlag-services/get?file=/frei/JEEMS_3_2013_409 (February 14, 2015).

8. *Source*: http://www.palgrave-journals.com/jibs/cfp_institutional_voids.html (October 26, 2014).

9. *Source*: http://www.palgrave-journals.com/jibs/cfp_global_state_own_si.html (October 26, 2014).

10. *Source*: http://www.journals.elsevier.com/journal-of-world-business/call-for-papers/emerging-market-multinationals-perspectives-from-latin-ameri/ (October 26, 2014).

REFERENCES

Aoki, M., Jackson, G., & Miyajima, H. (2007). *Corporate governance in Japan: Institutional change* and organizational diversity. New York, NY: Oxford University Press.

Banalieva, E. R. (2014). Embracing the second best? Synchronization of reform speeds, excess high-discretion slack, and performance of transition economy firms. *Global Strategy Journal*, *4*(2), 104–126.

Banalieva, E. R., Eddleston, K., & Zellweger, T. (2014). When do family firms have an advantage in transitioning economies? Toward a dynamic institution-based view. *Strategic Management Journal*. doi:10.1002/smj.2288

Braga de Macedo, J., & Martins, J. O. (2008). Growth, reform indicators, and policy complementarities. *Economics of Transition*, *16*(2), 141–164.

Chari, M., & Banalieva, E. R. (2014). How do pro-market reforms impact firm profitability? The case of India under reform. *Journal of World Business*. Retrieved from http://dx.doi.org/10.1016/j.jwb.2014.05.004

Chari, M., & David, P. (2012). Sustaining superior performance in an emerging economy: An empirical test in the Indian context. *Strategic Management Journal*, *33*(2), 217–229.

Ciravegna, L., Fitzgerald, R., & Kundu, S. (Eds.). (2014). *Operating in emerging markets: A guide to management and strategy in the new international economy*. Upper Saddle River, NJ: FT Press.

Cuervo-Cazurra, A. (2012). Extending theory by analyzing developing country multinational companies: Solving the "goldilocks" debate. *Global Strategy Journal*, *2*, 153–167.

Cuervo-Cazurra, A., & Dau, L. (2009). Promarket reforms and firm profitability in developing countries. *Academy of Management Journal*, *52*, 1348–1368.

Cuervo-Cazurra, A., & Genc, M. (2011). Obligating, pressuring, and supporting dimensions of the environment and the non-market advantages of developing country multinational companies. *Journal of Management Studies*, *48*(2), 441–455.

Cuervo-Cazurra, A., Inkpen, A., Musacchio, A., & Ramaswamy, K. (2014). Governments as owners: State-owned multinational companies. *Journal of International Business Studies*, *45*, 919–942.

Cuervo-Cazurra, A. & Ramamurti, R. (Eds.). (2014). *Understanding multinationals from emerging markets*. Cambridge: Cambridge University Press.

Danis, W., Liu, L., & Vacek, J. (2011). Values and upward influence strategies in transition: Evidence from the Czech Republic. *Journal of Business Ethics*, *42*(2), 288–306.

Dau, L. (2012a). Learning across geographic space: Pro-market reforms, multinationalization strategy, and profitability. *Journal of International Business Studies*, *44*, 235–262.

Dau, L. (2012b). Pro-market reforms and developing country multinational corporations. *Global Strategy Journal*, *2*, 262–276.

Dau, L., & Cuervo-Cazurra, A. (2014). To formalize or not to formalize: Entrepreneurship and pro-market institutions. *Journal of Business Venturing*, *29*, 668–686.

Dunning, J., Kim, S.-H., & Park, S. (2008). Old wine in new bottles: A comparison of emerging market TNCs today and developed country TNCs thirty years ago. In K. Sauvant (Ed.), *The rise of transnational corporations from emerging markets: Threat or opportunity?* Northampton, MA: Edward Elgar.

Erb, C., Harvey, C., & Viskanta, T. (2000). The risk and expected returns of African equity investments. In P. Collier & C. Pattillo (Eds.), *Investment and risk in Africa*. Basingstoke: Macmillan.

Gates, S., Milgrom, P., & Roberts, J. (1996). Complementarities in the transition from socialism: A firm-level analysis. In J. McMillian & B. Naughton (Eds.), *Reforming Asian socialism: The growth of market institutions* (pp. 17–37). Ann Arbor, MI: University of Michigan Press.

Gelos, R., & Wei, S.-J. (2005). Transparency and international portfolio holdings. *Journal of Finance*, *LX*(6), 2987–3020.

Greeven, M., Yang, S., Heck, E., & Krug, B. (2010). The business network of the Alibaba Group: How the Alibaba Group's strategy and implementation in China is creating sustainable value for suppliers, partners, and customers? Case Development Center. Rotterdam School of Management, Erasmus University. Case #: 310-125-1.

Guillen, M., & Garcia-Canal, E. (2009). The American model of the multinational firm and the "new" multinationals from emerging economies. *Academy of Management Perspectives*, *23*, 23–35.

Hall, P., & Soskice, D. (2001). *Varieties of capitalism: The institutional foundations of comparative advantage*. Oxford: Oxford University Press.

Hall, P. A., & Soskice, D. (2001). *Varieties of capitalism: The institutional foundations of comparative advantage*. Oxford: Oxford University Press.

Halper, S. (2010). *The Beijing consensus: How China's authoritarian model will dominate the twenty-first century*. New York, NY: Basic Books.

Han, Y., Zheng, E., & Xu, M. (2014). The influence from the past: Organizational imprinting and firms' compliance with social insurance policies in China. *Journal of Business Ethics*, *122*, 65–77.

Hansen, M., Larsen, M., Pedersen, T., Petersen, B., & Wad, P. (Eds.). (2010). *Strategies in emerging markets: A case book on Danish multinational corporations in China and India*. Copenhagen: Copenhagen Business School Press.

Heybey, B., & Murrell, P. (1999). The relationship between economic growth and the speed of liberalization during transition. *The Journal of Policy Reform*, *3*(2), 121–137.

Hoskisson, R., Eden, L., Lau, C., & Wright, M. (2000). Strategy in emerging economies. *Academy of Management Journal*, *43*, 249–267.

Hoskisson, R., Johnson, R., Tihanyi, L., & White, R. (2005). Diversified business groups and corporate refocusing in emerging markets. *Journal of Management*, *31*, 941–965.

Hoskisson, R., Wright, M., Filatotchev, I., & Peng, M. (2013). Emerging multinationals from mid-range economies: The influence of institutions and factor markets. *Journal of Management Studies*, *50*(7), 1295–1321.

Huang, Y. (2010). Debating China's economic growth: The Beijing consensus or the Washington consensus. *Academy of Management Perspectives*, *24*(2), 31–47.

Khoury, T., & Peng, M. (2011). Does institutional reform of intellectual property rights lead to more inbound FDI? Evidence from Latin America and the Caribbean. *Journal of World Business*, *46*(3), 337–345.

Kim, H., Kim, H., & Hoskisson, R. (2010). Does market-oriented institutional change in an emerging economy make business group-affiliated multinationals perform better? An institution-based view. *Journal of International Business Studies*, *41*, 1141–1160.

Li, M., Cui, L., & Lu, J. (2014). Varieties in state capitalism: Outward FDI strategies of central and local state-owned enterprises from emerging economy countries. *Journal of International Business Studies*, *45*, 980–1004. Available online http://www.palgrave-journals.com/jibs/journal/v45/n8/full/jibs201414a.html.

Liang, H., Ren, B., & Sun, S. (2015). An anatomy of state control in the globalization of state-owned enterprises. *Journal of International Business Studies*, *46*, 223–240. Available online http://www.palgrave-journals.com/jibs/journal/v46/n2/full/jibs201435a.html.

Luo, Y., & Tung, R. (2007). International expansion of emerging market enterprises: A springboard perspective. *Journal of International Business Studies*, *38*, 481–498.

Marquis, C., & Tilcsik, A. (2013). Imprinting: Toward a multilevel theory. *Academy of Management Annals*, *7*, 193–243.

McKinnon, R. (2010). China in Africa: The Washington consensus versus the Beijing consensus. *International Finance*, *13*(3), 495–506.

McKinsey. (2013). *Urban world: The shifting global business landscape*. Retrieved from www.mckinsey.com/insights/urbanization/urban_world_the_shifting_global_business_land scape. Accessed on October 26, 2014.

MSCI Index of Emerging Markets. (2014). Retrieved from www.msci.com/products/indexes/country_and_regional/em. Accessed on October 26, 2014.

MSCI Market Classification Framework. (2014). Retrieved from http://www.msci.com/resources/products/indexes/global_equity_indexes/gimi/stdindex/MSCI_Market_Classi fication_Framework.pdf. Accessed on October 26, 2014.

Musacchio, A., & Lazzarini, S. (2014). *Reinventing state capitalism: Leviathan in business, Brazil and beyond.* Cambridge, MA: President and Fellows of Harvard College. Available online (http://www.amazon.com/Reinventing-State-Capitalism-Leviathan-Business/dp/0674729684#reader_0674729684)

Nolke, A. (Ed.). (2014). *Multinational corporations from emerging markets: State capitalism 3.0*. New York, NY: Pakgrave Macmillan.

Park, S., Li, S., & Tse, D. (2006). Market liberalization and firm performance during China's economic transition. *Journal of International Business Studies*, *37*, 127–147.

Peng, M. W., Wang, D. Y. L., & Jiang, Y. (2008). An institution-based view of international business strategy: A focus on emerging economies. *Journal of International Business Studies*, *39*, 920–936.

Ramamurti, R. (2009). What have we learned about emerging market MNEs? In R. Ramamurti & J. Singh (Eds.), *Emerging multinationals from emerging markets*. Cambridge, MA: Cambridge University Press.

Ramamurti, R. (2012). What is really different about emerging market multinationals? *Global Strategy Journal, 2*(1), 41–47.

Ramamurti, R., & Singh, J. (Eds.). (2009). *Emerging multinationals in emerging markets.* Cambridge: Cambridge University Press.

Ramo, J. (2004). *The Beijing consensus.* London: The Foreign Policy Centre.

Rugman, A. (2010). Do we need a new theory to explain emerging market MNEs? In K. Sauvant, W. Maschek, & G. McAllister (Eds.), *Foreign direct investments from emerging markets: The challenges ahead.* New York, NY: Palgrave McMillan.

Sauvant, K. (Ed.). (2008). *The rise of transnational corporations from emerging markets: Threat or opportunity?* Cheltenham: Edward Elgar Publishing Limited.

Shinkle, G., & Kriauciunas, A. (2012). The impact of current and founding institutions on strength of competitive aspirations in transition economies. *Strategic Management Journal, 33*, 448–458.

Shleifer, A., & Vishny, R. (1998). *The grabbing hand: Government pathologies and their cures.* Cambridge, MA: Harvard University Press.

Stinchcombe, A. (1965). Social structure and organizations. In J. G. March (Ed.), *Handbook of organizations* (pp. 142–193). Chicago, IL: Rand McNally and Co.

Tihanyi, L., Devinney, T., & Pedersen, T. (Eds.). (2012). Institutional theory in international business and management. In *Advances in International Management* (Vol. 25). Bingley, UK: Emerald Group Publishing Limited.

Tihanyi, L., & Hegarty, H. (2007). Political interests and the emergence of commercial banking in transition economies. *Journal of Management Studies, 44*(5), 788–813.

Webb, J., Bruton, G., Tihanyi, L., & Ireland, D. (2013). Research on entrepreneurship in the informal economy: Framing a research agenda. *Journal of Business Venturing, 28*(5), 598–614.

Webb, J., Tihanyi, L., Ireland, D., & Sirmon, D. (2009). You say illegal, I say legitimate: Entrepreneurship in the informal economy. *Academy of Management Review, 34*(3), 492–510.

Williamson, J. (2010). What Washington means by policy reform. In J. Williamson (Ed.), *Latin American adjustment: How much has happened?* Washington, DC: Institute for International Economics.

Williamson, J., & Haggard, S. (1994). The political conditions for economic reform. In J. Williamson (Ed.), *Political economy of policy reform* (pp. 527–596). Washington, DC: Institute for International Economics.

Williamson, P., Ramamurti, R., Fleury, A., & Fleury, M.-T. (eds.). (2013). *The competitive advantage of emerging market multinationals.* New York, NY: Cambridge University Press.

World Bank. (2014). *Country and lending groups.* Retrieved from http://data.worldbank.org/about/country-and-lending-groups#Low_income. Accessed on October 26, 2014.

Wyrwich, M. (2013). Can socioeconomic heritage produce a lost generation with regard to entrepreneurship? *Journal of Business Venturing, 28*, 667–682.

Xin, K., Nie, W., & Pucik, V. (2012). Alibaba vs. eBay: Competing in the Chinese C2C market (B) (Abridged). Case #: IMD-3-2319.

Xu, D., & Meyer, K. (2013). Linking theory and context: "Strategy research in emerging economies" after Wright et al. (2005). *Journal of Management Studies, 50*(7), 1322–1346.

THE CO-EVOLUTION OF PRO-MARKET REFORMS AND EMERGING MARKET MULTINATIONALS

Alvaro Cuervo-Cazurra

ABSTRACT

I study the relationship between pro-market reforms and the expansion of emerging market multinational companies (EMNCs). Extending institutional economics, I propose a co-evolutionary process, whereby pro-market reforms in emerging markets induce the transformation of domestic firms into EMNCs, and the global expansion of EMNCs in turn facilitates the deepening of pro-market reforms in the home country. Specifically, I first explain how pro-market reforms lead to the emergence of EMNCs via international competitiveness, upgrading needs, and escape; I then explain how the global expansion of EMNCs leads to a deepening of pro-market reforms at home via learning, spillovers, and lobbying. I complement these explanations with a discussion of contingencies at the firm (private vs. state, domestic vs. foreign firms),

Emerging Economies and Multinational Enterprises
Advances in International Management, Volume 28, 71–94

ISSN: 1571-5027/doi:10.1108/S1571-502720150000028007

industry (global vs. local industries), and country (developing vs. transition countries) levels.

Keywords: Pro-market reforms; emerging markets; multinationals; co-evolution; institutions; international business

INTRODUCTION

Emerging market multinationals (EMNCs) have become an important phenomenon in the 21st century. Although there have been EMNCs for over a century, it was not until the 2000s that significant flows of outward foreign direct investment (OFDI) originated from emerging markets. By 2013, the share of OFDI flows from emerging countries reached over one quarter of the world total, and the share of OFDI stocks reached over one tenth; these are significant numbers in comparison with the numbers from as recent as 2000, when both were about five percent (UNCTAD, 2014).

A puzzle about these firms is what drove them to emerge now, and not before or later. One traditional explanation is that as countries develop, their companies generate increasingly advanced products and technologies to satisfy their more sophisticated consumers, enabling the firms to expand abroad to sell to other sophisticated consumers (Dunning, 1981; Vernon, 1966). However, we now witness many emerging countries spawning multinationals at low levels of development. Hence, I argue that one important driver of the emergence of EMNCs in the 2000s has been the implementation of pro-market reforms in emerging economies in the 1980s and 1990s. I explain how these pro-market reforms dramatically altered the competitive conditions in emerging economies, leading domestic firms to become EMNCs via three mechanisms: (1) international competitiveness, in which the liberalization of actions brought by pro-market reforms enables firms to move toward levels of international competitiveness and compete abroad as EMNCs; (2) upgrading needs, in which increased competition brought by the reforms induces domestic firms to invest abroad and obtain sophisticated resources needed to face the increased competition at home; and (3) escape, in which the reduction of constraints on outward foreign direct investment that follows pro-market reforms enables domestic firms to become MNCs and escape weaknesses of the home country.

I also argue that the transformation of domestic firms into EMNCs and their global expansion results in a deepening of pro-market reforms in the home country. This is done via three mechanisms: (1) learning, in which

EMNCs learn more sophisticated rules and governance practices abroad, which they then apply in their relationships with customers, distribution channels, and suppliers at home, improving rules and norms of behavior in the home country; (2) spillovers, in which EMNCs become sources of spillover of better governance capabilities to home-country competitors via demonstration, employee mobility, and training of common suppliers and distribution channels; and (3) lobbying, in which EMNCs lobby their home governments to deepen the pro-market reforms from which they benefit.

These two processes, the influence of pro-market reforms on the creation of EMNCs and the influence of EMNCs on the deepening of pro-market reforms, generate a co-evolution of pro-market reforms and EMNCs. This co-evolutionary process linking the environment in which the firm operates with the actions of the firm (Baum & Singh, 1994; Madhok & Liu, 2006) provides a nuanced extension to institutional economics (North, 1990). It complements the top-down approach that has commonly argued that pro-market reforms alter the institutional environment of firms and firms modify their behavior as a result, with a bottom-up approach in which firm behavior results in changes in institutions in the home country. These two processes result in a reinforcing cycle or co-evolution.

The rest of the paper is organized as follows. In the next section, I briefly review the concepts and literature. I then explain how pro-market reforms lead to the creation of EMNCs, and how the global expansion of EMNCs leads to the deepening of pro-market reforms. After this I explain contingencies that modify the relationships and conclude the paper.

CONCEPTS AND RELATED LITERATURE

Pro-Market Reforms

Pro-market reforms are the transformations in the norms, rules, and regulations that influence the behavior of economic actors toward supporting market interactions. Pro-market reforms have been discussed in the literature under different names, such as structural reforms, institutional change, or the Washington consensus (Williamson, 1990, 2004). I use the term pro-market reforms to denote both the objective and directionality of changes in institutions. The term includes not only economic liberalization that enables market interactions but also improvements in national governance that facilitate market interactions (Cuervo-Cazurra & Dau, 2009a).

Pro-market reforms spread throughout the world in the 1980s and 1990s and have taken different forms depending on the type of country that undertook them. I distinguish three broad types. First, in advanced economies, pro-market reforms resulted in a movement from mixed economies, in which the governments took an active role after the economic crisis of 1929 and especially during reconstruction after the Second World War, toward free-market economies with limited government intervention. The governments retrenched from the economy, privatizing state-owned companies, deregulating industries and liberalizing prices (Yergin & Stanislaw, 1998). Second, in developing countries, pro-market reforms replaced the import substitution models of economic development (Bruton, 1998), which had been implemented in the 1940s, with export-led models. Governments stopped being the main drivers of economic development and instead let private investors and markets operate freely, opening the countries to imports and foreign investors. In addition to retrenching from the economy, privatizing state-owned companies, deregulating industries, and liberalizing prices, governments implemented sound macroeconomic policies that reduced inflation and leverage (Kuczynski & Williamson, 2003). Third, in transition economies, pro-market reforms replaced communist economic systems with capitalistic ones. Governments changed from being the only driver of the economy, deciding production levels and setting prices, to being one driver in collaboration with a newly emerging private sector. Pro-market reforms included not only the privatization of state-owned companies, deregulation of industries, and liberalization of prices, but also much deeper transformations of the economic systems, such as allowing private ownership of means of production, establishing commercial and contract laws, and creating financial markets (Blanchard, 1997; Kornai, 1992; Peng & Heath, 1996; Uhlenbruck, Meyer, & Hitt, 2003).

The analysis of pro-market reforms in management studies has generated a growing literature.[1] For example, some studies have analyzed the impact of pro-market reforms on profitability (Banalieva, 2014; Chari & David, 2011; Cuervo-Cazurra & Dau, 2009a; del Sol & Kogan, 2007; Park, Li, & Tse, 2006), internationalization (Cuervo-Cazurra & Dau, 2009b; Cuervo-Cazurra & Stal, 2011) or competitiveness upgrading (Kumaraswamy, Mudambi, Saranga, & Tripathy, 2012). Here I integrate ideas from these studies to analyze the impact on EMNCs.

Emerging Market Multinationals

EMNCs are multinationals, or firms with value added activities abroad, from emerging countries, which in this paper I consider to be the countries not classified as advanced by the IMF.[2] What sets EMNCs apart from the experiences of advanced economy MNCs, which underlay most theories of the MNC, is the influence of their country of origin (Cuervo-Cazurra, 2012). Emerging economies are characterized by underdeveloped economic and institutional conditions that affect firm behavior (Khanna & Palepu, 2010).

The literature on EMNCs started in the 1970s, analyzing the expansion of mostly state-owned companies in natural resources and light industries (Lall, 1983; Wells, 1983). In the 2000s, a new wave of EMNCs and related literature emerged, analyzing the expansion of private companies in high-tech industries, as well as state-owned firms (see, e.g., papers in the special issues edited by Aulakh, 2007; Cuervo-Cazurra, 2012; Gammeltoft, Barnard, & Madhok, 2010; Luo & Tung, 2007). Much of this literature focused on the factors and processes that enabled these companies to achieve levels of international competitiveness and, in some cases, become leaders in their industries (Awate, Larsen, & Mudambi, 2012; Kumaraswamy et al., 2012; Luo & Tung, 2007; Mathews, 2006). Other literature has focused on the determinants of internationalization (Cuervo-Cazurra, 2008; Guillen & Garcia-Canal, 2009; Luo & Wang, 2012). (For a more detailed assessment of research on EMNCs see contributions in Cuervo-Cazurra & Ramamurti, 2014a).

The analysis of EMNCs can serve as the basis for extending theory and solving the goldilocks debate (Cuervo-Cazurra, 2012), in which some studies argue that existing theories can be used to explain the behavior of EMNCs (Rugman, 2009; Rugman & Nguyen, 2014), other studies argue that new theories are needed to explain their behavior (Luo & Tung, 2007; Mathews, 2006), and yet other studies propose that EMNCs can be used as a laboratory for extending existing theories (Cuervo-Cazurra, 2012; Ramamurti, 2009, 2012). I follow the third route and extend institutional economics by looking at how changes in institutions in emerging markets via pro-market reforms affect EMNCs, and how these firms in turn affect the pro-market reforms, resulting in a co-evolution.

THE CO-EVOLUTION OF PRO-MARKET REFORMS AND EMNCS

I build the arguments on institutional economics (North, 1990) and its view of institutions as constraints on human behavior. Individuals and firms are free to operate within the institutional framework of the country. Institutions establish both limitations on the freedom of action as well as incentives on behavior.

I extend the theory by proposing a co-evolutionary explanation of the relationship between institutions and firm behavior. Most of the work on institutional economics and pro-market reforms follows a top-down approach, arguing that pro-market reforms implemented by the government alter the institutional and operational environment of firms and as a result modify their behavior (e.g., Banalieva, 2014; Chari & David, 2011; Cuervo-Cazurra & Dau, 2009a; Park et al., 2006); in our case this is the transformation of domestic firms into EMNCs. I complement this top-down approach with a bottom-up approach, in which the global expansion of EMNCs becomes the driver of a deepening of pro-market reforms in the home country. These two processes result in a reinforcing cycle or co-evolution. Fig. 1 illustrates the co-evolution between pro-market reforms and EMNCs and the contingencies that modify this process.

Pro-Market Reforms' Influence on EMNCs

I first analyze the top-down approach, in which country-level institutions, in our case pro-market reforms, affect firm-level behavior, in our case

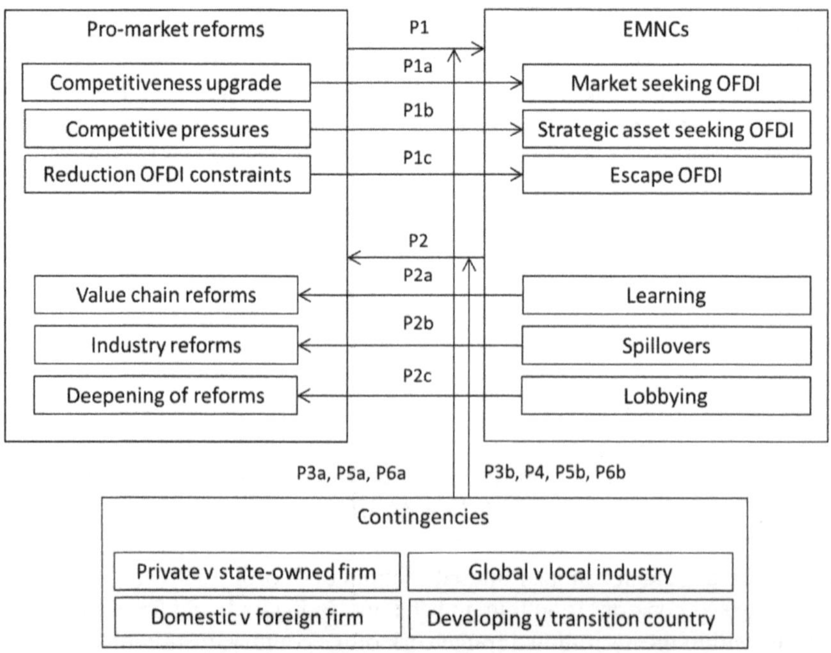

Fig. 1. The Co-Evolution of Pro-Market Reforms and EMNCs.

OFDI by emerging market firms which leads to the transformation of domestic firms into EMNC. I explain how pro-market reforms lead to the emergence and growth of EMNCs via three mechanisms: international competitiveness, upgrading need, and escape. The influence of these three mechanisms combined can be summarized in the following proposition:

> **Proposition 1.** Pro-market reforms have a positive impact on the emergence and growth of EMNCs.

The first mechanism is international competitiveness, in which the liberalization of actions brought by pro-market reforms enables firms to upgrade their competitiveness toward the international frontier, which helps them become EMNCs and serve customers in foreign countries in competition with local firms. This causality chain is enabled by the reduction of regulatory constraints, the liberalization of prices, and the privatization of state-owned companies (see a review in Armstrong & Sappington, 2006). First, the deregulation of the industry leads to an increase in competition, as entrepreneurs are free to enter the industry and foreign products and companies are allowed to enter the country and compete (Edwards, 1993; Tirole, 1988). In response to the increase in competition, incumbent companies undertake the upgrading of their capabilities (Kumaraswamy et al., 2012), helped in part by the deregulation of the industry that allows them to undertake the strategic actions they deem best rather than those allowed by the regulatory framework. This upgrading of capabilities toward the international frontier can be useful not only to face domestic and foreign competitors, but also to compete in other countries as companies reach the international frontier and internationalize (Cuervo-Cazurra & Dau, 2009b). Second, the liberalization of prices provides companies with incentives to upgrade capabilities and to innovate products and services that consumers demand and for which they can be paid a premium price. Companies that create new products can demand and obtain premium pricing now that they are free to set their own prices and no longer are constrained by government price controls. This creation of innovative products can help the firm not only serve domestic customers better but also serve customers abroad (Vernon, 1966). Third, the privatization of state-owned companies provides companies with new assets they can use to compete (Ramamurti, 2000; Vickers & Yarrow, 1995). Private firms can obtain complementary assets that were formerly in the hands of the state and increase the efficiency of these assets, improving their overall competitiveness (Cuervo & Villalonga, 2000; Megginson & Netter, 2001). Moreover, the privatization of state-owned firms leads to the creation of new private competitors that can move abroad to serve new customers instead of being constrained to achieving social objectives in the home country. These mechanisms result in a set of domestic companies with higher levels of competitiveness than before the reforms; those that are unable to upgrade their capabilities disappear (Kumaraswamy et al., 2012), while the reduction of constraints on actions enables companies to select actions they deem best to upgrade capabilities. As domestic companies arrive at international levels of competitiveness, they can use their sophisticated capabilities and innovative products to serve customers in new markets, increasing their profitability (Cuervo-Cazurra & Dau, 2009a). I summarize these arguments in the following proposition:

> **Proposition 1a.** The deregulation of actions that follows pro-market reforms has a positive impact on capability upgrading and subsequent OFDI to serve customers abroad (market-seeking OFDI).

The second mechanism is upgrading needs, in which the increased competition brought by the reforms induces domestic firms to become EMNCs to obtain sophisticated resources abroad to face the increased competition at home. As I discussed before, pro-market reforms lead to an increase in competitive pressures from new domestic entrants in the industry and from foreign products and firms that force domestic firms to upgrade their capabilities. However, emerging economies have weaker innovation systems than those prevalent in advanced economies, with lower levels of investment in R&D, fewer patents, less innovative universities, and less sophisticated education systems (OECD, 2014). These weaker innovation systems constrain the ability of domestic firms to upgrade capabilities, as they cannot rely as much on the environment for sophisticated employees, collaborators, or inputs (Khanna & Palepu, 2010). Thus, while emerging market firms can and do improve their capabilities to international levels, they still suffer some weaknesses such as in product innovation (Awate et al., 2012). A solution to the limitations of the home country in the provision of sophisticated technology to the firm is foreign expansion and the acquisition of such sophisticated technology from abroad (Luo & Tung, 2007; Mathews, 2006). Thus, emerging market firms become EMNCs and acquire companies in advanced economies to obtain sophisticated technological, managerial, and organizational capabilities they lack at home (Madhok & Keyhani, 2012). After the acquisition of the advanced economy firm, they can then transfer these sophisticated capabilities back to the home country to upgrade operations there and face the higher levels of competition brought by pro-market reforms. Hence, I propose that:

> **Proposition 1b.** The increased competition that follows pro-market reforms has a positive impact on OFDI in search of sophisticated capabilities (strategic asset seeking OFDI).

The third mechanism is escape, in which the reduction of constraints on OFDI that follows pro-market reforms enables domestic firms to become EMNCs and escape unfavorable institutional conditions in the home country. Some emerging market firms undertake escape investments that are facilitated by the reduction of constraints on foreign investment. Governments in emerging economies constrain the foreign exchange available to firms because investments abroad deplete foreign reserves in the country (Luo, Xue, & Han, 2010). For example, as recently as 2013 the Indian government restricted the foreign exchange that individuals and companies could take out of India to limit the depreciation of the Rupee (*BBCNews*, 2013). As pro-market reforms liberalize the exchange rate and firms are able to transfer money abroad, they engage in foreign direct investment. Although many do so to invest in the development of facilities to serve new markets and to acquire new capabilities, some may choose to invest abroad to escape the liabilities that companies suffer because they come from emerging markets. These escape investments can take several forms (Cuervo-Cazurra & Ramamurti, 2014b). First, institutional escape, in which the company establishes operations in countries with stronger institutions and a better rule of law to protect assets and contracts (Witt & Lewin, 2007). Second, transparency escape, in which the company invests in countries with higher privacy laws and less intrusive governments that enable the firm to disguise its identity. Some of these investments later become round tripping FDI (Geng, 2004), when the firm invests back in the home country and obtains benefits reserved for foreign investors. Third, discriminatory escape, in which the company seeks to reduce the connection with the country of origin by relocating its headquarters to an advanced country that has a better country-of-origin image (Barnard, 2014). Finally, the traditional tax escape, in which the company invests in offshore financial centers to reduce the tax burden the firm has to pay at home (Desai, Foley, & Hines, 2006). All these are facilitated by the reduction in restrictions on OFDI. I summarize these arguments in the following proposition:

Proposition 1c. The reduction of restrictions on OFDI that follows pro-market reforms has a positive impact on OFDI to escape the weak conditions of the home country (escape OFDI).

EMNCs' Influence on Pro-Market Reforms

I now analyze the bottom-up approach, in which firm-level actions, in our case the existence of EMNCs operating abroad, affect country-level actions, in our case pro-market reforms in the home country. I propose that the transformation of domestic companies into EMNCs and their presence abroad has a positive impact on the diffusion and deepening of pro-market reforms at home. A more detailed discussion of these ideas and mechanisms appears in Cuervo-Cazurra (2015). This is done via three channels: a learning mechanism, a lobbying mechanism, and a spillover mechanism. The combined influence of these three mechanisms can be summarized in the following proposition:

Proposition 2. EMNCs have a positive impact on the deepening of pro-market reforms in the home country.

The first mechanism is learning, in which EMNCs learn more sophisticated rules and governance practices abroad, which they then apply in their relationships with customers, distribution channels, and suppliers at home, improving rules and norms of behavior in the domestic environment. EMNCs are exposed to a variety of pro-market conditions in their foreign operations (del Sol & Kogan, 2007). In the particular case of EMNCs with operations in countries with higher levels of pro-market reforms, they have to learn and improve their institutional resources (Oliver, 1997) to be able to operate in those countries. This is challenging for many, as the institutional practices learned at home are difficult to unlearn abroad. For example, diplomats working in New York City who come from high corruption countries have more parking tickets, as parking tickets cannot be enforced thanks to diplomatic immunity (Fisman & Miguel, 2007). Nevertheless, managers do not enjoy such diplomatic immunity and thus need to behave according to the higher institutional standards or face penalties in countries with better institutions. EMNCs that want to operate in countries with stronger pro-market institutions have to adopt many of these pro-market institutions, including higher and stronger governance standards. For example, companies that list in advanced capital markets need to follow those stronger institutions and adopt higher standards of conduct (Coffee, 2002), which apply not only to the reporting and transparency in foreign operations but also to the whole company. These higher standards of conduct can be implemented not only within the company but also in its relationships with suppliers, distributors, and customers in the home country. For example, companies that issue financial instruments in US capital markets are subject to the Foreign Corrupt Practices Act (FCPA) and become subject to criminal penalties if they bribe abroad (Cuervo-Cazurra, 2006), providing them with an incentive to reduce corruption in the home country.

Alternatively, the desire to achieve efficiency in global operations induces companies to adopt similar superior practices across countries (Prahalad & Doz, 1987). Thus, even if the EMNC operates in other emerging markets where it is not exposed to higher levels of pro-market reforms, the exposure to a variety of levels of reforms across countries induces the EMNC to develop superior practices to manage efficiently across borders. The practices not only help other subsidiaries but also can be implemented in operations in the home country (Yang, Mudambi, & Meyer, 2008). Thus, for example, the process used by the Mexican Cement firm Cemex for improving efficiency in foreign operations, in which the practices of a target firm were analyzed and the best ones retained and diffused to other subsidiaries, was later implemented in the home operation, resulting in significant savings (Lessard & Reavis, 2009). In this way, the EMNC becomes an actor promoting pro-market reforms in its home country by implementing higher standards of rules and regulations within itself and in its relationships with customers, distributors, and suppliers. It has learned these standards from its exposure to countries with deeper pro-market reforms or from its development of practices to manage efficiently across borders, even if it only operates in other emerging countries. I summarize these ideas in this proposition:

> **Proposition 2a.** The advanced capabilities and governance practices that EMNCs learn abroad have a positive impact on the deepening of value chain pro-market reforms in the home country.

The second mechanism is spillovers, in which EMNCs become sources of better governance capabilities to home-country competitors. EMNCs can have a positive impact on the reforms at home via spillovers to their competitors; this is similar to the spillover that foreign MNCs have on domestic firms (Meyer, 2004; Spencer, 2008), but in our case among firms from the same country. This is done via three mechanisms (Blomstrom & Kokko, 1998): demonstration, training of joint suppliers, and employee mobility. First, in the demonstration effect, both competitive capabilities and more advanced institutional capabilities developed from the exposure to higher pro-market reforms abroad may diffuse among domestic companies via the direct copying by competitors of the practices. Competitors keep track of the practices and policies implemented by other companies to prevent them from gaining a first-mover advantage (Lieberman & Montgomery, 1988). EMNCs that bring more advanced governance techniques from their exposure to other countries may witness the diffusion of such techniques among competitors, which become indirectly exposed to the practices developed to deal with pro-market reforms in other countries via imitation of the EMNC. Second, in the training effect, pro-market reforms in other countries become diffused among home-country competitors via the training of joint suppliers and distribution channels by the EMNC. The EMNC implements better practices in its home operations and in the manner in which it collaborates with suppliers and distribution channels to improve its own efficiency and advantage (Kotabe, Martin, & Domoto, 2003). These better practices that suppliers and distribution channels receive from the EMNC help them not only provide better products and services to the EMNC but also to other competitors served by them. As a result, competitors indirectly obtain advanced governance practices from the EMNC. Third, employee mobility is another channel by which the EMNC transfers pro-market reforms to competitors in the home operation. As the EMNC trains its employees in the more advanced pro-market practices that it has learned abroad, some of those employees can be poached by competitors or can decide to leave the firm to create their own entrepreneurial ventures. These employees bring the practices learned in the EMNC with them and diffuse them to competitors (Somaya, Williamson, & Lorinkova, 2008). As the practices of the EMNC are implemented by competitors, they become embedded in the interactions among competitors, becoming institutions that deepen the pro-market reforms. In sum, I propose that:

> **Proposition 2b.** Spillovers of advanced institutional capabilities from the global exposure of EMNCs to domestic competitors via the demonstration, training of joint suppliers and distributors, and employee mobility mechanisms have a positive impact on the deepening of industry-level pro-market reforms in the home country.

The third mechanism is lobbying, in which EMNCs lobby their home governments to deepen pro-market reforms that benefit them. Some EMNCs can take an active political stance (Baron, 1995; Boddewyn, 1988) and lobby the government for the deepening of pro-market reforms directly. This is in contrast to learning and spillovers, in which the deepening of pro-market practices is done indirectly as they become embedded in the norms of interactions among economic actors. As EMNCs realize the benefits of operating in countries with higher levels of pro-market reforms and create superior practices from their exposure to a variety of pro-market reforms, managers may realize that better pro-market institutions in the home country can further the efficiency of their firms. Thus, managers of EMNCs can decide to speed up the deepening of pro-market reforms at home by lobbying the home-country government for the implementation of additional reforms. Since EMNCs tend to be the better companies in the country, additional pro-market reforms can help them push ahead of domestic competitors that are not prepared for deeper reforms. Even if the lobbying is biased toward their particular interests, the reduction of controls over firm behavior in areas such as regulation of action and price controls can lead to higher pro-market reforms for all firms. As MNCs, EMNCs have a credible threat of leaving the country or investing more abroad if the government does not provide a supporting environment (Stopford & Strange, 1992; Vernon, 1971), which can include deeper pro-market reforms. This flexibility in investment enables EMNCs to lobby hard for the deepening of pro-market reforms at home. I summarize these arguments in the following proposition:

> **Proposition 2c.** Lobbying by EMNCs that benefit from pro-market reforms has a positive impact on the deepening of pro-market reforms in the home country.

CONTINGENCIES ON THE CO-EVOLUTION OF PRO-MARKET REFORMS AND EMNCs

The co-evolution of pro-market reforms and EMNCs that I propose is subject to several contingencies that can explain the particular co-evolutionary processes of countries and companies. The start of pro-market reforms by politicians does not mean that a co-evolutionary process will automatically follow. There are incentives within companies and the government to limit the co-evolutionary process. Whereas the benefits of pro-market reforms and the internationalization of companies are uncertain and may take some time to realize, the costs of these reforms and internationalization are more certain and much more likely to be immediate. Hence, companies that are unable to upgrade capabilities to face increased competition will likely oppose pro-market reforms and lobby for protection, while government officials that have strong ties with protected and incompetent incumbent firms will likely limit pro-market reforms (Grossman & Helpman, 1994; Hillman, 1989). I discuss potential contingencies that can explain differences in the co-evolutionary process at three levels of analysis: firm, industry and country.

Private versus State-Owned Firms

At the firm level, there are likely to be differences between private and state-owned companies both in their internationalization as well as in how these companies influence pro-market reforms. First, private companies are more likely to react more positively to the influence of pro-market reforms and internationalize than state-owned firms. The former can upgrade their capabilities more easily, because they are free to focus on serving customers better and do not have to take into account any social objectives in their decision-making, something that state-owned firms must do (Cuervo-Cazurra & Dau, 2009a). Additionally, state-owned companies may be constrained in their ability to become MNCs because investments abroad may be perceived as substitutes for investments in the home country and may be opposed by some citizens and politicians (Stevens & Lipsey, 1992). Hence, I propose that:

> **Proposition 3a.** Private companies are more likely to become EMNCs with pro-market reforms than state-owned companies.

Second, in terms of the influence of EMNCs on pro-market reforms, private EMNCs are more likely to influence pro-market reforms at home via learning and spillovers than state-owned EMNCs, because they have more to gain from the expanded opportunity set that follows governmental retrenchment from the economy. State-owned EMNCs benefit from their connections to the government and their privileges as state-owned firms (Cuervo-Cazurra, Inkpen, Musacchio, & Ramaswamy, 2014), and thus have more to lose from promoting pro-market reforms at home (Chari & Gupta, 2008). Managers of state-owned firms may at most push to achieve autonomy from the government in their decision-making (Aharoni, 1982; Musacchio & Lazzarini, 2014), while keeping the benefits that come from connections to the government in the form of soft budgets and favorable regulation (Kornai, 1980), thus being less likely to promote additional pro-market reforms. I summarize these arguments in the following proposition:

> **Proposition 3b.** Private EMNCs are more likely to push for a deepening of pro-market reforms than state-owned EMNCs.

Domestic versus Foreign Firms

At the firm level, there are also likely to be differences between domestic and foreign-owned firms in how they push for pro-market reforms. However, in this contingency I can only analyze the impact of being a multinational on pro-market reforms. I cannot analyze the differential impact of pro-market reforms on the internationalization of these two types of firms because foreign-owned firms, by definition, are already multinationals. Foreign firms, especially those coming from countries with more sophisticated and stable institutions, are more likely to have a higher impact on the deepening of pro-market reforms than domestic EMNCs. Foreign firms are at a disadvantage over domestic firms as they suffer liabilities of foreignness (Zaheer, 1995) and outsidership (Johanson & Vahlne, 2009). These can be partially solved when they operate in an institutional framework that is more market friendly, because in such conditions competition tends to be on the basis of the competitive capabilities of the firms, rather than on the basis of the institutional capabilities and connections with the government, and companies have to respond to these new conditions (Ghemawat & Khanna, 1998). Thus, foreign firms have a larger incentive to lobby the government to deepen the pro-market reforms in the host country and move it toward a more level playing field. Additionally, foreign firms are subject to higher scrutiny in their global operations, especially advanced economy multinationals that operate in emerging countries, with non-governmental organizations (NGOs) keeping track of their environmental, labor, or development behavior (Vachani, Doh, & Teegen, 2009), and announcing the breach of norms in the home country, even when such norms may be acceptable in the emerging country. This can include, for example, implementing lower pollution controls in emerging markets or employing underage workers, which although legal in some emerging countries are not acceptable practices in advanced societies. Thus, foreign firms from advanced economies have a stronger incentive than domestic firms to deepen the pro-market reforms and establish better governance practices. These ideas can be summarized in the following proposition:

Proposition 4. Foreign-owned EMNCs are more likely to push for a deepening of pro-market reforms than domestic firms.

Global versus Local Industries

At the industry level, there are likely to be large differences among industries that are more globalized or more locally responsive. In terms of pro-market reforms leading to the creation of EMNCs, firms in industries that are more globalized are more likely to become EMNCs, in order to be able to face the entry of foreign companies that accompanies pro-market reforms. In a global industry, capabilities can not only be transferred but also applied successfully across countries, while firms with a presence in multiple countries benefit from the efficiency and learning across countries (Doz, Santos, & Williamson, 2001; Prahalad & Doz, 1987). Domestic firms may need to become EMNCs to be able to achieve efficiency levels that enable them to compete in their home country against incoming foreign products and firms. In contrast, companies operating in local industries do not have as many pressures to expand abroad even if they upgrade their capabilities to international levels after pro-market reforms. They can become strong incumbents in their home country and fend off foreign competitors because the capabilities of the latter are not as applicable across countries and there are limited benefits to global integration (Dawar & Frost, 1999). Therefore, I propose that:

Proposition 5a. Companies in global industries are more likely to become EMNCs with pro-market reforms than companies in local industries.

Regarding the deepening of pro-market reforms by EMNCs, EMNCs that operate in global industries are more likely to lobby for additional pro-market reforms in their home country than firms in local industries, in order to be able to compete on equal terms against foreign competitors. EMNCs in global industries benefit from the standardization of practices across countries (Prahalad & Doz, 1987). One way to improve the standardization of practices is to face similar conditions across countries, which can be partially achieved by deepening reforms in the home country. Thus, EMNCs in global industries may push for deeper pro-market reforms to reduce the variability in country conditions that limits their global efficiency. In contrast, EMNCs that operate in local industries may not have the incentive to push as hard for pro-market reforms at home because they would obtain fewer benefits from standardization across countries. In local industries, firms have to adapt practices to the local condition (Prahalad & Doz, 1987) and thus the practices developed in one country may not be of much use in others. These arguments can be summarized in the following proposition:

> **Proposition 5b.** EMNCs in global industries are more likely to promote the deepening of pro-market reforms than EMNCs in local industries.

Developing versus Transition Countries

Within the set of countries considered emerging, there are important differences between developing countries, which had capitalistic systems even when their economies were under high levels of government control (e.g., much of Latin America, Africa, and South Asia) (Bruton, 1998), and transition countries, which had communist economic systems in place before they moved toward capitalism (e.g., Eastern Europe, China, and former Soviet Republics) (Peng & Heath, 1996; Uhlenbruck, Meyer & Hitt, 2003). This results in differences in the impact of pro-market reforms on EMNCs. Companies operating in developing countries are more likely to become EMNCs with pro-market reforms because they already operated as private companies, with faster and less politically influenced decision-making, and were exposed to competition in the home country, even if this was constrained by government regulations. Although unusual, some may have already become EMNCs before the reforms (Cuervo-Cazurra, 2008). In contrast, companies operating in transition economies are less likely to become EMNCs with pro-market reforms, notwithstanding government mandates to expand abroad like in China (Luo, Xuer, & Han, 2010), because these companies have less experience operating as private companies; before the reforms, all firms were state-owned. They also have less experience competing openly; in command economies there is no competition because production and prices are mandated by government officials. These differences are temporary, however. With sustained pro-market reforms, transition and developing countries eventually converge in their conditions of operations, becoming emerging economies, and the ability and incentive to internationalize with additional reforms become similar in both countries. I summarize these ideas in the following proposition:

Proposition 6a. Companies from developing countries are more likely to become EMNCs with pro-market reforms than companies from transition economies, especially at the beginning of the pro-market reforms.

In terms of the influence of EMNCs on pro-market reforms, EMNCs from developing countries are more likely to continue pushing for additional pro-market reforms, because they are more used to operating under competition as private firms in a capitalistic system, even if previously the system was subject to high levels of government control. Continued reductions of government control over their operations help them improve efficiency and competitiveness in global operations (Cuervo-Cazurra & Dau, 2009a; Kumaraswamy, 2012). In contrast, EMNCs in transition economies have to learn to compete under the new rules of a capitalistic country; beforehand they only operated in a communist system (Peng & Heath, 1996; Uhlenbruck, Meyer & Hitt, 2003). They also have to learn to operate in a variety of countries with very different institutional conditions from home, unless they only expand into other transition economies. Thus, managers may be more reluctant to push for a deepening of pro-market reforms as they may face challenges in adapting to the new conditions of operation. Nevertheless, over time, developing and transition countries converge and EMNCs in both types of country may have similar incentives to deepen pro-market reforms. Therefore, I propose that:

Proposition 6b. EMNCs from developing countries are more likely to push for additional pro-market reforms than EMNCs from transition economies, especially at the beginning of the pro-market reforms.

CONCLUSIONS

Pro-market reforms and EMNCs are becoming two important phenomena, spanning large literatures. In this paper, I joined these two research streams and explained how they are connected. Specifically I proposed a co-evolutionary process, whereby pro-market reforms lead to the emergence of EMNCs, and those firms in turn lead to the deepening of pro-market reforms. I explained how this co-evolutionary process is driven by specific mechanisms. First, pro-market reforms in emerging markets induce the transformation of domestic firms into EMNCs via international competitiveness, upgrading needs, and escape. Second, the expansion of EMNCs leads to a deepening of pro-market reforms at home via learning, spillovers, and lobbying. The co-evolutionary process provides a dynamic view to our understanding of pro-market reforms and EMNCs, going beyond traditional studies that have analyzed how one concept influences the other, but have rarely considered subsequent changes over time.

These arguments contribute to a better understanding of institutional economics (La Porta, Lopez-de-Silanes, Shleifer, & Vishny, 1999; North, 1990). They provide an explanation not only of the influence of institutions on firm behavior, or the top-down approach that has been the usual focus of the literature, but also of the influence of firms on institutions, or a bottom-up approach. Thus, the traditional view of institutions as rules and regulations that constraint economic actors (North, 1990) can be rethought, since these economic actors can in fact modify the constraints on their behavior, not only via nonmarket strategies (Baron, 1995) but also via their competitive strategies.

Future studies can provide depth to the mechanisms described in this paper, measuring the variables and analyzing how the different contingencies play a role in the virtuous circle in which pro-market reforms enable the emergence and growth of EMNCs, which in turn lead to a deepening of pro-market reforms at home, which further support the global expansion of EMNCs. They can also explore the conditions under which this co-evolutionary process ceases to continue, for example, analyzing how incumbent firms and politicians who lose from the deepening of the reforms may block their implementation.

NOTES

1. There is a large literature on the determinants and impact of pro-market reforms at the country level (e.g., Henisz, Zelner, & Guillen, 2005; Kuczynski & Williamson, 2003; Williamson, 1990) that I will not review. Instead, I focus on the relationship between pro-market reforms and firms.

2. Countries classified as advanced by the IMF are the following (IMF, 2014): Australia, Austria, Belgium, Canada, Cyprus, Czech Republic, Denmark, Estonia, Finland, France, Germany, Greece, Hong Kong SAR, Iceland, Ireland, Israel, Italy, Japan, Korea, Latvia, Luxembourg, Malta, Netherlands, New Zealand, Norway, Portugal, San Marino, Singapore, Slovak Republic, Slovenia, Spain, Sweden, Switzerland, Taiwan Province of China, the United Kingdom, and the United States.

ACKNOWLEDGMENTS

I thank Ellie Banalieva, Tim Devinney, Torben Pedersen, Laszlo Tihanyi, and reviewers for useful suggestions for improvement and the Walsh

Research Professorship and the Robert Morrison Fellowship for financial support. All errors are mine.

REFERENCES

Aharoni, Y. (1982). State-owned enterprise: An agent without a principal. In L. P. Jones (Ed.), *Public enterprise in less-developed countries* (pp. 67–76). New York, NY: Cambridge University Press.

Armstrong, M., & Sappington, D. E. M. (2006). Regulation, competition, and liberalization. *Journal of Economic Literature, 44*, 325–366.

Aulakh, P. S. (2007). Emerging multinationals from developing economies: Motivations, paths, and performance. *Journal of International Management, 13*, 338–355.

Awate, S., Larsen, M., & Mudambi, R. (2012). EMNE catch-up strategies in the wind turbine industry: Is there a trade-off between output and innovation capabilities? *Global Strategy Journal, 2*, 205–223.

Banalieva, E. R. (2014). Embracing the second best? Synchronization of reform speeds, excess high-discretion slack, and performance of transition economy firms. *Global Strategy Journal, 4*, 104–126.

Barnard, H. (2014). Migrating EMNCs and the theory of the multinational. In A. Cuervo-Cazurra & R. Ramamurti (Eds.), *Understanding multinationals from emerging markets* (pp. 195–223). Cambridge, UK: Cambridge University Press.

Baron, D. P. (1995). Integrated strategy: Market and nonmarket components. *California Management Review, 37*, 47–65.

Baum, J. A. C., & Singh, J. V. (1994). Organization-environment coevolution. In J. A. C. Baum & J. V. Singh (Eds.), *Evolutionary dynamics of organizations* (pp. 379–402). Oxford: Oxford University Press.

BBCNews. (2013). India restricts foreign exchange to halt rupee slide. *BBCNews*, August 15. Retrieved from http://www.bbc.com/news/business-23709330. Accessed on November 2.

Blanchard, O. J. (1997). *The economics of post-communist transition*. New York, NY: Oxford University Press.

Blomstrom, M., & Kokko, A. (1998). Multinational corporations and spillovers. *Journal of Economic Surveys, 12*, 247–277.

Boddewyn, J. J. (1988). Political aspects of MNE theory. *Journal of International Business Studies, 19*, 341–363.

Bruton, H. J. (1998). A reconsideration of import substitution. *Journal of Economic Literature, 36*, 903–936.

Chari, A., & Gupta, N. (2008). Incumbents and protectionism: The political economy of foreign entry liberalization. *Journal of Financial Economics, 88*, 633–656.

Chari, M., & David, P. (2011). Sustaining superior performance in an emerging economy: An empirical test in the Indian context. *Strategic Management Journal, 33*, 217–229.

Coffee, J. C., Jr. (2002). Racing towards the top? The impact of cross-listings and stock market competition on international corporate governance. *Columbia Law Review, 102*, 1757–1831.

Cuervo, A., & Villalonga, B. (2000). Explaining the variance in the performance effects of privatization. *Academy of Management Review, 25*, 581–590.

Cuervo-Cazurra, A. (2006). Who cares about corruption? *Journal of International Business Studies, 37*, 803–822.

Cuervo-Cazurra, A. (2008). The multinationalization of developing country MNEs: The case of multilatinas. *Journal of International Management, 14*, 138–154.

Cuervo-Cazurra, A. (2012). How the analysis of developing country multinational companies helps advance theory: Solving the Goldilocks debate. *Global Strategy Journal, 2*, 153–167.

Cuervo-Cazurra, A. (2015). *The impact of emerging market multinationals on pro-market reforms*. Working Paper. Northeastern University.

Cuervo-Cazurra, A., & Dau, L. A. (2009a). Pro-market reforms and firm profitability in developing countries. *Academy of Management Journal, 52*, 1348–1368.

Cuervo-Cazurra, A., & Dau, L. A. (2009b). Structural reform and firm exports. *Management International Review, 49*, 479–507.

Cuervo-Cazurra, A., Inkpen, A., Musacchio, A., & Ramaswamy, K. (2014). Governments as owners: State-owned multinational companies. *Journal of International Business Studies, 45*, 919–942.

Cuervo-Cazurra, A., & Ramamurti, R. (Eds.). (2014a). *Understanding multinationals from emerging markets*. Cambridge, UK: Cambridge University Press.

Cuervo-Cazurra, A., & Ramamurti, R. (2014b). Conclusion: An agenda for future research. In A. Cuervo-Cazurra & R. Ramamurti (Eds.), *Understanding multinationals from emerging markets* (pp. 271–300). Cambridge, UK: Cambridge University Press.

Cuervo-Cazurra, A., & Stal, E. (2011). The investment development path and FDI from developing countries: The role of pro-market reforms and institutional voids. *Latin American Business Review, 12*, 209–231.

Dawar, N., & Frost, T. (1999). Competing with giants. *Harvard Business Review, 77*(2), 119–129.

del Sol, P., & Kogan, J. (2007). Regional competitive advantage based on pioneering economic reforms: The case of Chilean FDI. *Journal of International Business Studies, 38*, 901–927.

Desai, M. A., Foley, C. F., & Hines, J. R. (2006). The demand for tax haven operations. *Journal of Public Economics, 90*, 513–531.

Doz, Y. L., Santos, J., & Williamson, P. J. (2001). *From global to metanational: How companies win in the knowledge economy*. Boston, MA: Harvard Business School Press Books.

Dunning, J. H. (1981). Explaining the international direct investment position of countries: Towards a dynamic or developmental approach. *Weltwirtschaftliches Archiv, 117*, 30–64.

Edwards, S. (1993). Openness, trade liberalization, and growth in developing countries. *Journal of Economic Literature, 31*, 1358–1396.

Fisman, R., & Miguel, E. (2007). Corruption, norms and legal enforcement: Evidence from diplomatic parking tickets. *Journal of Political Economy, 115*, 1020–1048.

Gammeltoft, P., Barnard, H., & Madhok, A. (2010). Emerging multinationals, emerging theory: Macro- and micro-level perspectives. *Journal of International Management, 16*, 95–101.

Geng, X. (2004). *Round-tripping foreign direct investment in the People's Republic of China: Scale, causes and implications*. ADB Institute Research Paper Series No. 58. Tokyo: Asian Development Bank Institute.

Ghemawat, P., & Khanna, T. (1998). The nature of diversified business groups: A research design and two case studies. *Journal of Industrial Economics, 46*, 35–61.

Grossman, G. M., & Helpman, E. (1994). Protection for sale. *American Economic Review*, *84*(4), 833–850.

Guillen, M. F., & Garcia-Canal, E. (2009). The American model of the multinational firm and the "new" multinationals from emerging economies. *Academy of Management Perspectives*, *23*, 23–35.

Henisz, W. J., Zelner, B. A., & Guillen, M. F. (2005). The worldwide diffusion of market-oriented infrastructure reform, 1977–1999. *American Sociological Review*, *70*, 871–897.

Hillman, A. E. (1989). *The political economy of protection*. New York, NY: Harwood Academic Publishers.

IMF. (2014). *World economic and financial surveys*. World Economic Outlook. Database—WEO Groups and Aggregates Information. Retrieved from http://www.imf.org/external/pubs/ft/weo/2014/01/weodata/groups.htm. Accessed on September 13, 2014.

Johanson, J., & Vahlne, J.-E. (2009). The Uppsala internationalization process model revisited: From liability of foreignness to liability of outsidership. *Journal of International Business Studies*, *40*, 1411–1431.

Khanna, T., & Palepu, K. G. (2010). *Winning in emerging markets: A road map for strategy and execution*. Boston, MA: Harvard Business Press.

Kornai, J. (1980). *Economics of shortage*. Amsterdam: North Holland.

Kornai, J. (1992). *The socialist system: The political economy of communism*. Princeton, NJ: Princeton University Press.

Kotabe, M., Martin, X., & Domoto, H. (2003). Gaining from vertical partnerships: Knowledge transfer, relationship duration and supplier performance improvements in the U.S. and Japanese automotive industries. *Strategic Management Journal*, *24*, 293–316.

Kuczynski, P. P., & Williamson, J. (2003). *After the Washington consensus. Restarting growth and reform in Latin America*. Washington, DC: Institute for International Economics.

Kumaraswamy, A., Mudambi, R., Saranga, H., & Tripathy, A. (2012). Catch-up strategies in the Indian auto components industry: Domestic firms' responses to market liberalization. *Journal of International Business Studies*, *43*, 368–395.

La Porta, R., Lopez-de-Silanes, F., Shleifer, A., & Vishny, R. W. (1999). The quality of government. *Journal of Law, Economics, and Organization*, *15*, 222–279.

Lall, S. (1983). *The new multinationals: The spread of third world enterprises*. New York, NY: Wiley.

Lessard, D. R., & Reavis, C. (2009). *CEMEX: Globalization "The CEMEX Way"*. MIT Sloan School case study 09-039. Retrieved from https://mitsloan.mit.edu/LearningEdge/CaseDocs/09%20039%20CEMEX%20%20Lessard.pdf. Accessed on November 1, 2014.

Lieberman, M. B., & Montgomery, D. B. (1988). First-mover advantages. *Strategic Management Journal*, *9*(Summer), 41–58.

Luo, Y., & Tung, R. L. (2007). International expansion of emerging market enterprises: A springboard perspective. *Journal of International Business Studies*, *38*, 481–498.

Luo, Y., & Wang, S. L. (2012). Foreign direct investment strategies by developing country multinationals: A diagnostic model for home country effects. *Global Strategy Journal*, *2*, 244–261.

Luo, Y., Xue, Q., & Han, B. (2010). How emerging market governments promote outward FDI: Experience from China. *Journal of World Business*, *45*, 68–79.

Madhok, A., & Keyhani, M. (2012). Acquisitions as entrepreneurship: asymmetries, opportunities, and the internationalization of multinationals from emerging economies. *Global Strategy Journal*, *2*, 26–40.

Madhok, A., & Liu, C. (2006). A coevolutionary theory of the multinational firm. *Journal of International Management, 12*, 1–21.
Mathews, J. A. (2006). Dragon multinationals: New players in 21st century globalization. *Asia Pacific Journal of Management, 23*, 5–27.
Megginson, W., & Netter, J. (2001). From state to market: A survey on empirical studies on privatization. *Journal of Economics Literature, 39*, 321–389.
Meyer, K. E. (2004). Perspectives on multinational enterprises in emerging economies. *Journal of International Business Studies, 34*, 259–277.
Musacchio, A., & Lazzarini, S. G. (2014). *Reinventing state capitalism. Leviathan in business, Brazil and beyond.* Boston, MA: Harvard University Press.
North, D. C. (1990). *Institutions, institutional change and economic performance.* Cambridge: Cambridge University Press.
OECD. (2014). *OECD science, technology and industry outlook 2013.* Paris: Organization for Economic Cooperation and Development.
Oliver, C. (1997). Sustainable competitive advantage: Combining institutional and resource-based views. *Strategic Management Journal, 18*, 697–713.
Park, S. H., Li, S., & Tse, D. K. (2006). Market liberalization and firm performance during China's economic transition. *Journal of International Business Studies, 37*, 127–147.
Peng, M. W., & Heath, P. S. (1996). The growth of the firm in planed economies in transition: Institutions, organizations, and strategic choice. *Academy of Management Review, 21*, 492–528.
Prahalad, C. K., & Doz, Y. L. (1987). *The multinational mission.* New York, NY: The Free Press.
Ramamurti, R. (2000). A multilevel model of privatization in emerging economies. *Academy of Management Review, 25*, 525–550.
Ramamurti, R. (2009). What have we learned about emerging-market MNEs? In R. Ramamurti & J. V. Singh (Eds.), *Emerging multinationals from emerging markets.* New York, NY: Cambridge University Press.
Ramamurti, R. (2012). What is really different about emerging market multinationals? *Global Strategy Journal, 2*, 41–47.
Rugman, A. M. (2009). Theoretical aspects of MNEs from emerging economies. In R. Ramamurti & J. V. Singh (Eds.), *Emerging multinationals from emerging markets.* New York, NY: Cambridge University Press.
Rugman, A. M., & Nguyen, Q. T. K. (2014). Modern international business theory and emerging market multinational companies. In A. Cuervo-Cazurra & R. Ramamurti (Eds.), *Understanding multinationals from emerging markets* (pp. 53–80). Cambridge: Cambridge University Press.
Somaya, D., Williamson, I. O., & Lorinkova, N. (2008). Gone but not lost: The different performance impacts of employee mobility between cooperators versus competitors. *Academy of Management Journal, 51*, 936–953.
Spencer, J. W. (2008). The impact of multinational enterprise strategy on indigenous enterprises: Horizontal spillovers and crowding out in developing countries. *Academy of Management Review, 33*, 341–361.
Stevens, G. V. G., & Lipsey, R. E. (1992). Interactions between domestic and foreign investment. *Journal of International Money and Finance, 11*, 40–62.
Stopford, J., & Strange, S. (1992). *Rival states, rival firms: Competition for world market shares.* New York, NY: Cambridge University Press.
Tirole, J. (1988). *The theory of industrial organization.* Cambridge, MA: MIT Press.

Uhlenbruck, K., Meyer, K. E., & Hitt, M. A. (2003). Organizational transformation in transition economies: Resource-based and organizational learning perspectives. *Journal of Management Studies*, *40*, 257–282.

UNCTAD. (2014). *UNCTADStat*. Retrieved from http://unctadstat.unctad.org/ReportFolders/reportFolders.aspx?sRF_ActivePath=p,5&sRF_Expanded=,p,5. Accessed on September 13.

Vachani, S., Doh, J. P., & Teegen, H. (2009). NGOs' influence on MNEs' social development strategies in varying institutional contexts: A transaction cost perspective. *International Business Review*, *18*, 446–456.

Vernon, R. (1966). International investment and international trade in the product cycle. *Quarterly Journal of Economics*, *80*, 190–207.

Vernon, R. (1971). *Sovereignty at Bay: The multinational spread of U.S. enterprises*. New York, NY: Basic Books.

Vickers, J., & Yarrow, G. (1995). *Privatization: An economic analysis*. Cambridge, MA: The MIT Press.

Wells, L. T., Jr. (1983). *Third world multinationals: The rise of foreign investments from developing countries*. Cambridge, MA: MIT Press.

Williamson, J. (Ed.). (1990). *Latin American adjustment: How much has happened?* Washington, DC: Institute for International Economics.

Williamson, J. (2004). The strange history of the Washington Consensus. *Journal of Post Keynesian Economics*, *27*, 195–206.

Witt, M. A., & Lewin, A. Y. (2007). Outward foreign direct investment as escape response to home country institutional constraints. *Journal of International Business Studies*, *38*, 579–594.

Yang, Q., Mudambi, R., & Meyer, K. E. (2008). Conventional and reverse knowledge flows in multinational corporations. *Journal of Management*, *34*, 882–902.

Yergin, D., & Stanislaw, J. (1998). *The commanding heights. The battle for the world economy*. New York, NY: Touchstone.

Zaheer, S. (1995). Overcoming the liability of foreignness. *Academy of Management Journal*, *38*, 341–363.

A RESOURCE ENVIRONMENT VIEW OF COMPETITIVE ADVANTAGE

Heechun Kim and Robert E. Hoskisson

ABSTRACT

Our study proposes a resource environment view (REV) of competitive advantage by unpacking the environmental origins of a firm's competitive advantage. The key tenet of the REV is that the heterogeneity and imperfect mobility of strategic factor markets and institutions across countries explain how firms based in different countries would likely both create and sustain a competitive advantage. In particular, our study introduces the notion of "the paradox of environmental embeddedness." The paradox lies in the fact that the same environmental conditions – in terms of strategic factor markets and institutions – that enable firms to create a competitive advantage can paradoxically also create a situation in which it is more difficult for these firms to sustain an advantage. Another important aspect of our study is that, to enhance our understanding of how firms manage the paradox of environmental embeddedness, our study specifies the resource environmental conditions under which firms' internal and external resource-oriented strategies – that is, the development of dynamic capabilities and

Emerging Economies and Multinational Enterprises
Advances in International Management, Volume 28, 95–140

ISSN: 1571-5027/doi:10.1108/S1571-502720150000028008

interventions in the country resource environment – are more beneficial when managing the environmental paradox. Overall, our theorizing has important implications for strategic management theory and practice.

Keywords: Competitive advantage; strategic factor markets; institutions; resource environment view

INTRODUCTION

Both creating and sustaining competitive advantage simultaneously might well be considered the core of the success or failure of firms competing in the hypercompetitive global marketplace. As such, the origins and sustainability of competitive advantage have been at the heart of research in strategic management. There have been the two established models of competitive advantage in the literature: industrial organization economics (IOE) and the resource-based theory (RBT). Proponents of IOE working from the structure-conduct-performance paradigm argue that the origin of competitive advantage is the structure of an industry and firm positioning relative to industry competition (e.g., Porter, 1981). A second view (RBT) examines firm resource heterogeneity and mobility relative to firms in the industry as the critical source of competitive advantage (e.g., Barney, 1991; Dierickx & Cool, 1989; Peteraf, 1993; Wernerfelt, 1984).

Nonetheless, these two established models still fall short of providing a more complete answer to one of the four fundamental questions of strategy identified by Rumelt, Schendel, and Teece (1994, p. 2, italics added): "What determines the success or failure of the firm in *international competition*?" The implication is that, although firms and industries are nested in larger external environments, the two established models assuming away differences in external country resource environments of industries and firms have paid relatively scant attention toward understanding how the external resource environment affects not only the industry (e.g., Capron & Chatain, 2008; Chesbrough, 1999; Markman, Gianiodis, & Buchholtz, 2009) but firm-level competitive advantage (e.g., Ahuja & Yayavaram, 2011; Ingram & Silverman, 2002; Khanna & Palepu, 1997; Kim, Hoskisson, & Lee, 2015; Oliver, 1997; Peng, Wang, & Jiang, 2008; Porter, 1990, 1991; Wan, 2005; Wan & Hoskisson, 2003). We define competitive advantage as a unique advantage that helps a firm earn higher returns than its competitors in an industry.

In their cross-country study comparing firm performance persistence, a predictor of a sustainable competitive advantage, in West Germany, the United Kingdom, and France, Geroski and Jacquemin cautiously concluded that "countrywide factors have turned out to be more discriminating than firm or industry specific ones" (1988, p. 388). As such, the RBT and IOE are likely to yield an incomplete understanding of the origins and sustainability of competitive advantage without adequate attention being channeled to the external *country resource environment* in which firms and industries are nested. By country resource environments, we mean country-level resource environmental conditions that provide geographically embedded firms not only with environmental opportunities and constraints for resource acquisition and accumulation but also with the environmental basis for the dynamics of competition within an industry.

Although some strategy scholars have recognized the importance of the external resource environment (e.g., Hoskisson, Wright, Filatotchev, & Peng, 2013; Wan & Hoskisson, 2003), there are two important gaps that remain unfilled. First, scholarship has become bifurcated into the two camps associated with two distinct types of resource environments – that is, strategic factor markets (e.g., Barney, 1986; Chesbrough, 1999; Khanna & Palepu, 1997; Kim et al., 2015; Porter, 1990) and institutions (e.g., Ingram & Silverman, 2002; Oliver, 1997; Peng et al., 2008). Little scholarly engagement between the two camps may yield an incomplete understanding of the environmental origins of competitive advantage. Second, and more importantly, while the IOE model of competitive advantage (Barney, 1991, p. 100; Porter, 1981, p. 610) and the environmental embeddedness argument (Caeldries, 1996; Oliver, 1996) involve important paradoxical tensions between opportunities/benefits and threats/costs, little research has employed the environmental paradox to understand how the two different types of external resource environments could be both facilitative and disruptive origins of competitive advantage.

Our study introduces the concept of the *paradox of environmental embeddedness* of strategic factor markets and institutions in order to better address the sustainability of competitive advantage. The paradox of environmental embeddedness denotes the paradoxical challenges of creating and sustaining a competitive advantage induced by institutions and strategic factor markets in which firms are deeply embedded. Specifically, the same resource environmental conditions – in terms of strategic factor markets and institutions – that enable firms to create a competitive advantage can make it more difficult for these firms to sustain it. This situation is what we call "the paradox of environmental embeddedness." By recognizing the two opposing sides of the external resource environment, our treatise employs internal and external resource-oriented strategies – namely, the development of dynamic capabilities and interventions in the country resource environment – to offer theoretical and practical insights into how firms manage the environmental paradox. In doing so, our study specifies the resource environmental conditions under which these two types of resource-oriented strategies are more beneficial when managing the environmental paradox.

Our paper makes several contributions to the strategic management literature. First, our study advances a resource environment view (REV) of competitive advantage by proposing an integrative model of competitive advantage, showing that the origins of competitive advantage arise in part from the external resource environments. In particular, our multilevel theory sheds light on how the REV presented here is systematically connected with the two established models – that is, IOE and the RBT – of competitive advantage.[1] While the two established models have tended to treat the country-level external resource environment as exogenous to competitive advantage, our study brings it more directly into strategy research on the origins and sustainability of competitive advantage in international competition. Second, our study uses the concept of the paradox of environmental embeddedness to move beyond an overly simplified role of external environment contingency. While cognizance of the paradoxical challenges of creating and sustaining a competitive advantage is not new, previous studies have largely documented the paradox of organizational capabilities without consideration of the environment (e.g., Lado, Boyd, Wright, & Kroll, 2006; Leonard-Barton, 1992). In contrast, our study shifts scholarly attention to the environmental paradox and provides new insights into how firms manage this paradox by employing internal and external resource-oriented strategies.

Our paper is organized as follows. In the next section, we develop the REV by addressing the nature of the paradox of environmental embeddedness and its implications for the firm's competitive advantage. After that, we propose internal and external resource-oriented strategies as logical options for managing the paradox of environmental embeddedness. We finally discuss the implications of our exposition for strategic management theory and practice.

A RESOURCE ENVIRONMENT VIEW OF COMPETITIVE ADVANTAGE

As noted earlier, we advance the REV of competitive advantage, putting forth the idea that the origins of competitive advantage arise in part from the external resource and institutional environments consisting of strategic factor markets and institutions. Fig. 1 illustrates how the REV of competitive advantage is related to the two established models of competitive advantage (i.e., IOE and the RBT) and outlines our theoretical framework for understanding the origins and sustainability of competitive advantage. Rather than providing a detailed review of IOE and the RBT (see Hoskisson, Hitt, Wan, & Yiu, 1999 for a review), we simply point to the core arguments of these two widely accepted models regarding the origins of competitive advantage.

The central tenet of IOE is that the structure of an industry in which a firm operates and competes not only influences the conduct of firms but also serves as the main determinant of the collective performance of the

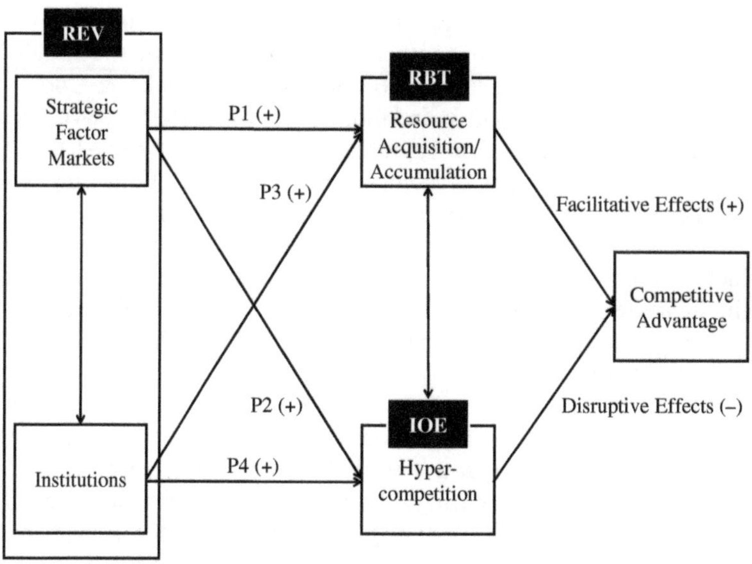

Fig. 1. An Integrative Model of Competitive Advantage: A Linkage of the Resource Environment View, Industrial Organization Economics, and the Resource-Based Theory as the Origins of Competitive Advantage.

firms in the same industry and performance differences across industries (e.g., Bain, 1956, 1968; Mason, 1939).[2] The key elements of industry structure identified as important to performance include structural barriers to entry and industry concentration. In fact, barriers to entry that include government regulation enable large, incumbent firms to create competitive advantage and earn above-normal profits while creating competitive disadvantage for potential new entrants such as entrepreneurial start-ups, diversifying entrants from another industry, and foreign entrants from another country (or multinational enterprises or MNEs). Because entry barriers limit industry competition and play a prominent role in a firm's competitive advantage, industry incumbents may well attempt to erect strategic entry barriers, which are among the most important isolating mechanisms at the industry level, by investing in strategic resources (Caves & Porter, 1977; Mahoney & Pandian, 1992).

When attempting to understand sources of a firm's competitive advantage, strategy scholars find it infeasible to evaluate industry attractiveness or hypercompetition independent of the resources a firm brings to that industry. While the IOE model focuses externally on the industry and product markets, the RBT focuses internally on the firm and its resources. Specifically, the RBT addresses the fundamental question of why some firms within the same industry outperform others and how they might sustain a competitive advantage (e.g., Barney, 1991; Dierickx & Cool, 1989; Peteraf, 1993; Sirmon, Hitt, & Ireland, 2007; Wernerfelt, 1984). Viewing the firm as a collection of firm resources, Barney (1991) argued that these resources are a key source of competitive advantage. Following Barney (1991) and Helfat et al. (2007), our study defines resources as all tangible and intangible resources that a firm can use to choose and implement its product market strategies. Yet, we refer to strategic resources that firms acquire in strategic factor markets as external resources to distinguish them from strategic resources that already exist in the firm, which we call internally accumulated resources.

As we will explain more in Propositions 1 and 3, a firm's competitive advantage stems from its ability to combine externally acquired and internally accumulated resources in a way that creates value for customers and wealth for shareholders (Barney, 1986, 1991; Dierickx & Cool, 1989; Maritan & Peteraf, 2011). Assuming that resource heterogeneity can be long lasting, RBT scholars have contended that a firm's competitive advantage is sustainable insofar as its strategically valuable resources are inimitable, rare, and nonsubstitutable (e.g., Barney, 1991; Dierickx & Cool, 1989; Reed & DeFillippi, 1990). As further developed in Propositions 2 and 4, the sustainability of the firm's competitive advantage is contingent upon the strategic isolating mechanisms (Rumelt, 1984) such as barriers to imitation of its strategic resources and the rarity of strategic resources among its competitors. Barriers to imitation refer to the degree to which current or potentially competing firms encounter difficulties in replicating or substituting a focal firm's strategic resources on their own. Furthermore, the rarity of strategic resources is defined as the extent to which competitors face difficulties in acquiring the same strategic resources possessed by the focal firm.

As noted earlier, our study offers an integrative model of competitive advantage by putting forth the REV. A fundamental premise of the REV is that strategic factor markets (for cross-country index, see Kim et al., 2015) and institutions (for cross-country index, see Chan, Isobe, & Makino, 2008; Hoskisson et al., 2013), which are heterogeneous and imperfectly mobile across countries and thereby create path-dependent trajectories, provide a valuable basis for a firm's competitive advantage. In the following subsection, we briefly examine the key concepts of our study.

Strategic Factor Markets

The concept of strategic factor markets, which refer to external resource markets, such as the labor market, the capital market, and the market for natural resources, where firms buy the external resources necessary to implement their product market strategies within industries and to create a competitive advantage, dates back to Ricardo (1817). Specifically, the classical Ricardian theory of comparative advantage pointed to the role of the factors of production (or input resources) of land, labor, and capital that are heterogeneous and imperfectly mobile across countries. Compared to product markets, strategic factor markets could be considered to be a country's input markets such as labor and capital markets (Khanna & Palepu, 1997; Kim et al., 2015; Wan & Hoskisson, 2003).[3] In regard to the development of strategic factor markets, it is important to note that there are the two dimensions of strategic factor markets – that is, efficiency and munificence – that are independent, capturing wholly different aspects of strategic factor markets. Because neither is sufficient to completely characterize the country resource environment, they must be considered together.

The degree of market efficiency plays a crucial role in information asymmetries and the resulting resource and transaction costs in Barney's (1986) strategic factor market theory. To illustrate why the efficiency of strategic factor markets matters, we consider the market for corporate control – that is, buying and selling companies – an example of a strategic factor market employed by Barney (1986). Research has suggested that the market for corporate control is a critical part of a dynamic process through which firms develop strategic resources to create a competitive advantage (e.g., Capron, Mitchell, & Swaminathan, 2001). Yet if strategic factor markets fail to function efficiently, there exist significant information asymmetries between buyers and sellers, increasing transaction costs associated with acquiring bad target firms. That is, the adverse selection problem will become so prevalent that firms would not have strong incentives to rely on the market for corporate control if strategic factor markets are inefficient.

The munificence of strategic factor markets matters as well. Very recently, Kim et al. (2015) demonstrated how so-called "new" MNEs especially from South Korea performed differently in resource-poorer versus resource-richer host countries than the home country in terms of the endowment of strategic factor markets.[4] While Kim et al. (2015) used the notion of endowment of strategic factor markets, that notion is largely interchangeable with the munificence of strategic factor markets in the present study. According to Castrogiovanni (1991, p. 542), environmental munificence refers to "the scarcity or abundance of critical resources needed by (one or more) firms operating within an environment." Such environmental munificence is a critical contingency factor for competitive firms in their industries because it is the objective condition of an environment not only to support their sustained growth and stability but also to affect their resource management (Sirmon et al., 2007). While all firms could access some strategic resources made available by munificent strategic factor markets in a certain country, their counterparts in another country might not have access to equivalent resources (Khanna & Palepu, 1997; Wan & Hoskisson, 2003). As a result, firms operating within highly munificent strategic factor markets differ substantially from their counterparts operating within highly scarce strategic factor markets, regardless of the industries in which they are competing (Kim et al. 2015).

Institutions

As Davis and North (1971) and North (1990) suggest, the institutional environment composed largely of both formal institutions (i.e., political and legal institutions) and informal institutions (i.e., social institutions) refers to the set of political, legal, and social rules that establishes the basis for production, exchange, and distribution. Because institutions play a significant role in reducing uncertainty and affecting the performance of the economy, it is hardly controversial that institutional development matters for organizations as players in the game defined by institutions (North, 1990). For example, Hill (1995, p. 120) argued that resource costs, which refer to "the cost of the resource inputs (land, labor, capital) required to produce a given output," are determined by the institutional structure of a society that can either increase or decrease transaction costs. Furthermore, institutions differ markedly from country to country, so some countries such as developed economies end up with more fully developed institutions than others such as emerging economies (North, 1990).

While institutions are less tangible than factor markets (Wan & Hoskisson, 2003), Peng et al. (2008) recently declared that institutions, which are referred to as "the humanly devised constraints that shape human interaction" or "the rules of the game in a society" (North, 1990, p. 3), are no longer background conditions – rather, they affect the potential for firms to create a competitive advantage (Oliver, 1997) and influence rents (or institutional rents) that are the extra profits that firms earn from their influence over institutions (Ahuja & Yayavaram, 2011). It is also important to note that, because there is the persistent variation in institutions among countries, and barriers to entry and barriers to imitation of resources that firms face differ across countries, industry structure varies by country (Kogut, 1991). In a similar vein, Bogner and Barr (2000) observed that social institutions are related to the extent to which the airline, banking, and telecom industries are hypercompetitive in different countries such as the United States, Europe, and Japan, because some countries' social institutions impose more constraints on creating competitive turbulence than others'. Furthermore, Ingram and Silverman (2002) pointed out that, because firms and industries are embedded in the institutional environment, strategy scholars need to consider the role of institutions in creating a competitive advantage to understand what determines success and failure in international competition.

Key characteristics of strategic factor markets and institutions are summarized in Table 1, although we will explain more later.[5] Unfortunately, these two theoretical camps are often treated as competing explanations of a firm's competitive advantage because strategy scholars have failed to integrate these two fundamental but different pillars of the broader external environment. In this paper, we thus attempt to integrate and extend these camps to gain a better understanding of the origins and sustainability of competitive advantage. In fact, combining them is appropriate in the sense

Table 1. A Comparison of Strategic Factor Markets and Institutions.

Characteristics	Strategic Factor Markets	Institutions
Definition	Resource markets whereby firms buy and sell external resources necessary to implement product market strategies	The humanly devised constraints that structure political, economic, and social interactions
Main actors	Firms as combiners of external resources	Institutions (or the rules of the game) and organizations (or major players of the game including political bodies and economic bodies)
Components	Resource inputs such as labor, capital, and raw materials	Formal (political and legal) and informal (social) institutions
Key decision constraints	Resource and transaction costs associated with information asymmetries	Resource and transaction costs associated with institutional uncertainty and information asymmetries involved in transactions
A firm's internal and external resource-oriented strategies	• Acquire good (or undervalued) external resources and avoid acquiring bad (or overvalued) external resources based on superior information • Reduce quantity or effectiveness of external resources available to its competitors	• Accumulate internal resources that fit best with the institutional environment but that may or may not be economically useful in product markets • Exert control over its competitors' external resources by manipulating institutions in its favor

that they share the compatible underlying assumption that institutions and strategic factor markets are heterogeneous and imperfectly mobile across countries. While building on previous studies, our study deviates from them in that it speaks not only of the paradox of environmental embeddedness but also of internal and external resource-oriented strategies necessary to manage the environmental paradox.

The Paradox of Environmental Embeddedness: Strategic Factor Markets and Institutions as Facilitators and Disruptors of Competitive Advantage

In the strategy literature, the concept of embeddedness has been generally defined as the interconnections between an organization and its larger environmental context within which the organization is deeply embedded and in which its economic action and strategy are initially implemented (Eisenhardt & Brown, 1996; Oliver, 1996). In a related vein, our study sheds light on how the paradox of environmental embeddedness may or may not translate into a firm's competitive advantage. The paradox of environmental embeddedness of strategic factor markets and institutions refers to the two opposing sides of strategic factor markets and institutions – grounded in tensions between the facilitating and disruptive effects of strategic factor markets and institutions.

The first of these sides is in facilitating the creation of a focal firm's competitive advantage through resource development. Here, our study responds to Maritan and Peteraf's (2011) call for bridging two separate mechanisms widely thought to explain how firms come to develop heterogeneous resources: external resource acquisition (Barney, 1986) and internal resource accumulation (Dierickx & Cool, 1989). In doing so, our study conceptualizes how heterogeneous, imperfectly mobile strategic factor markets and institutions that develop differently across countries have an enduring impact on the way that firms embedded in different resources environments develop heterogeneous resources that facilitate the creation of a competitive advantage. Specifically, we highlight the respective roles that strategic factor markets and institutions play in external resource acquisition and internal resource accumulation.

The second is in stimulating the emergence of hypercompetition, promoting competitive dynamics changing the rules of the game in the industry, and eroding the focal firm's competitive advantage. In our study, hypercompetition refers to a situation in which there are industrial dynamics of strategic maneuvering and rivalry among current competitors and between established firms and new entrants. In hypercompetition, product markets are changing very quickly due in large part to Schumpeterian competition, so it is highly challenging for firms to sustain a competitive advantage for very long (Christensen, 1997; D'Aveni, 1994; Schumpeter, 1942). In particular, our study illuminates how hypercompetition and competitive dynamics at the industry level are the natural result of the dissolution of strategic isolating mechanisms.

The Facilitative Effect of Strategic Factor Markets via External Resource Acquisition

In their resource dependence model, Pfeffer and Salancik (1978) highlighted the necessity of organizations acquiring important resources from their environment. In this regard, Porter (1991, p. 110) claimed that "[t]he proximate [or local] environment will define many of the input (factor) markets the firm has to draw on, ... Competitive advantage, then, may reside as much in the environment as in an individual firm." Regarding firms as combiners of inputs made available by strategic factor markets, Conner (1991) also observed that firms exist to combine factors of production (or productive inputs or resources) available in strategic factor markets and to sell the goods produced by these factors in product markets. Furthermore, Collis (1991) pointed out that because firms primarily acquire external resources from their domestic factor markets, they build core competences around factors with which the country is relatively well endowed. Building on this line of theoretical logic, we argue for the facilitative effect of strategic factor markets on the ability of firms to acquire external resources that help them create a competitive advantage.

While Barney (1986) focused exclusively on the costs of acquiring external resources in strategic factor markets that are not perfectly efficient, our study embraces the two dimensions of strategic factor markets presented earlier. Because the efficiency of strategic factor markets may vary from country to country, firms embedded in countries with more efficient strategic factor markets are more capable of searching for external resources without incurring significant resource and transaction costs than their counterparts in countries with less efficient strategic factor markets.

The munificence of strategic factor markets plays a critical role in creating a competitive advantage as well. Firms may find it more costly or less efficient in developing and accumulating strategically valuable resources internally unless strategic factor markets exist to provide these firms with an opportunity to acquire external resources such as human and financial capital. Moreover, our study recognizes that the extent to which external strategic resources are available to all firms across industries in a certain country varies considerably by country (e.g., Chacar & Vissa, 2005; Chesbrough, 1999; Khanna & Palepu, 1997). When countries are more richly endowed with strategic factor markets such as capital and labor markets, meaning that such strategic factor markets are more munificent, firms embedded in these countries are better able to gain access to the external resources necessary to implement product market strategies, thereby creating a competitive advantage more effectively (e.g., Khanna & Palepu, 1997; Kim et al., 2015; Porter, 1990).

In a related manner, previous research provides an indication that that strategic factor markets could be an important source of competitive advantage for firms competing in product markets. Consistent with the RBT, one would argue that the firm pursues a profitable innovation strategy by engaging in internal R&D activities, including new product development, to generate its competitive advantage. While firms are intent on developing an efficient internal labor market to facilitate the utilization of human resources who specifically conduct R&D activities (Lado & Wilson, 1994), they may not achieve their ambitions without purchasing some of human resources from strategic factor markets (e.g., Chesbrough, 1999; Khanna & Palepu, 1997). For example, Khanna and Palepu (1997) suggest that because the United States is endowed with better external labor markets than India, firms in the United States are more capable of and more efficient at obtaining external human resources compared to their counterparts in India.

Another interesting case that illustrates the importance of strategic factor markets is found in privatized firms in transition economies. When these firms attempt to obtain strategic resources from factor markets to upgrade relatively poor accumulated resources, the relative underdevelopment of strategic factor markets often limits their ability to do so (e.g., Peng & Heath, 1996; Uhlenbruck, Meyer, & Hitt, 2003). Because the external resources available to all firms embedded in a particular country affect the ability of firms to efficiently and effectively develop heterogeneous, hard-to-imitate resources necessary to implement product market strategies, the development of efficient and munificent strategic factor markets within a country is an important contingency factor determining a firm's competitive advantage.

Proposition 1. While competing in the same industry, firms operating in countries with higher levels of strategic factor market development are more likely to acquire external strategic resources that enable them to create a competitive advantage.

The Disruptive Effect of Strategic Factor Markets via Hypercompetition

The IOE model generally addresses industry competition among firms vying with one another in their own product markets (Bain, 1956, 1968; Mason, 1939). As such, some strategy scholars have addressed how product market rivalry in the competitive environment can dampen the ability of firms to sustain a competitive advantage (e.g., Miller & Shamsie, 1996). According to the IOE model, : "within-industry competition is the most significant competitive threat" (McGrath, 2013, p. 9). As McGrath (2013, p. 9) pointed out, however, "In more and more markets, we are seeing industries competing with other industries."

For example, because navigation apps and cameras are preloaded on each smartphone, smartphone makers such as Apple compete not only with navigation product makers such as Garmin and Magellan but also with digital camera makers like Kodak and Canon (Downes & Nunes, 2013). Moreover, consider the two exemplary companies that are arguably developing dynamic capabilities to achieve a series of temporary competitive advantages: Apple and Google. While Apple and Google had long competed in different product markets, direct competition between them began to emerge in the smartphone business. In fall 2009, both Apple and Google attempted to acquire AdMob (currently AdMob Google), the leader in the U.S. nascent mobile advertising industry, to strengthen ecosystems for mobile applications and devices that play a critical role in generating their competitive advantage (Burrows, 2010). Additional examples include increasing rivalry between Apple and Microsoft in the smartphone business as the latter entered the former's business by acquiring Nokia's Devices and Services business in 2013.

While various explanations can be offered for this emerging phenomenon, Markman et al. (2009) recently argued that some firms even from unrelated product markets in different industries can eventually become direct competitors or leapfrog industry incumbents' resource advantages through factor market rivalry over external resources. In fact, Ergas (1987), in his comparative study of seven industrialized countries such as the United States and Japan, suggested that the functioning of labor and capital markets determine the degree of competition and industrial structures in product markets. Therefore, it is important not to overlook the role of strategic factor markets in determining the dynamics of industry competition and structure. In particular, our study contends that the isolating mechanisms in industries, such as barriers to entry, barriers to imitation of strategic resources, and the rarity of strategic resources that not only impede hypercompetition by entry or imitation but also facilitate a sustainable competitive advantage, are more likely to break down in countries where strategic factor markets are more fully developed. As a result, one would expect that there will be more frequent entries and exits in an industry in a country endowed with more fully developed strategic factor markets than in a country with less fully developed strategic factor markets (e.g., Ergas, 1987).

For example, while the market for corporate control through mergers and acquisitions (M&As) is a typical example of reducing the immobility and inimitability of strategic resources (Chi, 1994), competitive firms embedded in countries where strategic factor markets are more fully developed would use M&As more frequently by acquiring the whole firm or the part of the firm in which strategic resources reside. Chacar, Newburry, and

Vissa (2010) found that the availability of skilled workers (e.g., senior managers) in labor markets reduced the sustainability of firms' competitive advantage. This might be because part of internal strategic resources were more or less mobile and thus partly imitated by a focal firm's competitors, so the firm's source of a competitive advantage dissipated among competitors where skilled workers transfer easily.

On the other hand, firms operating in highly inefficient and scarce strategic factor markets may engage in head-to-head competition less frequently in product markets because the strategic resources necessary to implement product market strategies are neither abundantly available nor cost-effective to acquire externally and/or accumulate internally. In some extreme cases, strategic factor markets are literally nonexistent. When Western MNEs set up their subsidiaries in Brazil, they learned that few Brazilian firms could offer global quality audit services (Khanna, Palepu, & Sinha, 2005). This implies that industry structures are relatively stable or at the best moderately dynamic in countries where strategic factor markets are inefficient and scarce because of formidable barriers to entry, and high barriers to imitation of strategic resources, and the rarity of external resources. To further illustrate and corroborate our point of view, we examine the following two cross-country comparative case studies.

In his study of Brazil, Mexico, and the United States in the textile industries, 1830–1930, Haber (1991) found that the development of financial capital markets such as securities markets and credit intermediaries that allowed established firms and new entrants to mobilize financial resources necessary to pursue strategies had a powerful influence on the degree of industrial concentration and the structure of the industry. Specifically, he found that constraints placed on the formation of financial capital markets in Brazil and Mexico led to more formidable barriers of entry and possibly barriers to imitation of resources against new entrants in the Brazilian and Mexican textile industries compared to the United States. Therefore, established textile firms in Brazil and Mexico could maintain their market power for far longer periods than their counterparts in the United States creating stiffer competition in the industry because more firms had easy access to capital in U.S. financial markets.

Another study by Chesbrough (1999) found the extent to which dominant incumbents in the same industry based in different countries were able to sustain a competitive advantage depended on differences in their countries' strategic factor markets. Specifically, incumbent U.S. firms in the hard disk drive industry failed to sustain their competitive advantage in the face of disruptive technological change affecting the industry's competitive dynamics. This was because the development of the technical labor market and the venture capital market in the United States allowed new entrants easy access to external resources. In fact, these new entrants armed with disruptive innovation (Christensen, 1997) could cause instantaneous decay in the barriers to imitation (Reed & DeFillippi, 1990). In the presence of threats from newly competing firms, it is thus more difficult for established firms to sustain a competitive advantage because of lower barriers to entry and barriers to imitation of strategic resources. On the other hand, this was not the case for incumbent Japanese firms. Because the technical labor market and the venture capital market in Japan were not as efficient and munificent as those of the United States, there were fewer new entrants able to successfully challenge incumbent firms in Japan. In fact, such differences in functioning of labor and capital markets may also partly explain more entries and exits in the flat panel industry in the United States than in Japan (Ergas, 1987; Spencer, 2003).

Proposition 2. While competing in the same industry, firms operating in countries with higher levels of strategic factor market development are more likely face hypercompetitive industry structures in which it will be more difficult for them to sustain a competitive advantage because the isolating mechanisms are more likely to break down.

The Facilitative Effect of Institutions via Internal Resource Development

North (1990, p. 5) noted that "[b]oth what organizations come into existence and how they evolve are fundamentally influenced by the institutional framework." In this regard, Oliver (1996, 1997) and Barney, Wright, and Ketchen (2001) stressed the critical importance of combining institutional and resource-based views in the strategy literature, arguing that because a firm's resource heterogeneity and competitive advantage depend on its ability to manage the institutional environment in which its resource decisions are embedded, scholars need to incorporate the institutional context. Echoing this view, Griffiths and Zammuto (2005, p. 824) pointed out that "various national institutional regimes create cultural and institutional policies and practices that structure competitiveness and firm and industry responses."

While institutions often develop as a result of strategic or political considerations, the widely held belief (or the efficient institutions view) is that societies choose the institutions that are socially efficient (Acemoglu, Johnson, & Robinson, 2005). As a result, because firms constructing business strategies take institutional opportunities and constraints into account

(North, 1990), they may find it legitimate to accumulate internal resources that fit best with their institutional policies and practices (e.g., Griffiths & Zammuto, 2005; Hoskisson, Eden, Lau, & Wright, 2000; Oliver, 1997). That is why while firms operating in developed economies, where institutions are relatively well-developed, have historically tended to accumulate market-oriented resources that are globally transferable. Their counterparts in emerging economies, where institutions are comparatively less developed, are likely to have relied more on nonmarket-oriented capabilities such as political connections that help take advantage of institutional voids but are less transferable and thus less valuable in the global marketplace (Guillén, 2000; Hoskisson et al., 2000; Peng, 2003).

As an example, consider advertising expenditures. According to the RBT, advertising expenditures could be viewed as investments in intangible marketing capabilities that in turn serve as the basis for competitive advantage (e.g., Dierickx & Cool, 1989). However, Spicer and Pyle (2002) found that, in post-communist Russia in the 1990s, advertising expenditures of newly established private commercial banks that were supposed to serve as a signal of quality or credibility and to attract new depositors had either little relationship, or even a negative relationship, with their product quality. These authors interpreted this finding as evidence of institutional malfunctioning. Because the unstable sociopolitical environment made it difficult for new private commercial banks to build long-term trusting relationships with Russian households who had remained loyal to *Sberbank* (the state-owned savings bank with a dominant market position), a large number of these private banks that engaged in heavy advertising struggled to survive and were perceived as failing to honor their obligations to depositors. As a result, households grew to distrust new private commercial banks.

Oliver (1997) claimed that firms competing in a particular regulatory environment are under pressure to obtain socially acceptable resources as inputs and, consequently, the way these inputs are combined and deployed is constrained by social expectations among competing firms. From this perspective, while marketing capabilities could be socially desirable resources in countries with well-developed institutions, the same capabilities could be considered socially undesirable in countries with less-developed institutions. Along the same lines, Hoskisson et al. (2000, p. 256) argued that "[l]ike most resources that create competitive advantage, resources for competitive advantage in emerging economies are, on the whole, intangible. However, they are not necessarily product-market-based." In these economies, nonmarket-oriented political resources that allow preferential access to business opportunities regulated by home governments could be a source of a short-term competitive advantage (e.g., Guillén, 2000; Peng, 2003; Wan, 2005). Although internally accumulating strategically valuable resources is necessary to create a competitive advantage in product markets in a way that generates value for customers and wealth for shareholders (Barney, 1991; Dierickx & Cool, 1989; Sirmon et al., 2007), this may be difficult to accomplish in institutionally underdeveloped countries.

Several studies noted below confirm our idea that that the institutional environment plays a paramount role in internally accumulating strategic resources that enable firms to create a competitive advantage. According to the RBT (e.g., Barney, 1991; Dierickx & Cool, 1989), one source of the firm's competitive advantage lies in its ability to pursue a profitable innovation strategy by engaging in internal R&D activities. It is essential that legal institutions be in place that protect intellectual property rights for firms to engage in internal R&D activities and new product development (Foss & Foss, 2005; Hirsch, 1975; Mahmood & Rufin, 2005). For example, Foss and Foss (2005) claimed that property rights, which are a component of legal institutions, are important to a resource owner. In fact, without property rights, firms will neither have the incentive to invest in strategic resources nor have a proper opportunity to appropriate value from their superior resources. Murmann (2003) found that, in the synthetic dye industry between 1877 and 1914, German firms that set up corporate R&D laboratories devoted exclusively to search for new technological capabilities outperformed British and American firms in the industry because Germany's institutions on intellectual property rights protection were superior to those of Britain and the United States In a similar vein, Bowen and De Clercq (2008), in their study of 40 countries, found that corruption in political institutions has a negative impact on the allocation of entrepreneurial effort directed toward high-growth activities.

Proposition 3. While competing in the same industry, firms operating in countries with higher levels of institutional development are more likely to accumulate internal strategic resources that enable them to create a competitive advantage.

The Disruptive Effect of Institutions via Hypercompetition

Paradoxically, however, institutions that help firms develop internal strategic resources in generating a competitive advantage can also make it more difficult for these firms to sustain it because countries with more fully developed institutions will likely set up lower institutional barriers to entry and to imitation of resources than countries with less developed institutions.

According to the IOE model, entry barriers impeding hypercompetition exist when incumbent firms are at a competitive advantage relative to new entrants. Consistent with the RBT, it is no wonder that incumbents have incentives to make entry barrier-raising investments in strategic resources (Caves & Porter, 1977). The most effective barriers to imitation of resources are achieved when new entrants encounter information asymmetries in regard to where incumbents' competitive advantage comes from (Reed & DeFillippi, 1990). However, new entrants are more likely to reduce such information asymmetries, wearing down barriers to entry and to imitation of resources more quickly in countries with higher levels of the development of legal, political, and social institutions.

Moreover, while Reed and DeFillippi (1990) argued that incumbent firms need to heighten reinvestment in strategic resources as a means of resisting decay in the barriers to imitation, Caves and Porter (1977) warned that entry barrier-raising investments in strategic resources can do incumbents firms harm rather than good. In a similar vein, Rumelt (1987) pointed out that the dark side of incumbents' advantage is that incumbent firms faced with the new product cannibalism problem (e.g., a new product cannibalizing sales of a recent but older product) often fail to see the emergence of substitute resources possessed by new entrants and thus prefer to deal with existing rather than potential competition. If an institutional framework in place reduces information asymmetries, adverse selection, and transaction costs facing new entrants often armed with a new bundle of strategic resources, then entry barriers may not be as formidable or effective as they appear. This is because these new entrants often strategically negate the value of strategic resources of industry incumbents by shifting bases of competitive advantage, making the isolating mechanisms that act to preserve a competitive advantage of incumbents irrelevant or invalid (e.g., Christensen, 1997; Schumpeter, 1942).[6] In fact, the dark side of incumbents' advantage manifests itself in the form of the paradox of organizational capabilities wherein core capabilities turn into core rigidities (e.g., Lado et al., 2006; Leonard-Barton, 1992).

In contrast, consider other countries with lower levels of institutional development, where new entrants lacking incentives to invest in strategic resources may be discouraged to challenge established firms that may tactically intervene in political, legal, and social institutions to control the market (e.g., Acemoglu et al., 2005; Caeldries, 1996; Rajan & Zingales, 2003). There is no dearth of examples – especially in emerging markets.

In China and Vietnam where the government tends to favor large domestic incumbents, for example, small new ventures are very frequently denied access to banks and stock exchange markets, two main sources of capital financing, due to various forms of legal and regulative discrimination against them (Yamakawa, Peng, & Deeds, 2008). In Russia, entrepreneurs and new entrepreneurial firms alike often experience an institutional atmosphere where they are seen as "speculators" or deemed "criminals for making a profit" and, consequently, their entrepreneurial activities are significantly suppressed across the country (Aidis, Estrin, & Mickiewicz, 2008, p. 658). Yet it is also true that only those in the inner circle of Russian elite groups are able to capitalize on emerging business opportunities, whereas others face extreme difficulty in accessing scarce resources as well as in establishing strong network ties that would help overcome bureaucratic costs.

Furthermore, previous research has suggested that, when formal, legal institutions such as contract enforcement and antitrust laws are underdeveloped, informal, social institutions such as trust and civic norms facilitate, rather than inhibit, arbitrary behavior and collusion among members in a society (Chacar et al. 2010; Knack & Keefer, 1997). In this regard, the anticompetitive actions that established firms often use to dampen industry competition are more likely when these firms are embedded in countries associated with underdeveloped institutions than in countries with fully developed institutions. This is because political strategies including lobbying would be more frequently deployed in the former than in the latter (Chacar et al., 2010; Mahmood & Rufin, 2005; Puffer & McCarthy, 2011). In Russia, for example, due to the lack of legitimate formal institutions, managers with severely limited strategic choices often pay protection money and bribes, which in turn "limit resources for product, market, and technology development, essentially limiting company competitiveness" (Puffer & McCarthy, 2011, p. 27). This case illustrates the possibility that weak formal institutions can give rise to flawed or distorted patterns of resource allocation.

Furthermore, when institutions are not functioning properly, new entrants cannot escape high levels of information asymmetries and the resulting transaction costs, which are not only important impediments to market efficiency but also significant sources of entry barriers (Yao, 1988). Oliver (1996, p. 169) introduced the concept of institutional impediments to market efficiency, arguing that "[i]nstitutional impediments exist when institutions impede perfect competition. … [i]nstitutional impediments are the causes of market failure." Because such institutional impediments help established firms with market power erect formidable barriers to entry and to imitation of strategic resources against new entrants (Mahoney & Pandian, 1992), firms are less likely to face hypercompetitive industry structures in countries with less-developed institutions.

Proposition 4. While competing in the same industry, firms operating in countries with higher levels of institutional development are more likely to face hypercompetitive industry structures in which it will be more difficult for them to sustain a competitive advantage because the isolating mechanisms are more likely to break down.

So far, we have addressed the paradoxical challenges of creating and sustaining a competitive advantage by examining the facilitative and disruptive effects of heterogeneous and imperfectly mobile institutions and strategic factor markets on the firm's competitive advantage, respectively. That is, we have discussed how these institutions and strategic factor markets can enable firms to create a competitive advantage, on the one hand, and how they can also complicate the ability of these firms to sustain a competitive advantage, on the other hand. According to Poole and Van de Ven (1989), researchers need to come to terms with seemingly incompatible, contradictory explanations to build more comprehensive theories and to generate new theoretical insights. In the following subsection, we thus address how firms manage these paradoxical tensions caused by the external resource environment in which firms are deeply embedded. In fact, understanding this issue is important because "companies may succeed or fail based on differences in their capabilities to *manage* paradox" (Lado et al., 2006, p. 115, italic in original). Our study takes into account the effects of internal and external resource-oriented strategies that influence the ability of firms to manage the paradox of environmental embeddedness.

Managing the Paradox of Environmental Embeddedness

Internal and External Resource-Oriented Strategies

For an internal resource-oriented strategy, our study employs a dynamic capabilities perspective to understand how firms manage the paradox of environmental embeddedness. More importantly, our treatise specifies the resource environmental conditions under which dynamic capabilities are more beneficial when managing the environmental paradox. Following Helfat et al. (2007, p. 4, italic added), our study defines dynamic capabilities as "the capacity of an organization to *purposefully* create, extend, or modify its resource base."[7] Anecdotally, Apple is a good example of how a firm develops its dynamic capabilities – not to mention companies like Google and IBM. Since Steve Jobs came back to Apple as interim CEO in 1997, the company has reinvested itself over and over again thanks to its dynamic capabilities.

Some strategy scholars have devoted their attention to the development and exercise of dynamic capabilities to address conceptually the notion of rapidly changing competitive environments (e.g., Eisenhardt & Martin, 2000; Helfat et al., 2007; Teece, 2007; Teece, Pisano, & Shuen, 1997; Winter, 2003). Furthermore, there is a growing consensus that, with the ongoing renewal available through their dynamic capabilities, firms are more capable of achieving a temporary (or transient) competitive advantage as a reality rather than being able to seek a sustainable competitive advantage, thereby shaping hypercompetition itself rather than just coping with it (e.g., D'Aveni, 1994; Eisenhardt & Martin, 2000; McGrath, 2013). Previous studies have implicitly assumed that dynamic capabilities are situated in the competitive environment at the industry level (Eisenhardt & Martin, 2000; Teece et al., 1997). Along the same lines, Zahra, Sapienza, and Davidsson (2006, p. 931) argued that "development and use of dynamic capabilities will vary with the rate of change in the industry itself." In contrast, our study argues that dynamic capabilities are, in part, necessitated more broadly in the resource environment at the country level.

In addition to an internal resource-oriented strategy, an external resource-oriented strategy can be pursued as well. While the sustainability of competitive advantage depends in part on firms' efforts to upgrade their own resource base by developing dynamic capabilities, Capron and Chatain (2008) contended that it also stems from their competitive interventions in the resource environment, which aim to degrade the resource position of their rivals or raise rivals' costs (cf. Oliver & Holzinger, 2008). Our study extends Capron and Chatain (2008) and claims that the degree to which firms favor one resource-oriented strategy over the other depends on resource environmental conditions. Our rationale behind this claim is that paradoxical tensions are subject to country-specific institutional and factor market differences which influence the likelihood that firms will develop dynamic capabilities and intervene in the country resource environment. Specifically, we show how different resource environmental conditions would mandate distinct mixtures of the development of dynamic capabilities and interventions given different strategic factor markets and institutions.

To illustrate our argument, our study develops a four-cell typology of resource environmental conditions and internal and external resource-oriented strategies. As depicted in Table 2, our study identifies four

Table 2. A Typology of Resource Environmental Conditions and Resource-Oriented Strategies.

Strategic factor market development		Institutional Development: High	Institutional Development: Low
	High	Cell 1 *Characteristics*: ○ Resource and transaction costs are low ○ External resources are abundantly available ○ Hypercompetition is most likely due to low barriers to entry and imitation ○ The value of internal resources is very high in product markets ○ Countries: The United States, Germany *Resource-oriented strategies*: ○ The need to develop dynamic capabilities is very high ○ Interventions in resource environments are least likely to help create and sustain a competitive advantage	Cell 2 *Characteristics*: ○ Resource and transaction costs are moderate ○ External resources are generally available ○ Hypercompetition is likely due to moderate barriers to entry and imitation ○ The value of internal resources is high in product markets ○ Countries: Japan, South Korea *Resource-oriented strategies*: ○ The need to develop dynamic capabilities is high ○ Interventions in resource environments are more likely to help create and sustain a competitive advantage
	Low	Cell 3 *Characteristics*: ○ Resource and transaction costs are high ○ External resources are generally scarce ○ Hypercompetition is less likely due to high barriers to entry and imitation ○ The value of internal resources is moderate in product markets ○ Countries: Chile, Poland *Resource-oriented strategies*: ○ The need to develop dynamic capabilities is moderate ○ Interventions in resource environments are less likely to help create and sustain a competitive advantage	Cell 4 *Characteristics*: ○ Resource and transaction costs are very high ○ External resources are seriously scarce ○ Hypercompetition is least likely due to very high barriers to entry and imitation ○ The value of internal resources is low in product markets ○ Countries: Russia, Venezuela *Resource-oriented strategies*: ○ The need to develop dynamic capabilities is low ○ Interventions in resource environments are most likely to help create and sustain a competitive advantage

different resource environmental conditions that influence the degree to which firms need to develop dynamic capabilities and intervene in the resource environment.[8] While firms in Cells 1 and 2 can be found mostly in developed economies, firms in Cells 3 and 4 are most likely to be found in emerging economies. We contend that firms in Cell 1 are more likely to develop dynamic capabilities, followed by firms in Cell 2, firms in Cell 3, and firms in Cell 4. On the other hand, although all firms in Cells 1–4 have incentives to intervene in the resource environment, firms in Cell 4 are more likely to do so, followed by firms in Cell 2, firms in Cell 3, and firms in Cell 1. Fig. 2 shows an expanded model of competitive advantage.

Development of Dynamic Capabilities versus Interventions in the Country Resource Environment

We begin by examining the two cells on the diagonal of Table 2: Cells 1 and 4 where there are the stark differences in the incentives for firms to develop dynamic capabilities and intervene in the resource environment. In Cell 1 countries such as the United States and Germany are characterized both by high levels of institutional development and by high levels of

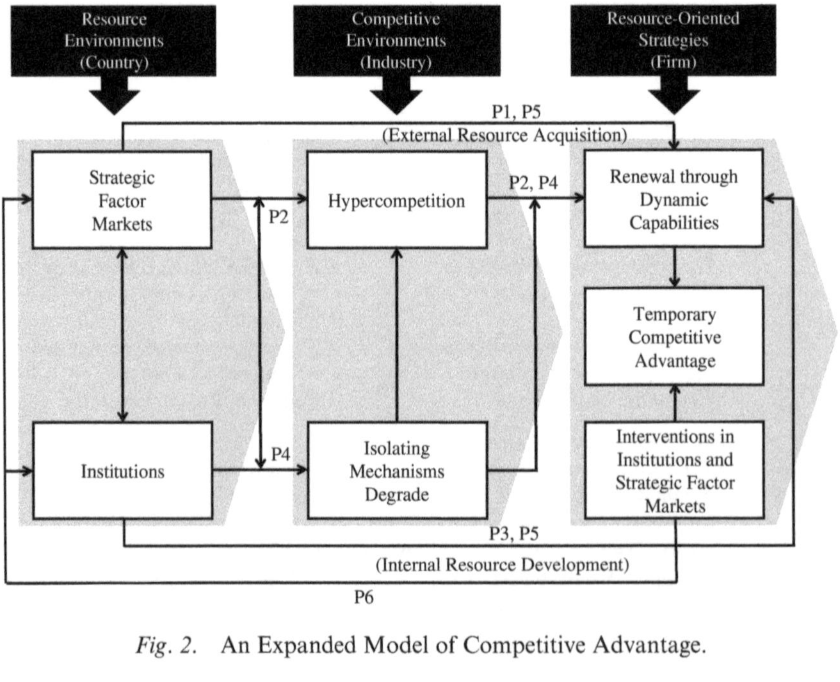

Fig. 2. An Expanded Model of Competitive Advantage.

strategic factor market development. Under these environmental conditions, it is logical to argue that operating in these countries is most likely to cause competitive firms to develop dynamic capabilities.

For example, although legal institutions such as those of intellectual property rights can help industry incumbents erect entry barriers that impede imitation of certain resources, new entrants that benefit greatly from accessing abundant external resources available in strategic factor markets and incurring low resource costs often undertake disruptive innovations, negating the value of critically acclaimed resources possessed by incumbents (e.g., Christensen, 1997). In response, industry incumbents are prompted to develop new resources and regain a competitive advantage, even though some may fail to do so (Lado et al., 2006). Participating in continuous and escalating hypercompetition will eventually render all firms in nearly all industry segments unable to sustain a competitive advantage, thereby encouraging them to develop dynamic capabilities. In the U.S. mobile handset industry, the rise and fall of global companies like Motorola, Nokia, and BlackBerry (formerly known as Research in Motion) vividly illustrate the necessity of dynamic capabilities (Binns, Harreld, O'Reilly, & Tushman, 2014).

At the same time, firms in Cell 1 are least likely to intervene in the resource environment for two reasons (Capron & Chatain, 2008). First, because the resource environment is already very well-structured, firms may have very limited latitude in shaping it to their advantage. Second, when market competition is increasingly more intense, focal firms are becoming less cost-effective in intervening in resource environments because it is more difficult for them to make sense of newly emerging, threatening resources and weaken the resource position of a large number of competitors. In fact, Bonardi, Hillman, and Keim (2005) argued that rivalry in product markets can naturally translate into rivalry in resource environments. As such, the chances of success for any individual company can be greatly reduced when rivalry in resource environments is intense. Overall, when the resource environment is already very well-structured, influencing it becomes less attractive or less effective for focal firms because any competitive advantage gained through such an external resource-oriented strategy may be minimal or shortly marginalized by competitors' dynamic capabilities in product markets.

Now we turn our attention to firms in Cell 4 where countries such as Russia and Venezuela are characterized by low levels of institutional development and low levels of strategic factor market development. Under these environmental conditions, competing firms will least likely need to develop dynamic capabilities for two reasons – especially given the fact that many established firms may be affiliated with business groups or controlled by states or oligarchs.[9]

First, newly competing firms in Cell 4 may find it hardest to replicate a competitive advantage of entrenched firms because these new entrants will face multiple obstacles to acquiring and utilizing superior resources in a cost-effective way. For example, institutional impediments to market efficiency (Oliver, 1996) can erect entry barriers against new entrants that may not be able to escape transaction costs because they will not know, with certainty, how accurate their information and expectations about external resources are (Barney, 1986). Also, when it comes to accessing financing, new entrants in Cell 4 are at a disadvantage due to capital market imperfections. Moreover, resource market imperfections in countries in Cell 4 with weak property rights protection will likely mitigate the incentives for new entrants to develop dynamic capabilities because they might benefit less from doing so (Foss & Foss, 2005).

Second, the costs of developing dynamic capabilities may exceed the benefits. While firms are required to develop dynamic capabilities in the dynamic competitive environment, Zahra et al. (2006) pointed out that when the competitive environment is relatively stable, the firm's efforts to repeatedly develop dynamic capabilities may harm firm performance. This is due to what might be called organizational costs associated with disrupting the firm's resource base and routines in the processes of acquiring, integrating, and divesting resources to adapt to its environment. In a similar vein, Winter (2003, p. 993) argued that "[a]ttempting too much change – perhaps in a deliberate effort to exercise the dynamic capability – can impose additional costs when the frequent disruption of the underlying capability outweighs the competitive value of the novelty achieved." In particular, this may be the case for firms whose competitive environment is not highly volatile. Unless competitive threats put a firm's competitive advantage at risk, its attempts to develop dynamic capabilities will be prohibitively costly under situations of low levels of institutional and strategic factor market development.

While both incumbent firms and new entrants in Cell 4 are least likely to develop dynamic capabilities on a regular basis, they may be strongly motivated to intervene in institutions and factor markets that are still in a nascent stage of evolution, but for different reasons. Incumbent firms in Cell 4 that may take preemptive actions to keep their market power and resource base intact, these firms are certainly motivated to maintain structural entry barriers against new entrants by purposefully exerting control over potential competitors' resources and by engaging in anticompetitive conduct in the resource environment (e.g., Acemoglu et al., 2005; Capron & Chatain, 2008; Rajan & Zingales, 2003). It follows that there will be a small number of competitors with a strong resource base in product markets that may prompt them not only to collude explicitly or implicitly but also to impede hypercompetition by reducing the quantity and quality of resources available to potential competitors in strategic factor markets (Capron & Chatain, 2008; Puffer & McCarthy, 2011). What all this means is that incumbent firms take concerted actions and do their best to effectively erect formidable barriers to imitation of their resource base and thus sustain a competitive advantage (Peng, 2003; Peng & Heath, 1996).

On the other hand, new entrants – many of which may be foreign MNEs – in Cell 4 intervene in the resource environment by exerting influence over strategic factor markets and institutions in a way that facilitates easy entry into their industries and/or alters the contexts in strategic factor markets and institutions in their favor. As an example, consider the experience of Chase Manhattan Bank (currently JPMorgan Chase) in Russia. In 1994, two licensed American banks, Chase Manhattan Bank and Citibank, were prohibited from serving institutional clients and retail customers alike while other foreign banks from Europe and China were allowed to operate without restrictions. In the midst of Russian top bankers' opposition, Chase Manhattan Bank successfully lobbied and worked closely with the Russian government to lift restrictions on the company's operations in the following year (Puffer, McCarthy, & Zhuplev, 1998). More critically, there have been numerous examples suggesting that a firm's government relations are more important than its own dynamic capabilities in countries in Cell 4 where governments often have every intention of slowing down or reversing market-oriented reforms (Conklin & Cadieux, 2009; Li, Peng, & Macaulay, 2013). During his years at the helm of Venezuela, for example, Hugo Chávez expropriated or nationalized private properties owned by domestic firms and foreign MNEs involved in a variety of industries and sectors such as food production, banking, energy, and the media (Conklin & Cadieux, 2009).

Let us now turn our attention to firms in the two off-diagonal cells in Table 2: Cells 2 and 3. Consider first Cell 2 where firms are embedded in countries such as Japan and South Korea characterized by low levels of institutional development and by high levels of strategic factor market development. While countries pertaining to Cell 2 are characterized by low levels of institutional development, legal institutions in these countries are relatively well-developed but political and social institutions are generally less-developed and still influential (Kim, Kim, & Hoskisson, 2010; Peng, Lee, & Wang, 2005). However, the development of strategic factor markets may lead to reduced resource and transaction costs and the development of legal institutions may strongly incentivize firms to develop internal resources, both of which may combine to render the marketplace hypercompetitive.

More importantly, RBT scholars have argued that Ricardian rents arising from competitive advantage are associated with strategic factor markets (e.g., Makadok, 2001; Sirmon et al., 2007). This implies that the existence of well-developed strategic factor markets may be a necessary condition for firms to develop dynamic capabilities through the upgrading of strategic resources. While firms in Cell 2 benefiting from munificent strategic factor markets have an opportunity to create a competitive advantage, they may need to fiercely compete for external resources in strategic factor markets (Barney, 1986; Markman et al., 2009). As Markman et al. (2009) suggest, it follows that factor market competition among firms spills over to product market competition in their industries. As can be easily seen, competitive firms are thus likely to face hypercompetition in industries like automobiles and electronics in Japan and South Korea. At the same time, it comes as no surprise that powerful incumbents very frequently resort to their outward resource-oriented strategy implemented through interventions in the resource environment in order to erect formidable entry barriers against new entrants.

Now consider Cell 3 where firms operate in countries such as Chile and Poland characterized by high levels of institutional development and by low levels of strategic factor market development. We begin by recognizing that Chile and Poland have arguably performed impressive institutional reforms in Latin America and Eastern Europe, respectively, and that the outcomes of these market-oriented reforms are prevalent in many business transactions. For example, research suggests that legal and regulatory institutions in Chile were reformed to improve market efficiency while reducing transaction costs (Dau, 2012; Stone, Levy, & Paredes, 1996). Consequentially, Chilean firms found it relatively easy to enter industries partly because they ended up allocating fewer resources to regulatory compliance activities. Yet, the development of institutions alone may not suffice to create hypercompetitive markets across the board. As an example, consider Poland. While legal, political, and social institutions have increasingly stabilized since 1990, the progress in market-oriented institutional change has not been matched through improved strategic factor markets (DeDee & Frederickson, 2004).

Although strategic factor markets and institutions tend to remain relatively stable within countries over time (Kogut, 1991; North, 1990), the pace of their changes in strategic factor markets generally lags behind the pace of changes in institutions (DeDee & Frederickson, 2004; Khanna & Palepu, 1999). Even when external shocks foster institutional improvements, resource and transaction costs associated with acquiring external resources may not be lowered significantly without an adequate development of strategic factor markets (Hoskisson et al., 2013). In fact, the underdevelopment of strategic factor markets such as the lack of capital and poorly developed labor markets would likely discourage new entrants because access to critical or substitute resources necessary to erode established firms' competitive advantage may not be available.

In a nutshell, firms in Cell 3 are less likely than firms in Cell 2 to face hypercompetition and, consequently, the former have reduced motivation to pursue dynamic capabilities compared to the latter. This means that the former will likely have weaker incentives to influence the resource environment in their favor in order to keep their current assets and competences intact than the latter (Oliver & Holzinger, 2008). Conversely, because institutions in Cell 2 are shaped and influenced more by a firm's external resource-oriented, political strategy than those in Cell 3 (Capron & Chatain, 2008), firms in Cell 2 are more likely than their counterparts in Cell 3 to intervene in the resource environment not only to protect their market positions but also to gain greater access to strategic resources necessary to upgrade existing resources and capabilities.

Because environmental embeddedness in four distinct resource environmental contexts differentially influences the extent to which firms benefit from developing dynamic capabilities and intervening in the resource environment, we put forth the following propositions to help manage the environmental paradox:

Proposition 5. While competing in the same industry, firms operating in countries with high levels of both institutional and strategic factor market development (pertaining to Cell 1) are more likely to develop dynamic capabilities to achieve a temporary competitive advantage, followed by firms in Cell 2, firms in Cell 3, and firms in Cell 4.

Proposition 6. While competing in the same industry, firms operating in countries with low levels of both institutional and strategic factor market development (pertaining to Cell 4) are more likely to intervene in the resource environment to achieve a temporary competitive advantage, followed by firms in Cell 2, firms in Cell 3, and firms in Cell 1.

DISCUSSION

Our objective in establishing the REV was to unpack more concretely the environmental sources of competitive advantage. As such, building on both the IOE and the RBT, we demonstrated how the environment influences these two models as well. Central to the REV is that because firms are nested in industries, which are in turn nested in larger external environments, the resource environment in which firms are deeply embedded plays a significant role in the ability of these firms to create and sustain a competitive advantage. Viewing institutions and strategic factor markets as the two fundamental but different pillars of our theoretical underpinning, our model conceptualizes the paradox of environmental embeddedness that encompasses both the facilitative and disruptive effects of institutions and strategic factor markets. Furthermore, our study also adds value to the dynamic capabilities perspective by justifying more fully the need for this perspective and suggesting that it helps firms manage the environmental paradox to create and sustain a competitive advantage. We discuss next further implications of the REV for theory and practice and then offer suggestions for applying the model in future research.

Implications for Theory

Our study has three important implications for theory and research. First, the REV offers a broader framework for explaining and understanding the origins of a firm's competitive advantage by providing a stronger theoretical foundation for both IOE and the RBT, as illustrated in Figs. 1 and 2 and summarized in Table 3. While proponents of IOE have been concerned with why industries in the same country perform differently, RBT scholars have long addressed why firms in the same industry perform differently. As noted earlier, however, these two established models have largely ignored the broader external environment in which firms and industries are embedded. In this regard, our study develops the REV of competitive advantage to put forward the idea that the success or failure of the firm in international competition rests in part on the country resource environment in which the firm is inherently embedded.

Although there have been attempts and calls for paying simultaneous attention to IOE and the RBT as complementary views (e.g., Collis, 1991; Conner, 1991; Mahoney & Pandian, 1992), their primary interests have

Table 3. A Summary of the Characteristics of the Resource Environment View, Industrial Organization Economics, and the Resource-Based Theory.

Characteristics	REV	IOE	RBT
Unit of analysis	• Country	• Industry	• Firm
Research questions	• Why does the same industry perform differently across countries? • Why do firms in the same industry based in different countries perform differently?	• Why do industries in the same country perform differently?	• Why do firms in the same industry perform differently?
Core concepts	• Institutional development and strategic factor market endowments	• Industry structure and firm conduct (or strategy)	• Valuable, rare, inimitable, and nonsubstitutable resources
Role of external environment	• Substantially influences firm conduct and performance	• Industry structure determines firm conduct and performance	• Influences firm conduct and performance
Key assumptions	• Institutions and strategic factor markets are heterogeneous and imperfectly mobile across countries • External resources are equally available to all firms in the same industry based in the same country unless some firms manipulate the external resource environment to exert control over others' resources • The resource heterogeneity among firms in different countries is greater than the resource heterogeneity among firms in the same country	• Firms within an industry or a strategic group are homogeneous in terms of the resources they possess and the strategies they pursue • Firms are heterogeneous across industries and strategic groups	• Firms in the same industry based in the same country are heterogeneous in terms of externally acquired and internally accumulated resources • Internally accumulated resources in combination with externally acquired ones are imperfectly mobile across firms
Origins of competitive advantage	• A firm's ability to access and reconfigure firm resources given favorable institutions and strategic factor markets • A firm's ability to develop dynamic capabilities necessary to reconfigure resources	• A firm's market power and industry entry barriers	• A firm's ability to acquire external resources and accumulate internal resources to generate heterogeneous, hard-to-imitate resources • A firm's ability to exploit existing external and internal resources and explore new ones

focused on the competitive environment and firm behavior in the product market. As we move from left to right across Figs. 1 and 2, however, it is apparent that the country resource environment affects the competitive environment and firm behavior in the product market. Therefore, we argue that the REV is not only complementary to the two established theoretical perspectives of IOE and the RBT but it also offers an integrative framework for explaining and understanding the origins of a firm's competitive advantage. In fact, a striking feature of the REV of competitive advantage is its ability to span three levels of aggregation: the country, the industry, and the firm.

It is well recognized that institutions and strategic factor markets matter. Institutions and strategic factor markets play a key role in changing the structure of the industry of which firms are an integral part and intensifying the fierce competition in the industry. For example, Murmann (2003) and Chesbrough (1999) have shown that industry dynamics and patterns of industry evolution vary significantly across countries with different national institutions and strategic factor markets. Moreover, institutions and strategic factor markets are argued to have a significant impact on the ability of these firms to develop firm-specific resources. Hoskisson et al. (2000) and Oliver (1997), among others, have argued that institutions influence the firm's resource heterogeneity. Equally important, RBT scholars, drawing on the Ricardian perspective, have argued that Ricardian rents accrue to the owners of abundant external resources that are used intensively in firm-specific resource accumulation and deployment (e.g., Kim et al. 2015; Makadok, 2001; Peteraf, 1993; Sirmon et al., 2007).

However, neither approach alone is adequate for explaining how and why institutions and strategic factors alike matter not only for the firm itself and the industry but also for competitive advantage. Moreover, the strategy literature has placed little emphasis on the mechanisms through which institutions and strategic factor markets actually contribute (positively and negatively) to competitive advantage. In this regard, our study proposes an integrative model of competitive advantage by suggesting the combined effects of institutions and strategic factor markets and by exploring the environmental mechanisms by which firms are incentivized to develop dynamic capabilities and in turn achieve a temporary (or transient) competitive advantage (D'Aveni, 1994; Eisenhardt & Martin, 2000; McGrath, 2013), as illustrated in Fig. 2.

Second, our study, drawing on two concepts of the paradox of environmental embeddedness and dynamic capabilities, provides a new rationale regarding the sustainability of competitive advantage. Previous studies have suggested that firms deeply embedded in an external network of suppliers, customers, communities, investors, and so on, to which they have made strategic commitments affect their ability to sustain a competitive advantage (e.g., Chesbrough, 1999; Christensen, 1997; Sull, Tedlow, & Rosenbloom, 1997). Compared to these studies, our study shifts the focus of attention to the external resource environment in which firms are inherently embedded to offer new insights into the sustainability of competitive advantage. Specifically, the basic thesis of our study is that the nature of paradoxical tensions imposed by the country resource environment is that the environmental embeddedness that provides firms with opportunities to create a competitive advantage can potentially provide the same firms with constraints that inhibit their ability to sustain a competitive advantage.

Finally, our treatise extends our understanding of dynamic capabilities by suggesting that country boundaries establish different incentives for developing dynamic capabilities in terms of institutions and strategic factor markets. There have been studies in the strategy literature showing why firms need to develop dynamic capabilities in changing or hypercompetitive environments at the industry level (e.g., D'Aveni, 1994; Miller & Shamsie, 1996; Teece et al., 1997). In this regard, Eisenhardt and Martin (2000, p. 1110) suggest a boundary condition of dynamic capabilities by pointing out that "[t]he pattern of effective dynamic capabilities depends upon [product] market dynamism." However, previous studies have also been cognizant of differences in the hypercompetitive status in the same industry across countries (e.g., Bogner & Barr, 2000; Chesbrough, 1999; Haber, 1991). Our study extends this line of reasoning to suggest country boundaries for dynamic capabilities by arguing that firms deeply embedded in countries associated both with more fully developed and efficient institutions and with more efficient and munificent strategic factor markets will be more compelled to develop dynamic capabilities, whereas this may not always be the case for firms embedded in countries associated both with less fully developed institutions and strategic factor markets.

Implications for Practice

The general applicability of the REV to top managers in firms deserves our attention. Several studies have shown why firms, when faced with radical environmental changes within a given industry, should manage the organizational paradox of success (e.g., Audia et al., 2000; Christensen, 1997). Comparatively, our study indicates that when creating and sustaining a competitive advantage, firms should examine more closely the paradoxical tensions caused by resource environments. One important implication of our theorizing is that firms in countries associated both with better functioning institutions and with more munificent strategic factor markets may be more susceptible to Schumpeterian competition or hypercompetition. As such, these firms need to consider not only developing dynamic capabilities but also seeking to achieve a series of temporary competitive advantages rather than seeking to enjoy a sustainable competitive advantage by defending their market position in the industry.

While proponents of the dynamic capabilities perspective have ascribed the necessity of dynamic capabilities to the dynamics of product market competition (e.g., Eisenhardt & Martin, 2000; Teece, 2007; Teece et al., 1997; Winter, 2003), our study takes a different lens to explain why firms need to develop dynamic capabilities. While making sense of, and acting within, hypercompetitive environments is a critical part of the strategic leader's job (Bogner & Barr, 2000), our study also urges corporate executives to pay attention to two potential blind spots – institutions and strategic factor markets that we argue influence a company's resource base and market position in a given industry. As previously illustrated in the Apple versus Google case (Burrows, 2010), it is apparent that some firms even from unrelated product markets can eventually become direct competitors through factor market rivalry over resources (Markman et al., 2009). Therefore, top managers who underestimate the significance of strategic factor markets by focusing too much on product markets per se may make strategic errors, finding a firm's dynamic capabilities underdeveloped and incapable of creating a series of temporary competitive advantages.

Our study also has practical implications for top managers of MNEs who may wish to ask themselves, "What determines the success or failure of the firm in international competition?" (Rumelt et al., 1994, p. 2). There have been two notable multinationalizing trends over the past decade or so. While a growing number of developed market MNEs (DMNEs) have shifted their strategic attention from other developed to emerging markets like China (e.g., Cell 1 → Cell 4 in Table 2), some (but not all) emerging market MNEs (EMNEs) have made forays into developed markets such as the United States (e.g., Cell 4 → Cell 1 in Table 2). While we generally suggest that both DMNEs and EMNEs formulate and execute internal and external resource-oriented strategies that fit emerging or developed markets, we first discuss what top executives of DMNEs need to consider when doing business in emerging markets.

Of course, the extent to which dynamic capabilities developed at home are readily transferable to emerging markets is a compelling question for top executives of DMNEs. As argued earlier, however, it is not an exaggeration to say that possessing dynamic capabilities per se does not necessarily determine the success or failure of DMNEs in emerging markets because dynamic capabilities are less important for DMNEs entering emerging markets. Rather, they are required to develop two complementary and equally important external resource-oriented strategies that fit emerging markets to at the very least establish a foothold in emerging markets.

First, DMNEs' active intervention in the resource environment is a reasonable consideration as an external resource-oriented strategy if it aims to shape the resource environment in a way that reduces the additional costs of doing business abroad (Baron, 1995; Capron & Chatain, 2008). The fact that the resource environment remains underdeveloped means that competitive threat is obviously limited. Nonetheless, it is important to keep in mind that local players take a variety of actions to oppose the entry of DMNEs, as was the case with Russian banks' opposition against the entry of foreign banks (Puffer et al., 1998). As a matter of fact, because the resource environment has been in flux in many emerging markets, DMNEs may be able to find more opportunities to preempt or control resources (Capron & Chatain, 2008).

A second external resource-oriented strategy DMNEs can execute is to work around the voids of the resource environment (Khanna et al., 2005). Yet there is a caveat associated with this strategy; DMNEs may incur the additional costs of doing business that might not have accrued to them in developed markets – what we call resource costs of doing business in emerging markets. As an example, consider Intel in Vietnam. In 2006, Intel decided to build its largest foreign facility in Vietnam because of the nation's cheap workforce and its location in the heart of Southeast Asia. Yet the company soon realized that the labor market did not supply a sufficient number of talented engineers, thereby launching its Intel Vietnam Study Abroad Program in 2009. Since then Intel has spent $7 million in sponsoring Vietnamese engineering students at Portland State University in the United States to help prepare them for a career in the company's facility in Ho Chi Minh City (Einhorn & Kharif, 2014).

McDonald's in Russia offers a similar example (Khanna et al., 2005). Even though McDonald's currently operates one of the world's busiest and biggest restaurants in Russia, it incurred substantial costs to work around the voids in local factor markets when it entered Russia in 1990. At the time McDonald's outsourced most of its supply chain operations in the

United States, but it could not do so in Russia because reliable suppliers were virtually nonexistent. With the help of its global supplier networks, the company thus decided to vertically integrate supply chain operations by producing beef, potatoes, dairy products, ketchup, mustard, and the like, as well as by setting up a trucking fleet to deliver supplies to restaurants.

We next discuss what top executives of EMNEs need to consider when entering developed markets. It is obvious that EMNEs face a different set of challenges when entering developed markets (Bartlett & Ghoshal, 2000; Hoskisson, Kim, White, & Tihanyi, 2004; Kim et al., 2015). Consider the situation faced by Cemex, Mexico's largest cement company and the world's fourth largest producer. In the late 1980s, the company established distribution facilities in Southern states such as California, Arizona, and Florida and served the U.S. cement market profitably by importing cements from Mexico. Yet eight U.S. cement producers and two unions filed an antidumping petition against Cemex that resulted in the U.S. agencies' imposition of a 58% duty on Cemex's imports. In response, Cemex decided to withdraw from markets like Florida where cement prices were relatively low while remaining in markets like California and Arizona where cement prices were much higher. At the same time, the company launched multiple appeals in an antidumping case, but its appeal failed (Baron, 1995).

It may be fair to say that Cemex is more the exception than the rule in the sense that the company experienced an immediate success in developed markets like the United States, which caused local firms to resort to national politics and political institutions. In general, it would take some time and deliberate efforts for EMNEs to capitalize on opportunities that exist in developed markets. And entering developed markets successfully in a rapidly changing marketplace requires more than just tweaking their home market resource-oriented strategies and low cost advantages (Dawar & Frost, 1999). Of course, EMNEs have an opportunity of developing a long-term competitive advantage by gaining access to well-developed resource environments. Paradoxically, however, they are often unable to sustain the pace of strategic change required. Just consider the competitive situation faced by EMNEs like Huawei, ZTE, and HTC competing in the U.S. smartphone industry, not to mention Samsung Electronics and LG Electronics. To compete and survive in developed markets, such EMNEs must be able to develop dynamic capabilities that are usually seen as less necessary or more costly at home.

Policy makers can also adopt and apply the REV by recognizing the importance of advancing both institutions and strategic factor markets.

Although the resource environment could be characterized by the nature of paradoxical tensions that involve the opposing sources of a firm's competitive advantage, public policy makers should stay mindful of the necessity to develop and enhance a country's competitiveness. Pursuing better competitiveness is in line with Porter (1990) and Kogut (1991) who argued for the long-lasting impact of home country advantages. As a large body of research illustrates, for example, emerging economies have implemented institutional change and moved toward more market-oriented economies (e.g., Kim et al., 2010; Spicer et al., 2000; Spicer & Pyle, 2002; Uhlenbruck et al., 2003). Although firms have a better opportunity to create their competitive advantage using their improved institutional conditions, they may not take full advantage of such market-oriented institutional change because it may not be automatically accompanied by advances in the efficiency and munificence in strategic factor markets. Therefore, policy makers should pay as much attention to strategic factor markets as to institutions. Likewise, policy makers need to keep in mind that in doing so, they will induce significant strategic changes on firms because such changes induce the environmental paradox, not only the opportunity for better resources, but also they will invite more hypercompetition, which also can be dysfunctional, especially if firms do not choose to develop potentially costly dynamic capabilities necessary to compete in hypercompetitive markets.

Applying the Resource Environment View in Future Research

It is important to validate and elaborate the REV presented in this treatise. Therefore, future research should test the boundaries of generalizability of our integrative model of competitive advantage. First, future research should test the contextual boundaries of our propositions. Although our propositions may apply to all types of countries, they may be more relevant for some countries than for others. In addition, some countries such as China may have regional variance in the institutional development and factor markets (Chang & Wu, 2013) making strategy formulation more complex. Moreover, our model generally assumes that our research propositions are relevant for all types of firms and industries because a country's institutions and strategic factor markets presumably have a universal impact on them in the same country. However, some empirical studies have found that this may not be the case (e.g., Hirsch, 1975). This implies that our propositions may be more relevant for some types of firms and industries than for others within a country. In a related vein, there is a caveat on the REV that comprise institutions and strategic factor markets as the two pillars of its theoretical underpinning. As Porter (1990) suggests, a firm's competitive advantage is also influenced by other variables such as related and supporting industries and demand conditions. For example, Japanese firms' strengths and global dominance in the automobile industry are in part driven by their strong ties with suppliers and by strong demand for fuel-efficient compact cars in Japan that needs to import oil and to manage territorial congestion. Yet if the REV includes all of these and other variables, then it might make it more difficult to establish its contextual boundaries.

Second, while our theorizing generally takes a cross-sectional perspective, future research should take into account a longitudinal perspective (e.g., Miller & Shamsie, 1996) and examine how changes in institutions and/or strategic factor markets influence the way firms, while coping with these changes, create and sustain a competitive advantage over time (e.g., Kim et al., 2010). As Collis (1991) observed, for example, there were the ups and downs of the United States, European, and Japanese firms in the global bearings industry between the mid 1950s and the late 1990s. An intriguing question is to examine how the dynamics of changes in institutions and/or strategic factor markets affect the dynamics of product market competition.

Finally, future research should investigate whether there are systematic differences between MNEs and purely domestic firms in the same industry based in the same country in terms of the way they create and sustain a competitive advantage. Our conjecture is that while MNEs are more capable than domestic firms in taking advantage of the heterogeneity of institutions and strategic factor markets between home and host countries, MNEs are more susceptible than domestic firms to changes and differences in institutions and strategic factor markets across countries.

CONCLUSION

The REV presented here points to the environmental origins of a firm's competitive advantage in international competition. Our theoretical model highlights the impact of the country resource environment on the ability of firms to create and sustain a competitive advantage. It also highlights the extent to which firms need to develop dynamic capabilities to address the paradoxical nature of the resource environment. We believe that the REV could be complementary to the two established theoretical perspectives on the origins and sustainability of competitive advantage – IOE and the RBT. We hope the REV set forth in this paper is useful to strategy and international scholars to develop theoretical and empirical work in this area, as well as to managers in firms who desire to create competitive advantage and deal with competitive disadvantage.

NOTES

1. Because firms are nested in industries, which are in turn nested in resource environments, it is important to recognize the stark differences in country-specific features of the national environment in which firms and industries are nested. Hitt, Beamish, Jackson, and Mathieu (2007) contend that the multilevel nesting arrangement has important implications for management theory and research. In building and specifying multilevel theory, our study follows Klein, Dansereau, and Hall's (1994) guidelines, assuming the homogeneity of industries and firms within countries and the heterogeneity of industries and firms between countries because our focus is on variation between countries in terms of strategic factor markets and institutions.

2. While the IOE model has largely assumed that industry structure viewed as exogenous influences firm conduct (strategy), but not vice versa, some industrial organization studies have recognized the effect of firm conduct on industry structure (see Porter, 1981), as depicted in the double arrow line in Fig. 1. In the strategy literature, however, research has shown that new entrants often change the structure of industries dramatically, displacing incumbent firms (e.g., Christensen, 1997; D'Aveni, 1994). That is, strategy scholars view industry structure as endogenous.

3. Markman et al. (2009) suggest that different terms such as strategic factor markets (Barney, 1986), production factors (Ricardo, 1817), and factor conditions (Porter, 1990) used in the strategy literature are interchangeable with each other.

4. According to Guillén and García-Canal (2009), new MNEs are based in (a) upper/middle income economies such as South Korea, Spain, Portugal, and Taiwan; (b) emerging economies such as Brazil, Chile, Mexico, China, India, and Turkey; (c) developing countries such as Egypt, Indonesia, and Thailand; and (d) oil-rich countries such as the United Arab Emirates, Nigeria, and Venezuela.

5. While the examination of a causal relationship between strategic factor markets and institutions is beyond the scope of our study, previous studies (e.g., Peng & Heath, 1996; Rajan & Zingales, 2003) have indicated a mutually dependent, reciprocal relationship between them, as depicted in the double arrow line in Fig. 1.

6. We are aware that legal institutions such as those of intellectual property rights can help industry incumbents set entry barriers that impede imitation of certain resources. However, Rumelt (1984, p. 569) recognized that "[m]ore fundamental shocks act to change the very structure of the industry, altering the nature and magnitudes of the isolating mechanisms at work."

7. The "resource base" includes the 'tangible, intangible, and human assets (or resources) as well as capabilities which the organization owns, controls, or has access to on a preferential basis' (Helfat et al. 2007, p. 4).

8. Four legend ratings are classified at low, moderate, high, and very high to evaluate the relative significance of items across cells. Also, those who are interested in classifying countries based on resource environmental conditions would refer to studies by Chan et al. (2008), Hoskisson et al. (2013), Kim et al. (2015), and Wan and Hoskisson (2003).

9. A business group is a collection of legally independent firms bound together in a variety of formal and informal ways. Because firms operate in countries in which strategic factor markets are underdeveloped, they tend to develop internal strategic factor markets within a business group to reduce resource and transaction costs (e.g., Guillén, 2000; Hoskisson et al., 2000; Khanna & Palepu, 1997). In Russia, for example, oligarchs are those "who gained control of many of the country's most valuable assets at a fraction of their value" during the country's privatization process after the collapse of the Soviet Union on December 31, 1991 (Puffer & McCarthy, 2011, p. 24).

ACKNOWLEDGMENTS

We are very grateful for the helpful comments and suggestions of Rajiv Nag and Qian Gu.

REFERENCES

Acemoglu, D., Johnson, S., & Robinson, J. A. (2005). Institutions as a fundamental cause of long-run growth. In P. Aghion & S. N. Durlauf (Eds.), *Handbook of economic growth* (pp. 385–472). Amsterdam: Elsevier.

Ahuja, G., & Yayavaram, S. (2011). Explaining influence rents: The case for an institutions-based view of strategy. *Organization Science*, *22*, 1631–1652.

Aidis, R., Estrin, S., & Mickiewicz, T. (2008). Institutions and entrepreneurship development in Russia: A comparative perspective. *Journal of Business Venturing*, *23*, 656–672.

Audia, P. G., Locke, E. A., & Smith, K. G. (2000). The paradox of success: An archival and a laboratory study of strategic persistence following radical environmental change. *Academy of Management Journal*, *43*, 837–853.

Bain, J. S. (1956). *Barriers to new competition*. Cambridge, MA: Harvard University Press.

Bain, J. S. (1968). *Industrial organization* (2nd ed.). New York, NY: Wiley.

Barney, J., Wright, M., & Ketchen, D. J. (2001). The resource-based view of the firm: Ten years after 1991. *Journal of Management*, *27*, 625–641.

Barney, J. B. (1986). Strategic factor markets: Expectations, luck, and business strategy. *Management Science*, *32*, 1231–1241.

Barney, J. B. (1991). Firm resources and sustained competitive advantage. *Journal of Management*, *17*, 99–120.

Baron, D. P. (1995). Integrated strategy: Market and nonmarket components. *California Management Review*, *37*(2), 47–65.

Bartlett, C. A., & Ghoshal, S. (2000). Going global lessons from late movers. *Harvard Business Review*, *78*(2), 132–142.

Binns, A., Harreld, J. B., O'Reilly, C., & Tushman, M. L. (2014). The art of strategic renewal. *MIT Sloan Management Review*, *55*(2), 21–23.

Bogner, W. C., & Barr, P. S. (2000). Making sense in hypercompetitive environments: A cognitive explanation for the persistence of high velocity competition. *Organization Science*, *11*, 212–226.

Bonardi, J.-P., Hillman, A. J., & Keim, G. D. (2005). The attractiveness of political markets: Implications for firm strategy. *Academy of Management Review*, *30*, 397–413.

Bowen, H. P., & De Clercq, D. (2008). Institutional context and the allocation of entrepreneurial effort. *Journal of International Business Studies*, *39*, 747–767.

Burrows, P. (2010). Apple vs. Google. *Bloomberg BusinessWeek*, January 25, pp. 28–34.

Caeldries, F. (1996). The institutional embeddedness of strategy: Predation through legislation (or, see you in court). *Advances in Strategic Management*, *13*, 215–246.

Capron, L., & Chatain, O. (2008). Competitors' resource-oriented strategies: Acting on competitors' resources through interventions in factor markets and political markets. *Academy of Management Review*, *33*, 97–121.

Capron, L., Mitchell, W., & Swaminathan, A. (2001). Asset divestiture following horizontal acquisitions: A dynamic view. *Strategic Management Journal*, *22*, 817–844.

Castrogiovanni, G. J. (1991). Environmental munificence: A theoretical assessment. *Academy of Management Review*, *16*, 542–565.

Caves, R. E., & Porter, M. E. (1977). From entry barriers to mobility barriers: Conjectural decisions and contrived deterrence to new competition. *Quarterly Journal of Economics*, *91*, 241–261.

Chacar, A., & Vissa, B. (2005). Are emerging economies less efficient? Performance persistence and the impact of business group affiliation. *Strategic Management Journal*, *26*, 933–946.

Chacar, A. S., Newburry, W., & Vissa, B. (2010). Bringing institutions into performance persistence research: Exploring the impact of product, financial, and labor market institutions. *Journal of International Business Studies*, *41*, 1119–1140.

Chan, C. M., Isobe, T., & Makino, S. (2008). Which country matters? Institutional development and foreign affiliate performance. *Strategic Management Journal*, *29*, 1179–1205.

Chang, S. J., & Wu, B. (2013). Institutional barriers and industry dynamics. *Strategic Management Journal*, *35*(8), 1103–1123.

Chesbrough, H. (1999). The organizational impact of technological change: A comparative theory of national institutional factors. *Industrial and Corporate Change*, *8*, 447–485.

Chi, T. (1994). Trading in strategic resources: Necessary conditions, transaction cost problems, and choice of exchange structure. *Strategic Management Journal*, *15*, 271–290.

Christensen, C. M. (1997). *The innovator's dilemma: When new technologies cause great firms to fail*. Boston, MA: Harvard Business School Press.

Collis, D. J. (1991). A resource-based analysis of global competition: The case of the bearings industry. *Strategic Management Journal*, *12*(Summer special issue), 49–68.

Conklin, D. W., & Cadieux, D. (2009). Hugo Chavez's public policy vision for Venezuela: Rooted in the past, doomed in the future. Ivey case No. 9B06M059.

Conner, K. (1991). A historical comparison of resource-based theory and five schools of thought within industrial organization economics: Do we have a new theory of the firm? *Journal of Management*, *17*, 121–154.

Dau, L. A. (2012). Pro-market reforms and developing country multinational corporations. *Global Strategy Journal*, *2*, 262–276.

D'Aveni, R. A. (1994). *Hypercompetition: Managing the dynamics of strategic maneuvering*. New York, NY: The Free Press.

Davis, L. E., & North, D. C. (1971). *Institutional change and American economic growth*. Cambridge: Cambridge University Press.

Dawar, N., & Frost, T. (1999). Competing with giants: Survival strategies for local companies in emerging markets. *Harvard Business Review*, *77*(2), 119–129.

DeDee, J. K., & Frederickson, P. (2004). Poland: What U.S. managers need to know. *Thunderbird International Business Review*, 46, 293–316.

Dierickx, I., & Cool, K. (1989). Asset stock accumulation and sustainability of competitive advantage. *Management Science*, *35*, 1504–1511.

Downes, L., & Nunes, P. F. (2013). Big-bang disruption. *Harvard Business Review*, *91*(3), 44–56.

Einhorn, B., & Kharif, O. (2014). Intel's big push for Vietnamese engineers. *Bloomberg Businessweek*, June 30, pp. 34–36.

Eisenhardt, K. M., & Brown, S. L. (1996). Environmental embeddedness and the constancy of corporate strategy. *Advances in Strategic Management*, *13*, 187–214.

Eisenhardt, K. M., & Martin, J. A. (2000). Dynamic capabilities: What are they? *Strategic Management Journal*, *21*, 1105–1121.

Ergas, H. (1987). Does technology policy matter? In B. R. Guile & H. Brooks (Eds.), *Technology and global industry: Companies and nations in the world economy* (pp. 191–245). Washington, DC: National Academy Press.

Foss, K., & Foss, N. J. (2005). Resources and transaction costs: How property rights economics furthers the resource-based view. *Strategic Management Journal*, *26*, 541–553.

Geroski, P. A., & Jacquemin, A. (1988). The persistence of profits: A European comparison. *Economic Journal*, *98*, 375–389.

Griffiths, A., & Zammuto, R. F. (2005). Institutional governance systems and variations in national competitive advantage: An integrative framework. *Academy of Management Review*, *30*, 823–842.

Guillén, M. F. (2000). Business groups in emerging economies: A resource-based view. *Academy of Management Journal*, *43*, 362–380.

Guillén, M. F., & García-Canal, E. (2009). The American model of the multinational firm and the "new" multinationals from emerging economies. *Academy of Management Perspectives*, *23*(2), 23–35.

Haber, S. H. (1991). Industrial concentration and the capital markets: A comparative study of Brazil, Mexico, and the United States, 1830–1930. *Journal of Economic History*, *51*, 559–580.

Helfat, C. E., Finkelstein, S., Mitchell, W., Peteraf, M., Singh, H., Teece, D., & Winter, S. (2007). *Dynamic capabilities: Understanding strategic change in organizations*. Oxford: Blackwell.

Hill, C. W. L. (1995). National institutional structures, transaction cost economizing and competitive advantage: The case of Japan. *Organization Science*, *6*, 119–131.

Hirsch, P. M. (1975). Organizational effectiveness and the institutional environment. *Administrative Science Quarterly*, *20*, 327–344.

Hitt, M. A., Beamish, P. W., Jackson, S. E., & Mathieu, J. E. (2007). Building theoretical and empirical bridges across levels: Multilevel research in management. *Academy of Management Journal, 50*, 1385–1399.
Hoskisson, R. E., Eden, L., Lau, C. M., & Wright, M. (2000). Strategy in emerging economies. *Academy of Management Journal, 43*, 249–267.
Hoskisson, R. E., Hitt, M. A., Wan, W. P., & Yiu, D. (1999). Theory and research in strategic management: Swings of a pendulum. *Journal of Management, 25*, 417–456.
Hoskisson, R. E., Kim, H., White, R. E., & Tihanyi, L. (2004). A framework for understanding international diversification by business groups from emerging economies. *Advances in International Management, 16*, 137–163.
Hoskisson, R. E., Wright, M., Filatotchev, I., & Peng, M. W. (2013). Emerging multinationals from mid-range economies: The influence of institutions and factor markets. *Journal of Management Studies, 50*, 1295–1321.
Ingram, P., & Silverman, B. S. (2002). Introduction: The new institutionalism in strategic management. *Advances in Strategic Management, 17*, 1–30.
Khanna, T., & Palepu, K. (1997). Why focused strategies may be wrong for emerging markets. *Harvard Business Review, 75*(4), 41–50.
Khanna, T., & Palepu, K. (1999). Policy shocks, market intermediaries, and corporate strategy: The evolution of business groups in Chile and India. *Journal of Economics and Management Strategy, 8*, 271–310.
Khanna, T., Palepu, K., & Sinha, J. (2005). Strategies that fit emerging markets. *Harvard Business Review, 83*(6), 63–76.
Kim, H., Hoskisson, R. E., & Lee, S.-H. (2015). Why strategic factor markets matter: "New" multinationals' geographic diversification and firm profitability. *Strategic Management Journal, 36*, 518–536.
Kim, H., Kim, H., & Hoskisson, R. E. (2010). Does market-oriented institutional change in an emerging economy make business-group-affiliated multinationals perform better? An institution-based view. *Journal of International Business Studies, 41*, 1141–1160.
Klein, K. J., Dansereau, F., & Hall, R. J. (1994). Levels issues in theory development, data collection, and analysis. *Academy of Management Review, 19*, 195–229.
Knack, S., & Keefer, P. (1997). Does social capital have an economic payoff? A cross-country investigation. *Quarterly Journal of Economics, 112*, 1251–1288.
Kogut, B. (1991). Country capabilities and the permeability. *Strategic Management Journal, 12*, 33–47.
Lado, A. A., Boyd, N. G., Wright, P., & Kroll, M. (2006). Paradox and theorizing within the resource-based view. *Academy of Management Review, 31*, 115–131.
Lado, A. A., & Wilson, M. C. (1994). Human resource systems and sustained competitive advantage: A competency-based perspective. *Academy of Management Review, 19*, 699–727.
Leonard-Barton, D. (1992). Core capabilities and core rigidities: A paradox in managing new product development. *Strategic Management Journal, 13*, 111–125.
Li, Y., Peng, M. W., & Macaulay, C. D. (2013). Market-political ambidexterity during institutional transitions. *Strategic Organization, 11*, 205–213.
Mahmood, I. P., & Rufin, C. (2005). Government's dilemma: The role of government in imitation and innovation. *Academy of Management Review, 30*, 338–360.
Mahoney, J. T., & Pandian, R. (1992). The resource-based view within the conversation of strategic management. *Strategic Management Journal, 13*, 363–380.

Makadok, R. (2001). Toward a synthesis of the resource-based and dynamic-capability views of rent creation. *Strategic Management Journal, 22*, 387–401.

Maritan, C. A., & Peteraf, M. A. (2011). Building a bridge between resource acquisition and resource accumulation. *Journal of Management, 37*, 1374–1389.

Markman, G. D., Gianiodis, P. T., & Buchholtz, A. K. (2009). Factor-market rivalry. *Academy of Management Review, 34*, 423–441.

Mason, E. S. (1939). Price and production policies of large-scale enterprise. *America Economic Review, 29*, 61–74.

McGrath, R. G. (2013). *The end of competitive advantage: How to keep your strategy moving as fast as your business*. Boston, MA: Harvard Business Review Press.

Miller, D., & Shamsie, J. (1996). The resource-based view of the firm in two environments: The Hollywood film studios from 1936 to 1965. *Academy of Management Journal, 39*, 519–543.

Murmann, J. P. (2003). *Knowledge and competitive advantage: The coevolution of firms, technology, and national institutions*. Cambridge: Cambridge University Press.

North, D. C. (1990). *Institutions, institutional change and economic performance*. Cambridge: Cambridge University Press.

Oliver, C. (1996). The institutional embeddedness of economic activity. *Advances in Strategic Management, 13*, 163–186.

Oliver, C. (1997). Sustainable competitive advantage: Combining institutional and resource-based views. *Strategic Management Journal, 18*, 697–713.

Oliver, C., & Holzinger, I. (2008). The effectiveness of strategic political management: A dynamic capabilities perspective. *Academy of Management Review, 33*, 496–520.

Peng, M. W. (2003). Institutional transitions and strategic choices. *Academy of Management Review, 28*, 275–296.

Peng, M. W., & Heath, P. S. (1996). The growth of the firm in planned economies in transition: Institutions, organizations, and strategic choice. *Academy of Management Review, 21*, 492–528.

Peng, M. W., Lee, S.-H., & Wang, D. Y. L. (2005). What determines the scope of the firm over time? A focus on institutional relatedness. *Academy of Management Review, 30*, 622–633.

Peng, M. W., Wang, D., & Jiang, Y. (2008). An institution-based view of international business strategy: A focus on emerging economies. *Journal of International Business Studies, 39*, 920–936.

Peteraf, M. A. (1993). The cornerstones of competitive advantage: A resource-based view. *Strategic Management Journal, 14*, 179–191.

Pfeffer, J., & Salancik, G. R. (1978). *The external control of organizations: A resource dependence perspective*. New York, NY: Harper & Row.

Poole, M. S., & Van de Ven, A. H. (1989). Using paradox to build management and organization theories. *Academy of Management Review, 14*, 562–578.

Porter, M. E. (1981). The contributions of industrial organization to strategic management. *Academy of Management Review, 6*, 609–620.

Porter, M. E. (1990). *The competitive advantage of nations*. New York, NY: The Free Press.

Porter, M. E. (1991). Towards a dynamic theory of strategy. *Strategic Management Journal, 12*(Winter special issue), 95–117.

Puffer, S. M., & McCarthy, D. J. (2011). Two decades of Russian business and management research: An institutional theory perspective. *Academy of Management Perspectives, 25*, 21–36.

Puffer, S. M., McCarthy, D. J., & Zhuplev, A. V. (1998). Doing business in Russia: Lessons from early entrants. *Thunderbird International Business Review*, *40*, 461–484.

Rajan, R. G., & Zingales, L. (2003). *Saving capitalism from the capitalists: Unleashing the power of financial markets to create wealth and spread opportunity*. New York, NY: Crown Business.

Reed, R., & DeFillippi, R. J. (1990). Causal ambiguity, barriers to imitation, and sustainable competitive advantage. *Academy of Management Review*, *15*, 88–102.

Ricardo, D. (1817). *Principles of political economy and taxation*. London: John Murray.

Rumelt, R. P. (1984). Towards a strategic theory of the firm. In R. B. Lamb (Ed.), *Competitive strategic management* (pp. 556–570). Englewood Cliffs, NJ: Prentice-Hall.

Rumelt, R. P. (1987). Theory, strategy, and entrepreneurship. In D. J. Teece (Ed.), *The competitive challenge: Strategies for industrial innovation and renewal* (pp. 137–158). Cambridge, MA: Ballinger.

Rumelt, R. P., Schendel, D. E., & Teece, D. J. (Eds.). (1994). *Fundamental issues in strategy: A research agenda*. Boston, MA: Harvard Business School Press.

Schumpeter, J. A. (1942). *Capitalism, socialism and democracy*. New York, NY: Harper & Brothers.

Sirmon, D. G., Hitt, M. A., & Ireland, R. D. (2007). Managing firm resources in dynamic environments to create value: Looking inside the black box. *Academy of Management Review*, *32*, 273–292.

Spencer, J. W. (2003). Global gatekeeping, representation, and network structure: A longitudinal analysis of regional and global knowledge-diffusion networks. *Journal of International Business Studies*, *34*, 428–442.

Spicer, A., McDermott, G. A., & Kogut, B. (2000). Entrepreneurship and privatization in Central Europe: The tenuous balance between destruction and creation. *Academy of Management Review*, *25*, 630–649.

Spicer, A., & Pyle, W. (2002). Institutions and the vicious circle of distrust in the Russian household deposit market, 1992–1999. *Advances in Strategic Management*, *19*, 373–398.

Stone, A., Levy, B., & Paredes, R. (1996). Public institutions and private transactions: A comparative analysis of the legal and regulatory environment for business transactions in Brazil and Chile. In L. J. Alston, T. Eggertsson, & D. C. North (Eds.), *Empirical Studies in Institutional change: Political economy of institutions and decisions* (pp. 95–128). Cambridge: Cambridge University Press.

Sull, D. N., Tedlow, R. S., & Rosenbloom, R. S. (1997). Managerial commitments and technological change in the US tire industry. *Industrial and Corporate Change*, *6*, 461–500.

Teece, D. J. (2007). Explicating dynamic capabilities: The nature and micro foundations of (sustainable) enterprise performance. *Strategic Management Journal*, *28*, 1319–1350.

Teece, D. J., Pisano, G., & Shuen, A. (1997). Dynamic capabilities and strategic management. *Strategic Management Journal*, *18*, 509–533.

Uhlenbruck, K., Meyer, K. E., & Hitt, M. A. (2003). Organizational transformation in transition economies: Resource-based and organizational learning perspectives. *Journal of Management Studies*, *40*, 257–282.

Wan, W. P. (2005). Country resource environments, firm capabilities, and corporate diversification strategies. *Journal of Management Studies*, *42*(1), 161–182.

Wan, W. P., & Hoskisson, R. E. (2003). Home country environments, corporate diversification strategies, and firm performance. *Academy of Management Journal*, *46*, 27–45.

Wernerfelt, B. (1984). A resource-based view of the firm. *Strategic Management Journal*, *5*, 171–180.

Winter, S. G. (2003). Understanding dynamic capabilities. *Strategic Management Journal*, *24*, 991–995.

Yamakawa, Y., Peng, M. W., & Deeds, D. L. (2008). What drives new ventures to internationalize from emerging to developed economies? *Entrepreneurship Theory and Practice*, *32*, 59–82.

Yao, D. A. (1988). Beyond the reach of the invisible hand: Impediments to economic activity, market failures, and profitability. *Strategic Management Journal*, *9*, 59–70.

Zahra, S. A., Sapienza, H. J., & Davidsson, P. (2006). Entrepreneurship and dynamic capabilities: A review, model and research agenda. *Journal of Management Studies*, *43*, 917–955.

THE EFFECTIVENESS OF THE STATE IN CHINESE OUTWARD FOREIGN DIRECT INVESTMENT: THE "GO GLOBAL" POLICY AND STATE-OWNED ENTERPRISES

Wenxin Guo and Joseph A. Clougherty

ABSTRACT

We question whether the Chinese state has played an effective role in promoting outward foreign direct investment via its "Go Global" policies. Using the literature in International Management as our framing, we observe three inter-related stylized realities. First, it is state-owned enterprises (SOEs) – not private enterprises – that tend to principally benefit from the favorable "Go Global" policies. Second, SOEs tend to pay much higher acquisition premiums in outward FDI as compared to non-SOEs. Third, SOEs tend to be less effective as compared to non-SOEs in gaining synergies and enhancing competitiveness as a result of these cross-border experiences. These results yield clear policy implications for the Chinese government: first, more effective public policy would involve enhanced targeting of private enterprises as the recipients of policies

Emerging Economies and Multinational Enterprises
Advances in International Management, Volume 28, 141–159

ISSN: 1571-5027/doi:10.1108/S1571-502720150000028009

promoting outward FDI; second, the Chinese government should continue along the path toward privatization of SOEs. The continued bolstering of economic and social development in China is contingent upon efforts to reduce the state's active role in outward FDI.

Keywords: Emerging markets; China; public policy; state-owned enterprises; FDI; MNEs

INTRODUCTION

With the onset of the open-door policy in 1978, China has grown to become one of the largest world players in terms of both inward and outward foreign direct investment (FDI). With a large population and competitive labor costs, China represents an attractive location for foreign investment by developed-nation multinational enterprises (MNEs) that wish to either expand their market territory or reduce production costs. Unsurprisingly, a large number of highly competitive MNEs have taken advantage of liberalization by entering the Chinese market in order to set up production facilities, form alliances with indigenous firms, and expand their local-market presence (Buckley et al., 2007). Yet, the opening up of the Chinese economy to world trade and foreign investment has created substantial challenges for indigenous Chinese firms, as many of these firms had productivity levels that lagged behind the most-efficient global firms. Morck, Yeung, and Zhao (2008) point out how inward FDI in the Chinese context has increased capacity and intensified price competition which in turn has led to reduced profit margins. In response to such pressures, Chinese firms have found it expedient to internationalize in order to seek external markets and develop capabilities that help them effectively compete in their home markets (Sauvant, Maschek, & McAllister, 2009).

In contrast to developed nations where firm activities are primarily driven by market forces, state support has been an important factor in Chinese outward FDI over the past two decades. The Chinese government represents an important player in that it sets the conditions which incentivize businesses to go abroad. In fact, the Chinese central government initiated the "Go Global" policy in 1999 so as to promote and support the foreign-investment efforts of Chinese firms (Buckley et al., 2007). The aim of this policy was the enhancement of capabilities via international experiences that resulted in advanced knowledge and strategic assets (i.e., technology, talents, management expertise, brands) being obtained from abroad. Interestingly, the ultimate driver of these policy efforts to upgrade the competitiveness of Chinese firms goes back to the need to compete more effectively with foreign rivals in both domestic and global markets (Luo & Tung, 2007; Ramamurti, 2008).

Beyond its policymaker role, the Chinese government is actively engaged in cross-border investment activity as a large number of Chinese MNEs are actually state-owned enterprises (SOEs).[1] Although corporatization and privatization of Chinese SOEs have been on-going since the 1990s (Ramamurti, 2000), most of the shares in Chinese publicly listed companies are still controlled by the state (Lau, Fan, Young, & Wu, 2007). For instance, Chen and Young (2010) report that the Chinese government represents the largest shareholder in the acquiring firm for many of the cross-border acquisitions aimed at accessing the foreign target's entire package of products, processes, and resources. Accordingly, the Chinese government is arguably the most important player when it comes to outward FDI as it not only sets the policy conditions which are instrumental in encouraging and incentivizing outward FDI, but also has a direct ownership stake – and control – in many of the Chinese firms engaged in such cross-border investments.

It is then the role of the Chinese state in outward FDI which we would like to consider here in detail. In particular, we are interested in whether the state has been effective in guiding outward FDI, and whether the ultimate aims of these policies have been achieved. The "Go Global" policies are non-trivial, as economic liberalization and government support have led to a surge of international expansion by Chinese firms. Indicative of China becoming a significant source of global FDI outflows, Chinese outward investment went from $2.7 billion in 2002 to some $101 billion in 2013 when China became the third-largest source of global FDI.[2] Moreover, we analyze this important policy area by taking a novel approach that embraces concepts and recent research in International Management (IM). Taking an IM perspective for policy analysis stands in contrast to the customary approach of invoking economics to analyze public policy effectiveness. The IM approach is particularly appropriate to analyze the effectiveness of the "Go Global" policy, as the policy is ultimately predicated on the ability of Chinese management in both SOEs and private enterprises to efficiently learn from cross-border investment experiences. If the Chinese firms engaging in cross-border investments are unable to learn and upgrade their capabilities as a result of these foreign experiences, then the subsidies involved with the "Go Global" policies represent sub-optimal and wasteful expenditures on the part of the Chinese government.

In order to follow through on the above aims to analyze the effectiveness of the "Go Global" policies, we structure the paper as follows. First, we consider whether SOEs receive disproportional support via the "Go Global" policies to engage in foreign-investment activities. Second, we consider whether SOEs in the Chinese context tend to overpay for foreign investments as compared to private enterprises. Third, we consider whether SOEs and private enterprises from China tend to gain synergies and enhance competitiveness as a result of their foreign-investment experiences. Finally, we conclude by reviewing the evidence and discussing the impact of our analysis for effective Chinese public policy; that is, we provide some normative implications for the future of the "Go Global" policies. In short, we will contend that the inherent managerial inefficiency associated with SOEs suggests that the Chinese government should continue and hasten its efforts to transition toward an economy dominated by private enterprises.

PREFERENTIAL TREATMENT OF SOEs

Chinese state assistance for outward FDI tends to come in the form of access to inexpensive financing, research and development expertise, and general policy support – all of which have been instrumental in easing the costs for Chinese firms engaging in outward FDI. Particular policies which support FDI activity include access to long-term/mid-term loans from state-owned banks, interest subsidies, special funds dedicated to foreign trade development and foreign aid projects, export credits, simplified foreign exchange procedures, and other measures of support. Financial incentives are focal to policy assistance; and Musacchio and Flores-Macias (2009) further observe that state-owned development banks tend to serve as conduits of cheap loans to politically connected firms. This suggests that in the emerging-market context it is firms with connections which will receive the great majority of policy benefits, while firms without such connections will be less likely to receive subsidies.

While both SOEs and private firms engage in cross-border investment activities, one concern expressed by managers from Chinese private enterprises is that the SOEs receive preferential treatment from the government (Li, Li, & Wen, 2009). Accordingly, the claim is that SOEs are able to fully take advantage of the various policy instruments associated with the "Go

Global" policies, as these subsidies are generally available to SOEs, but are less available to Chinese private enterprises as compared to SOEs. The structure formulated to support the "Go Global" policy was certainly designed to help all Chinese MNEs; but in reality, SOEs often receive more support from the government than do private enterprises (Li et al., 2009). This is particularly the case in terms of favorable financing, as the government is reported to provide SOEs with preferential access to foreign reserves; hence, SOEs potentially face fewer financial constraints than do private enterprises. In addition to privileged financial conditions, SOEs have also been reported to receive tax privileges, favorable insurance terms, and foreign industrial guidance – assistance that private enterprises have been less likely to receive. The extent of policy support for private enterprises has been more in terms of minor conveniences in the realms of customs inspections and overseas protection. The above patterns suggest favoritism in public policy toward SOEs at the expense of private enterprises (Ahlstrom, Chen, & Yeh, 2010; Huang, 2003). In this regard, the "Go Global" policy might seemingly be more beneficial to SOEs than to private enterprises, as the large investment by the Chinese government to subsidize cross-border investment activity is characterized by the great majority of these resources going toward SOEs.

We can provide some evidence here in line with the idea that the Chinese government provides preferential access to SOEs at the expense of private enterprises. If one considers the Chinese economy as a whole, then some 73% of Chinese listed firms involved state ownership in 2000 but this dropped to some 27% of firms by 2010. Hence, state ownership went from the dominant governance mode for listed firms to a minority governance mode in the span of a decade. Fig. 1 reflects the rapidity of change and increased privatization of the Chinese economy over this period. However, Fig. 1 also illustrates that SOEs engaged in somewhere between 41% and 78% of the cross-border M&As undertaken by Chinese publicly listed firms over the 2000–2010 period. While the role of SOEs in cross-border acquisition activity shows a steady decline in recent years (e.g., 78% of acquirers in outward investments were SOEs in 2006 but this reduced to 41% in 2010), it is clear that firms controlled by the Chinese government still represent a healthy percentage of the activity taking place. Moreover, it is also clear that SOEs disproportionally take part in cross-border acquisitions as compared to private enterprises, as the percentage of SOEs engaging in cross-border M&A activity always exceeds the percentage of SOEs in Chinese listed firms. For instance, 27% of Chinese listed firms involved state ownership in 2010; yet, 41% of Chinese listed firms engaging in

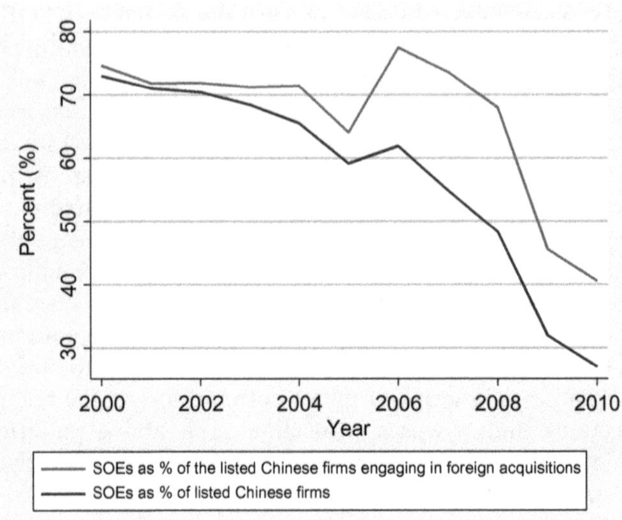

Fig. 1. SOEs as a Percentage of All Listed Chinese Firms, and as a Percentage of All Listed Chinese Firms Engaging in Foreign Acquisitions, 2000–2010. *Source*: Matched Chinese Acquirer dataset from Thomson SDC Platinum database and the China RESSET database.

cross-border acquisitions in 2010 involved state ownership. As an aside, the tick up in SOE activity manifested between 2005 and 2006 might be attributed to a spike in pure Chinese transactions where many SOEs acquired non-SOEs, or to a spike in the number of SOEs being partially listed on stock exchanges.

Consequently, the Chinese government has a strong hand in affecting the decision making concerning cross-border investment activities, as it can choose which types of firms are targeted for subsidies. Furthermore, the Chinese government has multiple and inter-related influences on outward FDI: first, the government is the key external player as it provides policy benefits that support and incentivize cross-border investments; second, the government represents a key internal decision maker when it comes to SOEs, as the government is often the biggest – or most important – shareholder in many Chinese firms; third, the above two roles do not show a significant degree of separation, as the government subsidies involved with the "Go Global" policy tend to be favorably available to SOEs and less available to private firms. As Peng, Wang, and Jiang (2008) point out, it is the institutional (under)development that shapes firm's strategic choices in the Chinese context. Thus, when it comes to the application of state-sponsored subsidies to Chinese firms engaging in outward cross-border investment, it does appear that it is the state-controlled firms which receive the lion's share of these benefits.

OVERPAYING FOR FOREIGN INVESTMENTS BY SOEs

A number of observers (e.g., Peng, 2012) have commented that Chinese investors have been systematically overpaying for foreign investments; though, it should be pointed out that such tendencies are quite characteristic of emerging-market MNEs in general (Hope, Thomas, & Vyas, 2011). For instance, The Economist (2010) reports that Chinese firms are never beaten on price when it comes to bidding for foreign assets and resources. Such observations regarding systematic overpayment by investors that are relatively new to the global marketplace for target firms are potentially akin to the surge of US investments by Japanese firms in the 1980s where the buyers substantially overpaid for many US assets. Sony's \$3.4 billion acquisition of Columbia pictures in 1989 – which resulted in a \$2.7 billion write-off in 1994 – represents one of the more notable examples of overpaying for foreign assets (Makino & Roehl, 2010).

While unfamiliarity with the global marketplace for corporate control is one explanation behind a tendency to overpay for foreign assets, another explanation for this behavior in the Chinese context may reside in the magnified role of the state. In particular, the substantial amount of policy support for SOEs – particularly the privileged access to finance provided by the government – means that SOEs potentially face a "soft budget constraint" (Kornai, Maskin, & Roland, 2003). Accordingly, the privileged access to finance and the fact that the state is always there to bail out an unprofitable SOE means that SOEs – as compared to private enterprises – can be far more aggressive and cavalier with respect to price when engaging in foreign-investment activities. Indicative of the ability to not be deterred by price, a number of Chinese SOEs have undertaken cross-border acquisitions of considerable size: for example, Lenovo's \$1.25 billion acquisition of IBM's PC division in 2005, Sinopec Group's \$7.16 billion acquisition of Switzerland's Addax Petroleum Corporation in 2009, and Shuanghui's \$4.7 billion acquisition of Smithfield in 2013.

In line with the idea that Chinese firms often overpay for foreign-investment opportunities is the observation by some observers (e.g., Chen & Young, 2010; Peng, 2012) that Chinese cross-border mergers involve significant "acquisition premiums."[3] Recall that SOEs are considered the principal beneficiaries of Chinese government support for outward FDI. It should also be noted that many government funds have been dedicated to strictly supporting Chinese cross-border M&As. Combining these facts with the idea that Chinese SOEs face soft budget constraints that alleviate bottom-line pressures to deliver profitable investments suggests that SOEs might pay much higher prices for foreign assets as compared to private enterprises. For instance, Guo, Clougherty, and Duso (2014) contend – and empirically support – that the relatively high premiums paid by Chinese acquirers for foreign targets is symptomatic of SOEs and not so symptomatic of private enterprises engaging in cross-border investments.

We can provide some evidence here in support of these conclusions, as we assembled data on the average acquisition premiums paid by Chinese acquirers (SOEs and private enterprises) when engaging in cross-border acquisitions of North American target firms over the 1990–2011 period. We find that Chinese SOEs engaging in North American acquisitions pay relatively high premiums of 96% on average.[4] As a benchmark, the average premiums paid for US target firms generally range from 30% to 50% (Varaiya & Ferris, 1987; Walkling & Edmister, 1985). In contrast to this tendency for SOEs to overpay, Chinese private enterprises paid premiums of 31% on average for North America targets during this same period – an average premium which falls in the lower range of premiums paid by other acquirers of North American targets. These stylized facts conform to pre-existing priors that Chinese SOEs have a tendency to pay a good bit more for foreign investments as compared to the pre-existing value of these investments. Furthermore, the evidence suggests that Chinese private enterprises are more price conscious and frugal, as they do not exhibit systematic overpayment in their North American investments.

Management scholars (e.g., Sirower, 1997) point out that high premiums are potentially damaging for investment value, as the "overpayment" consumes from the expected synergies that must be achieved to sustain the investor's market value. In short, the payment of high premiums can ensure that an investment is value-destroying, as it is nearly impossible to create sufficient synergies to compensate for overpaying in the first place. This draws our attention as to why Chinese SOEs may be willing to pay such high premiums. High premiums might be justified if SOEs are able to obtain economic gains via cross-border investments that offset the losses resulting from overpayment. In this case, high premiums represent upfront investments that secure the resources needed for the firm's capability development; hence, such investments could make strategic sense when taking into consideration the firm's long-run desire to develop and upgrade. Yet, if such overpayment cannot bring future economic gains to Chinese SOEs, then it suggests that Chinese SOEs are not reaping adequate returns for their cross-border investments. In this case, overpayment would be indicative of the SOE's inherent organizational inefficiency as compared to private firms. For these reasons, our analysis now turns to considering the success of Chinese cross-border investment activities by both SOEs and private enterprises.

CROSS-BORDER INVESTMENTS & UPGRADING OF DOMESTIC OPERATIONS

Cross-border investments by developed-nation MNEs are often undertaken in order to establish market power, create immediate synergies, and obtain instant growth. The cross-border investments undertaken by emerging-market MNEs, however, are generally considered to be driven by goals that are long term in nature (Kumar, 2009). For instance, Luo and Tung (2007) point out that learning from foreign experiences, developing global competencies, and upgrading domestic operations represent the primary aims of emerging-market firms when engaging in foreign investment. The growing Chinese market requires growth in home production capabilities in order to meet the increasing needs of consumers and in order to compete against foreign firms which are penetrating the domestic market. Chinese firms have certainly accumulated considerable financial and operational assets, upgraded technological and process management skills, and developed certain capabilities and learning experiences as a result of inward FDI (Young, Huang, & McDermott, 1996). Yet despite this upgrading of Chinese firms via spillovers from inward FDI, many Chinese firms still face competitive disadvantages with regard to advanced knowledge when compared with developed-nation MNEs. Accordingly, outward cross-border investments are a means for emerging-market MNEs to secure strategic natural resources (e.g., oil and gas, metals), obtain advanced technologies, acquire significant brands, and gain access to consumers in key foreign markets (Chari, Chen, & Dominguez, 2012).

We can provide some evidence here consistent with the idea that Chinese investors are motivated by the potential to learn from foreign-investment experiences. Table 1 breaks down Chinese cross-border acquisition activity over the 2000–2011 period by target nation, and classifies the target nations into the level of economic development: that is, developing, developed, and newly industrialized nations. If the primary motivation of Chinese investors is to learn, then disproportionate interest in target firms based in developed and newly industrial nations would seem to be in order. In line with these priors is the fact that Chinese MNEs appear to primarily acquire target firms based in developed nations (48.8%) and to a lesser degree target firms based in newly industrialized nations (31.5%). Accordingly, cross-border investments in nations that are relatively more developed as compared to China equate to some 80.3% of Chinese outward cross-border M&A activity. Stylized facts which are in line with the prior that Chinese firms are motivated by learning, as target firms in those nations should provide opportunities for upgrading and learning.

In addition to the proclivity of Chinese MNEs to make investments in nations where the potential exists for learning and upgrading, the industrial sectors targeted by outward FDI can also provide some insight with respect to the priorities and motivations of Chinese investors. China's current role as the "Manchester" of the world (Rowen, 2003) would indicate that manufacturing is an obvious sector of importance where learning from global best practices would be valuable. Yet the lack of abundant natural resources represents a salient challenge for China and its role as the world's manufacturer (Buckley et al., 2007). Accordingly, outward cross-border investments driven by the motivation to upgrade the domestic operations of Chinese MNEs would seemingly target the manufacturing and natural resource sectors at the expense of other sectors. Table 2 provides evidence in support of these priors, as the lion's share of Chinese outward cross-border M&A activity takes place in the manufacturing (35.12%) and natural resource (34.78%) sectors. Hence, the patterns of Chinese outward FDI – both in terms of nations and sectors targeted – are in line with the idea that learning and upgrading are primary motivations behind such activities.

While the motive to engage in cross-border investments that lead to domestic upgrading certainly exists, the complexities involved with such investments in various international settings suggests that learning and upgrading may not always result. In other words, it is not evident that Chinese MNEs can consistently achieve their learning objectives. Building on the perspectives of asset exploration and exploitation (March, 1991),

Table 1. Chinese Cross-border Acquisitions by Target Nation, 2000–2011.

Developing Nations									Newly Industrialized Nations		
Target Nation	Frequency	Percent	Target Nation	Frequency	Percent	Target Nation	Frequency	Percent	Target Nation	Frequency	Percent
Argentina	1	0.17	Kazakhstan	5	0.87	Australia	92	15.9	Hong Kong	153	26.5
Azerbaijan	1	0.17	Lesotho	1	0.17	Austria	1	0.17	Singapore	18	3.11
Barbados	2	0.35	Liberia	1	0.17	Belgium	3	0.52	South Korea	7	1.21
Belarus	1	0.17	Macau	3	0.52	British Virgin	2	0.35	Taiwan	4	0.69
Bermuda	1	0.17	Malaysia	4	0.69	Canada	44	7.61	Total	182	31.5
Brazil	8	1.38	Mexico	3	0.52	Cayman Islands	2	0.35			
Chile	4	0.69	Mongolia	3	0.52	Denmark	1	0.17			
Colombia	1	0.17	Nigeria	3	0.52	Finland	1	0.17			
Cyprus	1	0.17	Peru	2	0.35	France	9	1.56			
Czech Republic	1	0.17	Philippines	2	0.35	Germany	11	1.9			
Dem Rep Congo	1	0.17	Poland	2	0.35	Italy	10	1.73			
Ecuador	1	0.17	Portugal	1	0.17	Japan	17	2.94			
Egypt	2	0.35	Romania	1	0.17	Netherlands	7	1.21			
Estonia	1	0.17	Russian Fed	6	1.04	New Zealand	4	0.69			
Greece	1	0.17	Sierra Leone	1	0.17	Norway	5	0.87			
Guinea	1	0.17	South Africa	4	0.69	Spain	1	0.17			
Haiti	1	0.17	Sri Lanka	2	0.35	Sweden	4	0.69			
Hungary	4	0.69	Syria	1	0.17	Switzerland	2	0.35			
India	3	0.52	Tajikistan	1	0.17	United Kingdom	16	2.77			
Indonesia	7	1.21	Thailand	11	1.9	United States	50	8.65			
Iran	1	0.17	Ukraine	2	0.35	Total	282	48.8			
Israel	2	0.35	Vietnam	3	0.52						
Jamaica	2	0.35	Zambia	1	0.17						
Jordan	1	0.17	Zimbabwe	2	0.35						
Total	114	19.7									

Source: Matched Chinese Acquirer dataset from Thomson SDC Platinum database and the China RESSET database.

Table 2. Chinese Cross-border M&As by Target Industry, 2000–2011.

Target Industry	Frequency	Percent
Manufacturing	203	35.12
Natural Resources	201	34.78
Services	90	15.57
Financial	50	8.65
Trade	30	5.19
Other	4	0.69
Total	578	100

Source: Matched Chinese Acquirer dataset from Thomson SDC Platinum database and the China RESSET database.

absorptive capacity theory (Cohen & Levinthal, 1990), and the knowledge-based view of multinationals (Kogut & Zander, 1993), it would nevertheless seem then that Chinese firms have the potential to upgrade their domestic operations as a result of cross-border experiences. In support of this dynamic, Bertrand and Capron (2015) find that French firms engaging in outward cross-border investments are able to upgrade the productivity of their domestic operations. And closer to the subject at hand, Guo and Clougherty (2014) find evidence that Chinese acquirers tend to learn from foreign targets when they engage in outward cross-border acquisition activities. In particular, they find that upgrading and learning are evident when developed-nation targets are acquired, but this is not the case when developing-nation targets are acquired. Accordingly, it does appear that Chinese MNEs are generally able to assimilate the knowledge from foreign investments in developed nations and transfer this knowledge to domestic operations so as to upgrade the competitiveness of these operations. Thus, the foundational logic behind China's "Go Global" policy is relatively sound, as outward cross-border experiences can involve salient learning and upgrading mechanisms that lead to enhanced efficiency and productivity in home-market operations.

The next obvious question revolves around whether it is the SOEs or private enterprises from China which are generally able to learn from foreign experiences; thus, a closer examination of how state ownership affects the learning via cross-border M&A activities is called for. A review of the existing literature reveals that government ownership of these MNEs actually decreases the effectiveness of learning via cross-border M&As, as state-owned enterprises do not indicate systematic evidence of upgrading as a response to outward cross-border investment experiences. Instead, it is private enterprises that are learning and enhancing their domestic productivity via cross-border investment activities (Guo, 2014). This finding indicates that SOEs are less efficient in terms of learning as compared to private enterprises. More importantly, it is the private enterprises – rather than the SOEs – which are successfully achieving the ultimate aim of the "Go Global" policy.

We can provide some additional evidence that it is the private enterprises and not the SOEs which tend to upgrade their domestic capabilities in response to cross-border investment activity. Fig. 2 presents the domestic labor productivity of Chinese acquirers (both state-owned and non-state-owned) with respect to the frequency of cross-border M&A activity in the prior two to four years. Accordingly, the slopes of the two lines in Fig. 2 capture the marginal gain to domestic labor productivity due to engaging in an additional cross-border acquisition. Evident from the figure is the fact that private enterprises elicit a much higher gain to labor productivity as compared to SOEs, thus indicative of the prior that private enterprises are better able to assimilate knowledge from foreign targets and successfully

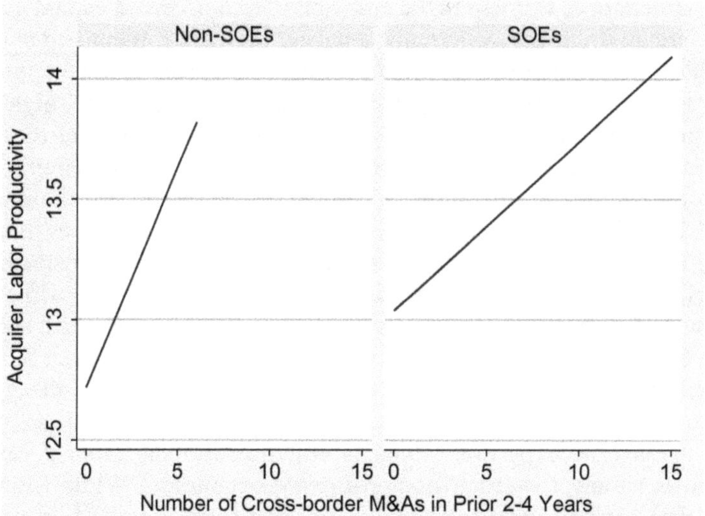

Fig. 2. Acquirer's Domestic Labor Productivity with respect to Number of Cross-Border Acquisitions in the Prior Two to Four Years, 2000–2011. *Source*: Matched Chinese Acquirer dataset from Thomson SDC Platinum database and the China RESSET database.

transfer that knowledge to their domestic operations. In light of the fact that SOEs tend to be favored by Chinese public policies encouraging outward FDI, our empirical findings indicate some challenging realities. Although SOEs represent the leading force and primary financial beneficiary of "Go Global" policies, SOEs appear to be less effective in achieving the ultimate goal of this policy.

NORMATIVE IMPLICATIONS FOR FUTURE CHINESE POLICIES

SOEs, as the implementer of a nation's economic, social, and political missions, take on very important roles in the process of emerging-market MNEs' internationalization. As supported, SOEs in the Chinese context disproportionately receive the benefits of public policies intended to subsidize outward FDI activity. Moreover, MNEs from emerging markets – and China in particular – tend to overpay when they engage in cross-border investment activity. While the determinants of this overbidding are not completely understood, Chinese SOEs enjoy privileged access to capital and policy preference from the government; hence, they have much softer budget constraints as compared to private enterprises when conducting cross-border investments. Accordingly, Chinese SOEs tend to pay very high acquisition premiums in order to secure foreign targets; yet, despite these high premiums Chinese SOEs do not seem to outperform private enterprises in terms of learning and upgrading of domestic operations even though these SOEs have privileged access to government subsidies. This implies that overpaying for foreign investment is not economically justified. Instead, there appears to be inherent organizational inefficiency involved with SOEs. Moreover, this means that the government is engaged in wasteful spending by consistently supporting the international expansion activities of SOEs.

The organizational inefficiency of SOEs may result from the government-influence over corporate governance and from the lack of professional managerial expertise. China is still transitioning from a centrally planned economy toward a market-oriented economy. While China has undertaken several major governance reforms since the 1990s in order to decentralize governmental control and delegate responsibilities to managers (Ramamurti, 2000), the influence of the party is still quite substantial in corporate decision making and daily operations. In this vein, SOEs are generally considered to be less effective as compared to private enterprises when it comes to making sound corporate decisions (Boardman, Eckel, & Vining, 1986; Boardman & Vining, 1989; Chen & Young, 2010; Megginson, Nash, & van Randenborgh, 1994). Government intervention in SOEs via majority state ownership and via the appointment of politically connected managers tends to distort financial investment behavior and harm investment efficiency. Furthermore, SOEs may be subject to substantial internal conflicts due to the differing objectives of government ownership and minority-shareholder ownership (Chen & Young, 2010; Dharwadkar, George, & Brandes, 2000; Young, Peng, Ahlstrom, Bruton, & Jiang, 2008). Such corporate inefficiencies would lead in turn to relatively inefficient cross-border investment activity as compared to private enterprises. Whereas private enterprises are considered to be more efficient in dealing with risks due to their being free of government intervention and masters of their own financial health; thus, they deploy cash in a more agile manner and hedge against risks. The use of funds by SOEs, on the other hand, must go through an elaborate process of examination and approval by different layers of the hierarchy – including the government. Also, the selection of many SOE managers is often not done on a performance basis, but instead driven by government-nomination (Zhang & Parker, 2002). Many SOE managers are still party appointees from government hierarchies, and by consequence are not specialized in firm operations (Fan, Wong, & Zhang, 2007; Kato & Long, 2006). Furthermore, the compensation of SOE managers is not closely tied to firm performance. Hence, the incentives for Chinese SOE managers to strive for shareholder value will be relatively weak – particularly when compared to the incentives of managers in private enterprises. Accordingly, SOEs are likely to be less effective in terms of learning from cross-border investments as compared to private enterprises.

It is indeed interesting that private enterprises substantially learn from cross-border investment experiences, as it is these organizations which receive comparatively little government support that are the major force in achieving the objectives (i.e., learning and upgrading of domestic operations) embedded in China's "Go Global" policy. Thus, the success of the "Go Global" policy appears to be accidental in that the major institutional vehicle (i.e., state-owned multinationals) via which this policy has been carried out does not appear to be successfully doing so. Instead, it is the private enterprises – which receive comparatively little government support – which appear to be successfully engaging in outward cross-border investments that ultimately lead to the enhancement of domestic operations and in turn domestic welfare.

Our results and analysis yield clear implications for the current debates within China regarding the future role of the state in the economy (Li, Wang, Cheung, & Jiang, 2011). If the ultimate aim of the Chinese government is to support cost-effective foreign-investment behavior that leads to the upgrading of domestic capabilities, then the Chinese state should further advance down the path toward greater privatization of SOEs. Simply put, it is the private enterprises which appear to be uniquely able to evaluate and properly price foreign investments, and then subsequently learn from these investment activities by transferring best practices back to home operations. The ultimate advancement of Chinese economic development seemingly depends then on the continued privatization of Chinese MNEs. In addition, the "Go Global" policy needs to enhance its financial and policy support for private enterprises engaging in cross-border investment activities. Specifically, private enterprises should be provided long-run/low-interest loans, eased policy constraints, and tax incentives to invest abroad. In essence, the continued bolstering of economic and social development in China is contingent upon efforts to reduce the state's active role in outward FDI, and enhance the role of private enterprises in outward FDI.

Empirical and theoretical studies on emerging-market outward FDI are still in their infancy. A number of scholars have argued that existing theories are quite adequate in explaining emerging-market MNE internationalization (Narula, 2006). This study, however, suggests that traditional theories largely built on the evidence of developed nations may not be sufficient in explaining the internationalization of emerging-market MNEs (Cuervo-Cazurra, 2012; Luo & Tung, 2007; Ramamurti, 2012). More specifically, we enrich the extant literature in International Management by making clear that Chinese outward investments are shaped by their distinct attributes. Namely, the role of government policy and the involvement of government ownership are salient attributes that impact which firms receive policy preferences, the prices paid for foreign investment, and the learning and upgrading involved with such outward cross-border activities.

China is arguably the most important emerging-market nation, as it has become the "world's factory" and has consequently taken up a significant proportion of the world's inward and outward FDI. Accordingly, change in the nature of the international activities of Chinese firms and changes in their productivity have a profound influence on other emerging-market economies as well as the world economy. The evidence we review and present here regarding the role of the Chinese state in outward FDI is sobering. The governments of many emerging-market nations often take on roles beyond simple policymaking, as these governments take active roles that involve direct ownership and governance of their indigenous global businesses. Our findings, however, suggest that such actions come at a substantial cost. In particular, the prices paid for foreign investments indicate a significant degree of overpayment and waste of precious capital resources, and the ultimate learning objectives of these cross-border investments may well not be achieved. Our findings regarding the "Go Global" policies and the role of SOEs suggest that the Chinese state – and possibly other emerging-market states – faces a clear incentive to advance the pace of reform regarding privatization of SOEs.

NOTES

1. We categorize state-owned enterprises here as firms that are listed in China, but also have an element of government ownership.
2. *Source*: United Nations Conference on Trade and Development, World Investment Report 2014, July 3, 2014.
3. Acquisition premium is a percentage measure that captures the price paid for a target firm with respect to the estimated value of the target firm prior to the acquisition.
4. *Source*: Based on data from Thomson SDC Platinum database.

REFERENCES

Ahlstrom, D., Chen, S., & Yeh, K. S. (2010). Managing in ethnic Chinese communities: Cultures, institutions, and context. *Asia Pacific Journal of Management*, *27*(3), 341–354.

Bertrand, O., & Capron, L. (2015). Productivity enhancement at home via cross-border acquisitions: The roles of learning and contemporaneous domestic investments. *Strategic Management Journal*, *36*(5), 640–658.

Boardman, A. E., Eckel, C., & Vining, A. R. (1986). The advantages and disadvantages of mixed enterprises. In A. R. Negandhi, H. Thomas, & K. L. K. Rao (Eds.), *Multinational corporations and state-owned enterprises: A new challenge in international business* (Vol. 1). *Research in International Business and International Relations.* Greenwich, CT: JAI Press.

Boardman, A. E., & Vining, A. R. (1989). Ownership and performance in competitive environments: A comparison of the performance of private, mixed, and state-owned enterprises. *Journal of Law and Economics*, *32*(1), 1–33.

Buckley, P. J., Clegg, J. L., Cross, A. R., Liu, X., Voss, H., & Zheng, P. (2007). The determinants of Chinese outward foreign direct investment. *Journal of International Business Studies*, *38*, 499–518.

Chari, A., Chen, W., & Dominguez, K. (2012). Foreign ownership and firm performance: Emerging-market acquisitions in the United States. *IMF Economic Review*, *60*, 1–42.

Chen, Y. Y., & Young, M. N. (2010). Cross-border mergers and acquisitions by Chinese listed companies: A principal-principal perspective. *Asia Pacific Journal of Management*, *27*(3), 523–539.

Cohen, W. M., & Levinthal, D. A. (1990). Absorptive capacity: A new perspective on learning and innovation. *Administrative Science Quarterly*, *35*(1), 128–152.

Cuervo-Cazurra, A. (2012). Extending theory by analyzing developing country multinational companies: Solving the Goldilocks debate. *Global Strategy Journal*, *2*(3), 153–167.

Dharwadkar, R., George, G., & Brandes, P. (2000). Privatization in emerging economies: An agency theory perspective. *Academy of Management Review*, *25*(3), 650–669.

Fan, J. P. H., Wong, T. J., & Zhang, T. (2007). Politically connected CEOs, corporate governance, and Post-IPO performance of China's newly partially privatized firms. *Journal of Financial Economics*, *84*(2), 330–357.

Guo, W. (2014). *How corporate governance matters for emerging-market acquirers' productivity gains via cross-border mergers and acquisitions: Evidence from Chinese acquirers.* Working paper.

Guo, W., & Clougherty, J. A. (2014). *Emerging-market acquirers' productivity gains via cross-border mergers and acquisitions: Evidence from Chinese acquirers.* Working paper.

Guo, W., Clougherty, J. A., & Duso, T. (2014). *Do state-owned enterprises pay more? Evidence from outward Chinese cross-border mergers and acquisitions.* Working paper.

Hope, O. K., Thomas, W., & Vyas, D. (2011). The cost of pride: Why do firms from developing countries bid higher? *Journal of International Business Studies*, *42*, 128–151.

Huang, Y. (2003). *Selling China.* New York, NY: Cambridge University Press.

Kato, T., & Long, C. (2006). CEO turnover, firm performance, and enterprise reform in China: Evidence from micro data. *Journal of Comparative Economics*, *34*(4), 796–817.

Kogut, B., & Zander, U. (1993). Knowledge of the firm and the evolutionary theory of the multinational corporation. *Journal of International Business Studies*, *24*(4), 625–645.

Kornai, J., Maskin, E., & Roland, G. (2003). Understanding the soft budget constraint. *Journal of Economic Literature*, *41*(4), 1095–1136.

Kumar, N. (2009). How emerging giants are rewriting the rules of M&A. *Harvard Business Review*, *87*(5), 115–121.

Lau, C. M., Fan, D. K. K., Young, M. N., & Wu, S. (2007). Corporate governance effectiveness during institutional transition. *International Business Review*, *16*(4), 425–448.

Li, K., Wang, T., Cheung, Y. L., & Jiang, P. (2011). Privatization and risk sharing: Evidence from the split share structure reform in China. *Review of Corporate Finance Studies*, *24*(7), 2499–2525.

Li, P., Li, Y., & Wen, T. (2009). Characteristics, driving forces, and influential factors of Chinese cross-border mergers and acquisitions. *Exploration in Economics*, *2*, 74–79.

Luo, Y., & Tung, R. L. (2007). International expansion of emerging market enterprises: A springboard perspective. *Journal of International Business Studies*, *38*(4), 481–498.

Makino, S., & Roehl, T. (2010). Learning from Japan: A commentary. *Academy of Management Perspectives*, *24*(4), 38–45.

March, J. G. (1991). Exploration and exploitation in organizational learning. *Organization Science*, *2*, 71–87.

Megginson, W. L., Nash, R. C., & van Randenborgh, M. (1994). The financial and operating performance of newly privatized firms: An international empirical analysis. *The Journal of Finance*, *49*(2), 403–452.

Morck, R., Yeung, B., & Zhao, M. (2008). Perspectives on China's outward foreign direct investment. *Journal of International Business Studies, 39*, 337–350.

Musacchio, A., & Flores-Macias, F. (2009). The return of state-owned enterprises: Should we be afraid? *Harvard International Review*, (April). Retrieved from http://hir.harvard.edu/the-return-of-state-owned-enterprises. Accessed on September 2, 2013.

Narula, R. (2006). Globalization, new ecologies, new zoologies, and the purported death of the eclectic paradigm. *Asia Pacific Journal of Management, 23*(2), 143–151.

Peng, M. W. (2012). The global strategy of emerging multinationals from China. *Global Strategy Journal, 2*(2), 97–107.

Peng, M. W., Wang, D. Y. L., & Jiang, J. (2008). An institution-based view of international business strategy: A focus on emerging economies. *Journal of International Business Studies, 39*(5), 920–936.

Ramamurti, R. (2000). A multilevel model of privatization in emerging economies. *The Academy of Management Review, 25*(3), 525–550.

Ramamurti, R. (2008). Why study emerging-market MNEs? In R. Ramamurti & J. V. Singh (Eds.). *Emerging multinationals in emerging markets*. Cambridge, UK: Cambridge University Press.

Ramamurti, R. (2012). What is really different about emerging market multinationals? *Global Strategy Journal, 2*(1), 41–47.

Rowen, H. S. (2003). Will China take over world manufacturing? *The International Economy, 17*(1), 72.

Sauvant, K. P., Maschek, W. A., & McAllister, G. (2009). *Foreign direct investment by emerging market multinational enterprises, the impact of the financial crisis and recession and challenges ahead.* Part of the official conference documentation for the OECD Global Forum on International Investment VIII (December 2009), Background material for Session 2.3. Retrieved from http://www.oecd.org/investment/globalforum/

Sirower, M. L. (1997). *The synergy trap: How companies lose the acquisition game*. New York, NY: Free Press.

The Economist. (2010). Being eaten by the dragon. *The Economist*, November 13, pp. 77–79.

Varaiya, N. P., & Ferris, K. R. (1987). Overpaying in corporate takeovers: The winner's curse. *Financial Analysts Journal, 9*(43), 64–70.

Walkling, R. A., & Edmister, R. D. (1985). Determinants of tender offer premiums. *Financial Analysts Journal, 41*(1), 27–37.

Young, M. N., Peng, M. W., Ahlstrom, D., Bruton, G. D., & Jiang, Y. (2008). Corporate governance in emerging economies: A review of the principal-principal perspective. *Journal of Management Studies, 45*(1), 196–220.

Young, S., Huang, C. H., & McDermott, M. (1996). Internationalization and competitive catch-up processes: Case study evidence on Chinese multinational enterprises. *Management International Review, 36*(4), 295–314.

Zhang, Y. F., & Parker, D. (2002). The impact of ownership on management and structures in the Chinese electronics industry. *Asia Pacific Business Review, 8*(3), 95–114.

HOW EXTERNAL AND INTERNAL SOURCES OF KNOWLEDGE IMPACT NOVEL AND IMITATIVE INNOVATION IN EMERGING MARKETS: EVIDENCE FROM COLOMBIA

Sandra Corredor, Clemente Forero and Deepak Somaya

ABSTRACT

This paper examines the extent to which different sources of ideas for innovation are associated with novelty of innovation outcomes. We measure the novelty of product innovation using three well-established categories, ranging from highly novel new-to-world products to new-to-firm products that are essentially imitative, with products that are new-to-country (but not the world) being an intermediary category. In turn we investigate how knowledge derived from different external and internal (within-firm) sources of ideas can help firms increase innovation with different degrees of novelty. Our empirical analyses are conducted on a

Emerging Economies and Multinational Enterprises
Advances in International Management, Volume 28, 161–199

ISSN: 1571-5027/doi:10.1108/S1571-502720150000028010

large sample of manufacturing firms from the South American emerging market of Colombia and show that many of the same sources of knowledge – such as scientific sources, production departments and managers – are associated with higher innovation in all three categories of novelty. However, some sources – notably external clients and internal interdisciplinary groups – are more significantly associated with more novel innovation than imitation. The implications of these findings for the literatures on innovation and imitation, and innovation by emerging market firms are discussed.

Keywords: Emerging markets; sources of knowledge; internal; external; innovating firms; novel innovation

INTRODUCTION

With emerging countries' continuing high growth rates, emerging market firms (EMFs) increasingly face opportunities and pressures to innovate. Specifically, innovative firms in emerging markets can better cope with increasing international competition, increase efficiencies in their operations, and counteract higher costs of capital and difficulties in property rights protection (Wright, Filatotchev, Hoskisson, & Peng, 2005). At the same time, more innovative EMFs can benefit from developments in their domestic markets, such as increasing collective R&D expenditures and a booming middle class that demands differentiated products and not just competitive prices (Khanna & Palepu, 2006). While prior research has noted that EMFs have been increasingly relying on technology and innovation to succeed (Khanna & Palepu, 2010), the literature has also recognized that innovative knowledge is less readily available in emerging markets (Hoskisson, Kim, White, & Tihanyi, 2004), and that access to such knowledge is plagued by market inefficiencies, information problems and skilled labor shortages (Hoskisson, Eden, Lau, & Wright, 2000). EMFs that succeed in overcoming these challenges can gain a competitive edge by accessing knowledge, innovating and upgrading their capabilities (Giuliani & Bell, 2005; McDermott, Corredoira, & Kruse, 2009; Moran & Ghoshal, 1999).

An expanding stream of innovation research, drawing on ideas relating to absorptive capacity (Cohen & Levinthal, 1990) and open innovation (Chesbrough, 2003) provides robust evidence that access to knowledge is key for firm innovation. Accessing knowledge through different contractual and partnering arrangements (Fey & Birkinshaw, 2005), from external or internal knowledge spaces (Katila, 2002), and across a wide range of external actors and sources (Laursen & Salter, 2006) has proven to help firms achieve and sustain innovation. Extant research also recognizes the importance of accessing knowledge during "early" phases of the innovation process, when idea generation occurs, as providing significant improvement opportunities for innovation (Backman, Börjesson, & Setterberg, 2007). This paper investigates the impact of different – external and internal – sources of ideas on innovation. In particular, we consider two main debates in the literature, namely, the effect of external sources of ideas (from outside the firm) on innovation versus the effect of internal sources of ideas (within the firm) on innovation. These two main strands have been studied on both developed and emerging markets. We focus our attention on emerging markets as companies in emerging markets may overcome the innovation challenge that they face by actively sourcing knowledge from different sources outside and within the firm, especially for their idea-generation processes. We also provide a more nuanced perspective on the relationship between knowledge sources on innovation by concurrently analyzing different drivers (internal and external) on different types of innovation – that is, new to world, to country and to firm – in the context of a second-generation emerging market, Colombia. Thus, in the emerging market context, we contribute to the understanding of how different types of knowledge drivers matter for different types of innovation.

Within the emerging markets literature, sources of knowledge have been primarily associated with inter-firm transactions. Such interactions have been shown to enable EMFs to build relationship and social capital (Nahapiet & Ghoshal, 1998; Xu & Meyer, 2013) expand their resource and knowledge bases (McDermott & Corredoira, 2010), realize collective efficiencies (Mesquita & Lazzarini, 2008) and accelerate their knowledge flows (Mu, Peng, & Love, 2008). However, what has perhaps received less empirical attention is a systematic investigation of how multiple external knowledge sources – such as suppliers, clients, competitors, and universities – impact innovation in emerging markets. In contrast, several studies have extensively investigated these patterns in European and other developed country contexts using data gathered from multiple country-level innovation surveys (Belderbos, Carree, & Lokshin, 2006; Santamaría, Nieto, & Barge-Gil, 2009; Tether, 2002; Tomlinson, 2010). Two possible exceptions in emerging market contexts are a study of Taiwanese firms (Tsai, 2009), although many observers no longer regard Taiwan to be an emerging market, and a study spanning six Latin American countries that associates external knowledge sources with innovation expenditures (but not outcomes) (Crespi & Zuniga, 2012). In this paper, we seek to fill this gap in the literature by shedding light on the relationship between knowledge flows from different external sources and innovation by firms in an emerging market.

Although previous research has largely focused on firms accessing *external* sources of knowledge, firms can also innovate by developing and using *internal* sources of knowledge, which may come from different functional areas and different hierarchical levels in the organization. Extant research posits that knowledge generated by different individuals and groups within a firm can be more easily accessed and transacted for internally, which also explains why knowledge-creating activities are often internalized by firms (Kogut & Zander, 1992; Mowery, 1983; Nonaka, Toyama, & Nagata, 2000). Moreover, because emerging markets usually have fragmented and regionalized demands, different individuals or units within EMFs may have a better understanding of different local demands (Dawar & Frost, 1998) and thus sourcing ideas from within the firm can help to develop innovations that better satisfy customers' needs. Therefore, it is palpable that internal knowledge sources may be valuable for EMFs' innovation, and we seek to contribute to the literature by examining these relationships and simultaneously contrasting them with the impacts of external knowledge sources on innovation. A particularly important question for both research and practice is whether internal and external knowledge sources have independent effects on innovation or whether they are fundamentally confounded and represent different facets of the same process.

Because not all innovation is identical, we need to understand how different internal and external knowledge sources affect different types of innovation objectives. For instance, prior research has noted that innovation may vary in their degree of technological or market novelty. Based on the extent to which innovations differ from existing technologies they can be classified into categories that vary in their novelty, ranging from truly novel "new to the world" innovation to intermediate "new to the country" innovation and finally largely imitative innovations that are simply "new to the firm" (OECD, 1995). This characterization has been widely used in prior studies of innovation in different contexts. For example, firms that undertake novel innovation have been linked to less hierarchical organizational culture (Naranjo-Valencia, Jiménez-Jiménez, & Sanz-Valle, 2011) and more developed economic contexts (Shinkle & McCann, 2014). By contrast, more imitative firms are believed to benefit greatly from knowledge spillovers, lower development costs, and risk reduction (Ordanini,

Rubera, & DeFillippi, 2008), among others. Moreover, it is not clear that firms separate cleanly into novel and imitative innovators – for example, they may adopt multi-dimensional innovative approaches that simultaneously yield both types of innovations (Chen, 1996). In turn, different knowledge sources may not only impact each type of innovation but they may also do so differentially. In this paper, we seek to advance the literature by not only examining the joint impact of external *and* internal knowledge sources on innovation in an emerging market context but also by distinguishing between these impacts on more novel *versus* more imitative innovation. An important question for research on innovation by emerging market firms is whether imitative innovation builds on similar knowledge sources as novel innovation and thus enables firms to sequentially build innovation capabilities by first imitating and then pursuing more novel innovation.

The current study examines the relationships between novel versus imitative innovation and external and internal sources of knowledge within a large sample of firms in the Colombian manufacturing industry. Colombia is a mid-tier emerging market in South America with a per capita GDP of 11,890 US dollars (PPP) in 2013 and growth rates of between 4% and 8% over the last decade (World Bank, 2014). Colombia is also a part of the S&P's CIVETS index (Colombia, Indonesia, Vietnam, Egypt, Turkey, and South Africa), a second-generation emerging markets index comprising the next tier of promising growth economies after the BRICs (Brazil, Russia, India, and China). Colombia is an active member of several trading blocks, including the Latin American Free Trade Association, the Southern Cone Common Market, the Andean Community Countries, and the Group of Three (Colombia–Mexico and Venezuela), along with many other bilateral agreements. The Colombian economy is highly diversified, with the manufacturing sector accounting for about 20% of economic activity, and food, beverages, textiles, and chemicals contributing the largest shares of GDP. Exports account for approximately 18% of the country's GDP, with imports also at approximately the same level (World Bank, 2014).

Research on firms and innovation in Latin American contexts is still at a nascent stage. However, prior research on innovation systems in Latin American economies suggests that knowledge sources are more scant and concentrated as a result of geo-political issues, and thus access to them could provide firms with a distinct competitive edge (Katz, 2001). Moreover, interactions between businesses and government support organizations and academia also appear to be weak in Latin American countries, including Colombia (Alcorta & Peres, 1998). Furthermore, key sectors of the Colombian economy are characterized by inter-firm conflicts along the value chain, resulting in un-coordinated buyer-supplier relationships (Business Monitor, 2010), suggesting additional challenges for innovation. Thus, our study not only fills an important gap in research on innovation by Latin American firms but also examines potential contributors to innovation that could be quite significant in this context.

The remainder of this paper is structured as follows. First we describe the details of our data source, the Colombian Innovation Survey, and the sample of firms that we study in our empirical work. Second, we discuss prior research on the sources of external and internal knowledge, and novel and imitative innovation, and describe the measurement of these key constructs in the Colombia Innovation Survey. Third, we present findings from our empirical analyses of firm-level survey responses from Colombian manufacturing firms. Finally, we discuss our key findings and the potential implications of our research for different audiences.

THE COLOMBIAN INNOVATION SURVEY

The current study uses the Colombian Innovation Survey (Encuesta de Desarrollo e Innovación Tecnológica – EDIT) that was administered by the Colombian Bureau of Statistics (Departamento Nacional de Estadística – DANE) to the population of all Colombian manufacturing firms in 2005 as part of the country's manufacturing census. The 2005 Colombian manufacturing census included a special annex requesting information on technology and innovation, which comprises the Colombian Innovation Survey. The purpose of this survey, inspired by the OECD's Oslo Manual, was to examine innovation-related activities undertaken by Colombian industrial firms. The Innovation Survey was thus administered to the same firms as the manufacturing census; namely, the population of officially registered manufacturing firms in the country with 130.5 million Colombian pesos (approximately 81,250 US dollars) or more in annual revenues. Within this population, all geographical areas and firm sizes are covered by the survey. These data are accessible to on-site researchers and were made available to the authors by the Colombian Bureau of Statistics (DANE) as part of an arrangement to participate in an academic advising committee for the survey design.

The data were collected through the regional offices of the Bureau of Statistics and the surveys were conducted by trained interviewers, each of whom completed an average of 20 surveys per month. The owner or manager of each firm was the first point of contact for the survey, but depending on the information required in each subsection of the survey, division managers can also be involved in answering specific survey sections. All 6,670 formally registered manufacturing establishments were included in the manufacturing census for the year 2005. The innovation survey was administered to each firm in the manufacturing census and requested information about innovation inputs and outputs, human capital, and organizational features. Out of the 6,670 firms surveyed, complete information on variables related to sources of ideas and types of innovation (novel versus imitative) are only available for 4,820 firms, which forms our core sample for empirical analysis. Table 1 describes the distribution of the survey sample we employ in this paper relative to the population of Colombian manufacturing firms surveyed by industry and firm size. These data suggest that the population of firms (i.e., the Colombian manufacturing census) and the firms in our sample (i.e., firms with complete data required for our study) are similarly distributed by industry and size. As Table 1 shows, the distribution of firms in the survey is concentrated in a few sectors, with about 41% of firms in the "food and beverages" and "textiles and apparel" industries. While the industry-wise distributions of the sample and population are similar, we note that our sample contains a smaller percentage of micro (<10 employees) and large (>200 employees) manufacturing firms relative to the overall population.

NOVEL VERSUS IMITATIVE INNOVATION

The degree of novelty in emerging market firms' innovation is an important barometer of their ability to compete in national and international markets. Because most firms in emerging markets are far from their industry's technological frontier, they may be inclined to simply reverse engineer technologies previously developed by other firms operating either in their local market or in more advanced countries. Despite being less novel, such innovation may enable emerging market firms to introduce new products into the marketplace and even allow them to gain a local advantage by moving closer to the global technology frontier. However, less novel innovation can also handicap firms from truly differentiating themselves and from developing a reputation for technological excellence. Engaging in more imitative innovation may be especially less desirable if it hinders firms from

Table 1. Population and Sample Statistics.

(a) Industry statistics

Industry	Population Frequency	Population Percent (out of 6,670)	Sample Percent (out of 4,820)	Average: "New to World" Innovation	Average: "New to Country" Innovation	Average: "New to Firm" Innovation
Food and beverages	1,336	20.0	20.5	1.1	2.8	3.7
Textiles and apparel	1,412	21.2	20.4	1.4	2.3	2. 9
Lumber, wood, and furniture	564	8.5	8	1.3	2.5	3.1
Paper and printing	635	9.5	9.5	1.3	2.8	3.5
Petroleum and chemicals	561	8.4	8.9	1.8	3.6	3.9
Rubber, miscellaneous plastics	512	7.7	7.8	1.3	2.9	3.5
Stone, clay, glass, concrete	310	4.6	4.6	1.3	3.2	4.2
Metal products	550	8.2	8.2	0.9	2.0	2.5
Machinery, electronics equipment, computers	533	7.9	8.3	1.6	3.1	3.6
Measurement instruments	49	0.7	0.7	1.7	4.4	6.2
Automotive and other transportation equipment	208	3.1	3.2	1.8	3.3	4.1
TOTAL	6,670	100	100	1.3	2.8	3.4

(b) Size statistics

Size	Population Frequency	Population Percent (out of 6,670)	Sample Percent (out of 4,820)	Average: "New to World" Innovation	Average: "New to Country" Innovation	Average: "New to Firm" Innovation
Micro: <10 employees	978	14.7	10.9	0.5	1.4	2.1
Small: <50 employees	3,115	46.7	48.9	0.8	2.3	3.0
Medium: <200 employees	1,543	23.1	28.4	1.7	3.2	3.8
Large: >200 employees	1,034	15.5	11.8	3.4	4.9	5.6
TOTAL	6,670	100.0	100.0	1.3	2.8	3.4

Note: The population of manufacturing firms (n = 6,670) comprises the set of firms that were surveyed in the Colombian Innovation Survey, whereas the sample we employ (n = 4,820) consists of those firm-surveys that had no missing data required for our analyses. The "Population Percent" and "Sample Percent" columns suggest that firms in the population and in our sample are similarly distributed, by industry (Table 1a) and size (see Table 1b.).

developing the ability to produce more novel innovation in the future. Interestingly, however, prior research finds that emerging market firms often learn about innovation more generally through their experiences with imitation (Kim, 1999; Naude, 2010).

Studies of the imitative behavior of firms in highly uncertain environments have concluded that organizational and competence-related characteristics may affect the likelihood of imitation (Semadeni & Anderson, 2010). Thus, organizational characteristics, including the sourcing of knowledge from different internal and external contexts, are likely to affect firms' imitative innovation in uncertain environments (such as emerging markets). Whereas external actors can play a central role as a source of ideas for firms to learn and imitate, extant research has also shown that firms introducing more novel innovations are also more likely to have access to a wider range of knowledge sources to develop their products (Amara & Landry, 2005). Consistent with the evolutionary theory of the firm (Nelson & Winter, 1982), breakthrough innovations in particular (a high-impact subset of novel innovations) may require the firm to entirely reconsider its innovation path(s), which is facilitated by sourcing more external knowledge than relying on internal ideas. Because novelty is likely to depend on higher levels of technological complexity, uncertainty, and financial risk (Belderbos et al., 2006), there may even be a stronger relationship between external sources of knowledge and more novel innovation, as compared to their relationship with more imitative innovation.

While prior research suggests that access to external sources of knowledge can position EMFs to achieve more novel as well as more imitative innovations, it sheds less light on how internal knowledge sourcing matters for the novelty of innovation. Another less studied topic in the literature is how *particular* external and internal sources of knowledge are associated with novel *versus* imitative innovation. Mansfield, Schwartz, and Wagner (1981) found that the cost and capacity profiles are similar for firms engaged in novel innovation and imitation, which may suggest that the impacts of different knowledge sources may also be similar for both types of innovation. However, the degree of novelty of emerging market companies' innovations might also be differentially associated with particular (internal or external) sources of innovation ideas.

The *Oslo Manual* (OECD, 1995) operationalizes the degree of novelty in innovation by distinguishing between products introduced that are (in decreasing order of novelty) "new to the world," "new to the country" and "new to the firm." New-to-world innovation can create entirely new product markets and have a global market but is at the same time associated with higher uncertainties. At the other end of the spectrum, new-to-firm innovation allows companies to enter and compete in existing markets with their own products, whereas new-to-country innovations allow companies to engage in global technological arbitrage and tap into local demand for products already introduced in the global market. As Table 1 show, firms in our sample – on average – achieve more new-to-firm innovation than new-to-country innovation, which are in turn both higher than their levels of new-to-world innovation. While the average level of 1.3 new-to-world product innovations may seem high, it is important to bear in mind that these are not necessarily radical or breakthrough (or indeed successful) products but simply something that is novel to the global market.

EXTERNAL SOURCES OF KNOWLEDGE

In view of the general trend toward more collaborative knowledge development by firms and the opening up of firm boundaries for innovation (Chesbrough, 2003; Cohen & Levinthal, 1990), firms seem to be increasingly relying on external sources of ideas. By external sources of knowledge, we specifically refer to entities, communities, or artifacts outside the firm that contribute ideas to the innovation process. Early research streams in the innovation literature focused on particular external actors like customers or suppliers (Utterback, 1994) as drivers of innovation. Not surprisingly, in prior empirical studies of external knowledge sourcing, research on specific external sources and their impacts on innovation has been the most common approach (Caloghirou, Kastelli, & Tsakanikas, 2004; Faems, Van Looy, & Debackere, 2005; Tsai & Wang, 2009). For example, suppliers are presumed to bring different insights into innovative components, organization of production, and other functions of technological development (Kessler & Chakrabarti, 1996). Similarly, customers (or users) can enhance innovation by becoming a valuable source of information about market opportunities and allowing firms to discover new user needs that are often a key source of innovation ideas (Gupta, Wilemon, & Atuahene-Gima, 2000; von Hippel, 1998).

While suppliers and customers may serve as valuable sources of "vertical knowledge" along the firm's value chain, horizontal sourcing of knowledge can also be equally important. For example, competitors can be important for innovation (Tether, 2002) as their actions frequently hint at significant market trends, new developments, and technical problems. Knowledge exchange may also occur between firms and organizations engaged in public science such as universities and public research laboratories, which can be actively involved in providing scientific research inputs to businesses. Extant research has shown that this university-firm link is strong in developed economies (Belderbos, Carree, & Lokshin, 2004; Hemmert, 2004; Laursen & Salter, 2004); however, surveys in developing countries show that fewer firms have cooperation agreements with research institutions (OECD, 2005). Business groups are also fairly common phenomena outside the developed world, including in Latin American and Asian emerging economies (Khanna & Rivkin, 2001). Companies within the same business group are expected to cooperate and create synergies for the conglomerate (Yiu, Bruton, & Lu, 2005); thus, it is quite likely that these firms exchange knowledge that serve as sources of ideas for innovation. In prior research, firms affiliated to business groups have been found to innovate more (Belenzon & Berkovitz, 2010; Sea-Jin, Chi-Nien, & Mahmood, 2006) and perform better at joint ventures (Lu & Xufei, 2008). Furthermore, business associations like industry bodies and chambers of commerce frequently provide technical and market information to their members, which in turn might create innovative opportunities. Finally, secondary sources of innovative ideas, such as seminars, magazines, and internet, are also being increasingly used by firms to access external knowledge due to the extended global reach of information technology.

Empirically, although external sources of knowledge have been increasingly studied as determinants of firm innovation (Belderbos et al., 2004; Lööf & Heshmati, 2002; Nieto & Santamaría, 2010; Tsai, 2009), a notable feature of this literature is that findings regarding the impact of particular partners – that is, clients, suppliers, competitors – on firm innovativeness have been mixed (see Table 2). For example, in their research on Swedish manufacturing firms, Lööf and Heshmati (2002) find that cooperating with universities and competitors has a positive effect on innovation effect on productivity; however, they observe that relationships with customers have a negative association. Belderbos et al. (2004), using data on Dutch innovating firms, finds that cooperation with universities and research centers has a strong positive effects on innovation, but interactions with competing firms have a weak effect. Nieto and Santamaría (2007) examine results for the Spanish innovation survey and suggest that R&D investments and cooperation with suppliers have a positive impact on innovations with both low and high degrees of novelty. These mixed results suggest that the effect of individual sources on innovation may not be straightforward, and depend, among others, on the context in which

Table 2. Summary of Literature on Knowledge Sources and Innovation.

Study	Country	Dependent Variable	Sources of Knowledge	Relationship
Gupta et al. (2000)	United States: 68 high-R&D-effective firms; 49 low-R&D-effective firms	Mean differences for split sample: by firm's *perception* of R&D effectiveness (high – low)	Customer Manufacturing Sale Senior management	Mean differences for all sources are significantly larger for firms perceived as having high R&D effectiveness
Lööf and Heshmati (2002)	Switzerland: 619 observations	(1) Probability of having one innovation output (2) Growth rate in labor productivity	Suppliers	(1) Positive (2) Positive
			Competitors	(1) Positive (2) Positive
			Customers	(1) Negative (2) Negative
			Secondary sources	(1) Weakly negative (2) Not significant
			Universities	(1) Not significant (2) Weakly positive
			Business groups	(1) Weakly positive (2) Positive
			Any source within the firm	(1) Positive (2) Positive
Belderbos et al. (2004)	The Netherlands: 2056 observations	Growth of new to the market innovations – sales per employee	Supplier Competitors Customers Universities	Not significant Weak and positive Not significant Positive
Hemmert (2004)	Japan: 109 observations Germany: 49 observations	Number of patent applications for (1) Japan (2) Germany	Factor loadings: a. Tech level of suppl., customers and competitors.	(1) a. Not significant b. Positive c. Not significant d. Not significant (2) a. Positive b. Not significant

Table 2. *(Continued)*

Study	Country	Dependent Variable	Sources of Knowledge	Relationship
			b. Tech level of universities, and R&D labs. c. Existence of ties to suppliers, customers and competitors. d. Skills R&D personnel	c. Not significant d. Positive
Santamaría et al. (2009)	Spain: 4,580 observations	Split sample for high and low tech firms. Probability of having at least one innovation: (1) Product (2) Process	Suppliers pressure	(1) Negative high & low tech (2) Not significant (for both)
			Competitors pressure	(1) Positive high & low tech (2) Positive only low-tech
			Clients pressure	(1) Negative only low tech (2) Not significant (for both)
Vega-Jurado, Gutiérrez-Gracia, and Fernández-de-Lucio (2009)	Spain: 675 observations	(1) Probability of having at least one Product Innovation (2) Probability of having at least one Process Innovation	Sum of scores given to: a. Other firms, clients, suppliers, and competitors. b. R&D Labs, tech centers, universities.	(1) a. Weakly positive only on supplier-based ind. b. Weakly positive only on science-based ind. (2) a. Not significant b. Not significant
Köhler et al. (2012)	Europe: 4,933 observations	Share of sales related with products that are (1) new to market (2) new to firm	a. Suppliers and secondary sources b. Customers and competitors c. Scientific institutions: R&D labs and universities	(1) a. Positive for new to market b. Not significant c. Positive only for new to market (2) a. Not significant for new to firm b. Positive for new to firm

				c. Not significant for new to firm
Belenzon and Berkovitz (2010)	Europe: 12,389 observations	Number of patent applications of innovative firms	Business Groups	Positive
Fitjar and Rodríguez-Pose (2013)	Norway: 1,602 observations	Probability of having at least one: (1) Product Innovation (2) Radical Product Innovation (3) Process Innovation	Suppliers	(1) Positive (2) Positive (3) Positive
			Competitors	(1) Negative (2) Negative (3) Not significant
			Customers	(1) Positive (2) Positive (3) Not significant
			Universities	(1) Positive (2) Positive (3) Not significant
			Business Groups	(1) Positive (2) Not significant (3) Not significant
Tsai and Wang (2009)	Taiwan: 1,346 observations	Firms' turnover linked to improved or new products	Suppliers	Not significant
			Competitors	Not significant
			Customers	Not significant
			University	Negative
Crespi and Zuniga (2012)	Argentina (1,192), Chile (1,151), Colombia (5,934), Costa Rica (352), Panama (481), and Uruguay (813)	Innovation expenditure per employee	Other (external) spillovers	Positive for Argentina and Colombia. Negative for Panama.
			Secondary sources	Not significant for any country.
			Scientific sources	Positive and significant only for Costa Rica

innovation is developed. Additionally, there is less systematic evidence about the association between different external knowledge sources and innovation novelty, especially in emerging market contexts.

INTERNAL SOURCES OF KNOWLEDGE

To obtain a more complete picture of the impact of different sources of ideas on innovation, we seek to further investigate the role of internal sources of ideas. A strong internal knowledge base is often considered key to innovation (Prahalad & Hamel, 1990). Moreover, because the costs of sourcing knowledge from outside the firm are often quite high (Parmigiani & Rivera-Santos, 2011), resource-constrained EMFs may need to rely on knowledge flows from their internal sources in order to innovate. Prior research has highlighted the important role of internal within-firm factors for innovation in a number of ways. For example, prior studies have examined the role of firm-level attributes, resources and strategies (Galende & de la Fuente, 2003), skills of R&D personnel (Hemmert, 2004), technological competences (Vega-Jurado, Gutiérrez-Gracia, Fernández-de-Lucio, & Manjarrés-Henríquez, 2008), as well as the firm's innovation objectives (Leiponen & Helfat, 2010) on innovation. However, what has perhaps received less attention is the extent to which different sources of knowledge within the firm individually contribute to innovation, and how these knowledge sources may differentially impact the degree of novelty in innovation.

In many firms, several actors within the organization may be called on to contribute ideas to the innovation process. In addition to their formal R&D departments, firms can source in-house ideas for innovation by drawing on the knowledge of their various internal departments, functional areas, and even interdisciplinary teams. Additionally, firms may also obtain relevant innovation ideas from different hierarchical levels within the organization, such as from their managerial cadres and rank and file employees. Because firms are widely considered to be efficient structures for both communicating and transacting for knowledge (Kogut & Zander, 1992; Mowery, 1983; Nonaka et al., 2000), internally sourced knowledge may have a particularly impactful effect on innovation outputs. Prior research suggests that different subunits of the firm may be particularly important for environmental sense-making and for communicating this knowledge within the firm, especially in emerging market contexts where external environments can be both highly differentiated and dynamic (Dawar & Frost, 1998). Additionally, emerging markets often lack smooth information channels and institutional structures through which innovation-related knowledge can flow, and so internally sourced knowledge may be an effective substitute for sourcing innovation ideas from outside sources. Among the hierarchical levels from which knowledge may flow, managerial knowledge may be critical for innovative activity because managers can more easily identify and exploit innovative opportunities within the firm's internal context (Thorpe, Holt, Macpherson, & Pittaway, 2005). However, lower level employees may also be important in the environmental sensing function noted above, as well as in identifying operational opportunities for innovation in the course of their daily work.

EMPIRICAL METHODS

The goal of our empirical analyses is to shed light on the role of different sources of knowledge, both internal and external to the firm, on the extent to which firms achieve novel and imitative innovation objectives in emerging market firms. The dependent variables in our study – counts of novel and imitative achieved innovation objectives – are non-negative integer count variables, and we therefore use negative binomial regression models. OLS models are inappropriate for count data that both have a lower bound of zero and have a discrete distribution. While the Poisson regression model may be used to model count data, it suffers from having a somewhat rigid distributional specification whereby the mean and variance of the distribution are designed to be equal. By contrast, the negative binomial distribution can accommodate over-dispersed data (the variance being larger than the mean), which are common in innovation samples. Therefore, negative binomial models are less likely to under-estimate the coefficients' standard errors (Cameron & Trivedi, 1998). Additionally, because the standard error estimates may not be consistent if the data do not have a true negative binomial distribution, we estimate and report consistent Huber-White semi-robust standard errors. We describe the measurement of our dependent and independent variables, below.

Measures: Dependent Variables

In this paper, the dependent variable measures firm-level novel versus imitative innovation using the counts of achieved product innovation objectives. The Colombian Innovation Survey asks manufacturing firms to report the product innovation objectives they have achieved, categorizing these objectives according to their degree of innovativeness. Specifically, respondents indicate whether their establishment has achieved any product innovation objectives during the preceding two years (2003–2004), and further specify which fall into each of the following categories: "new to the world," "new to the country," and "new to the firm." Thus, our dependent variables are the count of product innovations achieved in each of the following categories:

i. *New to World*: Products that are new or significantly improved to the international market.
ii. *New to Country*: Products that are new or significantly improved to the national market.
iii. *New to Firm*: Products that are new or significantly improved to the firm.

Table 3 shows the summary statistics of our main dependent, independent, and control variables.

Table 3. Summary Statistics (Dependent and Control Variables).

Variable Name	Variable Description	Mean	S.D.	Min.	Max.
New-to-world innovation	Count of achieved "New to World" innovation objectives	1.3	3.8	0.0	38.0
New-to-country innovation	Count of achieved "New to Country" innovation objectives	2.8	4.3	0.0	44.0
New-to-firm innovation	Count of achieved "New to Firm" innovation objectives	3.4	5.3	0.0	41.0
Patent or license (dummy)	Dummy variable for the acquisition of patents or licenses	0.2	0.4	0.0	1.0
Firm size	Number of employees	107.6	269.4	1.0	6510.0
% Professional employees	Percentage of employees with a professional degree	14.2	13.0	0.0	100.0
% Technical employees	Percentage of employees with a technical degree	15.1	16.9	0.0	100.0
External R&D funding	Amount (in US dollars) of R&D funding from external funding sources	7.9E+04	7.4E+05	0.0	2.7E+07
Internal R&D funding	Amount (in US dollars) of R&D funding from internal funding sources	1.2E+05	1.5E+06	0.0	5.9E+07
Observations		4,820			

For the subsequent regressions, firm size, % professional employees, % technical employees, external R&D funding, internal R&D funding, are logged in the form $\ln(1+x)$.

Measures: Key Independent Variables

External Sources of Knowledge

In the Colombian Innovation Survey, each surveyed firm is asked to assess the importance of each of the following external sources of ideas for their innovation on a scale from 0 to 4:

i. clients
ii. suppliers
iii. competitors
iv. universities
v. companies from the firm's business group
vi. business associations
vii. secondary sources (seminars, conferences, magazines, and internet)
viii. scientific sources (patent and copyright banks, scientific databases)

Internal Sources of Knowledge

The Colombian Innovation Survey measures the role of six internal sources of ideas by asking survey respondents to rate the importance of each source for innovation on a 0–4 scale. Four of these internal sources are horizontally differentiated, as follows:

i. R&D department
ii. production department
iii. marketing department and
iv. interdisciplinary groups.

Two internal sources of ideas for innovation are vertically differentiated, as follows:

i. managers and
ii. workers.

Each of these variables may be seen as proxies for the firm's knowledge resources, which may in turn facilitate different types of innovation objectives. Table 4 presents summary statistics as well as pair-wise correlations of the key independent variables in our sample. Table 4 indicates that, on average, firms consider secondary sources and clients to be their most important external sources of ideas for innovation, and managers and production departments as their most important internal sources of ideas for innovation. In general, internal sources have higher importance scores as

Table 4. Summary Statistics and Correlation Table (Key Independent Variables).

	Variables	(1)	(2)	(3)	(4)	(5)	(6)	(7)	(8)
	External sources:								
(1)	Suppliers	1							
(2)	Competitors	0.45	1						
(3)	Clients	0.42	0.40	1					
(4)	Universities	0.34	0.32	0.25	1				
(5)	Business group	0.25	0.24	0.19	0.28	1			
(6)	Business associations	0.39	0.35	0.30	0.41	0.21	1		
(7)	Secondary sources	0.41	0.38	0.43	0.35	0.23	0.39	1	
(8)	Scientific sources	0.39	0.36	0.32	0.46	0.30	0.44	0.51	1
	Internal sources:								
(9)	R&D department	0.25	0.25	0.21	0.33	0.26	0.19	0.25	0.31
(10)	Production department	0.28	0.25	0.27	0.28	0.23	0.24	0.32	0.32
(11)	Marketing department	0.33	0.34	0.34	0.34	0.25	0.31	0.38	0.42
(12)	Interdisciplinary groups	0.28	0.24	0.21	0.29	0.30	0.23	0.27	0.34
(13)	Managers	0.08	0.10	0.04	0.06	−0.01	0.06	0.05	0.08
(14)	Employees	0.37	0.29	0.33	0.29	0.26	0.28	0.35	0.37
	Mean	0.85	0.73	1.26	0.46	0.45	0.72	1.68	0.81
	Standard deviation	1.49	1.39	1.74	1.14	1.17	1.4	1.83	1.46
	Min.	0.00	0.00	0.00	0.00	0.00	0.00	0.00	0.00
	Max.	4.00	4.00	4.00	4.00	4.00	4.00	4.00	4.00

	Variables	(9)	(10)	(11)	(12)	(13)	(14)
	External sources:						
(1)	Suppliers						
(2)	Competitors						
(3)	Clients						
(4)	Universities						
(5)	Business group						
(6)	Business associations						
(7)	Secondary sources						
(8)	Scientific sources						
	Internal sources:						
(9)	R&D department	1					
(10)	Production department	0.32	1				
(11)	Marketing department	0.41	0.50	1			
(12)	Interdisciplinary groups	0.38	0.30	0.36	1		
(13)	Managers	0.00	0.02	0.05	−0.08	1	
(14)	Employees	0.29	0.36	0.41	0.33	0.09	1
	Mean	0.56	1.55	1.13	0.75	3.29	1.19
	Standard deviation	1.27	1.8	1.66	1.42	1.32	1.65
	Min.	0.00	0.00	0.00	0.00	0.00	0.00
	Max.	4.00	4.00	4.00	4.00	4.00	4.00

sources of innovation ideas, as compared to external sources. Yet, there is a high variance in the importance that firms give to each source.

Measures: Control Variables

We also include a number of control variables that have been identified in previous research as being important to innovation. These include controls for "Patent or License," which is a dummy variable equal to one when the focal firm has acquired a patent or a license; "Firm Size" measured as the log of the number of employees; "% of Professional Employees" measured as the percentage of total employees with a professional degree; "% of Technical Employees" measured as the percentage of total employees with a technical degree; "External R&D Funding" measured as the amount of innovation funding that the focal firm obtains from outside sources; and "Internal R&D Funding" measured as the amount of innovation funding that the focal firm invests from its own resources. All our models employ a full set of industry dummies in each model to account for industry-level idiosyncrasies in innovation.

RESULTS

In our empirical analyses, we seek to examine how the rated importance of different sources of ideas for innovation – for example, clients, suppliers, universities, scientific sources, different internal departments, managers and workers, among others – help manufacturing firms achieve different types of innovation objectives (more novel versus more innovative). The results are presented in Table 5 as four negative binomial models for each type of innovation representing a different degree of novelty, that is, "New to world," "New to country" and "New to firm." The first model for each type of innovation (models 1, 5, and 9) includes only the control variables, the second and third models (2, 6, and 10, and 3, 7, and 11) include the variables associated with external and internal sources of innovation ideas, respectively, and the fourth model (4, 8, and 12) includes all the variables simultaneously. In each of these models, we follow recommended best practice and log (continuous or count) independent variables to yield a log-log model specification (Chauradia & Somaya, 2015). For variables that can take on zero values we add one before taking logs. Coefficients from these

Table 5. External and Internal Sources of Ideas and Product Innovation by Innovativeness Category in Colombia.

	New-to-World Innovation				New-to-Country Innovation				New-to-Firm Innovation			
	(1)	(2)	(3)	(4)	(5)	(6)	(7)	(8)	(9)	(10)	(11)	(12)
Patent or license (dummy)	0.194*	0.136	0.144	0.149	0.244***	0.166***	0.149**	0.145**	0.177***	0.110*	0.119**	0.104*
	(0.109)	(0.112)	(0.121)	(0.116)	(0.065)	(0.063)	(0.064)	(0.064)	(0.057)	(0.057)	(0.057)	(0.058)
Firm size	0.524***	0.476***	0.442***	0.438***	0.224***	0.181***	0.161***	0.155***	0.177***	0.141***	0.120***	0.119***
	(0.037)	(0.039)	(0.041)	(0.041)	(0.021)	(0.021)	(0.023)	(0.023)	(0.018)	(0.018)	(0.019)	(0.020)
% Professional employees	0.263***	0.224***	0.221***	0.213***	0.168***	0.135***	0.132***	0.125***	0.078***	0.046*	0.048**	0.040*
	(0.050)	(0.053)	(0.052)	(0.053)	(0.028)	(0.028)	(0.028)	(0.028)	(0.024)	(0.024)	(0.024)	(0.023)
% Technical employees	0.021	0.015	−0.004	0.005	0.043*	0.036	0.022	0.025	0.024	0.018	0.010	0.013
	(0.043)	(0.042)	(0.044)	(0.041)	(0.023)	(0.023)	(0.023)	(0.023)	(0.020)	(0.019)	(0.020)	(0.019)
External R&D funding	0.083***	0.075***	0.078***	0.075***	0.069***	0.061***	0.065***	0.061***	0.068***	0.060***	0.064***	0.061***
	(0.012)	(0.011)	(0.012)	(0.011)	(0.006)	(0.006)	(0.006)	(0.006)	(0.006)	(0.006)	(0.006)	(0.006)
Internal R&D funding	0.055***	0.057***	0.064***	0.062***	0.043***	0.044***	0.046***	0.045***	0.049***	0.046***	0.050***	0.047***
	(0.016)	(0.014)	(0.016)	(0.014)	(0.009)	(0.008)	(0.008)	(0.008)	(0.008)	(0.007)	(0.007)	(0.007)
Industry dummy	*Yes*	*Yes*	*Yes*	*Yes*	*Yes*	*Yes*	*Yes*	*Yes*	*Yes*	*Yes*	*Yes*	*Yes*
External sources												
Suppliers		0.215**		0.140		0.093*		0.040		0.091**		0.044
		(0.087)		(0.089)		(0.050)		(0.053)		(0.041)		(0.042)
Competitors		0.067		0.016		0.103**		0.066		0.059		0.037
		(0.087)		(0.083)		(0.052)		(0.054)		(0.044)		(0.045)
Clients		0.164**		0.150**		0.085**		0.056		0.033		0.000
		(0.071)		(0.071)		(0.041)		(0.042)		(0.034)		(0.035)
Universities		0.118		0.030		0.090		0.022		0.104*		0.054
		(0.093)		(0.095)		(0.058)		(0.059)		(0.055)		(0.056)
Business group		0.085		0.046		0.069		0.035		0.022		−0.015
		(0.089)		(0.093)		(0.050)		(0.053)		(0.043)		(0.044)
Business associations		−0.102		−0.137		−0.057		−0.094*		−0.046		−0.055
		(0.084)		(0.087)		(0.051)		(0.052)		(0.042)		(0.043)

Secondary sources		0.058		0.018		0.135***		0.106**		0.154***		0.128***
		(0.074)		(0.075)		(0.041)		(0.043)		(0.035)		(0.036)
Scientific sources		0.265***		0.214**		0.184***		0.114**		0.173***		0.120***
		(0.083)		(0.091)		(0.049)		(0.052)		(0.042)		(0.044)
Internal sources												
R&D dept.			0.041	−0.002			0.085*	0.045			0.054	0.021
			(0.076)	(0.079)			(0.047)	(0.047)			(0.043)	(0.044)
Production dept.			0.277***	0.252***			0.171***	0.148***			0.183***	0.161***
			(0.072)	(0.070)			(0.042)	(0.042)			(0.035)	(0.035)
Marketing dept.			0.019	−0.053			0.101**	0.049			0.046	−0.003
			(0.080)	(0.083)			(0.044)	(0.046)			(0.038)	(0.039)
Interdisciplinary groups			0.295***	0.264***			0.132***	0.112**			0.085**	0.058
			(0.076)	(0.076)			(0.047)	(0.049)			(0.041)	(0.043)
Managers			0.265***	0.221***			0.168***	0.159***			0.107**	0.094**
			(0.080)	(0.079)			(0.053)	(0.052)			(0.047)	(0.046)
Employees			0.210***	0.103			0.210***	0.143***			0.213***	0.148***
			(0.072)	(0.070)			(0.041)	(0.042)			(0.038)	(0.039)
Constant	*Yes*	*Yes*	*Yes*	*Yes*	*Yes*	*Yes*	*Yes*	*Yes*	*Yes*	*Yes*	*Yes*	*Yes*
Observations	4,820	4,820	4,820	4,820	4,820	4,820	4,820	4,820	4,820	4,820	4,820	4,820
BIC	11051.2	11033	10980.5	11017.6	18755.7	18706.9	18629.7	18673	21553.8	21491.3	21395.4	21430.7

Standard errors in parentheses; $^{*}p < 0.10$, $^{**}p < 0.05$, $^{***}p < 0.01$.

Firm size, % professional employees, % technical employees, external R&D funding, internal R&D funding, external sources and internal sources of ideas are logged in the form $\ln(1 + x)$.

log-log models can essentially be interpreted as elasticities (percentage changes in y for each percentage change in x).

Results: Novel Innovations

The first panel in Table 5 examines how the importance of different external and internal sources of knowledge is associated with the number of truly novel new-to-world innovation objectives achieved by the firm. The results show that, among external knowledge sources, scientific sources (patent banks, scientific databases) are strongly associated with new-to-world innovation comes, which is statistically significant at the 0.05 level (in the full model, model 4). Likewise, clients is an external source of ideas with a statistically significant association (at the 0.05 level in model 4) with novel innovation. Although scientific sources seem to facilitate "new to world" innovation, other secondary sources that are more market-oriented (e.g., seminars, magazines, internet) do not seem to be associated with firms achieving "new to world" objectives. Thus, even in this emerging market context, scientific sources seem to be providing firms with cutting edge knowledge that promotes the most novel innovations. In model 2 (which includes external knowledge sources but excludes internal knowledge sources, and is therefore arguably more comparable with prior work), novel innovation is also positively associated with external knowledge from suppliers (p-value = 0.05), consistent with previous findings from radical innovation likelihood in more developed economies, for example, Norway (Fitjar & Rodríguez-Pose, 2013).

Among internal sources of knowledge, knowledge from the production department and knowledge from interdisciplinary groups are strongly associated (p-value = 0.01) with novel innovation. These findings indicate that building strongly on knowledge related to unique production processes may be an important route to achieving highly novel innovation, and that internal structures which bring together employees from diverse functional backgrounds, such as interdisciplinary groups, may foster knowledge recombinations that seem to be important for achieving more novel innovation objectives (p-value = 0.01 in model 4). Managers, which are vertically differentiated internal knowledge sources, are significantly associated with new-to-world innovation. In particular, the effect of managers' ideas is strong and positive even in model 4 (the full model specification).

Results: Imitative Innovations

Empirical analyses of how different external and internal sources of knowledge are associated with less novel, new-to-country and new-to-firm, innovations are presented in the middle and last panels of Table 5 (models 5–12). Among our control variables, the main difference between the two is the lower and less statistically significant impact of the patent and license dummy and percentage of professional employees on new-to-firm innovations relative to new-to-country innovations, which is arguably consistent what we might expect. Additionally, the impacts of interdisciplinary groups on new-to-firm innovation is weaker (and less significant) than new-to-country innovation, which we discuss further below.

With regards to external sources of ideas, we find that scientific sources are again strongly and statistically significantly associated with both types of "less novel" innovations (at the 0.05 and 0.01 levels for new-to-country and new-to-firm innovation, respectively, in the full model). Thus, scientific publications appear to be a significant source of knowledge for firms to achieve innovations with any degree of novelty. Interestingly, we also find a similar and strong association between secondary knowledge sources (such as seminars, conferences and the internet, which are more "market-oriented") and both of these types of more imitative innovation (at the 0.05 and 0.01 levels for new-to-country and new-to-firm innovation, respectively, in the full model). This finding is somewhat surprising because previous studies have found that secondary sources have a weak or negative overall association with innovation outputs – undifferentiated by novelty – for developed economy firms (Lööf & Heshmati, 2002), and have no significant effect on innovation inputs (e.g., innovation expenditure) for emerging market firms (Crespi & Zuniga, 2012). Moreover, knowledge from clients – which is associated with novel new-to-world innovations in our sample – is not significantly related to either new-to-firm or new-to-country innovations (in the full models, 8 and 12). However, in models without the internal knowledge sources variables external knowledge from both competitors and clients are significantly associated with new-to-country innovation (p-value = 0.05; model 6), and knowledge from suppliers is significantly associated with new-to-firm innovations (p-value = 0.05; model 10).

Among internal sources of knowledge, our findings for these less novel types of innovations are similar to new-to-world innovations in that knowledge from both production departments and managers are positively and significantly associated with innovation (p-value = 0.01, except p = 0.05 for managers in model 12). Ideas from R&D continue to have no significant association with innovation, but one must bear in mind that the models already control for firm size, professional and technical personnel, and R&D spending, which are correlated with this variable. Interestingly, knowledge from interdisciplinary teams is strongly associated (p-value = 0.05) with new-to-country innovations in the full model (model 8), but it is not significant in the full model for new-to-firm innovations. Along the vertical internal dimension, ideas from employees, which was not significantly associated with new-to-world innovations in the full model, are significantly associated with both types of more imitative innovation (p-value = 0.01 in models 8 and 12). In the partial model (model 7) that only included internal sources of ideas, but not in the full model (model 8), ideas from the marketing department are significantly associated with new-to-country innovations.

In summary, we find a number of similarities in the sources of ideas that impact the ability of firms to achieve innovation objectives at all levels of novelty. Specifically, scientific sources, production departments, and managers are significantly associated with all three categories of innovation novelty. In general, the magnitudes of coefficients are graduated in such a way as to indicate that relevant knowledge sources either become steadily less important or more important as one transitions from less novel to more novel types of innovation. Thus, on many (but not all) dimensions, new-to-country innovation is "intermediate" between new-to-world and new-to-firm innovation. However, in terms of statistical significance, only four knowledge sources stand out as being different in their impacts on the most novel new-to-world innovations versus the most imitative new-to-firm innovations (at a p-value of at least 0.10). Of these, knowledge from clients and interdisciplinary groups are more strongly associated with new-to-world innovations (model 4) at conventional statistical significance levels of 0.05, whereas knowledge from secondary sources is more important for new-to-firm inventions and knowledge from managers has a bigger impact on new-to-world innovation, but both only at the 0.10 level. Interestingly, in the first two cases, clients and interdisciplinary groups, the association with imitative new-to-firm innovations is statistically insignificant, suggesting that at least for these two sources firms may need to develop new capabilities and knowledge channels to engage in truly novel innovation. Despite these findings, one may need to interpret the results for external knowledge sources with care in light of the additional analyses reported below.

Post-Hoc Analyses: Combining (Some) Sources of Ideas

One of the interesting features of our results is the support that we see for some of the sources of innovative ideas, both internal and external, in the partial models but these results decrease in significance in the full models. One of the potential explanations for a lack of stronger support may be that firms tend to use multiple sources of knowledge at the same time, so that the effects are conflated and we may not be able to cleanly separate the impact of some individual knowledge sources. The high correlations between some of the sources of knowledge (see Table 2) provide further evidence that supports this possibility. To further explore this issue in our data, we conducted factor analyses to examine how some external or internal sources of knowledge may be often used together by firms. We found that some external sources of innovation ideas, but not internal sources, tended to be used together by firms and loaded on the same factor. Accordingly, we combined the use of these groups of external sources into "composite variables" by computing their means. Specifically, we coded three variables that combined the importance of the following external knowledge sources: (a) external firms, which is the average importance score of clients, suppliers, and competitors, (b) external institutions, which is the average importance score of universities, business groups, and business associations, and (c) second-hand knowledge, which is the average importance score of secondary sources and scientific sources. In addition to being suggested by our factor analyses, these combined variables also have intuitive appeal.

Table 6 reports the results from negative binomial models using these grouped composite variables, which are reported in three panels in the same way as before. With respect to external sources, we find no statistical support for the institutional sources of knowledge (see models 4, 8, and 12), and second-hand sources appear to matter about equally for all types of innovation objectives (arguably due to a blending of the contrasting effects of secondary and scientific sources). However, ideas from external firms appear to have a graduated effect, with the strongest impact on new-to-world innovations (p-value = 0.01 in model 4), a weaker impact on new-to-country innovations (p-value = 0.05 in model 8), and no significant impact on new-to-firm innovations (model 12). Again, the implication is that emerging market firms may need to develop a new ability to learn from other firms in order to engage in more novel types of innovation. We find (in Table 6) that all our remaining results remain substantially the same as in Table 5.

Table 6. External (Grouped) and Internal Sources of Ideas and Product Innovation by Innovativeness Category in Colombia.

	New-to-World Innovation				New-to-Country Innovation				New-to-Firm Innovation			
	(1)	(2)	(3)	(4)	(5)	(6)	(7)	(8)	(9)	(10)	(11)	(12)
Patent or license (dummy)	0.194*	0.123	0.144	0.139	0.244***	0.163***	0.149**	0.140**	0.177***	0.107*	0.119**	0.099*
	(0.109)	(0.112)	(0.121)	(0.118)	(0.065)	(0.063)	(0.064)	(0.064)	(0.057)	(0.057)	(0.057)	(0.057)
Firm size	0.524***	0.481***	0.442***	0.443***	0.224***	0.186***	0.161***	0.160***	0.177***	0.143***	0.120***	0.120***
	(0.037)	(0.038)	(0.041)	(0.040)	(0.021)	(0.021)	(0.023)	(0.023)	(0.018)	(0.018)	(0.019)	(0.019)
% Professional employees	0.263***	0.224***	0.221***	0.215***	0.168***	0.135***	0.132***	0.126***	0.078***	0.044*	0.048**	0.038
	(0.050)	(0.053)	(0.052)	(0.053)	(0.028)	(0.028)	(0.028)	(0.028)	(0.024)	(0.023)	(0.024)	(0.023)
% Technical employees	0.021	0.009	−0.004	0.000	0.043*	0.033	0.022	0.023	0.024	0.016	0.010	0.011
	(0.043)	(0.043)	(0.044)	(0.043)	(0.023)	(0.023)	(0.023)	(0.023)	(0.020)	(0.019)	(0.020)	(0.019)
External R&D funding	0.083***	0.073***	0.078***	0.073***	0.069***	0.060***	0.065***	0.061***	0.068***	0.060***	0.064***	0.061***
	(0.012)	(0.011)	(0.012)	(0.011)	(0.006)	(0.006)	(0.006)	(0.006)	(0.006)	(0.006)	(0.006)	(0.006)
Internal R&D funding	0.055***	0.055***	0.064***	0.061***	0.043***	0.044***	0.046***	0.045***	0.049***	0.046***	0.050***	0.047***
	(0.016)	(0.014)	(0.016)	(0.015)	(0.009)	(0.008)	(0.008)	(0.008)	(0.008)	(0.007)	(0.007)	(0.007)
Industry dummies	*Yes*	*Yes*	*Yes*	*Yes*	*Yes*	*Yes*	*Yes*	*Yes*	*Yes*	*Yes*	*Yes*	*Yes*
External sources												
Firms average score		0.424***		0.292***		0.262***		0.142**		0.153***		0.050
		(0.101)		(0.107)		(0.063)		(0.068)		(0.052)		(0.056)
Institutions average score		0.151		−0.013		0.129*		−0.011		0.153**		0.064
		(0.136)		(0.148)		(0.076)		(0.082)		(0.073)		(0.080)
Secondary knowledge average score		0.426***		0.295**		0.441***		0.299***		0.459***		0.350***
		(0.134)		(0.139)		(0.080)		(0.084)		(0.071)		(0.074)

Internal sources												
R&D dept.			0.041	–0.004			0.085*	0.052			0.054	0.020
			(0.076)	(0.078)			(0.047)	(0.047)			(0.043)	(0.044)
Production dept.			0.277***	0.246***			0.171***	0.149***			0.183***	0.162***
			(0.072)	(0.071)			(0.042)	(0.042)			(0.035)	(0.035)
Marketing dept.			0.019	–0.062			0.101**	0.046			0.046	–0.007
			(0.080)	(0.083)			(0.044)	(0.046)			(0.038)	(0.040)
Interdisciplinary			0.295***	0.269***			0.132***	0.106**			0.085**	0.052
groups			(0.076)	(0.078)			(0.047)	(0.048)			(0.041)	(0.043)
Managers			0.265***	0.221***			0.168***	0.155***			0.107**	0.095**
			(0.080)	(0.080)			(0.053)	(0.052)			(0.047)	(0.047)
Employees			0.210***	0.111			0.210***	0.144***			0.213***	0.149***
			(0.072)	(0.071)			(0.041)	(0.042)			(0.038)	(0.040)
Constant	*Yes*	*Yes*	*Yes*	*Yes*	*Yes*	*Yes*	*Yes*	*Yes*	*Yes*	*Yes*	*Yes*	*Yes*
Observations	4,820	4,820	4,820	4,820	4,820	4,820	4,820	4,820	4,820	4,820	4,820	4,820
BIC	11051.2	10999.8	10980.5	10984.9	21553.8	21458.0	21395.4	21396.7	18755.7	18673.6	18629.7	18638.7

Standard errors in parentheses; $^{*}p < 0.10$, $^{**}p < 0.05$, $^{***}p < 0.01$.

Firm size, % professional employees, % technical employees, external R&D funding, internal R&D funding, external sources and internal sources of ideas are logged in the form $\ln(1+x)$.

CONCLUSIONS AND DISCUSSION

Whereas extant research, focusing mostly on developed economies, has considered that ideas for innovation can come from many (mainly external) sources, we sought to assess the comparative impact of different knowledge sources on innovation with different degrees of novelty within a relatively less studied context – emerging market economies. We differentiate between external knowledge sources – that is, suppliers, competitors, clients, universities, business group, business association, secondary sources and scientific sources – and internal knowledge sources – that is, R&D, production and marketing departments, as well as interdisciplinary groups, managers, and employees. Using data from an innovation survey administered during the 2004 census of Colombian manufacturing firms, we examine the impact of these different knowledge sources on the extent to which firms achieve innovation objectives with different degrees of novelty – that is, new-to-world, new-to-country, and new-to-firm innovations.

Our empirical findings provide support for the general view that firms obtaining knowledge from various external and internal sources engage in more innovative activities; however, it also suggests a number of nuances about these relationships that have not been highlighted in prior research. We found that for those knowledge sources that have a significant association with innovation, the relationship is always positive; in contrast to previous studies in developed country contexts that have found negative relationships between some knowledge sources and innovation – for example, suppliers (Santamaría et al., 2009), customers (Lööf & Heshmati, 2002), competitors (Fitjar & Rodríguez-Pose, 2013), and universities (Caloghirou et al., 2004). This difference may be attributed to the unique context of this study. In response to institutional voids in emerging market economies, companies in these contexts may find it beneficial for innovation to tap into different business relationships and knowledge sources to offset the lack more formalized structures that support innovation (e.g., Miller, Lee, Chang, & Le Breton-Miller, 2009).

One of the unique contributions of our study is the analysis of a more complete set of innovation drivers by simultaneously assessing the innovation impacts of both internal and external knowledge sources alongside each other. Overall, we find that accounting for both types of knowledge sources – as compared to extant work that focuses mostly on external sources – helped to better identify knowledge sources that are truly more valuable for innovation. Among internal knowledge sources, ideas from R&D and Marketing departments are (surprisingly) not associated with innovation of any type when other internal and external knowledge sources are included in the model; however, ideas from marketing are significantly associated with new-to-country innovation when external sources are not included in the model. Furthermore, in contrast with previous anecdotal and theoretical evidence (e.g., von Hippel, 1987), we find that sourcing ideas from clients, competitors, and suppliers (after controlling for knowledge from different internal sources) are not always associated with innovation in the full models (4, 8, and 12) despite showing some promise in partial models that do not include both internal and external knowledge sources. For example, suppliers are significantly associated with novel and imitative innovation when only external sources are included in the analysis (see models 2 and 10, Table 5), but this effect fades away when internal sources of knowledge are taken into account (models 4 and 12, Table 5). There are similar non-robust associations between ideas sourced from competitors and clients with new-to-country innovation (model 6, Table 5), which are no longer significant when internal sources of knowledge are included in the model (model 8, Table 5). In general, these findings indicate that empirical models which include only one set of knowledge sources may be underspecified, and highlight the importance of modeling internal and external knowledge sources simultaneously to assess their true associations with innovation outputs.

Finally, while some knowledge sources appear to matter for innovation generally, affecting both imitative and novel innovation, our results also indicate that not all sources matter for all types of innovation. For example, while ideas from clients and interdisciplinary groups are associated with more novel new-to-world innovation (model 4 in Table 5), they do not have a significant effect on the most imitative new-to-firm innovation (model 12 in Table 5). Similarly, non-scientific secondary knowledge sources are associated with less novel types of innovation but not with new-to-world innovation. In turn, these findings have important implications for theories about innovation by emerging market firms, for managerial practice, and for public policy, which we discuss further below.

Theoretical Implications

Overall, our results are consistent with an "open innovation" paradigm, in which firms adopting ideas from external sources as well as from internal sources are able to innovate more. Our findings suggest that such knowledge sourcing is an important mechanism for emerging market firms in particular to overcome the innovation challenges they face. However, consistent with extant arguments suggesting that firms selectively employ their open innovation approaches (West & Bogers, 2014), this paper finds that firms do not benefit equally from all sources of knowledge in achieving innovation objectives.

In this paper, we particularly contribute to understanding the antecedents, in terms of the different knowledge sources, of novel versus imitative innovation. Similar to previous studies in developed economies (see Fitjar & Rodríguez-Pose, 2013; Köhler, Sofka, & Grimpe, 2012), we found that some external knowledge sources – as well as some internal sources, on which prior research has shed less light – have a similar impact for both more novel and more imitative innovation. Knowledge sourcing from scientific sources, production departments, and managers have positive and statistically significant associations with more novel as well as more imitative types of innovation. Thus, to an extent, our findings are consistent with prior work which suggests that imitation can be a first step in many EMFs' innovation paths (Kim, 1999) and function as stepping stones toward achieving more novel innovation objectives. Relationships with some knowledge sources that are important for imitation can thus be repurposed to achieve more novel innovation as well.

However, there are also some important differences in the associations between knowledge sources and novelty of innovation outcomes. Among external sources, for example, knowledge from clients is more significantly associated with novelty, whereas secondary sources are more significantly associated with imitation. Our findings regarding the impact of knowledge from clients are consistent with the literature on user innovation (Von Hippel, 1986) but run counter to research claiming that excessive user-focus may inhibit firms from developing breakthrough innovations (Christensen, 1997; Slater & Narver, 1998). Our findings are consistent with prior research suggesting that suppliers may have a weak (Eisenhardt & Tabrizi, 1995) or insignificant (Sánchez & Pérez, 2003) impact on innovation performance and this does not appear to vary by the degree of novelty. However, our results may add some nuance to prior findings on secondary sources – such as seminars, magazines, and internet – that have been somewhat mixed (Crespi & Zuniga, 2012; Lööf & Heshmati, 2002). As these prior studies do not discriminate between novel and imitative innovation, they are likely to find a net effect of secondary sources on total innovation that is confounded by the different impacts on distinct innovation types.

Among internal sources, we find that interdisciplinary groups are more important for achieving more novel innovation objectives (e.g., models 4 and 8 in Table 5), but not new-to-firm innovation (model 12). A potential explanation is that heterogeneous interdisciplinary groups are effective at creating significant recombination opportunities, which are likely to yield more novel innovation, but such groups may also entail coordination costs that attenuate more routine imitative innovation. Finally, ideas from employees seem to matter only for more imitative new-to-country and new-to-firm innovation (models 8 and 12, respectively), and not for novel innovation (model 4). In general, these results suggest that more novel innovation is not always achieved by simply extending linkages and capabilities related to knowledge sources that also yield more imitative innovation. Thus, emerging market firms may also face some barriers in migrating from imitative innovation to novel innovation.

Managerial Implications

A central challenge for managers, particularly in resource-strapped emerging market contexts, is how to distribute their attention among different sources of knowledge in order to help their own firms to innovate. Because each source likely requires the allocation of firm's resources and not all sources of knowledge support innovation to the same extent, our study provides guidance on which sources of knowledge are more worthwhile for innovation, and furthermore on how their effects vary based on whether the innovation is more novel or imitative. Overall, our findings indicate that building a platform for innovation requires sourcing knowledge from both internal and external sources, and EMFs' managers could help increase innovation by developing the human capital and idea sharing advancements that foster knowledge flows from these sources. However, they may also benefit by being somewhat selective in their approach. For example, our results indicate that firms need to reach out beyond the usual R&D-marketing nexus to scientific sources, production departments and managers for generating innovation in general.

Moreover, managers should recognize that some sources such as secondary external sources and employees may provide useful ideas to achieve more imitative types of innovation, but are less useful for more novel innovation by emerging market firms. Similarly, clients and interdisciplinary teams are not as useful for imitative innovation but more useful for truly novel innovation. Because different knowledge sources are sometimes needed for more versus less novel innovation, managers should consciously make this transition in "upskilling" their firms' R&D capabilities and pursuing more novel innovation goals. Thus, EMFs' managers could develop the relationships and capabilities to source ideas from clients and interdisciplinary teams more heavily when they are ready to implement a more novel approach to innovation. In other words, our findings suggest that firms may need to shift strategies and access different knowledge sources or de-emphasize others in order to achieve more novel innovation outcomes.

Policy Implications

Governments and policy makers in developing countries generally recognize that innovation, and particularly novel path-breaking innovation, can help domestic firms compete more effectively in global markets and help generate positive spillovers for the economy as a whole. However, a notable challenge in fostering innovation by domestic firms is helping them to overcome the limitations in firm-level resources as well as deficits in broader institutional supports for innovation. Our research suggests that a variety of external and internal knowledge links might help emerging market firms overcome these challenges, which creates the potential for targeted policies that enable firms to develop links with and learn to source ideas from different knowledge sources. For example, teaching firms how to source ideas from second-hand sources, as well as encouraging cooperation with clients and suppliers, can prove to be a useful policy for promoting more innovation.

For many emerging market firms, a relatively easy and attractive first step would be to engage in "catch up" types of innovation that are less novel, and imitate products introduced by other firms in the domestic or international markets. At the same time, there is a risk that firms may get locked into this type of imitative innovation and never advance into creating truly novel innovations. If there are inherent tradeoffs between the requirements for novel and imitative innovation, it posed a dilemma for policy makers because it becomes unclear which type of innovation they should seek to support. However, an important lesson from our findings is that imitative and novel innovations do not involve inherent tradeoffs in the knowledge sources that firms may draw on for each, and that some of the same knowledge sources associated with imitative innovation are also associated with novel innovation. Thus, policies designed to support more imitative innovation in the beginning can also support novel innovation in the long run. However, our findings also suggest that a change in emphasis is required as firms and economies transition from greater imitation to greater novelty in their innovative activities. Therefore, policy makers should be ready to support the need for accessing new types of knowledge sources (e.g., clients, interdisciplinary teams) or reducing/increasing reliance on some knowledge sources in order to foster more novel innovation. Overall, our findings support the proposition that emerging market firms may learn to innovate through their experiences with imitation, but also suggests the need for developing new linkages and capabilities to complete this transition.

REFERENCES

Alcorta, L., & Peres, W. (1998). Innovation systems and technological specialization in Latin America and the Caribbean. *Research Policy*, *26*, 857–881.

Amara, N., & Landry, R. (2005). Sources of information as determinants of novelty of innovation in manufacturing firms: Evidence from the 1999 statistics Canada innovation survey. *Technovation*, *25*, 245–259.

Backman, M., Börjesson, S., & Setterberg, S. (2007). Working with concepts in the fuzzy front end: exploring the context for innovation for different types of concepts at Volvo Cars. *R&D Management*, *37*, 17–28.

Belderbos, R., Carree, M., & Lokshin, B. (2004). Cooperative R&D and firm performance. *Research Policy*, *33*, 1477–1492.

Belderbos, R., Carree, M., & Lokshin, B. (2006). Complementarity in R&D cooperation strategies. *Review of Industrial Organization*, *28*, 401–426.

Belenzon, S., & Berkovitz, T. (2010). Innovation in business groups. *Management Science*, *56*, 519–535.

Business Monitor. (2010). Colombia Business Forecast Report: Business Monitor International Research.

Caloghirou, Y., Kastelli, I., & Tsakanikas, A. (2004). Internal capabilities and external knowledge sources: Complements or substitutes for innovative performance? *Technovation*, *24*, 29–39.

Cameron, A. C., & Trivedi, P. K. (1998). *Regression analysis of count data*. Cambridge: Cambridge University Press.

Chauradia, A., & Somaya, D. (2015). Count data models in strategic management research: A review of critical issues.

Chen, R. (1996). Technological expansion: The interaction between diversification strategy and organizational capability. *Journal of Management Studies*, *33*, 649–666.

Chesbrough, H. W. (2003). *Open innovation: The new imperative for creating and profiting from innovation*. Boston, MA: Harvard Business School Press.

Christensen, C. M. (1997). *The innovator's dilemma: When new technologies cause great firms to fail*. Boston, MA: Harvard Business School Press.

Cohen, W. M., & Levinthal, D. A. (1990). Absorptive capacity: A new perspective on learning and innovation. *Administrative Science Quarterly*, *35*, 128–152.

Crespi, G., & Zuniga, P. (2012). Innovation and productivity: Evidence from Six Latin American countries. *World Development*, *40*, 273–290.

Dawar, N., & Frost, T. (1998). Competing with giants. Survival strategies for local companies in emerging markets. *Harvard business review*, *77*, 119–129.

Eisenhardt, K. M., & Tabrizi, B. N. (1995). Accelerating adaptive processes – Product innovation in the global computer industry. *Administrative Science Quarterly*, *40*, 84–110.

Faems, D., Van Looy, B., & Debackere, K. (2005). Interorganizational collaboration and innovation: Toward a portfolio approach*. *Journal of Product Innovation Management*, *22*, 238–250.

Fey, C. F., & Birkinshaw, J. (2005). External sources of knowledge, governance mode, and R&D performance. *Journal of Management*, *31*, 597–621.

Fitjar, R. D., & Rodríguez-Pose, A. (2013). Firm collaboration and modes of innovation in Norway. *Research Policy*, *42*(1), 128–138.

Galende, J., & de la Fuente, J. M. (2003). Internal factors determining a firm's innovative behaviour. *Research Policy*, *32*, 715–736.

Giuliani, E., & Bell, M. (2005). The micro-determinants of meso-level learning and innovation: Evidence from a Chilean wine cluster. *Research Policy*, *34*, 47–68.

Gupta, A. K., Wilemon, D., & Atuahene-Gima, K. (2000). Excelling in R&D. *Research-Technology Management*, *43*, 52–58.

Hemmert, M. (2004). The influence of institutional factors on the technology acquisition performance of high-tech firms: Survey results from Germany and Japan. *Research Policy*, *33*, 1019–1039.

Hoskisson, R. E., Eden, L., Lau, C. M., & Wright, M. (2000). Strategy in emerging economies. *The Academy of Management Journal*, *43*, 249–267.

Hoskisson, R. E., Kim, H., White, R. E., & Tihanyi, L. (2004). A framework for understanding international diversification by business groups from emerging economies. *Advances in International Management*, *16*, 137–163.

Katila, R. (2002). New product search over time: Past ideas in their prime? *Academy of Management Journal*, *45*, 995–1010.

Katz, J. (2001). Structural reforms and technological behaviour: The sources and nature of technological change in Latin America in the 1990s. *Research Policy*, *30*, 1–19.

Kessler, E. H., & Chakrabarti, A. K. (1996). Innovation speed: A conceptual model of context, antecedents, and outcomes. *Academy of Management Review*, *21*, 1143–1191.

Khanna, T., & Palepu, K. G. (2006). Emerging giants: Building world-class companies in developing countries. *Harvard Business Review*, *84*, 60–69.

Khanna, T., & Palepu, K. G. (2010). *Spotting and responding to institutional voids*, winning in emerging markets. Boston, MA: Harvard Business Press.

Khanna, T., & Rivkin, J. W. (2001). Estimating the performance effects of business groups in emerging markets. *Strategic Management Journal*, *22*, 45.

Kim, L. (1999). Building technological capability for industrialization: Analytical frameworks and Korea's experience. *Industrial and Corporate Change*, *8*, 111–136.

Kogut, B., & Zander, U. (1992). Knowledge of the firm, combinative capabilities, and the replication of technology. *Organization Science*, *3*, 383–397.

Köhler, C., Sofka, W., & Grimpe, C. (2012). Selective search, sectoral patterns, and the impact on product innovation performance. *Research Policy*, *41*, 1344–1356.

Laursen, K., & Salter, A. (2004). Searching high and low: What types of firms use universities as a source of innovation? *Research Policy*, *33*, 1201–1215.

Laursen, K., & Salter, A. (2006). Open for innovation: The role of openness in explaining innovation performance among U.K. manufacturing firms. *Strategic Management Journal, 27*, 131–150.

Leiponen, A., & Helfat, C. E. (2010). Innovation objectives, knowledge sources, and the benefits of breadth. *Strategic Management Journal, 31*, 224–236.

Lööf, H., & Heshmati, A. (2002). Knowledge capital and performance heterogeneity: A firm-level innovation study. *International Journal of Production Economics, 76*, 61–85.

Lu, J. W., & Xufei, M. A. (2008). The contingent value of local partners' business group affiliations. *Academy of Management Journal, 51*, 295–314.

Mansfield, E., Schwartz, M., & Wagner, S. (1981). Imitation costs and patents: An empirical study. *The Economic Journal, 91*, 907–918.

McDermott, G., & Corredoira, R. (2010). Network composition, collaborative ties, and upgrading in emerging-market firms: Lessons from the Argentine autoparts sector. *Journal of International Business Studies, 41*, 308–329.

McDermott, G. A., Corredoira, R. A., & Kruse, G. (2009). Public-private institutions as catalysts of upgrading in emerging market societies. *Academy of Management Journal, 52*, 1270–1296.

Mesquita, L. F., & Lazzarini, S. G. (2008). Horizontal and vertial relationships in developing economies: Implications for SMEs' acces to glocal markets. *Academy of Management Journal, 51*, 359–380.

Miller, D., Lee, J., Chang, S., & Le Breton-Miller, I. (2009). Filling the institutional void: The social behavior and performance of family vs non-family technology firms in emerging markets. *Journal of International Business Studies, 40*, 802–817.

Moran, P., & Ghoshal, S. (1999). Markets, firms, and the process of economic development. *The Academy of Management Review, 24*, 390–412.

Mowery, D. C. (1983). The relationship between intrafirm and contractual forms of industrial research in American manufacturing, 1900–1940. *Explorations in Economic History, 20*, 351–374.

Mu, J., Peng, G., & Love, E. (2008). Interfirm networks, social capital, and knowledge flow. *Journal of Knowledge Management, 12*, 86–100.

Nahapiet, J., & Ghoshal, S. (1998). Social capital, intellectual capital, and the organizational advantage. *Academy of Management Review, 23*, 242–266.

Naranjo-Valencia, J. C., Jiménez-Jiménez, D., & Sanz-Valle, R. (2011). Innovation or imitation? The role of organizational culture. *Management Decision, 49*, 55–72.

Naude, W. (2010). Entrepreneurship, developing countries, and development economics: New approaches and insights. *Small Business Economics, 34*, 1–12.

Nelson, R. R., & Winter, S. G. (1982). *An evolutionary theory of economic change*. Cambridge, MA: Belknap Press of Harvard University Press.

Nieto, M., & Santamaría, L. (2007). The importance of diverse collaborative networks for the novelty of product innovation. *Technovation, 27*, 367–377.

Nieto, M. J., & Santamaría, L. (2010). Technological collaboration: Bridging the innovation gap between small and large firms. *Journal of Small Business Management, 48*, 44–69.

Nonaka, I., Toyama, R., & Nagata, A. (2000). A firm as a knowledge-creating entity: A new perspective on the theory of the firm. *Industrial and corporate change, 9*, 1–20.

OECD. (1995). *Interpreting technological innovation data (Oslo Manual)*. Paris: DSTI/OECD: Organization for Economic Co-operation and Development.

OECD. (2005). *University research management: Developing research in new institutions*. Paris: OECD.

Ordanini, A., Rubera, G., & DeFillippi, R. (2008). The many moods of inter-organizational imitation: A critical review. *International Journal of Management Reviews*, *10*, 375–398.

Parmigiani, A., & Rivera-Santos, M. (2011). Clearing a path through the forest: A meta-review of interorganizational relationships. *Journal of Management*, *37*, 1108–1136.

Prahalad, C. K., & Hamel, G. (1990). The core competence of the corporation. *Harvard Business Review*, *68*, 79–91.

Sánchez, A. M., & Pérez, M. P. (2003). Flexibility in new product development: A survey of practices and its relationship with the product's technological complexity. *Technovation*, *23*, 139–145.

Santamaría, L., Nieto, M. J., & Barge-Gil, A. (2009). Beyond formal R&D: Taking advantage of other sources of innovation in low- and medium-technology industries. *Research Policy*, *38*, 507–517.

Sea-Jin, C., Chi-Nien, C., & Mahmood, I. P. (2006). When and how does business group affiliation promote firm innovation? A tale of two emerging economies. *Organization Science*, *17*, 637–656.

Semadeni, M., & Anderson, B. S. (2010). The follower's dilemma: Innovation and imitation in the professional services industry. *Academy of Management Journal*, *53*, 1175–1193.

Shinkle, G. A., & McCann, B. T. (2014). New product deployment: The moderating influence of economic institutional context. *Strategic Management Journal*, *35*, 1090–1101.

Slater, S. F., & Narver, J. C. (1998). Customer-led and market-oriented: Let's not confuse the two. *Strategic Management Journal*, *19*, 1001–1006.

Tether, B. S. (2002). Who co-operates for innovation, and why: An empirical analysis. *Research Policy*, *31*, 947–967.

Thorpe, R., Holt, R., Macpherson, A., & Pittaway, L. (2005). Using knowledge within small and medium-sized firms: A systematic review of the evidence. *International Journal of Management Reviews*, *7*, 257–281.

Tomlinson, P. R. (2010). Co-operative ties and innovation: Some new evidence for UK manufacturing. *Research Policy*, *39*, 762–775.

Tsai, K. (2009). Collaborative networks and product innovation performance: Toward a contingency perspective. *Research Policy*, *38*, 765–778.

Tsai, K.-H., & Wang, J.-C. (2009). External technology sourcing and innovation performance in LMT sectors: An analysis based on the Taiwanese technological innovation survey. *Research Policy*, *38*, 518–526.

Utterback, J. M. (1994). *Mastering the dynamics of innovation: How companies can seize opportunities in the face of technological change*. Cambridge, MA: Harvard Business School Press.

Vega-Jurado, J., Gutiérrez-Gracia, A., & Fernández-de-Lucio, I. (2009). Does external knowledge sourcing matter for innovation? Evidence from the Spanish manufacturing industry. *Industrial and Corporate Change*, *18*, 637–670.

Vega-Jurado, J., Gutiérrez-Gracia, A., Fernández-de-Lucio, I., & Manjarrés-Henríquez, L. (2008). The effect of external and internal factors on firms' product innovation. *Research Policy*, *37*, 616–632.

Von Hippel, E. (1986). Lead users: A source of novel product concepts. *Management Science*, *32*, 791–805.

von Hippel, E. (1987). Cooperation between rivals: Informal know-how trading. *Research Policy*, *16*, 291–302.

von Hippel, E. (1998). Economics of product development by users: The impact of 'sticky' local information. *Management Science*, *44*, 629–645.

West, J., & Bogers, M. (2014). Leveraging external sources of innovation: A review of research on open innovation. *Journal of Product Innovation Management*, *31*, 814–831.

World Bank. (2014). World Development Indicators database.

Wright, M., Filatotchev, I., Hoskisson, R. E., & Peng, M. W. (2005). Strategy research in emerging economies: Challenging the conventional wisdom. *Journal of Management Studies*, *42*, 1–33.

Xu, D., & Meyer, K. E. (2013). Linking theory and context: 'Strategy research in emerging economies' after Wright et al. (2005). *Journal of Management Studies*, *50*, 1322–1346.

Yiu, D., Bruton, G., & Lu, Y. (2005). Understanding business group performance in an emerging economy: Acquiring resources and capabilities in order to prosper. *Journal of Management Studies*, *42*, 183–206.

MANAGING INNOVATION IN EMERGING ECONOMIES: ORGANIZATIONAL ARRANGEMENTS AND RESOURCES OF FOREIGN MNEs IN THE CHINESE PHARMACEUTICAL INDUSTRY

Vittoria Giada Scalera, Alessandra Perri and Ram Mudambi

ABSTRACT

To investigate the impact of knowledge-intensive FDI in the Chinese pharmaceutical industry, this study analyzes the activity of foreign MNEs operating in this context by exploring their innovative background, the organizational arrangements they use for local knowledge creation and the performance of their local innovative processes. Based on the analysis of the universe of USPTO pharmaceutical patents applied for between 1975 and 2010 and granted to foreign assignees

Emerging Economies and Multinational Enterprises
Advances in International Management, Volume 28, 201–233

ISSN: 1571-5027/doi:10.1108/S1571-502720150000028011

utilizing the work of Chinese inventors, our results show that, while the presence of foreign MNEs in the Chinese pharmaceutical industry entails a strong potential for positive externalities that could enhance the performance of the local innovation system, such externalities do not completely materialize yet, likely because of local actors' limited absorptive capacity.

Keywords: Multinational enterprises; knowledge-intensive foreign direct investment; R&D internationalization; innovative performance; China; pharmaceutical industry

INTRODUCTION

Recent research suggests that emerging markets are gaining mounting importance in the global innovation systems (Govindarajan & Ramamurti, 2011; Zeng & Williamson, 2007). Accordingly, the patenting activity originating from these contexts is growing substantially (National Science Board, 2014). Multinational enterprises (hereafter, MNEs) from the advanced world play a crucial role in this process. In fact, they increasingly engage in knowledge-intensive FDI in emerging countries, thus contributing in several ways to the local innovative activity through what have been called "spillover processes" (Mudambi, 2008). While literature has already explored specific aspects related to the management of knowledge and innovation in emerging countries (Lewin, Massini, & Peeters, 2009; Zhao, 2006), there are a number of unanswered questions regarding the profile and characteristics of MNEs' R&D activities in these contexts. Addressing these questions is critical to evaluate the extent to which the involvement of these companies in emerging countries' innovation may contribute to their technological catch-up. In the FDI spillovers literature, foreign MNEs have been linked to improved innovative performance of the domestic innovation system (e.g., Blomström & Kokko, 1998), particularly in emerging markets (Buckley, Clegg, & Wang, 2002, 2007; Hu & Jefferson, 2002). More specifically, it has been suggested that foreign investors' heterogeneity helps explain the differences in the size of the technology spillovers that host-country firms may attain from the presence of foreign MNEs (Giroud, 2012). Building on this literature, we study the nature and extent of the innovative activity carried out by foreign MNEs in emerging countries in order to gain insights on how this affects the technological development of domestic firms.

Specifically, we analyze the innovative activity of foreign MNEs operating in the Chinese pharmaceutical industry by exploring (1) their innovative background, (2) their investment choices and the organizational arrangements they use for local knowledge creation, and (3) the performance of their local innovative processes. In doing so, we focus on the role of geography that – either exogenously or endogenously – influences the outcomes of MNEs' strategic behavior.

Our empirical strategy is based on the analysis of the population of pharmaceutical patents issued by the USPTO between 1975 and 2010 and granted to foreign assignees utilizing the scientific work of Chinese inventors. Given that agents affiliated to the pharmaceutical industry extensively use patents as a way to protect their innovation output and intellectual property (IP), patent information is a reliable and rather comprehensive data source in this context, allowing for the analysis of several aspects that are relevant to our objectives.

The focus of our analysis on the Chinese pharmaceutical industry has a twofold justification. First, it is well-known that patent data represent a key source of innovation in the pharmaceutical industry (Henderson & Cockburn, 1994). Second, China is one of the largest pharmaceutical markets in the world (KPMG, 2011). While the Chinese government has been putting a great deal of emphasis on the attraction of foreign pharmaceutical MNEs, the role of IP is still an open issue in this context, since it has been documented that the Chinese environment presents some concerns about IP rights protection (Zhao, 2006), and this may influence the innovative process of foreign MNEs. All these conditions contribute to make the Chinese pharmaceutical industry a very interesting context to be investigated.

CONCEPTUAL FRAMEWORK

Emerging markets are complex environments whose high growth rates have strongly attracted MNEs investments in the last years. While MNEs from the advanced world have often entered these contexts with the primary objective to access a huge and fast-growing demand that could counterbalance the stagnation in their traditional markets, these contexts have soon demonstrated to be able to offer much more than just market opportunities. In fact, emerging economies grant to investing foreign firms extensive learning opportunities, arising not only from the fundamental diversity – in terms of economic conditions, institutions and business practices (Meyer, 2004) – between them and the traditional world, but also from their unique resource endowment, and notably their high skilled labor, available at a very convenient cost (Lewin et al., 2009).

Beside the multiple opportunities that emerging countries can offer to foreign firms, FDI spillover research suggests that also such host-economies could attain positive consequences from the presence of advanced MNEs (Blomström & Kokko, 1998; Görg & Greenaway, 2004). In particular, in the last two decades, the study of the impact of MNEs on emerging economies has gained renewed attention in international business (hereafter, IB) literature (Meyer, 2004), as scholars have highlighted that IB theoretical perspectives are critical to understand the extent to which the contact between foreign and local firms may contribute to host-countries' technological development (Perri & Peruffo, forthcoming).

Traditional IB research assumes that FDI spillovers materialize as a consequence of MNEs' superior technological endowment. According to the eclectic theory, MNEs are provided with ownership advantages, which may stem from the availability of distinctive assets as well as from their ability to manage a geographically distributed network of resources and activities (Dunning, 1981). As MNEs invest in foreign countries, their subsidiaries receive a knowledge infusion from technologically advanced headquarters (Awate, Larsen, & Mudambi, 2015), which lays the basis for the local spillover effect (Hymer, 1976).

More recently, IB perspectives have suggested that foreign investors' heterogeneity fundamentally influences the dynamics of FDI-assisted technological development (Driffield & Love, 2007; Giroud, 2012; Perri & Andersson, 2014). Specifically, research has demonstrated that the relationship between MNEs' endowment with an ownership advantage and their beneficial effects on host-countries is not as automatic as it has been long depicted (Marin & Bell, 2006), for several reasons. On one hand, MNEs' advantages are not homogeneous (Giroud, 2012), and their investment decisions may be explained by different motivations, which may influence the technological profile of foreign subsidiaries (Driffield & Love, 2007). On the other hand, foreign subsidiaries may also differ in terms of the activities they carry out in the host-country (Marin & Sasidharan, 2010) and the strategies they use to protect their assets from external appropriation on the part of local competitors (de Faria & Sofka, 2010). Hence, there is a double source of heterogeneity, both at the MNE and at the subsidiary level.

In order to evaluate the extent to which MNEs can contribute to the technological upgrading of emerging countries and to the development of the local innovation system, it is therefore critical to account for the different sources of heterogeneity involving the foreign investing firm. In particular, while it is vital to analyze the technological profile of MNEs, it is equally important to investigate the role of subsidiaries and, more specifically, the way in which their local technological activities are organized.

MNE-level technological heterogeneity may impact primarily MNEs' location choices. In fact, according to the strategic deterrence perspective, leading and lagging MNEs tend to pursue different location patterns, depending on the net spillover – as resulting from the difference between inward and outward spillovers – they would obtain once established in a foreign country (Alcacer & Chung, 2007; Shaver & Flyer, 2000). More specifically, this literature stream predicts that leading MNEs will avoid to agglomerate with less developed local firms which, due to their relative technological backwardness, could act only as knowledge recipients but not as knowledge sources.

At the subsidiary level, it is critical to recognize that MNE subsidiaries operating in emerging economies may structure their innovative activities by following different patterns of interaction with local firms. In fact, literature has documented the existence of varying degrees of integration between foreign and local firms. On one hand, the externally controlled plant model (Watts, 1981) depicts a situation in which subsidiaries lack autonomy thus being unable to develop any kind of relationship with the host-environment. On the other, the embedded subsidiary model (Andersson, Forsgren, & Holm, 2002) implies that subsidiaries become real insiders of the local business network, thus instigating high value-added linkages with local firms.

A critical form of interaction between local and foreign firms takes place when these agents cooperate when conducting their R&D activities. R&D collaborations are important because they may act as conduits through which capabilities are developed, and knowledge is exchanged among partners. Through R&D collaborations, partner firms may develop sophisticated technologies (Baumol, 2002), share the risks and the costs arising from the innovation process, and tap into each other's tacit knowledge (Hagedoorn, 1993).

Existing literature has also investigated the relationship between R&D collaborations and spillovers. Research demonstrates that cooperative R&D agreements are plagued by a problem of imperfect appropriability of the outcomes of the innovation process (Cassiman & Veugelers, 2002), which originates two contrasting effects: inward and outward spillovers. On one hand, firms may have an incentive to undertake joint R&D activities, when they are able to intercept high incoming spillovers from partner and non-partner organizations. Simultaneously, firms' R&D investment in joint research projects may generate positive knowledge externalities for agents who are external to the agreement (Greenlee & Cassiman, 1999), leading to free-riding behaviors (Kesteloot & Veugelers, 1995). In sum, R&D collaborations are considered to represent an effective channel for the occurrence of spillovers, to both partner and non-partner firms (Cassiman & Veugelers, 2002).

From the MNE perspective, R&D collaborations with local firms represent a crucial mean to access the local expertise. Local firms are in fact a vital source of information regarding local market needs and the functioning of the local business environment. Through inter-firm interaction and joint problem-solving processes associated with R&D collaborations, MNEs can acquire tacit and complex knowledge (McEvily & Marcus, 2005), thus overcoming the barriers to knowledge sourcing across distance (Frost & Zhou, 2005; Lahiri, 2010). Accordingly, research has demonstrated that, over the last decades, MNEs have progressively developed research-based partnerships with local suppliers and distributors, competitors and knowledge institutions (Archibugi & Iammarino, 1999; Dunning, 1994).

Besides the benefits that MNEs could achieve through a research-based agreement with local firms, the other face of the coin – that is, the spillover process to local firms – is also extremely relevant as far as the technological catch-up process of emerging economies is concerned. In fact, as it has previously been highlighted, the effects of R&D partnerships are not necessarily bounded to the firms directly involved in the agreement. As an example, it has been suggested that cross-regional collaborations may act as a mean through which the network of co-located agents gathers fresh knowledge inputs through the mechanism of localized spillovers (Zhao & Islam, 2007), due to the interaction between long-distance partners. Hence, beyond contributing to MNEs' ability to explore and take advantage of the local firms' information endowment, R&D collaborations are also important in that they generate externalities that feed the local innovative processes.

Beside the role of the R&D organizational arrangements, the impact of MNE presence on emerging host-economies also depends on the type of technological activities implemented by local subsidiaries and research centers (Marin & Bell, 2006; Marin & Sasidharan, 2010). R&D foreign subsidiaries are largely focused on two strategies, that is, competence-exploitation and competence-creation (Cantwell & Mudambi, 2005, 2011). Foreign subsidiaries with a competence-exploitation mandate mainly replicate the technological knowledge developed in the headquarters. On the other hand, competence-creation subsidiaries contribute to the knowledge base of the MNE through the generation of new capabilities that need to be transferred to the headquarter (and eventually to the other subsidiaries). Host-country characteristics and the different types of local knowledge sources play a crucial role in determining the type of mandate assigned to the foreign subsidiaries (Cantwell & Mudambi, 2005). MNE subsidiaries might source knowledge from the external environment by collaborating with local suppliers or buyers, through employees' turnover or by interacting with scientists across firms and research centers (Chung & Yeaple, 2008). Overall, the availability of knowledge sources that are heterogeneous in terms of typology and geographical origin can benefit MNEs' knowledge base both in terms of stock and in terms of quality, for example, technical diversity (Cantwell, 1989; Cantwell & Janne, 1999). In turn, the mandate given by the headquarters to each subsidiary is expected to influence both the quality and the quantity of knowledge produced abroad (Phene & Almeida, 2008).

The IB literature stream investigating subsidiary heterogeneity has been mainly focused on the analysis of competence-creation subsidiaries, since they fulfill the primary aim of R&D internationalization, which is the creation of new capabilities and the enhancement of the MNE's product/process portfolio (e.g., Birkinshaw, Hood, & Jonsson, 1998; Song & Shin, 2008). This has also occurred because, traditionally, R&D internationalization literature has analyzed advanced economy multinationals (AMNEs), and their strategic-asset seeking FDI toward other advanced economies (Dunning & Narula, 1995).

However, the growing importance of emerging economies is gradually shifting the locus of global innovation towards countries such as China and India, and recently this is getting recognition (Govindarajan & Ramamurti, 2011; Immelt, Govindarajan, & Trimble, 2009). Traditionally, AMNEs seldom joined emerging economies through the set-up of a new R&D facility, but in more recent times their innovative presence in these markets has become increasingly more common. This trend has been favored also by the openness policies in destination countries, which have started to welcome FDI by AMNEs, especially when the latters operate in knowledge-intensive industries. Innovation generated by emerging economies is on average not breakthrough, but involves original combinations of the existing knowledge and is driven by the need to solve local problems (Govindarajan & Ramamurti, 2011).

R&D subsidiaries established in emerging countries by foreign, mainly advanced, MNEs are intended to leverage knowledge created in the home country and adapt domestic technologies to the local needs. Specifically, they are required to develop products that are suitable for the local markets and for the requests of the target customers, which are generally very different from the ones of the home market (Cuervo-Cazurra & Genc, 2008). The low per capita income and the institutional voids in the host-environment require that innovations addressed to emerging economies should be relatively cheap and easy to operate (Ramamurti & Singh, 2009). While pursuing these objectives, foreign R&D subsidiaries also need to protect themselves from unintended knowledge leakage, very likely to occur in weak IP regimes, such as China (Zhao, 2006). Ultimately, this risk may also limit the reservoir of technological capabilities made available by the headquarters to their emerging markets' subsidiaries. In fact, MNEs may perceive the spillover of their core competences as too risky, thus opting for the exclusive use of such resources at home (or at least in stronger IP regimes).

Even if adaptation is probably the most common mandate of R&D subsidiaries in China, reverse innovation to headquarter could be a secondary outcome of the presence in emerging economies. As suggested by Govindarajan and Ramamurti (2011), AMNEs may launch new products that later can be targeted at consumers in advanced economies, where they can leverage market position already held. In fact, when the improvements of the technology underlying low-cost products reach satisfactory levels, the product can be addressed to more demanding mainstream consumers (Christensen & Bower, 1996). This is, for instance, the case of General Electric's portable ultrasounds, originally developed in China and later used for high-end radiology and obstetrics applications (Govindarajan & Ramamurti, 2011; Immelt et al., 2009). However, AMNEs' R&D subsidiaries in China may have to face internal resistance to transfer radical and/or incremental innovation from emerging economies.

MANAGING INNOVATION IN THE GLOBAL PHARMACEUTICAL INDUSTRY

The global pharmaceutical industry is a technologically dynamic context (DeCarolis, 2003), which has long proved to be disseminated with relevant profit opportunities (Ghemawat, 2010). Although profitability in this sector has been found to correlate with sustained innovation (Roberts, 1999), and performance is driven by the discovery and commercialization of novel drugs (DeCarolis, 2003), profit opportunities come along with relevant risks arising precisely from the specificities of the pharmaceutical innovation process. Such process requires in fact massive investments and lengthy drug discovery and development procedures (DiMasi, Hansen, Grabowski, & Lasagna, 1991).

More specifically, the pharmaceutical innovation process is made up of a sequence of stages, which may overlap (DiMasi, Hansen, & Grabowski, 2003), and whose architecture tends to be heavily regulated (Gambardella, 1995). Each stage is aimed at examining the features of particular compounds, which – if considered feasible – can enter the following stage (Gambardella, 1995), leading to very slow dynamics. Typically, the innovation process starts when a company identifies a general target area (as an example, a type of disease) (Sharma & Lacey, 2004), thus initiating a discovery program whose outcome is the synthesis of compounds that need to be tested. Subsequently, in the preclinical R&D, molecules are evaluated in the laboratory, based on their potential therapeutic effectiveness and toxicity. After this stage, which may last up to three years, a small portion of the initial set of molecules goes through clinical trials. Clinical trials encompass different types of test of compounds on patients and may take from 2 to 10 years (Gambardella, 1995). If the clinical trials are positive, and the drug proves to be sufficiently safe and effective, the last stage of marketing approval begins (DiMasi et al., 2003), and it may last up to seven years.

The choice of the breadth of the knowledge base which firms are willing to develop is crucial in the pharmaceutical industry (Bierly & Chakrabarti, 1996). In fact, while pursuing new drugs in one therapeutic field allows for enhanced learning which can be useful in other areas, focusing on narrow research trajectories may result in limitative strategies leading to lock-in situations and impeding the development of broader pipelines and portfolios of potential new molecules (DeCarolis, 2003). In this regard, Henderson and Cockburn (1994) conclude that the integration of a differentiated range of disciplines in the pharmaceutical innovation process helps firms improve their drug research productivity. Similarly, Pisano (1994) highlights the importance of combining diverse knowledge areas across the stages of a new drug manufacturing process. In this regard, it is worth noting that because the successful exploitation of the rents arising from innovation requires also access to some complementary assets, firms operating in the global pharmaceutical industry have to be provided not only with technological capabilities, but also with marketing and regulatory competences (Bogner & Thomas, 1994; Cool & Schendel, 1987; Henderson & Cockburn, 1994; Hill & Hansen, 1991; Thomas, 1990). Hence, the value of a firm's set of competences and resources also depends on the specificities of the market environment in which it operates.

In terms of patenting process, while pharmaceutical companies usually patent a new molecular compound at the time of discovery in order to obtain some protection, the long lead-time between this moment and the actual commercialization implies that patents are almost expired when products are finally brought to the market (Pisano, 1997).

In current times, several challenges are altering the competitive scenario in which pharmaceutical companies operate. First, while originally big pharmaceutical firms could rely on "blockbuster" drugs' profits, the discovery of new breakthrough molecules is becoming increasingly rare (Bruche, 2012, p. 5). Moreover, while traditionally pharmaceutical companies were used to build upon organic chemistry and pharmacology knowledge bases (DeCarolis, 2003) and to discover through processes of trial and error, starting from the 1980s, the progress in biotechnology and genetics eased the entry of new, specialist organizations in the industry, requiring established companies to develop new capabilities in terms of "rational drug design." This made a compelling case for using external technology sources (Cockburn, 2004). Finally, the approval of the Watchman-Hax Act – in the United States first, and in many other countries subsequently – has allowed imitative companies to file "Abbreviated New Drug Applications" even before the patent expiration date. They could do so by simply demonstrating that the new drug was "bioequivalent" to the original patented one, thus skipping many costly and time-consuming clinical trials. This led to the rapid development of a "generic drugs market segment," populated by firms engaged in the production of imitator drugs (Bruche, 2012). Hence, the dynamics of innovation have started to follow two distinct processes: while the search for original branded drugs requires explorative R&D, the development of generic drugs is based on exploitative R&D.

These processes, far from being separated, increasingly co-exist within the same company (The Economist, 2012). In fact, the discovery of entirely new chemical entities nowadays covers only a part of the innovative activities in the sector, as firms extensively involve in imitation, "inventing around" and development of new combination of existing molecules (Malerba & Orsenigo, 2002). As a consequence, global competition ceased to be played only on the ground of new product introductions, and started to depend also on incremental improvements and imitation. In this scenario, high growth markets, such as the emerging ones, allow for the survival of firms following both paths.

THE RISE OF EMERGING ECONOMIES AND THE CHANGING GEOGRAPHY OF KNOWLEDGE

The major changes described above have strongly influenced the geography of competition and innovation in the pharmaceutical industry. In fact, while for decades continents like North America, Europe, and Japan have governed the marketplace, accounting for more than 80% of the world pharmaceutical sales (KPMG, 2011), the global competitive landscape is currently experiencing the entry of emerging economies like India, China, and Brazil both as producers and consumers of drugs. It is no surprise that the economic and research activities are gradually migrating from advanced to emerging countries, where market opportunities are huge in terms of both size and growth rate. While emerging countries were originally considered as mere final markets where Western pharmaceutical firms could sell their products, in recent years this view started to be challenged, as it appears that these locations can host not only manufacturing sites but also R&D facilities. Accordingly, one major trend that can be observed among big pharmaceutical companies is the increasing recourse to low-cost locations that nonetheless offer sophisticated physical and human resources. Advanced economy firms take advantage of the cost-effective resources in such locations to outsource production and to locate or contract R&D activities (Bruche, 2012). Initially, outsourcing and contract R&D was limited to standardized activities, such as compounds synthesis and preclinical testing (Friedman, 2010). However, as the level of pharmaceutical innovation in emerging countries improves, the volume and value of the activities performed in these locations could also increase.

It is worth noting that there are crucial differences amongst emerging countries in terms of the opportunities and challenges they represent for developed economy MNEs. In fact, some of them, such as India and Brazil, have a much stronger position in generic drugs development and commercialization, thus giving developed economy MNEs serious concerns in terms of IP protection. On the other hand, in countries like China, local capabilities are still weak and the quality of the locally manufactured generic versions of Western drugs is very low. For foreign MNEs, this reduces the competitive risks of knowledge leakage while simultaneously allowing for the application of a high mark-up in the local market.

The Chinese Pharmaceutical Industry: New Actors in a Dynamic Scenario

The Chinese pharmaceutical industry is highly fragmented and characterized mainly by domestic companies (Yuanjia, Geng, Ying, & Yitao, 2007). Domestic pharmaceutical firms lack research and production sophistication, and found their domestic competitive advantage on manufacturing generics and active pharmaceutical ingredients (API) (KPMG, 2011). About 90% of the Chinese drug manufacturers are small or medium-sized enterprises, and the top domestic players are mainly state-owned enterprises (SOEs), whose capabilities are often dragged down by overproduction and financial losses. The Chinese pharmaceutical market is yet to mature and is characterized by a complex system of regional markets dominated by non-branded generics and over the counter drugs (OTC). Hospitals remain the main outlets for the distribution of pharmaceuticals, but the scenario is slowly changing with the growing number of retail pharmacy outlets. The price of pharmaceuticals is decreasing steadily and the central government fixes and adjusts products' prices in order to control their affordability and the profit margins of drug companies (KPMG, 2011).

The main problems underlying the inefficiency of the domestic industry are the lack of (1) IP rights protection, (2) transparency with regard to the drug approval procedures, (3) effective governmental incentives, and (4) homogeneous policies for local and foreign companies (Deloitte, 2011). In general, the industry is small-scale and inefficiencies arise from the difficulty to exploit advantages of economies of scale because R&D and manufacturing activities are geographically widespread throughout the country and scattered across several (especially domestic) manufacturers, which lack competences and financial resources to develop their own brand. This inefficiency could be worsened by the privatization of hospitals and provision of drugs, which may sustain non-branded generics and OTC.[1] In 2009, the Chinese government has started to reorganize the industry by upgrading the existing innovation system and infrastructures, favoring the integration of local companies with foreign MNEs, enlarging insurance coverage and reducing the costs of medical services (Rein, 2009; Spigarelli & Wei, 2012).

Further, China's entry in the World Trade Organization (WTO) in December 2001 has positively influenced the domestic pharmaceutical market and fostered the integration of the country into the global economy. An array of improvements has been introduced, such as a stronger patent system, a more diffused medical insurance system, and more transparent and reliable commercial legal procedures. China's WTO commitments include the strengthening of IP regulations, tariff concessions, and market access of non-domestic distributors of pharmaceutical products. Further improvements have been introduced in full compliance with the requirements of the TRIPS. As a result, pharmaceutical MNEs from the United States and Europe have increasingly invested in China as they recognize the growing potential of the Chinese market. Among the top 10 pharmaceutical companies in China half are multinationals, but none of them controls more 2.5% of the total market (Kwok & Lyn, 2010). The Chinese generic segment represents the strategic lever for the global success of MNEs from advanced countries, which aim at acquiring domestic generic drug companies to compensate for the loss of income from expiring patents (KPMG, 2011). KPMG (2011) highlights that foreign MNEs have invested more than a billion dollars in China since 2009, building R&D centers as well as manufacturing facilities. Novartis, and other big pharmaceutical MNEs from advanced countries are increasingly choosing China to establish new R&D bases for drug development and testing. As a consequence, pharmaceutical R&D is rapidly growing in the country and especially the Shanghai area is becoming one of the most important global centers.

High competition, high costs, shortage of skilled workforce make it harder to pursue the old way of drug research, concentrated in wealthy countries. Western drug companies first moved their manufacturing and marketing facilities to China, but finding not only a cheaper labor force but also a less expensive patient pool and talented scientists, they have decided to invest in R&D and innovative collaborations with local companies and universities. Compared to their local counterparts, foreign companies from Western economies can leverage brand awareness and a trusted image, because Chinese consumers tend to trust foreign brands more, especially for long-run treatment (Yuanjia et al., 2007). Yet, foreign companies still face numerous challenges arising primarily from the strong competition from the local drug-makers, which have a deeper knowledge of the complex and heterogeneous domestic market as well as impressive distribution networks. In addition, the strong regulatory regime and the price control by the central government hamper foreign entry into the Chinese market. Overall, Chinese government welcomes foreign investors operating in high tech sectors, such as pharmaceuticals, because they are believed to promote China export and to enhance local competences, while simultaneously obstructing the entry of foreign competitors whose main objective is selling in the Chinese domestic market.

DATA DESCRIPTION

In order to study the profile of MNEs in the Chinese pharmaceutical industry and their influence on the local innovative production, we used patent data as a proxy for innovative output. We focus on the United States Patent and Trademark Office (USPTO) data, in order to use a reliable and established data source, which is also able to assure that the innovations we analyze are original and valuable (Archibugi & Coco, 2005). This would probably not have been possible if we had focused on the Chinese patent office, that is, the State Intellectual Property Office of the P.R.C. (SIPO), for several reasons. For example, the significant changes occurred in the Chinese patent system make Chinese data inconsistent over time. The choice of relying exclusively on USPTO data is also related to the well-known issues arising from the lack of consistent quality across national patent systems and homogeneity in approval procedures and time. It is indeed common practice to use data from a single patent office (Jaffe & Trajtenberg, 2002) to standardize the measure of innovation (Singh, 2007), as already done by Branstetter, Li, and Veloso (2013)[2] using USPTO patents as an indicator of innovative activity in China and India.

In addition to the reasons explained by Griliches (2000), we chose to use patent data as source of information on MNEs R&D activities for three main motives in line with Zhao (2006). First, patents are the output of R&D and, compared with input measures, they represent a more refined measure of the efficient utilization of human capital (e.g., R&D expenditure or number of scientists). Second, through the use of patents, we measure R&D outputs taking into account only innovations considered valuable by the company. In fact, applying for a patent implies non-trivial costs and time investment and a firm will likely go through this process only if the underlying technology can potentially enhance the value of the company. Finally, patents provide detailed information on the inventor team, favoring the identification of collaborations among inventors and their geographical distribution.

In order to build our initial sample, we selected all USPTO patents that: (1) have at least one Chinese inventor; (2) were granted between 1975 and 2010; (3) are representative of the pharmaceutical industry, referring to the Drug and Medical technological fields defined by Hall, Jaffe, and Trajtenberg (2001);[3] and (4) are assigned to an organization, thus excluding patents assigned to individuals. We also included design patents mentioning the technological class "Pharmaceutical Devices" (D24). We define the patents that display all these characteristics as Chinese pharmaceutical patents. The sample thus generated consists of 996 patents.[4] For the purpose of our study, we selected from the initial sample only patents assigned to MNE parents or their subsidiaries, thus obtaining a final sample of 333 patents.

MNE Parent-Subsidiary Data

In order to ascertain whether a specific innovation should be considered as originating from an MNE, we need to identify the ownership structure of the firm, which allows to distinguish between MNE and single-location firm or national group. Starting from the initial sample, for each assignee mentioned in the patent document we analyzed first the institutional typology and then, in the case of firms, the ownership structure, manually inspecting the assignees and relying on information from *BvD Orbis*, companies' websites and other on-line resources. In particular, with regard to the institutional typology of the assignee, we first identified and retained patents which were assigned to firms, thus excluding those innovations pertaining, for instance to universities or research centers. To further classify the assignee of the selected patents, we defined as MNE any firm that has at least one foreign subsidiary by looking at the family tree for every firm in our sample. Because patents may be assigned either to the MNE parent company or to one of its subsidiaries for unobservable reasons (Cantwell & Mudambi, 2005), we considered each multiunit firm as an integrated strategic agent, following the approach of Zhao (2006). Finally, we distinguished between Chinese and foreign MNEs, using the location of the parent company in the case of MNEs' subsidiaries. A Chinese MNE in this study includes a parent company registered in China and all its subsidiaries at home as well as abroad. On the other hand, a foreign MNE is intended as a parent company headquartered outside China and all its subsidiaries located at the home-country and abroad, included in China.

MAJOR FINDINGS

Foreign MNEs Innovative Background

As recalled above, IB literature suggests that the potential impact of foreign MNEs on emerging countries' technological performance depends primarily on the level of innovativeness of these firms. To investigate the innovative background of foreign MNEs in the Chinese pharmaceutical industry, we first offer a description of these actors and then analyze their patent portfolio.

Among the top foreign assignees in our sample by number of patents involving at least one Chinese inventor, there are very well-known Western MNEs, such as the F. Hoffmann–La Roche (Switzerland), Bayer (Germany), and DuPont (the United States) (Table 1). These companies have increasingly invested in China in order to establish new R&D bases for drug discovery, testing and development. As an example, F. Hoffmann–La Roche SA started its Chinese R&D center in 2004 in Zhangjiang Hi-Tech Park in Shanghai, where about 100 scientists work to support the activities of drug discovery of the group, and have become a center of excellence in the fields of oncology, virology, and metabolic diseases, while other 110 people are involved in the development of new medicines not only for China, but for the global market. The Development Center, in particular, is the first "*comprehensive Clinical Development Organization in Asia Pacific (excluding Japan) of Roche*," and as such is the only pharmaceutical company in China that is able to "*design, conduct and analyse clinical studies to meet the registration needs*" (Biotechine, 2013). The Zhangjiang Hi-Tech Park also hosts the Chinese R&D center of DuPont, which was established in 2005 with the objective of supporting all key activities of the group in the region, such as design, development, licensing, training, and technology transfer (DuPont, 2013), as well as of promoting the collaboration with major Chinese and Asian research centers and universities, and which currently involve around 250 researchers. Bayer innovative activities are instead located in Beijing, where the company performs drug development for the whole Asia region with the aim of systematically accounting for Asian patients' needs earlier in the global drug development process (Industry Watch, 2009).

Fig. 1 shows that the great majority of foreign MNEs conducting R&D and patenting in China are US-based companies, followed by Swiss and Japanese companies.

Table 1. Top Foreign Assignee of Chinese-Based Pharmaceutical Patents.

Assignee_name	Number of Patents
Roche holding AG	21
BAYER AG	12
The Procter & Gamble Company	12
IRM LLC	10
Schering Corporation	9
E. I. DU PONT DE NEMOURS AND COMPANY	7
Lonza AG	7
NOVOZYMES, A/S	7
Siemens Aktiengesellschaft	7
CONAIR CORPORATION	6

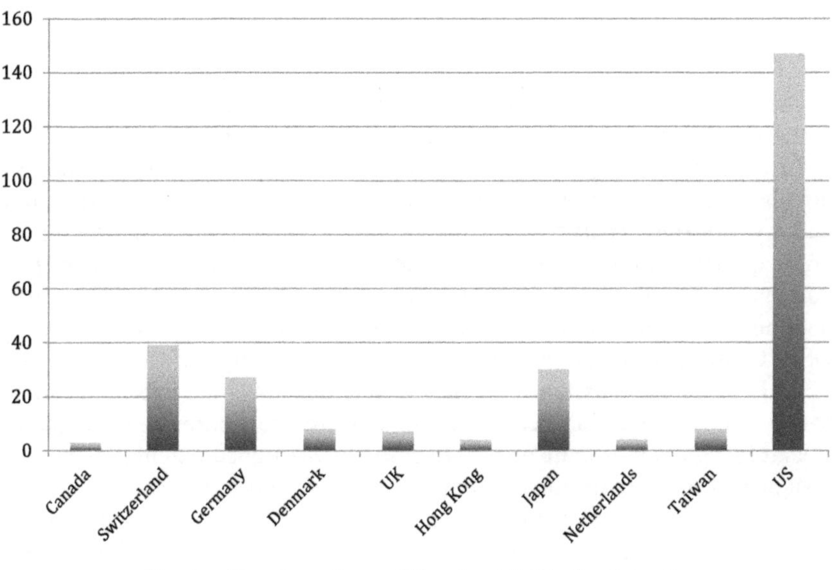

Fig. 1. Top Locations of Foreign MNEs (by Patent).

Fig. 2 depicts the number of patents granted to both Chinese and foreign MNEs over time. The number of foreign MNEs' patents is steadily higher over time, and it seems to grow more rapidly. The stable growing trend starts in the late 1990s for foreign MNEs, and at the beginning of 2000 for the Chinese. However, in the last years of our sample, the number

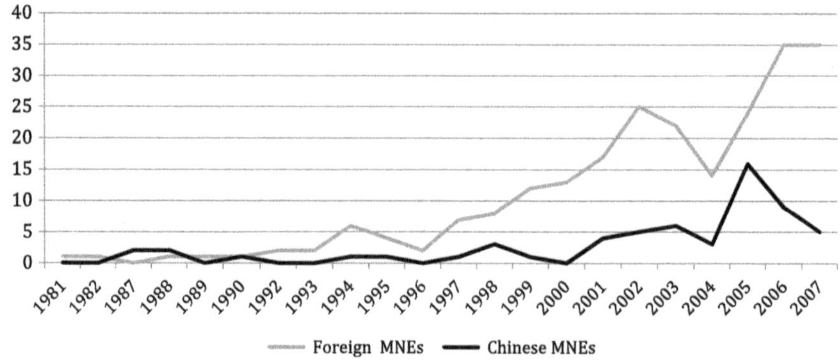

Fig. 2. Number of Chinese Patents Granted to Foreign and Chinese MNEs (by Application Year[7]).

of foreign MNEs' patents remains stable, as opposed to Chinese MNEs' patents, which tend to rapidly decline starting from 2006.

In order to investigate the degree of innovativeness of foreign multinationals conducting R&D in the Chinese pharmaceutical industry, we built a dummy variable, *Leader*, which takes the value of 1 for assignees in the upper quartile of the global pharmaceutical industry in terms of patent production in the year previous to the patent application ($t-1$). Patent production is measured as the natural logarithm of the cumulative number of USPTO pharmaceutical patents[5] issued by each assignee in the period 1975 $- t-1$. In case the assignee belongs to a group or is the subsidiary of an MNE, the variable has been calculated using the pharmaceutical patent stock of its global ultimate owner. In case of co-assigned patent (i.e., patents assigned to more than one organization), *Leader* takes the value of 1, if at least one of the co-assignees is in the upper quartile. Our data suggests that the 68.7% of foreign assignees utilizing the work of Chinese inventors is indeed a technological leader in the global pharmaceutical industry. This confirms the belief according to which China is currently a priority market for advanced pharmaceutical multinationals. On the other hand, this also suggests that the innovative activity performed in China by foreign companies is associated with a high learning potential for local inventors, which on average come into contact with leading innovators from the developed world, which operate at the research frontier and therefore may act as a critical channel for spillovers.

Foreign MNEs Investment Choices and Organizational Arrangements Used for Local Knowledge Creation

Beside their innovative background, a second factor influencing foreign MNEs' potential contribution to the development of emerging countries' innovation system is their interaction behavior with local actors. MNEs' location choices can be used as a first proxy of the extent to which they are open to the contact with local firms. Firms that agglomerate are certainly more available to develop different types of relationships with the local business network, as opposed to firms that tend to isolate. In order to explore this issue, we have analyzed the Chinese cities that foreign MNEs choose to set up their R&D activities, by representing the locations of foreign MNEs' Chinese inventors in a map. As we can observe in Fig. 3, the most common locations of foreign MNEs are Shanghai and Beijing, and more in general the great majority of MNEs' inventive activity is localized in the coastal area. Far from being isolated locations, these places seem to

Fig. 3. Chinese Locations of Foreign MNEs' Inventive Activity.

offer the highest opportunity to connect with local firms. In fact, as it appears from our data, Shanghai and Beijing are the most important inventor locations also for Chinese firms (about 43% of Chinese MNEs' inventors is in fact concentrated in the two cities). This result seems to suggest that when investing in emerging countries, foreign MNEs do not seek isolate research locations, but rather they tend to co-locate, most likely to gain access to talented local human resources and geographically concentrated experience and knowledge of the local industry. Simultaneously, such agglomeration dynamics seem to pave the way for knowledge outflows in the opposite direction, that is, from foreign MNEs to local firms, thus contributing to the diffusion of innovative best-practices, problem-solving routines, and advanced technologies.

Although location choices may act as a proxy of the *potential* patterns of interaction between foreign MNEs and local firms in the host-environment, the extent to which these agents will actually share knowledge depends on the *realized* contacts, which in turn depend critically on the organizational arrangements foreign MNEs use to create new technological knowledge in the host-location. In order to explore this issue, we rely on two types of data. First, at the inventor level, we use the information on foreign MNEs' inventor team composition, in order to single out the extent to which Chinese inventors who offer their scientific work to foreign firms are actually exposed to the knowledge and capabilities of inventors from the advanced world. Second, at the assignee level, we use the information on the so-called "co-assigned patents," in order to ascertain whether foreign MNEs formally cooperate with local firms to develop innovation, thus activating effective channels for spillover.

In order to analyze the characteristics of the inventor teams of Chinese patents granted to foreign MNEs, in Table 2 we show the number and locations of their inventors, and compare them with the characteristics of local MNEs' inventor teams. Almost 84% of inventors of Chinese patents granted to MNEs work for foreign MNEs. Compared to Chinese MNEs, foreign MNEs have bigger inventors teams. On average, the ratio inventors/patent is 4 and 1.62 for foreign and Chinese MNEs, respectively. Further, it can be noted that the number of inventors of foreign MNEs' patents is growing more rapidly, compared to inventors of Chinese MNEs' patents. The former are substantially increasing starting from 2001. On the other hand, the latter show a stable trend.

As regards the inventor locations, almost 67% of the inventors working for foreign MNEs are from advanced countries and almost 33% are from China.[6] For Chinese MNEs, 93% of inventors are home-based and the rest

Table 2. Inventors' Number and Location of Chinese Patents Granted by Foreign- and China-Based MNEs.[a]

Application Year	Inventors Working for Foreign MNEs					Inventors Working for Chinese MNEs				
	Located in advanced countries		Located in China		Total	Located in advanced countries		Located in China		Total
1987	0	–	0	–	0	0	–	8	100%	8
1988	6	75%	2	25%	8	0	–	2	100%	2
1989	2	67%	1	33%	3	0	–	0	–	0
1990	4	80%	1	20%	5	0	–	2	100%	2
1992	0	0%	3	100%	3	0	–	0	–	0
1993	14	88%	2	13%	16	0	–	0	–	0
1994	33	77%	10	23%	43	0	–	7	100%	7
1995	4	25%	12	75%	16	0	–	2	100%	2
1996	8	73%	3	27%	11	0	–	0	–	0
1997	28	72%	11	28%	39	1	33%	2	67%	3
1998	17	65%	9	35%	26	1	13%	7	88%	8
1999	26	50%	25	48%	52	3	60%	2	40%	5
2000	23	53%	19	44%	43	0	–	0	–	0
2001	49	66%	25	34%	74	9	45%	11	55%	20
2002	76	65%	41	35%	117	2	11%	16	89%	18
2003	67	59%	43	38%	113	0	–	30	100%	30
2004	56	72%	20	26%	78	0	–	8	100%	8
2005	83	69%	38	31%	121	0	–	44	100%	44
2006	118	72%	47	28%	165	0	–	21	100%	21
2007	137	71%	56	29%	193	0	–	11	100%	11
Total	751	67%	368	33%	1126	17	7%	214	93%	231

[a]In case of foreign MNEs, the total may be adjusted considering inventors located in other emerging countries.

is located in advanced economies. Hence, Chinese MNEs mainly utilize the scientific work of local inventors. This may be either explained as an attempt to minimize possible inefficiencies due to the high cultural distance which separates them from colleagues located in advanced countries, or as the result of an insufficient absorptive capacity, which hinders the collaboration with external peers. On the contrary, foreign MNEs can likely leverage more sophisticated capabilities to manage dispersed and large innovation networks, due also to previous experience in international collaborations. Our findings only partially support the arguments of Branstetter et al. (2013), which highlight the importance of international co-invention partnerships between Chinese (and Indian) inventors with Western inventors as a mean to accumulate high-level skills. We found that foreign MNEs, compared to Chinese ones, are more capable to favor fruitful international coinvention partnerships, which can be expected to play an important role in fostering the enhancement of the technical skill of local inventors in China.

To better understand where inventors collaborating in Chinese patents granted to foreign MNEs come from, we analyze their top locations, based on the inventor's address provided by the UPSTO. Fig. 4 shows that

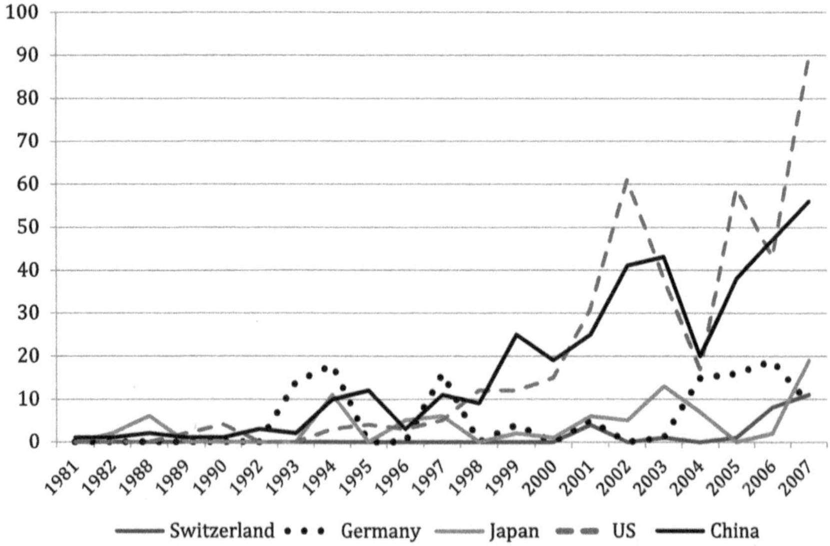

Fig. 4. Top Inventors' Locations of Chinese Patents Granted by Foreign MNEs (by Application Year).

inventors of foreign MNEs' patents are mainly US- and China-based. From 1993 to 1999 the number of Chinese inventors is higher than the number of US inventors, which is growing especially starting from the beginning of 2000. Other foreign inventors participating in foreign MNEs' patents mainly originate from advanced countries, in particular from Japan, Germany and Switzerland. There is a quite predictable overlap between the home-country of foreign MNEs and locations of their non-Chinese inventors. Domestic inventors seem to act as a bridge between HQ and foreign R&D subsidiaries.

In order to further analyze the organizational arrangements utilized by foreign firms to conduct R&D activities in China, we focus on R&D collaborations. To explore this phenomenon, we analyze the cases in which a technological innovation as represented by a patent is assigned to more than one company, suggesting that it has been developed as a result of a cooperation. We refer to these patents as to "R&D collaborations," pointing to technical activities undertaken jointly by two or more organizations. Just like the involvement of Chinese inventors in research teams lead by advanced foreign multinationals is an opportunity for Chinese actors to be exposed to superior knowledge and best-practices, whenever the collaboration occurs between foreign firms and local organizations, it may represent an effective catch-up opportunity for the latter. In order to identify R&D collaborations, we looked at those patents within our main sample that reported more than one assignee. As highlighted in Table 3, R&D collaborations started in 1996 but they never assumed a constant trend over time. In fact, these forms of joint-innovative activities are very limited in their overall number (23 in the whole period covered by our analysis) and do not seem to increase over time.

In order to understand whether R&D collaborations – in spite of their limited number – may in reality act as channel for outward spillover to the Chinese local context, it is necessary to explore who are the partners involved in such cooperative activities. Many advanced MNEs, for instance, declare that their R&D investment in China is driven by the desire to carry out cooperative technical activities with important universities in the host-location. To further investigate this issue, we explored (1) the type of partner, distinguishing between MNEs, universities or research centers, and single-location firms and (2) the geographic origin of the partner. As far as the first aspect is concerned, it can be noticed from Table 4 that the majority of R&D collaborations involve only private firms. More specifically, the majority of them occur between MNEs (10 over 23), while in 8 cases over 23 MNEs collaborate with single-location companies. Regarding

Table 3. Number of Co-Practices in the Chinese Pharmaceutical Industry.

Year	Number of Co-Practices
1996	1
1997	0
1998	0
1999	1
2000	1
2001	0
2002	4
2003	3
2004	0
2005	1
2006	1
2007	9
2008	0
2009	1
2010	1
Total	*23*

Table 4. Type of Partners Involved in Co-Practices in the Chinese Pharmaceutical Industry.

Partner Type	Number of Co-Practices
MNE	10
MNE and universities/research centers	5
MNE and single-location firm	8

the collaboration with partners other that companies, it can be noticed that only 5 co-assigned patents over 23 involve a university or research center. This suggests that although the structure of these partnerships is actually one that highlights the combination of a MNE and a university or research center, these agreements are not so frequent as one may expect. Another potential explanation is that MNEs and universities do collaborate in the Chinese pharmaceutical industry, but not very often this collaboration results in a technological innovation meriting the protection of a US patent.

The second aspect that we have analyzed is the geographic origin of the assignees involved in R&D collaborations. Table 5 suggests that Chinese organizations are never involved in this kind of cooperative activities, which instead occur among partners originating mainly from the United

Table 5. Country Origin of Assignees Involved in Co-Practices in the Chinese Pharmaceutical Industry.

Country Mix	Number of Co-Practices
The United States	13
Taiwan	3
China and the United States	3
The United Kingdom and the United States	1
Hong Kong and the United States	1
The United Kingdom and Japan	1
Japan	1

States, Taiwan, and Switzerland. This excludes the possibility that such activities can act as a direct channel for knowledge spillover to local organizations. As a consequence, it seems that the only mechanism through which these R&D collaborations can contribute to the diffusion of advanced knowledge to the Chinese pharmaceutical industry refers to a situation in which the technology and knowledge shared between the collaboration's partners finds its way to external Chinese organizations, through mediated contacts.

In several cases, the combination of partners involved in the R&D collaboration seems to repeat itself. For instance, Schering Corporation and Pharmacopeia Drug Discovery have realized seven co-assigned patents over the period covered by our analysis. This information is useful because the extent to which one collaboration leads to valuable knowledge sharing and capability building also depends on the repetitiveness and extensive interaction of the cooperative activity. As far as the degree of technological development of the partners involved in the R&D collaborations is concerned, it is possible to single out that only in 22% of the cases, at least one collaborating partner has the status of a global technological leader, suggesting that the content of the knowledge flowing through these relationships may often be of limited innovativeness.

Foreign MNEs' Local Innovative Performance

Beside the number of patents, a complementary aspect to consider when evaluating firms' innovative performance using patent data is the quality of the patent production. In particular, following the established literature on this issue, we consider two different measures of patent quality, that is, the citations to non-patent literature and the number of forward citations. Non-patent literature consists of peer-reviewed scientific papers, conference proceedings, and databases, and other relevant literature. The use of these documents as knowledge sources in the innovative process may reflect how close a patented invention is to scientific knowledge and help depict the proximity of technological and scientific developments (Callaert, van Looy, Verbeek, Debackere, & Thijs, 2006). Cassiman, Veugelers, and Zuniga (2008) suggest that patents that cite science may contain more complex and fundamental knowledge, and this in turn may influence the generality of the patents. On the other hand, the number of citations received, that is, forward citations, measures the technological importance of the patents and prior literature has empirically demonstrated that the forward citations are highly correlated with the quality of the invention (Harhoff, Narin, Scherer, & Vopel, 1999; Jaffe, Trajtenberg, & Fogarty, 2000; Trajtenberg, 1990). The underlying relationship is that more valuable inventions are more frequently cited by subsequent patents, such that the number of forward citations can be employed as a proxy for the quality of each patent. Since it takes time for patent citations to occur (Hall et al., 2001), we count the cumulative number of citations Chinese patents have received as of the end of 2013, that is, two years later our current focal patents dataset ends.

Fig. 5 shows the cumulative number of references to non-patent literature cited by Chinese patents granted to Chinese and foreign MNEs. Patents granted to the latter cite on average a larger number of non-patent documents (except for the period 2002–2004). As such, Chinese MNEs seem to undertake more incremental and codified research, compared to

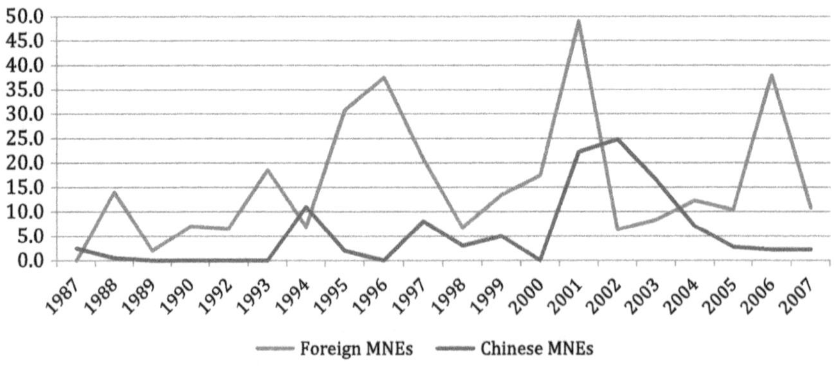

Fig. 5. Number of Non-Patent Literature Citations of Chinese Patents Granted by Foreign and Chinese MNEs (by Application Year).

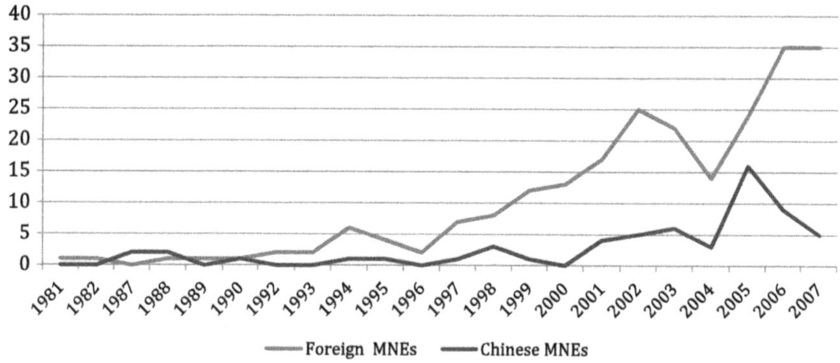

Fig. 6. Number of Forward Citations of Chinese Patents Granted by Foreign and Chinese MNEs (by Application Year).

their foreign counterparts, which on the contrary more frequently leverage basic knowledge to create innovative outputs. As regards the number of citations received by Chinese patents, foreign MNEs' patents are on average more heavily cited (Fig. 6), suggesting that Chinese patents granted to foreign MNEs possess on average a higher quality compared to the ones granted to Chinese MNEs.

CONCLUSIONS

This study aims to improve our understanding of how foreign MNEs manage innovation in a country with relatively weak protection of IPRs, unstable institutional environment and unevenly developed infrastructures, and of how this affects the performance of the local system of innovation. The availability of low-cost skilled human capital and the importance of the local market in the global scenario make China one of the favorite location for knowledge-intensive FDI undertaken by MNEs, especially from advanced countries, which have traditionally played a crucial role in pushing forward the global pharmaceutical industry's innovative frontier. Yet, although the FDI spillover literature suggests that the presence of these companies may enhance local firms' innovation, such beneficial effects are not automatic.

Our results show that the Chinese pharmaceutical industry is actually populated by a number of extremely competitive MNEs from the advanced world, which involve in R&D activities locally and whose presence represents an extraordinary learning opportunity for local firms. The knowledge produced by foreign MNEs is on average characterized by higher quality compared to the knowledge produced by the Chinese local peers, both in terms of scientific content and in terms of impact. Because these foreign companies also tend to locate their R&D labs close to the Chinese research clusters, their posture toward the local business environment seems to be open for interaction, rather than signaling a willingness to isolate. Yet, our results suggest that the realized patterns of interaction with local firms are not as extensive as expected. Foreign MNEs interact with local actors, that is, inventors, universities, and firms, and with the local innovative system through two different channels. On one hand, they act as pipelines favoring the collaboration between local and foreign scientists. On the other hand, they engage in shared R&D projects with other firms or universities. While the first channel seems to offer Chinese inventors the opportunity to be exposed to peers from advanced technological contexts, such as the United States, the channel of R&D collaborations, as represented by co-assigned patents, turned out to be extremely infrequent. Overall, these findings seem to suggest that while the preconditions for the occurrence of FDI-mediated learning processes do exist in the Chinese pharmaceutical industry, local firms may still be unable to fully benefit from the presence of advanced MNEs, likely because they are not yet provided with sufficient absorptive capacity to successfully internalize advanced technology or conduct joint research activities with MNEs from developed countries.

Therefore, we conclude that the presence of advanced MNEs in the Chinese pharmaceutical industry is associated with a strong potential for positive externalities that could be highly beneficial for the local innovation system. However, such externalities do not fully materialize yet. Local firms still need to invest in the build-up of higher absorptive capacity which may allow them to exploit the manifold opportunities associated with the growing presence of advanced foreign firms and the increasing integration of the local industry with global value chains. Whether the current trends and dynamics of local innovative processes in China will allow it to make the leap and reach the technology frontier in the pharmaceutical industry is, of course, a different and more complex question.

NOTES

1. We are grateful to Wexing Guo for the comment.

2. The authors provide a comprehensive analysis of potential problems arising from the use of US patents as an indicator of innovative output of another country, specifically of China.

3. The Drug and Medical category as defined by Hall et al. (2001) includes four sub-categories: Drugs (sub-category code 31); Surgery and Medical Instruments (32); Biotechnology (33); and Miscellaneous – Drugs and Medicine (39).

4. We excluded patents assigned to individuals or unassigned.

5. Defined as described in Section DATA DESCRIPTION.

6. A residual small number of inventors comes from other emerging economies.

7. We present the patent production trend from 1981 to 2007, excluding the last three years in order to avoid truncation problems, which generally affect patent data.

REFERENCES

Alcacer, J., & Chung, W. (2007). Location strategies and knowledge spillovers. *Management Science*, *53*, 760–776.

Andersson, U., Forsgren, M., & Holm, U. (2002). The strategic impact of external networks – Subsidiary performance and competence development in the multinational corporation. *Strategic Management Journal*, *23*, 979–996.

Archibugi, D., & Coco, A. (2005). Measuring technological capabilities at the country level: A survey and a menu for choice. *Research Policy*, *34*, 175–194.

Archibugi, D., & Iammarino, S. (1999). The policy implications of the globalization of innovation. *Research Policy*, *28*, 317–336.

Awate, S., Larsen, M., & Mudambi, R. (2015). Accessing vs. sourcing knowledge: A comparative study of R&D internationalization between emerging and advanced economy firms. *Journal of International Business Studies*, *46*, 63–86.

Baumol, W. J. (2002). *The free-market innovation machine*. Princeton, NJ: Princeton University Press.

Bierly, P., & Chakrabarti, A. (1996). Generic knowledge strategies in the U.S. pharmaceutical industry. *Strategic Management Journal*, *17*, 123–135.

Biotechine. (2013). *Roche in China*. Retrieved from http://biotechine.blogspot.it

Birkinshaw, J., Hood, N., & Jonsson, S. (1998). Building firm-specific advantages in multinational corporations: The role of subsidiary initiative. *Strategic Management Journal*, *19*, 221–242.

Blomström, M., & Kokko, A. (1998). Multinational corporations and spillovers. *Journal of Economic Surveys*, *12*, 247–277.

Bogner, W. C., & Thomas, H. (1994). Core competence and competitive advantage: A model and illustrative evidence from the pharmaceutical industry. In G. Hamel & A. Heene (Eds.), *Competence based competition*. Chichester: Wiley.

Branstetter, L., Li, G., & Veloso, F. (2013). The rise of international co-invention. In A. B. Jaffe & B. Jones (Eds.), *The changing frontier: Rethinking science and innovation policy*. Chicago, IL: University of Chicago Press.

Bruche, G. (2012). Emerging Indian pharma multinationals: Latecomer catch-up strategies in a globalised high-tech industry. *European Journal of International Management*, *6*, 300–322.

Buckley, P., Clegg, J., & Wang, C. (2002). The impacts of FDI on the performance of Chinese manufacturing firms. *Journal of International Business Studies*, *33*, 637–655.

Buckley, P., Clegg, J., & Wang, C. (2007). Is the relationship between inward FDI and spillover effect linear? An empirical examination of the case of China. *Journal of International Business Studies*, *38*, 447–459.

Callaert, J., van Looy, B., Verbeek, A., Debackere, K., & Thijs, B. (2006). Traces of prior art: An analysis of non-patent references found in patent documents. *Scientometrics*, *69*, 3–20.

Cantwell, J. (1989). *Technological innovation and multinational corporations*. London: Basil Blackwell.

Cantwell, J., & Janne, O. (1999). Technological globalisation and innovative centres: The role of corporate technological leadership and locational hierarchy. *Research Policy*, *28*, 119–144.

Cantwell, J., & Mudambi, R. (2005). MNE competence-creating subsidiary mandates. *Strategic Management Journal*, *26*, 1109–1128.

Cantwell, J., & Mudambi, R. (2011). Physical attraction and the geography of knowledge sourcing in multinational enterprises. *Global Strategy Journal*, *1*, 206–232.

Cassiman, B., & Veugelers, R. (2002). R&D cooperation and spillovers: Some empirical evidence from Belgium. *American Economic Review*, *92*, 1169–1184.

Cassiman, B., Veugelers, R., & Zuniga, P. (2008). In search of performance effects of (in)direct industry science links. *Industrial and Corporate Change*, *17*, 611–646.

Christensen, C. M., & Bower, J. L. (1996). Customer power, strategic investment, and the failure of leading firms. *Strategic Management Journal*, *17*, 197–218.

Chung, W., & Yeaple, S. (2008). International knowledge sourcing: Evidence from US firms expanding abroad. *Strategic Management Journal*, *29*, 1207–1224.

Cockburn, I. M. (2004). The changing structure of the pharmaceutical industry. *Health Affairs*, *23*, 10–22.

Cool, K., & Schendel, D. (1987). Strategic group formation and performance: The case of the U.S. pharmaceutical industry. *Management Science*, *33*, 1102–1124.

Cuervo-Cazurra, A., & Genc, M. (2008). Transforming disadvantages into advantages: Developing-country MNEs in the least developed countries. *Journal of International Business Studies*, *39*, 957–979.

de Faria, P., & Sofka, W. (2010). Knowledge protection strategies of multinational firms – A cross-country comparison. *Research Policy*, *39*, 956–968.

DeCarolis, D. M. (2003). Competencies and imitability in the pharmaceutical industry: An analysis of their relationship with firm performance. *Journal of Management*, *29*, 27–50.

Deloitte. (2011). *The next phase: Opportunities in China's pharmaceuticals markets*. Beijing: Deloitte Touche Tohmatsu CPA Ltd.

DiMasi, J., Hansen, R., & Grabowski, H. (2003). The price of innovation: New estimates of drug development costs. *Journal of Health Economics*, *22*, 151–185.

DiMasi, J., Hansen, R., Grabowski, H., & Lasagna, L. (1991). Cost of innovation in the pharmaceutical industry. *Journal of Health Economics*, *10*, 107–142.

Driffield, N., & Love, H. J. (2007). Linking FDI motivation and host-economy productivity effects: Conceptual and empirical analysis. *Journal of International Business Studies*, *38*, 460–473.

Dunning, J. H. (1981). *International production and the multinational enterprise*. London: Allen and Unwin.

Dunning, J. H. (1994). Multinational enterprises and the globalization of innovatory capacity. *Research Policy*, *23*, 67–89.

Dunning, J. H., & Narula, R. (1995). The R&D activities of foreign firms in the United States. *International Studies of Management & Organization*, *25*, 39–74.

DuPont. (2013). *Fact sheet greater China*. Retrieved from www.dupont.com

Friedman, Y. (2010). Location of pharmaceutical innovation: 2000–2009. *Nature Reviews Drug Discovery*, *9*, 835–836.

Frost, T. S., & Zhou, C. (2005). R&D co-practice and 'reverse' knowledge integration in multinational firms. *Journal of International Business Studies*, *36*, 676–687.

Gambardella, A. (1995). *Science and innovation: The US pharmaceutical industry in the 1980s*. Cambridge, MA: Cambridge University Press.

Ghemawat, P. (2010). *Strategy and the business landscape*. Upper Saddle River, NJ: Pearson.

Giroud, A. (2012). Mind the gap: How linkages strengthen understanding of spillovers. *The European Journal of Development Research*, *24*, 20–25.

Görg, H., & Greenaway, D. (2004). Much ado about nothing? Do domestic firms really benefit from foreign direct investment? *World Bank Research Observer*, *19*, 171–197.

Govindarajan, V., & Ramamurti, R. (2011). Reverse innovation, emerging markets, and global strategy. *Global Strategy Journal*, *1*, 191–205.

Greenlee, P., & Cassiman, B. (1999). Product market objectives and the formation of research joint ventures. *Managerial and Decision Economics*, *20*, 115–130.

Griliches, Z. (2000). *R & D, education, and productivity*. Boston, MA: Harvard University Press.

Hagedoorn, J. (1993). Understanding the rationale of strategic technology partnering: Interorganizational modes of cooperation and sectoral differences. *Strategic Management Journal*, *14*, 371–385.

Hall, B. H., Jaffe, A. B., & Trajtenberg, M. (2001). *The NBER patent citation data file: Lessons, insights and methodological tools*. NBER Working Paper No. 8498.

Harhoff, D., Narin, F., Scherer, F. M., & Vopel, K. (1999). Citation frequency and the value of patented inventions. *Review of Economics and Statistics*, *81*, 511–515.

Henderson, R., & Cockburn, I. (1994). Measuring competence? Exploring firm effects in pharmaceutical research. *Strategic Management Journal*, *15*, 63–84.

Hill, C., & Hansen, G. (1991). A longitudinal study of the cause and consequences of changes in diversification in the U.S. pharmaceutical industry 1977–1986. *Strategic Management Journal*, *12*, 187–199.

Hu, A. G. Z., & Jefferson, G. H. (2002). FDI impact and spillover: Evidence from China's electronic and textile industries. *World Economy*, *25*, 1063–1076.

Hymer, S. H. (1976). *The international operations of national firms: A study of foreign direct investment*. Cambridge, MA: MIT Press.

Immelt, J. R., Govindarajan, V., & Trimble, C. (2009). How GE is disrupting itself. *Harvard Business Review*, *87*, 56–65.

Industry Watch. (2009). *Bayer Schering pharma to invest 100 million euro in China to build a global R&D center*. Retrieved from www.asiabiotech.com

Jaffe, A. B., & Trajtenberg, M. (2002). *Patents, citations, and innovations: A window on the knowledge economy*. Cambridge, MA: MIT press.

Jaffe, A. B., Trajtenberg, M., & Fogarty, M. S. (2000). *Knowledge spillovers and patent citations: Evidence from a survey of inventors*. NBER/Sloan Project report, 21.

Kesteloot, K., & Veugelers, R. (1995). Stable R&D cooperation with spillovers. *Journal of Economics and Management Strategy*, *4*, 651–672.

KPMG. (2011). *China's pharmaceutical industry – Poised for the giant leap*. Beijing: KPMG Advisory China Limited.

Kwok, D., & Lyn, T. E. (2010). Analysis global drug firms take aim at made-for-China healthcare. *Reuters*. Retrieved from http://www.reuters.com/article/2010/09/21/us-china-pharma-idUSTRE68K1EM20100921. Accessed on September 21.

Lahiri, N. (2010). Geographic dispersion of R&D units: How does it help innovation? *Academy of Management Journal*, *53*, 1194–1209.

Lewin, A. Y., Massini, S., & Peeters, C. (2009). Why are companies offshoring innovation? The emerging global race for talent. *Journal of International Business Studies*, *40*, 901–925.

Malerba, F., & Orsenigo, L. (2002). Innovation and market structure in the dynamics of the pharmaceutical industry and biotechnology: Toward a history friendly model. *Industrial and Corporate Change*, *11*, 667–703.

Marin, A., & Bell, M. (2006). Technology spillovers from foreign direct investment: The active role of MNC subsidiaries in Argentina in the 1990. *Journal of Development Studies*, *42*, 678–697.

Marin, A., & Sasidharan, S. (2010). Heterogeneous MNC subsidiaries and technological spillovers: Explaining positive and negative effects in India. *Research Policy*, *39*, 1227–1241.

McEvily, B., & Marcus, A. (2005). Embedded ties and the acquisition of competitive capabilities. *Strategic Management Journal*, *26*, 1033–1055.

Meyer, K. E. (2004). Perspectives on multinational enterprises in emerging economies. *Journal of International Business Studies*, *35*, 259–276.

Mudambi, R. (2008). Location, control and innovation in knowledge-intensive industries. *Journal of Economic Geography*, *8*, 699–725.

National Science Board. (2014). Industry, technology, and the global marketplace. *Science and engineering indicators*. Arlington, VA: National Science Foundation.

Perri, A., & Andersson, U. (2014). Knowledge outflows from foreign subsidiaries and the tension between knowledge creation and knowledge protection: Evidence from the semiconductor industry. *International Business Review*, *23*, 63–75.

Perri, A., & Peruffo, E. (forthcoming). Knowledge spillovers from FDI: A critical review from the international business perspective. *International Journal of Management Reviews*, doi:10.1111/ijmr.12054

Phene, A., & Almeida, P. (2008). Innovation in multinational subsidiaries: The role of knowledge assimilation and subsidiary capabilities. *Journal of International Business Studies*, *39*, 901–919.

Pisano, G. (1994). Knowledge integration and the locus of learning: An empirical analysis of process development. *Strategic Management Journal*, *15*, 85–100.

Pisano, G. (1997). *The development factory: Unlocking the potential of process innovation*. Boston, MA: Harvard Business School Press.

Ramamurti, R., & Singh, J. V. (2009). *Emerging multinationals in emerging markets*. Cambridge: Cambridge University Press.

Rein, S. (2009). Health-Care reform, China style. *Bloomberg Businessweek*. Retrieved from http://www.businessweek.com/globalbiz/content/aug2009/gb20090821_005732.htm. Accessed on August 21.

Roberts, P. W. (1999). Product innovation, product-market competition, and persistent profitability in the U.S. pharmaceutical industry. *Strategic Management Journal, 20*, 655–670.

Sharma, A., & Lacey, N. (2004). Linking product development outcomes to market valuation of the firm: The case of the US pharmaceutical industry. *Journal of Product Innovation Management, 21*, 297–308.

Shaver, J. M., & Flyer, F. (2000). Agglomeration economies, firm heterogeneity, and foreign direct investment in the United States. *Strategic Management Journal, 21*, 1175–1193.

Singh, J. (2007). Asymmetry of knowledge spillovers between MNCs and host country firms. *Journal of International Business Studies, 38*, 764–786.

Song, J., & Shin, J. (2008). The paradox of technological capabilities: A study of knowledge sourcing from host countries of overseas R&D operations. *Journal of International Business Studies, 39*, 291–303.

Spigarelli, F., & Wei, H. (2012). *The rising Chinese pharmaceutical industry: Local champions vs global players*. c.MET Working paper 06/2012.

The Economist. (2012). *Battling borderless bugs*. Retrieved from http://www.economist.com/node/21542410. Accessed on January 7.

Thomas, L. G. (1990). Regulation and firm size: FDA impacts on innovation. *Rand Journal of Economics, 21*, 497–517.

Trajtenberg, M. (1990). A penny for your quotes: Patent citations and the value of innovations. *Rand Journal of Economics, 21*, 172–187.

Watts, H. D. (1981). *The branch plant economy*. London: Longman.

Yuanjia, H., Geng, F., Ying, B., & Yitao, W. (2007). The Chinese pharmaceutical market: Perspectives of the health consumer. *Journal of Medical Marketing: Device, Diagnostic and Pharmaceutical Marketing, 7*, 295–300.

Zeng, M., & Williamson, P. (2007). *Dragons at your door: How Chinese cost innovation is disrupting global competition*. Boston, MA: Harvard Business School Press.

Zhao, M. (2006). Conducting R&D in countries with weak intellectual property rights protection. *Management Science, 52*, 1185–1199.

Zhao, M., & Islam, M. (2007). Cross-regional ties within firms: Promoting knowledge flow or discouraging knowledge spillover? Mimeo.

DETERMINANTS OF BOARD ROLES IN IJVS IN CHINA: CONTROL AND COLLABORATION

Xuanli Xie, Jeffrey J. Reuer and Elko Klijn

ABSTRACT

Despite the growing interest in IJVs and their governance, systematic research is limited on the board of directors and their roles in international joint ventures in emerging markets. In this study, we draw from corporate governance research that suggests that the levels of control and collaboration by boards are influenced by organizational complexity. While joint ventures possess several similarities compared to unitary firms, they also have unique sources of complexity given the fact that two or more international partners collaborate within JVs under an incomplete contract. Based on a sample of 114 IJVs, we argue and show four separate conditions that influence the functions that boards undertake as well as how control and collaboration as two separate functions are interrelated. Our findings address calls for research to open the black box of what boards actually do as well as to bring corporate governance theory to new organizational forms such as joint ventures.

Keywords: International joint venture; board of directors; corporate governance; emerging markets

Emerging Economies and Multinational Enterprises
Advances in International Management, Volume 28, 235–265

ISSN: 1571-5027/doi:10.1108/S1571-502720150000028012

INTRODUCTION

While considerable research attention has been dedicated to joint venture governance and the adoption of contracts as formal governance solutions in particular, little is known about the board of directors of these organizational forms in emerging markets. Joint ventures are separate legal organizational entities that are partially held by parent firms originating from different countries (Shenkar & Zeira, 1987), and they have been a popular mode for organizations to enter emerging markets due to their potential cost advantages, shared risks, and access to complementary resources (Contractor & Lorange, 2002). Joint ventures have boards of directors as a "formal organ" (Hewitt, 1987) that is responsible for overseeing the business to realize these benefits for parent firms.

Governing IJVs in emerging markets is challenging for parent firms and IJV success rates have been mixed (Beamish, 1988; Chang, Chung, & Moon, 2013; Sim & Ali, 1998; Vanhonacker, 1997), so it is important to study the functions of boards in particular and investigate the black box of what boards actually do in this type of collaborations (Daily, 1996). The literature on joint ventures has often highlighted the importance of boards as an administrative control mechanism (Balakrishnan & Koza, 1993; Geringer & Hebert, 1989), yet it is striking that so little systematic research has been undertaken on them. Corporate governance scholars, on the contrary, have extensively studied the roles of boards in unitary organizations but have failed to study what boards do in this particular hybrid organizational form. As a result, recent calls for corporate governance research exist that discuss the need to investigate other organizational forms such as joint ventures (Krause et al., 2014; Reuer, Klijn, & Lioukas, 2014).

We believe that there is value in bringing in corporate governance research to the theory of joint venture governance given the fact that IJVs are different organizational forms that present some similarities and differences compared to unitary organizations. International joint ventures are separate legal entities that are established by multiple international partners under an incomplete contract, and we argue that complexities that stem from this particular organizational form can influence boards to undertake their functions differently compared to unitary organizations. For instance, IJV boards not only monitor and advise management (e.g., Forbes & Milliken, 1999), but they also function as information-processing channels for parents or as a platform for conflict resolution. Hence, boards not only represent partners' interests, but also aim to enhance the strategic and operational effectiveness of the collaboration between the parent firms.

Boards undertake a variety of tasks, but generally these responsibilities can be categorized as control and collaboration (Sundaramurthy & Lewis, 2003). The control role of boards stresses discipline and monitoring by directors (Kosnik, 1987), while the collaborative approach focuses on services and calls for board-management ties to foster trust and consultation (Westphal, 1999). The control and collaboration roles are often interrelated (Adams, Hermalin, & Weisbach, 2009), yet within the context of joint ventures it remains interesting to investigate the relation between these two roles. This is due to the fact that IJVs are hybrid organizations between international partners prone to opportunism (Hennart, 1988; Williamson, 1985) and other collaboration challenges (Kogut & Zander, 1992). Thus, while some JV characteristics might influence the intensity of boards to be engaged in monitoring, in other cases directors need to place emphasis on collaboration.

While the execution of these dual tasks of board control and collaboration might apply to most joint ventures, we also expect that these two functions may not be equally important across all joint ventures. In addition, some recent studies began to examine IJV boards in developed countries (e.g., Klijn et al., 2013; Reuer et al., 2014), but research is needed on boards of directors in emerging markets in particular. It is therefore the aim of this study to address this gap in the literature by examining the functions of IJV boards in China. We develop four JV-specific drivers that influence the functioning of boards and show that control and coordination by JV boards are influenced by the cultural distance between partners, the type of assets involved, and by the learning capabilities of partners. As such, we make several contributions to the theory of JV governance and boards in joint ventures in particular.

First, we address recent calls for research to study the governance of organization forms besides the modern corporation (e.g., Krause et al., 2014). The literature on corporate governance is extensive, but most of these studies tend to look at the board of unitary firms or those of family firms (Daily, Dalton, & Cannella, 2003; Dalton, Daily, Ellstrand, & Johnson, 1998; Hambrick, Werder, & Zajac, 2008; Hillman & Dalziel, 2003). The context of joint ventures is important to study given the number of deals formed over the last decade. In addition, JV partners have multiple governance solutions at their disposal (e.g., informal governance, contracts) and it is interesting to see how the board undertakes its control and collaboration functions while controlling for additional governance solutions that parents can implement as well. For example, rather than having a diffuse set of equity investors, the prototypical joint venture has two direct owners. This concentrated ownership structure on the one hand will increase the incentive of owners to monitor and reduce traditional principal–agent conflicts. Yet on the other hand, because owners' motives and their interests outside of IJV can diverge greatly, principal–principal conflict tends to rise. This is likely to influence the control and collaboration roles of boards in this particular setting.

Second, while corporate governance research has extensively studied the structure and performance implications of the board by using secondary data, we use primary data to offer detailed insights on the engagement by boards in their control and collaboration functions. As such, we address calls for research to investigate the black box of what boards actually do (Daily, 1996). We argue that JV boards are also responsible for maintaining and improving the relationship between the IJV partners. Some scholars have pointed out that IJV boards have a "buffering function" and serve as a communication and information-processing channel between the parents and the IJV (Kumar & Seth, 1998; Shenkar & Zeira, 1992). This can potentially imply boards of JVs in emerging countries face different pressures to engage in control and collaboration as well because language or cultural barriers exist.

This chapter is structured as follows. First, we review the literature on IJV governance and in particular the roles of boards. We then discuss the Chinese context and present the hypotheses development. The chapter proceeds with an explanation of the research methods and this is followed by analyses and results. We finish with theoretical and practical implications of our study as well as a discussion of future research directions.

LITERATURE REVIEW

Background Theory

Emerging market IJVs are often formed between foreign multinational enterprises (MNEs) and local companies in developing countries. In such collaborations, MNEs typically contribute advanced technology, manufacturing skills, and managerial expertise, and local companies contribute local market knowledge, distribution channels, and networks (Yan & Gray, 1994). The board of directors plays an important role in overseeing these different inputs from these partners. Not only do they need to control whether the partners keep their promises regarding what they had agreed to bring in to the joint venture (Hennart, 1988), but they also need to collaborate with management to ascertain how these inputs must be implemented and managed. As such, the control and collaboration functions are important for boards to be engaged in (Li, Zhou, & Zajac, 2009).

Both agency theorists as well as transaction cost scholars have called for the importance of the control role undertaken by directors. Boards are regarded as an administrative control mechanism (Williamson, 1985) and are involved in controlling management when opportunism occurs. In a similar vein, agency theorists have called for the need to control when principal–agent conflicts are likely to occur. Employees are more likely to engage in self-seeking behavior when they understand they are not being monitored (Eisenhardt, 1989). Finally, joint venture boards can also be involved in control activities when principal–principal conflicts are likely to arise. This tends to be the case when partners commit superior organizational competences or when there is high goal incongruence between the parent firms (Luo, Shenkar, & Nyaw, 2001).

While much of the IJV literature highlights the control aspect of governance, there is a growing acknowledgment of the importance of collaboration within boards. The collaboration function is rooted in the stewardship theory (Davis, Schoorman, & Donaldson, 1997) and emphasizes the board as a mechanism to create value, advise management, and help management to make informed decisions (Finkelstein & D'Aveni, 1994). For instance, from the knowledge-based perspective (Kogut & Zander, 1992), IJVs are formed for the purpose to create, store, and apply knowledge. Beyond simply transferring knowledge from the parent to the joint venture, resources and competences from both parents need to be combined (e.g., advanced technology combined with the knowledge of local consumer needs) and jointly created in order to achieve IJV success. IJV employees come from different organizations and are used to their own organization's routines and policies (Geringer & Hebert, 1989). As such, the advisory function of boards is important because it holds the potential to smoothen interorganizational collaboration, increase both parties' commitment and engagement, facilitate the combination of knowledge and resources, and create higher IJV productivity (Li et al., 2009).

Boards of Directors: The Dual Role of Control and Collaboration

While the control and collaboration activities have not been systematically analyzed in joint ventures and researched as two functions that boards can undertake, the corporate governance literature has acknowledged the importance of these two functions. First, the directors' control role is to ensure corporate growth and protect shareholders' interests by evaluating the company's and CEO's performance (Zahra & Pearce, 1989). For example, according to agency perspectives, as firms grow large and management and ownership diverge, conflicts of interest arise (Jensen & Meckling, 1976); so, the primary responsibility of boards is to ensure that a CEO's decisions and actions are consistent with the interest of the corporation's owners (Beatty & Zajac, 1994; Oviatt, 1988). When managers' personal preferences regarding firm strategies and policies conflict with the interests of shareholders, boards can intervene to ensure that shareholders' interests are protected (Hermalin & Weisbach, 1988; Hill & Snell, 1988). Another source of conflict of interest may arise from the different preferences between owners, and such conflicts take on particular salience in the case of IJVs. At the extreme, if one owner owns a large percentage of shares in the firm, this partner is able to direct the JV to pursue its private interest at the expense of other owners' interests (Luo et al., 2001). Facing this principal–principal conflict, IJV boards provide administrative controls that can help mitigate partner opportunism that may harm a collaborative agreement (Geringer & Hebert, 1989; Mjoen & Tallman, 1997; Oxley & Sampson, 2004; Petrovic, Kakabadse, & Kakabadse, 2006).

Participating in strategy formulation and advising management on strategic issues is another role of boards. This view is supported by resource-dependence theorists (Pfeffer & Salancik, 1978) as well as strategic management researchers (Lorsch & MacIver, 1989; Mace, 1971; Stiles, 2001). Boards are engaged in collaboration when they are involved in company strategy by rendering counsel and advice to the CEO or senior management, by initiating their own analysis or by suggesting alternatives, and by providing access to essential resources through linkages to the external environment (Gulati & Westphal, 1999). Under this perspective, the relationship between the board of directors and the management as well as the collaboration across directors on the board can foster trust, helping executives to seek greater input from directors and give directors more confidence to offer feedback (Westphal, 1999). In IJVs, the collaboration function of the board can entail additional functions that boards in unitary organizations are not engaged in. For instance, due to the fact that board members are representatives of the partner firms, they are often engaged in the formulation of strategy with management collectively (Ravasi & Zattoni, 2006; Yan & Gray, 1994), and boards also offer a potential venue for conflict resolution, coordination of activities, and trust-building (Shenkar & Zeira, 1992).

In summary, given that the joint venture literature has emphasized control and collaboration as major concerns of parent firms, and recent corporate governance literature has also featured these two aspects of governance in the board context, this chapter provides a strong theoretical basis for joining these two literatures. On the one hand, the IJV board's role is to control the performance and operations of an IJV and its management, making sure the parents' (owners') interests are protected. On the other hand, IJV board members need to collaborate with the CEO, management, and other board members in order to foster trust, enhance the decision quality, and reduce conflicts that might emerge. In the following section, we will introduce Chinese IJVs as the empirical context for our study and develop hypotheses that identify key antecedents of board control and collaboration for IJVs.

The Chinese Context

Since the adoption of the "reform and open-door policy" in 1978, China has emerged from a centrally planned to a more market-oriented system with an annual growth rate of over 8 percent per year (Child & Tse, 2001). In 2006, China also became one of the largest recipients of foreign direct investment (FDI). Due to the potential advantages of IJVs and the influence of Chinese governmental policies, IJVs have become a frequent form of market entry for foreign investors in China (Beamish, 1993; Walsh, Wang, & Xin, 1999). Although there are tremendous opportunities for foreign investors to access resources and markets in China, several issues present challenges for partners intending to cooperate by means of IJVs.

First, IJVs in China face significant uncertainty because of the underdeveloped institutions in China, which could elevate transaction costs of doing business for foreign firms (Khanna & Palepu, 1997). For example, not only are the laws for IJVs different compared to domestic partners, requirements might also be different depending on who has control and what assets are provided by whom (Meyer, 2011; Peng, 2003). The Chinese legal system is further complicated by a lack of consistency that allows individual judges leeway in determining rights and wrongs (Si & Bruton, 1999).

Furthermore, Guanxi (connections) play an important role in the Chinese society. Sometimes, Guanxi could be the substitute for formal institutions, especially when the formal institution is lacking or unclear (e.g., Tsui, Schoonhoven, Meyer, Lau, & Milkovich, 2004; Zhang & Keh, 2010). Thus, foreign partners would value local partners' local market knowledge, place great emphasis on gaining access to partners' knowledge of local markets and networks, and seek to learn how to do business in China (Beamish, 1993; Dong & Glaister, 2006; Yan & Gray, 1994).

On the other hand, the goal of Chinese firms forming IJVs is to learn technology and management skills from foreign partners (Si & Bruton, 1999). These capabilities are usually proprietary, difficult to imitate in developed countries, and are lacking in emerging economies (Yan & Gray, 1994). In fact, absorbing advanced technology through forming IJVs with MNEs has been the strategy of the Chinese government to foster economic development (Beamish, 1993; Meyer, 2004). However, foreign firms may not want to transfer their proprietary knowledge to IJVs due to concerns regarding the suboptimal use of the technology by the IJV as well as the misuse of the technology by the local partner (Mjoen & Tallman, 1997), especially given the weak protection of intellectual property in China (Zhang, Li, Hitt, & Cui, 2007).

The inherent goal incongruence between foreign and Chinese partners can make their alliances particularly vulnerable. For example, research on Chinese IJVs found that the Chinese parent's goal tends to be to acquire foreign technology more quickly and effectively, but foreign parents want to increase their market share and improve their competitive position in the local market (Yan & Gray, 1994). Both sides would strive for control in order to protect their own interests, yet collaboration is also necessary to achieve the expected mutual learning and knowledge transfer. Because insufficient legislative protections in China offer foreign investors limited safeguards from local partners' opportunistic behaviors, compared to those in a developed country (Khanna & Palepu, 1997), the board of directors became an important control mechanism to improve the functioning of the IJV.

Research Hypotheses

According to corporate governance research, boards might strive to simultaneously control and collaborate, while they might emphasize one approach over the other at a point in time (Sundaramurthy & Lewis, 2003).

Boards have a finite amount of time and must use this as efficiently as possible (Tuggle, Sirmon, Christopher, & Bierman, 2010). The control and collaboration functions of boards are driven by the organizational complexities of the venture and can therefore differ among joint ventures (Reuer et al., 2014). For example, studies by Luo et al. (2001) argue that the IJV board of directors is part of the overall control mechanisms of governance. Yan and Gray (2001) view boards as an instrument of strategic control, which is at a higher level of hierarchy than operational and structural control. Similarly, boards are also found to be a major mechanism for collaboration. They act as a communication channel and a major conduit for relationship development and enhancement between the parents and the IJV (Hambrick, Li, Xin, & Tsui, 2001; Shenkar & Zeira, 1992).

Members of the board of directors, as representatives from their parent firms, are likely to look to interparent behavior norms for guidance for their own behavior (Pearce, 2001). If the IJV parents view reduction of misappropriation of proprietary assets as the major task, then the board may emphasize its control function, while those IJV parents that view IJV as a way to learn and create knowledge tend to develop the attitude for collaboration (Li et al., 2009), so their boards will tend to be more collaboration-oriented.

Asset Specificity

Previous literature identified asset specificity as a key factor that will increase partner opportunistic behavior (Klein, Crawford, & Alchian, 1978; Williamson, 1985). In a joint venture, asset specificity refers to the situation when one or more partners must make transaction-specific investments, or investments in the joint venture which have less value outside. While joint ventures as a hybrid organizational form can partially reduce the transaction cost compared to market transactions, they do not offer the extensive safeguards provided by hierarchical organization (Chi, 1994; Hennart, 1991). When a firm makes transaction-specific investments, the other partner can threaten to terminate the alliance in order to capture more value. To avoid the value loss from such hold-up behavior, alliance partners have an incentive to enhance the formal governance mechanism to mitigate such risks (Poppo & Zenger, 2002; Reuer & Arino, 2007). The board offers monitoring advantages and administrative controls to counter the risk of opportunism. Since boards have a finite amount of time in which they need to undertake both control and coordination (Tuggle et al., 2010), when partners have invested transaction-specific assets, the board will place more emphasis on control in order to make sure that partners do not engage in opportunism. This leads to our first hypothesis:

Hypothesis 1. The greater the level of asset specificity, the greater the control exercised by the IJV board.

Knowledge-Based Assets

IJV parents contribute resources and competences to create an IJV's bundle of strategic resources that ultimately serve as a source of competitive advantage. Resource contributions by parent firms are of various types and can be classified into property-based and knowledge-based resources (Miller & Shamsie, 1996). Property-based resources are financial capital, physical assets, patents, and brands, which are protected by contracts and laws. Knowledge-based resources refer to the know-how and skills, such as technological and managerial expertise (Das & Teng, 2001). These resources are protected by knowledge barriers such as tacitness, complexity, and causal ambiguity.

Another unique characteristic of knowledge-based resources is that they cannot be easily measured and divided, and have to be integrated in the collaboration to generate competitive advantage (Chen, Park, & Newburry, 2009). For example, to successfully transfer knowledge as intended, both the teacher and the learner must make efforts. Both need to work together and be involved in venture operations to enforce knowledge contributions and learn from each other. The frequent interactions between parents facilitate cross-firm knowledge flow and help develop a common understanding and trust. Under these situations, collaboration-based governance can better facilitate the process. For instance, prior research has found that relational governance mechanisms and social control are more desirable than formal governance mechanism when substantial knowledge-based assets are involved in an alliance (Chen et al., 2009; Hoetker & Mellewigt, 2009). A collaborative board can help directors contribute more knowledge and work cohesively with the IJV management, enhancing knowledge assimilation and knowledge creation (Forbes & Milliken, 1999; Sundaramurthy & Lewis, 2003). In addition, since many of these knowledge-based assets are tacit, face-to-face meetings with boards and management are needed to facilitate the boards to provide advice on how the knowledge can be used. This leads us to our second hypothesis:

Hypothesis 2. The greater the partners' contribution of knowledge-based resources, the greater the collaboration exhibited by the IJV board.

Acquisitive IJV

Joint ventures may be formed by one parent firm acquiring a stake in an existing business of another firm, or by greenfield investment when the parent firms form a new business. Certain opportunistic actions are likely to emerge when the joint venture is formed by one partner acquiring assets from the other partner, for several reasons. First, acquisition contracts are inherently lacking total binding power to guarantee complete transfer of all acquired assets in the business in question. The indigenous firms that previously owned the acquired assets will have information and location advantages to behave opportunistically. This indicates that ex-post governance mechanisms must be in place to safeguard the execution of the transfer. The board needs to engage more in control in order to reduce this threat of opportunism. Secondly, joint ventures formed by acquisitions require the foreign partner to face the labor forces and managerial systems inherited from the host country partner, which will increase the complexity in the collaboration (Chen, 2008; Jemison & Sitkin, 1986). Monitoring by boards is important under these conditions, because it enables the board to detect issues where advice is needed (Adams et al., 2009). We therefore posit:

> **Hypothesis 3.** Compared to joint ventures formed by greenfield investment, joint ventures formed by acquisitions will exhibit greater control exercised by the IJV board.

Cross-National Distance

Another factor that might affect boards' collaboration function more than the control role is the cross-national distance between partners. The field of international business has paid much attention to the impact of cross-national distance on the decision to enter specific countries (Holburn & Zelner, 2010), the choice of entry mode (Xu & Shenkar, 2002; Yiu & Makino, 2002), and performance of foreign firms (Gaur & Lu, 2007). Despite these contributions we have an incomplete understanding of how cross-national differences might affect the governance in joint ventures and in particular the functions that the IJV board of directors undertakes. Since administrative practices, organizational practices, and systems vary widely across countries, board members from distant countries will have different leadership styles and different ways to respond to strategic issues (Hennart & Zeng, 2002; Schneider & de Meyer, 1991). This will create difficulty for IJV boards to improve mutual understanding and trust building (Parkhe, 1991) and restrain the social capital development between boards and management as well as between board members (Currall & Inkpen, 2002).

By contrast, the IJV board collaboration will likely be greater when fewer cross-national differences exist between partners. Under these circumstances, it is easier to transfer information between the board and managers as well as form a collaborative relationship. The advice and counsel of directors will also be more useful and relevant for joint venture management (Reuer et al., 2014). Thus, similar partners can rely on social exchange norms to govern daily activities (Luo, 2007; Nooteboom, 1996), and the board collaboration will be more feasible and effective when cross-national differences are high. Therefore, we hypothesize:

Hypothesis 4. The less the cross-national differences between parent firms, the greater the collaboration exhibited by the IJV board.

METHODS

Data

We collected primary data by means of a large-scale survey from a group of international joint ventures formed in China. In order to identify a population of IJVs, we used the China Industrial Enterprise Statistical Database as well as the SDC database to identify Chinese firms forming joint ventures with foreign firms. After identifying potential key respondents, we used the alumni database of a prominent Chinese business school. The alumni list was developed by four research assistants to ensure whether the respondents that were alumni of the university also worked in a senior position in the JV. Once identified, respondents were asked about their ability to participate in the survey on joint venture governance, or whether they could direct us to an executive within their firm who was directly involved in these deals. After the identification process, 504 alumni were selected. Five well-trained research assistants made initial contacts with them through phone calls.

Preliminary versions of the questionnaire were reviewed by business scholars to ensure face validity. The survey was translated into Chinese and reviewed by two Chinese-speaking researchers. The translated survey was pretested by four Chinese executives experienced in IJVs. As deemed necessary, minor changes were made after pretesting the survey. The final

Chinese version was then reverse-translated into English by a person unfamiliar with the study, and there was a high degree of correspondence between the Chinese and English versions (Saunders, Thornhill, & Lewis, 2009). Out of the total 504 distributed surveys, we received 128 responses (25%). The response rate may be the result of the efforts taken to identify potential respondents, to motivate alumni to participate, to initiate follow-up procedures of sending emails and making supplemental phone calls, and to assure confidentiality (e.g., Dillman, 1978). After the exclusion of uncompleted responses, the final sample included 114 IJVs. The sampled IJVs are distributed across 12 sectors, with the majority in manufacturing industry (53%), and information technology (10%). These ventures are also spread across 19 different provinces in China (including Hong Kong and Taiwan) and the partners are distributed across six continents, and the three highest counts are from Europe (30%), Asia (27%), and North America (23%).

We adopted a key informant approach for collecting the data. In order to ensure the quality of the key informants and reduce informant bias, we developed a respondent profile in the survey (e.g., Campbell, 1995) to ensure that the respondent was eligible to participate in the study. Results show that the respondents' average year of involvement with the IJV is 8.84 years making them knowledgeable in responding to the questionnaire.

We also performed a number of tests to assess the quality of the data. In order to access potential nonresponse bias, we tested for possible differences between early and late respondents, under the assumption that late respondents are more similar to nonrespondents (Armstrong & Overton, 1977). In particular, we tested for differences in firm size based on the number of employees, and the industry distribution of international joint ventures. ANOVA tests showed no difference between the sectoral and temporal distributions across early and late respondents ($F < 0.65$, n.s., and $F < 12.33$, n.s., respectively). Data collection by means of a self-administered survey can also result in the possibility of a common method bias as well as generate social desirability effects. In order to test for common method bias, we used Harman's (1967) single-factor analysis to ensure whether a significant amount of common variance exists in the data. Unrotated factor analysis using the eigenvalue-greater-than-one criterion revealed more than one factor ($n = 7$), and none of the factors explained a significant percent of the variance in the data, indicating that the findings cannot be attributed to common method bias.

Measures

Control and Collaboration

Prior research on boards has shown that control and collaboration can be two distinct categories of board functions (Forbes & Milliken, 1999; Westphal, 1999). Based on these works (e.g., Gulati & Westphal, 1999; Westphal, 1999; Westphal & Stern, 2007), we measure board control and board collaboration by five items, respectively. We adopted the scales by Westphal and Stern (2007) in order to measure the control and collaboration functions of boards. Details on the measurement scales appear in the Appendix. The Cronbach alpha coefficient for the scale is 0.74 for control and 0.80 for collaboration, so both are above the threshold of 0.70 to indicate construct reliability (Nunnally, 1978).

Independent Variables

Existing joint venture governance research argues that formal governance increases when alliance-specific investments are made. We follow Reuer and Arino (2007) and measure asset specificity by means of a six-item scale. The Cronbach alpha for this scale is 0.73, demonstrating satisfactory reliability (Nunnally, 1978; e.g., *asset specificity*). In order to test our second hypothesis, we adopted a scale used by Miller and Shamsie (1996) which classified knowledge-based resources into (a) technological know-how, (b) managerial expertise, (c) market knowledge, and (d) local knowledge. Respondents were first asked to evaluate the extent to which the abovementioned resources were contributed by each parent firm to the IJV. Second, we required them to rate the importance of each resource to the IJV operations on a five-point Likert scale. The overall knowledge-based assets were then calculated by taking the weighted average of knowledge-based assets contributed by the parent firm (i.e., *knowledge-based assets*). Our third hypothesis argues that acquisitive JVs require more control, whereas greenfield joint ventures can require more coordination. Given the fact that greenfield joint ventures require boards to be engaged in collaboration because new employees and other resources need to be brought into the joint venture, operating policies need to be designed, routines need to be developed (Chen, 2008; Harzing, 2002), we created a dummy variable to identify whether the JV is formed by means of a greenfield or acquisitive JV. A code "1" was given when the JV was acquisitive, and "0" otherwise. (i.e., *acquisitive IJV*). Finally, to test our final hypothesis, we measures differences across countries along four dimensions. First, we measured the cultural distance scores obtaining the GLOBE practice scores. There are nine dimensions of cultures in the GLOBE study (House, Hanges, Javidan, Dorfman, & Gupta, 2004). The formula is:

$$\text{Cultural distance} = \sum_{j,k} \frac{\left\{\sum_{i=1}^{9} \left\{ (I_{ij} - I_{ik})^2 / V_i \right\} / 9 \right\}}{(n/2)}$$

where n is the number of partners; I_{ij} and I_{ij} denote the index for the ith cultural dimension for partner j and k's home countries, and V_i is the variance of the index for the ith cultural dimension (i.e., *cultural distance*). Second, we used the administrative distance measured by differences in bureaucratic patterns due to colonial ties, language, and religion (Ghemawat, 2001). The administrative distance between two countries ranges from 0 (sharing colonial ties, language, and religion) to a maximum of 3 (sharing no colonial tie, language, and religion; i.e., *administrative distance*). Our third measure, global connectedness distance which is measured by the connectedness of a country with the rest of the world (Ghemawat, 2001). Following the literature (Berry, Guillen, & Zhou, 2010), we capture this dimension using the average of country differences in international tourism expenditures as a percentage of GDP, international tourism receipts as a percentage of GDP, and Internet users as a percentage of the population (i.e., *global connectedness distance*). Finally, economic distance is captured by country differences in GDP per capita, inflation rates, and intensity of trade with the rest of the world (Berry et al., 2010). An average is then taken when calculating the overall economic distance (i.e., *economic distance*).

Control Variables

We incorporated several controls in the models in order to account for other factors that might be related to the extent that directors are engaged in control and collaboration. First, we followed existing research in corporate finance which argues that the net benefits of monitoring as well as advice increase when firms grow larger (Linck, Netter, & Yang, 2008). Our measure for firm size was the number of employees presently working in the joint venture. Given the positive skewness, we used a log transformation (i.e., *JV size*). Second, we included board size as a second control because when boards expand, so does the chance for free-riding of individual directors implying that directors are less engaged in control and collaboration for a given number of IJV directors (Boone, Field, Karpoff, & Raheja, 2007; Coles, Daniel, & Naveen, 2008: Judge & Zeithaml, 1992;

Linck et al., 2008; i.e., *JV board size*). We also included three variables that capture additional joint ventures characteristics that can also potentially affect their governance. First, we controlled for the number of partners in the joint venture, because an increase in the number of partners can bring greater conflicts and coordination needs (Gong, Shenkar, Luo, & Nyaw, 2007; Gulati & Singh, 1998; Li, Eden, Hitt, Ireland, & Garrett, 2012; Parkhe, 1993; i.e., *number of partners*). Second, we included a dummy measure for CEO duality. CEO duality was coded as "1," if the CEO served both as the CEO and chairman, and as "0" otherwise. Third, we included shared ownership of Chinese partners in order to capture power considerations and the need for shared decision-making (Finkelstein & D'Aveni, 1994; Li et al., 2009; Rechner & Dalton, 1991; i.e., *shared ownership*). We used two variables to control for alternative means of governance (e.g., Hoetker & Mellewigt, 2009; Poppo & Zenger, 2002; Reuer & Arino, 2007). To capture formal governance mechanisms, we controlled for contract complexity of IJVs. Specifically, we used Parkhe's (1993) measure and asked respondents to indicate whether or not each of the eight types of contractual provisions was included in the formal agreement. The equation to calculate the measure is:

$$\text{Contractual complexity} = \frac{1}{36}\sum_{i=1}^{8} D_i$$

where D_i equals i if the ith provision was employed, and zero otherwise (Parkhe, 1993; i.e., *contractual complexity*). Second, we use the partners' prior collaborations to capture relational governance since it can potentially influence the need for board control and collaboration. We asked the respondents to report the number of prior alliances formed with the same partner (Gulati, 1995; i.e., *prior ties*). Partner joint venture experience is measured by the number of prior joint ventures formed by the partners (i.e., *JV experience*). Finally, we included industry fixed effects in the models.

RESULTS

Table 1 provides descriptive statistics as well as the correlation matrix for the variables in the regression models. The highest correlation is 0.29 and the maximum VIF of 2.1 in the estimated models also indicates that the

Table 1. Descriptive Statistics and the Correlation Matrix.[a]

Variable	Mean	SD	1	2	3	4	5	6	7
1. Board control	3.63	0.61							
2. Board collaboration	3.44	0.63	0.73						
3. IJV size	6.13	1.99	0.09	0.03					
4. IJV board size	7.23	4.42	0.01	−0.08	0.48				
5. Ownership split	48.62	18.47	0.21	0.26	0.01	−0.09			
6. Number of partners	1.09	0.31	0.16	0.13	0.17	0.05	−0.01		
7. CEO duality	0.20	0.40	−0.13	0.00	−0.11	−0.14	−0.03	0.07	
8. Prior ties	1.82	2.54	0.11	0.10	0.07	0.07	−0.06	0.05	0.04
9. Contractual complexity	0.67	0.36	0.07	0.13	0.07	−0.22	0.02	0.00	−0.07
10. IJV experience	6.42	9.87	0.00	−0.03	0.11	0.03	−0.01	−0.04	−0.13
11. Asset specificity	3.28	0.56	0.23	0.36	0.12	0.01	0.19	−0.18	−0.04
12. Acquisitive IJV	0.27	0.45	0.11	0.00	0.17	0.03	0.09	−0.05	0.23
13. Knowledge-based assets	3.31	0.84	0.29	0.29	0.13	0.06	0.01	0.14	−0.18
14. Cultural distance	1.77	0.67	0.03	−0.08	0.10	0.11	0.01	0.54	0.05
15. Administrative distance	1.81	0.62	0.00	0.05	−0.21	−0.13	0.06	0.04	0.10
16. Connectedness distance	0.71	0.21	0.09	0.15	−0.01	0.00	0.05	−0.15	−0.03
17. Economic distance	6.38	9.94	−0.12	−0.17	0.17	0.05	−0.11	0.08	0.01

Variable	8	9	10	11	12	13	14	15
1. Board control								
2. Board collaboration								
3. IJV size								
4. IJV board size								
5. Ownership split								
6. Number of partners								
7. CEO duality								
8. Prior ties								
9. Contractual complexity	0.03							
10. IJV experience	0.10	−0.05						

Table 1. *(Continued)*

Variable	8	9	10	11	12	13	14	15	
11. Asset specificity	−0.02	0.02	0.11						
12. Acquisitive IJV	−0.07	0.03	−0.11	−0.07					
13. Knowledge-based assets	0.13	0.26	0.07	0.15	−0.12				
14. Cultural distance	0.11	−0.03	0.06	−0.15	0.02	0.18			
15. Administrative distance	−0.02	0.13	−0.05	−0.17	0.12	0.12	0.19		
16. Connectedness distance	0.00	0.09	−0.09	0.02	−0.16	0.07	−0.29	0.17	
17. Economic distance	0.03	−0.24	0.06	0.01	0.12	−0.18	0.03	−0.64	−0.51

[a] $N = 114$. $p < 0.05$ for correlation above 0.19.

results are not affected by multicollinearity. On an average, there are about seven board members on IJV boards. Only about 20% of IJVs have CEOs who also hold the position of the Chairman of the board. Table 2 presents the results of multiple regressions. We estimate the equations with board control and board collaboration as dependent variables simultaneously in STATA using seemingly unrelated regression (rho = 0.71, $p < 0.001$). The positive correlation among the disturbances indicates that unobservables leading to greater board control also increase board collaboration. Model 1 and Model 3 are the baseline models that consist of the control variables. Model 2 and Model 4 are full models testing board control and board collaboration respectively ($p < 0.001$).

In terms of specific hypotheses, Hypothesis 1is about the effect of asset specificity, which we posited will be positively related to board control. The positive and significant coefficient estimate ($p < 0.01$) in Model 2 lends support to Hypothesis 1. In Model 4, asset specificity also shows a significant positive relationship ($p < 0.001$) with board collaboration, suggesting that boards will increase both control and collaboration to deal with asset specificity for the venture to create value and also protect parent firms' investments.

Our second hypothesis is concerned with the influence of knowledge-based assets on the collaboration function of boards. The results provide strong support for the hypothesis given the significant positive coefficient ($p < 0.05$) of knowledge-based assets in Model 4. Interestingly, knowledge-based assets are also positively related to board control ($p < 0.05$), perhaps because such assets can also be prone to opportunistic behavior and require more extensive oversight and formal governance.

Hypothesis 3 suggests that acquisitive IJVs are more likely to emphasize board control. The positive sign of the coefficient ($p < 0.01$) for acquisitive IJV in Model 2 confirms our hypothesis. Interestingly, this variable has neither a positive nor negative influence on collaboration by the board, suggesting that greenfield versus acquisitive ventures do not have greater coordination requirements necessitating collaboration, as might be anticipated.

Finally, cross-country differences were argued to be negatively associated with board collaboration in Hypothesis 4. Among the four types of differences across parent firms' nations, only cultural distance turned to be significant ($p < 0.05$), lending support for this hypothesis. Economic distance, on the other hand, shows a marginal negative effect ($p < 0.10$) on board control. We will further discuss these results in the following section.

Table 2. Seemingly Unrelated Regressions on Board Control and Collaboration.[a]

	Board Control				Board Collaboration			
	Model 1		Model 2		Model 3		Model 4	
Intercept	1.84*	(0.65)	0.57	(0.81)	1.78*	(0.67)	−0.55	(0.79)
Sector fixed effects	Incl.	–	Incl.	–	Incl.	–	Incl.	–
IJV size	0.03	(0.03)	0.01	(0.03)	0.02	(0.03)	0.01	(0.03)
IJV board size	−0.01	(0.01)	−0.01	(0.01)	−0.01	(0.01)	−0.01	(0.01)
Shared ownership	0.01*	(0.00)	0.00	(0.00)	0.01**	(0.00)	0.01*	(0.00)
Number of partners	0.33†	(0.18)	0.52**	(0.19)	0.22	(0.18)	0.56**	(0.19)
CEO duality	−0.25†	(0.14)	−0.23†	(0.13)	−0.05	(0.15)	0.01	(0.13)
Prior ties	0.02	(0.02)	0.03	(0.02)	0.02	(0.02)	0.03	(0.02)
Contractual complexity	0.13	(0.15)	−0.10	(0.15)	0.24	(0.16)	0.01	(0.15)
IJV experience	0.01	(0.01)	0.01	(0.01)	0.01	(0.01)	0.00	(0.00)
Asset specificity (H1)	–	–	0.28**	(0.09)	–	–	0.44***	(0.09)
Knowledge-based assets	–	–	0.18*	(0.13)	–	–	0.14*	(0.12)
Acquisitive IJV	–	–	0.37**	(0.07)	–	–	0.13	(0.07)
Cultural distance	–	–	−0.08	(0.09)	–	–	−0.20*	(0.09)
Administrative distance	–	–	−0.11	(0.11)	–	–	0.05	(0.11)
Collectedness distance	–	–	0.09	(0.28)	–	–	0.26	(0.28)
Economic distance	–	–	−0.01†	(0.01)	–	–	−0.01	(0.01)
R^2	0.19		0.36***		0.19		0.42***	

[a] $N = 114$. †$p < 0.10$; *$p < 0.05$; **$p < 0.01$; ***$p < 0.001$.

Results for the control variables also indicate that both the control and collaboration functions of the board tend to be greater as the number of partners in the joint venture increase, as might be anticipated given the greater governance and administrative complexity of such international collaborations.

DISCUSSION AND CONCLUSION

Contributions and Implications

While JV governance research has long acknowledged the importance of boards as an administrative control mechanism that partners in IJVs have at their disposal, little systematic and empirical research has been devoted to them. While recent research has investigated the involvement of IJV boards as well as their performance consequences (Klijn et al., 2013; Reuer et al., 2014), the roles that boards undertake when they are involved have not yet been systematically investigated. In this chapter, we have built upon corporate governance research that stresses the importance of boards undertaking control as well as collaboration functions (e.g., Hillman & Dalziel, 2003; Sundaramurthy & Lewis, 2003). Based on the assumption that directors have a finite amount of time and organize their tasks effectively (i.e., Tuggle et al., 2010), we predicted that certain conditions affect JV boards' involvement in control and collaborative activities. Given the unique context of IJVs in emerging markets, it is interesting to study the conditions when boards are engaged in particular functions. Not only does this provide new insights into the control and collaboration roles of IJV boards, it also provides new insights for managers operating in cross-national collaborations with a Chinese partner in particular.

In line with existing work in corporate governance research, our results confirm that board control and board collaboration are driven by organizational attributes as well as the contexts in which IJVs operate. More specifically, greater investments in specific assets or when the IJV is acquisitive in nature are associated with an IJV board exerting greater control over the venture. On the other hand, when partners invest in knowledge-based assets or are culturally similar, the board will engage more in collaboration rather than focusing on control.

While research on unitary organizations has shown that the control and collaboration functions of boards are inversely related given the finite amount of time (Tuggle et al., 2010), our results show that in IJVs these functions might be interrelated. For instance, asset specificity or knowledge-based assets also require boards to be engaged in collaboration whilst at the same time they are engaged in control. A potential argument can be that dedicated investments, once brought into the joint venture, are context-specific and require boards to be engaged in giving advice in order to make them useful. In addition, possible reasons for knowledge-based assets stimulating greater control might be that these assets are related to the core competence of a firm or otherwise lead to opportunism concerns, so partners would like to monitor the joint venture as well. As such, in contrast to the governance of unitary organizations our findings imply that the unique setting of joint ventures can lead to boards to be engaged in both functions.

A second contribution of this chapter is that we extend research on contracting and formal governance mechanisms in alliances (e.g., Hoetker & Mellewigt, 2009; Li, Poppo, & Zhou, 2010; Luo, 2002) by investigating boards as an ex-post governance mechanism. While equity ownership as well as contractual safeguards might function as important ex-ante governance mechanisms, boards undertake control and collaboration functions in order to monitor the IJV ex post. Our study, therefore, calls for the inclusion of boards in future studies on IJV governance, since it is an important mechanism that partners have at their disposal as well and important opportunities exist to develop theories of corporate governance in the setting of international joint ventures.

Finally, this chapter directly examines board control and collaboration, which advances beyond conceptual treatments of directors' roles or indirect proxies that are commonly used in previous empirical research (e.g., board size or composition). As such, we are able to address calls for research that opens up and investigates the black box of what boards actually do (e.g., Daily, 1996) and also study board functions in other organizational contexts besides unitary organizations (e.g., Krause et al., 2014). By collecting primary data to investigate what boards do, we are able to provide more detailed insights into the individual functions of boards.

Limitations and Future Research Directions

Despite the usefulness of collecting primary data in order to investigate the functions of boards, this chapter does have some noteworthy limitations that extensions to this study might examine. First, our measures for board control and board collaboration were both adapted from corporate governance studies that have investigated these functions in unitary organizations. Given the fact that IJVs have multiple international partners involved who collaborate under an incomplete contract, IJV boards can engage in additional control and collaboration functions. Our current measures do not take this into account and future research can adjust the scales to better accommodate the context of joint ventures and the unique control and collaboration requirements presented by this organizational form.

Another limitation of our study is that we have relied on single-key informants and it can be valuable to collect multiple responses per collaboration. The collection of multiple responses not only enables the triangulation of our results, but they can also reveal differences (i.e., such as in dedicated investments) that partners bring into their joint venture and how the composition of boards is potentially influenced by this. Finally, while our focus was on the determinants of board roles, we have not examined the actual performance consequences of these functions to investigate how boards matter for IJVs. It would also be interesting to know how joint venture characteristics potentially moderate the relationship between board functions and IJV performance to understand specific situations when the involvement of IJV boards is particularly important.

CONCLUSION

Research on the roles of IJV boards in China remains limited and a new research opportunity for corporate governance scholarship exists. In this chapter, we aim to investigate several determinants that shape the control and collaboration roles that IJV directors undertake. We argue that joint ventures possess similarities compared to unitary organizations as an organizational form, and they also have unique sources of complexity that can potentially influence the control and collaboration functions of IJV boards in China. By arguing and showing unique conditions that affect the roles that IJV boards undertake, we are able to address calls for research to open the black box of what boards actually do, as well as address the need to bring corporate governance theory to new organizational forms such as joint ventures. We hope this study encourages additional research that joins together the corporate governance and IJV governance literatures, which have largely developed independently to date.

ACKNOWLEDGMENTS

We would like to thank the Associate Editor Laszlo Tihanyi and anonymous reviewers for offering useful insights during the review process. We acknowledge the funding support provided by Guanghua-Cisco Leadership Research Institute and National Science Foundation of China (Grant 71132002).

REFERENCES

Adams, R. B., Hermalin, B. E., & Weisbach, M. S. (2009). *The role of boards of directors in corporate governance: A conceptual framework and survey*. Unpublished manuscript, Center for Responsible Business, University of California, Berkeley.

Armstrong, J. S., & Overton, T. S. (1977). Estimating nonresponse bias in mail surveys. *Journal of Marketing Research*, *14*, 396–403.

Balakrishnan, S., & Koza, M. (1993). Information asymmetry, adverse selection and joint venture: Theory and evidence. *Journal of Economic Behavior and Organization*, *20*(1), 99–117.

Beamish, P. W. (1988). *Multinational joint ventures in developing countries*. London: Routledge.

Beamish, P. W. (1993). The characteristics of joint ventures in the People's Republic of China. *Journal of International Marketing*, *1*(2), 29–48.

Beatty, R. P., & Zajac, E. J. (1994). Top management incentives, monitoring, and risk-sharing: A study of executive compensation, ownership and board structure in initial public offerings. *Administrative Science Quarterly*, *39*, 313–336.

Berry, H., Guillen, M. F., & Zhou, N. (2010). An institutional approach to cross-national distance. *Journal of International Business Studies*, *41*, 1460–1480.

Boone, A. L., Field, L. C., Karpoff, J. M., & Raheja, C. G. (2007). The determinants of corporate board size and composition: An empirical analysis. *Journal of Financial Economics*, *85*, 66–101.

Campbell, D. T. (1995). The informant in quantitative research. *American Journal of Sociology*, *60*, 339–342.

Chang, S. J., Chung, J., & Moon, J. J. (2013).When do wholly owned subsidiaries perform better than joint ventures? *Strategic Management Journal*, *34*, 317–337.

Chen, D., Park, S. H., & Newburry, W. (2009). Parent contribution and organizational control in international joint ventures. *Strategic Management Journal*, *30*, 1133.

Chen, S. F. S. (2008). The motives for international acquisitions: Capability procurements, strategic considerations, and the role of ownership structures. *Journal of International Business Studies*, *39*(3), 454–471.

Chi, T. (1994). Trading in strategic resources: Necessary conditions, transaction cost problems, and choice of exchange structure. *Strategic Management Journal*, *15*, 271–290.

Child, J., & Tse, D. K. (2001). China's transition and its implications for international business. *Journal of International Business Studies*, *32*(1), 5–21.

Coles, J. L., Daniel, N. D., & Naveen, L. (2008). Boards: Does one size fit all? *Journal of Financial Economics*, *87*, 329–356.

Contractor, F. J., & Lorange, P. (2002). Why should firms cooperate? The strategy and economics basis for cooperative ventures. In F. J. Contractor & P. Lorange (Eds.), *Cooperative strategies in international business* (pp. 3–30). Oxford: Elsevier.

Currall, S. C., & Inkpen, A. C. (2002). A multilevel approach to trust in joint ventures. *Journal of International Business Studies*, *33*(3), 479–495.

Daily, C. M. (1996). Governance patterns in bankruptcy reorganizations. *Strategic Management Journal*, *17*(5), 355–375.

Daily, C. M., Dalton, D. R., & Cannella, A. A. (2003). Corporate governance: Decades of dialogue and data. *Academy of Management Review*, *28*, 371–382.

Dalton, D. R., Daily, C. M., Ellstrand, A. E., & Johnson, J. L. (1998). Meta-analytic reviews of board composition, leadership structure, and financial performance. *Strategic Management Journal*, *19*, 269–290.

Das, T. K., & Teng, B. (2001). A resource-based theory of strategic alliances. *Journal of Management*, *26*(1), 31–61.

Davis, J. H., Schoorman, F. D., & Donaldson, L. (1997). Toward a stewardship theory of management. *Academy of Management Review*, *22*, 20.

Dillman, D.(1978). *Mail and telephone survey: The total design method.* New York, NY: Wiley.

Dong, L., & Glaister, K. W. (2006). Motives and partner selection criteria in international strategic alliances: Perspectives of Chinese firms. *International Business Review*, *15*(6), 577–600.

Eisenhardt, K. M. (1989). Agency theory: An assessment and review. *Academy of Management Review*, *14*(1), 57–74.

Finkelstein, S., & D'Aveni, R. A. (1994). CEO duality as a double-edged sword: How boards of directors balance entrenchment avoidance and unity of command. *Academy of Management Journal*, *37*, 1079–1108.

Forbes, D. P., & Milliken, F. J. (1999). Cognition and corporate governance: Understanding boards of directors as strategic decision-making groups. *Academy of Management Review*, *24*, 485–505.

Gaur, A. S., & Lu, J. W. (2007). Ownership strategies and survival of foreign subsidiaries: Institutional distance and experience. *Journal of Management*, *33*(1), 84–110.

Geringer, J. M., & Hebert, L. (1989). Control and performance of international joint ventures. *Journal of International Business Studies*, *19*, 235–254.

Ghemawat, P. (2001). Distance still matters. *Harvard Business Review*, *79*(8), 137–149.

Gong, Y., Shenkar, O., Luo, Y., & Nyaw, M. K. (2007). Do multiple parents help or hinder international joint venture performance? The mediating roles of contract completeness and partner cooperation. *Strategic Management Journal*, *28*, 1021–1034.

Gulati, R. (1995). Does familiarity breed trust? The implications of repeated ties for contractual choice in alliances. *Academy of Management Journal*, *38*, 85–112.

Gulati, R., & Singh, H. (1998). The architecture of cooperation: Managing coordination costs and appropriation concerns in strategic alliances. *Administrative Science Quarterly*, *43*, 781–814.

Gulati, R., & Westphal, J. D. (1999). Cooperative or controlling? The effects of CEO-board relations and the content of interlocks on the formation of joint ventures. *Administrative Science Quarterly*, *44*, 473–506.

Hambrick, D. C., Li, J., Xin, K., & Tsui, A. (2001). Compositional gaps and downward spirals in international joint venture management groups. *Strategic Management Journal, 22*, 1033.

Hambrick, D. C., Werder, A., & Zajac, E. J. (2008). New directions in corporate governance research. *Organization Science, 19*, 381–385.

Harman, H. H. (1967). *Modern factor analysis*. Chicago, IL: University of Chicago Press.

Harzing, A.-W. (2002). Acquisitions versus greenfield investments: International strategy and management of entry modes. *Strategic Management Journal, 23*, 211–227.

Hennart, J. F. (1988). A transaction cost theory of equity joint ventures. *Strategic Management Journal, 9*, 361–374.

Hennart, J. F. (1991). The transaction cost theory of joint ventures: An empirical study of Japanese subsidiaries in the United States. *Management Science, 37*(4), 483–497.

Hennart, J. F., & Zeng, M. (2002). Cross-cultural differences and joint venture longevity. *Journal of International Business Studies, 33*, 699–716.

Hermalin, B. E., & Weisbach, M. S. (1988). The determinants of board composition. *Rand Journal of Economics, 19*, 589–606.

Hewitt, I. (1987). *Joint ventures* (1st ed.). London: Sweet and Maxwell.

Hill, C. W. L., & Snell, S. A. (1988). External control, corporate strategy, and firm performance in research-intensive industries. *Strategic Management Journal, 9*, 577–590.

Hillman, A. J., & Dalziel, T. (2003). Boards of directors and firm performance: Integrating agency and resource dependence perspectives. *Academy of Management Review, 28*, 383–396.

Hoetker, G., & Mellewigt, T. (2009). Choice and performance of governance mechanisms: Matching alliance governance to alliance type. *Strategic Management Journal, 30*, 1025–1044.

Holburn, G. L. F., & Zelner, B. A. (2010). Political capabilities, policy risk and international investment strategy: Evidence from the global electric power generation industry. *Strategic Management Journal, 31*(12), 1290–1315.

House, R. L., Hanges, P. W., Javidan, M., Dorfman, P., & Gupta, V. (2004). *Culture, leadership, and organizations: The GLOBE study of 62 societies*. Beverly Hills, CA: Sage.

Jemison, D. B., & Sitkin, S. B. (1986). Corporate acquisitions: A process perspective. *Academy of Management Review, 11*(1), 145–163.

Jensen, M. C., & Meckling, W. H. (1976). Theory of the firm: Managerial behavior agency costs and capital structure. *Journal of Financial Economics, 3*(4), 305–360.

Judge, W. Q., & Zeithaml, C. P. (1992). Institutional and strategic choice perspectives on board involvement in the strategic decision process. *Academy of Management Journal, 35*, 766–794.

Khanna, T., & Palepu, K. (1997). Why focused strategies may be wrong for emerging markets. *Harvard Business Review, 75*(4), 41–51.

Klein, B., Crawford, R. A., & Alchian, A. A. (1978). Vertical integration, appropriable rents, and the competitive contracting process. *Journal of Law and Economics, 21*, 297–326.

Klijin, E., Reuer, J. J., Van den Bosch, F. A. J., & Volberda, H. W. (2013). Performance implications of IJV boards: A contingency perspective. *Journal of Management Studies, 50*(7), 1245–1266.

Kogut, B., & Zander, U. (1992). Knowledge of the firm, combinative capabilities and the replication of technology. *Organization Studies, 3*, 383–397.

Kosnik, R. D. (1987). Greenmail: A study of board performance in corporate governance. *Administrative Science Quarterly*, *32*, 163–185.

Krause, R., Semadini, M., & Cannella, A. A., Jr. (2014). CEO duality: A review and research agenda. *Journal of Management*, *40*(1), 256–286.

Kumar, S., & Seth, A. (1998). The design of coordination and control mechanisms for management joint venture-parent relationships. *Strategic Management Journal*, *19*, 579–599.

Li, D., Eden, L., Hitt, M. A., Ireland, R. D., & Garrett, R. P. (2012). Governance in multilateral R&D alliances. *Organization Science*, *23*, 1191–1210.

Li, J., Poppo, L., & Zhou, K. (2010). Relational mechanisms, formal contracts, and local knowledge acquisition by international subsidiaries. *Strategic Management Journal*, *31*, 349–370.

Li, J., Zhou, C., & Zajac, E. (2009). Control, collaboration, and productivity in international joint ventures: Theory and evidence. *Strategic Management Journal*, *30*, 865.

Linck, J. S., Netter, J. M., & Yang, T. (2008). The determinants of board structure. *Journal of Financial Economics*, *87*, 308–328.

Lorsch, J. W., & MacIver, E. (1989). *Pawns or potentates: The reality of America's corporate boards*. Boston, MA: Harvard Business School Press.

Luo, Y. (2002). Capability exploitation and building in a foreign market: Implications for multinational enterprise. *Organization Science*, *13*(1), 48.

Luo, Y. (2007). Are joint venture partners more opportunistic in a more volatile environment? *Strategic Management Journal*, *38*, 39–60.

Luo, Y., Shenkar, O., & Nyaw, M. K. (2001). A dual-parent perspective on control and performance in international joint ventures: Lessons from a developing economy. *Journal of International Business Studies*, *32*(1), 41–58.

Mace, M. L. (1971). *Directors: Myth and reality*. Boston, MA: Harvard University.

Meyer, K. E. (2004). Perspectives on multinational enterprises in emerging economies. *Journal of International Business Studies*, *35*(4), 259–276.

Meyer, M. W. (2011). Is it capitalism? *Management and Organization Review*, *7*(1), 5–18.

Miller, D., & Shamsie, J. (1996). The resource-based view of the firm in two environments: The Hollywood firm studios from 1936–1965. *Academy of Management Journal*, *39*, 519–543.

Mjoen, H., & Tallman, S. (1997). Control and performance in international joint ventures. *Organization Science*, *8*, 257–274.

Nooteboom, B. (1996). Trust, opportunism and governance: A process and control model. *Organization Studies*, *17*(6), 985–1010.

Nunnally, J. C. (1978). *Psychometric theory* (2nd ed.). New York, NY: McGraw-Hill.

Oviatt, B. M. (1988). Agency and transaction cost perspectives on the manager-shareholder relationship: Incentives for congruent interests. *Academy of Management Review*, *13*(2), 214–226.

Oxley, J. E., & Sampson, R. C. (2004). The scope and governance of international R&D alliances. *Strategic Management Journal*, *25*, 723–749.

Parkhe, A. (1991). Interfirm diversity, organizational learning and longevity in global strategic alliances. *Journal of International Business Studies*, *22*(4), 579–601.

Parkhe, A. (1993). Strategic alliance structuring: A game theoretic and transaction cost examination of interfirm cooperation. *Academy of Management Journal*, *36*, 794–829.

Pearce, R. (2001). Looking inside the joint venture to help understand the link between inter-parent cooperation and performance. *Journal of Management Studies*, *38*(4), 557.

Peng, M. W. (2003). Institutional transitions and strategic choices. *Academy of Management Review*, *28*(2), 275–296.

Petrovic, J., Kakabadse, A., & Kakabadse, N. K. (2006). International joint venture directors' contribution to board effectiveness: Learning from the literature. *Management Decision*, *44*(3), 346.

Pfeffer, J., & Salancik, G. R. (1978). *The external control of organizations: A resource dependence perspective*. New York, NY: Harper & Row.

Poppo, L., & Zenger, T. (2002). Do formal contracts and relational governance function as substitutes or complements? *Strategic Management Journal*, *23*, 707–725.

Ravasi, D., & Zattoni, A. (2006). Exploring the political side of board involvement in strategy: A study of mixed-ownership institutions. *The Journal of Management Studies*, *43*(8), 1671.

Rechner, P., & Dalton, D. (1991). CEO duality and organizational performance: A longitudinal analysis. *Strategic Management Journal*, *12*, 155–160.

Reuer, J. J., & Arino, A. (2007). Strategic alliance contracts: Dimensions and determinants of contractual complexity. *Strategic Management Journal*, *28*, 313–330.

Reuer, J. J., Klijn, E., Lioukas, C. S. (2014). Board involvement in international joint ventures. *Strategic Management Journal*, *35*(11), 1626–1644.

Saunders, M. K. T., Thornhill, A., & Lewis, P. (2009). *Research methods for business students* (5th ed.). UK: Prentice Hall.

Schneider, S. C., & de Meyer, A. (1991). Interpreting and responding to strategic issues: The impact of national culture. *Strategic Management Journal*, *12*, 307–320.

Shenkar, O., & Zeira, Y. (1992). Role conflict and role ambiguity of chief executive officers in international joint ventures. *Journal of International Business Studies*, *23*(1), 55.

Shenkar, O., & Zeira, Y. (1987). Human resources management in international joint ventures: Directions for research. *Academy of Management Review*, *12*, 546–557.

Si, S. X., & Bruton, G. D. (1999). Knowledge transfer in international joint ventures in transitional economies: The China experience. *Academy of Management Executive*, *13*(1), 83.

Sim, A. B., & Ali, Y. (1998). Performance of international joint ventures from developing and developed countries: An empirical study in a developing country context. *Journal of World Business*, *33*(4), 357–377.

Stiles, P. (2001). The impact of the board on strategy: An empirical examination. *Journal of Management studies*, *38*(5), 627–649.

Sundaramurthy, C., & Lewis, M. (2003). Control and collaboration: Paradoxes of governance. *Academy of Management Review*, *28*(3), 397.

Tsui, A. S., Schoonhoven, C. B., Meyer, M. W., Lau, C.-M., & Milkovich, G. T. (2004). Organization and management in the midst of societal transformation: The People's Republic of China. *Organization Science*, *15*(2), 133–144.

Tuggle, C. S., Sirmon, D. G., Christopher, R. R., & Bierman, L. (2010). Commanding board of director attention: Investigating how organizational performance and CEO duality affect board member's attention to monitoring. *Strategic Management Journal*, *31*(10), 946–968.

Vanhonacker, W. (1997). Entering China: An unconventional approach. *Harvard Business Review*, *75*(2), 130–140.

Walsh, J. P., Wang, E. P., & Xin, K. R. (1999). Same bed, different dreams: Working relationships in Sino-American joint ventures. *Journal of World Business*, *34*, 69–93.

Westphal, J. (1999). Collaboration in the boardroom: Behavioral and performance consequences of CEO-board social ties. *Academy of Management Journal*, *42*, 7–25.

Westphal, J. D., & Stern, I. (2007). Flattery will get you everywhere (especially if you are a male Caucasian): How ingratiation, boardroom behavior, and demographic minority status affect additional board appointments at U.S. companies. *Administrative Science Quarterly*, *50*, 207–288.

Williamson, O. E. (1985). *The economic institutions of capitalism*. New York, NY: Free Press.

Xu, D., & Shenkar, O. (2002). Institutional distance and the multinational enterprise. *Academy of Management Review*, *27*(4), 608–618.

Yan, A., & Gray, B. (1994). Bargaining power, management control and performance in international joint ventures: A comparative case study. *Academy of Management Journal*, *37*(6), 1478.

Yan, A., & Gray, B. (2001). Antecedents and effects of parent control in international joint ventures. *Journal of Management Studies*, *38*(3), 393.

Yiu, D., & Makino, S. (2002). The choice between joint venture and wholly owned subsidiary: An institutional perspective. *Organization Science*, *13*(6), 667–683.

Zahra, S. A., & Pearce, J. A. (1989). Boards of directors and corporate financial performance: A review and integrative model. *Journal of Management*, *15*(2), 291–334.

Zhang, J., & Keh, H. T. (2010). Interorganizational exchanges in China: Organizational forms and governance mechanisms. *Management and Organization Review*, *6*(1), 123–147.

Zhang, Y., Li, H., Hitt, M. A., & Cui, G. (2007). R&D intensity and international joint venture performance in an emerging market: Moderating effects of market focus and ownership structure. *Journal of International Business Studies*, *38*, 944–960.

APPENDIX: MEASUREMENT SCALES

Board Control

To measure board control within the IJV, respondents were asked, "To what extent are joint venture board members involved in the following?" The five-point scale was anchored at either extreme using the labels "no extent" and "very large extent." Respondents answered this question for the following five activities:

1. Deferring manager's judgment on final strategic decisions
2. Seeking information from management or other director for the purpose of evaluating the performance of JV management
3. Constructively criticizing strategic proposal put forth by management
4. Suggesting revisions to strategic proposal put forth by management
5. Exert control overall management decision-making

Board Collaboration

To measure board collaboration within the IJV, respondents were asked, "To what extent are joint venture board members involved in the following?" The five-point scale was anchored at either extreme using the labels "no extent" and "very large extent." Respondents answered this question for the following five activities:

1. Providing advice and counsel in discussions outside of board meetings
2. Providing information or expertise in regards to strategy or policy issue
3. Answering questions from the management about strategy or policy issue
4. Socializing with the IJV manager
5. Being acquaintances or friends of IJV general manager

Asset Specificity

Respondents were asked to evaluate on a five-point scale ranging from "negligible" to "substantial" for the following six statements:

1. Our investment in dedicated personnel specific to this venture is…
2. Our investment in dedicated facilities to this venture is…

3. If we decided to stop this venture, the difficulty we would have in redeploying our people and facilities presently serving the venture to other uses would be…
4. The time required to learn about our partner's style has been…
5. The time and effort of coordination with our partner required to perform our tasks in the venture have been…
6. If this venture were to dissolve, our nonrecoverable investments in equipment, people, etc. would be…

Contractual Complexity

Respondents were asked, "Which safeguards listed below were put into the formal agreement of this venture? (tick all that apply)"

1. Periodic written reports of all relevant transactions
2. Prompt written notice of any departures from the agreement
3. The right to examine and audit all relevant records through a firm of CPAs
4. Designation of certain information as proprietary and subject to confidentiality provisions of the contract
5. Nonuse of proprietary information even after termination of agreement
6. Termination of agreement
7. Arbitration clauses
8. Lawsuit provisions

SOURCES OF COMPETITIVENESS AND MULTINATIONALITY: EMERGING MARKET FIRMS IN THE ELECTRONICS INDUSTRY

Sumon Kumar Bhaumik, Nigel Driffield and Ying Zhou

ABSTRACT

The extant literature on emerging market multinationals (EMNEs) suggest that they derive their advantages from factors such as economies of scale, and that they internationalise, in large measure, to access technology. However, support for this framework typically comes from analysis of static data, comparing EMNEs and OECD MNEs at a point in time. Little attention is paid to their development paths in a dynamic setting. We examine these propositions directly using an approach that enables us to decompose productivity growth of firms into its components, namely, changes in scale economies, technological progress and technical efficiency. We compare Chinese MNEs with their non-MNE domestic counterparts and developed country MNEs that have operations in China. We demonstrate that Chinese MNEs continue to derive much of their productivity growth from changes in scale economies, while

Emerging Economies and Multinational Enterprises
Advances in International Management, Volume 28, 267–296

ISSN: 1571-5027/doi:10.1108/S1571-502720150000028013

developed country MNEs continue to have an advantage with respect to technical progress. Both these types of MNEs have a significant advantage over Chinese non-MNE domestic firms.

Keywords: Competitive advantage; firm-specific advantage; country-specific advantage; Chinese MNEs; technological progress

INTRODUCTION

Emerging market multinational enterprises (EMNEs) continue to pose a conceptual challenge to international business (IB) scholars because they cannot be conceptualised as possessing the forms of ownership advantages that are assumed to drive internationalisation within the OLI-eclectic paradigm (Meyer & Peng, 2005; Meyer & Xia, 2012; Ramamurti, 2008). It has been argued that they enjoy instead country-specific advantages (CSAs) such as access to natural resources as oil and minerals, access to cheap labour and capital, and proximity to domestic governments (Ramamuti & Singh, 2009). The literature on EMNEs further emphasises home market size, and resulting economies of scale, as a key country-specific advantage explaining EMNEs. The popular wisdom concerning EMNEs is that they leverage these CSAs to internationalise and, thereafter, use internationalisation to develop traditional technological capabilities. Their foreign direct investment (FDI) is therefore characterised as technology-capability seeking (Mathews, 2002, 2006).[1] A complementary line of analysis of EMNEs proposes that the advantage of these firms lies in the fact that they are adept at working within contexts of institutional voids and market failures (Bhaumik, Driffield, & Pal, 2010; Khanna & Palepu, 2010).[2]

While the existing literature on EMNEs is possibly sufficient to explain internationalisation without firm-specific advantages (FSAs), our understanding of EMNEs is incomplete. To begin with, there is little empirical evidence to substantiate the argument that CSAs play a significant role as an enabler of overseas investment of emerging market firms. It is largely a conjecture. Further, CSAs do not constitute proprietary advantages, by definition, and some of them, such as scale economies and cheap labour, are potentially available to all firms, including developed country MNEs that have large operations in emerging market economies. This, in turn, raises two related but slightly different questions. First, how is it that only a small fraction of emerging market firms are able to leverage CSAs to internationalise? Second, what implications does this have for the sustainability of CSA-based competitive advantage, especially vis-à-vis developed country MNEs that have traditional ownership advantages?

This, in turn, has several implications for the development on the literature on EMNEs. Even if the importance of CSAs relative to traditional ownership advantages were to be established, one cannot look at EMNEs in isolation, as a distinct group, or, where comparisons are undertaken, compare them with developed country MNEs alone. Indeed, it is necessary to compare EMNEs not merely with developed country MNEs but also with non-MNE domestic firms in their own country in order to fully understand the source of their competitive advantage. Without this comparison, a theory about the internationalisation of emerging market firms is incomplete. Specifically, in the absence of traditional ownership advantages, CSAs may be necessary for internationalisation of emerging market firms but they may not be sufficient, as evident from the internationalisation of a tiny minority of emerging markets firms. A theory of internationalisation, by contrast, should be able to say how necessary and sufficient conditions for internationalisation of these firms may be met. Further, one has to take a dynamic view of these firms, and examine how CSAs and traditional ownership advantages manifested through technological progress change over time for EMNEs and their domestic and foreign peer groups. Such an analysis would provide a dynamic view of competitive advantage.

The reason for this gap in the literature is the absence of methodological approaches that can clearly demonstrate that relative ability of EMNEs and their non-MNE counterparts to exploit CSAs such as scale economies as well as FSAs such as technological progress better than others within the same context and industry. Further, the literature fails to exploit data which can facilitate appropriate methodology to explore this in dynamic terms. An understanding about the competitive advantages of EMNEs in the short run as well as over time would be incomplete unless there is (a) a comparison of EMNEs, their non-MNE counterparts and developed country MNEs, and (b) an examination of the changes in CSA-based advantages (e.g. scale economies) and traditional ownership advantages (viz., technological progress) over time.

Typically, the literature on EMNEs is somewhat loosely based on the concept of resource dependency, with FDI from emerging markets assumed to be associated with knowledge or technology sourcing (Gaffney, Kedia, & Clampit, 2013; Kedia, Gaffney, & Clampit, 2012). Following Driffield and Love (2005) and De Propris and Driffield (2006), it is possible to argue that the learning that occurs between the foreign and domestic sectors in a given country, or between inward investors in a given location is essentially technologically neutral, including agglomeration effects (capturing external economies of scale), learning by doing, demonstration effects, as well as classic technology transfer. This is likely to be particularly true of EMNEs, given their distance from the global technological frontier. However, to the best of our knowledge, while there is literature on the dynamics of changing competitive advantage of EMNEs (Athreye, Kale, & Ramani, 2009; Chittoor, Sarkar, Ray, & Aulakh, 2009) and on the impact of capabilities on performance (Ethiraj, Kale, Krishnan, & Singh, 2005), there is as yet no empirical evidence concerning the relative importance of knowledge acquisition and initial CSAs in explaining subsequent EMNE performance. A better understanding of the relationship between multinationality, scale economies, and technological progress is not only essential to facilitate for the presumptions on the basis of which theories about EMNEs are being developed, it also has implications for the related literature on global value chains. If productivity growth in EMNEs continues to be based on scale efficiencies, despite outward investment, then the competitive advantage of EMNEs is likely to remain restricted to industries that require large sunk costs (e.g. energy and metals) and where competitive advantage is closely associated with scale economies.

Our paper makes three significant contributions to the literature on EMNEs. First, using a novel methodology that is well tested in the literature on productivity analysis, but is yet unused in the IB literature, we explore the drivers of EMNE performance. We demonstrate that scale economies, a proxy for CSAs, dominate sources of traditional ownership advantages such as technological progress in a large emerging market economy. Second, we provide a heuristic explanation about why not all emerging market firms are able to exploit CSAs to internationalise. Finally, we provide empirical evidence about the changes in scale economies and technological progress of EMNEs and their developed market competitors over time, thereby providing prima facie evidence about the dynamic aspects of EMNEs' competiveness relative to their global competitors.

We extend the existing literature by comparing the changing contributions of scale economies and technological progress to productivity of Chinese firms, both MNEs and non-MNEs, with those of western MNEs, within the electronics industry. This offers the opportunity to apply our method to a well-defined sector[3] that accounted for 10% of China's GDP growth and about 35% of China's foreign trade at the end of the last decade (APCO, 2010). The paper proceeds by discussing the research setting, and thereafter building on the existing theoretical analysis of EMNEs within the context of their internationalisation and performance to develop a set of hypotheses that enable us to make the aforementioned contribution ('Competitive Advantage of Emerging Market Firms' section). We also present in detail the novel methodological approach that enables us to distinguish between technological progress, the basis for traditional firm-specific ownership advantages in MNEs, and other drivers of productivity growth such as change in scale economies, which is considered to be an important component of country-specific advantages that are enjoyed by emerging market firms ('Methodology and Data' section).

THE RESEARCH SETTING

The focus of our analysis is the electronics sector, an industry in which it is accepted that China has significant comparative and competitive advantage, at least in terms of production. This is fuelled in part by the high levels of both inward investment and outsourcing to China by western firms, and significant economies of scale.

From 2001 to 2008 the Chinese electronics sector generated double digit growth rates, peaking in 2005 with a growth rate of 45%. Based on Ministry of Industry and Information Technology (MIIT) figures, the industry grew at 6% even in 2010, recovering from the decline on global demand through the crisis. The sector also accounts for some 30% of total exports, exceeding $520 billion in 2009. Equally, imports exceeding $130 billion in 2009. The United States is the largest export market, followed by Japan and the European Union, led by Germany and the Netherlands. This shows clear evidence of export penetration into the most technologically advanced electronics markets, though domestic demand is also very strong, with home sales growth outstripping export growth over the period. This is boosted by government intervention, encouraging adoption of newer more energy efficient consumer electronics domestically.[4]

However, at the same time, there has been much talk of the position of Chinese manufacturing within global supply chains, and the 'smile of value creation', suggesting that China dominates by volume but not by value. The financial crisis has therefore placed significant pressure on the margins of Chinese exporters, who as a result are seeking to move up the value chain, with internationalisation playing a key role in this (Wei, Zheng, Liu, & Lu, 2014).

As such therefore, this industry is one that may be expected to be an industry that can spawn 'traditional' EMNEs whose competitive advantage lie in economies of scale and other country-specific advantages, but also provide a comparison in terms of both the global technology frontier in terms of the large number of MNEs from OECD firms, and a large domestic Chinese sector who have not internationalised. This provides therefore a focus for our analysis, concerning the differences between domestic firms that rely on that competitive advantage and Chinese MNEs that have to build on CSAs and potentially move up the value chain.

Table 1 illustrates the distribution of firms across the sector, with Chinese firms more prevalent in components (2611), circuit boards (2612) and consumer electronics. These typically represent activities higher up the supply chain, and lower down the value chain, than emerging for example optical media (2680) or electric medical equipment (2660). These are also sectors where economies of scale, rather than for example internal innovation are key drivers of productivity.

Fig. 1 presents this contrast in more detail. It reports the average size of Chinese MNEs and non-MNEs, as well as that of developed country (OECD member countries[5]) MNEs, by 4-digit industries within the electronics sector. Size is captured by both value of output (Panel A) and employment (Panel B). The figure suggests that both Chinese MNEs (where they are present) and developed country MNEs are significantly larger than Chinese domestic non-MNEs. This gives a good deal of credence to the

Table 1. Distribution of Firms by Types and 4-Digit Industries.

NACE 4 Digit	Industry Name	Chinese MNE	Chinese Non-MNE	OECD MNE
2611	Electronic components	0.30	1.69	10.03
2612	Loaded electronic boards	–	2.16	7.08
2620	Computers and peripheral equipment	0.14	0.60	2.32
2630	Communication equipment	0.41	0.82	5.05
2640	Consumer electronics	0.54	1.62	6.20
2651	Instruments and appliances for measuring, testing, and navigation	0.05	0.10	4.66
2652	Watches and clocks	–	–	6.07
2660	Irradiation, electrometrical, and electrotherapeutic equipment	–	0.16	2.88
2670	Optical instruments and photographic equipment	0.17	0.17	3.70
2680	Magnetic and optical media	–	–	3.14

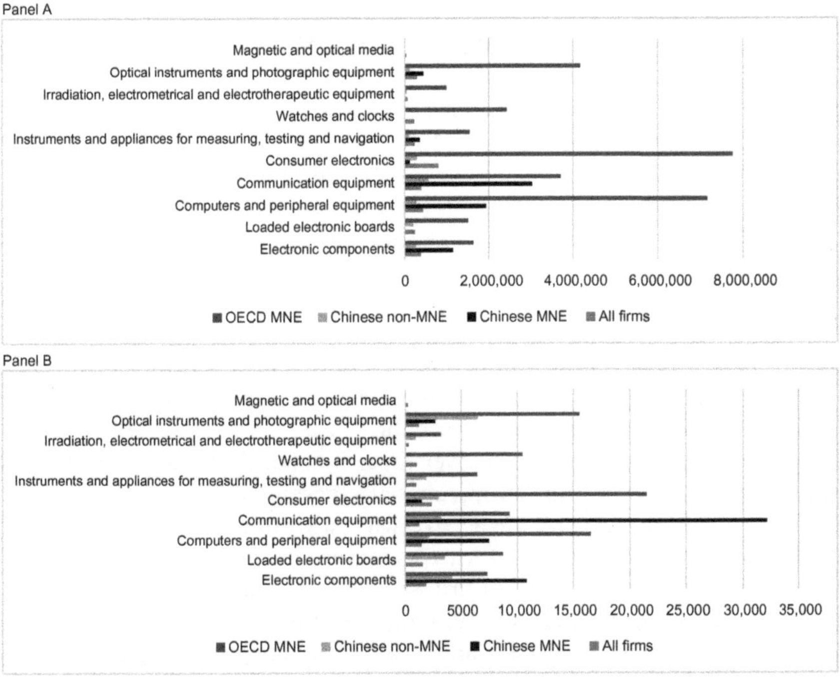

Fig. 1. Relative Size of Firms by Firm Type. Panel A: By output. Panel B: By Employment.

'scale economies' explanation of FDI from emerging markets, and also points to significant differences between Chinese MNEs and Chinese non-MNEs in terms of their ability to harness economies of scale. The scale dominance of Chinese MNEs over non-MNEs is particularly visible in industries such as communication equipment, and computers and peripheral equipment. Importantly, developed country MNEs have value of output and employment levels that are comparable to those of Chinese MNEs, lending credence to our research question as to whether the CSA-based competitive advantage of EMNEs is sustainable in the long run.

However, from these headline numbers, it is difficult to make a case for either the importance of CSAs in emerging market contexts or the dynamics of competitiveness of EMNEs vis-à-vis their developed market competitors over time. It is also not possible to get a sense of why Chinese non-MNEs do not have the same scale as the Chinese MNEs in sectors where the latter are present. This requires a more finely grained analysis.

COMPETITIVE ADVANTAGE OF EMERGING MARKET FIRMS

Ramamurti (2008), Sauvant, Mascheck, and McAllister (2010), Guillen and Garcia-Canal (2009) and Meyer, Mudambi, and Narula (2011) highlight what they argue to be the essential difference between EMNEs and developed country MNEs. They argue that in contrast to developed country MNEs, who develop firm-specific advantages in the form of new technology or knowledge, Asian and other emerging market MNEs have developed advantages based on economies of scale and the ability to deliver relatively standard products at very low cost.[6] Ramamurti (2008) argues that in part this could be an outcome of a late mover advantage whereby emerging market firms can choose the largest scale available ex ante, presumably with the benefit of the information acquired by the industry/sector about optimal production scales over time. Further, Bhaumik et al. (2010) argue that more important is operational efficiency and market power at home as key drivers of their overseas investment, such that non-technological advantages are at least as important as technological advantages when explaining sources of firm-specific advantages of EMNES.

This analysis then requires a more detailed understanding of the nature of the interaction between FSA and CSA in the context of both emerging markets and EMNEs. For example, Bhaumik and Driffield (2011) demonstrate that market leadership in such countries is a feature of the ability to successfully imitate global market leaders, and to operate successfully in an environment characterised by institutional voids. However, they also show that the ownership structures, with cross holdings, and the use of internal labour and capital markets that support this market position, do not necessarily lend themselves to the degree of transparency required for FDI. We therefore argue that the ability to lever CSAs into internationalisation requires not only CSAs, and the ability to operate successfully in the context of institutional voids, but to do this in a way that is consistent with internationalisation.

Subsequently, the literature argues that firms seek to leverage these into technology sourcing abroad. Meyer and Xia (2012), for example, focus on technology acquisition and the use of cash flow generated at home to facilitate this,[7] while Mathews (2002, 2006) emphasises the importance of 'learning' in the narrative concerning the internationalisation of emerging market firms. This view is influenced by high profile acquisitions of high technology developed country firms by their emerging market counterparts, such as Tata's acquisition of Jaguar Land-Rover and Lenovo's acquisition of IBM's personal computer business.[8] There is also wider evidence about the centrality of acquisition of intangible resources (or 'knowledge') in the overseas acquisition strategies of EMNEs (Gaffney et al., 2013; Kedia et al., 2012).

It is reasonable therefore to hypothesise that CSAs account for a much greater share of the competitive advantage of emerging market firms, especially EMNEs, than traditional ownership advantages. If productivity growth is taken as the basis for competitive advantage, CSAs such as scale efficiencies should, therefore, contribute to a greater share of this growth than proxies of traditional advantages such as technological progress.

While this explanation may be valid, it is but part of a more complex story. The popular wisdom about CSA-based competitive advantage of EMNEs does not provide an explanation as to why some emerging market firms become MNEs while others do not. Indeed, as mentioned earlier in this paper, the literature on EMNEs typically relies on explanations that are linked to the literature on institutional voids and missing markets, see for example Kim et al. (2010). Explanations include for example preferential access to government contracts, or access to finance that is more generally restricted to imperfect capital markets, or finally a lack of managerial resources. An important question therefore is whether, controlling for country of origin, there is also evidence of FSAs when comparing EMNEs with purely domestic firms from the same country. These can take the form of scale economies, but may include technological capacity.

Our conjecture concerning the relationship between CSAs and FSAs whose interaction facilitate internationalisation of emerging market firms is captured in Fig. 2. The crucial link here between market leadership in a domestic setting, and the ability to leverage this into internationalisation are the drivers of performance. Even in the absence of what may be considered 'traditional' FSAs in a western MNE sense, we suggest that at the firm level successful EMNEs must possess two key features. The first, as we outline above, is the ability to operate successfully in an environment characterised by institutional voids, and the second is the ability to assimilate and even imitate existing externally sourced technology. These two features are key to market leadership in emerging markets, along with economies of scale and the other CSAs discussed above, but are also key for successful internationalisation. It is the ability to harness these that sets EMNEs apart from domestic firms at a similar scale.

FSAs that enable firms to advanced technology, and to better exploit CSAs are difficult to quantify, or even to characterise, as they generally

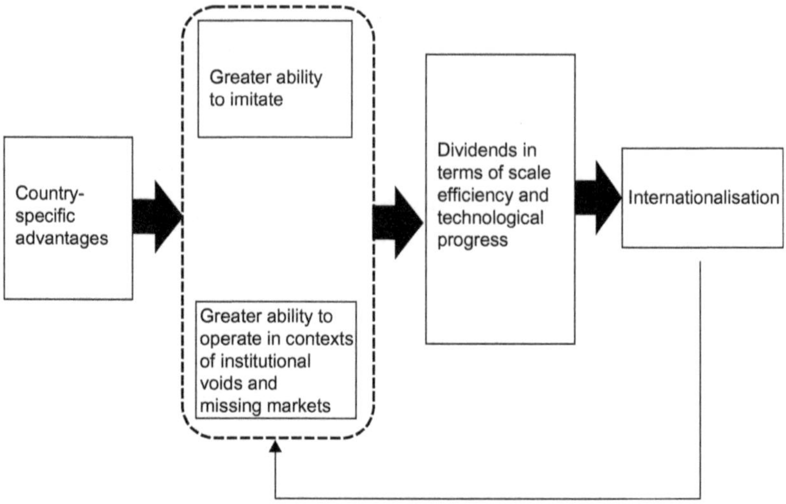

Fig. 2. Interaction of CSAs and FSAs of Emerging Market Firms and Internationalisation.

remain embedded in the managerial-entrepreneurial teams and could be path dependent on past experiences of organisations. However, we should be able to observe significant differences in not just scale economies but other measurable outcomes such as technical progress of the firms that presumably have this capacity and hence can internationalise, and their non-MNE domestic counterparts. On the basis of this discussion, we propose the following:

H1a. CSAs such as scale economies contribute to competitive advantage of emerging market firms more than traditional FSAs that are reflected in technological progress.

H1b. Firms in emerging markets that internationalise are better able to exploit CSAs and, in part, this is reflected in observable measures such as technical progress.

The product life-cycle hypothesis of Vernon (1966) suggests that developed country MNEs move operations to emerging market economies only after their products have been standardised, at which point competitiveness is dependent on cost advantages as opposed to technological advantages. In his re-evaluation of the hypothesis, Vernon (1979) acknowledges that, at least in principle, firms may strategically decide to standardise the products on a world basis, to 'reduce or avoid the costs of processing and interpreting the information that bears on the distinctive needs of individual markets; and [to] capture the scale economies of production and marketing on a global scale' (p. 262). Even if production is organised differently, through an integrated network of firms that take into consideration peculiarities of local demand (Bartlett & Ghoshal, 1998), the core of the products is standardised to generate economies of scale (Bartlett & Ghoshal, 2002). This resonates with theories purporting to explain how firms choose to own foreign value added facilities to capture scale related production economies (Caves, 1982, 1996; Teece, 1981, 1984).

Once firms have internationalised there are a number of advantages associated with being an MNE, that are not reliant on technology sourcing, including the ability to expand production into new markets thus exploiting scale economised still further; the possibility of identifying new markets, new opportunities in global supply chains, and strengthening the brand, through it becoming identified with host country brands, thus overcoming the liability of foreignness. Note that all of these are potentially linked to efficiency but are technologically neutral.

The above discussion suggests that EMNEs are likely to not only enjoy significant advantages of scale economy ex ante but may also earn significant returns to the newly acquired capabilities from FDI ex post. Kogut (1985) suggests that firms at the early stage of internationalisation rely heavily on home country-specific advantages, but over time this merely becomes a safety net, and interactions between firm-specific advantages and home country-specific advantages take over. A key issue here is how such firms can access global technology. Bhaumik et al. (2010) for example argue that EMNEs are a select group of companies within their home country, whom through superior management and better resources are better able to assimilate technology. As such actively seeking new technology is a superior strategy than relying on inward investment or the importing of capital goods to generate spillovers effects in the home market. This suggests that EMNEs are likely to experience much more rapid technological progress than their home country counterparts that do not have an international presence. However, the wider literature on intra-firm technology transfer suggests that such learning is not automatic and acquisition of (or access to) technology is therefore not synonymous with its absorption and assimilation, never mind transfer between affiliate and parent. Driffield, Love, and Menghinello (2010) highlight the limits to the process, even in the presence of knowledge sourcing by affiliates, while Mudambi and

Navarra (2004) explore incentives that affiliates may have to not transfer knowledge to the parent. An important question in the context of south-north FDI, therefore, is whether the interaction between the technology-sourcing emerging market firms and the host country environment facilitates creation of firm-specific ownership advantages (Dunning, 1998). Ramamurti (2008) suggests that EMNEs may be in a better position to use any acquired technology more efficiently, in part because they can use the newly acquired technology optimally from the start, without having to re-engineer or restructure their production process to ease out older technology. Jing, Chen, and Shapiro (2010) argue that EMNEs assimilate advanced knowledge overseas by increasing their R&D investments at home.

The problems in facilitating international technology transfer are well understood, though there is significant evidence that technology sourcing does lead to technological upgrading at the firm level (does this need a reference), and that this holds for MNEs from developing countries as well as from richer countries. Therefore, while frictions can restrict the 'transfer capacity' (of tacit knowledge) of developed country MNEs to their network of subsidiaries (Martin & Salomon, 2003), similar frictions are also likely to affect flow of knowledge about newly acquired technology within EMNEs. We therefore expect some catch up by EMNEs in terms of technical progress, but that this will be restricted to only the leading EMNEs. This gives us our second hypothesis:

H2. EMNEs catch up with developed country MNEs over time, but the catch up is greater in terms of efficiency than in terms of technology.

METHODOLOGY AND DATA

Productivity, Technological Progress and Scale Economies

In order to address the gaps in our understanding highlighted in the section 'Competitive Advantage of Emerging Market Firms', we decompose productivity growth in our three groups of firms into its different components. This enables us to focus on scale economies, as the important aspect of country-specific advantages of emerging markets, and technological progress as the central aspect of firm-specific advantages of traditional developed country MNEs. We apply the stochastic frontier approach to modelling production, which identifies differences in efficiency by isolating the deterministic component of firm level efficiency from the random one. In this methodology, realised output is seen as bounded from above by the stochastic frontier (Schmidt & Sickles, 1984) and technical inefficiency is seen as the amount by which a firm's actual output falls short of the efficiency frontier. This has been used in the context of both transition and developing economies, exporting, inward investment and internationalisation through imports of capital goods, see for example Driffield and Kambhampati (2003) and Henry, Kneller, and Milner (2009).

Thereafter, the Malmquist total factor productivity (TFP) index to measure the performance evolution at firm level identifies firm level scale effect, technical progress and efficiency improvement. The Malmquist TFP index allows the decomposition of TFP growth into three distinctive sources, which are: change in scale economies; technological progress; and technical efficiency change (Coelli, Rao, O'Donnel, & Battese, 2005). The change in scale economies measures how firm level production diverges from constant return to scale (CRS), with economic theory suggesting that in the long run a firm doing business in a competitive market should operate at the minimum point of the long run average cost curve, that is at constant returns to scale. The value of change in scale economies measures the extent to which a firm's static returns to scale have changed over time. If for example returns to scale increase, then the value would be greater than 1, if they decrease it would be less than 1. Technological progress is measured by the increase in output production resulted from pure technology improvement without any change in inputs. This would be positive if a firm can produce more output with the same inputs used as before, whilst negative otherwise. Finally, a firm is said to be technically efficient if it cannot sustain an output level by reducing *one* of the factor inputs such as labour unless it increases *another* factor input such as capital. Measures of changes in technical efficiency are derived by comparing firm level technical efficiency across the period of interest. It is easily seen therefore how the adoption of this methodology enables us to examine the hypotheses developed in the previous section.

The starting point, therefore, is to estimate a production function in which a firm's output (Y) is dependent on (or a function of) two factor inputs, namely, labour (L) and capital (K). It is stylised in the literature to use a translog production function in which (log) output is a nonlinear function of (log) labour and (log) capital. Once the production function has been estimated using this stochastic frontier approach, we can estimate the inefficiency parameter u_{it} following Jondrow, Materov, Lovell, and

Schmidt (1982). After estimating the coefficients for stochastic frontier function and efficiency level, we construct and decompose the Malmquist TFP index into efficiency change (EC), technical progress (TC) and scale change (SC) as in Coelli et al. (2005) and Malmquist TFP index is the geometric mean of these three components. Further details about this methodology can be found in the appendix.

As evident from our discussion in the previous section, we shall focus on SC and TC that are closely aligned with the competitive advantage of firms, and MNEs in particular. Note also that, as indicated earlier, *technical change* and *technical efficiency* are not one and the same thing. Technical change indicates technical (or technological) progress whereas technical efficiency is a measure of whether a firm is operating efficiently, that is whether is capable of increasing output without increasing at least one of the inputs.

Data

The focus therefore is the NACE 26 industry (i.e. Computer, Electronic and Optical products) manufacturing firms, and the data are obtained from the Orbis company information dataset from Bureau van Dijk. Data from Orbis have been used widely for empirical studies involving firms from more than one country; see for example Bhaumik et al. (2010) for India, Yong, Martins, and Driffield (2013) for a multi-country study, and Greenaway et al. (2014) for a paper on China.

All firms in the industry with valid annual data on output and inputs between 2005 and 2009 are included. Prior to this there were too few Chinese MNEs for meaningful comparison. A total of 13,107 firms around the world and 65,535 observations over the period of five years are included.[9] Chinese MNEs account for over 10% of total Chinese output over the period, growing to 12% in the final year. Table 2 reports the key variables used for stochastic frontier estimation. As the basis of our analysis is the derivation and comparison of total factor productivity using the stochastic frontier approach, the focus then becomes the measures of output and inputs, and the need for them to be internationally comparable. Our proxy for output is US dollar value of sales. Our measure of the capital input is US dollar value of capital. Our measure of the labour input, on the other hand, is the employment figure reported by the firms.[10] The descriptive statistics and correlations among the input and output variables are reported in Table 3. The high correlation

Table 2. Summary Statistics and Correlation.

Variable	Obs.	Mean[a]	Std. Dev.	Turnover	Asset	Employee
			Full sample			
Output[b]	65,535	250,006	2,994,043	1		
Capital	65,535	280,787	3,801,338	0.9128	1	
Employee	65,535	969	10,686	0.9003	0.8118	1
			Chinese MNEs			
Output	120	2,144,876	3,749,464	1		
Capital	120	1,721,883	2,799,651	0.8745	1	
Employee	120	16,177	25,407	0.6484	0.8301	1

[a]The arithmetic mean values.
[b]The value of output and capital are converted into US dollar at end of year exchange rate.

Table 3. Summary Statistics and Correlation.

Variable	Obs.	Mean[a]	Std. Dev.	Turnover	Asset	Employee
			Full sample			
Output[b]	65,535	250,006	2,994,043	1		
Capital	65,535	280,787	3,801,338	0.9128	1	
Employee	65,535	969	10,686	0.9003	0.8118	1
			Chinese MNEs			
Output	120	2,144,876	3,749,464	1		
Capital	120	1,721,883	2,799,651	0.8745	1	
Employee	120	16,177	25,407	0.6484	0.8301	1

[a]The arithmetic mean values.
[b]The value of output and capital are converted into US dollar at end of year exchange rate.

between the two inputs – capital and labour – is stylised and consistent with the literature on production function estimation.

Although subsequent analysis involves comparison of various groups, the determination of the frontier, and the estimates of total factor productivity (TFP) overall is done on all firms, irrespective of nationality or location. There is, in other words, a single global efficiency frontier for highly tradable goods such as electronic products, this ensures that the estimated frontier is truly a globally efficient frontier.

Subsequent to estimating TFP for the full sample of firms, we decompose the drivers of TFP into its components, focussing on technological progress and scale efficiency. It is easily seen that these two terms map directly on to the drivers of internationalisation: scale economies are a proxy for are CSAs, especially for emerging market economies with large domestic markets, while advantages of traditional MNEs are based on ownership advantages a reasonable proxy for which is technological progress.

RESULTS AND IMPLICATIONS FOR HYPOTHESES

To begin with, we estimate the translog production function, but since it merely provides the basis for the computation of productivity growth and its two key components, changes in scale efficiencies and technological progress, we do not report the results of the coefficient estimates themselves. We then examine the distribution of the three groups of firms within the quintiles of the distributions of scale efficiency and technical progress. These are illustrated in Table 4. This illustrates for each of the three types of firms – Chinese MNE, Chinese non-MNE and developed country MNE – the percentage of firms within a 5×5 matrix. Each cell of a matrix reports the proportion of a certain type of firm in the *m*th quintile of the distribution of scale efficiency change and the *n*th quintile of the distribution of technological progress. For example, in 2006 (Panel A), 13% of Chinese MNEs are in the 5th quintile of the distribution for technological progress and 1st quintile of the distribution for change in scale efficiencies. In 2009 (Panel B), the proportion of Chinese MNEs in the same relative positions in the two distributions rise to 17%.

In Table 4, the Chinese MNEs largely conform to the expected pattern of EMNEs. Nearly half (47%) of the Chinese MNEs in our sample occupy just 4 cells in the bottom left hand corner of the distribution, with high values for scale efficiency, and low values for technical progress. In addition, another 17% of firms have average values for scale efficiency, but are in the lowest quintiles for technical progress. Overall, 76% of Chinese MNEs are in the lowest two quintiles for technological progress, with only 12% in the top two quintiles. In comparison, the developed country MNEs have only 33% of firms in the bottom two quintiles of technical progress and some 46% in the top two quintiles. In contrast, however, Chinese MNEs have only 16% of firms in the bottom two quintiles for scale efficiency, while developed country MNEs have more than double that percentage. Overall, this would suggest that the stylised facts concerning EMNEs are correct; such firms are built on CSAs, and compete with their more technologically advanced firms from the west by exploiting sectoral level scale economies.

Table 4. Changes in Scale Efficiency and Technological Progress over Time (By Firm Type).

		Technical Progress									
		Chinese MNEs					Chinese Non-MNEs				
		Panel A: 2006									
Scale efficiency change		5th	4th	3rd	2nd	1st	5th	4th	3rd	2nd	1st
	5th	0	0	0	0	0	0.07	0.07	0.02	0.03	0.01
	4th	0.04	0.04	0.00	0.00	0.00	0.11	0.07	0.01	0.00	0.00
	3rd	0.17	0.04	0.00	0.00	0.00	0.15	0.03	0.06	0.00	0.01
	2nd	0.04	0.17	0.00	0.00	0.04	0.10	0.06	0.03	0.01	0.01
	1st	0.13	0.13	0.04	0.04	0.04	0.07	0.03	0.02	0.00	0.00
		Panel B: 2009									
		5th	4th	3rd	2nd	1st	5th	4th	3rd	2nd	1st
	5th	0.00	0.04	0.00	0.04	0.04	0.08	0.09	0.00	0.00	0.00
	4th	0.13	0.08	0.00	0.04	0.00	0.07	0.05	0.02	0.00	0.02
	3rd	0.00	0.00	0.00	0.00	0.00	0.07	0.04	0.03	0.01	0.02
	2nd	0.00	0.13	0.00	0.00	0.00	0.13	0.08	0.03	0.03	0.02
	1st	0.17	0.13	0.13	0.00	0.08	0.05	0.07	0.03	0.03	0.00

		Technical Progress				
		Developed Country MNEs				
		Panel A: 2006				
Scale efficiency change		5th	4th	3rd	2nd	1st
	5th	0.03	0.02	0.03	0.06	0.06
	4th	0.07	0.04	0.03	0.03	0.03
	3rd	0.03	0.05	0.04	0.04	0.03
	2nd	0.01	0.04	0.05	0.04	0.03
	1st	0.01	0.03	0.05	0.07	0.08
		Panel B: 2009				
		5th	4th	3rd	2nd	1st
	5th	0.02	0.03	0.04	0.04	0.06
	4th	0.05	0.05	0.04	0.03	0.02
	3rd	0.07	0.04	0.04	0.03	0.02
	2nd	0.02	0.04	0.04	0.06	0.02
	1st	0.01	0.01	0.04	0.07	0.10

This analysis therefore offers direct support for H1a, in that EMNEs are, compared with traditional MNEs, more reliant on CSAs for their competitive advantage. This, in turn, leads us to perhaps the more interesting question. If by definition CSAs are available to all firms operating in the country, what distinguishes EMNEs from non-MNEs in the same country? More than half of Chinese non-MNEs are in the bottom quintile for technical progress and only 7% in the top two quintiles, and less than half of these firms are in the top two quintiles for scale efficiency. Recall that only 16% of Chinese MNEs are in the bottom two quintiles for changes in scale efficiencies, that is they are able to leverage their CSA-based advantages better than their non-MNE counterparts. These EMNEs also seem to enjoy a technological advantage. While EMNEs lag some way behind developed country MNES in terms of technical progress, therefore, they are some way ahead of their domestic non-MNE competitors. In other words, there is at least partial or *prima facie* evidence to support H1b, namely, that emerging market firms that transform themselves into EMNEs are able to do so because they have some FSA-related advantage over their non-MNE counterparts. In part, this is manifested through greater technical progress that is conceptually correlated with greater ability to assimilate and adapt technology.

The analysis then explores dynamics of these processes over time, as a test of hypothesis two. While Chinese MNEs in general improve their position in the table through the period, both in terms of technology and scale economies, there is very little movement between 2006 and 2009 in the distributions of developed country MNEs and Chinese domestic firms. The most notable move is the increase in the proportion of Chinese MNEs that are in the top quintile for scale efficiency. Between 2006 and 2009, there was an increase from 38% to 50%. This is then double the percentage of developed country MNEs in this category. This provides direct support for H2; while CSAs are theoretically available to all firms in a given country, these appear more important for local MNEs than for foreign affiliates. Further, these CSAs in the form of scale economies are directly linked to performance and internationalisation of EMNEs. This is illustrated by the fact that the most significant change over the period is the doubling of the number of Chinese MNEs that are in the top quintile in both dimensions, and a doubling of the number of firms in the second highest quintile for technical progress. Overall, there is a general shift of Chinese MNEs to higher quintiles for both aspects, for firms in the bottom right corner or the 2006 block of Chinese MNEs. These firms show significant catch up in technical progress, and a move to higher quintiles for scale efficiency.

While the improvements in scale efficiency among Chinese MNEs are striking, the moves in terms of technical progress are noticeable but smaller. The proportion of Chinese MNEs in the top two categories for technical progress increased from 12% to 21%, suggesting significant catch up in terms of technical progress, even if the figures are not as marked as for scale economies. This would suggest, therefore, that, holding other CSAs constant (i.e. comparing Chinese MNEs and non-MNEs) EMNEs should demonstrate not only greater scale economies (Fig. 1) but also a greater increase in scale economies over time. Equally, in the absence of cutting edge technology, then scale economies should be more important for Chinese MNEs, than for traditional MNEs from the developed countries, for whom new technology and local input linkages may overcome lower scale economies at the firm level.

Taken together the results suggest that EMNEs performance is related to efficiency as much as to the more tightly defined definition of technology. Compared with the earlier literature, which focussed merely on FSAs and CSAs, this finding is an important contribution. It highlights the key nature of the FSAs that are demonstrated by EMNEs that enable them to compete effectively abroad. It also demonstrates that the analysis of FSAs more generally needs to focus on the wider definition than merely technology when explaining multinationality.

CONCLUSIONS

The purpose of this paper is to extend the existing literature on EMNEs by examining their technological progress, and comparing it with scale economies in driving productivity growth (and hence competitive advantage) over time. The performance of EMNEs is compared both with firms who have potentially the same access to country-specific advantages associated with scale economies but less access to technology (i.e. Chinese non-MNEs), and with a set of firms that may be considered to be represent the technological frontier of the industry but have imperfect access to the aforementioned sources of scale economies (i.e. developed country MNEs). Using a large firm level dataset and an established yet sophisticated methodology, we are able to compare technological progress and change in scale economies of all three types of firms over time. Our sample period traces these changes in scale efficiency and technological progress both before the onset of the financial crisis in 2008 and for one year into the crisis. To the best of our knowledge no one has compared EMNEs and OECD MNES in this way.

It has been commented on elsewhere, in well-known studies of iconic brands such as first IBM, and then Apple, as well as in consumer electronics, that the main driver of profitability is innovation, while the main driver of productivity is scale efficiency at the firm level; it dominates technological progress, on average, in each of the years in the same period. Extending this casual empiricism, our results are consistent with the hypotheses that EMNEs have an advantage with respect to scale economies but that developed country MNEs continue to have an advantage with respect to technological progress. Overall, therefore, the EMNEs and developed country MNEs in our sample can convert factor inputs into output with (roughly) the same degree of efficiency, and both groups are much more efficient than the Chinese non-MNEs. A notable difference between the two groups, however, is in the distribution of firms across sectors: developed country MNEs achieve efficiency gains in less standardised sectors while EMNEs' advantage relates to the production of relatively standard components.[11]

Finally, it is worth noting that since the Chinese MNEs are concentrated in high end of production chain and low end of value chain, they suffered more from the adverse external shock of the financial crisis period than both the developed country MNEs and the Chinese non-MNEs. This is indicated by the mean efficiency change between 2007 and 2008. Chinese non-MNEs were least affected by the financial crisis, due mainly to the domestic electronic upgrading initiative promoted by the Chinese government. Considerable subsidies were paid during the period to domestic electronic producers to sell in the less developed regions in the country (APCO, 2012). This allowed them to utilise their spare production capacity and provided more leeway in adjusting to the fall in external demand. This also encouraged an improvement in technical efficiency in these firms. Although Chinese MNEs could also benefit from this initiative at home, their foreign subsidiaries were excluded, which explains them being outperformed by domestic firms. Comparing the performance of developed country MNEs and EMNEs it is clear that during crisis the developed country MNEs were better are adjusting their production scales than the EMNEs, which reflects the higher ability of developed country MNEs in learning and adapting to the changing environment.

Taken together, these findings represent an important contribution over the existing literature, which is based on the ad hoc assumption that EMNEs invest overseas in search of technology to enhance their competitiveness. Our results suggest that even subsequent to internationalisation the main source of competitiveness of EMNEs remains their ability to generate growth of scale efficiencies. On the other hand, while developed country MNEs are not able to match the ability of EMNEs to benefit from scale efficiencies their advantage with respect to technological progress keeps them competitive vis-à-vis these emerging market competitors.

An equally important question is why some Chinese firms are able to succeed through internationalisation while others may not. This has implications for the extent to which emerging market firms might, in the future, be able to leverage their country-specific advantages to become global competitors of developed country MNEs. It is clear from a comparison of Chinese MNEs and domestic firms, all of whom potentially have the same country-specific advantages, that the key difference is one of scale, as Chinese MNEs are significantly larger than their domestic counterparts (Fig. 1) and therefore are able to better leverage this country-specific advantage than their domestic non-MNE counterparts. These are number of explanations of this, which suggest future avenues of research. First, it is plausible that the EMNEs are the most successful of the emerging market firms in terms of process innovation; they are those that have overcome the organisational and other problems of operating efficiently at very large scale. Secondly, EMNEs may have succeeded in accessing finance required for such large scale operations much more than their domestic competitors. In the context of emerging market firms, this hints at for example family connections, political patronage, government contracts, or perhaps foreign investment facilitating access to global capital and goods markets. Exploration of these conjectures would add significantly to the literature of EMNEs. There is much less evidence however of technological superiority over domestic competitors. This represents an interesting departure from the existing literature, which suggests that while CSAs are crucial in allowing emerging market firms to compete internationally, there is still a degree of technological superiority at home.

In the context of technological progress on the other hand, the question is how or why developed country MNEs retain advantage over EMNEs. Product innovation in the electronics sector is still relatively concentrated in a few leading locations, and there is little evidence that internationalisation by EMNEs is changing that status quo. This may in part be related to the sectors in which Chinese firms are distributed, in components and peripherals for example, but our findings suggest that internationalisation in these sectors may not be facilitating EMNEs to move up the value chain. As such, therefore, internationalisation is a not a key part of technology transfer at the product level, but may be linked to technology transfer at the process level. These results demonstrate that long run competitive advantage of EMNEs perhaps needs to be grounded in technical progress. In the absence of technological progress, developed country MNEs would be able to compensate for any scale economy related disadvantage with technology related advantage, thereby preserving any initial gap between the two types of MNEs. However, our results also demonstrate that EMNEs are better able to assimilate technology than their non-MNE domestic counterparts and hence the technological advantage of the developed country MNEs will not necessarily be preserved in the long run. The sources of CSAs are varied. We have focussed here on a case where emerging market economies have large domestic markets (another example may be Indian generic drug companies), with CSAs taking the form of scale economies. In cases (e.g. for Russian oil and gas firms), they centre on access to natural resources such as oil and gas, and minerals, in general. In some other cases (e.g. Chinese state-owned companies), it could be access to inexpensive credit and relationships with powerful governments. In yet other cases (e.g. Indian IT companies), it could be access to cheap semi-skilled or skilled labour. In the words of Rugman (2005), '[i]n Porter (1990) terminology, the CSAs form a global platform from which the multinational firm derives a home-base 'diamond' advantage in global competition' (p. 35).

Our results also suggest that being 'average' is not sustainable for EMNEs. EMNES that are in the median groups for scale economies at the start of the period do not retain that position. Such firms have to improve in at least one dimension, or fall behind. It is these firms who face perhaps the greatest threat from liability of foreignness in international markets, and therefore need to maximise their exploitation of CSAs over time. In other words, while the average EMNE has greater capability to leverage CSAs than the average non-EMNE at any given point in time, the discipline in terms of having and managing processes that internationalisation forces upon these firms (following Bartlett & Ghoshal, 2002) is a key step in putting them on a path on which competitiveness cannot just be generated sporadically but it can also be sustained in the long run.

The analysis presented here, in addition to highlighting the two dimensions to firm performance in the context of emerging markets, also highlights the need for more work at the firm level to explore the precise nature of the interaction between CSAs and FSAs. This requires a greater understanding of the precise nature of CSAs with emerging markets, and in particular a better understanding of how/why some firms lever these into internationalisation and others do not. Indeed, one could characterise the ability to lever CSAs into internationalisation is in itself and FSA. This, we suggest is a feature of human capital as well as knowledge capital, but requires more analysis, perhaps through cases (including firms that appear on the surface to be ripe for internationalisation but choose not to) and surveys.

While there is some scope for speculation about these issues, what we can say with much more confidence, on the basis of our results is that while internationalisation does not guarantee technological progress to match developed country MNEs, it is a more reliable route than dependence on spillover effects in the home market. In other words, if developing countries want to develop competitive advantages based on technological progress, they should perhaps focus on creating environments that facilitate overseas investment by domestic firms than on environments that attract inward FDI.

NOTES

1. Some empirical studies have brought this wisdom into question. For example, research suggests that the ICT sector that was responsible for 29% of Indian overseas acquisitions between 2000 and 2006 is largely focussed on servicing overseas clients on location in developed countries (Niosi & Tschang, 2009; Singal & Jain, 2012) and providing 'end-to-end business services' (Thite, 2012). Similarly, Tiwari and Herstatt (2009) find that Indian outward foreign direct investment (OFDI) in Germany is largely market-seeking, with many Indian MNEs in Germany motivated by the presence of their competitors in the German market.
2. The obvious implication of this argument is that when EMNEs do internationalise they are more likely to invest in other emerging markets and/or developing economies than in developed economies where the absence of institutional voids and market failures make these firms lose (part of) their competitive advantage. Bhaumik and Driffield (2011) demonstrate that EMNE family firms from emerging markets, which are generally most adept at working in contexts of weak institutions, may indeed have greater exposure to developing countries than to developed countries.
3. For further discussion of this sector, and its global value chain, see Dedrick, Kraemer, and Linden (2010), Sturgeon and Kawakami (2010) and Tung and Wan (2013).
4. The best known examples of this are the 'home appliances to the countryside' and 'Household Appliance Replacement' programmes, and the 'energy saving products benefits people' project.
5. For these purposes we use the OECD membership of countries for our sample period of 2005–2009. However, we recognise that some OECD member countries (e.g. Czech Republic, Korea, Hungary, Mexico, Poland, Slovakia and Turkey) were classified as emerging markets by the International Monetary Fund during the same time period.
6. For further discussion of this in the context of the notable example of Ranbaxy, see Kedron and Bagchi-Sen (2012).

7. For example, according to recent reports, just the four largest IT companies in India have total cash reserve in excess of USD 9 billion (http://news.in.msn.com/business/indias-top-4-it-firms-build-rs-56000-crore-cash-chest-infosys-leads). A 'going out' strategy of the Chinese companies, many of which are state-owned, is similarly backed by a significant fraction of China's USD 3.4 trillion reserves (http://www.bbc.co.uk/news/business-22567974).

8. See Sauvant et al. (2010) for a discussion of emerging market investments and the concentration of outward investment of ex-China BRICS firms in the United States and the EU.

9. All firms from India are excluded from the sample due to unobserved employee data.

10. Note that it is perfectly normal for input values to be highly correlated to not only the output but also to each other in a production function set up, because of the very nature of a production function. The correlations reported in Table 2 are therefore not a manifestation of the usual multicollinearity problem.

11. In our sample, the Chinese MNEs are generally concentrated in industries with standardised product such as electronic components and computers and peripheral equipment, while the OECD MNEs are concentrated in industries with less standardised product such as instruments and appliances for measuring, testing and navigation and irradiation, electrometrical and electrotherapeutic equipment. For example, while over 20% of Chinese MNEs are concentrated in computers and peripheral equipment, which has a fairly standardised product and where average firm size is 1447 employees, over 20% of OECD MNEs are concentrated in industries such as Instruments and appliances for measuring, testing and navigation in which products are arguably less standardised and where average firm size is only 965.

12. The models by Schmidt and Sickles (1984), Kumbhakar (1990), Kumbhakar and Heshmati (1988) and Pitt and Lee (1982) have been criticised for assuming firm level inefficiency to be time invariant. Others have assumed that inefficiency decreases over time at a constant rate (Battese & Coelli, 1995), but it has been argued that such an assumption is also restrictive and could lead to extreme results (Greene, 1995).

13. Same method has been adopted by Pieres and Garcia (2012) to study the productivity of countries around the world.

14. Consider two firms A and B. Both these firms can be technically efficiency, that is neither of these firms may be able to sustain its output level if one of the factor inputs such as labour is reduced without increasing the use of the other factor input (in this case, capital). However, Firm A may have greater managerial ability that enables it to generate more output per unit of input than Firm B, and in this sense the two firms may be different. Our methods enables us to capture this type of heterogeneity, after accounting for exogenous changes that impact of all firms simultaneously using a time trend. We assume the firm level heterogeneity affects firm production in a time-invariant fashion but that it is independent of firm level time-varying technical efficiency. This means the possible production capacity of firms might vary significantly even if they have the same technical efficiency level – on account of unobserved factors such as management capacity – and would therefore affect the level of output.

ACKNOWLEDGEMENT

Nigel Driffield acknowledges gratefully the support of the Leverhulme Trust.

REFERENCES

APCO. (2010). *Market analysis report: China's electronics industry*. APCO Worldwide. Retrieved from http://www.export.gov.il/uploadfiles/03_2012/marketelectronics.pdf

APCO Worldwide. (2012). Market analysis report: China's electronics industry. Presented to Israel Ministry of Industry, Trade and Labor and Isreal Export & International Cooperation Institute. Retrieved from http://www.export.gov.il/uploadfiles/03_2012/marketelectronics.pdf

Athreye, S., Kale, D., & Ramani, S. V. (2009). Experimentation with strategy and the evolution of dynamic capability in the Indian pharmaceutical sector. *Industrial and Cultural Change*, *18*, 729–759.

Bartlett, C., & Ghoshal, S. (1998). *Managing across borders the transnational solution* (2nd ed.). London: Random House.

Bartlett, C., & Ghoshal, S. (2002). Building competitive advantage through people. *MIT Sloan Management Review*, *43*(2), 34–41.

Battese, G. E., & Coelli, T. J. (1988). Prediction of firm level efficiencies with a generalized frontier production function and panel data. *Journal of Econometrics*, *38*, 387–399.

Battese, G. E., & Coelli, T. J. (1992). Frontier production functions, technical efficiency and panel data: With applications to paddy farmers in India. *Journal of Productivity Analysis*, *3*, 153–169.

Battese, G. E., & Coelli, T. J. (1995). A model for technical inefficiency effects in a stochastic frontier production function for panel data. *Empirical Economics*, *20*, 325–332.

Bhaumik, S., & Driffield, N. (2011). Direction of outward FDI of EMNEs: Evidence from the Indian pharmaceutical sector. *Thunderbird Review of IB*, *53*, 615–628.

Bhaumik, S., Driffield, N. L., & Pal, S. (2010). Does ownership concentration affect MNE operations? The case of Indian automobiles and pharmaceuticals. *Journal of International Business Studies*, *41*, 437–450.

Caves, R. E. (1982). *Multinational enterprise and economic analysis*. Cambridge: Cambridge University Press.

Caves, R. E. (1996). *Multinational enterprise and economic analysis* (2nd ed.). Cambridge: Cambridge University Press.

Chittoor, R., Sarkar, M. B., Ray, S., & Aulakh, P. S. (2009). Third-world copycats to emerging multinationals: Institutional changes and organizational transformation in the Indian pharmaceutical sector. *Organization Science*, *20*, 187–205.

Coelli, T., Rao, D., O'Donnel, C., & Battese, G. (2005). *An introduction to efficiency and productivity analysis* (2nd ed.). New York, NY: Springer.

Dedrick, J. K., Kraemer, L., & Linden, G. (2010). Who profits from innovation in global value chains?: A study of the iPod and notebook PCs. *Industrial and Corporate Change*, *19*, 81–116.

De Propris, L., & Driffield, N. (2006). FDI, clusters and technology sourcing. *The Cambridge Journal of Economics*, *30*, 277–291.

Driffield, N., Love, J. H., & Menghinello, S. (2010). The multinational enterprise as a source of international knowledge flows: Direct evidence from Italy. *Journal of International Business Studies*, *41*, 350–359.

Driffield, N. L., & Kambhampati, U. S. (2003). Efficiency of firms in Indian industry: The effect of reforms. *Review of Development Economics*, *7*, 419–430.

Driffield, N. L., & Love, J. H. (2005). Who gains from whom? Spillovers, competition and technology sourcing in the foreign-owned sector of UK manufacturing. *The Scottish Journal of Political Economy*, *52*(5), 663–686.

Dunning, J. H. (1998). Location and the multinational enterprise: A neglected factor? *Journal of International Business Studies*, *29*, 45–66.

Ethiraj, S. K., Kale, P., Krishnan, M. S., & Singh, J. V. (2005). Where do capabilities come from and how do they matter? A study in the software services industry. *Strategic Management Journal*, *26*, 24–45.

Gaffney, N., Kedia, B., & Clampit, J. (2013). A resource dependence perspective of EMNE FDI strategy. *International Business Review*, *22*, 1092–1100.

Greenaway, D., Guariglia, A., & Yu, Z. (2014). The more the better? Foreign ownership and corporate performance in China. *The European Journal of Finance*, *20*(7–9), 681–702.

Greene, W. (2003). *Econometric analysis*. Upper Saddle River, NJ: Prentice Hall.

Greene, W. H. (1995). *LIMDEP, version 7.0, users manual*. Australia: Econometric Software, Inc.

Guillen, M. F., & Garcia-Canal, E. (2009). The American model of the multinational firm and the "new" multinationals from emerging economies. *Academy of Management Perspectives*, *23*, 23–35.

Henry, M., Kneller, R. A., & Milner, C. R. (2009). Trade, technology transfer and national efficiency in developing countries. *European Economic Review*, *53*, 237–254.

Jing, L., Chen, D., & Shapiro, D. M. (2010). Product innovations in emerging economies, the role of foreign knowledge access channels and internal efforts in Chinese firms. *Management and Organization Review*, *6*, 243–266.

Jondrow, J., Materov, I., Lovell, K., & Schmidt, P. (1982). On the estimation of technical inefficiency in the stochastic frontier production function model. *Journal of Econometrics*, *19*, 233–238.

Kedia, B., Gaffney, N., & Clampit, J. (2012). EMNEs and knowledge-seeking FDI. *Management International Review*, *52*, 155–173.

Kedron, P., & Bagchi-Sen, S. (2012). Foreign direct investment in Europe by multinational pharmaceutical companies from India. *Journal of Economic Geography*, *12*, 809–839.

Khanna, T., & Palepu, K. (2010). *Winning in the emerging economies. A road map for strategy and execution*. Cambridge, MA: Harvard Business Press.

Kim, H., Kim, H., & Hoskisson, R. E. (2010). Does market-oriented institutional change in an emerging economy make business group-affiliated multinationals perform better? An institution-based view. *Journal of International Business Studies*, *41*, 1141–1160.

Kogut, B. (1985). Designing global strategies: Comparative and competitive value-added chains. *Sloan Management Review*, *6*, 15–28.

Kumbhakar, S. (1990). Production frontiers and panel data and time varying technical efficiency. *Journal of Econometrics*, *46*, 201–211.

Kumbhakar, S. C., & Heshmati, L. (1988). *Efficiency measurement using rotating panel data: An application to Swedish dairy farms 1976–1988*. Manuscript, Department of Economics, University of Texas.

Martin, X., & Salomon, R. (2003). Knowledge transfer capacity and its implications for the theory of the multinational corporation. *Journal of International Business Studies, 34*, 356–373.

Mathew, J. A. (2006). Dragon multinationals: New players in 21st century globalisation. *Asia Pacific Journal of Management, 23*, 5–27.

Mathews, J. A. (2002). *Dragon multinationals: A new model of global growth*. New York, NY: Oxford University Press.

Meyer, K. E., Mudambi, R., & Narula, R. (2011). Multinational enterprise and local contexts: The opportunities and challenges of multiple-embeddedness. *Journal of Management Studies, 48*, 235–252.

Meyer, K. E., & Peng, M. W. (2005). Probing theoretical into Central and Eastern Europe: Transactions, resources and institutions. *Journal of International Business Studies, 24*, 527–534.

Meyer, K. E., & Xia, H. (2012). British entrepreneurs: Global versions. *Business Strategy Review, 23*, 52–57.

Mudambi, R., & Navarra, P. (2004). Is knowledge power? Knowledge flows, subsidiary power and rent-seeking within MNCs. *Journal of International Business Studies, 35*, 385–406.

Niosi, J., & Tschang, F. T. (2009). The strategies of Chinese and Indian software multinationals: Implications for internationalization theory. *Industrial and Corporate Change, 18*, 269–294.

Pires, J. O., & Garcia, F. (2012). Productivity of nations: A stochastic frontier approach to TFP decomposition. *Economics Research International, 2012*, 19 p.

Pitt, M., & Lee, L. (1982). The measurement and sources of technical inefficiency in Indonesian weaving industry. *Journal of Development Economics, 9*, 43–64.

Porter, M. E. (1990). *The competitive advantage of nations*. London: Macmillan.

Ramamurti, R. (2008). What have we learned about EMNEs. In R. Ramamurti & J. Singh (Eds.), *Emerging multinationals from emerging markets*. Cambridge, UK: Cambridge University Press.

Ramamurti, R., & Singh, J. V. (Eds.). (2009). *Emerging multinationals in emerging markets*. Cambridge: Cambridge University Press.

Rugman, A. M. (2005). *The regional multinationals: MNEs and global strategic management*. Cambridge: Cambridge University Press.

Sauvant, K. P., Mascheck, W. A., & McAllister, G. (2010). Foreign direct investment by emerging market multinational enterprise, the impact of the financial crisis and recession and challenges ahead. In K. P. Sauvant, G. McAllister, & W. A. Mascheck (Eds.), *Foreign direct investments from emerging markets: The challenges ahead* (pp. 3–30). New York, NY: Palgrave Macmillan.

Schmidt, P., & Sickles, R. (1984). Production frontiers with panel data. *Journal of Business and Economic Statistics, 2*, 367–374.

Singal, A., & Jain, A. K. (2012). Outward FDI trends from India: Emerging MNCs and strategic issues. *International Journal of Emerging Markets, 7*(4), 443–456.

Sturgeon, T., & Kawakami, M. (2010). *Global value chains in the electronics industry: Was the crisis a window of opportunity for developing countries?* World Bank Policy Research Working Paper Series No. 5417, The World Bank, Washington, DC.

Teece, D. J. (1981). Internal organization and economic performance: An empirical analysis of the profitability of principal firms. *Journal of Industrial Economics*, *30*, 173–199.

Teece, D. J. (1984). Economic analysis and strategic management. *California Management Review*, *26*, 87–110.

Thite, M. (2012). Strategic global human resource management: Case study of an emerging Indian multinational. *Human Resource Development Journal*, *15*, 239–247.

Tiwari, R., & Herstatt, C. (2009). *The emergence of Indian multinationals: An empirical study of motives, status-quo and trends of Indian investments in Germany*. Working Paper No. 56. Technologie- und Innovationsmanagement, Technische Universitat, Hamburg.

Tung, A.-C., & Wan, H. (2013). Chinese electronics export; Taiwanese contract manufacturing – The win–win outcome along the evolving global value chain. *World Economy*, *36*, 827–842.

Vernon, R. (1966). International investment and international trade in the product cycle. *Quarterly Journal of Economics*, *80*, 190–207.

Vernon, R. (1979). The product cycle hypothesis in a new international environment. *Oxford Bulletin of Economics and Statistics*, *41*, 255–267.

Wei, Y., Zheng, N., Liu, X., & Lu, J. (2014). Expanding to outward foreign direct investment or not? A multi-dimensional analysis of entry mode transformation of Chinese private exporting firms. *International Business Review*, *23*, 356–370.

Yong, Y., Martins, P. S., & Driffield, N. L. (2013). Multinational performance and the geography of FDI: Evidence from 46 countries. *Management International Review*, *53*, 763–794.

APPENDIX: DECOMPOSING PRODUCTIVITY GROWTH INTO ITS COMPONENTS

Recapitulate from the section 'Productivity, Technological Progress and Scale Economies' that the starting point is to estimate a production function in which a firm's output (Y) is dependent on (or a function of) two factor inputs, namely, labour (L) and capital (K). It is stylised in the literature to use a translog production function in which (log) output is a nonlinear function of (log) labour and (log) capital. An important econometric issue that has to be addressed during the estimation of this production function is that it has to be able to capture firm-specific heterogeneities that might affect output. Although Pitt and Lee (1982), Schmidt and Sickles (1984), Kumbhakar and Heshmati (1988), Kumbhakar (1990) and Battese and Coelli (1988, 1992, 1995) have provided different solutions to this important issue, an improved method was proposed by Greene (2003) to overcome their drawbacks.[12] We therefore follow Greene (2003) and employ a true random effect panel stochastic frontier.[13] The random effects approach, of course, has the added advantage of being able to accommodate time-invariant variables such as industry or location dummies.[14]

This estimation method is particularly suitable therefore for the electronics industry because firm characteristics such as size varies significantly within the computer, electronic, and optical products manufacturing sectors. The stochastic frontier estimation as proposed by Greene (1995) in this case can be written as follows:

$$\ln Y_{it} = (\beta_0 + w_i) + \beta_L \ln L + \beta_K \ln K + \frac{1}{2}\beta_{LK} \ln L \ln K + \beta_t t + \beta_{tL} t \ln L$$
$$+ \beta_{tK} t \ln K + \frac{1}{2}\beta_{tt} t^2 + v_{it} - u_{it} \quad (1)$$
$$\text{where} \quad v_{it} \sim N[0, \sigma_v^2], \ u_{it} \sim N^+[0, \sigma_u^2], \ w_i \sim N[0, \sigma_w^2]$$

where $N^+[0, \sigma_u^2]\sigma_u^2$ is a truncated normal distribution with mean 0 and variance σ_u^2.

In Eq. (1) above, Y_{it} denotes the output produced by firm i at time period t, L, and K denote the labour and capital inputs of firm i at time t. v_{it} represents the normal error term, u_{it} denotes the measure for firm i's inefficiency at time t and w_i denotes a random firm-specific effect that is invariant across time. In this paper the total number of firms is i = 13,107 and, as we shall see later, we have data for a 5-year period, that is $T = 5$. Finally, v_{it}, u_{it} and w_i denote the error term inefficient terms and individual random effect.

Once the production function has been estimated using this stochastic frontier approach, we can estimate the inefficiency parameter u_{it} following Jondrow et al. (1982). Given the translog specification in Eq. (1) the efficiency level (i.e. TE) of each individual i at time t can be calculated as:

$$\mathrm{TE}_{it} = \mathrm{Exp}\left(-\hat{E}[u_{it}|\varepsilon_{it}]\right) \tag{2}$$

As explained in the paper, after estimating the coefficients for stochastic frontier function and efficiency level, we construct and decompose the Malmquist TFP index into efficiency change (EC), technical progress (TC) and scale change (SC) as in Coelli et al. (2005) and Malmquist TFP index is the geometric mean of these three components.

CORRUPTION AND FOREIGN DIRECT INVESTMENT: A STUDY OF GUATEMALA

José Godinez and Mauricio Garita

ABSTRACT

This study researched how corruption affects the attraction of foreign direct investment (FDI). With the help of a qualitative methodology, the results of the analysis show that firms headquartered in countries where corruption is high have an advantage when operating in a foreign country with a similar institutional environment. The reason for this advantage is that such firms may possess knowledge of how to cope with the arbitrary and pervasive dimensions of corruption at home. On the other hand, firms from countries with lower corruption levels than the host country are more affected by corruption in a highly corrupt host country. Finally, even though this study found evidence that all firms operating in a highly corrupt country might participate in corrupt deals, those headquartered in highly corrupt countries are more willing to do so. This claim is based on the fact that firms from less corrupt countries might face stronger pressures from their headquarters to not engage in corrupt deals, whereas firms from more corrupt countries might not encounter such pressures.

Keywords: Corruption; FDI; institutional theory; firm-level analysis

Emerging Economies and Multinational Enterprises
Advances in International Management, Volume 28, 297–326

ISSN: 1571-5027/doi:10.1108/S1571-502720150000028014

INTRODUCTION

Corruption has been defined as the abuse of public power for personal gain (Rodriguez, Uhlenbruck, & Eden, 2005). In the International Business (IB) field, the issue of corruption has only recently gained prominence, especially regarding how it affects the attraction of foreign direct investment (FDI) to a specific location (Cuervo-Cazurra, 2006; Habib & Zurawicki, 2001). However, the vast majority of these studies have only focused on whether or not corruption in the host country deters the entry of foreign firms, without explaining how it affects the operation of existing foreign companies operating in a highly corrupt host location. One reason for this apparent dearth of argumentation might be the illegal and secretive nature of corruption. Nevertheless, corruption matters. In fact, MNEs have a greater probability of encountering corruption abroad than other issues such as the threat of expropriation (Doh et al., 2003). Therefore, in order to understand how corruption might affect FDI, this study will look at the issue from the perspective of the firm.

Studies analyzing how corruption affects FDI have taken a look at the issue from a macroeconomic level (e.g., Cuervo-Cazurra, 2008; Habib & Zurawicki, 2002; Wei, 1997). However, in order to better understand the issue, analyses at different levels are needed. We investigate the effect of corruption on FDI at the firm level in this paper. To better understand the firm-level implications of corruption, we differentiate between pervasive corruption (corruption that is widespread and certain), and arbitrary corruption – corruption that is uncertain (Cuervo-Cazurra, 2008) in this paper. Drawing from 32 semi-structured interviews with managers with FDI decision-making authority located in Guatemala, we suggest that the level of corruption in the home country compared to that of the host country is that might affect the attraction of FDI.

We argue that firms based in highly corrupt home countries might be better prepared to cope with the arbitrary and pervasive dimensions of corruption of the host country based on the experience acquired at home. In contrast, firms from countries with lower corruption levels than the host country are more affected by corruption in a highly corrupt host country. Furthermore, those based in highly corrupt countries are more willing to participate in corrupt deals. The next section provides a theoretical background of corruption and its effect on foreign investors, followed by results, exploration of the data, and future recommendations.

LITERATURE REVIEW

Corruption

If high corruption exists in a given location, detrimental effects will be reflected not only on firms but also on an entire economy (Rose-Ackerman, 2008). By rewarding unproductive firms, those firms without government connections or firms unwilling to participate in corrupt deals will be penalized (Rodriguez et al., 2005). Through this vision, a firm could become motivated by the schemes of corruption that will give control over profits and stability in the long run. On the other hand, a firm might choose to not partake in corrupt deals and forfeit potential gains.

However, not all firms will have the same experience in dealing with foreign corrupt officials. Within this context, firms located in countries with high levels of corruption might not mind corruption abroad. On the other hand, firms located in countries with low levels of corruption might be negatively affected by this issue when doing business abroad (Cuervo-Cazurra, 2006). Therefore, it could be argued that those firms headquartered in countries with high levels of corruption might have an advantage when operating in similarly corrupt foreign locations than those located in countries with low levels of corruption.

Studies have researched the influence of corruption and national economies (Ades & Di Tella, 1997; de Vaal & Ebben, 2011), concluding that corruption is detrimental for all aspects of a society. Others have considered corruption an ethical issue (Li, 2009; Tan & Wang, 2011) reaching similar conclusions. However, fewer efforts have been made to assess its impact on firms (Collins, Uhlenbruck, & Rodriguez, 2008; Demirbag, Glaister, & Tatoglu, 2007), especially at the decision-making level. Nonetheless, the probabilities of multinational enterprises (MNEs) facing corruption abroad are higher than the likelihood of encountering problems due to other host country risks such as expropriation (Doh et al., 2003). One plausible explanation for the apparent dearth of research toward the issue is the secretive and illegal nature of corruption, which makes collecting managers' opinions on the subject challenging. Nonetheless, despite the inherent difficulties of studying corruption, this issue matters. The characteristics of corruption could become institutionalized and hence, become part of a location's institutional environment (Collins & Uhlenbruck, 2004) despite its illegal nature. Therefore, it is necessary to understand how managers perceive corruption and devise plans to minimize its detrimental effects.

The study of corruption is paramount since it is a global phenomenon that affects all countries (Charap & Harm, 1999), especially those in the developing world (Li, 2005; Svensson, 2005). However, in developing countries, corruption might be more rampant. Corruption is prevalent in countries where the administrative mechanism possesses excessive discretionary power, and where legal procedures lack transparency (LaPalombara, 1994; Tanzi, 1998). Furthermore, corruption is increased by income inequalities and deficiency of economic development (Alam, 1995). According to Li (2005), corruption is an important informal institution that is embedded in the institutional context in which formal institutions are not well developed. Moreover, scholars have argued that institutional quality (and hence corruption) is formed by economic factors (Demsetz, 1967). Therefore, a country's income level is responsible for its institutional development, which can also explain its levels of corruption.

Corruption and Foreign Direct Investment (FDI)

The study of corruption has only recently gained prominence as firms from developed countries engaged in operations in emerging and transition economies (Rodriguez, Siegel, Hillman, & Eden, 2006). However, despite the recent popularity of the subject, the issue of how corruption affects the attraction of foreign direct investment to a highly corrupt location is still not fully evaluated in the extant literature, especially at the firm-level. Understanding how corruption affects the decision-making process of investing in a foreign country is important. MNEs may use care when choosing host countries for their foreign subsidiaries because of their concern for the additional uncertainty and operational costs associated with corruption (Kwok & Tadesse, 2006).

Corruption has, consequently, been considered as deterrence to FDI (Judge, McNatt, & Xu, 2011). A contrary view, however, does exist and has seen corruption as a necessary evil, a lubricant for transactions (Meon & Weill, 2010) particularly when "institutional voids" are prevalent in developing economies (Khana & Palepu, 1997). The "grease the wheels" hypothesis, for example, asserts that corruption may improve efficiency by alleviating the distortions caused by ill-functioning institutions and inefficient bureaucracy (Huntington, 1968).

Corruption varies across different locations as well as in the degree of uncertainty it creates (Uhlenbruck, Rodriguez, Doh, & Lorraine, 2006). Thus, not all MNEs perceive and respond to corruption in the same manner. In that sense, the degree of uncertainty and the costs associated with corruption may vary depending on the country of origin of the foreign investors (Cuervo-Cazurra, 2006). For this reason, recent studies have concluded that MNEs located in countries with low levels of corruption would avoid investing in highly corrupt countries (Habib & Zurawicki, 2001). With little knowledge and skills for dealing with this phenomenon at home (Pajunen, 2008), they are more likely to be deterred by high levels of corruption as well as their unfamiliarity with it abroad (Driffield, Jones, & Crotty, 2013). On the other hand, firms which originated in highly corrupt environments may not be as sensitive to high corruption levels abroad; they may be attracted by the environment and even take advantage of corrupt activities (Suchman, 1995).

One reason why the extant literature, however, has not yet fully understood how corruption affects the attraction of FDI may be because of the approach taken to understand this phenomenon. Yackee (2010) says that most studies dealing with how corruption affects FDI follow a common design. A corruption perception index is used as the independent variable and it is regressed against country-level FDI flow data. Unfortunately, according to Yackee (2010), the results of these various and gradually more complex statistical exercises are inconsistent due to their reliance on secondary data. Therefore, Yackee (2010) proposes to return to the less sophisticated, but potentially more enlightening methodologies of interviews and surveys.

Corruption and FDI in Latin America

Corruption has been seen as one of the most pressing problems within Latin America (Selingson, 2006). While analyzing corruption in Latin America, Weyland (1998) argues that corruption has grown in alarming rates since these countries began their transition into democracies. The spread of corruption can be explained by the dispersion of power that was once concentrated in a few dictators. In other words, while the reforms in the region liberalized once closed economies, such reforms also caused local economies to be vulnerable to corrupt actions. Furthermore, Latin America shows inequality levels, lack of transparency, and inefficient economic development that are amongst the worse in the world (Ferreira & Gignoux, 2011). Therefore, in Latin America corruption has found fertile grounds to grow and spread. Paradoxically, despite its high levels of corruption, Zhan (2013) points out that the Latin American region is the second largest recipient of FDI in the developing world behind Asia.

In spite the importance of the region in terms of attraction of FDI, it still remains under researched. Few attempts have been made to understand how corruption affects the attraction of FDI to the region. Such studies show that countries that can curve corruption and crime might receive more FDI than those that do not (Gaviria, 2002). Also, Biglaiser and De Rouen (2006) point out that those Latin American countries that can maintain low corruption levels can attract more FDI in the region. Viewing the issue from a different lens, Godinez and Liu (2014) argue that it is not the corruption level of the host countries what might deter FDI to Latin America, but the distance and direction between corruption levels of the home and host countries. However, such studies have followed a macroeconomic methodology, leaving the question of how corruption affects FDI widely unanswered.

In order to address this gap in the literature, a firm-level analysis of how corruption affects the attraction of FDI is needed. While a firm-level study analyzing the whole Latin American region would be ideal, carrying such a study out would be daunting. Therefore, choosing a representative sample would be advisable. In order to analyze this issue, this study looks at foreign firms investing in Guatemala.

CORRUPTION AND ITS EFFECT ON FOREIGN DIRECT INVESTMENT AT THE FIRM-LEVEL SEEN THROUGH THE INSTITUTIONAL THEORY LENS

Institutions have been defined as the formal and informal "rules of the game" (North, 1990). In his work, North (1990) states that formal institutions are explicit rules that constrain human economic behavior (such as laws and regulations), while informal institutions are tacit constraints (such as self-imposed codes of conduct or social conventions). In this sense, this study utilizes institutional theory because it provides a theoretical justification for MNE reactions to government actions (Westney, 1993). Furthermore, to analyze how the dimensions of corruption affect the allocation of foreign investment depending on the corruption level of the host country, institutional theory is adequate since it provides contextual factors that affect this process.

Grounded on institutional theory, Kostova and Zaheer (1999) argue that MNEs face a conflicting situation when trying to achieve legitimacy in the different markets where they operate. According to Kostova and Zaheer (1999), headquarters' managers often inflict pressure to their foreign subsidiaries to replicate practices used at the home when conducting operations abroad. Nonetheless, subsidiary managers might resist such pressure if they perceive that the practices endorsed by headquarters go against local expectations (Kostova & Roth, 2002). In the context of this study, this claim means that a foreign subsidiary might face substantial host country pressure to partake in corrupt practices abroad. However, the pressure might be different depending on the level of corruption of the home country as compared to that of the host country.

Furthermore, Kostova, Roth, and Dacing (2008) argue that firms might experience stronger pressures to conform to certain practices from internal constituencies rather than from external host country expectations. Nevertheless, local subsidiaries might resist such pressures in order to conform to local practices that might not be in accordance to the guidelines imposed by the headquarters (Kostova & Roth, 2002).

In the context of high levels of corruption in the host country, this means that foreign firms might encounter pressures to conform to local corrupt practices while facing instructions from headquarters to avoid such corrupt practices (Spencer & Gomez, 2011). However, such pressure might be different depending on the level of corruption of the host country. In other words, those firms located in countries with high levels of corruption might not mind a similar corrupt situation when operating in a foreign country.

Scholars researching institutional environments and how they affect organizations have long argued that legitimacy is a critical issue that MNEs face when operating in various institutional environments (Parsons, 1956; Pfeffer & Dowling, 1975). Suchman (1995, p. 574) defines legitimacy as a "generalized perception or assumption that the actions of an entity are desirable, proper, or appropriate, within some socially constructed system of norms, values, beliefs, and definitions." Furthermore, this issue has intensified once MNEs began to conduct operations in developing countries (Gardberg & Fombrun, 2006).

Recent studies have made evident the challenges resulting from firms attempting to gain legitimacy across varied institutional environments (Kraatz & Block, 2008). Moreover, when facing conflicting pressures between headquarters and foreign subsidiaries, MNEs would opt for a *negotiation process* between all the parties involved (Kostova et al., 2008).

Kraatz and Block (2008) observed that MNEs might deal with the conflicting pressures via one of the following four strategies: (1) by eliminating the struggle by denying the validity of the subsidiary's demands; (2) MNEs might isolate the different identities of the subsidiaries and deal with them independently; (3) by finding a cooperative solution to the tensions; and (4) foreign subsidiaries might arise as institutions in their own right and gain legitimation. Given the diversity of how firms might handle institutional diversity, it is necessary to understand how corruption affects the operations of foreign firms, based on the corruption level of their home countries. Nevertheless, these studies have not analyzed how the level of corruption of the host country might predict how a firm from a highly corrupt home country reacts to corruption abroad.

If a firm is able to control the political risk abroad and maintain utilities based on unmerited contracts gained through corruption, such firm will maintain a long-term commitment with the country. The reason is that in an environment of pressure, a firm will search for the reduction of variability. Therefore, corruption will enhance when its prevalence in such a country is higher and this behavior could lead to an act of imitation between firms (Uhlenbruck et al., 2006). However, some firms might have a better idea of how to deal with this situation depending on their experience of dealing with corrupt officials at home. On the other hand, those firms with lower levels of corruption at home might not have developed knowledge of how to deal with corruption abroad, or they might face greater pressures to not partake in corrupt dealings in a foreign country.

Dimensions of Corruption at the Transaction Level

Several types of corruption have been identified at the transaction level in literature. Shleifer and Vishny (1993) make a distinction of corruption with or without theft. When considering corruption with theft, the authors say that the corrupt official keeps the amount of the bribe and provides the amount of the service to the government. On the other hand, in the corruption with theft context the official keeps the whole amount paid. In this study the authors show how corruption increases transaction costs.

Rose-Ackerman (1978) differentiates between bribery to modify existing rules and bribery to shape the application of such rules; Rose-Ackerman also concludes that corruption increases costs and, thus, creates inefficiencies. One problem encountered with these classifications is that they were considered at the transaction level as opposed to the country level

(Cuervo-Cazurra & Genc, 2008). To account for this problem, scholars have distinguished between two dimensions of corruption: Arbitrariness and Pervasiveness (Doh et al., 2003; Rodriguez et al., 2005).

Dimensions of Corruption at the Decision-Making Level

Arbitrariness of Corruption

Corruption changes widely across different locations in its scope in an economy as well as in the level of uncertainty it creates (Uhlenbruck et al., 2006). The uncertainty created by corruption is also called arbitrariness (Wei, 1997), which echoes the amount of ambiguity linked with corrupt deals in any given location (Rodriguez et al., 2005). Arbitrary corruption is viewed as the uncertainty created by corruption regarding how to operate in a given location (Uhlenbruck et al., 2006). In this sense, foreign investors, when operating in a country with high arbitrary corruption, will not know whether or not they will be asked for illegal payments or if the service agreed on will be delivered after making the illegal payment.

A high level of arbitrary corruption can be described as "disorganized corruption" where different parties across the public sector may ask for illegal payments independently from one another (Shleifer & Vishny, 1993). As a result from this, a foreign investor cannot be certain that, after making an illegal payment to a local official, another payment will be required for the same service or if additional payments will need to be made. This leads to what Uhlenbruck et al. (2006) define as ineffectual corrupt transactions.

Arbitrary corruption negatively impacts FDI due to the fact that it creates operational ambiguity in a foreign location (Cuervo-Cazurra, 2008). However, not all foreign investors are equal (Cuervo-Cazurra, 2006). Therefore, it is possible that foreign investors from highly corrupt countries use their knowledge of how to deal with corruption as a competitive advantage (Cuervo-Cazurra & Genc, 2008). Therefore, these kind of investors may not be as affected by the levels of arbitrary corruption as those without such knowledge.

Pervasiveness of Corruption

Pervasive corruption is defined as the likelihood of an MNE to encounter corruption in a foreign location (Rodriguez et al., 2005). Pervasive corruption increases the costs of operating in a country. In other words, pervasive corruption represents the known costs of host country corruption and thus,

MNEs have an idea of what to expect from corrupt public officials (Cuervo-Cazurra, 2008). Also, in countries with high levels of pervasive corruption, the chances of facing consequences for corrupt activities are lower (Lee, Oh, & Eden, 2010). Furthermore, Murphy, Shleifer, and Vishny (1993) argue that corrupt behavior can be institutionalized and thus becoming a normal practice in certain locations.

The pervasiveness level of corruption in a location is likely to affect each MNE's assessment of the costs and benefits of participating in corrupt deals (Doh et al., 2003). However, not all MNEs perceive corruption in the same manner. MNEs have organizational practices defined at their founding that will be replicated overseas (Kogut, 1993). For this reason recent studies have concluded that MNEs located in countries with low levels of corruption would avoid investing in highly corrupt countries (Habib & Zurawicki, 2001). Nevertheless, high pervasiveness of corruption enables foreign MNEs to gain access to local government without the need of a local partner (Uhlenbruck et al., 2006). This could imply that countries used to operating in pervasive environments might have a competitive advantage when operating in similar environments. Furthermore, MNEs located in countries considered corrupt might carry over their own practices when investing abroad. Hence, such firms may not avoid investing in corrupt locations.

RESEARCH DESIGN AND DATA COLLECTION

Setting

In order to analyze how the dimensions of corruption, at the decision-making level, affect the decision-making process of allocating FDI to a highly corrupt foreign country, Guatemala was chosen as our setting. A developing country, such as Guatemala, is an appropriate location to analyze corruption and its effects due to the high corruption levels that the country suffers (Transparency International has ranked Guatemala in the 123rd place globally, out of 177 countries) (Transparency International, 2013).

Guatemala is the largest economy in Central America with a GDP of US$53.80 billion in 2014, and the second largest recipient of FDI of the region with US$1.308 in the same year (World Bank, 2014). Despite its economic performance, Guatemala's economic freedom has deteriorated, according to the Heritage Foundation (2014). The reason for this deterioration is because of the expansion of government spending and high levels of taxation. Also, the country has seen a double-digit decline in property rights. Drug-trafficking and related violence are increasing in alarming rates. Furthermore, the judiciary system is troubled by inefficiency, capacity shortages, and intimidation of judges, prosecutors, and witnesses (Heritage Foundation, 2014), which has made settlements by corrupt means more appealing in all sectors of the country.

The levels of corruption within Guatemala can be explained due to several reasons. Firstly, Guatemala presents high levels of inequality, which, according to Rose-Ackerman (2008), can be a predictor of corruption. In fact, the country is ranked within the top 20 countries with the most unequal income distribution in the world (UNDP, 2009). Secondly, relevant literature argues that states transitioning after an internal conflict usually have very weak institutions and a rising influx of foreign investment, which is the case of Guatemala: it suffered from a 40-year civil war that ended in 1996. These two circumstances, according to Rose-Ackerman (2008), provide incentives to local officials to make corrupt deals for their personal gain. This can be explained because the conflict might have nurtured a culture of impunity and secrecy on which illegal acts are fairly easy to cover. Furthermore, the end of such conflict might not encourage the enactment of a transparent government with accountability for its actions, especially if those who benefitted financially from the conflict remain in power. Hence, even though incentives to participate in corrupt deals exist everywhere, the frequency and magnitude of corruption may be especially elevated in post-conflict countries (Rose-Ackerman, 2008), which is the case of Guatemala.

Sampling

Due to the nature of the study, a purposive sampling was used. This was the most appropriate method to study how corruption and its dimensions affect the decision-making process of allocating FDI to a highly corrupt foreign location. The potential respondents were identified as managers with decision-making authority of MNEs who had invested in Guatemala during the time of 2008–2013.[1] Interviewees were selected based on the following criteria: (a) respondents should be managers of MNEs operating in Guatemala, and (b) respondents should have direct involvement on foreign investment decisions in their companies. As presented in Table 1,

Table 1. Characteristics of Respondents.

Firm	Level of Corruption of Home Country Compared to Host Country[a]	Role of Respondent	Operations in Latin America	Industry
1	Less corrupt	Guatemalan Director[b]	6	Banking
2	Less corrupt	SM: Strategy[c]	9	Banking
3	Less corrupt	SM: Business[b] Development	7	Electricity
4	Less corrupt	MD: Operations[c]	6	Infrastructure
5	Less corrupt	SM: Strategy[c]	4	Manufacturing
6	Less corrupt	SM: Strategy[c]	9	Manufacturing
7	Less corrupt	SM: Business Development[b]	12	Manufacturing
8	Less corrupt	SM: Strategy[b]	8	Manufacturing
9	Less corrupt	SM: Strategy[c]	10	Manufacturing
10	Less corrupt	SM: Business Development[b]	5	Mining and Oil
11	Less corrupt	Guatemalan Director[c]	7	Mining and Oil
12	Less corrupt	Guatemalan Director[b]	5	Mining and Oil
13	Less corrupt	Guatemalan Director[c]	8	Telecommunications
14	Less corrupt	SM: Business[c] Development	15	Telecommunications
15	Less corrupt	MD: Operations[c]	8	Telecommunications
16	Less corrupt	SM: Strategy[b]	6	Telecommunications
		Average operations	*7.81*	
17	More corrupt	Guatemalan Director[c]	8	Agriculture
18	More corrupt	MD: Operations[b]	8	Agriculture
19	More corrupt	SM: Business Development[b]	8	Agriculture
20	More corrupt	Guatemalan Director[c]	5	Agriculture
21	More corrupt	Guatemalan Director[b]	7	Agriculture
22	More corrupt	Guatemalan Director[c]	7	Banking
23	More corrupt	MD: Operations[b]	6	Banking
24	More corrupt	Guatemalan Director[b]	5	Banking
25	More corrupt	SM: Business Development[c]	4	Food and Beverage
26	More corrupt	Guatemalan Director[b]	4	Food and Beverage
27	More corrupt	SM: Strategy[b]	6	Food and Beverage
28	More corrupt	MD: Operations[c]	5	Manufacturing
29	More corrupt	SM: Business Development[c]	9	Manufacturing
30	More corrupt	SM: Strategy[b]	6	Manufacturing
31	More corrupt	SM: Business Development[c]	6	Retail
32	More corrupt	MD: Operations[b]	8	Retail
		Average operations	*6.37*	

SM: Senior Manager.
MD: Managing Director.
[a]According to Rankings by Transparency International.
[b]Expatriate employee.
[c]Guatemalan employee.

respondents were divided in two groups: those whose firms were located in countries with lower corruption levels than Guatemala and those located in countries with higher corruption levels than Guatemala based on the CPI (Transparency International, 2013).

According to the Guatemalan Chamber of Commerce, as of 2013 there were 299 MNEs operating in the country and all firms were contacted to participate in the study. After sending the invitations, 32 managers with FDI decision-making responsibilities were interviewed using semi-structured interviews that were conducted from August 2013 to August 2014. The semi-structured interviews were used to ensure that the core themes identified by the literature review were addressed but at the same time, allowing for freedom of elaboration and clarification if needed.

According to Bryman and Bell (2011), when evaluating qualitative work, some of the main criteria that a researcher must use are credibility, transferability, dependability, and ease of confirmation. The credibility of this research was maintained through the scope of the initial literature review, the truthfulness and robustness of the data analysis, and by the large size of the sample group. The transferability of the research deals with how the results and conclusions can be applied in other settings. Since our study was performed only on managers of firms operating in Guatemala, we caution the reader that future research is needed to confirm the generalizability of our research beyond this context. However, we expect that our results are likely to hold for other developing countries with highly corrupt domestic environments like Guatemala. Additionally, to gauge transferability, the results in this study were compared to existing theory that was formulated in the current research context, as proposed by Luiz and Stewart (2014). Dependability in this context refers to whether or not the results can be applied at different points in time (Bryman & Bell, 2011). However, the nature of this research indicates that time might not be relevant to similar institutional stages. Finally, this research shows great levels of confirmability since it was designed to exclude personal values and biases of the researcher.

Interviews

In various areas of rigorous empirical investigation in International Business there is no satisfactory approach to substitute interviews (Parkhe, 2004; Yackee, 2010). However, the researcher must be cautious when conducting interviews since problems can arise. According to Parkhe (2004), there are several possible problems with conducting research interviews. Such problems range from self-reporting bias, language reporting context, and interpretation and so on.

Daniels and Cannice (2004) argue that before deciding to conduct interviews to study an issue in International Business, three requirements must be met: (1) the study must be exploratory, (2) there must be a small population of possible respondents, and (3) the interviews should allow a more in-depth interaction with respondents than the interaction provided by questionnaires. In order to analyze how corruption affected the attraction of FDI and subsequent operations in Guatemala, all three requirements will be met.

In this study, gaining access to managers of MNEs investing in Guatemala was extremely challenging. These difficulties are acknowledged in current International Business literature since according to Welch, Marschan-Piekkari, Penttinen, and Tahvanainen (2002) obtaining access to elite interviewees presents different challenges to those faced when studying non-elites. Notwithstanding the difficulties inherent in accessing top managers of MNEs investing in Guatemala, the task could be even more difficult when the only respondents suited to be interviewed are those managers who (a) had the power to make decisions regarding the allocation of FDI; and (b) were willing to share their views on how corruption in the host country affected their decision to invest in Guatemala and their subsequent operations.

Profile of Respondents

The results of the 32 interviews conducted provide an insight of how corruption affects the allocation of FDI in a highly corrupt host country. The profiles of the firms selected for the interview are provided in Table 1. Of the 32 interviews, 16 firms were headquartered in countries with higher levels of corruption than Guatemala, while the rest are located in a home country with lower corruption levels than the host country. The results of how corruption affects FDI to Guatemala depending on the corruption levels of the home country are provided below.

The main motivation of firms located in countries with higher corruption levels than Guatemala to invest in the country was to gain access to the host market. On the other hand, investors from countries with lower corruption levels than Guatemala declared that their motivations to invest in the country were to gain access to the market and natural resources of the country. Overall, managers of firms from more corrupt countries than the host country declared that making illegal payments to local officials was not morally acceptable, but they engaged in paying bribes to local official nevertheless. This was justified as a "means to an end" approach. Interestingly, all the interviewees from this group of investors justified paying bribes to local Guatemalan officials by saying that if they did not do this they would go out of business and their employees would suffer. These managers also acknowledged that personal connections with local officials were crucial to expedite processes to operate in the country.

On the other hand, managers of firms headquartered in countries with lower corruption levels than the host country declared that corruption was a very important problem to overcome, but not the only one. According to these respondents, they also had to adjust their strategies to operate in the country despite its high levels of insecurity. Another problem that was unanimously acknowledged was the poor infrastructure of Guatemala, especially its communications systems. Respondents reported that a vast amount of resources were used to manage the logistics in these challenging conditions.

Analysis

To understand the data we arranged it into a condensed, chronological account, as proposed by Miles and Huberman (1994), and coding each data source depending on its source. For each segment we indicated personal views on corruption (coded "C"), personal views to arbitrariness of corruption (coded "A"), and personal views on pervasiveness of corruption (coded "P"). This approach helped us to condense the events in a chronological manner. After the chronological account was established, the data was arranged to breakdown answers from respondents depending on the corruption level of their home country as compared to the host country (either more or less corrupt than the host country).[2] Following Strauss and Corbin (1994), the answers provided by the respondents were used as a "generative" plan.

After the data was coded it was studied firstly by identifying commonly used phrases by the respondents. For example, references to the uncertainty caused by corruption when deciding to invest in Guatemala and to what extent did the respondent knew how to operate in a highly corrupt foreign location were identified. Then, the researchers using their knowledge of the host country identified justificatory narratives (Greenwood, 2006). For example, most respondents on this study declared that corruption was a problem; however, their accounts differed when asked if they had actually taken part in a corrupt deal and why.

After the initial set of phrases and justificatory narratives were organized, they were carefully reviewed, consulting often with the original transcripts. At this point the coded data was studied in a latent manner in which the researchers interpreted the data based on what they knew about the subject and the context on which such data was collected (Berg, 2004). During several interactions with the raw data, summaries, and the theoretical foundations, three core dynamics were generated: Personal views on corruption, effect of arbitrary corruption on investment, and effect on pervasive corruption on investment.

RESULTS AND DISCUSSION

Perceptions of Corruption and Their Effect on FDI

In general, respondents in this research identified corruption as a significant characteristic of doing business in Guatemala. However, the uncertainty it created was perceived differently by foreign investors depending on the level of corruption of their home country as compared to the host country, as proposed by Cuervo-Cazurra (2006). In this sense, investors located in home countries with higher corruption levels than Guatemala seemed to have an advantage over those investors located in less corrupt home countries. For investors from countries with high corruption levels operating in Guatemala, the host country resembled their own home country environment, and therefore, the uncertainty levels created by corruption of the host country were not perceived as high. On the other hand, those firms located in home countries with lower corruption levels than Guatemala seemed more negatively affected by corruption in the host country as compared to those investors with home countries with high corruption levels.

When analyzing the responses from investors located in home countries with higher corruption levels than Guatemala it was obvious that corruption played an important role in their operations but they were better equipped to deal with this problem, confirming at the decision-making level the findings proposed by Cuervo-Cazurra and Genc (2008), but this time at the country level. For example, according to Investor 25, corruption, although detrimental for a society, is sometimes necessary to expedite processes. This respondent, concurring with respondent 28, argued that "although corruption should not exist, there is only so much a single company can do about it." These investors also declared that the uncertainty generated by corruption in Guatemala was minimal since "everybody knows the country is highly corrupt" and knowledge of how to deal with corruption in Guatemala could be obtained in the home country. Furthermore, this manager argued that if his company did not engage in corrupt deals, the well-being of the company and the employees could be in jeopardy. Furthermore, in the words of the interviewee:

> Corruption is morally wrong. However, sometimes managers have to engage in corrupt deals in order to be able to generate business. If I had a choice, of course I would not participate in corrupt deals, but the reality is that if you want to operate in Guatemala without engaging in corruption, you won't get very far.

The view expressed by Investor 25 was echoed by Investors 17, 24, 26, 29, and 31. According to these managers, corruption should not exist and it is detrimental for businesses as well as all sectors of a society. Nevertheless, these investors also argued that if they want to continue operating in Guatemala, they have to comply with the local "business culture." This view is explained by investor 20:

> I know corruption is a problem that increases our costs and damages a society, but if I don't participate in it, someone else will. I have an obligation to provide jobs to my employees and the only way I can do this is by playing by the local rules.

However, the general view among investors from countries with higher corruption levels than Guatemala argued that corruption in the host country did not increase uncertainty since they had familiarity of the possible illegal requirements requested by local public officials, echoing the findings proposed by Luiz and Stewart (2014). The one difference between these investors, however, is how they replied to the question regarding if they had acquired knowledge of how to deal with corruption at home.

While most investors from countries with higher levels of corruption than the host country declared that corruption was a problem, others claimed that corruption was just part of doing business. These results show how corruption has been institutionalized in Guatemala and has become unavoidable. As respondents 17, 29, and 31 said, "bribing local officials is how things are done." This view echoes the studies presented by Moore (2008) and Zyglindopulus, Fleming, and Rothenberg (2008) that say that some individuals might attempt to justify their actions by arguing that this problem is victimless and/or unavoidable. Other respondents taking the same approach argued that "it was not their fault" that corrupt actions were the norm in Guatemala, and they just "had to play by the local rules."

Surprisingly, not all investors from a country with higher levels of corruption than Guatemala "condoned" corruption. According to Investor 32, corruption does not have a logical reason to exist. According to this respondent, if the system were transparent and fair to all parties, public officials as well as companies would not have an incentive to participate in corrupt deals. Moreover, this investor declared that even though the experience at home might provide some knowledge about how to deal with corruption, no one can totally learn how to deal with corruption at one location and just replicate such knowledge in another one.

On the other hand, when talking to managers of MNEs headquartered in countries with a lower corruption level than Guatemala, there was consensus regarding how corruption affected the decision-making process of allocating of FDI in Guatemala. As respondents 8, 12, and 16 said, corruption was a serious factor to take into account but not the only factor. According to these managers, corruption delayed and increased prices of projects, but did not dictate whether or not investment was going to be made. The respondents also said that the corruption level of the host country could affect the duration of the project, the quality of the work performed, and the entry-mode used (either wholly owned subsidiary or joint venture), as argued by Rodriguez et al. (2005).

Considering corruption in Guatemala, all interviewed managers from countries with lower levels than the host country agreed that corruption was detrimental to doing business. However, some managers had stronger views regarding corruption than others. For instance, for investors 10, 13, and 15 "corruption is a very important factor to take into account when deciding to invest in a foreign location." Corruption, according to these respondents, was the root of all problems in the country because it divests private funds to a few government employees, increases inefficiencies, and hence deepens the poverty levels in the host country. Managers of MNEs from less corrupt countries than Guatemala also expressed that corruption is as an "evil force" that needs to be stopped. However, some of these managers admitted that in order to do business in a corrupt environment like Guatemala's, they needed to adapt to local social conventions that might not be acceptable in their home countries.

One interesting finding was that all the managers from less corrupt countries viewed corruption as a serious problem that needed to be eliminated; however, their operations in the host country told a different story. For example, investors 1, 8, and 12 argued that making illegal extra payments and providing kickbacks to local officials was, sometimes, necessary to keep the business going, even though these investors acknowledged that doing so was wrong. One important point to be raised is that the decision to invest in a foreign country does not depend only on the corruption levels of such location. Instead, as investor 8 puts it "the corruption levels would dictate the kind of investment and the length of the commitment."

Although investors from countries with lower level of corruption than Guatemala agreed that corruption was not acceptable, their views on several issues differ from one another. According to Investors 2, 3, 4, 10, 13, and 15, corruption is not only morally wrong but also the cause of the poverty around the world, and a cancer to society. Furthermore, these investors firmly declared not to engage in any corrupt deal in any market where the company operates. These managers also argued that the uncertainty levels that corruption generates can actually dictate whether or not a foreign investment is made, which is in line with the majority of studies analyzing corruption and how it affects FDI (e.g., Biglaiser & De Rouen, 2006; Cuervo-Cazurra, 2006; Habib & Zurawicki, 2002). These investors also declared that they did not have the opportunity to learn at home how to deal with high levels of corruption abroad. These investors also agreed that their home countries are not "corruption-free" but that this problem is mainly present in the public sector, and since they do not do business with their government, they can avoid corrupt deals.

On the other hand, there were interviewees from countries with lower corruption levels than Guatemala that did not "demonize" corruption. According to Investors 1, 8, 9, 11, 14, and 16, corruption is a major factor that might impede business, but it is not the only one. Furthermore, according to these respondents, corruption should be avoided when possible, but this cannot be done in all situations. Finally, Investor 5 declared that corruption is very predictable in Guatemala and even though it helps expedite processes it should be avoided when possible.

Perceptions of Pervasiveness of Corruption

This study furthers the knowledge regarding how corruption affects the attraction of FDI at the decision-making level taking into account the pervasiveness and arbitrariness of corruption. In this sense, this study presents empirical evidence that firms headquartered in highly corrupt countries may be better prepared to cope with the arbitrariness of corruption abroad because they have acquired knowledge of how to cope with that dimension of corruption at home, as declared by most respondents from these firms (except respondents 17, 29, 31, and 32). On the other hand, firms without such knowledge might be deterred by the uncertainty caused by arbitrary corruption abroad.

According to almost all respondents from countries with high levels of corruption (except respondents 17, 29, 31, and 32), knowledge of how to respond to corrupt officials can be acquired at home. These respondents argued that while public officials act differently in different countries, how to react and respond to corrupt demands is a "skill" that they had developed at home. On the other hand, respondents 17, 29, and 32 said that they did not acquire knowledge of how to deal with corruption at home, but they downplayed the importance of this problem as to a way to do business in developing countries.

This claim that knowing how to deal with the pervasiveness of corruption can be acquired at home is supported by responses to the questions asked about pervasiveness of corruption in a highly corrupt host country. According to investors from home countries with high levels of corruption, knowledge of how to deal with the known costs derived from host country corruption can be acquired at home. For instance, investors 17, 26, 29, and 30, argued that corruption in Guatemala resembled that of their home country, and therefore, "little adjustments' had to be made to operate in this foreign country. As investor 26 puts it:

> While every country is unique, the business environment in Guatemala is not that different than our home country. Therefore, getting used to dealing with the problems in Guatemala was not that difficult for us.

One of the most important factors to take into account when choosing a foreign location to establish operations is the institutional environment of such a location (Orr & Scott, 2008; Wu, Lawler, & Xiang, 2008). According to Cantwell, Dunning, and Ludan (2010), MNEs must adjust their strategies and structures to respond to uncertainty in a foreign environment. Furthermore, the institutional environment of a foreign location can determine the attraction of foreign investment since a good institutional environment may raise the productivity of foreign MNEs (Bénassy-Quéré, Coupet, & Mayer, 2007). On the other hand, a poor institutional environment abroad might increase the costs of operating in that location and thus deter FDI (Bénassy-Quéré et al., 2007). Nevertheless, building on the premise that not all foreign investors are equal (Cuervo-Cazurra, 2006), we argue that some firms have developed the knowledge of how to cope with corruption at home, and thus, the uncertainty created by corruption abroad might not affect all of them equally.

Investors from a home country with lower levels of corruption had differences when asked whether or not they had acquired knowledge at home about dealing with corruption abroad. Those investors that declared that corruption was a serious problem also claimed that they did not learn how to deal with corruption and they did not want to learn such "skill." On the other hand, for those who accepted participating in corrupt deals in Guatemala, it is evident that they did not have the opportunity of learning how to deal with corruption at home. Responses from investors 1, 8, and 12 tell us that although these respondents accepted paying bribes in Guatemala, they had to learn to do so while operating in that country. For instance, investor 8 says that

> Most people think that making an illegal payment is easy. They think that a local official requests an amount of money for a service and then the deal is done. However, local officials are not that direct. Furthermore, if you just offer them money for a service they get offended. It is only after a while of dealing with them when you learn how these dealings work.

Recently, authors have argued that it is not only the level of corruption abroad what might deter FDI corruption's different dimensions. According to Cuervo-Cazurra (2006), pervasive corruption deters FDI because it increases the known costs of investing in a highly corrupt location. This study furthers Cuervo-Cazurra's claim by analyzing the issue at the decision-making level. According to our respondents, the arbitrariness dimension of corruption has a detrimental effect on foreign investors when such investors' home countries have lower levels of corruption than the host country. On the other hand, those firms headquartered in home countries with higher levels of corruption than a highly corrupt host country might have developed knowledge at home of how to deal with corruption abroad.

Therefore, an important finding of this study is the fact that it appears that acquiring knowledge of how to deal with pervasiveness of corruption at home might help to cope with corruption abroad. This claim can be explained because MNEs based in highly corrupt home countries might not see corruption abroad as a deterrent for FDI since they are used to operating in such environments in their home country (Cuervo-Cazurra & Genc, 2008). Also, since corruption is the norm in the home country, these MNEs might not face pressures at home to abstain from investing in highly corrupt foreign locations (Spencer & Gomez, 2011). On the other hand, firms located in countries with low levels of corruption might be deterred by the uncertainty that corruption in the host country represents. Furthermore, these firms might also face pressures at home for not conducting business in foreign locations considered as highly corrupt.

Perceptions of Arbitrariness of Corruption

When analyzing arbitrary corruption, firms headquartered in countries with higher corruption levels than Guatemala seem to have another advantage over their counterparts based in countries with lower levels of corruption. Based on the responses from foreign investors in Guatemala, we argue that arbitrary corruption may not deter FDI when the home country is more corrupt than the host country. Therefore, this study provides an explanation of why high levels of corruption in the host country may not deter foreign investors from highly corrupt home countries.

Respondents from countries with higher levels of corruption than Guatemala argued that they were not excessively affected by the uncertainty derived from corruption of the host country. These respondents argued that the levels of "disorganized corruption" (Shleifer & Vishny, 1993) did not have a significant negative effect in their operations in Guatemala. Respondents 18, 19, 20, 21 26, 29, and 30, argued that while corruption in Guatemala exists, they had knowledge of how to deal with it. In fact, all of these respondents argued that part of such knowledge was developed at home, and the rest was, as Investor 29 said it: "common sense."

Arbitrariness of corruption, also known as ineffectual transactions (Uhlenbruck et al., 2006), is said to be more detrimental to foreign investors than the other dimension of corruption, pervasiveness. We found evidence of this claim but only when the foreign investor is located in a home country with lower levels of corruption than the host country. The reason for this result is twofold. Firstly, according to respondents from countries with lower levels of corruption than Guatemala, they did not have an opportunity to learn how to deal with arbitrariness of corruption at home. This view was shared by Investors 1, 8, 9, 11, 12, and 14. Secondly, other investors (Investor 8, 12, and 16) argued that they face strong pressures from their home constituencies to not engage in corruption abroad. This means that their chances to learn how to deal with this dimension of corruption at home are minimal.

This is an important finding because it helps explain why firms headquartered in highly corrupt countries might not be deterred by high levels of corruption in a foreign location. Based on this premise, this study proposes that firms based on highly corrupt countries have acquired knowledge not only about the known costs of corruption abroad, but also regarding whether or not extra payments will be needed or if the service will be delivered as promised. This result addresses a gap in the current literature by empirically demonstrating at the firm-level why firms from highly corrupt countries might not be deterred by high corruption abroad (Table 2).

Implications

These results make a contribution to literature in many levels. Firstly, it dealt with a problem that all MNEs face when operating abroad, especially in developing countries. Secondly, contextually, this study was conducted in a relatively unexplored geographic area. Thirdly, this study compared the decision-making process of managers of MNEs from developing countries and from developed countries investing in a highly corrupt foreign location, highlighting important differences in such process. Despite these contributions to literature, our study also has some drawbacks. One important limitation of our study is that it only analyzes one developing country; future research should look at comparing how the arbitrariness and pervasiveness of corruption affect the decision-making process of allocating FDI at a regional level in order to validate our results.

Another important finding is that managers from MNEs investing in a highly corrupt foreign location see themselves as "institution takers." In line with Luiz and Stewart (2014), we found that managers find themselves "forced" to accommodate to the rules of the game imposed by corruption in a foreign country. This finding suggests that managers underestimate their potential to bring change to a foreign location. Kwok and Tadesse (2006) demonstrated that MNEs can change the host country institutional environment where they operate. Therefore, both practitioners and policymakers should devote more effort to breaking the vicious cycle of complying with corruption abroad. These efforts could result in a decrease of corruption, which in turn would benefit the attractiveness of host countries and the bottom line of MNEs operating in them.

Table 2. Summary of Findings.

Corruption Level of Home Country as Compared to Host Country	Motivation for Investment	Personal Views on Corruption	Knowledge Gained at Home about How to Deal with Corruption	Pervasiveness of Corruption	Arbitrariness of Corruption
More corrupt than home country	Market-seeking	Morally wrong but justifiable	Knowledge about coping with corruption abroad can be acquired at home	Knowledge about dealing with pervasiveness of corruption abroad can be acquired at home	Knowledge about dealing with arbitrariness of corruption abroad can be acquired at home
Less corrupt than home country	Market-seeking and resource-seeking	Very important problem but not only one to be considered	Knowledge about coping with corruption abroad cannot be acquired at home	Knowledge about dealing with pervasiveness of corruption abroad cannot be acquired at home	Knowledge about dealing with arbitrariness of corruption abroad cannot be acquired at home

Source: Researchers' interviews.

CONCLUSIONS AND IMPLICATIONS FOR FUTURE RESEARCH, POLICYMAKERS AND PRACTITIONERS

Grounded on institutional theory, researchers have argued that the institutional environment of a foreign location is one of the most important factors to take into account when choosing to establish operations abroad (Orr & Scott, 2008; Wu et al., 2008). Therefore, MNEs must adjust their strategies and structures to respond to uncertainty in a foreign environment (Cantwell et al., 2010). However, since not all foreign investors are equal (Cuervo-Cazurra, 2006), we argue that some firms have developed the knowledge of how to cope with corruption at home, and thus, the uncertainty created by corruption abroad does not affect all of them equally.

On another aspect, pressures to not engage in corrupt deals differ based on the level of corruption of the home country. Firms based in countries with lower levels of corruption than a highly corrupt host country may get involved in corrupt deals; however, these firms tried to avoid direct contact with the local government. Instead, firms based in home countries with higher levels of corruption than an already highly corrupt host country actively engaged in business with the local government. This result may suggest that although all firms engage in some level of corrupt deals in the host country, those firms located in countries with lower levels of corruption than the host country face more pressures to not engage in corruption abroad.

We also studied how managers react to the perception of corruption when investing in a highly corrupt foreign location. However, different firms operating in different industries have different reactions to the issue of corruption. Future studies should analyze how corruption affects the attraction of FDI not only at the firm-level but also at the industry level. This distinction should be done because certain industries are more regulated than others and thus, some industries might be more plagued by corruption than others within the same country.

While we propose that those firms located in highly corrupt home countries might have an advantage when investing in host countries with similar institutions, the reality is that corruption is still a problem that needs addressing. Even though countries with high levels of corruption, such as Guatemala, might attract FDI from other highly corrupt countries, they do not achieve their full potential of attracting FDI due to corruption. This assertion is based on the fact that the largest sources of FDI in the world are countries with low levels of corruption. Therefore, policymakers should address the causes of corruption and try to combat it in order to attract more FDI into their countries.

Finally, this study has its limitations. Firstly, due to its nature this study relies in a relatively small number of participants. Future studies should research this issue trying to extend the respondent number in order to make it more generalizable. Also, although this study was conducted with firms operating in a highly corrupt host country, future studies should analyze different host countries to ample our knowledge of the subject.

NOTES

1. The five-year time frame was chosen for the investment to be representative but fairly recent in order for the event to still be in the mind of the decision-maker.
2. See Appendix for list of questions.

REFERENCES

Ades, A., & Di Tella, R. (1997). National champions and corruption: Some unpleasant interventionist arithmetic. *The Economic Journal*, *107*(443), 1023–1042.

Alam, M. (1995). Theory of limits on corruption and some applications. *Kyklos*, *48*, 419–435.

Bénassy-Quéré, A., Coupet, M., & Mayer, T. (2007). Institutional determinants of foreign direct investment. *The World Economy*, *5*(30), 764–782.

Berg, B. (2004). *Qualitative research methods for the social sciences*. Boston, MA: Allyn and Bacon.

Biglaiser, G., & De Rouen, K. (2006). Economic reforms and inflows of foreign direct investment in Latin America. *Latin American Research Review*, *41*, 51–75.

Bryman, A., & Bell, E. (2011). *Business research methods* (3rd ed.). New York, NY: Oxford University Press.

Cantwell, J., Dunning, J., & Ludan, S. (2010). An evolutionary approach to understanding international business activity: The co-evolution of MNEs and the institutional environment. *Journal of International Business Studies*, *41*, 567–586.

Charap, J., & Harm, C. (1999). *Institutionalized corruption and the Kleptocratic state*. Washington, DC: The International Monetary Fund.

Collins, J., & Uhlenbruck, K. (2004). How firms respond to government corruption: Insights from India. *Academy of Management Best Paper Proceedings* (pp. 1–6).

Collins, J., Uhlenbruck, K., & Rodriguez, P. (2008). Why firms engage in corruption: A top management perspective. *Journal of Business Ethics*, *87*, 89–108.

Cuervo-Cazurra, A. (2006). Who cares about corruption? *Journal of International Business Studies*, *37*, 807–822.

Cuervo-Cazurra, A. (2008). Better the devil you don't know: Type of corruption and FDI in transition economies. *Journal of International Management*, *14*(1), 12–27.

Cuervo-Cazurra, A., & Genc, M. (2008). Converting disadvantages into advantages: Developing country MNEs in the least developed countries. *Journal of International Business Studies*, *39*(6), 957–979.

Daniels, J., & Cannice, M. (2004). Interview studies in international business research. In W. C. Marschan-Piekkari (Ed.), *Handbook of qualitative research methods for international business* (pp. 185–206). Cheltenham: Edward Elgar Publishing Ltd.

de Vaal, A., & Ebben, W. (2011). Institutions and the relation between corruption and economic growth. *Review of Development Economics*, *15*(1), 108–123.

Demirbag, M., Glaister, K., & Tatoglu, E. (2007). Institutional and transaction cost influences on MNEs' ownership strategies of their affiliates: Evidence from an emerging market. *Journal of World Business*, *42*, 418–434.

Demsetz, H. (1967). Towards a theory of property rights. *American Economic Review*, *57*(2), 61–70.

Doh, J., Rodriguez, J., Uhlenbruck, K., Collins, J., & Eden, L. (2003). Coping with corruption in foreign markets. *Academy of Management Perspectives*, *17*(3), 114–127.

Driffield, N., Jones, C., & Crotty, J. (2013). International business research and risky investments, an analysis of FDI in conflict zones. *International Business Review*, *22*(1), 140–155.

Ferreira, F., & Gignoux, J. (2011). The measurement of inequality of opportunity: Theory and an application in Latin America. *The Review of Income and Wealth*, *57*(4), 622–657.

Gardberg, N., & Fombrun, C. (2006). Corporate citizenship: Creating intangible assets across institutional environments. *Academy of Management Review*, *31*(2), 329–346.

Gaviria, A. (2002). Assessing the effects of corruption and crime on firm performance: Evidence from Latin America. *Emerging Markets Review*, *3*(3), 245–268.

Godinez, J., & Liu, L. (2014). Corruption distance and FDI flows into Latin America. *International Business Review*, *24*, 33–42.

Greenwood, R. (2006). Institutional entrepreneurship in mature fields: The big five accounting firms. *Academy of Management Journal*, *49*(1), 27–48.

Habib, M., & Zurawicki, L. (2001). Country-level investments and the effect of corruption: Some empirical evidence. *International Business Review*, *10*(6), 687–700.

Habib, M., & Zurawicki, L. (2002). Corruption and foreign direct investment. *Journal of International Business Studies*, *33*(2), 291–307.

Heritage Foundation. (2014). *Index of economic freedom*. Retrieved from http://www.heritage.org/index/country/guatemala

Huntington, S. (1968). *Political order in changing societies*. New Haven, CT: Yale University Press.

Judge, W., McNatt, B., & Xu, W. (2011). The antecedents and effects of national corruption: A meta-analysis. *Journal of World Business*, *46*(1), 93–103.

Khana, T., & Palepu, K. (1997). Why focused strategies may be wrong for emerging markets. *Harvard Business Review*, *75*(4), 41–51.

Kogut, B. (1993). Learning, or the importance of being inert: Country imprinting and international competition. In S. Ghoshal & D. Westney (Eds.), *Organization theory and the multinational corporation* (pp. 136–154). New York, NY: St. Martin's Press.

Kostova, T., & Roth, K. (2002). Adoption of an organizational practice by subsidiaries of multinational corporations: Institutional and relational effects. *Academy of Management Journal*, *45*, 215–233.

Kostova, T., Roth, K., & Dacing, M. (2008). Institutional theory in the study of multinational corporations: A critique and new directions. *Academy of Management Review*, *33*, 994–1006.

Kostova, T., & Zaheer, S. (1999). Organizational legitimacy under conditions of complexity: The case of the multinational enterprise. *Academy of Management Review*, *24*, 64–81.

Kraatz, M., & Block, E. (2008). Organizational implications of institutional pluralism. In R. Greenwood, C. Oliver, K. Sahlin-Anderson, & R. Suddaby, (Eds.), *The handbook of organizational institutionalism* (pp. 243–275). London: Sage.

Kwok, C., & Tadesse, S. (2006). The MNC as an agent of change for host-country institutions: FDI and corruption. *Journal of International Business Studies*, *37*, 767–785.

LaPalombara, J. (1994). Structural and institutional aspects of corruption. *Social Research*, *61*(2), 325–350.

Lee, S., Oh, K., & Eden, L. (2010). Why do firms bribe? Insights from residual control theory into firms' exposure and vulnerability to corruption. *Management International Review*, *50*(6), 775–796.

Li, P. (2005). The puzzle of China's township-village enterprises: The paradox of local corporatism in a dual-track economic transition. *Management and Organization Review*, *1*, 197–224.

Li, P. (2009). The duality of crony corruption in economic transition: Toward and integrated framework. *Journal of Business Ethics*, *85*, 41–55.

Luiz, J., & Stewart, C. (2014). Corruption, South African multinational enterprises and institutions in Africa. *Journal of Business Ethics*, *124*, 383–398.

Meon, P., & Weill, L. (2010). Is corruption an efficient grease? *World Development*, *38*(3), 244–259.

Miles, M., & Huberman, M. (1994). *Qualitative data analysis: An expanded sourcebook* (2nd ed.). Newbury Park, CA: Sage.

Moore, C. (2008). Moral disengagement in process of organizational corruption. *Journal of Business Ethics*, *80*, 129–139.

Murphy, K., Shleifer, A., & Vishny, R. (1993). *Why is rent-seeking so costly to growth?* AEA Papers and Proceedings.

North, D. (1990). *Institutions, institutional change and economic performance*. Cambridge: Cambridge University Press.

Orr, R., & Scott, W. (2008). Institutional exceptions in global projects: A process model. *Journal of International Business Studies*, *39*(4), 562–588.

Pajunen, K. (2008). Institutions and inflows of foreign direct investment: A fuzzy-set analysis. *Journal of International Business Studies*, *39*, 652–669.

Parkhe, A. (2004). Interviews: A key data source in international business research. In R. Marschan-Piekkari & C. Welch (Eds.), *Handbook of qualitative research methods for international business*. Cheltenham: Edward Elgar Publishing Limited.

Parsons, T. (1956). Suggestions for a sociological approach to the theory of organizations. *Administrative Science Quarterly*, *1*(1), 63–88.

Pfeffer, J., & Dowling, J. (1975). Organizational legitimacy: Social values and organizational behavior. *Pacific Sociological Review*, *18*(1), 122.

Rodriguez, P., Siegel, D., Hillman, A., & Eden, L. (2006). Three lenses on the multinational enterprise: Politics, corruption, and corporate social responsibility. *Journal of International Business Studies*, *37*, 733–746.

Rodriguez, R., Uhlenbruck, K., & Eden, L. (2005). Government corruption and the entry strategies of multinationals. *Academy of Management Review*, *30*(2), 383–396.

Rose-Ackerman, S. (1978). *Corruption: A study in political economy*. New York, NY: Academic Press.

Rose-Ackerman, S. (2008). Corruption and government. *Journal of International Peacekeeping, Special Issue on Post-Conflict Peacebuilding and Corruption, 15*(3), 328–343.

Selingson, M. (2006). The measurement and impact of corruption victimization: Survey evidence from Latin America. *World Development, 34*(2), 381–404.

Shleifer, A., & Vishny, R. (1993). Corruption. *Quarterly Journal of Economics, 108*, 599–617.

Spencer, J., & Gomez, C. (2011). MNEs and corruption: The impact of national institutions and subsidiary strategy. *Strategic Management Journal, 32*, 280–300.

Strauss, A., & Corbin, J. (1994). Grounded theory methodology: An overview. In N. Dezin & S. Lincoln (Eds.), *Handbook of qualitative research* (pp. 273–285). Thousand Oaks, CA: Sage.

Suchman, M. (1995). Managing legitimacy: Strategic and institutional approaches. *Academy of Management Review, 20*, 571–611.

Svensson, J. (2005). Eight questions about corruption. *The Journal of Economic Perspectives, 19*(3), 19–42.

Tan, J., & Wang, J. (2011). MNC strategic responses to ethical pressure: An institutional logistic perspective. *Journal of Business Ethics, 98*, 373–390.

Tanzi, V. (1998). *Corruption around the world: Causes consequences, scope and cures.* IMF Working Papers WP/98/63, Washington, DC.

Transparency International. (2013). *Corruption perception index.* Retrieved from http://www.transparency.org/country#GTM_DataResearch_SurveysIndices. Accessed on June 16, 2014.

Uhlenbruck, K., Rodriguez, P., Doh, J., & Lorraine, E. (2006). The impact of corruption on the entry strategy: Evidence from telecommunication projects in emerging economies. *Organization Science, 17*(3), 402–414.

UNDP. (2009). *Humanity divided: Confronting inequality in developing countries.* New York, NY: United Nations Development Program.

Wei, S. (1997). *Why is corruption so much more taxing than tax? Arbitrariness kills.* Cambridge, MA: National Bureau of Economic Research.

Welch, C., Marschan-Piekkari, R., Penttinen, H., & Tahvanainen, M. (2002). Corporate elites as informants in qualitative international business research. *International Business Review, 11*(5), 611–628.

Westney, D. (1993). Institutionalization theory and the multinational corporation. In *Organization theory and the multinational corporation* (pp. 53–75). New York, NY: St. Martin's Press.

Weyland, K. (1998). The politics of corruption in Latin America. *Journal of Democracy, 2*, 108–121.

World Bank. (2014). *World development indicators.* Retrieved from http://data.worldbank.org/country/guatemala

Wu, C., Lawler, J., & Xiang, J. (2008). Overt employment discrimination in MNC affiliates: Home-country cultural and institutional effects. *Journal of International Business Studies, 39*(5), 772–794.

Yackee, J. (2010). How much do U.S. corporations know (and care) about bilateral investment treaties? Some hints from new survey evidence. *Perspectives on topical foreign direct investment issues by the Vale Columbia Center on Sustainable International Investment.*

Zhan, J. (2013). *Regional integration and foreign direct investment.* Geneva: UNCTAD.

Zyglindopulus, S., Fleming, P., & Rothenberg, S. (2008). Rationalization, overcompensation and the escalation of corruption in organizations. *Journal of Business Ethics, 84*, 65–73.

APPENDIX

Questions used during the interviews:

1. What was the main motive for your company to invest in Guatemala?
2. Is there corruption in Guatemala in the industry in which you operate?
3. How often do firms in your same industry engage in acts that might be perceived as corrupt?
4. Have you (or anyone in your firm) ever been requested a bribe by a Guatemalan public official?
5. When operating in Guatemala, do you have advance knowledge of how much an unofficial payment to a government official will be?
6. If you had such knowledge, was this knowledge obtained where your company's headquarters are located?
7. When operating in Guatemala, do you have advance knowledge of whether or not, after making an unofficial payment to an officer, another payment for the same service should be made to another officer?
8. If you had such knowledge, was this knowledge obtained where your company's headquarters are located?
9. When operating in Guatemala, do you have advance knowledge that after making an unofficial payment the service is delivered as agreed?

AN INTEGRATED MODEL OF UPGRADING AND CATCHUP BY EMERGING ECONOMY FIRMS

Murali D. R. Chari

ABSTRACT

One of the more important and interesting phenomena in international business in recent times is the upgrading and catchup of firms from emerging economies. How do these firms upgrade and catchup? This paper reviews and synthesizes the literature on upgrading and catchup by emerging economy firms and develops a model and testable propositions to advance research on the topic.

Keywords: Upgrading; catchup; emerging economy firms; integrated model

INTRODUCTION

Among the defining developments in international business in recent times is the rise of firms from rapidly growing developing countries (i.e., emerging

Emerging Economies and Multinational Enterprises
Advances in International Management, Volume 28, 327–349

ISSN: 1571-5027/doi:10.1108/S1571-502720150000028015

economies) that are upgrading their capabilities and emerging as significant competitors to advanced economy (AE) firms. A growing number of firms from emerging economies (EEs) now routinely make the lists of the largest firms in the world (Fortune, 2014). Firms from these economies are also among the significant competitors internationally in many industries (BCG, 2013). How do firms from EEs, which until recently were thought to lack sophisticated capabilities, upgrade and catchup with the competitiveness of AE firms?

There are several strands of literature that have attempted to address this question. The strands of literature, however, have evolved in silos (i.e., independently). As a result, the literature to date is deficient in certain respects. First, with each strand of literature focusing on different capabilities, it is unclear which capabilities are involved in the overall process of upgrading and catchup. Second, it is unclear whether the upgrading mechanism considered within each strand of literature may contribute to upgrading capabilities that lie outside the focus of that strand of literature. Third, knowledge of whether the process of upgrading and catchup proceeds in a particular sequence is lacking. The objective of this paper is to address these deficiencies. The paper will review and synthesize the different strands of literature and develop an overarching model of the upgrading and catchup process along with testable propositions.

CAPABILITIES INVOLVED IN THE PROCESS OF UPGRADING AND CATCHUP

Each strand of the literature on upgrading and catchup has focused on different capabilities, often to the exclusion of others. For example, one strand focusses on just the labor and total factor productivity of firms (e.g., Buckley, Clegg, & Wang, 2007), while another focusses on the ability to internationalize the firm (Mathews, 2006). As a result, a holistic understanding of the various capabilities involved in upgrading and catchup is wanting. The concept of catchup, which refers to achieving parity in capabilities with competitive AE firms, offers a basis to determine the relevant capabilities. Three types of capabilities are salient in competitive AE firms: production capability, project execution capability, and innovation capability (Bell & Pavitt, 1995; Nam, 2011). Consequently, the upgrading of all three should be part of a holistic model of what constitutes upgrading and catchup. Production capability refers to a firm's ability to monitor, maintain, and improve its existing operations to meet higher efficiency and quality standards (Nam, 2011). Project execution capability, also called investment capability, refers to a wide range of skills and knowledge required to successfully establish new operations or expand existing ones (Bell & Pavitt, 1995; Guillen, 2000; Nam, 2011). Innovation capability refers to a firm's capacity to create new knowledge and apply it to practical or commercial uses through ingenious combinations of pre-existing knowledge, skills, and other resources (Cohen & Levinthal, 1990; Nam, 2011). The three types of capabilities play different roles in the competitiveness of firms. Production capability is essential to produce products and be in business, while project execution capability is salient to grow and adapt the firm to changing circumstances. By enabling the introduction of new products and processes, innovation capability plays an important role in the firm's ability to stay ahead of competition and remain in business even as the relevant technologies in the industry advance. Given differences in their roles from the basics required to be in business, to the more advanced issues of growing and sustaining the firm over time, production, project execution, and innovation capabilities, in that order, can be thought of as representing lower to higher order capabilities (Winter, 2003).

EE firms have traditionally lagged behind AE firms in all three capabilities. Operations that meet higher efficiency and quality standards would be reflected as higher labor and total factor productivity of firms, and EE firms have been noted to lag behind AE firms with respect to both labor and total factor productivity (Buckley et al., 2007). The literature on EE firm internationalization notes that while competitive AE firms are able to invest and establish facilities both at home and internationally, EE firms lag behind in their ability to invest and establish facilities overseas (Luo & Tung, 2007). With respect to innovation, the literature on EE firms notes that these firms have the ability to replicate or adapt existing products and processes introduced by AE firms, but lag behind AE firms as they lack the ability to introduce new to the world products and processes. Catching up by EE firms, therefore, involves upgrading all three capabilities to match those of competitive AE firms. Fig. 1 depicts upgrading and catchup and how the capabilities of EE and competitive AE firms differ.

REVIEW OF THE LITERATURE ON UPGRADING AND CATCHUP

Four strands of literature have dealt with upgrading and catchup by EE firms. Three of the four share a key assumption that upgrading and

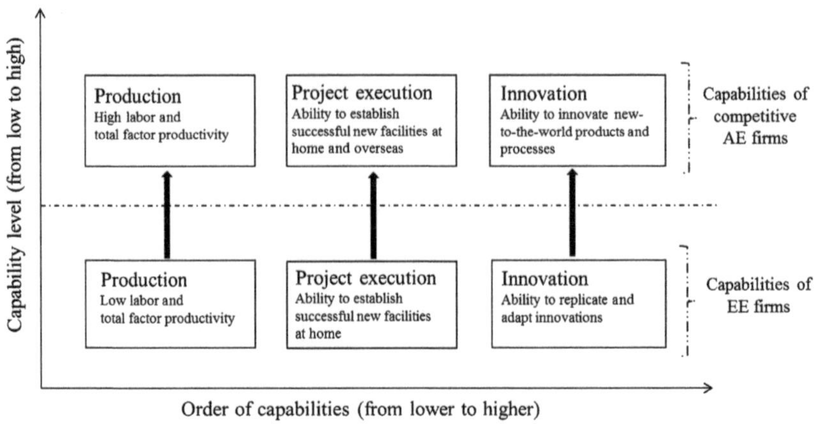

Fig. 1. What Upgrading and Catchup Entails.

catchup requires EE firms to learn from internationally competitive AE firms or MNCs (Multinational Corporations). This assumption is consistent with the literature on catchup of nations (Amsden, 1991) and with the investment led development path postulated for countries (Dunning, 1981; Dunning & Narula, 1996). The fourth strand holds that while learning from MNCs is beneficial, upgrading and catchup also requires internal R&D by EE firms. Each strand of literature is reviewed briefly below.

Upgrading through Spillovers

The premise of this strand is that the presence of MNCs in EE markets can help EE firms upgrade through demonstration effects, aided by employee mobility and competitive pressures. The literature in this strand is large and primarily empirical. The typical approach in this strand is to model MNC presence in the market as a driver of EE firms' labor productivity or total factor productivity. A positive coefficient for MNC presence from such regression models is then taken as evidence that MNC presence helps EE firms upgrade their productivity.

Early studies varied widely in their findings, with some finding a positive effect (i.e., positive coefficient for MNC presence), some finding a negative effect, and others finding no effect (Görg & Greenaway, 2004; Zhang, Li, & Li, 2014). More recent studies recognize the potential for negative effects due to the crowding-out of EE firms by MNCs. These studies propose an inverse U-shaped relationship with positive spillover effects at low to moderate levels of MNC presence and negative effects at higher levels of MNC presence (Altomonte & Pennings, 2009; Buckley et al., 2007). The literature has also identified other contingencies including vertical versus horizontal industries and the home country of MNCs. Studies find positive vertical spillovers (i.e., positive spillovers from the presence of MNCs in downstream industries), but limited horizontal spillovers (i.e., lower levels or even no spillovers from MNC presence in the same industry) (Altomonte & Pennings, 2009; Javorcik, 2004; Liu, Wang, & Wei, 2009), and greater spillovers from the presence of AE MNCs (Buckley et al., 2007).

Certain initial conditions, the literature finds, enhance the ability of firms to benefit from spillovers (Blalock & Simon, 2009; Zhang, Li, Li, & Zhou, 2010). Specifically, larger firms and firms with moderate levels of productivity gap with MNCs appear to benefit more from spillovers (Zhang et al., 2010). Both labor and total factor productivity represent efficiency in converting inputs to outputs (measured as sales), and hence indicate production capability.

Upgrading through Links (or Link and Learn)

The premise of this strand of literature is that EE firms can learn to upgrade through their links with MNCs as buyers of technology/capital equipment, contract manufacturers, and joint venture partners (Mathews, 2002, 2006; Nam, 2011).[1] Acquiring technology and capital equipment from technically advanced foreign firms or MNCs to overcome the lack of domestic technology sources, studies in this strand of literature note, has led EE firms to enhance their production capability (Amsden & Hikino, 1994; Hikino & Amsden, 1994). As Amsden (2009, p. 65) observed, "[f]oreign firms that are teachers tend to be vendors of parts and components ... they help by giving all their customers a road map to their industry." Serving as contract manufacturers or suppliers for MNCs has also been found to enhance the production capabilities of EE firms as the MNCs provide EE firms with managerial assistance in quality control and other production related areas to ensure that their output meets the MNC's high quality standards (Chen & Chen, 2002; Luo & Tung, 2007; McDermott & Corredoira, 2010). Joint ventures between MNCs and EE firms, the literature finds, enhance the production capabilities of EE firms as working closely with MNCs enables EE firms to learn from the MNC (Lane, Salk, & Lyles, 2001; Lyles & Salk, 1996; Nam, 2011).

In addition to upgrading production capability, the literature on EE firm internationalization has argued that when EE firms combine what they learn from their links and their indigenous advantages, the combination can be leveraged to offset the added costs and risks of establishing foreign facilities (Luo & Tung, 2007; Mathews, 2006). For example, links as buyers of foreign technology and as contract manufacturers help EE firms learn to manufacture products to the strict standards and specifications required for success in foreign markets. Combining these with their own indigenous advantages, for example in low cost production, ability to swiftly scale up production (Amsden, 2009), or operate under adverse conditions (Chari, 2013; Dawar & Frost, 1999; Ramamurti, 2009), enable EE firms to enter and establish operations/facilities in foreign countries. Early studies of internationalization by EE firms, for example, found that EE firms that combined imported technologies with their own capability to adapt such technologies to the particular needs of developing countries were able to overcome the risks and added costs of establishing production facilities in other developing countries (Lall, 1983). Similar accounts of EE firms combining what they learn from their links with MNCs and their own indigenous advantages to establish foreign facilities are provided by several recent studies including Bonaglia, Goldstein, and Mathews (2007), Karabag and Berggren (2014), Amsden (2009), and Mathews (2006). Thus, links with MNCs, the literature finds, contributes to project execution capability upgrading as well.

The literature on upgrading through links also notes that government policies that mandate local content and joint ventures enhance the opportunity for EE firm upgrading by incentivizing MNCs to train and teach EE firms (Mu & Lee, 2005; Nam, 2011). The type of link has also been noted to moderate upgrading, with links that provide greater engagement such as joint ventures providing more opportunity for upgrading than arms-length relationships (Kumaraswamy, Mudambi, Saranga, & Tripathy, 2012; McDermott & Corredoira, 2010; Nam, 2011). Finally, larger firms and firms that are more prominent in the local economy, the literature observes, are better positioned to forge links with MNCs (Amsden, 2009; Chari, 2013; Khanna & Palepu, 2000).

Upgrading through Acquisitions (or Acquire and Assimilate)

The premise of this strand is that EE firms can upgrade by acquiring AE firms and assimilating their capabilities. Studies frequently claim that acquiring advanced or higher order capabilities such as innovation capability is a motivation for EE firm acquisitions in AEs (Deng, 2009; Luo & Tung, 2007). The evidence on acquisitions of AE targets enabling EE firms to upgrade their capabilities however is very limited and is anecdotal or case based. Case studies show that many acquisitions of AE firms have failed (Williamson & Anand, 2013). Some studies find anecdotal evidence of EE firms upgrading their production capabilities aided by their acquisitions in AEs (Ramamurti, 2013; Williamson & Anand, 2013). There is however no evidence of innovation capability upgrading. Although EE firms do indeed obtain patents and technological products of target firms, what Williamson and Anand (2013, p. 276) call "hard technology and intellectual property" through acquisitions, gaining ownership of existing patents, and products is not the same as gaining the capability to innovate new-to-the-world products and processes (Awate, Larsen, & Mudambi, 2012).

Similarly, the acquisition of an AE target firm does indeed provide the EE firm with ownership of an already established foreign facility. However, gaining ownership of a foreign facility is not the same as gaining the capability to establish a foreign facility. Acquisition of an AE target firm may indeed be a source of gaining this capability if the EE firm is able to learn from the AE target how to perform the complex activities involved in establishing foreign facilities such as understanding foreign markets, developing relationships with stakeholders in the market, and managing operations in that market. Studies to date, however, have not empirically examined this possibility.

Upgrading through Internal R&D

In contrast to the previous three strands where upgrading is based on learning from MNCs, the premise of this strand of literature is that EE firms can upgrade their capabilities through internal R&D. At least two distinct arguments have been advanced to emphasize the need for internal R&D. First, because technologies including production methods developed in AEs may not be suitable for EE markets, EE firms would need to engage in internal R&D to develop new to the world products and processes that are suitable for their markets (Basu & Weil, 1998; Fu, Pietrobelli, & Soete, 2010). Second, since innovation capability is among their main sources of competitive advantage, MNCs will guard their innovation capability from possible leakage or diffusion to EE firms. EE firms would therefore need to engage in internal R&D to upgrade their innovation capability and move from imitation and adaptation of existing products and processes to innovating new-to-the-world products and processes (Bell & Pavitt, 1995; Fan, 2006; Fu et al., 2010; Karabag & Berggren, 2014; Lee & Lim, 2001, p. 476).

Supporting the importance of internal R&D to upgrade and better compete with the growing numbers of competitors in their markets following economic reforms, empirical studies have found that a greater proportion of EE firms invest in internal R&D after their governments open up their markets to foreign competition (Bowonder & Richardson, 2000; Pradhan, 2003), and that investment in R&D helps EE firms mitigate the competitive erosion of superior profits following economic reforms in their country (Chari & David, 2012). Studies have also found that internal R&D by EE firms enhances their uptake of external technologies (Aggarwal, 2000). Case studies support the position that MNCs are reluctant to provide EE firms with access to their innovation capabilities, requiring EE firms to engage in internal R&D to develop new-to-the-world products and processes (Fu et al., 2010; Karabag & Berggren, 2014; Lee & Lim, 2001).

SYNTHESIS, OVERALL MODEL, AND TESTABLE PROPOSITIONS

Table 1 shows a summary and synthesis of the four streams of literature on upgrading reviewed above. By highlighting similarities as well as key differences, the summary and synthesis can help develop an overall model of the upgrading and catchup process that goes beyond the scope of any one of the four strands of literature. As the table shows, the upgrading mechanisms differ in the main mode of learning involved, the nature of the firm's role in the process, and the resource commitment and associated risks involved. While differences in the main mode of learning and the firm's role are fairly straightforward, some explanation is required with respect to resource commitment and associated risks.

Resource commitment and associated risks in spillovers are mainly in the form of managerial resources to observe and adopt practices, and are low relative to those involved in the other mechanisms. Link and learn involves greater resource commitment than spillovers. Specifically, when linking with MNCs as a buyer of technologies or capital equipment, financial outlays are required for the acquisition and managerial resources are necessary to incorporate the technologies and capital equipment into the firm's operations. Financial outlays and managerial effort to upgrade

Table 1. A Synthesis of the Four Strands of Literature.

	Spillover	Link and Learn	Acquire and Assimilate	Internal R&D
Learning by	Observing the activities of MNCs	Performing activities jointly or with guidance/ assistance from MNCs	Integrating with and assimilating from AE target firms	Disciplined experimentation
EE firms' role	Relatively passive	Active	Active	Active
Resource commitment and associated risks	Low	Medium	Medium to high	High
Capability dealt with	Production	Production, project execution	Project execution, innovation	Innovation

production facilities, similarly, are required to meet the higher quality standards when linking with MNCs as original equipment manufacturers (OEMs) or suppliers. When links take the form of joint ventures, EE firms will need to commit their share of capital investments and managerial resources to the venture. While the resource commitment and associated risks in link and learn are significant, they are lower than that required for acquisitions and internal R&D. The resource commitment and associated risks for link and learn are therefore characterized as "medium" in Table 1.

Acquisitions of AE firms involve substantial financial outlays, much more than that required for forging shared ownership or arms-length links (Anderson & Gatignon, 1986). The managerial resource commitments required to perform due diligence, negotiate the deal, and manage the target firm's activities after acquisition are all substantial even in domestic acquisitions. Such managerial resource commitments are even greater in foreign acquisitions (Chari & Chang, 2009). The resource commitment and associated risks involved in acquire and assimilate are therefore characterized as "between medium and high" in Table 1. Internal R&D, in particular internal R&D required to develop new to the world products and processes, requires very large and sustained commitment of financial and managerial resources including investments in the necessary facilities, equipment, and highly skilled personnel (Karabag & Berggren, 2014). Such R&D efforts often span several years, soaking up very large investments, even as the outcome of such efforts are highly uncertain. The resource commitment and associated risks are therefore the highest for internal R&D among the upgrading mechanisms and are accordingly labeled "high" in Table 1.

As also shown in Table 1, each strand of the literature has implicitly focused on a subset of capabilities. The strands of literature, however, have not systematically considered why the mechanisms will or will not contribute to the upgrading of other capabilities. The strands of literature have also not considered whether upgrading of capabilities will progress in any particular sequence. The next section draws on relevant theories and the summary and synthesis presented above (and in Table 1) to develop an overall model of upgrading and catchup with testable propositions. The overall model of upgrading and catchup developed is shown in Fig. 2 and Table 2. The model portrays three sets of relationships with respect to which testable propositions are developed. First, drawing from the theoretical literature on learning, the section develops propositions relating each upgrading mechanism with one or more of the capabilities. Second, drawing on the behavioral theory of the firm, the section proposes that the upgrading process progresses in a particular sequence. Third, drawing on the relevant literature, the section proposes internal and external factors that moderate the relationship between upgrading mechanisms and capabilities upgraded.

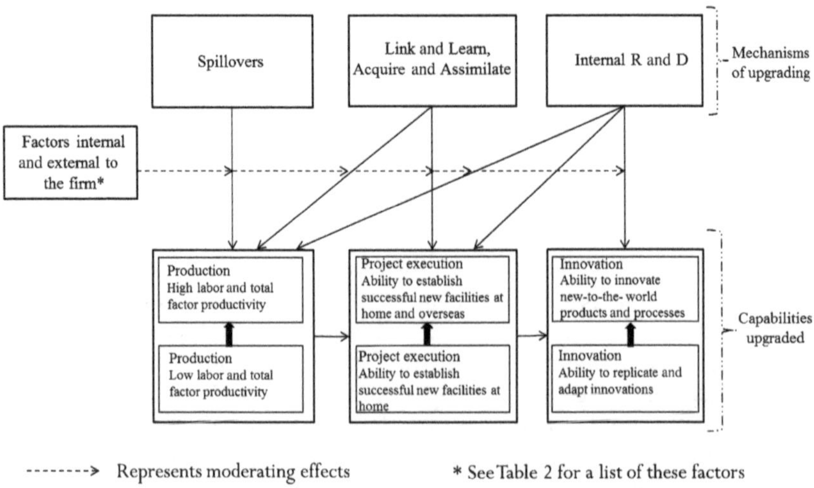

Fig. 2. The Integrated Model of Upgrading and Catchup.

Table 2. Internal and External Factors that Moderate the Efficacy of Upgrading through Each Mechanism.

Upgrading Mechanism	Internal and External Factors
Spillovers	EE firm size Productivity gap Extent of MNC presence Industry of MNC presence: Downstream versus horizontal Origin of MNCs: AEs versus other countries
Link and learn	EE firm size EE firm domestic market share EE government mandate on local content and joint ventures Type of link: Joint ventures versus arms-length
Acquire and assimilate	EE firm size EE country market size and growth
Internal R&D	EE firm size EE firm experience with imported technologies EE country institutional context for innovation

Relationship between Mechanisms and Capabilities Upgraded

This section draws from the theoretical literature on learning to analyze the relationship between the mechanisms of upgrading and the capabilities upgraded. As shown in Table 1, the primary mode of learning differs across the four mechanisms. Learning in spillovers is primarily by observing the practices of MNCs. Learning through observation, also referred to as vicarious learning in the learning literature, is effective for simple and routine activities since repetition enhances observability and simplicity aids the observers' understanding of cause-effect relationships (Barney, 1995; Huber, 1991). Of the three – production, project execution, and innovation – production involves activities that are the most routine with relatively simpler cause-effect relationships as evidenced by the presence of standardized and well codified production practices such as Six Sigma and Lean Manufacturing (Harry & Schroeder, 2005; Wilson, 2009). Spillovers therefore can contribute to production capability upgrading. Project execution and innovation, in contrast, are complex and nonroutine activities and hence are not suited for upgrading through spillovers.

Upgrading project execution capability involves learning to perform many complex activities including understanding the needs of the foreign market, producing products to the specifications and standards of the foreign market, building relationships with stakeholders in the foreign market, and managing operations in the foreign market (Johanson & Vahlne, 1977). Foreign market entry is also a nonroutine activity. Complex and nonroutine activities, because they are less amenable to codification, are best learned through more engaged learning processes such as performing the activities jointly or with assistance from a competent firm that can guide or tutor the novice firm (Kogut, 1988; Luo & Tung, 2007). Link and learn as well as acquire and assimilate enable learning through greater engagement between novice EE firms and more competent MNCs (Hamel, 1991; Huber, 1991; Kogut, 1988; Lyles & Salk, 1996). In link and learn for example, the MNC assists/tutors the EE firm in using more advanced technologies, in producing products for the higher standards and specifications of foreign markets, and/or in superior management practices, all of which can facilitate the expansion of EE firms to foreign markets (Amsden, 2009; Chen & Chen, 2002; Luo & Tung, 2007; McDermott & Corredoira, 2010). Managers from the acquired AE firm, similarly, can assist the EE firm in learning the needs and requirements of operating in foreign markets (Björkman, Stahl, & Vaara, 2007; Huber, 1991). Link and learn and acquire and assimilate therefore are suited for upgrading project execution capability.

Innovation is also an activity that is complex and nonroutine. Hence, in theory, innovation capability should be amenable for upgrading through the more engaging learning processes in link and learn and acquire and assimilate. In practice, however, link and learn and acquire and assimilate are unlikely to contribute to innovation capability upgrading in EE firms. This is because innovation capability is MNCs' main source of competitive advantage. MNCs as a result would be reluctant to link with EE firms for innovation activities for fear of losing their main source of advantage (Karabag & Berggren, 2014). In the case of acquisitions, engaging in joint research and development with a target firm or otherwise transferring the innovation capability, which by its nature is tacit, requires deep and sustained integration of the AE target firm and the EE acquirer – much more so than is required for the transfer of the relatively less tacit knowledge on how to establish foreign operations (Bresman, Birkinshaw, & Nobel, 1999; Huber, 1991; Karnani, 2010; Polanyi, 2009). Extant research however suggests that, perhaps due to their lack of international management experience, EE firms tend not to integrate their AE targets or do so only to a limited extent (Kumar, 2009; Williamson & Anand, 2013). In addition, the lack of sufficient absorptive capacity for innovation in EE firms will also hinder the effective transfer of innovation capability from AE targets to the

EE firms and dissuade MNCs from engaging in joint innovation through links. The more engaging learning processes can also contribute to upgrading capability in simple and routine activities. Hence, link and learn and acquire and assimilate can also contribute to production capability upgrading.

Complex capabilities such as innovation are amenable to upgrading through learning by doing, although the process can be arduous and time consuming since much of the learning has to occur with the firms' own efforts (Fu et al., 2010; Karabag & Berggren, 2014). Specifically, the firm will have to discover the cause-effect relationships between activities and their results on their own through trial and error which injects considerable uncertainty and time into the process. Upgrading through internal R&D, which involves a form of learning by doing – learning through disciplined experimentation – is therefore a viable albeit time consuming and arduous mechanism for upgrading EE firm innovation capability. By engaging in internal R&D, EE firms have been able to upgrade their innovation capabilities and move from imitating and adapting existing products and processes to innovating new-to-the-world products and processes (Karabag & Berggren, 2014). Although the learning by doing in internal R&D is focused on upgrading innovation capability it can also contribute to upgrading project execution capability and production capability. Specifically, internal R&D can deliver substantial enhancements to existing products and processes and thereby raise the firm's productivity (i.e., upgrade production capability). Substantial improvements in products and processes can also enhance the competitiveness of the firm in overseas markets and thereby lower the risks and liabilities associated with establishing foreign facilities (i.e., help upgrade project execution capability) (Zaheer, 2002).

> **P1.** The four upgrading mechanisms differ in their contribution to upgrading and catchup such that spillovers contribute to production capability upgrading, link and learn and acquire and assimilate contribute to project execution and production capability upgrading, and internal R&D contributes to innovation, project execution, and production capability upgrading.

Sequence of Capability Upgrading

This section draws on the behavioral theory of the firm to develop the proposition on the sequence of capability upgrading. Behavioral theory of the firm suggests that firms, made up of decision makers who are boundedly rational, attend to goals in a sequential fashion seeking to lower uncertainty and risk by prioritizing the resolution of short-term problems rather than long-term strategy (Cyert & March, 1963; Mahoney, 2004; Pierce, Boerner, & Teece, 2002). In the context of upgrading and catchup, upgrading of each capability can be seen as a goal that can be attended to one at a time. Additionally, the resource commitment and the associated risks/uncertainties vary across mechanisms that contribute to upgrading each of the three capabilities.

As argued in developing proposition 1, production capability can be upgraded through spillovers. Upgrading through spillovers (as shown in Table 1) involves the least amount of resource commitment and associated risks/uncertainties. Following tenets of the behavioral theory of the firm, one can therefore expect that managers of EE firms would prioritize and pursue production capability upgrading first. Since it is the more productive local firms that succeed in internationalizing their operations, managers are likely to consider raising firm productivity (or production capability upgrading) as a more immediate goal that can also reduce the greater risks and uncertainties associated with project execution capability upgrading (Greenaway & Kneller, 2007). Upgrading of project execution capability is therefore likely to be pursued after production capability upgrading. Internal R&D required to upgrade innovation capability (as shown in Table 1) involves the highest levels of resource commitment and associated risks/uncertainties. Consequently, following tenets of the behavioral theory of the firm, EE firms can be expected to pursue innovation capability upgrading last in the sequence of capability upgrading.

P2. The sequence of upgrading and catchup by EE firms is from production capability upgrading, to project execution capability upgrading, to innovation capability upgrading.

Influence of Internal and External Factors on Upgrading

There are differences across firms within EEs and also differences among EEs themselves. These differences are likely to moderate the efficacy of upgrading through the mechanisms. This section draws on relevant literatures to propose how internal and external factors moderate the efficacy of upgrading through each mechanism.

The empirical literature on spillovers is the most extensive of the four streams, and has identified internal and external factors that influence upgrading through spillovers. Internal factors that enhance upgrading thorough spillovers include productivity gap and firm size (Blalock & Simon, 2009; Zhang et al., 2010). EE firms that are neither too close to nor too far behind MNCs in their productivity levels are expected to have both the incentive and the necessary ability to observe and adopt superior practices (Zhang et al., 2010). Larger firms are expected to have the economies of scale and the complimentary resources necessary to benefit more from spillovers (Zhang et al., 2010). With respect to external factors, capability upgrading through spillovers is greater at low to moderate levels of MNC presence, greater from the presence of MNCs in downstream (vertical) industries than in the same (horizontal) industry, and greater from the presence of MNCs from AEs relative to MNCs from other countries (Altomonte & Pennings, 2009; Buckley et al., 2007; Javorcik, 2004; Liu et al., 2009).

P3a. Capability upgrading through spillovers is greater when the EE firm productivity gap with MNCs is moderate, when the EE firm is larger, when MNC presence is low to moderate in downstream (relative to horizontal) industries, and when MNCs are from AEs (relative to from other countries).

By attracting more and deeper links with MNCs, larger size and a more prominent position in the local economy are internal factors that would enhance EE firm upgrading through link and learn (Amsden, 2009; Khanna & Palepu, 2000). By inducing MNCs to forge links with local firms, EE government policies that mandate local content and joint ventures are external factors that would foster upgrading through link and learn (Mu & Lee, 2005). In addition, because they involve closer relationships with MNCs, joint ventures can be expected to foster greater upgrading than arms-length links such as buyer and supplier relationships.

P3b. Capability upgrading through link and learn is greater when the EE firm is larger, when the EE firm has a higher domestic market share, when the EE government policy mandates local content and joint ventures, and when the link is a joint venture rather than an arms-length relationship.

Unlike the case of upgrading through spillovers and link and learn, empirical research on upgrading through acquire and assimilate is very limited. The moderators proposed here have therefore received little or no empirical testing in extant research. With respect to internal factors, since larger firms are better able to afford the large costs and absorb the higher risks of acquiring target firms in AEs, larger EE firms can be expected to benefit more from upgrading through acquire and assimilate (Chari, 2013). With respect to external factors, there is anecdotal evidence that the prospect of greater access to large and growing home markets of acquiring EE firms motivate target firm managers from AEs to help with the transfer of capabilities to the EE firm (Williamson & Anand, 2013). The size and growth of the EE firm's home country market can therefore be expected to moderate upgrading through acquisitions.

P3c. Capability upgrading through acquire and assimilate is greater when the EE firm is larger and when the EE firm's home country market is large and growing.

The literature on innovation argues that certain internal and external factors would influence the efficacy of upgrading through internal R&D. In particular the literature suggests that larger firm size and greater absorptive capacity, developed for example through experience with imported technologies, are internal factors that can enhance a firm's internal R&D efforts (Chang, Chung, & Mahmood, 2006; Cohen & Levinthal, 1990). An institutional context that is supportive of innovation, the literature suggests, is an important external factor that facilitates upgrading through internal R&D (Hobday, 2005; Hu & Mathews, 2005; Nelson, 1993).

P3d. Capability upgrading through internal R&D is greater when the EE firm is larger, when the EE firm has greater absorptive capacity through greater experience with imported technologies, and when the institutional context of the EE firm's home country is more supportive of innovation.

DISCUSSION AND CONCLUSION

This paper reviewed four strands of literature on upgrading and catchup by EE firms, and developed an integrated overall model of the upgrading and catchup process with testable propositions. There are four notable features of the overall model developed in the paper. First, the overall model incorporates a clear articulation of the capabilities involved in upgrading and catchup. Second, the overall model develops theoretically based arguments to relate each upgrading mechanism with a set of capabilities upgraded.

Third, the overall model proposes how the sequence of upgrading and catchup is likely to proceed. Fourth, the overall model proposes that the efficacies of the four upgrading mechanisms are likely to vary with internal and external factors of the EE firm. Each of these features holds implications for, and contributes to, research in the area as discussed below.

With each strand of the literature focusing on different sets of capabilities, a unified understanding of the capabilities involved in the process of upgrading and catchup is lacking in the literature. This paper leveraged the notion that catchup refers to EE firms catching up with competitive AE firms to identify production, project execution, and innovation capabilities as the salient capabilities. Moreover, the paper drew from the literature on EE firms to clearly articulate the gap between EE firms and AE firms with respect to each capability that would need to be bridged by the process of upgrading and catchup. The clear articulation of the specific capabilities involved and the gap between EE firms and AE firms with respect to these capabilities should help advance research by enabling scholars to relate and test the efficacy of various mechanisms deemed helpful for the upgrading and catchup by EE firms.

Another aspect unclear from extant research is whether (and why) the mechanisms of upgrading dealt within each strand of literature may contribute to upgrading capabilities that lie outside the focus of that strand of literature. This paper, leveraging the fact that learning occurs differently in each upgrading mechanism, drew on learning theory to analyze and propose theoretically grounded relationships between each upgrading mechanism and capabilities upgraded. Specifically, spillover the paper proposed contributes to production capability, but not project execution or innovation capability upgrading. Link and learn and acquire and assimilate contribute to production and project execution capability upgrading, but not innovation capability upgrading. Internal R&D contributes to the upgrading of all three capabilities – production, project execution, and innovation. The value of developing these relationships based on a theoretical analysis can be seen in the fact that in some cases, the capabilities that the upgrading mechanisms are proposed to contribute to in this paper are different from the capabilities that has been the implicit focus of the literature within each stream (see Table 1).

A third unanswered question in the literature on upgrading and catchup is whether the process of upgrading and catchup proceeds in a particular sequence. Addressing this question is important to gain an integrated understanding of EE firm upgrading and catchup. The paper addressed this question by drawing on the behavioral theory of the firm along with differences in resource commitment and risks involved in the various upgrading mechanisms. The paper proposed that the process of upgrading and catchup progresses from production capability upgrading, to project execution capability upgrading, to innovation capability upgrading. The proposed sequence which expects EE firms to upgrade their project execution capability before they upgrade their innovation capability is consistent with the literature on EE firm internationalization. Specifically, the EE firm internationalization literature has noted that the possibility of learning through links with AE firms enables EE firms to internationalize their operations even in the absence of significant innovation capabilities that were considered important for the earlier internationalization of AE firms (Chari, 2013; Luo & Tung, 2007; Mathews, 2006; Ramamurti & Singh, 2009).

Lastly, the overall model proposed that internal and external factors moderate the effectiveness of upgrading mechanisms. This set of propositions is important and makes a contribution because, together with other aspects of the model, it can help predict which firms from which EEs are more likely to upgrade and catchup with AE firms. For example, since larger firms are more likely to afford the resources required for internal R&D and since internal R&D is indispensable for upgrading innovation capability, one can expect that larger EE firms are the ones that are more likely to fully catchup with AE firms. Similarly, since internal R&D is expected to be more effective in countries with supportive institutional infrastructure for innovation, firms from countries with such institutional contexts can be expected to have a higher likelihood of fully catching up with AE firms.

In conclusion, the study made substantial progress in developing an integrated, overall model of the process of upgrading and catchup. Four features of the model make specific contributions with implications for research in the area as discussed above. An important direction for further research is to empirically test the overall model and specific propositions developed in this paper. Testing the model would require a diverse sample of firms from a diverse set of EEs to ensure internal and external validity and avoid the problems of selection bias (Collinson & Rugman, 2007). Finally, abiding by the principles of parsimony, rather than develop multiple models, the paper developed an overall model with propositions that are expected to apply to EE firms on the average. It is possible that particular EE firms may vary from the relationships expected for the average EE firm in this paper. Identifying and studying such exceptions would also be important to uncover pioneering trends, or potential "blind spots" in the analyses presented in this paper.

NOTE

1. A rare exception is Lorenzen and Mudambi (2013) who explore the role of personal rather than firm level connections across-borders.

REFERENCES

Aggarwal, A. (2000). Deregulation, technology imports and in-house R&D efforts: An analysis of the Indian experience. *Research Policy*, *29*(9), 1081–1093.

Altomonte, C., & Pennings, E. (2009). Domestic plant productivity and incremental spillovers from foreign direct investment. *Journal of International Business Studies*, *40*(7), 1131–1148.

Amsden, A. H. (1991). Diffusion of development: The late-industrializing model of greater East Asia. *American Economic Review*, *81*(2), 282–286.

Amsden, A. H. (2009). Does firm ownership matter? POEs vs. FOEs in the developing world. In R. Ramamurti & J. V. Singh (Eds.), *Emerging multinationals in emerging markets* (pp. 64–77). Cambridge, UK: Cambridge University Press.

Amsden, A. H., & Hikino, T. (1994). Project execution capability, organizational know-how and conglomerate corporate growth in late industrialization. *Industrial and Corporate Change*, *3*, 111–147.

Anderson, E., & Gatignon, H. (1986). Modes of foreign entry: A transaction cost analysis and propositions. *Journal of International Business Studies*, *17*(3), 1–26.

Awate, S., Larsen, M. M., & Mudambi, R. (2012). EMNE catch-up strategies in the wind turbine industry: Is there a trade-off between output and innovation capabilities? *Global Strategy Journal*, *2*(3), 205–223.

Barney, J. B. (1995). Looking inside for competitive advantage. *The Academy of Management Executive*, *9*(4), 49–61.

Basu, S., & Weil, D. N. (1998). Appropriate technology and growth. *Quarterly Journal of Economics*, *113*, 1025–1054.

BCG. (2013). *Introducing the 2013 BCG global challengers*. Boston, MA: The Boston Consulting Group.

Bell, M., & Pavitt, K. (1995). The development of technological capabilities. In I.-U. Haque & M. Bell (Eds.), *Trade, technology and international competitiveness* (Vol. 22, pp. 69–101). Washington, DC: World Bank.

Björkman, I., Stahl, G. K., & Vaara, E. (2007). Cultural differences and capability transfer in cross-border acquisitions: The mediating roles of capability complementarity, absorptive capacity, and social integration. *Journal of International Business Studies*, *38*(4), 658–672.

Blalock, G., & Simon, D. H. (2009). Do all firms benefit equally from downstream FDI? The moderating effect of local suppliers' capabilities on productivity gains. *Journal of International Business Studies*, *40*(7), 1095–1112.

Bonaglia, F., Goldstein, A., & Mathews, J. A. (2007). Accelerated internationalization by emerging markets' multinationals: The case of the white goods sector. *Journal of World Business*, *42*(4), 369–383.

Bowonder, B., & Richardson, P. (2000). Liberalization and the growth of business-led R&D: The case of India. *R&D Management*, *30*(4), 279–288.

Bresman, H., Birkinshaw, J., & Nobel, R. (1999). Knowledge transfer in international acquisitions. *Journal of International Business Studies*, *30*, 439–462.

Buckley, P. J., Clegg, J., & Wang, C. (2007). Is the relationship between inward FDI and spillover effects linear? An empirical examination of the case of China. *Journal of International Business Studies*, *38*(3), 447–459.

Chang, S.-J., Chung, C.-N., & Mahmood, I. P. (2006). When and how does business group affiliation promote firm innovation? A tale of two emerging economies. *Organization Science*, *17*(5), 637–656.

Chari, M. D. R. (2013). Business groups and foreign direct investments by developing country firms: An empirical test in India. *Journal of World Business*, *48*(3), 349–359.

Chari, M. D. R., & Chang, K. (2009). Determinants of the share of equity sought in cross-border acquisitions. *Journal of International Business Studies*, *40*(8), 1277–1297.

Chari, M. D. R., & David, P. (2012). Sustaining superior performance in an emerging economy: An empirical test in the Indian context. *Strategic Management Journal*, *33*, 217–229.

Chen, H., & Chen, T.-J. (2002). Asymmetric strategic alliances: A network view. *Journal of Business Research*, *55*(12), 1007–1013.

Cohen, W. M., & Levinthal, D. A. (1990). Absorptive capacity: A new perspective on learning and innovation. *Administrative Science Quarterly*, *35*(1), 128–152.

Collinson, S., & Rugman, A. M. (2007). The regional character of Asian multinational enterprises. *Asia Pacific Journal of Management*, *24*(4), 429–446.

Cyert, R. M., & March, J. G. (1963). *A behavioral theory of the firm*. Upper Saddle River, NJ: Prentice-Hall Inc.

Dawar, N., & Frost, T. (1999). Competing with giants. *Harvard Business Review*, *77*(2), 119–129.

Deng, P. (2009). Why do Chinese firms tend to acquire strategic assets in international expansion? *Journal of World Business*, *44*(1), 74–84.

Dunning, J. H. (1981). Explaining the international direct investment position of countries: Towards a dynamic or developmental approach. *Weltwirtschaftliches Archiv*, *117*(1), 30–64.

Dunning, J. H., & Narula, R. (1996). The investment development path revisited. In *Foreign direct investment and governments: Catalysts for economic restructuring* (pp. 1–41). London: Routledge.

Fan, P. (2006). Catching up through developing innovation capability: Evidence from China's telecom-equipment industry. *Technovation*, *26*(3), 359–368.

Fortune. (2014). Global 500. *Fortune*. Retrieved from http://fortune.com/global500/

Fu, X., Pietrobelli, C., & Soete, L. (2010). *The role of foreign technology and indigenous innovation in emerging economies: Technological change and catching up*. Inter-American Development Bank Technical Notes No. IDB-TN-166.

Görg, H., & Greenaway, D. (2004). Much ado about nothing? Do domestic firms really benefit from foreign direct investment? *The World Bank Research Observer*, *19*(2), 171–197.

Greenaway, D., & Kneller, R. (2007). Firm heterogeneity, exporting and foreign direct investment. *The Economic Journal*, *117*(517), F134–F161.

Guillen, M. F. (2000). Business groups in emerging economies: A resource-based view. *Academy of Management Journal*, *43*(3), 362–380.

Hamel, G. (1991). Competition for competence and interpartner learning within international strategic alliances. *Strategic Management Journal*, *12*(S1), 83–103.
Harry, M., & Schroeder, R. (2005). *Six sigma: The breakthrough management strategy revolutionizing the world's top corporations*. New York, NY: Random House LLC.
Hikino, T., & Amsden, A. H. (1994). Staying behind, stumbling back, sneaking up, soaring ahead: Late industrialization in historical perspective. In W. J. Baumol, R. R. Nelson, & E. N. Wolf (Eds.), *Convergence of productivity: Cross-national studies and historical evidence* (pp. 285–315). New York, NY: Oxford University Press.
Hobday, M. (2005). Firm-level innovation models: Perspectives on research in developed and developing countries. *Technology Analysis & Strategic Management*, *17*(2), 121–146.
Hu, M.-C., & Mathews, J. A. (2005). National innovative capacity in East Asia. *Research Policy*, *34*(9), 1322–1349.
Huber, G. P. (1991). Organizational learning: The contributing processes and the literatures. *Organization Science*, *2*(1), 88–115.
Javorcik, B. S. (2004). Does foreign direct investment increase the productivity of domestic firms? In search of spillovers through backward linkages. *American Economic Review*, 605–627.
Johanson, J., & Vahlne, J.-E. (1977). The internationalization process of the firm-a model of knowledge development and increasing foreign market commitments. *Journal of International Business Studies*, *8*(1), 23–32.
Karabag, S. F., & Berggren, C. (2014). Joint ventures or independence? Alternative ways of R&D capability building at emerging economy firms. *DRUID Society conference 2014, CBS*, Copenhagen, June 16–18.
Karnani, A. (2010). *Dubious value of international acquisitions by emerging economy firms: The case of Indian firms*. Ross School of Business Working Paper 1140. University of Michigan.
Khanna, T., & Palepu, K. (2000). Is group affiliation profitable in emerging markets? An analysis of diversified Indian business groups. *Journal of Finance*, *55*(2), 867–891.
Kogut, B. (1988). Joint ventures: Theoretical and empirical perspectives. *Strategic Management Journal*, *9*(4), 319–332.
Kumar, N. (2009). How emerging giants are rewriting the rules of M&A. *Harvard Business Review*, *87*(5), 115–121.
Kumaraswamy, A., Mudambi, R., Saranga, H., & Tripathy, A. (2012). Catch-up strategies in the Indian auto components industry: Domestic firms' responses to market liberalization. *Journal of International Business Studies*, *43*(4), 368–395.
Lall, S. (1983). *The new multinationals: The spread of third world enterprises*. Chichester: Wiley.
Lane, P. J., Salk, J. E., & Lyles, M. A. (2001). Absorptive capacity, learning, and performance in international joint ventures. *Strategic Management Journal*, *22*(12), 1139–1161.
Lee, K., & Lim, C. (2001). Technological regimes, catching-up and leapfrogging: Findings from the Korean industries. *Research Policy*, *30*(3), 459–483.
Liu, X., Wang, C., & Wei, Y. (2009). Do local manufacturing firms benefit from transactional linkages with multinational enterprises in China. *Journal of International Business Studies*, *40*(7), 1113–1130.
Lorenzen, M., & Mudambi, R. (2013). Clusters, connectivity and catch-up: Bollywood and Bangalore in the global economy. *Journal of Economic Geography*, *13*, 501–534.
Luo, Y., & Tung, R. L. (2007). International expansion of emerging market enterprises: A springboard perspective. *Journal of International Business Studies*, *38*(4), 481–498.

Lyles, M. A., & Salk, J. E. (1996). Knowledge acquisition from foreign parents in international joint ventures: An empirical examination in the Hungarian context. *Journal of International Business Studies*, 877–903.

Mahoney, J. T. (2004). *Economic foundations of strategy*. London: Sage.

Mathews, J. A. (2002). Competitive advantages of the latecomer firm: A resource-based account of industrial catch-up strategies. *Asia Pacific Journal of Management*, *19*(4), 467–488.

Mathews, J. A. (2006). Dragon multinationals: New players in 21st century globalization. *Asia Pacific Journal of Management*, *23*, 5–27.

McDermott, G. A., & Corredoira, R. A. (2010). Network composition, collaborative ties, and upgrading in emerging-market firms: Lessons from the Argentine autoparts sector. *Journal of International Business Studies*, *41*(2), 308–329.

Mu, Q., & Lee, K. (2005). Knowledge diffusion, market segmentation and technological catch-up: The case of the telecommunication industry in China. *Research Policy*, *34*(6), 759–783.

Nam, K.-M. (2011). Learning through the international joint venture: Lessons from the experience of China's automotive sector. *Industrial and Corporate Change*, *20*(3), 855–907.

Nelson, R. R. (1993). *National innovation systems: A comparative analysis*. University of Illinois at Urbana-Champaign's Academy for Entrepreneurial Leadership Historical Research Reference in Entrepreneurship.

Pierce, J. L., Boerner, C. S., & Teece, D. J. (2002). Dynamic capabilities, competence and the behavioral theory of the firm. In *The economics of choice, change, and organization: Essays in memory of Richard M. Cyert* (pp. 81–95). Cheltenham, UK: Edward Elgar Publishing Ltd.

Polanyi, M. (2009). *The tacit dimension*. Chicago, IL: University of Chicago press.

Pradhan, J. P. (2003). Liberalization, firm size and R&D performance: A firm level study of Indian pharmaceutical industry. *Journal of Indian School of Political Economy*, *14*(4), 647–666.

Ramamurti, R. (2009). What have we learned about emerging market MNEs? In R. Ramamurti & J. V. Singh (Eds.), *Emerging multinationals in emerging markets* (pp. 339–426). Cambridge, UK: Cambridge University Press.

Ramamurti, R. (2013). Cross-border M&A and competitive advantage of Indian EMNEs. In P. J. Williamson, R. Ramamurti, A. Fleury, & M. T. L. Fleury (Eds.), *The competitive advantage of emerging market multinationals* (pp. 239–260). Cambridge, UK: Cambridge University Press.

Ramamurti, R., & Singh, J. V. (2009). *Emerging multinationals in emerging markets*. Cambridge, UK: Cambridge University Press.

Williamson, P. J., & Anand, R. P. (2013). Cross-border M&A and competitive advantage of Chinese EMNEs. In P. J. Williamson, R. Ramamurti, A. Fleury, & M. T. L. Fleury (Eds.), *The competitive advantage of emerging market multinationals* (pp. 261–277). Cambridge, UK: Cambridge University Press.

Wilson, L. (2009). *How to implement lean manufacturing*. New York, NY: McGraw Hill Professional.

Winter, S. G. (2003). Understanding dynamic capabilities. *Strategic Management Journal*, *24*(10), 991–995.

Zaheer, S. (2002). The liability of foreignness, redux: A commentary. *Journal of International Management*, *8*(3), 351–358.

Zhang, Y., Li, H., Li, Y., & Zhou, L. A. (2010). FDI spillovers in an emerging market: The role of foreign firms' country origin diversity and domestic firms' absorptive capacity. *Strategic Management Journal*, *31*(9), 969–989.

Zhang, Y. A., Li, Y., & Li, H. (2014). FDI spillovers over time in an emerging market: The roles of entry tenure and barriers to imitation. *Academy of Management Journal*, *57*(3), 698–722.

FRAMING INTERNATIONAL OPERATIONS MANAGEMENT: CONTRIBUTIONS FROM EMERGING COUNTRY MULTINATIONALS

Afonso Fleury, Yongjiang Shi,
Maria Tereza Leme Fleury, Silas Ferreira Jr.,
Jose Henrique Cordeiro and Xingkun Liang

ABSTRACT

Despite the seminal works of authors like Bartlett, Ghoshal, Nohria, Doz, Williamson, among others, because they focused on mature multinationals, newcomers in international markets find scarce information about the design and implementation of international operations networks. In this paper we analyze the internationalization process of Brazilian and Chinese firms to understand the evolution of their networks, a process influenced by factors inexistent in studies about developed country multinationals, namely global production networks (GPNs) and country-of-origin effects. The key characteristics of their

Emerging Economies and Multinational Enterprises
Advances in International Management, Volume 28, 351–377

ISSN: 1571-5027/doi:10.1108/S1571-502720150000028016

international operations networks seem to be well described by a stage-based approach where emerging country multinationals start as local optimizers and then evolve by taking different strategic positions within the GPN to which they are connected. That upgrading is possible when the implementation of the international operations network reaches a certain level of maturity.

Keywords: Internationalization; emerging country multinationals; International Operations Management; international operations networks

INTRODUCTION

A long list of international management models and typologies may be found in the literature, as those proposed by Bartlett and Ghoshal (1986), Nohria and Ghoshal (1997), Doz, Santos, and Williamson (2001), among others. As their object of study was mature multinationals, there is scarce evidence as to how those firms started to build their networks of subsidiaries in the early stages of internationalization.

The pioneers in the study of a multinationals' international structure were Chandler (1962) and Stopford and Wells (1972). However, those authors wrote about multinationals that had already evolved beyond the stage of international operations being coordinated by an International Division, which can be considered the simplest organizational arrangement. In other words, research has always been geared toward multinationals that already had complex structures. Recent publications, like Rugman, Verbeke, and Yuan (2010), identify a still higher degree of complexity to the issue. Acknowledging that previous authors considered aggregate national subsidiary roles only, Rugman et al. (2010) recall that current developments allow the multinational to fine slice its value chain and pinpoint each subsidiary in the location where it may best bundle its internal competences with available external resources. In other words, they observe that the number of factors to be considered in the design of international operations networks is higher than previously thought.

The aforementioned authors are looking for structural solutions which optimize global efficiency, national responsiveness, and worldwide learning simultaneously (Bartlett, Ghoshal, & Beamish, 2008). However, one must question to what extent the knowledge so consolidated contributes to newcomers in international markets, at a time when emerging multinationals start building their own international operations networks.

To address the research question – how do firms design and implement their international operations network to penetrate international markets – we looked at emerging country multinationals (EMNEs) that are in the early stages of internationalization (Ramamurti, 2009b). Are they able to cope with the simultaneous challenges and develop complex organizational architectures or do they adopt simpler solutions?

Compared to their predecessors, the developed country multinationals (DMNEs), the EMNEs' internationalization processes present two distinct dimensions. First, EMNEs usually grow as part of global production networks (GPNs) led by developed country multinationals, what creates specific drivers and constraints for international expansion (Gereffi, Humphrey, & Sturgeon, 2005; Fleury & Fleury, 2014). Second, their key competitive advantage stems from their production and operations competences rather than the marketing and research and development competences, with the latter supporting the early internationalization of developed country multinationals (Fleury, Fleury, & Borini, 2012; Ramamurti, 2009a). Moreover, as highlighted by authors such as Peng, Wang, and Jiang (2008), there is an extrinsic dimension influencing EMNEs' internationalization, namely the institutional environment where they were born. As these dimensions bear significant differences, they have to be properly qualified in the analysis.

The analytical framework combines the literature on International Business with that on International Operations Management (IOM), because IOM is especially important for firms that have production and operations competences as their key competitive asset. In the fieldwork two EMNEs from Brazil and two from China with comparable features were studied, following the comparative historical analysis procedures (Saka-Helmhout, 2010). The data was gathered through structured interviews in both their headquarters and subsidiaries operating in both developed and developing countries. Secondary sources of information were used for triangulation purposes and archival information was used to configure historical facts.

The structure of this paper is as follows. The literature review looks at specific topics in International Business and emerging country multinationals and International Operations Management. From that review three propositions emerge. The development of the analytical framework follows, providing the basic information for the presentation of the fieldwork, which has illustrative purposes. The final sections encompass an assessment of the usability of the framework, some preliminary conclusions about the factors that influence the process of designing and implementing international operations networks in EMNEs and suggestions for further research.

LITERATURE REVIEW

International Management Models

The first multinationals chose to organize their international activities either in one single International Division, or in divisions per products, or else per geographical regions. Stopford and Wells (1972) stated that the choice would depend on two factors: foreign product diversity and foreign sales. Later, a third factor was identified, namely the percentage of foreign manufacturing.

Since the mid-1980s, a new MNE organization logic was identified. Based on longitudinal studies of renowned global companies such as GE and Procter & Gamble, it was observed that the adopted organizational architecture became the one that best adjusted to the corporation's international strategy, which should respond both to pressures for local responsiveness and global integration. These studies lead to the identification of international management models, as presented in Table 1.

In the *multidomestic model*, subsidiaries have to serve their local markets in a differentiated way and there is little integration with the headquarters. This implies the existence of competences in subsidiaries that will guarantee a competitive edge to face local competition. Subsidiaries act as isolated companies that may receive investment from the parent company if their performance meets or exceeds expectations. Due to high autonomy and low integration between subsidiaries and headquarters and amongst the

Table 1. International Management Models.

Type	Key Features
Multidomestic	Autonomous subsidiaries; high responsiveness to local demands
Global	Build cost advantages through centralized global scale operations
Transnational	Exploit knowledge and competences through worldwide diffusion and adaptation
Metanational	Speed in combining knowledge from different parts of the world and roll out the results throughout the world

Sources: Bartlett and Ghoshal (1998), Doz et al. (2001).

subsidiaries themselves, competences developed in subsidiaries are exclusive, that is, they are not transferred.

In the *global model*, competence transfer follows a unidirectional path, from center to periphery. Strong communication, shared values, credibility deposited in subsidiaries, and world standards in the search for global efficiency are elements that facilitate competence transfer. However, the lack of autonomy, together with standardization, requires that subsidiaries use competences developed at headquarters. Subsidiaries may develop competences, but it is a development aligned and led by the parent company, which for some strategic reason is then developed in the subsidiary. This may be justified by lower development costs, adequate and cheaper external services, and tax-free research investments, among other reasons.

The third model is the *transnational*, which is capable of merging the global and multidomestic models in a configuration that accommodates different types of subsidiaries with different types of relationships with the headquarters. In the configuration of differentiated network, the relations between headquarters and subsidiaries are not uniform, which implies a more complex management style. The question of autonomy and integration, for example, is outlined differently: one subsidiary may present strong integration with the headquarters and little autonomy, whereas another may be highly autonomous and less integrated.

Finally, the *metanational model* proposes to solve two points left untouched by the previous models: the insertion of companies in global business networks as a source of knowledge and competences and the governance relationship between parent company and subsidiaries in competence development and transfer in subsidiaries. According to Doz et al. (2001), the greatest challenge faced by multinationals is developing global learning. In the metanational strategy, the multinational has the notion that the competitive advantage is not created by headquarters or major subsidiaries only, but rather by each and every subsidiary, including those that were typically global or multidomestic subsidiaries only a while ago. This goes against approaches that advocate determined roles for subsidiaries and supports the evolutionary theory of competence development in any kind of subsidiary without previous acknowledgment or authorization.

A critical differential of the metanational strategic model is its focus on discovering and exploring hidden knowledge all around the world, as opposed to the transnational strategy model, which defends learning from a particular subsidiary as being of greater strategic importance. Thus, competences in the metanational model are developed both at headquarters and at subsidiaries of multinationals, including branches that have not yet received a strategic role of global importance but have developed their own initiatives for the creation of competences. The metanational model acknowledges the importance of actors external to the corporate network: subsidiary partners and the context in which they are operating. In other words, the places where subsidiaries and headquarters operate become equally important for corporate strategy. Hence, competences may be created by both headquarters and subsidiaries and valued equally regardless its origin.

Along with those models, subsidiary roles typologies were also proposed. For example, Bartlett and Ghoshal (1989) suggested a four-fold typology depending on the relative importance of the market where the subsidiary is located and the level of competences it displays: implementer, contributor, black hole, and strategic leader. For Birkinshaw and Hood (1998), subsidiaries may develop initiatives that spill-over the assigned roles. According to the type of initiatives, subsidiaries can be categorized as implementer, contributor, or global mandate.

International Operations Management Frameworks

The field of International Operations Management brings important complementarities to the above mentioned models because, for the very nature of the field, the analysis is more detailed, more fine-grained, especially in what concerns the issue of international manufacturing networks. However, as their approaches focus on the manufacturing function the most strategic level addressed is international manufacturing strategy rather than the firm's internationalization strategy.

In 1998, the "Cambridge Approach" presented by Shi and Gregory (1998) expanded Hayes and Wheelwright's (1984) Factory Manufacturing System concept, toward international manufacturing networks. By considering geographic dispersion, coordination mechanisms (both horizontal and vertical) and factory's characteristics as key dimensions for analysis, the authors identified seven types of network configurations related to four types of network capabilities.

Configuration means the combination and interaction of all elements that define the network: geographic dispersion, governance, operations processes, and subsidiary roles. These are elements of the network design; their implementation will result in a network configuration. For Shi and Gregory (1998) seven possible network configurations exist: regional uncoordinated, home exporting, regional exporting, multidomestic, glocalised, global-integrated, and global-coordinated.

Network capability is the ability, derived from the network configuration, to deliver key outputs that fulfill the network's mission. Fleet and Shi (2005) and Srai and Gregory (2008) proposed a classification of network capabilities that includes cost efficiency, customer responsiveness, resource accessibility, agility, learning, risk management, and manufacturing mobility.

In regards to subsidiary roles, Ferdows (1997) proposed a six-type categorization: server, contributor, source, offshore, lead, and outpost, a typology congruent to Birkinshaw and Hood (1998).

The Analytical Framework Built from IMM and IOM Focusing on DMNEs

The combination of the constructs and concepts derived from studies of DMNEs, as previously mentioned, allows for the proposition of an analytical framework described in Table 2.

The complementary constructs are defined as follows.

Network Mission

In the IB literature, the traditional definition of network mission is global efficiency and local responsiveness. In the IOM literature, Zhang and Gregory (2011) admit that the network mission can be: (1) efficiency-oriented, when it seeks economies of scale/scope, international operations synergies, the leveraging of expertise or precious resources on a global scale, and the sharing and reuse of existing solutions; (2) innovation-oriented when it seeks customer intimacy, technology leadership, and market/technology-driven innovation, learning across disciplines or organizations; or (3) flexibility-oriented when it seeks flexible work approaches, mobile engineering resources, reconfigurable network structures, and local responsiveness.

Geographic Dispersion

Although dispersion is usually drawn by forces external to the company, especially new market opportunities, there is a full range of options from domestic to multinational manufacture (Shi & Gregory, 1998). Domestic means that all production is carried out in a single country serving both home and export markets. Regional approaches set up factories and

Table 2. Description of the IOM Analytical Framework.

Level	Design Element	International Management Model			
		Multidomestic	Global	Transnational	Metanational
HQ	Network mission	Local responsiveness	Global efficiency	Local responsiveness and global efficiency	Learning and worldwide competence development
Intra-firm network	Dispersion	Ruled by demand	Ruled by production	Ruled by specialization and differentiation	Ruled by integration
	Governance – coordination	Decentralized	Centralized	Contingent	Synergetic
	Flow processes	Locally defined	Standard – global	Formal/informal	Informal/formal
	Configuration	Regional uncoordinated or multidomestic	Globally integrated	Globally and locally coordinated	Globally integrated
	Capability	Customer responsiveness or resource accessibility	Cost efficiency	Cross national learning	Global learning
Subsidiary	Assigned role[a]	Contributor	Implementer	Contributor/leader	Contributor/leader
	Host country effects	Not considered	Not considered	Implicitly considered	Explicitly considered
	Local value networks	Not considered	Not considered	Implicitly considered	Explicitly considered
	Initiative/actual role[b]	Contributor	Implementer	Global mandate	Global mandate

[a]Based on Bartlett and Ghoshal typology.
[b]Based on Birkinshaw and Hood typology.

networks located in a particular geographical region, usually sharing similar cultural value systems. Multinational approaches, with trans-regional dispersion, involve factories located in several countries and continents.

Governance/Coordination

Once a business moves beyond a conventional single domestic operation it is obliged to establish authority structures and international coordination mechanisms, which refer to linking or integrating the production and distribution facilities in order to achieve the firms' strategic objectives or its network mission (Meijboom & Vos, 1997; Shi & Gregory, 1998). For Zhang and Gregory (2011), governance refers to the mechanisms that direct and control the network, including authority structures, performance measurement, and coordination mechanisms. In principle, there can be two generic orientations: multidomestic (weak coordination and more independent factories) and global (strong coordination and more interdependent factories, from either designed system structures or operations processes).

Emerging Country Firms' Internationalization Strategies

The first insight into EMNEs' strategizing was provided by Mathews with his linking-leveraging-learning approach. His arguments rely on the pluralistic character of the process of globalization, as contrasted with the conventional account that sees a trend toward uniformity and convergence. The author stressed that 21st century globalization allows a connectivity that facilitates international flows, conditions absent when incumbents internationalized. As these are being fully exploited by EMNEs, Mathews identified as their key features: accelerated internationalization, organizational innovation rather than technological innovation and implementation through strategic innovations.

However, it is problematic to generalize Mathews findings, because EMNEs are not a homogeneous group, the diversity being justified by country-of-origin effects mainly (Sethi & Elango, 1999). Among the BRIC countries, Brazil and Russia are rich in natural resources while China and India have large populations and scarce natural resources. That favors the development of nature-based companies in the former countries and labor-intensive type of industries in the latter. In regards to business ecosystems, the differences are also significant. The international expansion of Chinese multinationals has been supported by the local government through the "Go Global" project, among other initiatives, what led Ramamurti (2009b) to coin the term GSA – Government Specific Advantages. Conversely, both Brazilian and Indian governments show conservative attitudes in regards to the importance of their firms moving abroad. China and India are considered nations that cultivate entrepreneurship while Brazil is said to be more conservative and risk-averse. Russia has a very particular type of institutional environment favoring oligarchies.

Ramamurti's generic internationalization strategies (2009b) take into account those country-of-origin effects:

- Natural resources vertical integrator – firms located in countries rich in natural resources and large demand for such inputs, which internationalize to achieve forward integration to downstream markets and/or backward integration upstream to secure natural resources;
- Local optimizer – firms located in countries populated by low-income consumers and underdeveloped "hard" and "soft" infrastructures, having the ability to reengineer imported products, modifying them to better suit emerging markets;
- Low-cost partner – firms located in low-cost labor countries, where a large pool of skilled labor is available, which become global suppliers for GPNs and move up the value chain to increase value-adding and move down the value chain to diversify supply locations;
- Global consolidator – firms located in large and rapidly growing home markets where customers are price sensitive, which achieve manufacturing excellence and move internationally to achieve global scale through the acquisition of poorly performing companies;
- Global first-mover – firms located in countries characterized by large and rapidly growing demand in a new industry where design, engineering, and production are low cost, targeting the global market and internationalizing to acquire key technologies or capabilities and customer access.

Additionally, for many EMNEs, their internationalization processes stands from the role they perform global production networks. Fleury and Fleury (2007, 2014) identified four likely positions in GPNs, depending on the core competence and competitive advantage of the firm: manufacturer (core competence is manufacturing), developer (core competence is research and development), integrator of complex product systems (core competence is systems engineering) and service operators (core competence is service operations management). The concept of network governance – the control of the network by one particular firm while the remaining firms position themselves according to their core competences – is particularly relevant for the understanding of the impact of GPNs in EMNEs internationalization.

PROPOSITIONS

The variables involved in the design and implementation of international operations can be depicted in the following model.

The model first suggests a direct relationship between internationalization strategy, as previously defined, and international network design and implementation. Additionally, we propose that the baseline relationship in Fig. 1 will be further modified by two contingencies. Specifically, since EMNEs internationalize following a particular set of strategies, as formerly mentioned, the way in which they design and implement international operations networks and associated management systems will be influenced by the interactions within GPNs (the GPN Effect) and home countries (the country-of-origin effect).

The notion that structure follows strategy comes from the early works by Chandler (1962). In our case, we are focusing on a particular type of strategy – the internationalization strategy of an emerging country firm – and the way in which these firms organize their resources internationally to accomplish the strategy. Since emerging country firms may adopt different internationalization strategies:

> **P1.** EMNEs will configure different international operations networks depending on the adopted internationalization strategy.

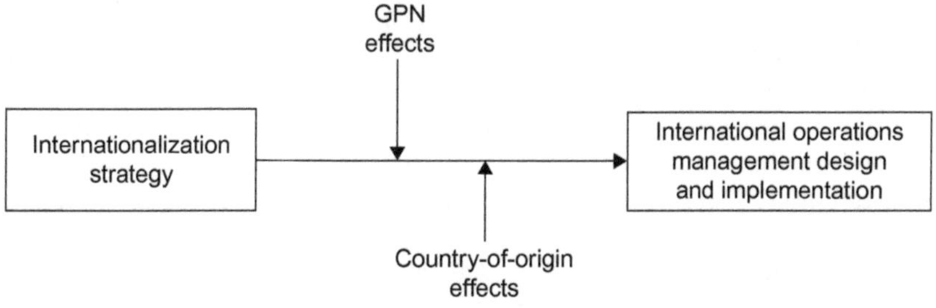

Fig. 1. The Model for Analyzing International Operations Design and Implementation.

Country-of-origin effects may stimulate or inhibit the internationalization process. Factors endowment will have both a vertical effect in what concerns the development of the types of industry which are more benefited by them (e.g., natural resources) or transversal when there are factors that benefit all industries like abundant qualified workforce. Cultural traces affect the propensity of firms toward internationalization and risk-taking. Governmental policies may provide support or barriers to investing abroad. Therefore, we propose that:

> **P2.** Country-of-origin effects will influence the design and implementation of international operations networks.

Usually, EMNEs engage in global value chains commanded by multinationals from developed countries and are expected to upgrade to survive and prosper (Bartlett & Ghoshal, 2000). Therefore, we propose that:

> **P3.** The upgrading of EMNEs in global production networks relates to the increasing capability of their international operations networks.

RESEARCH DESIGN AND FIELDWORK

In this study, comparative historical analysis (CHA) was adopted (Saka-Helmhout, 2010), a method that meets the challenge of dealing simultaneously with capturing the interactions and attaining causality in patterns of activities for generalizability. The objective is to identify patterns of causalities or regularities in the phenomenon embedded in historical contextual singularities across countries to improve the generalizability of cross-country comparisons. The approach combines detailed case studies with systematic comparison. Detailed accounts ensure that the context-embededness of the conditions underlying the phenomenon of interest is elicited. A systematic comparison allows for a significant theoretical leverage so that generalization is made possible. For such an analysis to serve as a theoretical lever, the cases must be theoretically sampled and comparable.

Two Brazilian multinationals, Alpha and Beta,[1] as well as two Chinese multinationals, Gamma and Delta, were examined according to three evolutionary stages of their lives. The analyses focused on the last 20 years of existence, which is when they expanded sales and production to global markets. The four firms were selected due to the following reasons. First, they are successful industrial firms with subsidiaries located in developing countries (besides their respective home countries) as well as developed countries (in Europe and North America). Second, we aimed to enhance the discriminatory power of the comparative analysis by pairing the firms according to the similarity of their respective industries (Alpha with Gamma and Beta with Delta). Third, they are largely connected to GPNs from their respective industries. Lastly, the evolution of their strategies and operations is largely documented.

Historical data was gathered and analyzed for further discussion with the company's executives at both the headquarters and subsidiaries, leading to the identification of potential contingency factors concerning network design and relationships between the network and strategic context. Due to the nature of the issue, very little documentation was available in the companies, thus making historical data and interviews as the main source of information. Triangulation was possible through the access to some related company presentation material.

Semi-structured questionnaires were used during the sessions, with opportunities for clarification as well as collecting supplementary information between sessions. Most of the meetings had two researchers, one leading the discussion and the other taking notes and asking questions for clarification. Notes were compared after the meetings and then shared with the executives for validation. Then, comparisons were made between the EMNEs.

Alpha: Creating the Capabilities to Internationalize

Alpha, a large Brazilian tech company, branches out internationally in eight countries, including China, France, Ireland, Portugal, Singapore, the United Arab Emirates, the United Kingdom, and the United States.

1969–1993 – The Local Producer of a Global Product

Initially as a state-owned enterprise, Alpha's mission was to produce high-tech products for the Brazilian market and contributing toward the development of the country. Having to negotiate with large DMNEs for the acquisition of technology, Alpha became a modest client in large GPNs. Also involved in partnerships with mid-sized Italian and American manufacturers, supplier for a large American manufacturer, the company created international links early in its history.

As part of a large governmental project, Alpha had the support of a research center and an engineering school. Besides, to make feasible the global sale of its products, Brazilian public banks created a financing plan.

Alpha's strategy initially focused on domestic demand and exports started in the late 1970s only. As a precondition for that, Alpha created a network of subsidiaries specialized in sales and after-sales.

Therefore, in the first stage of its history, Alpha was an isolated, vertically integrated tech manufacturer, using components imported from DMNEs, as well as selling its products all over the world. Alpha's ION configuration could then be categorized as home exporting manufacturing (Shi & Gregory, 1998), given that it had no international production subsidiaries, centralized manufacturing in home the country and operated a global logistic system (for the acquisition of supplies and provision of sales and after-sales services).

1994–2000 – Becoming the Leader of a Minor Global Production Network
Alpha was privatized in the early 1990s in its delicate financial situation. The government gradually withdrew direct support, maintaining indirect influence through a "golden share" stake. The newly empowered stakeholders gave Alpha a new strategic intent, redefining its corporate mission, from technology-oriented to market-oriented, and implemented a new culture and organization.

Alpha also headed a network of foreign partners who were, previously, ordinary suppliers. That is to say, the company reshaped its international network to maintain its position in international markets.

For the most part of the second stage of its history, Alpha's ION configuration remained as home exporting, because it still had no international production: manufacturing was kept centralized in the home country while risk-partners became key suppliers. Alpha's new products required increasingly complex inbound logistics and sales, thus justifying the expansion of that type of subsidiary.

The success of its new products consolidated Alpha as a complex product systems integrator and leader of a minor international production network. That arrangement provided extraordinary competitive edge for Alpha. Due to the flexibility of its international network, Alpha emerged as a new challenger in its industry.

2001-Present – Global First-Mover and GPN Leader
In the 2000s, Alpha changed into a global first-mover. Its previous experience in product development production and sales enabled the company to

set up a much more complex international network of production involving renowned DMNEs. At the same time, this newly assembled GPN made possible for Alpha to diversify its corporate strategy by entering into new businesses.

Alpha's ION gradually expanded, changing significantly its position in the GPN by "deverticalizing" production and strengthening its interface with suppliers, partners, and markets. Its ION can be categorized as a global-integrated manufacturing configuration (GMC3), according to Shi and Gregory (1998), but it has a regional orientation in what concerns sales and services. This configuration is meant to lead to capabilities of resources accessibility and learning ability, to satisfy the main mission of market presence.

In sum, as a global first-mover (Ramamurti, 2009b), the reasons for going abroad are to acquire global customers and scale as well as to acquire key missing technologies and capabilities. It occupies a unique leading position in its GPN, as a complex systems integrator. Companies such as Alpha, which operate in high technology, fast-moving global industries, are likely to develop innovative management models for their network-based organizations.

Beta: From Low-Cost Supplier to Global Consolidator of Industrial Equipment

Beta is one of the world's leading technology manufacturers. Its global presence embraces subsidiaries in nine countries besides Brazil: Argentina, Mexico, the United States, India, South Africa, Portugal, Austria, Germany, and China. Commercial offices are located in 28 other countries. Beta sells to over 100 countries and has over 100 authorized repair shops covering all continents.

1961–1990 – Beta's Growth in a Period of Imports Substitution Industrialization

Beta was founded in the 1960s with the mission to domestically produce technology cheaper than the imported technology. At that moment, the imports substitution was at its peak, therefore the government provided broad support to start business, as well as specific financial support for R&D activities.

Located in Southern Brazil, the prevalent European culture led Beta to develop a strong organizational culture and embrace a participative management system, where decisions are made by committees. The structure is highly vertically integrated, from assembly to sales and distribution.

Since the very beginning, Beta has had a global mindset. Modest exports to neighboring countries started in the 1970s, in order to sell excess production, but during the 1980s exports became priority. The Exportation Department was created with the mission to open new markets, and to export even when returns were negative. The main objective was to learn how to serve sophisticated foreign markets and thus reshape the company's strategies. The R&D department was also created at that time.

Therefore, in the first stage of its history, Beta was an isolated, vertically integrated manufacturer for domestic markets, but with increasing exports, first to neighboring markets and then to more demanding ones. The weaknesses of a strategy based on exporting through foreign distributors soon became evident, and Beta started to establish commercial branches, the first one in the United States. The Exportation Department was renamed International Department. The role of the commercial branches was to approach large clients while distributors would keep their role as suppliers to retailers. According to Shi and Gregory (1998), Beta's ION configuration would then be categorized as home exporting manufacturing, because it had no international manufacturing operations, centralized manufacturing in home country, and operated a global logistic system (for the acquisition of supplies and distribution of products).

1991–2003 – From Home-Exporter to Low-Cost Partner

In the early 1990s, with the new wave of globalization, Beta was ready to expand exports to a wide range of segments, from universal to make-to-order products. It was then categorized as a low-cost partner (Ramamurti, 2009b).

The mission of its ION was largely related to be present in preferential markets, but it became clear that it had to change its mission to dynamic responses, seeking closer relationship with its clients. The corporate supply chains are dispersed in many countries to access to the most optimized resources, markets and strategic capabilities according to the corporate strategic intentions. Beta used to distribute supply chains vertically and centralize each stage of process to reduce the duplication of manufacturing facilities. This configuration is meant to lead to capabilities of resources accessibility and learning ability, to satisfy the main mission of market presence. Thus, Beta moved to a global-integrated manufacturing configuration.

2004-Present – From Low-Cost Partner to Global Consolidator

In the 2000s, Beta decided to invest in foreign plants through acquisitions seeking, from the world's largest markets, those where legal and political stability prevailed. Beta has kept its main position as a world-class manufacturer, and its generic internationalization strategy shifted to global consolidator.

The mission of the network combines efficiency-orientation and flexibility-orientation. There is excess capacity and redundancy in different foreign plants, what was observed in the Chinese plant which exports almost half of its production to other subsidiaries. Recently, Beta changed its organizational structure: each subsidiary was relocated to one of the business units and the International Department became responsible for the commercial operations only. The aim of this change was to increase coordination and synergy between the foreign and Brazilian plants.

Dispersion of Beta's ION can be categorized as worldwide due to the high number of subsidiaries present in a large number of regions and countries, to serve five business units. Governance follows a global pattern since units are horizontally coordinated and there is no hierarchy among them. Processes are both standardized and ad-hoc due to the specifics of the products and the business units. Therefore, the configuration is global-coordinated and network capabilities combine manufacturing mobility and thriftiness ability, to satisfy the mission of global competitiveness.

In sum, Beta is characterized by a high level of strategic entrepreneurship. Also, it is a global consolidator in its internationalization strategy, the reasons for going abroad are to acquire global customers and scale as well as to acquire key missing technologies and capabilities. It occupies a traditional position in its GPN, as a manufacturer, although secondarily it is also a technology supplier and service.

Gamma: From Importer and Distributor to Global First-Mover in a Hi-Tech Industry

Gamma is a large telecommunication equipment and service provider, headquartered in China. The firm was founded in the 1980s as a private firm. It grew outstandingly, especially after 2001, with sales growth exceeding 25% annually. In 2013, Gamma had over 150,000 employees, among that over 20% are foreigners and 40% are R&D staff. The company runs over 100 sales offices and more than 20 research institutes worldwide. Having developed a very complex supply network, Gamma developed its own approach to governance mechanisms due to the increasing complexities in market demands, products and technologies.

1987–1997 – From Product Importer and Distributor to Local Optimizer

The company was founded as a distributor of technology products imported from Hong Kong, facing fierce competition from foreign multinational giants. The 1990s witnessed the fast growth of its local industry and Gamma realized that the company could not survive long if depending merely on selling products. Therefore, the company started to build up its own operations, prioritizing technology development.

At that time, national and industrial policies were focused on leveraging the growth of state-owned enterprises (SOEs), which relied on technology transfer, through joint ventures with foreign MNEs. Differently from those firms, Gamma's transformation started with R&D rather than production, based on the principle that to survive in a high-tech industry, firms must have their own technological advantages.

During its initial evolutionary stage, R&D activities focused on reverse-engineering, while the company invested much of its revenue to develop its own technology. As a dealer, Gamma had solid experience and knowledge on how to capture the demands of the Chinese market, what allowed the company to develop the capabilities to serve customers with the appropriate technologies. By 1990, Gamma has achieved its first breakthrough delivering the most advanced product of its local industry. Its huge success significantly improved Gamma's revenue.

Due to the increasing demand, Gamma centralized its production at home, where there was a better interaction with R&D in order to provide tailored solutions. The company targeted markets in rural areas neglected by the SOEs and MNEs. To serve those markets, Gamma built a hierarchical structure of sales and service network, from Province, to City and to Town. With the rising awareness that high technology is relevant to national security, Gamma, as a local manufacturer, was increasingly supported by national policy and developed good relationship with governments and military agencies. Gamma kept its operations network in China, while enhancing its technological capabilities.

1998-2004 – From Home-Exporter to Developer

In 1998, Gamma started a transformation aimed at changing the ways of managing to adapt to its growing size, to enable the domestic-market-focused company to be integrated for internationalization. Seeking to establish a Western management system the company integrated internal operations resources to improve the efficiency to respond to customer needs through integrated supply chain management (ISC), integrated product development (IPD), and integrated IT supporting system. ISC and IPD focused on standardizing internal processes from sourcing raw material to fulfilling customer needs whereas the IT systems were an enabler for the integration. In this way, Gamma established a fully integrated, responsive, and efficient global value chain covering the whole spectrum from R&D to sales.

In the late 1990s, Gamma won its first overseas bid, selling its products to a Hong Kong company. Two years after, Gamma established an R&D branch overseas where they could employ cheap software engineers. Since then, Gamma boosted its internationalization through building up new research centers in developed countries. These centers were actually used to scan and learn new technologies from competitors or universities or industrial clusters. On the other hand, Gamma reinforced its development capabilities in China by establishing new development centers in large Chinese cities. The development centers, albeit in China, are focused on transferring technologies or applied research in overseas centers into their product through ISC and IPD. Such development also emphasizes to meet home and overseas customers' specifications as much as possible.

Gamma centralized its IONs in China with global logistics for two reasons. Firstly, it provides global efficiency for the operations as a result of the scale and scope of economies. Secondly, Gamma integrates its supply network so that the company has more power and fewer risks in its global operations.

Until 2000, when the company moved its focus to overseas markets development, Gamma's major markets were China's neighboring countries. Huawei's ION configuration was regional exporting manufacturing (GMC2), because the company operated by the centralized production plant in China with a logistic system delivering to regional markets.

2005-Present – Global First-Mover in the Industry

Around 2000, Gamma first entered the European market. However, at that time, their business in Europe was based on very unstable sales, as few customers knew Gamma and its products. The main purpose to enter was to learn technologies and understand market needs in developed countries.

Gamma started to expand to the rest of the European market after 2005. Since 2005, Gamma has over 50% profits from overseas markets, an indicator of its successful internationalization strategy. Meanwhile, Gamma's new research centers overseas reinforced its capabilities in technological innovation. From 2008, Gamma has become one of the most innovative companies worldwide, as measured by its patent applications.

The expansion of European markets brought challenges for the company, one of which was on-time delivery due to the centralized production, huge complexity of products, and dynamic and uncertain needs. Gamma started to decentralize its ION by building greenfield investments in different regions.

Currently, Gamma has five foreign global supply centers that take charge of the production for each region while the home country plants are responsible for all the other markets. Together with its decentralized research facilities, the company is able to quickly transfer market needs into products. According to Shi and Gregory (1998), Gamma's current ION is the glocalised manufacturing configuration (MMC3).

Delta: The Rise of a Parts Supplier in a Traditional Global Industry

Delta started as a township-village enterprise in the late 1960s. Currently, it is specialized in the production of four categories of components. Its sales revenue in the domestic market exceeded US$ 3 billion, which indicated it became one of the largest components producer in China. Delta's internationalization trajectory can be described as follows.

1969–1992 – From Contract Manufacturer to Exporter

In the highly protected and regulated industry, it was very difficult for Delta to increase its domestic share, because production of components was centrally planned by the government, which assigned orders primarily to SOEs. Therefore, it began to export parts to the United States in the early 1980s, acting as a contract manufacturer a local company. By 2001 it expanded its exports to the United States substantially. Additional markets were opened in Europe, South America, and Japan.

1993–1999 – Establishing a Sales and Distribution Network Abroad

Delta created its first overseas subsidiary in the United States in the early 1990s. That subsidiary was active in building and extending the marketing and sales network across North America, South America, and Europe. Later Delta Europe and Delta South America were established as affiliates to the American corporation, to take charge of overseas business in Europe and South America. In the late 1990s, Delta bought majority shares in a local competitor in the United Kingdom, to market and sell its products in the European market. Worldwide, Delta has built an international sales network that covers over 60 countries.

2000-Present – Becoming a Low-Cost Partner and Global Follower
Since 2000, Delta entered international production, mainly through acquisitions. In 2000, it acquired its ex-partner in the American market, incorporating its equipment, brand, technology patents, and distribution channels. This and other acquisitions significantly enhanced Delta's businesses in North America.

Delta runs a number of manufacturing plants in the United States. From every factory, it transferred some capital-intensive production processes to China to achieve economies of scale; most labor-intensive production processes, such as component production process, were also transferred to China to make use of its low labor cost and to achieve economies of scale. All plants in the United States stayed in the front and bottom of its value chain, that is, its product design and customization and assembly, testing, and packaging, respectively. Table 3 summarizes the cases.

DISCUSSION

The comparative analysis of the four cases suggests that the design and implementation of IONs follows a stage-based model, as Galbraith (2000) already noticed in multinationals from other nationalities. Such evidence ratifies the importance of experiential learning in internationalization processes: the company must learn how to transfer its competitive advantages to other foreign subsidiaries while seeking to maximize its benefits for the whole of the network.

However, the stages described in all the cases seem to be specific examples for EMNEs. In the first stage, they may all be categorized as local optimizers, that is, they develop and produce products and services that provides them competitive edge in the domestic market and, at times, in other developing country markets. From then on, EMNEs start changing their positioning and internationalization strategies, as well as reconfiguring their IONs.

In the second stage, either the EMNE upgrades in the GPN, moving to a position in which its portfolio of activities has higher added-value (Alpha ratifying its position as Complex Product Systems Integrator and Gamma

Table 3. Summary of the Cases.

		Alpha	Gamma	Beta	Delta
First stage	*Time period*	*1969–1993*	*1987–1997*	*1961–1990*	*1969–1992*
	Internationalization strategy	Local optimizer/manufacturer	Local optimizer	Local optimizer and exporter	Local optimizer and exporter
	GPN position	Client of other GPNs	Isolated from GPNs	Isolated from GPNs	Isolated from GPNs
	COE	SOE	Huge local market needs	Imports substitution	Barriers to local expansion
	Network mission	Inbound and outbound logistics support	Technology hunting	Distribution – international exports	Distribution – international exports
	Configuration	Scattered business units	Scattered business units	Contracted distributors	Contracted distributors
	Coordination	Centralized	Centralized	Centralized	Centralized
	Subsidiary roles	Support imports and exports	Outposts (Ferdows, 1997)	Distribution	Local server (Ferdows, 1997)
Second stage	*Time period*	*1994–2000*	*1998–2004*	*1991–2003*	*1993–1999*
	Internationalization strategy	Local first-mover	Low-cost global supplier	Low-cost global supplier	Low-cost regional supplier (the United States)
	GPN position	Developer and leader small production network	Global supplier; developer for local markets	Manufacturer	Manufacturer and regional follower
	COE	Market opening and privatization	Government support for internationalization	Market opening and increased competition	Government support for scaling-up
	Network mission	Coordination of globally distributed design and manufacturing networks	Technology learning and regional manufacturing	Presence in preferential markets supplying GPN leaders	Improve quality and exports; supplying GPN leaders
	Configuration	According to partners	R&D centers worldwide; centralized manufacturing	Regional manufacturing plants; global assistance	Double-core centers
	Coordination	Project management	Integrated management systems	Centralized	Centralized
	Subsidiary roles	Support imports and exports	Technology hunting and regional manufacturing	Implementer	Distribution, Business seeker

Third and current stage	*Time period*	*2001-Present*	*2005-Present*	*2004-Present*	*2000-Present*
	Internationalization strategy	Global first-mover	Developer plus integrator and manufacturer	Global consolidator (manufacturer)	Global consolidator (manufacturer)
	GPN position	Leader of GPN	Global supplier	Global supplier	Global supplier
	COE	Strong but manageable	Strong but manageable	Increasingly independent from COEs through internationalization	Government support for internationalization
	Network mission	Global presence selling to customers	Global presence serving diversified global clients	Global presence in diversified markets	Supply the local industry
	Configuration	Product/market configuration	R&D labs in developing countries; manufacturing plants serving regional markets	Regional manufacturing plants; global assistance	Regional manufacturing plants
	Coordination	Project management and industry standards	Integrated management systems, industry standards	Centralized; participative managerial system; corporate standards	Decentralized, industry standards
	Subsidiary roles	Ranging from black hole to global mandate	Regional strategic leader	Contributors and global mandate	Contributors and reverse transfer of technology to China

its position as Developer), or keeps its role in the GPN and increases substantially its global reach. Examples here are the cases of Beta and Delta maintaining their manufacturer roles and growing internationally through acquisitions from incumbents, which withdrew from certain positions in the GPN (Fleury & Fleury, 2014).

The third and current stage has the EMNEs seeking to consolidate their positions in international markets through both acquisitions and organic growth. The increasing number and the diversification of subsidiary types, with amplified coordination needs, require a deep restructuring process at the company level.

The international management models adopted are hardly comparable to those in Table 1. These EMNEs have not been moving toward a multidomestic model because they have been striving to integrate their IONs in order to explore synergies and accelerate the expansion abroad. They have not been adopting a transnational model either, because they have not been exploiting their own knowledge and competences. On the contrary, they have been exploring new knowledge and competences through the foreign subsidiaries, usually in order bring them back to the headquarters. The Beta and Delta cases seem fit with the global model: both firms are building cost advantages through centralized global operations. However, the degree of centralization is relative because, as they are operating in markets which are more demanding and sophisticated than their home countries, the subsidiaries exert an important role in terms of knowledge development; it is different from the "in-house offshoring" (Contractor, Kumar, Kundu, & Pedersen, 2010) adopted by developed country multinationals with a global strategy. Finally, there are traces of the metanational model in all those firms, especially Alpha and Gamma because, coming from emerging countries, they seem to depart from the principle that competitive advantage is not created by headquarters but, rather, at each and every subsidiary. Differently from DMNEs which have purposefully moved to a metanational model, the traces observed in EMNEs seem to be justified by country-of-origin effects.

Therefore, the EMNEs' stages model shows little similarity to those described in the literature for the developed country multinationals because the rationale is influenced by specific factors, that is, the COE as well as the position in the GPN. The fact that their competitive advantage stems from their competence in production and operations also influences the internationalization pattern in what concerns the design and implementation of IONs.

CONCLUSIONS

The aim of this paper was to address the question: how do firms design and implement their operations network to penetrate international markets? The answer was sought through the study of emerging country multinationals.

In regards to the propositions, P1 is observed with an additional finding: EMNEs change their internationalization strategy as they expand internationally. The case evidence suggests that the outcome is associated to P3. In other words, the change in the internationalization strategy seems to be related to the process of capability building in international operations: there is a cyclical effect when the operations network associated to a given strategy achieves a certain capability level thus providing leverage for the multinational to redefine its strategy and redesign its network accordingly. As to P2, the cases brought evidences for this proposition as well.

From that outcome, four conclusions emerge. First, country-of-origin effects and relationships within the GPN affect both design and implementation especially in the initial stages of internationalization. Second, it is important to understand the firms' evolution in regards to design and implementation of international operations in stages, even though critiques to the stage model exist (Galbraith, 2000). Third, although the literature presents an extensive typology of international management models, the ones that are being developed by the new multinationals seem to keep specific features. The small size of the sample does not allow any attempt to specify new international management models but there are clues that their evolution would be better described by a version of the metanational model. Fourth, the analysis of the four cases brings a new perspective to Ramamurti's generic strategies in the sense that they show an evolutionary path. Emerging country firms start as local optimizers and then, depending on the relationships within the GPN, COEs and the effectiveness in the design and implementation of their international networks, they will adopt other generic strategies adequate for international expansion.

From the standpoint of theoretical development, the approach adopted widens the lens in the analysis of International Business by further integrating International Operations Management concepts to the analytical framework.

This study has implications for researchers in that we show that strategic and network decisions are strongly interrelated and need to be considered in an integrated fashion. Repositioning in the GPN, deliberate or not, cannot be taken in isolation. Instead, the relationship with the whole network must be considered. Further development of the analytical framework may provide guidance for the design and implementation of international operations networks in firms planning their internationalization.

NOTE

1. We use fictional names for the study to preserve the anonymity of our respondents.

REFERENCES

Bartlett, C., & Ghoshal, S. (1986). Tap your subsidiaries for global reach. *Harvard Business Review*, *64*, 87–94.

Bartlett, C., & Ghoshal, S. (1989). *Managing across borders. The transnational solution*. Boston, MA: Harvard Business School Press.

Bartlett, C., & Ghoshal, S. (1998). Beyond strategic planning to organization learning: Lifeblood of the individualized corporation. Strategy & Leadership, *26*(1), 34–39.

Bartlett, C., & Ghoshal, S. (2000). Going global: Lessons from late-movers. *Harvard Business Review*, March–April, *78*(2), 132–142.

Bartlett, C., Ghoshal, S., & Beamish, P. (2008). *Transnational management*. New York, NY: McGraw-Hill Irwin.

Birkinshaw, J., & Hood, N. (1998). Multinational subsidiary evolution: Capability and charter change in foreign-owned subsidiaries companies. *Academy of Management*, *23*, 773–795.

Chandler, A. (1962). *Strategy and structure: Chapters in the history of the industrial enterprise*. Boston, MA: MIT Press.

Contractor, F., Kumar, V., Kundu, S., & Pedersen, T. (2010). Reconceptualizing the firm in a world of outsourcing and offshoring: The organizational and geographical relocation of high-value company functions. *Journal of Management Studies*, *47*(8), 1417–1433.

Doz, Y., Santos, J., & Williamson, P. (2001). *From global to metanational*. Boston, MA: Harvard Business School Press.

Ferdows, K. (1997). Making the most of foreign factories. *Harvard Business Review*, March–April, *75*, 73–88.

Fleet, D., & Shi, Y. (2005). A practical approach to applying theoretical concepts in the design of global manufacturing networks. *Proceedings of 10th Cambridge International Manufacturing symposium*. September.

Fleury, A., & Fleury, M. T. (2007). The evolution of production systems and conceptual frameworks. *Journal of Manufacturing Technology Management*, *18*(8), 949–965.

Fleury, A., & Fleury, M. T. (2014). Emerging country firms acquiring in developed countries: The importance of local enablers of Business models. *Journal of Business Research*, *67*(4), 516–526.

Fleury, A., Fleury, M. T., & Borini, F. (2012). Is manufacturing the core competence for the internationalization of emerging country firms? *International Journal of Production Economics*, *140*, 339–349.

Galbraith, J. (2000). *Designing the global corporation*. San Francisco, CA: Jossey-Bass.

Gereffi, G., Humphrey, J., & Sturgeon, T. (2005). The governance of global value chains. *Review of International Political Economy*, *12*(1), 78–104.

Hayes, R. H., & Wheelwright, S. C. (1984). *Restoring our competitive edge: Competing through manufacturing*. New York, NY: Wiley.

Meijboom, B., & Vos, B. (1997). International manufacturing and location decisions: Balancing configuration and co-ordination aspects. *International Journal of Operations and Production Management*, *178*, 790–805.

Nohria, N., & Ghoshal, S. (1997). *The differentiated network: Organizing multinational corporations for value creation*. San Francisco, CA: Jossey-Bass.

Peng, M. W., Wang, D., & Jiang, Y. (2008). An institution-based view of international business strategy: A focus on emerging economies. *Journal of International Business Studies*, *39*, 920–936.

Ramamurti, R. (2009a). What have we learned about emerging country multinationals? In R. Ramamurti & J. Singh (Eds.), *Emerging multinationals from emerging markets*. Cambridge, UK: Cambridge University Press.

Ramamurti, R. (2009b). The theoretical value of studying Indian multinationals. *Indian Journal of Industrial Relations*, *45*(1), 101–114.

Rugman, A., Verbeke, A., & Yuan, W. (2010). Re-conceptualizing Bartlett and Ghoshal's classification of national subsidiary roles in the multinational enterprise. *Journal of Management Studies*, *48*(2), 253–277.

Saka-Helmhout, A. (2010). Organisational learning as situated routine-based activity in international settings. *Journal of World Business*, *45*(1), 41–48. doi:10.1016/j.jwb.2009.04.009

Sethi, S., & Elango, B. (1999). The influence of "country of origin" on multinational corporation global strategy: A conceptual framework. *Journal of International Management*, *5*, 285–298.

Shi, Y., & Gregory, M. (1998). International manufacturing networks: To develop global competitive capabilities. *Journal of Operations Management*, *16*, 195–214.

Srai, J., & Gregory, M. (2008). A supply network configuration perspective on international supply chain development. *International Journal of Operations and Production Management*, *28*(5), 386–411.

Stopford, J., & Wells, L. (1972). *Managing the multinational enterprise*. New York, NY: Basic Books.

Zhang, Y., & Gregory, M. (2011). Managing global network operations along the engineering value chain. *International Journal of Operations and Production Management*, *31*(7), 736–764.

BUSINESS GROUP EFFECTS ON THE INNOVATION-INTERNATIONALIZATION RELATIONSHIP: EVIDENCE FROM THE INDIAN PHARMACEUTICAL SECTOR

Saptarshi Purkayastha, Tatiana S. Manolova and Linda F. Edelman

ABSTRACT

We combine insights from the strategic management and international business literatures in order to explore the moderating role of business group characteristics on the link between innovation and internationalization in the context of the pharmaceutical sector in India. We test our three hypotheses on a sample of 219 Indian pharmaceutical firms affiliated with business groups, over a five-year period (2005–2010) in a panel of 1,096 firm-year observations. Results indicate that, contrary to our contention, research expenditure is negatively associated with export intensity, implying that firms in the Indian pharmaceutical sector may

Emerging Economies and Multinational Enterprises
Advances in International Management, Volume 28, 379–402

ISSN: 1571-5027/doi:10.1108/S1571-502720150000028017

face a trade-off between investing in innovation and international expansion. As expected, business group characteristics significantly impact the strength of the relationship between innovation and internationalization. Theoretical and practitioner implications are discussed.

Keywords: Innovation; R&D intensity; internationalization; emerging economies; ownership

INTRODUCTION

A long lineage of research in the international business literature, starting with Vernon's (1966) product life cycle theory, has coalesced around the dictum that R&D and innovation capabilities are positively associated with a firm's decision to export and subsequent export intensity. Vernon (1966, 1979) hypothesized that firms will initially innovate and produce for their home market, but will start moving into exports to exploit their market power in foreign markets because of the limits the domestic market poses in the early growth stage (Hirsch & Bijaoui, 1985). Innovation is positively associated with exporting because it allows the firm to exploit its competitive advantages globally (Chang, 1995; Hitt, Hoskisson, & Kim, 1997) thereby generating revenues on a larger scale and extending the product life cycle. Internationalization, in turn, provides exposure to demanding customers and capable competitors overseas, promotes knowledge spillovers (Görg & Greenaway, 2002; Salomon & Jin, 2008), and allows firms to learn-by-exporting, thus enhancing productivity and firm performance (Salomon & Shaver, 2005).

The link between innovation and internationalization in the context of emerging economies may be more tenuous and complex. Emerging economies are characterized by lower returns on R&D (Gorondichenko, Svejnar, & Terrell, 2008), prompting firms to engage more in imitation and adaptation of already created and tested innovations, rather than in generating new inventions (Gorondichenko et al., 2008; Minniti & Levesque, 2010). In other words, the type and scale of innovation activity by emerging market firms may not be of the caliber necessary to provide a source of sustainable advantage in global competition. Further, most emerging market firms still face significant financial constraints and need to make a choice between investing in innovation and investing in internationalization (Gorodnichenko & Schnitzer, 2010). Finally, emerging markets firms have to cope with home market imperfections and institutional voids (Peng,

2003; Yi, Wang, & Kafouros, 2013) which increase the risks and costs of doing business both domestically and internationally. Business groups, an organizational form that emerged to substitute market imperfections in emerging markets (Granovetter, 1994), may facilitate the process of internationalization of their affiliated companies through the establishment of an internal market for labor and capital, the support of linkages across their affiliated companies, or the provision of institutional support (Yiu, 2011).

In this study, we investigate the link between the R&D intensity and export intensity in the context of business group-affiliated firms in the Indian pharmaceutical sector. We ask the following research questions: (1) What is the link between the research and export intensity of business group-affiliated Indian pharmaceutical firms? and (2) What is the effect of the structural characteristics of the business group to which the firm is affiliated on the strength of the relationship between research and export intensity?

The results from our panel GLS estimations indicate that research expenditure is negatively associated with export intensity. This suggests that traditional, nonresearch-active firms are more active exporters compared to the research-active firms. Further, we find that the degree of business group diversification strengthens the negative effect of R&D investment on export intensity, whereas the degree of business group internationalization alleviates this negative effect.

Our study makes three contributions. First, while most studies on the internationalization of emerging market firms do control for the effect of business group membership, a deeper understanding of the specific mechanisms through which business group affiliation affects internationalization has been slower to emerge. We address this gap by examining the contingent effects of two structural characteristics of the business group: the degree of product diversification and the degree of internationalization (i.e., market diversification). Second, our exploration of the contingent effects of business group internationalization and product diversification integrates insights from the international business and strategic management literatures. These two literatures have studied different aspects of diversification, that is, market diversification versus product diversification, using different theoretical lenses. Third, we explore the case of the Indian pharmaceutical industry post 2005, when India shifted from a process patent to a product patent regime, creating a strong impetus for product innovation, which in our case is new drug discovery. Thus, our study provides fresh empirical evidence from a dynamic industry, which currently ranks fourth in volume and thirteenth in value globally (Chittoor, Sarkar, Ray, & Aulakh, 2009).

Our paper is structured as follows. We begin by developing our theoretical argument and formulating three hypotheses that guide our study. We next present the context of the study, describe our methodological approach, and report statistical results. We conclude by discussing the theoretical, practitioner, and public policy implications of our findings.

THEORETICAL PERSPECTIVES AND HYPOTHESIS DEVELOPMENT

Research Intensity and Exporting

Research intensity (an input into innovation) boosts the export intensity of the firm through several interrelated mechanisms. First, innovation directed toward the introduction of new products, creative design, higher quality, or other desirable product attributes, provides firms with a source of monopolistic competitive advantage through differentiation, which can be exploited on a global scale (Chang, 1995; Hitt et al., 1997). Investments in innovation increase the firm's ability to meet the demands of its changing domestic and international markets, thus making exporting more profitable for a firm (Zahra & Covin, 1994). Second, firms involved in innovation are motivated to increase their revenue base through exporting so they can recoup their R&D investments faster (Alvarez & Robertson, 2004). Finally, innovation provides a boost to productivity, which in turn facilitates export involvement (Cassiman & Golovko, 2011). Empirical evidence from developed economies has largely supported the positive association between R&D capability and exporting, utilizing samples from various national contexts (Basile, 2001; Cassiman & Golovko, 2011; Caves, Porter, Spence, & Scott, 1980; Girma, Gorg, & Hanley, 2008; Roper & Love, 2002; Tomiura, 2007) and at different levels of analysis (Basile, 2001; Caves et al., 1980; Roper & Love, 2002).

The link between endogenous R&D activity and export intensity in the context of emerging market firms is less clear. On the one hand, emerging market firms come from the position of latecomers, lacking the resources and capabilities of established multinationals from developed countries (Kumaraswamy, Mudambi, Saranga, & Tripathy, 2012). They need to constantly balance the need to develop internal capabilities with the desire for global reach (Chang & Rhee, 2011; Guillén & García-Canal, 2009). Thus, emerging market firms may choose to abstain from aggressive export expansion while they develop their internal capabilities until such a moment when they reach a major technological breakthrough or a certain size threshold.

On the other hand, investment in R&D facilitates the development of technological innovations and innovation capabilities and protects against profit erosion (Chari & David, 2012), thus improving the competitiveness of emerging market firms in the international arena. A longitudinal study of the determinants of R&D behavior of Indian enterprises over the 1990s documented that Indian firms directed their R&D activity primarily toward the assimilation of imported technology and to providing a backup to their outward expansion via exports and foreign direct investment (Kumar & Aggarwal, 2005). Indeed, a study of the strategic archetypes of Indian multinationals revealed that about 17% of them were "established internationalizers," large multinationals with high levels of investments, very similar to Western multinationals (Karna, Upadhyayula, & Kumar, 2014). Thus, we expect that the fundamental mechanisms translating a firm's R&D capabilities into higher export intensity will work in much the same way in emerging markets as in the context of developed markets. Formally:

> **H1.** Research expenditure will be positively associated with export intensity.

The Moderating Role of Business Group Characteristics

Khanna and Rivkin (2001, pp. 45–74) defined business groups as "firms which though legally independent, are bound together by a constellation of formal and informal ties and are accustomed to taking coordinated actions." Business groups have become ubiquitous in emerging economies (Carney, Gedajlovic, Heugens, van Essen, & van Oosterhout, 2011). They are known as *chaebols* in South Korea (Chang, 2003), *grupos economicos* in Latin America (Strachan, 1976), *hongs* in Hong Kong (Wong, 1996), *business houses* in India (Encarnation, 1989), *guanxiqiye* in Taiwan (Numazaki, 1996), and *qiye jituan* in China (Keister, 1988). This unique organizational form has a significant economic impact. For example, the top 100 business groups in Taiwan contribute up to 45% of the country's industrial output (Chung, 2004). As of 2000, business groups in India controlled about 75%

of the total industrial output in the private sector (Purkayastha, Manolova, & Edelman, 2012).

To explain their prevalence and dominance in different societies, researchers have adopted various theoretical perspectives, such as institutional theory (Khanna & Palepu, 1997), the resource-based perspective (Guillén, 2000), or a social network perspective (Adler & Kwon, 2002; Gerlach, 1992; Granovetter, 1994). Many theorists have argued that business group affiliation has performance-enhancing benefits (Yiu, Lu, Bruton, & Hoskisson, 2007). Business groups can be seen as a mechanism through which inter-firm transaction costs are lowered, efficient resource allocation is done, superior information about affiliate firms is obtained, and reduction in the possibility of contractual disputes is assured. Collectively, these factors improve the outcomes for affiliated firms (for a recent meta-analysis on the effect of business group affiliation on member-firms' performance, see Carney et al., 2011). Below, we argue how the performance-enhancing benefits stemming from the group's degree of product diversification and internationalization can facilitate the translation of research intensity into export intensity.

The Moderating Effect of the Business Group's Degree of Product Diversification

Firms affiliated with diversified business groups can enjoy substantial economies of scope from product diversification, generated by shared physical assets, shared external relations, or shared learning (Ghoshal, 1987). The diversified business group network can act as a conduit to transfer technological knowledge, thereby improving and directing the focal firm's R&D capability (Mahmood, Zhu, & Zajac, 2011). Through their interactions with sister affiliates, group-affiliated firms can identify potential clients for exports whose requirements can be met with the help of their increased R&D capability. Being tied up to a business group with operations in multiple industries can enable group firms to know more about the export sales opportunities in different product markets.

Being part of a diversified business group not only provides awareness of different export markets, but may also induce prospective clients to buy from the group-affiliated firms by lowering information asymmetries between buyers and sellers (Lamin, 2013). This is especially true in the case of high R&D products because of the intrinsic risk associated with them. Further, being part of a diversified business group can serve as a basis of establishing initial contact with potential clients across different industries by referring clients to sister affiliates or introducing affiliates to potential clients. Indirect referrals or contacts are valuable resources because they provide prospective clients with reliable information regarding a firm's capabilities and trustworthiness, enabling clients to evaluate a potential exchange partner. Furthermore, the more diversified the business group is, the broader scope of industries it can target as it can get the benefit of referrals from all those industries. Formally:

> **H2a.** The degree of business group diversification will strengthen the relationship between research expenditure and export intensity.

The Moderating Role of the Business Group's Degree of Internationalization

Firms affiliated with business groups can benefit from significant synergies arising from the utilization of common infrastructures, resources, and competencies in the process of their internationalization. For example, they can use the global subsidiary network of the business group, take advantage of foreign market intelligence and local contacts, recruit top talent globally and benefit from the established brand name recognition in international markets. Information about foreign market opportunities is likely to be shared within the business group structure, as group ties facilitate interaction and communication among managers of sister affiliates. Information gleaned through group ties enables group-affiliated firms to be aware of more international export possibilities based on their R&D capabilities. The more international the business group is, the more information about various foreign market opportunities can be channeled, thereby increasing the export intensity of the affiliated firm. Internationalization also allows business groups to exploit internalized intermediary institutions; for example, internal capital markets help groups allocate financial resources across different markets and thereby overcome international finance fluctuations (Hitt et al., 1997). Business group affiliation also plays a key role in buffering the company from the risks that are involved in creating and exploiting assets through internationalization (Becker-Ritterspach & Bruche, 2012).

In addition to the advantages of scope economies stemming from foreign market diversification, organizational learning theory suggests that exposure to different environments also speeds up learning processes, because the group can transfer, integrate, and create knowledge-based resources to cope with uncertainties in different environments (Sambharya, 1995). Importantly, firms can pool knowledge developed in different markets and learn from the internationalization experiences of other members of the business group. Formally:

H2b. The degree of business group internationalization will strengthen the relationship between research expenditure and export intensity.

METHODS

Research Context

The Indian pharmaceutical industry accounts for about 10% of global production. Since the liberalization of the Indian economy in 1991, the sector has grown at over 20% per annum, reaching about $22 billion in 2009–2010 (Dun & Bradstreet, 2012). The industry is fragmented with more than 10,000 manufacturers; the top 200 companies, however, control 70% of the market (PwC, 2012).

Upon its accession to the World Trade Organization (WTO) in 1995, India committed to a transition from a process patent to a product patent system over the following 10 year period, thereby providing legal protection to trade-related intellectual property rights by 2005. This decision constituted a major institutional shock for indigenous Indian pharmaceutical firms, which had traditionally thrived by manufacturing and selling imitations of patented drugs through reverse engineering. In light of these changes in the property rights regime, the prognosis for domestic firms in the Indian pharmaceutical industry was rather pessimistic. However, in sharp contrast to the predictions, the last decade has seen an industry-wide resurgence and emergence of the pharmaceutical industry as one of the key drivers of India's global competitiveness and export-led growth.

One of the main reasons for the transformation in the Indian pharmaceutical industry has been the steep growth in the degree of internationalization and percentage of revenues from foreign markets. The total exports of pharmaceuticals from India (primarily undertaken by indigenous Indian firms rather than subsidiaries of multinationals) has increased from $503.1 million in 1995 to more than $18.83 billion in 2010 (FICCI, 2012), for a compounded 27% annual growth rate. Another notable feature of internationalization of the Indian pharmaceutical industry is its breadth – a sizeable number of firms, instead of just a few large ones, are international – which indicates international expansion is an industry-wide phenomenon. Indian pharmaceutical companies also invest aggressively overseas in order to obtain a toehold in the large and growing generics markets in the United States and Europe (Athreye & Godley, 2009; KPMG, 2006), and to gain access to the patents and product lines of R&D-intensive pharmaceutical companies in developed economies (Bhaumik, Driffield, & Pal, 2009).

Sample Selection

Our sample is drawn from the Center for Monitoring the Indian Economy (CMIE) database, which includes all firms listed on India's major stock exchanges, including public sector enterprises and foreign firms. For the purpose of this study we considered only firms belonging to the Indian pharmaceutical industry and affiliated to business groups. Our sample is thus comprised of 219 firms belonging to 109 Indian business groups.

We followed the following steps to build our sample. First, we downloaded from the database all business group firms that are categorized under the four digit industry classification of drugs and pharmaceuticals, which provided us with a list of 262 firms. Second, we eliminated 23 subsidiaries of foreign firms and 8 firms that had been founded post 2005, the starting point in our sample. Finally, as the database had some missing values, we searched for data on those firms in competing databases such as Capital Line and Worldscope. Still, we were not able to find the complete information on our entire list of variables and thus had to exclude 12 firms. Finally we were left with 219 firms for a period of five years (2005–2010). We conducted a panel data regression analysis with 1,096 observations. All explanatory variables were lagged by one year.

VARIABLES

Dependent Variable

We measured the internationalization of the firm as the ratio of foreign sales to total sales (FSTS), also known as export intensity. Export intensity is considered the most common measure of internationalization (Chittoor et al., 2009). We chose the ratio of foreign sales to total sales over other possible measures, such as international geographic spread, growth in foreign sales, or foreign direct investment (FDI), for two reasons. First, the validity of any measure must be assessed on the basis of its potential explanatory power in the context of the theoretical assumptions on which it is based (Hassel, Hopner, Kurdelbusch, Rehder, & Zugehor, 2003). Because the majority of firms from emerging economies remain in the early stages of the internationalization process and use exporting as the dominant mode of international expansion (Aulakh, Kotabe, & Teegen, 2000), this measure is more contextually appropriate compared with other measures, such as FDI. Second, data availability on FDI is limited and there is a sizeable number of missing values, presenting problems with the validity and generalizability of our results.

Independent and Moderator Variables

The key explanatory variable for this study was firm's expenditure in R&D. The most direct measure taken from CMIE database is R&D intensity. However, as there were a large number of firms that did not have any R&D expenses, using a continuous measure would result in a sizeable error of estimation. We therefore used a dummy variable as a proxy for expenditure in R&D. The *R&D dummy* variable takes a value of 1 for firms which have R&D expenditure; 0 otherwise.[1] Other explanatory variables include group diversification (*Bus group div.*), and business group internationalization (*Bus group int.*). The *Bus group div.* measure uses the Jacquemin-Berry entropy measure of diversification (Jacquemin & Berry, 1979) and *Bus group int.* uses foreign sales to the total sales of the group. Finally, in order to test for the moderating effect of business groups' characteristics on the relationship between R&D intensity and firm internationalization, we allowed out explanatory variables to interact with the *R&D dummy* variable.

Control Variables

Ownership of the firm has been found to affect its degree of internationalization (Banalieva & Eddleston, 2011; Singla & George, 2013) and so we controlled for it. We controlled for different categories of ownership depending on the proportion (%) of equity held by each specific group. Family ownership (*Family*) refers to the proportion of shares held by the founding family, including those held by family members and family foundations, as well as those held by group firms. *Foreign corp.* refers to the percentage of common shares held by foreign corporations. The variable *Foreign inst.* refers to the percentage of common shares owned by foreign financial institutions. We also controlled for a number of firm-level characteristics. The size of the firm (*Sales*) constitutes a critical control variable, because larger firms may be better positioned to access international resources, whether technology or finance, as well as to internationalize their product markets. Firm size, measured as the natural logarithm of sales (to remedy potential over-dispersion), thus controls for size effects. The age of each firm (*Age*) since it was founded, in years, serves as a measure of experience. We also included current ratio (*Current Ratio*, measured as current assets over current liabilities) and leverage (*Leverage*, measured as debt over total assets) to control for the financial health of the company. Finally, prior-year performance may influence a firm's outlook about embarking on international expansion, so we used prior return on assets (*ROA*) of the firm lagged by one year, as our last control variable. Because the entire data set pertains to a single industry, no industry controls are needed. However, we introduced year dummies to control for exogenous shocks relative to the baseline year (2006). Descriptions of all variables entered in the regression estimations are presented in Table 1.

Table 1. Variable Definitions.

Internationalization measures
FSTS: Ratio of foreign sales to total sales
Explanatory variables
R&D dummy: A proxy for expenditure in R&D. The dummy variable takes a value of 1 for firms which have R&D expenditure; 0 otherwise
Bus group div.: Business group diversification, measured as Σi Piln(1/Pi), where Pi is the proportion of affiliated firm's sales over the total sales of the business group
Bus group int.: Business group foreign sales to the total sales of the group
Control variables
Family: Percentage of shareholding by founding member's family, including those held by family members and family foundations, as well as those held by group firms
Foreign corp.: Percentage of common shares held by foreign corporations
Foreign inst.: Percentage of common shares owned by foreign financial institutions
Sales: Natural logarithm of sales
Age: Years since the incorporation of the firm
Leverage: Leverage defined as the ratio of total debt to total assets
Current Ratio: Current assets by current liabilities
ROA: Return on assets, defined as operating profit before depreciation, taxes, interest and other amortization charges over total assets

Model Specifications

To test the hypotheses, we used a panel design with generalized least square estimation (GLS) on observations running from 2005 to 2010. GLS is better suited for our data structure as it allows estimation in the presence of autocorrelation within panels and cross-sectional correlation and heteroskedasticity across panels (Wooldridge, 2010). In order to mitigate endogeneity problems of the explanatory variables, following Bhaumik et al. (2009) and Yi et al. (2013) we lagged them by one time period such that, for example, the research expenditure in period $t-1$ affects export intensity in the period t. Our regression specification is given by the following:

$$\begin{aligned}\text{FSTS}_{ijt} = {} & \beta_0 + \beta_1\, \textit{R\&D dummy}_{ij,t-1} + \beta_2\, \text{Family}_{ij,t-1} \\ & + \beta_3\, \text{Foreign corp}_{ij,t-1} + \beta_4\, \textit{Foreign inst}_{ij,t-1} \\ & + \beta_5\, \textit{Bus group div}_{j,t-1} + \beta_6\, \textit{Bus group int}_{j,t-1} \\ & + \beta_7\, \text{Sales}_{ij,t-1} + \beta_8\, \text{Age}_{ij,t-1} + \beta_9\, \text{Leverage}_{ij,t-1} \\ & + \beta_{10}\, \text{Current Ratio}_{ij,t-1} + \beta_{11}\, \text{ROA}_{ij,t-1} + \beta_{12}\, I \\ & + \beta_{13}-\beta_{16}\, \text{Year dummies} + u_{ij} + \varepsilon_{ijt}\end{aligned}$$

where i refers to the ith firm belonging to the jth business group; t and $t-1$ refers to the time periods; I refers to the interaction term between the *R&D dummy* variable and the other explanatory variables; u_{ij} represents the firm-specific fixed effects and ε_{ijt} is the error term. Our hypotheses have the following implications for the coefficient estimates:

- *Hypothesis 1 implies* $\beta_1 > 0$
- *Hypothesis 2a implies* $\beta_{12} > 0$ *when I is the interaction between the R&D dummy variable and Bus group div.*
- *Hypothesis 2b implies* $\beta_{12} > 0$ *when I is the interaction between the R&D dummy variable and Bus group int.*

RESULTS

Table 2 contains the means and correlation matrix for all variables in the model. Almost none of the coefficients (cf. BGD and BGI) exhibit high correlations with other control variables, and none of the variance inflation factors exceed 10, the general threshold for detecting serious multicollinearity (Mendenhall & Sincich, 2003).

Table 2. Descriptive Statistics and Correlations.

Variables	Mean	S.D.	1	2	3	4	5	6	7	8	9	10	11
1. FSTS	0.37	0.24	1.00	–0.03	0.02	–0.05	–0.01	–0.14	0.01	0.05	–0.09	0.17	–0.16
2. Sales[a]	4,244	10,024		1.00	–0.02	0.12	0.49	0.08	0.01	–0.06	0.02	0.16	0.12
3. Family	64.97	20.79			1.00	0.01	–0.02	0.03	0.02	0.01	0.03	–0.00	–0.01
4. Foreign corp.	3.75	6.35				1.00	0.21	0.03	0.01	–0.05	0.02	0.17	0.02
5. *Foreign inst.*	1.59	5.03					1.00	0.15	–0.02	–0.02	–0.07	0.01	0.17
6. Age	25.30	15.65						1.00	–0.04	0.03	0.01	–0.11	0.02
7. Leverage	1.55	1.18							1.00	0.07	0.05	–0.04	0.21
8. Current Ratio	3.26	2.27								1.00	–0.07	0.03	–0.15
9. *Bus group div.*	1.06	1.64									1.00	–0.27	0.05
10. *Bus group int.*	0.23	0.19										1.00	0.04
11. ROA	0.31	0.57											1.00

$N = 219$, All correlations above 0.14 are significant at 0.05 or below.
[a]Measured in Indian Rupees in million.

The results of the panel data regression appear in Table 3. The results from the basic regression Model 1 (without interaction) reveal a negative, significant coefficient of R&D, suggesting that firms with R&D expenditure are poor internationalizers compared to firms without R&D expenditure. This result holds even after introducing the interaction terms (Models 2–4). Thus our hypothesis about the positive effect of R&D expenditure on export intensity is not supported.

Model 2 shows that the interaction effect between business group diversification and the *R&D dummy* is negative which is not in accordance with our Hypothesis 2a. Thus, Hypothesis 2a is not supported. In Model 3, the coefficient of the interaction term between business group internationalization and the *R&D dummy* is positive, which is in accordance with Hypothesis 2b. Both of these interaction effects are tested simultaneously

Table 3. Panel Data Estimation with Internationalization as the Dependent Variable.

Variable	Baseline Model	Interaction Models		
	Model 1	Model 2	Model 3	Model 4
Constant	0.171**	0.160**	0.197**	0.191**
	(0.033)	(0.032)	(0.032)	(0.032)
R&D dummy	−0.092**	−0.044*	−0.266**	−0.231**
	(0.019)	(0.022)	(0.028)	(0.033)
Bus group div.	−0.006	−0.008	−0.002	−0.003
	(0.005)	(0.006)	(0.005)	(0.005)
Bus group int.	0.197**	0.184**	0.024	0.031
	(0.040)	(0.040)	(0.044)	(0.044)
Family	0.000	0.000	0.000	0.000
	(0.000)	(0.000)	(0.000)	(0.000)
Foreign corp.	0.003*	0.002	0.002	0.002
	(0.001)	(0.001)	(0.001)	(0.001)
Foreign inst.	−0.001	−0.002	−0.004*	−0.004**
	(0.001)	(0.002)	(0.002)	(0.001)
Sales	0.027**	0.028**	0.028**	0.028**
	(0.004)	(0.004)	(0.004)	(0.004)
Age	−0.002**	−0.002**	−0.002**	−0.002**
	(0.000)	(0.000)	(0.000)	(0.000)
Leverage	−0.003	−0.004	−0.004	−0.004
	(0.005)	(0.006)	(0.006)	(0.005)
Current Ratio	0.006^{+}	0.004	0.005^{+}	0.004
	(0.003)	(0.003)	(0.003)	(0.003)
ROA	−0.024**	−0.024**	−0.023**	−0.022**
	(0.009)	(0.009)	(0.009)	(0.009)

Table 3. *(Continued)*

Variable	Baseline Model	Interaction Models		
	Model 1	Model 2	Model 3	Model 4
Diversification * *R&D dummy*		−0.039**		−0.018+
		(0.009)		(0.009)
Internationalization * *R&D dummy*			0.729**	0.675**
			(0.086)	(0.090)
Year effects				
2007	0.045*	0.045*	0.043*	0.043*
	(0.022)	(0.022)	(0.022)	(0.022)
2008	0.060**	0.060**	0.058**	0.058**
	(0.022)	(0.022)	(0.022)	(0.022)
2009	0.069**	0.068**	0.063**	0.064**
	(0.023)	(0.023)	(0.022)	(0.022)
2010	0.081**	0.0800**	0.074**	0.075**
	(0.023)	(0.022)	(0.022)	(0.022)
Wald Chi Square	147.95**	169.39**	229.42**	233.82**
No. of Obs.	1,095	1,095	1,095	1,095

Standard errors are in parentheses.
+$p < 0.10$; *$p < 0.05$; **$p < 0.01$.

in the fully subscribed Model 4 where the results are unchanged. In summary, R&D expenditure has a negative impact on export intensity, but business group internationalization positively moderates, while business group diversification negatively moderates this relationship.

To test the robustness of our results to alternative operationalizations of the independent variable, we re-ran our analysis with taking the natural log of the amount of R&D expenditure and R&D intensity (R&D expenditure as a percent of sales revenue). The results from the robustness tests were consistent with the reported results, though less statistically significant. They are reported in Table 4.

DISCUSSION

Internationalization patterns vary between developed and emerging markets. A well-established body of international business literature finds a positive correlation between innovation and exporting, but resource-constrained emerging market firms are more likely to have to make a

Table 4. Robustness Tests with Alternative Operationalizations of the Independent Variable.

Variable	With R&D/Sales	With ln(R&D)
	Model 1	Model 2
Constant	0.276*	0.421**
	(0.111)	(0.121)
R&D/Sales	−1.652+	
	(0.996)	
ln(R&D)		−0.012
		(0.014)
Bus group div.	−0.020	−0.015
	(0.013)	(0.016)
Bus group int.	0.521**	0.221
	(0.111)	(0.138)
Family	0.000	0.001
	(0.001)	(0.001)
Foreign corp.	0.001	−0.000
	(0.003)	(0.004)
Foreign inst.	−0.001	−0.001
	(0.001)	(0.001)
Sales	0.001	0.006
	(0.013)	(0.015)
Age	−0.002*	−0.003*
	(0.001)	(0.001)
Leverage	−0.007	−0.008
	(0.010)	(0.009)
Current Ratio	0.006	0.007
	(0.005)	(0.005)
ROA	−0.030	−0.024
	(0.025)	(0.024)
R&D/Sales * *Bus group div.*	−1.011+	
	(0.560)	
R&D/Sales * *Bus group int.*	4.0633+	
	(2.296)	
ln(R&D) * *Bus group div.*		−0.002
		(0.005)
ln(R&D) * *Bus group int.*		0.093**
		(0.027)
Year effects		
2007	0.004	0.004
	(0.018)	(0.016)
2008	0.030+	0.030+
	(0.018)	(0.017)
2009	0.040*	0.042*
	(0.019)	(0.018)
2010	0.038+	0.035+
	(0.019)	(0.019)
Wald Chi Square	113.28**	117.11**
Adj. R^2	0.194	0.265
No. of Obs.	238	238

+$p < 0.10$; *$p < 0.05$; **$p < 0.01$.

choice between pursuing a strategy of exporting or channeling resources into innovation. In this study, we built on arguments from the international business and strategic management literatures in order to explore the effect of innovation on internationalization in the context of emerging market firms. We were particularly interested in the moderating effects of business group membership as business groups have been theorized to significantly impact the strategies and performance of emerging market firms (Carney et al., 2011; Khanna & Palepu, 2006). The results from our statistical tests lead to two principal findings, which we discuss below.

Emerging Market Firm Still Face Strategic Trade-Offs between Investments in Innovation and Export Expansion

Our finding of a negative relationship between research expenditures (an input into the innovation process) and export intensity adds to the literature on the patterns of internationalization of technologically driven companies in the context of emerging economies. An argument has been made that firms in emerging economies are faced with numerous strategic trade-offs when internationalizing, making choices between foreign revenue exposure, country risk, and entry mode commitment in each country (Hashai, 2011). Under conditions of financial constraints, as the case is for the majority of emerging market firms, internationalization and innovation activities often become substitutes, although they are generally considered natural complements (Gorodnichenko & Schnitzer, 2010). Inputs in and outputs from the technology innovation process, in particular, may present conflicting tensions on internationalization patterns. While substantial research and development outlays create pressures to recoup the costs through increased revenue generation on a global scale, technological innovations (an output from innovation) which are sensitive to threats of competitive imitation or intellectual property rights infringements may create pressures to abstain from aggressive international expansion until a critical threshold in size or a technological breakthrough is reached.

Our findings support the arguments advanced by Kumar and Siddharthan (1994) in their study of the inter-firm variation in export behavior of Indian firms across 13 manufacturing industries. They argue that firms in developing or emerging markets are unlikely to achieve a competitive advantage from innovation because they are starting later, do not have the firm-specific knowledge or vertical integration economies, suffer from shorter product life-cycles under which to recoup investment, and generally are less geographically diversified. From this, they suggest that the level of technology in an industry matters in that firms competing in industries with relatively low technology may achieve a competitive advantage based on imitation, but in firms competing in higher technology industries, or in industries based on introducing innovative new products or services, imitation advantages matter less. Our findings of a negative relationship between innovation and export intensity also supports Bruche's (2011) analysis of the challenges faced by Indian pharmaceutical companies in their competition with major global pharmaceutical companies. Bruche (2011) concludes that in "fortress industries" such as pharmaceuticals, due to the interaction of global oligopolistic structures, complex and multiple complementary resource and capability requirements or intellectual property and brand walls, the catch-up process – if left to market forces – may take up much longer. In sum, our findings suggest that there is a significant tension between allocating scarce resources for internationalization and for research and development, and in the context of Indian pharmaceuticals, where imitation has been superseded by a mandate for innovation, this tension affects internationalization. We call on future research can extend this inquiry to other industry and national context for a broader corroboration of our findings.

The Link between Research and Export Intensity Is Contingent on the Structural Characteristics of the Business Group

In line with a long lineage of research on the important role of business groups in emerging markets (Carney et al., 2011), we found that the degree of diversification and the degree of internationalization of the business group significantly affect the strength of the innovation-internationalization relationship in the Indian pharmaceutical sector. However, business group diversification and internationalization create tensions that pull in opposite directions, as we discuss below.

The results from our statistical tests suggest that firms belonging to overly diversified business groups may not be able to translate their research expenditures into a corresponding increase of the share of exports in their revenues. We surmise that the over-extended use of shared resources and the distraction of managerial attention away from the core business may lead to loss of control over the sources of individual firms' competitive advantage (Khanna & Yafeh, 2007). In addition, overly embedded intra-group networks can encourage parochialism, xenophobia, isolationism, and inertia, which are detrimental to corporate performance and globalization (Chung, 2004). For example, Gaur and Kumar (2008) in their study based on a sample of Indian firms found that business group affiliation reduces the positive effect of internationalization on firm performance. To sum up, diversified business groups grapple with many drawbacks which may negatively impact the translation of research intensity into export intensity.

In contrast, the degree of internationalization of the business group alleviates the negative effect of R&D intensity on export intensity. This suggests that firms affiliated with internationalized business groups can derive significant synergies and learn from the internationalization experiences of other group members. The group-wide learning mechanisms can be instrumental in the translation of research intensity into export intensity. The empirical evidence from our panel industry study supports insights gleaned from prior case-based research on the internationalization of emerging market business groups such as China's Haier Group (Duysters, Jacob, Lemmens, & Jintian, 2009) or India's Tata Group (Becker-Ritterspach & Bruche, 2012).

Our findings of the opposing moderating effects of business group diversification and internationalization pose broader questions about emerging market business groups' ability to benefit from different sources of economies of scope and learn from experiences across different product markets and geographies of operation. Similarly, in their exploration of the effects of product and international diversification on innovation and performance, Hitt et al. (1997) theorized and found complex interaction effects of product and international diversification, highlighting the difficulties in the implementation of complex diversification strategies. We thus call for a more nuanced and finer-grained analysis of the mechanisms through which different business group characteristics affect the strength of the research intensity-export intensity relationship, particularly in the context of emerging market business groups.

Boundaries and Limitations

As with all research, our study has a number of limitations. Specifically, as is common to all single industry studies, the issue of generalizability beyond the context of the Indian pharmaceutical industry is of concern. While the conclusions that we draw from the study are applicable in the pharmaceutical industry, we suggest that our results may be applied to other industries, as well. For example, two other major industries in India that have a global presence are automotives and its ancillaries, and information technology. Future researchers may look into both of these industries to test the validity of our results. Second, our measure of internationalization (foreign sales to total sales) is coarse. More fine grained measures such as the entropy measures that incorporate both the breadth (number of countries) and the depth (relative importance of each market) of internationalization might lead to a better understanding of the relationships that we have explored in this study. Data limitations prevent us from using such measures. Similarly, our measure of R&D capabilities in terms of R&D expenditure is also rudimentary. Future studies may incorporate the effect of R&D expenditure in terms of new patents filed or new products introduced in the markets. Finally, as our study only looks at firms affiliated to business groups, future researchers may examine similar hypothesis related to unaffiliated firms.

IMPLICATIONS AND CONCLUSIONS

Limitations notwithstanding, our study seeks to make three contributions to the international business literature. First, we explore the link between innovation and internationalization in the context of an emerging economy, an area relatively unexplored by prior research. Next, we systematically investigate the moderating effect of different business group structural characteristics on the strength of this relationship. Last, but not least, we test our hypothesis using rich panel data, allowing us to track the dynamics of change over time.

Our study looks at the very root of globalization and liberalization in an emerging economy. Additional large-sample studies in multiple industries and different geographical and institutional contexts should attempt to refine and validate our hypotheses and formulate new ones. Such studies may go a long way to clarifying the important linkages between changes in innovation and capability configurations and internationalization. To practicing managers, our study fleshes out the tensions between investments in innovation and export intensity and brings to the fore the dynamics of capability creation and capability exploitation through the internationalization process. To public policy-makers, the implications from our study strongly suggest that public policy mechanisms need to be put in place in order to enhance the positive externalities of business group affiliation.

NOTE

1. We perform robustness checks using alternative measures of research intensity and report those in the "Results" section.

ACKNOWLEDGMENTS

A previous version of the paper was presented at the *2013 Strategic Management Society Special Conference on Strategic Leadership: An Emerging Market Perspective*, Mohali, India. The authors would like to thank Elitsa Banalieva and Laszlo Tihanyi for their thoughtful comments and recommendations on how to improve the manuscript. All errors and omissions remain our own.

REFERENCES

Adler, P., & Kwon, S. (2002). Social capital, prospects for a new concept. *Academy of Management Review*, *27*, 17–40.

Alvarez, R., & Robertson, R. (2004). Exposure to foreign markets and firm-level innovation: Evidence from Chile and Mexico. *Journal of International Trade and Economic Development*, *13*, 57–87.

Athreye, S., & Godley, A. (2009). Internationalization and technological leapfrogging in the pharmaceutical industry. *Industrial and Corporate Change*, *18*, 295–323.

Aulakh, P. S., Kotabe, M., & Teegen, H. (2000). Export strategies and performance of firms from emerging economies: Evidence from Brazil, Chile and Mexico. *Academy of Management Journal*, *43*, 342–361.

Banalieva, E. R., & Eddleston, K. A. (2011). Home-region focus and performance of family firms: The role of family vs non-family leaders. *Journal of International Business Studies*, *42*, 1060–1072.

Basile, R. (2001). Export behavior of Italian manufacturing firms over the nineties: The role of innovation. *Research Policy*, *30*(8), 1185–1201.

Becker-Ritterspach, F., & Bruche, G. (2012). Capability creation and internationalization with business group embeddedness: The case of Tata Motors in passenger cars. *European Management Journal*, *30*(3), 232–247.

Bhaumik, S. K., Driffield, N., & Pal, S. (2009). Does ownership structure of emerging-market firms affect their outward FDI? The case of the Indian automotive and pharmaceutical sectors. *Journal of International Business Studies*, *47*, 437–450.

Bruche, G. (2011, July 1). *Emerging challengers in knowledge-based industries? The case of Indian pharmaceutical multinationals*. Columbia FDI Perspectives [Electronic copy]. No. 41. Retrieved from http://academiccommons.columbia.edu/catalog/ac,137385. Accessed on January 10, 2013.

Carney, M., Gedajlovic, E. R., Heugens, P. P. M. A. R., van Essen, M., & van Oosterhout, J. H (2011). Business group affiliation, performance, context and strategy: A meta-analysis. *Academy of Management Journal*, *54*(3), 437–460.

Cassiman, B., & Golovko, E. (2011). Innovation and internationalization through exports. *Journal of International Business Studies*, *42*, 56–75.

Caves, R. E., Porter, M. E., Spence, M., & Scott, J. T. (1980). *Competition in the open economy: A model applied to Canada*. Cambridge, MA: Harvard University Press.

Chang, S. J. (1995). International expansion strategy of Japanese firms: Capability building through sequential entry. *Academy of Management Journal*, *38*, 383–407.

Chang, S. J. (2003). Ownership structure, expropriation, and performance of group-affiliated companies in Korea. *Academy of Management Journal*, *46*, 238–253.

Chang, S.-J., & Rhee, J. H. (2011). Rapid FDI expansion and firm performance. *Journal of International Business Studies*, *42*(8), 979–994.

Chari, M. D., & David, P. (2012). Sustaining superior performance in an emerging economy: An empirical test in the Indian context. *Strategic Management Journal*, *33*(2), 217–229.

Chittoor, R., Sarkar, M. B., Ray, S., & Aulakh, P. S. (2009). Third-world copycats to emerging multinationals: Institutional changes and organizational transformation in the Indian pharmaceutical industry. *Organization Science*, *20*, 187–205.

Chung, H. K. (2004). Business groups in Japan and Korea: Theoretical boundaries and future direction. *International Journal of Political Economy*, *34*, 67–98.

Dun & Bradstreet. (2012). *Industry overview. Section A, pharmaceutical industry* [Electronic copy]. Retrieved from http://www.dnb.co.in/SME_cluster_series2012_Indore/PDF/IndustryOverview.pdf. Accessed on January 10, 2013.

Duysters, G., Jacob, J., Lemmens, C., & Jintian, Y. (2009). Internationalization and technological catching up of emerging multinationals, a comparative case study of China's Haier group. *Industrial and Corporate Change*, *18*(2), 325–349.

Encarnation, D. (1989). *Dislodging multinationals, India's comparative perspective*. Ithaca, NY: Cornell University Press.

FICCI. (2012). *Competitiveness of the Indian pharmaceutical industry in the new product patent regime*. FICCI report for National Competitiveness Council, New Delhi, March.

Gaur, A. S., & Kumar, V. (2008). International diversification, business group affiliation and firm performance: Empirical evidence from India. *British Journal of Management*, *20*(2), 172–186.

Gerlach, M. L. (1992). *Alliance capitalism: The social organization of Japanese business*. Oakland, CA: University of California Press.

Ghoshal, S. (1987). Global strategy: An organizing framework. *Strategic Management Journal*, *8*(5), 425–440.

Girma, S., Gorg, H., & Hanley, A. (2008). R&D and exporting: A comparison of British and Irish firms. *Review of World Economics*, *144*, 750–773.

Görg, H., & Greenaway, D. (2002). *Much ado about nothing? Do domestic firms really benefit from foreign direct investment?* CEPR Discussion paper No. DP3485.

Gorodnichenko, Y., & Schnitzer, M. (2010). *Financial constraints and innovation: Why poor countries don't catch up* [Electronic copy]. IZA. Discussion paper No. 4786, Forschungsinstitut zur Zukunft der Arbeit (Institute for the Study of Labor), Bonn, Germany. Retrieved from http://ssrncom. Accessed on March 20.

Gorondichenko, Y., Svejnar, J., & Terrell, K. (2008). *Globalization and innovation in emerging markets* [Electronic copy]. Working paper No. 14481. Cambridge, MA, NBER. Retrieved from http://www.nber.org/papers/w14418. Accessed on January 11, 2013.

Granovetter, M. (1994). Business groups. In N. J. Smelser & R. Swedberg (Eds.), *Handbook of economic sociology* (pp. 453–475). Princeton, NJ: Princeton University Press.

Guillén, M. F. (2000). Business groups in emerging economies: A resource based view. *Academy of Management Journal, 43*, 362–380.

Guillén, M. F., & García-Canal, E. (2009). The American model of the multinational firm and the "new" multinationals from emerging economies. *The Academy of Management Perspectives, 23*(2), 23–35.

Hashai, N. (2011). Sequencing the expansion of geographic scope and foreign operations by "born global" firms. *Journal of International Business Studies, 42*, 995–1015.

Hassel, A., Hopner, M., Kurdelbusch, A., Rehder, B., & Zugehor, R. (2003). Two dimensions of the internationalization of firms. *Journal of Management Studies, 40*, 705–724.

Hirsch, S., & Bijaoui, I. (1985). R&D intensity and export performance: A micro view. *Weltwirtschaftliches Archiv, 121*, 238–251.

Hitt, M. A., Hoskisson, R. E., & Kim, H. (1997). International diversification: Effects of innovation and firm performance in product diversified firms. *Academy of Management Journal, 40*, 767–798.

Jacquemin, A. P., & Berry, C. H. (1979). Entropy measure of diversification and corporate growth. *The Journal of Industrial Economics, 24*, 359–369.

Karna, A., Upadhyayula, R., & Kumar, V. (2014). Strategic archetypes of emerging market multinationals: Analysis of outward FDI of Indian firms. In T. Pedersen, M. Venzin, T. M. Devinney, & L. Tihanyi (Eds.), *Orchestration of the global network organization* (Vol. 27, pp. 325–347). Advances in International Management. Bingley, UK: Emerald Group Publishing Limited.

Keister, L. (1988). Engineering growth, business group structure and firm performance in China's transition economy. *American Journal of Sociology, 10*, 404–440.

Khanna, T., & Palepu, K. G. (1997). Why focused strategies may be wrong for emerging markets. *Harvard Business Review, 77*, 3–10.

Khanna, T., & Palepu, K. G. (2006). Emerging giants: Building world-class companies in developing countries. *Harvard Business Review, 84*, 60–69.

Khanna, T., & Rivkin, J. W. (2001). Estimating the performance effects of business groups in emerging markets. *Strategic Management Journal, 22*, 45–74.

Khanna, T., & Yafeh, Y. (2007). Business groups in emerging markets: Paragons or parasites? *Journal of Economic Literature, 45*, 331–372.

KPMG. (2006). *The Indian pharmaceutical industry, collaboration for growth.* London: KPMG.

Kumar, N., & Aggarwal, A. (2005). Liberalization, outward orientation and in-house R&D activity of multinational and local firms: A quantitative exploration for Indian manufacturing. *Research Policy, 34*, 441–460.

Kumar, N., & Siddharthan, N. S. (1994). Technology, firm size and export behavior in developing countries: The case of Indian enterprises. *The Journal of Development Studies, 31*, 289–309.

Kumaraswamy, A., Mudambi, R., Saranga, H., & Tripathy, A. (2012). Catch-up strategies in the Indian auto components industry: Domestic firms' responses to market liberalization. *Journal of International Business Studies, 43*(4), 368–395.

Lamin, A. (2013). Business groups as information resource: An investigation of business group affiliation in the Indian software services industry. *Academy of Management Journal, 56*, 1487–1509.

Mahmood, I. P., Zhu, H., & Zajac, E. J. (2011). Where can capabilities come from? Network ties and capability acquisition in business groups. *Strategic Management Journal, 32*, 820–848.

Mendenhall, W., & Sincich, T. (2003). *A second course in statistics: Regression analysis* (6th ed.). Upper Saddle River, NJ: Prentice Hall.

Minniti, M., & Levesque, M. (2010). Entrepreneurial types and economic growth. *Journal of Business Venturing*, *25*(30), 305–314.

Numazaki, I. (1996). The role of personal networks in the making of Taiwan's *Guanxiqiye* (related enterprises). In G. Hamilton (Ed.), *Asian business networks* (pp. 71–86). Walter de Gruyter, Berlin, Germany.

Peng, M. W. (2003). Institutional transitions and strategic choices. *Academy of Management Review*, *28*, 275–296.

Pricewaterhouse Coopers (PwC). (2012). *India Pharma Inc.: Capitalising on India's growth potential* [Electronic copy]. Retrieved from http://www.pwc.in/assets/pdfs/pharma/PwC-CII-pharma-Summit-Report-22Nov.pdf. Accessed on January 10, 2013.

Purkayastha, S., Manolova, T. S., & Edelman, L. (2012). Diversification and performance in developed and emerging market contexts: A review of literature. *International Journal of Management Reviews*, *14*, 18–38.

Roper, S., & Love, J. H. (2002). Innovation and export performance: Evidence from the UK and German manufacturing plants. *Research Policy*, *31*, 1087–1102.

Salomon, R., & Jin, B. (2008). Does knowledge spill to leaders or laggards? Exploring industry heterogeneity in learning by exporting. *Journal of International Business Studies*, *39*, 132–150.

Salomon, R., & Shaver, J. M. (2005). Learning-by-exporting: New insights from examining firm innovation. *Journal of Economics and Management Strategy*, *14*(2), 431–461.

Sambharya, R. B. (1995). The combined effect of international diversification and product diversification strategies on the performance of US-based multinational corporations. *Management International Review*, *35*, 197–218.

Singla, C., & George, R. (2013). Internationalization and performance: A contextual analysis of Indian firms. *Journal of Business Research*, *66*, 2500–2505.

Strachan, H. W. (1976). *Family and other business groups in economic development: The case of Nicaragua*. Praeger, Santa Barbara, CA, USA.

Tomiura, E. (2007). Effects of R&D and networking on the export decision of Japanese firms. *Research Policy*, *36*, 758–767.

Vernon, R. (1966). International investment and international trade in the product cycle. *Quarterly Journal of Economics*, *80*, 190–207.

Vernon, R. (1979). The product cycle hypothesis in a new international environment. *Oxford Bulletin of Economics and Statistics*, *41*, 255–267.

Wong, G. (1996). Business groups in a dynamic environment: Hong Kong 1976–1986. In G. Hamilton (Ed.), *Asian business networks* (pp. 87–114). Walter de Gruyter, Berlin, Germany.

Wooldridge, J. M. (2010). *Econometric analysis of cross section and panel data* (2nd ed.). Cambridge, MA: MIT Press.

Yi, J., Wang, C., & Kafouros, M. (2013). The effects of innovative capabilities on exporting: Do institutional forces matter? *International Business Review*, *22*(2), 392–406.

Yiu, D. W. (2011). Multinational advantages of Chinese business groups: A theoretical exploration. *Management and Organization Review*, *7*(2), 249–277.

Yiu, D. W., Lu, Y., Bruton, G. D., & Hoskisson, R. E. (2007). Business groups: An integrated model to focus future research. *Journal of Management Studies*, *8*, 1551–1579.

Zahra, S. A., & Covin, J. G. (1994). Domestic and international competitive focus, technology strategy and firm performance: An empirical analysis. *Technology Analysis and Strategic Management*, *6*, 39–53.

WHAT DO WE KNOW ABOUT STATE-OWNED EMERGING-ECONOMY FIRMS, AND HOW? EVALUATING LITERATURE ABOUT INWARD AND OUTWARD MULTINATIONAL ACTIVITIES

Xavier Martin and Cha Li

ABSTRACT

In this paper, we conduct a conceptual and bibliographic analysis of the literature that deals with the international strategy of state-owned enterprises (SOEs), with particular attention to SOEs from emerging economies (EEs). We first review the state of the art in defining the concepts of EEs and SOEs. We then conduct a detailed bibliographic analysis of the literature pertaining to SOEs' involvement in international activities, whether as outward foreign investors or as potential local partners of inward-investing multinational enterprises. The analysis covers general trends in the literature, prominent research questions and outcome variables, use of theories, and choices pertaining to methodology (type of

Emerging Economies and Multinational Enterprises
Advances in International Management, Volume 28, 403–439

ISSN: 1571-5027/doi:10.1108/S1571-502720150000028018

research and effects, empirical contexts). We document a literature that is fast-growing and well balanced in some respects. In other respects, we advance recommendations pertaining to (a) consistency and precision in the use of the concepts of "state-owned enterprise" and "emerging economy"; (b) search for specific evidence on the outward activities of EE SOEs in less-developed economies and even in other EEs, and on their performance; (c) understanding of relative propensities of local SOEs and inward investors to collaborate, and what happens when SOEs encounter each other across borders; (d) opportunities to strengthen the theoretical foundations and contributions of this research; and (e) minding the mix of home and host countries in studies and avoiding undue generalization from what has become a predominantly China-centric literature.

Keywords: State-owned enterprises; emerging economies; international strategy; international business theory; foreign direct investment; China

INTRODUCTION

As emerging economies (EEs) gain a prominent, and even by some measure predominant role in global economic activities, questions about the activities and specificities of their firms require attention. It is commonly assumed that EEs are different, and therefore their firms must have some special characteristics too, though opinions differ as to whether these differences are of kind or of degree if at all. From an international or comparative business or management perspective (IB in short), the question arises of what this means for the behavior and performance of firms – both from an inward perspective (i.e., patterns and consequences of interactions within EEs between local firms and incoming multinational investors) and from an outward perspective (i.e., patterns and consequences of expansion abroad by firms from EEs). Although this entire topic is too much to address in one paper, we aim to address it with respect to one specific category of firms: state-owned or otherwise state-controlled enterprises (SOEs in short). SOEs are commonly assumed to play a relatively large role in EEs, whether as a legacy of more or less reformed communist or socialist systems in these countries (in particular the largest four EEs, so-called

BRICs) or as a matter of economic development strategy (e.g., during the rise of the Singaporean economy).

In this paper, we deal with the literature that relates SOEs with both inward and outward international business activities, with a focus on forms of foreign direct investment (FDI) and performance. We aim to identify trends and specificities of this literature as it pertains to SOEs from EEs. In so doing, we aim to make three contributions. First, we provide a comprehensive bibliometric review of the themes and trends in this literature. Second, we identify certain patterns that indicate over- or conversely under-representation of certain topics or countries in extant research. Third, accordingly we put forward recommendations for the future research that would stand to make the strongest contribution to this area of research, and to research on SOEs and EEs more generally.

The remainder of this paper is structured as follows. First, we describe our methodology and review the core definitions used. Second, we present a comprehensive bibliometric analysis of the management literature on SOEs. We identify what is specific about multinational activities of SOEs, and specifically about SOEs from EEs as compared with SOEs from developed economies. Third, we make a series of organized suggestions for research about the international activities of SOEs, especially those from EEs. We analyze, on one hand, literature that deals with the foreign investment activities and performance of SOEs, that is where they become multinational corporations undertaking FDI; and on the other hand, research on inward effects associated with SOEs, that is studies about the conduct and performance of a foreign multinational that encounters an SOE in the latter's home market, and about the conduct and performance of an SOE that cooperates and competes with multinational corporations. Accordingly, we make a series of recommendations for future research. Fourth, we provide a brief conclusion encompassing promising directions at the intersection of EEs and SOE activities.

METHODOLOGY AND CONCEPTS

Data Collection

Since our purpose is to review and evaluate the literature, we start with a comprehensive bibliometric analysis (Martin & van den Oever, 2013). To establish the sample for our review, we examined articles published in

16 academic journals in management during the past six decades. The list included 10 generalist journals, that is, *Academy of Management Journal*, *Academy of Management Review*, *Administrative Science Quarterly*, *Journal of Business Research*, *Journal of Management Studies*, *Long Range Planning*, *Management Science*, *Organization Science*, *Organization Studies*, and *Strategic Management Journal*; and 6 prominent journals specialized in international business and management, that is, *Global Strategy Journal*, *International Business Review*, *Journal of International Business Studies*, *Journal of International Management*, *Journal of World Business*, and *Management International Review*. The time span for the publications reviewed goes from 1954, the earliest publication year among the journals reviewed, to 2014, including forthcoming articles published online through October 2014.

We started by identifying all papers on SOEs, regardless of topics (i.e., whether dealing with an international management topic or not) and of the research context (i.e., whether in EEs or not). The criterion for inclusion was that the article contained in its title, abstract, or keywords any of the following terms:

- *State(-)owned, state owner, state ownership*;
- *Government(-)owned, government owner, government ownership*;
- *State(-)controlled, state control, state controller*;
- *Government(-)controlled, government control, government controller*;
- *State firm, state enterprise.*

This initial search resulted in a sample of 183 articles. After reading the abstract and introduction of these articles, we excluded two types of articles: (1) those that mentioned any of our search words simply to introduce background but without dealing with them substantively, and (2) those that focused on the discussion of privatization on an institution level, for example, investigating the institutional change during privatization, and thus did not provide insights into characteristics of SOEs. This left 169 articles.

Since the focus of this study was on the differences between SOEs and non-SOEs in EEs in terms of their international business activities (both outward investment and interactions with inward foreign investors), we further refined our set based on the topics of the articles. In a second stage, we excluded 112 articles that investigated non-IB topics, such as domestic strategy, corporate governance (again, domestically), and performance of SOEs. We also excluded two articles that investigated the exporting strategy of SOEs, since our focus in this article is on FDI activities, though alternatively including these two articles did not change our conclusions substantively. This left us with a final sample of 55 articles. Within that narrower sample, 41 articles examined SOEs from EEs markets, 7 articles examined SOEs from developed economies, and 7 articles examined SOEs in mixed or unspecified research settings. Although we are especially interested in examining SOEs from EEs markets, we maintained in our sample the 14 articles that discussed IB topics but not specifically on EEs. This allowed us to make comparisons between research in EEs and in other contexts and to enrich the inferences and conclusions that we could draw.

Core Concepts

International Strategy and Multinational Enterprises

International strategy refers to the activities of firms that cross national boundaries. As such international strategy research encompasses the determinants and consequences (performance) of various foreign entry (and exit) decisions, such as via establishment modes such as greenfield or acquisition, via wholly owned or jointly owned entry modes, and via other alternatives such as licensing (Hitt, Tihanyi, Miller, & Connelly, 2006; Martin, 2013; Martin, Swaminathan, & Tihanyi, 2007; Martin & van den Oever, 2013). In this paper, following the scope of this volume, we excluded exporting from the scope of the research examined, to focus instead on activities that entail the deployment of assets abroad. A separate literature speaks to exporting, which tends to be a more common and less distinctive activity where emerging economies are concerned (e.g., Campa & Guillén, 1999).

A multinational enterprise (MNE), or equivalently multinational corporation (MNC), is a firm that controls via ownership production facilities in two or more countries (Caves, 2007). This definition is well established (see also Buckley & Casson, 2002; Martin, 2014), and a large consensus has been reached both among supranational institutions such as the OECD and among academic researchers about the ownership level (typically 10%) that identifies ownership for the purpose of measuring FDI and thus MNE scope (Graham & Krugman, 1995; Vukmanic, Czinkota, & Ricks, 1985). This consensus, which may have resulted from a long tradition of research on MNEs and FDI (summarized in Caves, 2007; Dunning & Lundan, 2008; Martin, Mitchell, & Swaminathan, 1994), stands in contrast to the diversity of definitions of SOEs and even emerging economies, which we examine next.

Emerging Economies

We took as our starting point the IMF's (2012) view that emerging economies (EEs; also known as emerging markets) are national economies that have not reached the advanced stage of development, but that are displaying evidence of economic and institutional progress toward the advanced stage. Economic emergence thus reflects the development of national and institutional capabilities (Sen, 1989), which stand to interact with corporate activities in determining national and corporate advantage (Martin, 2014). The IMF definition separates EEs both from fully developed economies (DEs, the most advanced economies – roughly, the OECD members) and from economies that may be developing but that are poorer and less far along institutionally – which we refer to in short as less-developed economies (also known as least-developed economies, or sometimes as developing economies). Following this logic, we started with the IMF's lists to identify which papers deal with EEs, matching each paper's sampling timeframe with the evolving list. This led us, for instance, to consider some papers with early data about South Korea as dealing with an EE, but not later papers (South Korea joined the OECD in 1996 and is now by all accounts a high-income country with well-developed institutions). This also led us to classify as mixed samples those that included one or more EE alongside one or more less-developed (or developed) economy (e.g., a sample including Brazilian and Bolivian firms: Dau, 2012). Finally, in a small number of cases we accepted authors' claims that they were studying "emerging markets" if we found secondary support, even though the original authors did not back up their claim; for instance Vietnam (Meyer & Nguyen, 2005) is not on the IMF list of EEs but figures in the less rigorously defined "Next Eleven" and "CIVETS" lists (Moore, 2012).

Pointing out the ambiguities above is relevant because, aside from their real economic importance, EEs may be subject to a fad effect leading to both cross-sectional and longitudinal misclassification. The cross-sectional issue arises in particular when "emerging" serves as a euphemism for the poorest countries, leading to confusion between emerging and less-developed economies. The longitudinal issue arises when a former EE develops to the point of qualifying as developed rather than emerging (or conversely experiences decline, as for instance in the case of Greece), and researchers fail to adjust the classification of their sample countries or firms. Because state-firm interactions are also a function of the state's resources (Lazzarini, 2015; Martin, 2014), as indeed our proposed definition of SOE below recognizes, researchers should pay more attention to the basis on which they label economies as emerging. Specifically:

Recommendation 1: Authors should state explicitly on what basis they associate firms or countries in their sample with EEs. In multi-country or international samples, the classification should separate EEs both from less developed and from fully developed economies. This enables clear and meaningful comparisons in terms of national economic and institutional development, and also with respect to the strategies for MNEs investing to or from peer emerging, versus poorer, versus more advanced economies.

State-Owned or Controlled Enterprises

Our search terms (see above) encompassed both ownership and control by the state. Although ownership and control are separate concepts (Chi & Roehl, 1997), in practice most state ownership is meant and operates as a means of controlling the enterprise's action (Mazzolini, 1980a), so the terms are closely related. As it were, only one set of early papers by Mazzolini (e.g., 1979) used the term "government-controlled" – and even then, Mazzolini interchanged "state-owned" in later work (1980b). When it comes to defining state ownership, though, approaches differ strikingly among the papers in our sample. Half of the papers provide no definition or description of the measure, though a small subset of these state instead that they use a code provided in the SDC dataset – of which the criteria are not explicit or scientifically tested to our knowledge. Among papers that report how they measure state ownership, a minority use a continuous measure of the percentage of the firm's equity held by the state. The remainder use discrete measures, which again exhibit much variation. The minimum equity stake by the state to define an SOE ranges from as low as 10% (Li, Miller, Eden, & Hitt, 2012; although these authors stand out for reporting that they examined robustness for other thresholds) to 100% (Wei, Clegg, & Ma, 2015). Other papers use intermediate cutoffs, either absolute (e.g., 50%: Dau, 2012) or relative (largest shareholder: Meyer, Ding, Li, & Zhang, 2014). Precision in this respect is important because minority ownership by the state may affect firm behavior, but perhaps differently than majority ownership (Inoue, Lazzarini, & Musacchio, 2013).

A further sign of the need for conceptual clarity is that papers on SOEs vary in how they define firms that are not state-owned, using disparate labels including: private, non-state-owned, publicly owned (as in, traded on a public stock exchange), etc. Only if what is an SOE is clearly defined, is the alternative form or forms clear. A further subtlety in defining SOEs, in the case of China, pertains to whether to treat collectively owned enterprises as state-owned (Zhou & van Witteloostuijn, 2010) or as a separate group (Tan, 2002). We conclude that it is preferable to treat collectively owned firms as a separate group, given growing evidence of differences in their strategies (Peng, Tan, & Tong, 2004) and in their competitive impact and outcomes (Xu, Lu, & Gu, 2014).

Given the ambiguity in the literature, we propose a theory-based approach toward defining SOEs. Studies that provide no definition, or base their measurement on a potentially arbitrary cutoff, assume that any level of government ownership (or any above a threshold) fundamentally and homogeneously changes the nature of the firm or its behavior. We deem this insufficiently specific, from conceptual and empirical standpoints. Rather, our premise is that the threshold required for influence stands to vary with the nature and stage of the firm-state relationship (Martin, 2014). What matters, when examining the investments of a firm or its reaction toward other firms (in this paper, foreign MNEs), is whether the resources or the goals of the focal firm are substantially modified by state ownership. Thus, ownership is of relevance primarily if it leads the state to exert control over the firm's strategic decisions. In this respect one recent paper, Liang, Ren, and Sun (2015), stands out for its complete and theoretically coherent approach to measuring state ownership and control. Based on the above review, we provide a definition, and some recommendations for future research.

Definition: A state-owned or state-controlled enterprise (SOE) is a legally separate firm in which the state, through at least partial direct or indirect ownership or other means of direct control, has the ability to influence the strategic decisions of the firm.

This definition acknowledges that ownership may be indirect or via a pyramid structure (Liang et al., 2015). In practice, effective control will typically require that the state's (or aligned state entities') ownership be larger than that of any possible counteracting coalition of private shareholders (blockholders); or that lesser state ownership be accompanied by dependence of the firm upon other resources provided by the state, such as key employees, non-equity financing, or dependence on the state as a client. The effective use of the concept of SOE requires further attention to the measure and theoretical mechanisms than is apparent in some of the researches we reviewed. Accordingly, we allow ourselves a second recommendation:

Recommendation 2: Researchers should (a) describe explicitly and precisely how they define and measure state ownership or control as applied to their study; and (b) connect the construct to the causal mechanism(s) examined in their paper, that is explain *how* and *why* state ownership as conceptualized should make a difference. In addition, authors should relate their measures and definitions to previous literature, so a more coherent body of work may develop around the concept of SOE.

We return below to the importance of theorizing, based on a subsequent stage of our review. In the next section, we proceed to a quantitative overview of the literature on SOEs, EEs, and thus SOEs from EEs.

SOEs AND EMERGING ECONOMIES: A BIBLIOMETRIC ANALYSIS

In this section, we report a systematic analysis of the literature on SOEs, with specific attention to international business themes and to EEs. We first briefly review the overall pattern of research on SOEs in management journals, distinguishing between international management and other topics. We then examine trends pertaining to SOEs in EEs, both as home countries and as host countries. We examine patterns in the research questions addressed, research designs employed, and theories used or developed. Some distinctive lessons arise from this comprehensive overview.

Overview

Fig. 1 depicts the absolute number of articles on SOEs in each year, with the solid line for articles on IB topics, that is, on SOEs' outward foreign investment or their interactions with inward foreign investors at SOEs' home countries, and the dashed line for articles on other topics. The figure shows a clear growth in the absolute number of the articles on SOEs since 1968, when the first article on SOEs was published in the journals of interest. Noticeably, while an uptick appeared by the mid-1990s for research on non-IB topics of SOEs, research on IB topics of SOEs only began to surge in the last decade. Special issues in journals appear to play

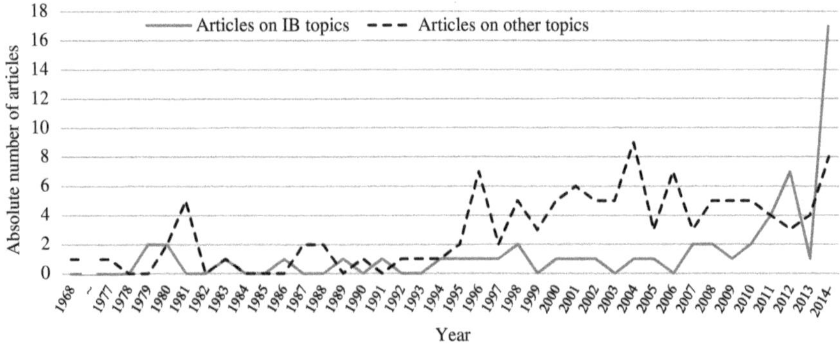

Fig. 1. Absolute Number of Articles on State-Owned Enterprises, per Year and Topic.

some role in explaining some of the peaks shown in Fig. 1. For example, the special issue on corporate transformation in China in *Organization Science* in 2004 and the special issue on state-owned multinational companies in *Journal of International Business Studies* in 2014 might account for, respectively, the peak in 2004 for research on non-IB topics and the peak in 2014 and onwards for research on IB topics. The 2004 *Organization Science* issue does not appear to have been followed by a surge of interest in the same journal, so this short-term impact does not imply that the journal issues created trends, though that would be a separate issue to examine.

To allow for a closer look at the composition of the articles on SOEs, Fig. 2 breaks down the studies not only by topic but also by research context, that is depending on whether a study examines SOEs in EEs or in other economies (non-EEs). Here, a non-EE context may be either a DE context or a mixed context that contains both EEs and DEs. We use black bars for articles on IB topics and gray bars for other topics, and use solid bars for articles specifically on EEs and striped bars for articles on other research contexts. Furthermore, we split studies that examine IB topics of EE SOEs, which are represented by the black solid bars, into studies specifically on China and studies on other EEs, respectively depicted by the solid line and the dashed line.

We can draw several conclusions from Fig. 2. First, the different waves of SOE studies on IB topics and on other topics observed in Fig. 1 seem to be mainly driven by studies on EEs. In contrast with the relatively stable amount of SOE studies on DEs or mixed contexts, research on EE

SOEs showed a clear upsurge between 1996 and 2006 for domestic topics and a recent uptick for IB topics. Second, the further decomposition of research on IB topics of EE SOEs shows a large imbalance between research on China and research on other EEs, revealing that the upward trend of research in this area is essentially due to the growing number of articles published about Chinese firms. Furthermore, since the trend in articles on SOEs may simply be due to the growth in the total number of articles published in the journals, we also replicated Fig. 2 but as the *proportion*, rather than the absolute number, of articles on SOEs out of the total number of articles published in each time period. An upward trend of research on SOEs in the past two decades can still be observed (figure available from the authors upon request).

Table 1 reports the distribution of articles on SOEs by the journals we reviewed. We first report the distribution of papers when pooling all topics together (columns 2 and 3), and then report the distribution only for papers on IB topics (columns 4 and 5). To shed further light on the trend by topics (IB vs. non-IB), we also report subtotals of articles for generalist journals and for IB-specialized journals. We observe some patterns in this table. First, the proportion of articles on EE SOEs (as opposed to non-EE SOEs) is comparable for articles on all topics (75%) and for articles on IB topics (71%). This shows that studies of EE SOEs are not inherently on IB topics. Second, while there are roughly as many articles on SOEs in generalist journals as in IB-specialized journals when pooling all topics together

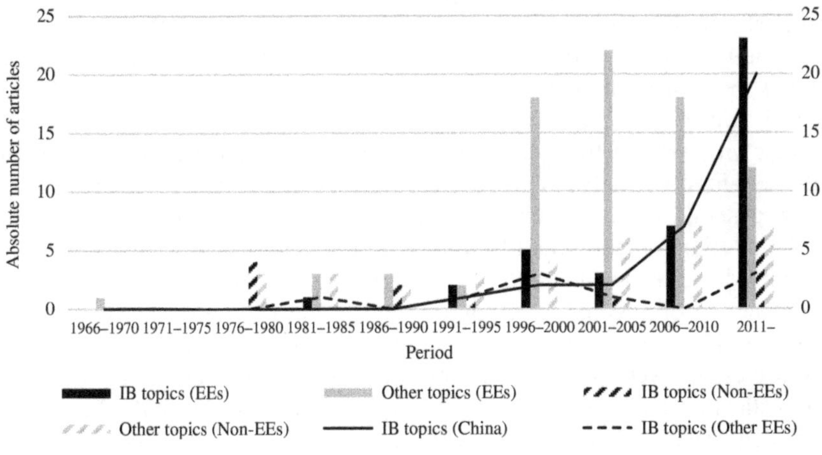

Fig. 2. Absolute Number of Articles on SOEs, per Period, Topic, and Context.

Table 1. Absolute Number of Articles on SOEs, per Journal.

Journal	All Topics		IB Topics	
	Papers in total	Papers on EEs	Papers in total	Papers on EEs
Academy of Management Journal	5	5	0	0
Academy of Management Review	4	2	0	0
Administrative Science Quarterly	2	1	1	0
Journal of Business Research	18	11	0	0
Journal of Management Studies	12	8	2	1
Long Range Planning	8	4	2	1
Management Science	5	3	0	0
Organization Science	7	5	0	0
Organization Studies	14	11	0	0
Strategic Management Journal	8	5	2	1
Subtotal	83	55	7	3
Global Strategy Journal	1	1	1	1
International Business Review	14	11	9	8
Journal of International Business Studies	35	23	25	17
Journal of International Management	6	6	4	4
Journal of World Business	11	10	4	4
Management International Review	19	14	5	4
Subtotal	86	65	48	38
Total	169	120	55	41

(83 vs. 86), studies examining the international activities of SOEs are found primarily in IB-specialized journals (IB journals accounting for 87% of that total). Moreover, the proportion of papers dealing with EEs is slightly higher in IB-specialized journals (76%) than in generalist journals (66%) for all topics, but the difference increases sharply when it comes to IB topics, with 79% of the articles on IB topics of SOEs pertaining to EEs in IB-specialized journals in contrast to only 43% in generalist journals.

In general, Table 1 shows that research investigating the IB topics of SOEs in EEs is predominantly found in IB-specialized journals. This may be considered as an indication of the openness of IB journals to EE phenomena and of possible foresight among the editors and reviewers of these journals. However, a more sobering interpretation is that EE research on IB topics has yet to reach the level of conceptual and methodological sophistication required in the top general management journals (Martin & van den Oever, 2013) – even relative to non-IB research on SOEs. To understand better why this would be, and how this research can reach a broader audience, in the analyses below we focus on the articles that deal with international behavior of SOEs, namely the 55 studies in the narrower final sample. We examine in detail what research questions are investigated, what theories are adopted, and what methodologies are employed in this literature.

Table 2 reports the distribution of articles by their general topics, that is, whether an article examines the outward investment of SOEs or their

Table 2. Distributions of Articles by Direction of International Activities (SOEs as Outward Foreign Investors vs. SOEs Dealing with Inward Foreign Investors).

Panel A: Distribution of articles on SOEs as outward foreign investors versus SOEs with inward foreign investors

Outward	Inward	Both	Total
30	23	2	55

Panel B: SOEs as outward foreign investors: Distribution of articles by home country type and host country type

Home Country of SOEs	Host Country of SOEs' Outward Foreign Investment					
	Emerging economies	Less-developed economies	Developed economies	Mixture	Not specified	Total
Emerging economies	0	1	3	10	6	20
Developed economies	0	0	1	1	4	6
Mixture	0	0	0	2	4	6
Total	0	1	4	13	14	32

Panel C: SOEs with inward foreign investors: distribution of articles by home country type of SOEs and inward foreign investors

Home Country of SOEs	Home Country of Inward Investors					
	Emerging economies	Less-developed economies	Developed economies	Mixture	Not specified	Total
Emerging economies	0	0	12	6	3	21
Developed economies	0	0	1	0	1	2
Mixture	0	0	1	0	1	2
Total	0	0	14	6	5	25

interactions with inward foreign investors at home. As shown in Panel A, 30 out of 55 studies investigate the outward investment of SOEs, 23 investigate the interaction of SOEs with inward foreign investors, and two examine both topics. There seems to be a good balance between studies on these two directions in general, although questions about inward effects may be inherently more heterogeneous (as we show later).

Panel B focuses on studies that examine the outward FDI of SOEs and classifies this group of studies by the type of home countries (by row) and host countries (by column). Out of the 32 articles on the outward topics (30 studies exclusively on outward topics plus two studies on both outward and the inward topics), 20 studies deal with SOEs from EEs, six deal with SOEs from DEs, and six investigate a mixed of economies or provide a general discussion.

The decomposition based on the type of *host* countries that SOEs enter reveals some gaps in the literature. First, we find no study that specifically investigates SOEs, especially EE SOEs, expanding into other EEs, although a few papers examine a mixed sample of host countries that include both emerging countries and developed host countries. Also, only one study – Xing, Liu, Tarba, and Cooper (2014) – examines EE SOEs investing in less-developed economies. This gap in the literature is worth noticing, given that prior literature suggests that EE firms prevalently expand into other EEs or into less-developed economies. For example, Morck, Yeung, and Zhao (2008) report that Asia, Latin America, and Africa account for 63.9%, 26.3%, and 3.4% of the stock of outward FDI made by Chinese firms by the end of 2006. Thus, the questions of how outbound EE SOEs behave particularly in other EEs or in less-developed economies, and how well those SOEs perform, seem important but under-researched. The lack of studies may owe partly to the difficulty of acquiring reliable data on EEs (except perhaps China, Cuypers & Martin, 2006a, 2006b, 2010) and less-developed economies as host locations.

Second, many papers in this group examine a mixed sample of host countries, or even do not specify the target countries of the outward investment. Among studies using mixed samples of host countries, only two – Duanmu (2012) and Wang, Hong, Kafouros, and Wright (2012) – hypothesize and test differences between a developed versus a "developing" host country (albeit at the risk of confusing emerging and less-developed countries). Much of the current literature may be ignoring specificities of various types of host countries, especially when addressing EE MNEs. Yet there are ample theoretical reasons to expect differences such as due to relative institutional and cultural proximity, and market similarities. For this reason, we suggest that future research in this area should pay more attention to specifying the destinations of the outward FDI. This will enable clear and meaningful comparisons in terms of national economic and institutional development, and also with respect to the strategies for MNEs investing to or from peer emerging versus poorer versus more advanced economies.

Recommendation 3: Authors of studies of outward investment by SOEs and other EE firms should state explicitly on what basis they examine developed, emerging or less-developed host countries. In multi-country or international samples, the classification should separate EEs both from less developed and from fully developed economies. Future research should theorize and test differences between these types of host countries with respect to the behavior and performance of investors from EEs (including SOEs).

In parallel with Panel B, Panel C presents the summary for research on SOEs' interactions with inward foreign investors in SOEs' home countries. Again, we classify the studies based on the home countries of SOEs (by row) and the home countries of incoming MNEs (by column). Among the 25 articles (23 studies exclusively on inward topics plus two studies on both outward and inward activities), 21 examine SOEs from EEs, two examine SOEs from DEs, and two investigate SOEs from mixed contexts or provide a general discussion.

A few interesting patterns emerge from Panel C. First, a plurality of the studies on EEs (12 out of 21) investigate local firms' interaction with MNEs from DEs, which corresponds to the widely shared interest in the literature regarding how MNEs from developed countries deal with EE firms. Second, we found no study where the firms dealing with SOEs in these SOEs' home countries were themselves EE firms. That is, there appear to be no study about outbound EE SOEs encountering other local SOEs – which parallels our previous comment but further demonstrates a gap in studying SOE-to-SOE interactions across borders. We did find one paper on DE-based SOEs, Fang, Fridh, and Schultzberg (2004), that investigates a situation where a SOE confronts another SOE. In that study, the authors look into a failed merger between a Norwegian SOE and a Swedish SOE and explore reasons for the failure. Unfortunately, the paper mainly draws upon a cross-cultural management perspective and does not discuss the role and influence of state ownership. Two more recent studies, Duanmu (2014) and Jandhyala and Weiner (2014), do not pertain to SOE-SOE relations but rather discuss how the home country government of SOEs may confront or negotiate with the host country government to mitigate the expropriation risks faced by outbound SOEs. Such research may shed some light on possible interactions between a local SOE and an inward SOE investor from another country, but only indirectly. The lack of research on interactions between SOEs is puzzling since it may be assumed that SOEs have an affinity for each other (as Vernon, 1979 postulated), perhaps because they repulse non-SOE partners; and because SOE-SOE encounters may be expected where the local firm and inward investors operate in the same sector that prompted state involvement (such as natural resources or defense). In fact, if the outward activities of SOEs are prone to generate supporting involvement by these SOEs' home governments (see also Lu, Liu, Wright, & Filatotchev, 2014; Luo, Xue, & Han, 2010), then cases where state-owned MNEs encounter local SOEs are even more interesting because they should also provide evidence about any propensity of host governments to become involved, and what happens when both governments thus interact via SOEs.

Research Questions and Dependent Variables

Next, we turn to another layer of analysis that may eventually help explain different specificities of SOEs' international activities, and how they depend on EE versus other contexts. We examine the research topics and outcomes addressed in the literature.

To gain a better understanding of the exact activities and aspects of SOEs examined in the papers in our sample, we summarized the studies by their research questions, or, more specifically, their dependent variables. This is reported in Table 3. Since one article may examine multiple research questions, the sum of each column may exceed the total number of articles in that group. Panel A classifies the research questions into firm choices and performance (Martin, 2013). A divergence can be observed when comparing research on outward topics (Column 2) and on inward topics (Column 3). While research on SOEs interacting with inward-investing MNEs is well balanced between studies of firm choices and performance, research on SOEs as outward investing MNEs is mostly on firm choices. This implies that we still have a limited understanding of the performance of state-owned MNEs.

In Panels B and C we present separate summaries for research on outward topics and inward topics, and unfold the types of firm choices examined in

Table 3. Distribution of Articles on SOEs by Research Question (Dependent Variable).

Panel A: Distribution of articles on SOEs by topic type

Question	SOEs as Outward Foreign Investors	SOEs with Inward Foreign Investors
Firm choices	27	12
Performance	6	16

Panel B: SOEs as outward foreign investors: Distribution of articles by research question

Question	SOEs from EEs	SOEs from DEs	SOEs from Mixture	Total
Propensity/extent	11	3	2	16
Entry process choice	5	0	3	8
Location/country diversity	3	2	2	7
Management control	2	1	0	3
Performance	2	1	3	6

Panel C: SOEs with inward foreign investors: Distributions of articles by research question

Question	SOEs from EEs	SOEs from DEs	SOEs from Mixture	Total
Entry mode choice	1	0	0	1
Location choice	1	0	0	1
Target choice	1	0	1	2
IJV-related choices	7	1	0	8
Equity ownership	2	0	0	2
Negotiation process	2	0	0	2
Control in IJV	2	0	0	2
Employee relations	1	0	0	1
Partner choice	0	1	0	1
Licensing choice	1	0	0	1
Performance	13	1	2	16

each literature. In Panel B, we divide the choices made by SOEs as outward investing MNEs into four categories: the propensity and extent of FDI, entry choices, location or country diversity choices, and management control choice. The entry process choice category contains choices made by firms as they enter the host country, including entry mode, equity ownership, partner/target choice, and business activity choice. The management control category includes questions relating to human resource management and management control systems. We further break the results down based on whether the SOEs studied come from EEs, DEs, or mixed contexts.

One pattern is especially noteworthy in panel B: There are relatively few studies of performance. Although this may indicate proper attention to the determinants of strategy given the potential endogeneity of performance (Caves, 1998; Martin, 2013; Shaver, 1998), this is unlikely to be the main reason given the prevalence of performance studies on the inward side (compare Panel C). Rather, we surmise that issues with data and the interpretation of outward performance effects amidst multiple potential levels of explanation may be a stronger explanation for this pattern (see also Peterson, Arregle, & Martin, 2012). Indeed, the dearth of research on performance outcomes is even more evident for SOEs from EEs, with only 2 out of the 20 articles addressing this question (column 2 of Panel B) as opposed to 4 out 17 studies for SOEs from DEs and mixed contexts. The study of the performance of outward investment from EEs requires more attention, including but not limited to the case of state-owned MNEs. We return to the issue of performance in a subsequent table.

Panel C of Table 3 presents the research questions in the inward part of the literature, that is where MNEs encounter SOEs in host countries. A large spectrum of firm choices have been studied in this area, including entry mode choice, location choice, acquisition target choice, international joint venture (IJV)-related choices by firms, and licensing. The IJV-related choice category includes firm decisions in terms of equity ownership, negotiation process, management controls, employee relations, and partner selection. Most of the choices examined in these studies are choices made by incoming MNEs, that is the focus is on the foreign party (which need not be an SOE). This may be explained by data considerations, though a single-sided focus risks missing fundamental aspects of an IJV transaction (Hennart, 2009). A few exceptions examine the choices of local SOEs. For instance, Choudhury and Khanna (2014) examine the choice of an Indian SOE regarding licensing patents to inbound MNEs, though this represents a bit of an unusual case where the local party possesses superior technology (Caves, 2007; Martin, 2014).

Parallel to Panel B, we report the breakdown based on research contexts in Panel C. We draw two further observations from this breakdown. First, from the standpoint of understanding SOEs, an interesting question is whether (and under what conditions) SOEs are favored partners for MNEs, or whether (and under what conditions) privately owned MNEs are put off by SOEs as potential IJV partners. Yet only one study (Ferris, Joshi, & Makhija, 1995) examines partner choices for IJVs. This study deals with DE-based SOEs. Thus, surprisingly, we find no empirical study on the pros and cons of EE SOEs as partners. Furthermore, Ferris et al.'s (1995) is a qualitative study of how MNEs should evaluate various SOEs as potential partners. Original though this study is, it does not shed light on the question of whether and under what conditions SOEs are favored partners for MNEs. Although the direct evidence is scant, findings in articles on MNEs' entry mode choices (e.g., Meyer & Nguyen, 2005) and on their performance (e.g., Pollitte, Miller, & Yaprak, 2015) may allow us to draw some inferences on the suitability of SOEs as IJV partners, provided due attention is paid to the self-selection issues.

Second, as mentioned earlier by comparison with the literature on outward activities of SOEs, a good many of articles on the inward topics investigate the performance consequence (45% of the total in Panel C). This makes sense as this cell counts both studies on the performance of MNEs and studies on the performance of SOEs (e.g., as local partners). Because these studies inherently deal with the consequences of an initial partnering choice, they are also subject to self-selection and other endogeneity problems (Krishnan, Martin, & Noorderhaven, 2006; Martin, 2013).

To take a closer look at whose performance is examined and what measures of performance are adopted, below we look in detail at the performance constructs used in current literature.

Table 4 summarizes articles that employ performance as (one of) their dependent variable(s), depending on the measure of performance and whose performance is examined. The columns, and likewise the rows, are not mutually exclusive since one study may adopt various performance measures and examine the performance of multiple actors. In terms of measurement, we find that a wide diversity of performance measures have been

Table 4. Distribution of Articles by Measure of Performance.

Measure	Total	Outward		Inward	
		Parent	Subsidiary	SOEs	MNEs
Perceptual-qualitative	1	0	0	0	1
Perceptual-survey	2	1	0	2	1
Survival	2	0	1	2	2
Sales	3	0	0	3	1
Profitability – ROA/ROE/ROS	3	1	0	0	2
Abnormal returns	4	0	0	3	1
Price paid for acquiring resources	2	2	0	0	0
Acquisition completion	2	1	0	0	1
Productivity	2	0	0	2	1
New product development	1	0	0	1	0
Global market access – export intensity	1	0	0	1	0
Theoretical discussion	1	0	0	0	1

employed, ranging from subjective to objective, and from financial to operational. However, perceptual measures were primarily used in earlier papers (published in 1983, 1986, and 2000, respectively), whereas recent studies make greater use of secondary data. As for whose performance is examined, we distinguish between the parent firm and the subsidiary for articles on the outward investment of SOEs, and between the local firm, which includes SOEs, and the MNE for articles on the interaction between SOEs and inward-investing MNEs. In the inward part of the literature, the performance of both SOEs and MNEs is well balanced and well covered, with 14 and 11 studies respectively. Conversely, research on performance is under-developed in the outward part of the literature, with a limited number of studies overall (six) but also a predominant focus on the performance of the parent firm. Only one outward study examines subsidiary performance, making use of a version of subsidiary survival data. Survival is a generally measurable and robust measure for measuring performance at the subsidiary level (e.g., Shaver, Mitchell, & Yeung, 1997). However, the one study of SOE subsidiary-level performance in Table 4 (Fang et al., 2004) may not be considered as examining the performance of the subsidiary in a typical sense; rather, it investigates the split-up of a cross-border merger of two SOEs. Thus, an under-explored question in the literature remains as to how well the foreign investments of SOEs, especially those of EE SOEs, perform. Given the relevance of this question to international strategy (Martin, 2014; Martin et al., 2007; Martin & van den Oever, 2013), this is a gap that researchers should aim to fill.

So far, we have reviewed what topics and specific research questions have been examined in the literatures on SOEs' outward investment and on their interaction with inbound MNEs. In summary, we find several areas to be under-researched. Our next set of recommendations addresses these.

Recommendation Set 4:

- In terms of SOEs' outward investment, first, researchers should aim to examine the activities of EE SOEs in less-developed economies or other EEs.
- Second, generally, studies should specify the destinations of SOEs' outward investment, and recognize if not leverage the potentially heterogeneous nature of expansion into less-developed economies versus EEs, versus DEs.
- Third, the overseas performance of outbound SOEs requires further examination.

- In terms of SOEs interaction with MNEs in SOEs' home countries, first, research should be conducted to answer the basic question of whether inbound MNEs are more, or less, prone to build IJVs with SOEs than with non-SOEs and how these IJVs differ from those of non-SOEs.
- Second, the same holds from the perspective of SOEs: Future research may thus examine whether SOEs, compared to non-SOEs, are more – or less – prone to collaborate with MNEs and how these collaborations differ.
- Third, there is so far limited understanding and few systematic studies of situations where one SOE encounters another SOE, whether in either firm's home market or in a third market (or globally). That is, the interaction between SOEs from different countries is an interesting area for future research.

Use of Theory

Next, we probe into the theories that were used to answer the research questions discussed above. This section follows the theory decomposition approach of Martin and van den Oever (2013). Before examining *what* theories are used, though, we find it necessary to discuss *whether* and to what extent theory is used in the literature of interest here.

We consider that an article employs theory if the use and name of a recognizable theory is explicitly mentioned or if foundational work of at least one theory is cited. We code the use of specific theories accordingly. Full details of the coding approach are available from the authors. Normally, the theories employed to explain SOE effects are a subset of those used to support the paper's overall argument. However, in some cases, we coded a theory only as pertains to the SOE argument when the theory was used narrowly to motivate the arguments regarding SOEs (the SOE-argument level) but was irrelevant to the main idea of the paper (the paper level). As a result, the frequency of some theories as pertains to the SOE-argument level may exceed their frequency as pertains to the whole papers. In addition, since one paper can build upon more than one theory, the total number of theories used may go beyond the sum of papers for a certain group.

Table 5 addresses the *whether theory* question. To facilitate the comparisons between articles on EE SOEs and on other SOEs, we also split the summary based on research contexts. Although the use of theory is not indispensable to making a research contribution, reliance on theory

Table 5. Theory Prevalence: Number and Proportion of Articles with Well-Defined Theory for SOE Arguments (AWDT).

Panel A: Theory prevalence: By time period

AWDT	1979–1988	1989–1998	1999–2008	2009–	Total Out of 55
Num	5	3	8	20	36
%	83	38	89	63	65

Panel B: Theory prevalence: By research context of SOEs

AWDT	EEs	DEs	Mixture	Total Out of 55
Num	27	7	2	36
%	66	100	29	65

Panel C: Theory prevalence: SOEs as outward foreign investors versus SOEs with inward foreign investors

AWDT	Outward	Inward	Both	Total Out of 55
Num	20	15	1	36
%	67	65	50	65

(including ex ante hypothesis building in deductive studies and ex post derivation of general propositions in inductive studies) ensures generalizability and durability of research arguments. Acknowledging that SOEs and especially EEs are relatively recent research topic, we may expect some atheoretical exploratory work to be present especially in early research. Panel A shows that this is true to some extent, but that the use of theory has not progressed markedly over time; indeed, it may have regressed in the last five years. A possible explanation for this can be found in Panel B: Papers that deal with EE contexts or mixed (and typically under-specified) ones, as opposed to DEs, are more likely to lack theory. This ongoing state of affairs is a cause for concern about the soundness and reliability of research on EE SOEs. Finally, Panel C shows that there is no remarkable difference between studies of outward and inward activities of SOEs. In that sense, it is the EE aspect, rather than the topical area, that tends to be accompanied by theoretical under-development.

Next, with Table 6, we examine the use of specific theories, this time contrasting the SOE arguments as well as the contexts. Table 6 shows that a wide range of theories has been used. A comparison between theory adoption at the paper level and at the SOE-related argument level, however, reveals that theory is less explicit when it comes to the SOE part of

Table 6. Distribution of Articles by Theory and Research Context of SOEs.

Theory	Paper Level								SOE-Related Argument Level							
	Total		EEs		DEs		Mixed		Total		EEs		DEs		Mixed	
	Num	Column %	Num	Column %	Num	Column %	Num	Column %	Num	Column %	Num	Column %	Num	Column %	Num	Column %
Organizational learning	2	2	2	3	0	0	0	0	2	4	2	5	0	0	0	0
Knowledge-based view	4	5	4	6	0	0	0	0	2	4	2	5	0	0	0	0
Institution-based view	8	9	7	11	0	0	1	11	3	6	3	8	0	0	0	0
Institutional theory (sociological)	10	12	8	12	1	10	1	11	7	14	6	16	0	0	1	17
Organizational control theory	1	1	1	2	0	0	0	0	0	0	0	0	0	0	0	0
Social exchange perspective	1	1	1	2	0	0	0	0	2	4	2	5	0	0	0	0
Transaction cost economics	6	7	5	8	0	0	1	11	4	8	3	8	0	0	1	17
Resource-based view	4	5	2	3	1	10	1	11	2	4	1	3	0	0	1	17
Resource dependence theory	8	9	6	9	0	0	2	22	5	10	4	11	0	0	1	17
Population ecology	1	1	1	2	0	0	0	0	0	0	0	0	0	0	0	0
Institutional economics	7	8	7	11	0	0	0	0	2	4	2	5	0	0	0	0
Agency theory	7	8	4	6	2	20	1	11	5	10	4	11	0	0	1	17
Behavioral theory of the firm	1	1	0	0	1	10	0	0	1	2	0	0	1	17	0	0
Uppsala model[a]	1	1	1	2	0	0	0	0	0	0	0	0	0	0	0	0
Internalization theory	2	2	2	3	0	0	0	0	1	2	1	3	0	0	0	0
OLI	3	4	3	5	0	0	0	0	0	0	0	0	0	0	0	0
Property rights theory	1	1	1	2	0	0	0	0	1	2	1	3	0	0	0	0
Upper echelon theory	1	1	0	0	1	10	0	0	0	0	0	0	0	0	0	0
Public choice/interest theory	1	1	1	2	0	0	0	0	1	2	0	0	1	17	0	0
Grounded theory (exploratory)	8	9	6	9	1	10	1	11	9	18	7	18	1	17	1	17
Crossvergence theory	1	1	1	2	0	0	0	0	0	0	0	0	0	0	0	0
Others	7	8	3	5	3	30	1	11	3	6	0	0	3	50	0	0

[a]Also known as the internationalization process model.

the papers than for the papers as a whole. More specifically, the total count of theories at the paper level adds up to 85, far exceeding the total number of articles in the sample. This is consistent with the use of multiple theories within most papers (see also Martin & van den Oever, 2013). However, the total for theories used at the SOE-argument level is only 50, suggesting that a fair number of papers are ad hoc, that is they do not explicitly use any theory to motivate their argument regarding SOEs. We will examine this aspect further when we come to Table 8.

We do not find much difference when comparing studies in EEs and in other contexts, especially when taking into account the limited number of papers on non-EE settings. Roughly the same theories are used in papers on EEs as in other papers, both at the paper level and as specifically pertains to SOE behavior. The most frequently used theories at the paper level are (sociological) institutional theory, institution-based view, resource dependence theory, and grounded theorizing (exploratory inductive studies). One pattern worth noticing is that, when it comes to EE SOEs, the most common theories used are (sociological) institutional theory, institution-based view, and institutional economics, that is three versions of institutional perspectives. This reflects the particular emphasis on institutions in research on EEs. At the SOE-argument level, the category with the highest frequency is grounded theory, followed by institutional theory, resource dependence theory, and agency theory. The ranking once again suggests that a notable proportion of papers have no preexisting theory for the behavior of SOEs.

We observe several interesting patterns when looking into individual theories. First, the knowledge-based view has a relatively low popularity, which is odd considering that this perspective could be useful to study the knowledge seeking intent or mandate sometimes attributed to SOEs, and especially EE SOEs (Luo & Tung, 2007; Morck et al., 2008). Second, whereas institution-based view and institutional economics are frequently used at the paper level, their popularity drops when it comes to SOE arguments. This implies that researchers do not deem these two perspectives as particularly useful to explain the behavior of SOEs; however, as we will see below, a specialized theory related with institutional economics (public choice theory) may be "splitting the credit." Third, the Uppsala model and the OLI framework, which are among the most distinctively "home-grown" theories in international business (Martin & van den Oever, 2013), are rarely used to explain SOE behavior. However, in contrast with these theories' relative decline in international strategy research overall (Martin & van den Oever, 2013), there may be a delayed upward trend in the use of these theories to study SOEs recently: Three of the four papers employing these two perspectives were published since 2012.

Finally, we want to call special attention to public choice theory and a related perspective, public interest. Originating in economics and political science (Schubert, 1957; Tullock, 2008), these two perspectives are particularly relevant in explaining the multiple goals faced by state entities and managers, including potentially SOEs. Many papers build their argument, at least implicitly, on the premise that SOEs have mixed motives (see below); indeed this may be one of their most defining characteristics (Cuervo-Cazurra, Inkpen, Musacchio, & Ramaswamy, 2014). Public choice theory has been used for some time to study topics related with SOEs (e.g., Caves, 1990). However, so far, just two papers in our sample journals – Benito, Lunnan, and Tomassen (2011) and Duanmu (2014) – have explicitly employed public choice theory. Of these, only Benito et al. (2011) used this theory to explain the distinctive behavior of SOEs, whereby SOEs pursue "vote-gaining goals instead of efficiency goals" (Benito et al., 2011, p. 381). One possible obstacle to the use of public choice theory is that it traditionally presumes that decisions are influenced by a full set of democratic institutions. This may make the theory less straightforward to apply in the context we documented as dominant in recent literature, namely China. However, public choice theory can accommodate and even explain alternative institutional setups. Thus it is a plausible complement, if not a better defined alternative, for research that uses a power perspective to examine dealings with Chinese firms – such as Pan (1996). Public choice theory could also be useful to raise attention to the local party in alliance research (Cuypers & Martin, 2007; Hennart, 2009).

Recommendation 5: Authors who study the behavior of SOEs, especially from EEs, should specify explicitly the theoretical foundations and consequences of their research. One potentially useful theory for this purpose is public choice theory. (See also Recommendation set 6 for an extension of Recommendation 5.)

We also tabulated the theory distribution separately for research on outward and inward topics, though we do not report the table here due to space limitation. One observation from this analysis is that, compared to the outward part of the literature, there is a more scattered mix of theories in the inward part. This makes sense considering that the inward literature contains a mix of papers from the perspective of the inward-investing MNEs and from the perspective of local partners (among them local

SOEs). In terms of individual theories on the SOE-argument level, institutional theory, institution-based view, resource-based view, and agency theory are used less in the inward part of the literature compared with the outward part, while knowledge-based view and organizational learning perspectives are employed more in the inward literature. This plausibly reflects the specific research questions and aspects of SOEs that the two parts of literature focus on. For example, the outward literature pays more attention to the institutional pressures that outbound SOEs may face in host countries, or to institutional distance (see also Martin, Salomon, & Wu, 2010), while the inward literature puts more emphasis on knowledge acquisition by SOEs when they interact with MNEs at home (see also Martin & Salomon, 2002, 2003).

Methodologies and Contexts

We next move on to discuss the methodologies used in current literature. First, Table 7 reports the distribution of articles by the type of research, namely whether studies are theoretical, qualitative, or quantitative. As in

Table 7. Distribution of Articles by Type of Research.

Panel A: Distribution of articles by type of research and time period

Type of Research	1979–1988	1989–1998	1999–2008	2009–	Total
Theoretical	1	2	1	1	5
Qualitative	4	3	2	2	11
Quantitative	1	3	6	29	39

Panel B: Distribution of articles by type of research and research context of SOEs

Type of Research	EEs			DEs	Mixture	Total
	Total	China	Others			
Theoretical	3	1	2	0	2	5
Qualitative	5	2	3	5	1	11
Quantitative	33	28	5	2	4	39

Panel C: Distribution of articles by type of research and topic

Type of Research	Outward	Inward	Both	Total
Theoretical	3	2	0	5
Qualitative	6	3	2	11
Quantitative	21	18	0	39

earlier tables, we report the distributions by period, research context, and topic in panels A, B, and C, respectively. According to Panel A, in contrast with the steady amount of theoretical articles and the downward trend in the number of qualitative studies, the number of quantitative studies increases over time, and especially sharply in the past five years. Panel B shows that research on China is highly quantitative, accounting for most of the quantitative research in the sample – indeed quantitative research on China accounts for just over half of all papers in the sample – and conversely includes only one context-theoretical paper. By contrast, research on other EEs is more balanced in types of research. The relative difficulty of obtaining secondary firm-level data, even for a large English-speaking economy such as India, may explain this pattern and might also eventually induce higher quality (if more difficult) survey and qualitative data collection where non-Chinese cases are concerned (Cappelli, Singh, Singh, & Useem, 2010; Krishnan et al., 2006). In Panel C, the distribution is comparable between the outward part and the inward part of the literature, again suggesting a balance between the two parts of research in this regard.

Table 8 focuses on the quantitative papers just discussed and reports the distribution of these articles by role of the SOE variable, that is, whether

Table 8. Distribution of Articles by Role of SOE Variables.

Panel A: Distribution of articles by role of SOE variables and time period

Role of SOE Variables	1979–1988	1989–1998	1999–2008	2009–	Total	Total-Column %
Main (independent)	2	1	3	16	22	56
Moderator	0	0	3	13	16	41
Dependent variable	0	0	0	1	1	3

Panel B: Distribution of articles by role of SOE variables and research context of SOEs

Role of SOE Variables	EEs	DEs	Mixture	DEs and mixture	Total	Total-Column%
Main (independent)	17	2	3	5	22	56
Moderator	15	0	1	1	16	41
Dependent variable	0	0	1	1	1	3

Panel C: Distribution of articles by role of SOE variables and topic

Role of SOE Variables	Outward	Inward	Both	Total	Total-Column%
Main (independent)	10	12	0	22	56
Moderator	11	5	0	16	41
Dependent variable	0	1	0	1	3

the SOE construct is included as a direct predictor (main effect), moderator, or dependent variable. One study – Jory and Ngo (2014) – used the SOE variable both as a dependent variable and as an independent variable, as they employ a Heckman two-stage regression. We excluded one quantitative study from this analysis because its sample consisted entirely of SOEs, so that SOE status was not an identifiable variable. Panel A summarizes the distribution by period. Earlier studies mainly focused on the main effect of state ownership, while later on there was a growing proportion of research on state ownership moderating another effect. This does not necessarily suggest that the role of state ownership becomes less central in research, but rather is consistent with research getting more sophisticated with its use of moderation in testing contingent arguments (Martin & van den Oever, 2013). Panel B presents the distribution by research context. Given the limited number of articles on DEs and mixed contexts, we added a column that pooled the two groups together to facilitate comparison. The overall pattern is that all but one moderated analysis have pertained to EEs, which is also consistent with the younger vintage (and rapid development) of EE research on SOEs. Combined with the observation from Panel B of Table 5, this leads to a mixed diagnosis: Quantitative research on EEs is comparatively sophisticated in its use of contingent predictions, yet it is also quite prone *not* to use explicit theory. Since moderation is a form of synthesis of ideas (Martin & van den Oever, 2013), the proper development of moderation hypothesis should be all the more prone to use theory – indeed often more than one theory. Absent this systematic connection, we may conclude that the journals where the EE research has been published upheld lower standard of theorizing (consistent with Table 1), and that some studies came up with interaction effects that may not stand the test of replication. This is a cause for concern if EE research (on SOEs) is to make a lasting impact and influence on other research. Panel C reports the distribution by topic. Here, there is a bit of a difference between inward and outward research: moderated SOE arguments pertain more to outward studies (11 of 21 such studies) than to inward studies (5 of 17 such studies, excluding one where SOE partner choice is a first-stage dependent variable). This implies that research on SOE's investments abroad is more prone not to look at state ownership as a principal cause of difference in international strategy, but rather as a firm characteristic that affects sensitivity to other effects such as resource base (Cui, Li, Meyer, & Li, 2014) and institutional environment (e.g., Cui & Jiang, 2012; Dau, 2012). Conversely, research on how incoming MNEs and local SOEs deal with each other is more likely to treat SOEs as a distinct category. This makes sense insofar as part of the inward literature is written from the standpoint of the MNE. However, this also suggests that there is room for greater sophistication in distinguishing among various types of state ownership and influence, as exemplified by Liang et al. (2015).

Having already identified the large share of China research in our sample (Fig. 2 and Panel B of Table 7), we next turn to a more detailed breakdown by home and host country to identify what *other* EE countries or regions have been studied, or conversely may be understudied. Table 9 provides this information based on the empirical research on EEs, including both qualitative and quantitative studies. One article may count more than once when it covers more than one country or region in the table; for example, the article by Li et al. (2012) is counted four times as it examines the BRIC countries. In general, the EE countries or regions covered by current research include China, India, Vietnam, Latin America, and Eastern Europe. The Latin American countries covered include Costa Rica, Mexico, and mixes of South American countries. The studies of Eastern Europe include Russia, Hungary, and Romania. A first remark at this level is that the research sampled here – dealing with SOEs – has so far ignored some important EEs in Asia (such as Indonesia, Pakistan, the Philippines, to mention a few of the largest) and Europe (such as the Ukraine and Poland), and it has not been extensive in separating out various Latin American countries (e.g., Brazil vs. Colombia, Argentina, etc.).

On a more detailed level, Panel A of Table 9 reports the distribution of the countries researched by period. It further confirms what we observed in Fig. 2: The rising amount of research on the IB topics of EE SOEs is largely driven by research on China. No other country was studied more than twice. This implies a dual threat to validity: first, that EEs other than China are not deeply understood in the sense of scientific replication; and second, that any claim that studies of China are broadly representative of EEs must be made cautiously and supported carefully, as empirically that can at best be based on limited evidence of cross-setting robustness. In general, claims to generalizability should be argued specifically rather than taken for granted, whether in studies of FDI from or into a given country (e.g., Martin, Mitchell, & Swaminathan, 1995; Martin, Swaminathan, & Mitchell, 1998) or in comparative studies (e.g., Kotabe, Martin, & Domoto, 2003).

Panel B summarizes the distribution for articles on outward investment by EE SOEs. The columns classify the studies based on host countries of outbound SOEs. The panel shows that research on outward topics has been almost exclusively about Chinese SOEs. Besides, we found only one paper specifically about EE firms investing in less-developed economies,

Table 9. Distribution of Empirical Articles by Researched Country.

Panel A: Distribution of empirical articles by researched country and time period

Type of Research	1979–1988	1989–1998	1999–2008	2009–	Total
China	0	3	5	24	32
India	0	0	0	2	2
Vietnam	0	0	1	0	1
Latin America	1	0	1	2	4
Eastern Europe	0	1	0	1	2

Panel B: SOEs as outward foreign investors: Distribution of empirical articles by researched country and host country type

Home Country of SOEs	Host Country of SOEs' Outward Foreign Investment					
	Emerging economies	Less-developed economies	Developed economies	Mixture	Not specified	Total
China	0	1	3	9	5	18
Latin America	0	0	0	0	1	1

Panel C: SOEs with inward foreign investors: Distribution of empirical articles by researched country and home country type of inward foreign investors

Home Country of SOEs	Home Country of Inward Investors					
	Emerging economies	Less-developed economies	Developed economies	Mixture	Not specified	Total
China	0	0	7	5	2	14
India	0	0	0	1	1	2
Latin America	0	0	2	1	0	3
Vietnam	0	0	0	1	0	1
Eastern Europe	0	0	1	1	0	2

Panel D: Distribution of empirical articles by researched country and study type

Home Country of SOEs	Qualitative	Quantitative			Total
		Total	Secondary data	Survey	
China	3	29	24	5	32
India	0	2	2	0	2
Vietnam	0	1	0	1	1
Latin America	1	3	1	2	4
Eastern Europe	1	1	1	0	2

namely Xing et al. (2014) on Chinese firms investing in Africa; and none specifically dealing with EEs as host countries for state-owned MNEs. Panel C presents the distribution for articles on the inward topics, that is, on SOEs interacting in their home countries with incoming MNEs. The columns list the home countries or regions of the MNEs. Here, China research remains the majority, but there is more diverse representation of other EEs where MNEs may encounter SOEs. This implies, though, that the literature still largely treats non-Chinese SOEs as part of the host country environment, rather than as potential foreign investors themselves. Yet the work edited by Ramamurti and Singh (2010) shows the potential to study SOEs from other EEs as outward investors too.

One potentially disturbing pattern arises in both Panel B and Panel C: In both the outward and the inward literature, most studies used rather undifferentiated mixes of target countries, or even fail altogether to report in what countries the FDI is occurring. Although this does not preclude the use of some types of measures, such as distance, this sample under-specification (or at least under-reporting) precludes both scientific replication and the detailed comparison between EEs, DEs, and less-developed economies that would be most powerful in understanding the specificities of EEs (see also Recommendation 1). Finally, Panel D presents the distribution by data collection method, combining studies on outward and inward topics. We further classified quantitative studies by the source of their data, namely secondary data or surveys. The panel shows that there is some diversity of sources among non-Chinese studies, as there is among Chinese studies, but we conclude again that replication is lacking as no country other than China has been studied more than twice with any given type of data. Overall, based on Tables 7–9, we draw a few recommendations:

Recommendation set 6:

- Authors should specify the mix of home and host countries in their studies, to allow replication.
- Researchers should take into account the mix of home and host countries in their studies to draw inferences about the relative effects for firms from and encountering EE, DE, or less-developed-country firms and environments.
- Extending and specifying Recommendation 5: Researchers who make contingent predictions, including moderated and mediated relationships, should make an extra effort to specify on what theories these predictions build, and what conceptual consequences the results have.

- Authors should motivate specifically, rather than assume, the generalizability of their predictions or results from one EE to others. Although the body of evidence for China is large, studies centered on China (on the inward or outward side) do not suffice to ensure such generalizability given the scarcity of research for other EEs.
- Studies on EEs other than China should be encouraged, to complement the large and growing body of evidence about China.
- Studies that distinguish among types of SOEs and examine heterogeneity in SOE behavior should be encouraged.

CONCLUSIONS

As EEs become a larger part of the global economy, and SOEs gain more attention, the literature on SOEs from EEs can be expected to grow in quantity, but it should also gain in quality and impact. Our analysis shows that a growing literature on SOEs specifically deals with their international strategy – whether outwards as MNEs or inwards as local partners of foreign MNEs – and that SOEs from EEs are increasingly being studied. We found the literature well developed in some respects – for instance, there is a better overall balance of inward and outward balance than we initially expected – but still largely confined to IB journals. With a view to elevating the impact of this research, we reach several conclusions and make corresponding recommendations.

Overall, we urge greater precision in identifying what firms operate in EEs. This will allow greater insights from understanding differences with other country groups, and also among EEs. Likewise, this literature can grow to yield more systematic insights into heterogeneity among SOEs (Lazzarini, 2015; Martin, 2014), and we propose a definition that may help toward this end. We also urge greater attention to theory and conceptual development, starting with the diagnosis that less theoretical attention is apparent where studies of EEs are concerned. The upshot from this would be firmer foundations for predictions that are often complex – such as about contingencies for SOE FDI and performance effects, and about propensities to interact among MNEs and domestic SOEs. Finally, we urge greater attention to the geographic representativeness of samples. We document a dominant China-centric character to recent research, which is not in itself an issue – plausibly being a reflection of data and demographic factors that offer unusual opportunities – but which makes it difficult to assume that the rest of EEs can be understood in this light. Together, efforts at conceptual, theoretical, and sample precision should ensure more compelling explanations, sounder claims to generalizability, and ultimately greater impact. Such effort would be well justified given the academic and practical importance of research on SOEs and EEs.

REFERENCES

Benito, G. R. G., Lunnan, R., & Tomassen, S. (2011). Distant encounters of the third kind: Multinational companies locating divisional headquarters abroad. *Journal of Management Studies*, *48*(2), 373–394.

Buckley, P. J., & Casson, M. C. (2002). *The future of the multinational enterprise* (25th anniversary ed.). Basingstoke: Palgrave Macmillan.

Campa, J. M., & Guillén, M. F. (1999). The internalization of exports: Firm- and location-specific factors in a middle-income country. *Management Science*, *45*(11), 1463–1478.

Cappelli, P., Singh, H., Singh, J. V., & Useem, M. (2010). The India way: Lessons for the U.S. *Academy of Management Perspectives*, *24*(2), 6–24.

Caves, R. E. (1990). Lessons from privatization in Britain: State enterprise behavior, public choice, and corporate governance. *Journal of Economic Behavior and Organization*, *13*(2), 145–169.

Caves, R. E. (1998). Research in international business: Problems and prospects. *Journal of International Business Studies*, *29*(1), 5–19.

Caves, R. E. (2007). *Multinational enterprise and economic analysis* (3rd ed.). Cambridge: Cambridge University Press.

Chi, T., & Roehl, T. W. (1997). The structuring of interfirm exchanges in business know-how: Evidence from international collaborative ventures. *Managerial and Decision Economics*, *18*(4), 279–294.

Choudhury, P., & Khanna, T. (2014). Toward resource independence – Why state-owned entities become multinationals: An empirical study of India's public R&D laboratories. *Journal of International Business Studies*, *45*(8), 943–960.

Cuervo-Cazurra, A., Inkpen, A., Musacchio, A., & Ramaswamy, K. (2014). Governments as owners: State-owned multinational companies. *Journal of International Business Studies*, *45*(8), 919–942.

Cui, L., & Jiang, F. M. (2012). State ownership effect on firms' FDI ownership decisions under institutional pressure: A study of Chinese outward-investing firms. *Journal of International Business Studies*, *43*(3), 264–284.

Cui, L., Li, Y., Meyer, K., & Li, Z. (2014). Leadership experience meets ownership structure: Returnee managers and internationalization of emerging economy firms. *Management International Review*, 1–33. Retrieved from http://dx.doi.org/10.1007/s11575-014-0221-8.

Cuypers, I. R. P., & Martin, X. (2006a). Strategic alliance governance: An extended real options perspective. In A. Arino & J. J. Reuer (Eds.), *Strategic alliances: Governance and contracts* (pp. 111–121). Houndmills, Basingstoke: Palgrave Macmillan.

Cuypers, I. R. P., & Martin, X. (2006b). What makes and what does not make a real option? A study of international joint ventures. *Academy of Management Best Paper*

Proceedings, Business Policy and Strategy Division (pp. QQ1–QQ6). New York, NY: Academy of Management.

Cuypers, I. R. P., & Martin, X. (2007). Joint ventures and real options: An integrated perspective. In J. J. Reuer & T. W. Tong (Eds.), *Advances in strategic management* (Vol. 24, pp. 107–148). St Louis, MO: Elsevier.

Cuypers, I. R. P., & Martin, X. (2010). What makes and what does not make a real option? A study of equity shares in international joint ventures. *Journal of International Business Studies*, *41*(1), 47–69.

Dau, L. A. (2012). Pro-market reforms and developing country multinational corporations. *Global Strategy Journal*, *2*(3), 262–276.

Duanmu, J. L. (2012). Firm heterogeneity and location choice of Chinese Multinational Enterprises (MNEs). *Journal of World Business*, *47*(1), 64–72.

Duanmu, J. L. (2014). State-owned MNCs and host country expropriation risk: The role of home state soft power and economic gunboat diplomacy. *Journal of International Business Studies*, *45*(8), 1044–1060.

Dunning, J. H., & Lundan, S. M. (2008). *Multinational enterprises and the world economy* (2nd ed.). Cheltenham: Edward Elgar.

Fang, T., Fridh, C., & Schultzberg, S. (2004). Why did the Telia–Telenor merger fail? *International Business Review*, *13*(5), 573–594.

Ferris, S. P., Joshi, Y. P., & Makhija, A. K. (1995). Valuing an East European company. *Long Range Planning*, *28*(6), 48–60.

Graham, E. M., & Krugman, P. (1995). *Foreign direct investment in the United States* (3rd ed.). Washington, DC: Institute for International Economics.

Hennart, J.-F. (2009). Down with MNE-centric theories! Market entry and expansion as the bundling of MNE and local assets. *Journal of International Business Studies*, *40*(9), 1432–1454.

Hitt, M. A., Tihanyi, L., Miller, T., & Connelly, B. (2006). International diversification: Antecedents, outcomes, and moderators. *Journal Of Management*, *32*(6), 831–867.

IMF. (2012). *World economic outlook update: New setbacks, further policy action needed.* Washington, DC: International Monetary Fund. Retrieved from http://www.imf.org/external/pubs/ft/weo/2012/update/02/pdf/0712.pdf

Inoue, C. F. K. V., Lazzarini, S. G., & Musacchio, A. (2013). Leviathan as a minority shareholder: Firm-level implications of state equity purchases. *Academy of Management Journal*, *56*(6), 1775–1801.

Jandhyala, S., & Weiner, R. J. (2014). Institutions sans frontières: International agreements and foreign investment. *Journal of International Business Studies*, *45*(6), 649–669.

Jory, S. R., & Ngo, T. N. (2014). Cross-border acquisitions of state-owned enterprises. *Journal of International Business Studies*, *45*(9), 1096–1114.

Kotabe, M., Martin, X., & Domoto, H. (2003). Gaining from vertical partnerships: Knowledge transfer, relationship duration and supplier performance improvement in the U.S. and Japanese automotive industries. *Strategic Management Journal*, *24*(4), 293–316.

Krishnan, R., Martin, X., & Noorderhaven, N. G. (2006). When does trust matter to alliance performance? *Academy of Management Journal*, *49*(5), 894–917.

Lazzarini, S. G. (2015). Strategizing by the government: Can industrial policy create firm-level competitive advantage? *Strategic Management Journal*, *36*(1), 97–112.

Li, D., Miller, S. R., Eden, L., & Hitt, M. A. (2012). The impact of rule of law on market value creation for local alliance partners in BRIC countries. *Journal of International Management*, *18*(4), 305–321.

Liang, H., Ren, B., & Sun, S. L. (2015). An anatomy of state control in the globalization of state-owned enterprises. *Journal of International Business Studies*, *46*(2), 223–240.

Lu, J., Liu, X., Wright, M., & Filatotchev, I. (2014). International experience and FDI location choices of Chinese firms: The moderating effects of home country government support and host country institutions. *Journal of International Business Studies*, *45*(4), 428–449.

Luo, Y., & Tung, R. L. (2007). International expansion of emerging market enterprises: A springboard perspective. *Journal of International Business Studies*, *38*(4), 481–498.

Luo, Y., Xue, Q., & Han, B. (2010). How emerging market governments promote outward FDI: Experience from China. *Journal of World Business*, *45*(1), 68–79.

Martin, X. (2013). Solving theoretical and empirical conundrums in international strategy research: Linking foreign entry mode choices and performance. *Journal of International Business Studies*, *44*(1), 28–41.

Martin, X. (2014). Institutional advantage. *Global Strategy Journal*, *4*(1), 55–69.

Martin, X., Mitchell, W., & Swaminathan, A. (1994). Recreating and extending buyer-supplier links following international expansion. In P. Shrivastava, A. Huff, & J. Dutton (Eds.), *Advances in strategic management* (Vol. 10B, pp. 47–72). Greenwich, CT: JAI Press.

Martin, X., Mitchell, W., & Swaminathan, A. (1995). Recreating and extending Japanese automobile buyer-supplier links in North America. *Strategic Management Journal*, *16*(8), 589–620.

Martin, X., & Salomon, R. (2002). Knowledge transfer capacity and cooperative strategies: When should firms leverage tacit knowledge through licensing and alliances? In F. J. Contractor & P. Lorange (Eds.), *Cooperative strategies and alliances* (pp. 729–748). New York, NY: Pergamon/Elsevier Science.

Martin, X., & Salomon, R. (2003). Knowledge transfer capacity and its implications for the theory of the multinational corporation. *Journal of International Business Studies*, *34*(4), 356–373.

Martin, X., Salomon, R. M., & Wu, Z. (2010). The institutional determinants of agglomeration: A study in the global semiconductor industry. *Industrial and Corporate Change*, *19*(6), 1769–1800.

Martin, X., Swaminathan, A., & Mitchell, W. (1998). Organizational evolution in an interorganizational environment: Incentives and constraints on international expansion strategy. *Administrative Science Quarterly*, *43*(3), 566–601.

Martin, X., Swaminathan, A., & Tihanyi, L. (2007). Modeling international expansion. In D. J. Ketchen & D. D. Bergh (Eds.), *Research methodology in strategy and management* (Vol. 4, pp. 101–117). Amsterdam: Elsevier.

Martin, X., & van den Oever, K. (2013). Progress, maturity or exhaustion? Sources and modes of theorizing on the international strategy–performance relationship (1990–2011). In T. M. Devinney, T. Pedersen, & L. Tihanyi (Eds.), *Advances in international management* (Vol. 26, pp. 331–361). Advances in International Management. Bingley, UK: Emerald Group Publishing Limited.

Mazzolini, R. (1979). European government-controlled enterprises – Explaining international strategic and policy decisions. *Journal of International Business Studies*, *10*(3), 16–27.

Mazzolini, R. (1980a). European government-controlled enterprises – An organizational politics view. *Journal of International Business Studies*, *11*(1), 48–58.
Mazzolini, R. (1980b). The international strategy of state-owned firms – An organizational process and politics perspective. *Strategic Management Journal*, *1*(2), 101–118.
Meyer, K. E., Ding, Y., Li, J., & Zhang, H. (2014). Overcoming distrust: How state-owned enterprises adapt their foreign entries to institutional pressures abroad. *Journal of International Business Studies*, *45*(8), 1005–1028.
Meyer, K. E., & Nguyen, H. V. (2005). Foreign investment strategies and sub-national institutions in emerging markets: Evidence from Vietnam. *Journal of Management Studies*, *42*(1), 63–93.
Moore, E. (2012). Civets, BRICs and the next 11. *Financial Times*. Retrieved from http://www.ft.com/intl/cms/s/0/c14730ae-aff3-11e1-ad0b-00144feabdc0.html
Morck, R., Yeung, B., & Zhao, M. (2008). Perspectives on China's outward foreign direct investment. *Journal of International Business Studies*, *39*(9), 337–350.
Pan, Y. (1996). Influences on foreign equity ownership level in joint ventures in China. *Journal of International Business Studies*, *27*(1), 1–26.
Peng, M. W., Tan, J., & Tong, T. W. (2004). Ownership types and strategic groups in an emerging economy. *Journal Of Management Studies*, *41*(7), 1105–1129.
Peterson, M. F., Arregle, J.-L., & Martin, X. (2012). Multilevel models in international business research. *Journal of International Business Studies*, *43*(5), 451–457.
Pollitte, W. A., Miller, J. C., & Yaprak, A. (2015). Returns to US firms from strategic alliances in China: A knowledge-based view. *Journal of World Business*, *50*(1), 144–148.
Ramamurti, R., & Singh, J. V. (Eds.). (2010). *Emerging multinationals in emerging markets*. New York, NY: Cambridge University Press.
Schubert, G. A. (1957). "The public interest" in administrative decision-making: Theorem, theosophy, or theory? *American Political Science Review*, *51*(2), 346–368.
Sen, A. (1989). Development as capability expansion. *Journal of Development Planning*, *19*(1), 41–58.
Shaver, J. M. (1998). Accounting for endogeneity when assessing strategy performance: Does entry mode affect FDI survival? *Management Science*, *44*(4), 571–585.
Shaver, J. M., Mitchell, W., & Yeung, B. (1997). The effect of own-firm and other-firm experience on foreign direct investment survival in the United States, 1987–92. *Strategic Management Journal*, *18*(10), 811–824.
Tan, J. (2002). Impact of ownership type on environment–strategy linkage and performance: Evidence from a transitional economy. *Journal of Management Studies*, *39*(3), 333–354.
Tullock, G. (2008). Public choice. In S. N. Durlauf & L. E. Blume (Eds.), *The new Palgrave dictionary of economics (online)*. Basingstoke: Palgrave Macmillan.
Vernon, R. (1979). The international aspects of state-owned enterprises. *Journal of International Business Studies*, *10*(3), 7–15.
Vukmanic, F. G., Czinkota, M. R., & Ricks, D. A. (1985). National and international data problems and solutions in the empirical analysis of intra-industry direct foreign investment. In A. Erdilek (Ed.), *Multinationals as mutual invaders: Intra-industry direct foreign investment* (pp. 160–184). New York, NY: St Martin's Press.
Wang, C. Q., Hong, J., Kafouros, M., & Wright, M. (2012). Exploring the role of government involvement in outward FDI from emerging economies. *Journal of International Business Studies*, *43*(7), 655–676.

Wei, T., Clegg, J., & Ma, L. (2015). The conscious and unconscious facilitating role of the Chinese government in shaping the internationalization of Chinese MNCs. *International Business Review*, *24*(2), 331–343.

Xing, Y., Liu, Y., Tarba, S. Y., & Cooper, C. L. (2014). Intercultural influences on managing African employees of Chinese firms in Africa: Chinese managers' HRM practices. *International Business Review*. Retrieved from http://dx.doi.org/10.1016/j.ibusrev.2014.05.003

Xu, D., Lu, J. W., & Gu, Q. (2014). Organizational forms and multi-population dynamics: Economic transition in China. *Administrative Science Quarterly*, *59*(3), 517–547.

Zhou, C., & van Witteloostuijn, A. (2010). Institutional constraints and ecological processes: Evolution of foreign-invested enterprises in the Chinese construction industry, 1993–2006. *Journal of International Business Studies*, *41*(3), 539–556.

WHY DO THE TURKISH FIRMS INVEST IN MAINLAND EUROPE?

Sathyajit R. Gubbi and Sinan A. Sular

ABSTRACT

Outward foreign direct investments (FDI) by Turkish firms in the new millennium show intriguing geographic distribution pattern and unlike the predictions of classical theories of FDI. In this study we contribute by linking the observed pattern of outward FDI with Turkish firms' motivation for investment across national borders. We enrich research by collecting and analyzing FDI motivation data at the firm-level for a very important but less researched developing country: Turkey. Content analysis of text material on the foreign investments made by 211 Turkish firms reveals that Turkish firms primarily perform FDI in European developed countries for reasons other than conventional, namely, market- and strategic-asset-seeking motivations. More importantly, Turkish firms seem to be using the European countries to (1) present themselves as a European Union company, (2) make use of special features of these countries to expand their businesses within and to other countries and, (3) make use of the favorable tax treatment policies available to foreign investors. Surprisingly, our analysis shows that in spite of its small size, the Netherlands is a preferred destination for Turkish FDI over other

Emerging Economies and Multinational Enterprises
Advances in International Management, Volume 28, 441–470

ISSN: 1571-5027/doi:10.1108/S1571-502720150000028019

Western European countries due to its strategic location and favorable investment policies.

Keywords: Outward foreign direct investments; Turkish multinational firms; motivation for investment; host market characteristics

INTRODUCTION

Global patterns of FDI are changing and changing quickly. Even though developed countries still remain the leaders of outward foreign direct investments (OFDI), developing countries are fast catching up: from about 5% in the early 1990s, developing countries accounted for over 30% of the global FDI outflows in 2012 (UNCTAD, 2013). While the sharp rise in the value of OFDI by developing countries has caught attention of policy-makers and researchers alike, the nuances of OFDI by developing countries in terms of geographic distribution and forms of investment requires further scrutiny. In particular, the strategic behavior of emerging market multinational enterprises (EMNEs) in the present era of rapid globalization has much to offer in terms of advancing our knowledge of FDI.

Conventional motivations for FDI, largely based on the experiences of Anglo-American firms, emphasize the superior resources and the capabilities of the investing firm to expand internationally (Bonaglia, Goldstein, & Mathews, 2007). In contrast, EMNEs lacking in resources such as proprietary technology, financial capital, brands, and experienced management pursue internationalization paths different from those of established Western EMNEs (Guillén & García-Canal, 2009; Zaheer & Mosakowski, 1997). These EMNEs have used and leveraged various kinds of strategic and organizational innovations in order to establish a presence in the world market. The manner in which these firms have internationalized has often been incongruent with the predictions of classic theories of FDI (Luo & Tung, 2007; Ramamurti, 2008), thus, invoking a need for a reassessment (Gammeltoft, Pradhan, & Goldstein, 2010). In this paper we deal with the OFDI by firms from one of the prominent but relatively underresearched emerging economy: Turkey.

While there are several studies on the inward FDI in Turkey, as acknowledged by Sauvant, Maschek, and McAllister (2009), only a few studies have dealt with the outward FDI of Turkish EMNEs. And even among these, most rely on macro-level reasoning to account for the FDI flows (e.g., Kayam & Hisarciklilar, 2009) or use data prior to 2003 (e.g., Culpan & Akcaoglu, 2003; Erdilek, 2003; Uray, Vardar, & Nacar, 2012). The broad macro features of Turkish OFDI, as outlined below and in Fig. 1, in fact provide the motivation and the need for us to undertake a detailed firm-level analysis, as we do in this paper.

Turkey has been an economy with much promise since 2001 according to the International Monetary Fund. After a huge financial crisis in 2000, it has recovered impressively to record economic growth rate of 5% in 2013, leaving the Euro-zone behind which is still facing a financial crisis (UNCTAD, 2012). During the period of 2001–2010, Turkey's OFDI flows increased by 26% and was the second highest among developing countries after those of India (UNCTAD, 2010). In value terms, the total OFDI of Turkey was 200 million USD in the beginning of the new millennium. However, within a short span of one decade it had crossed nearly 3 billion USD. An intriguing feature of the OFDI by Turkish firms is the fact that while bulk of the investments in the last decade went into the advanced country markets of Western Europe, the Netherlands was found to be the most desired country by Turkish EMNEs followed by others like Germany, United Kingdom, Italy, Belgium, and France (TCMB, 2013). Out of the nearly 109 destination countries where the Turkish firms invested, the Netherlands alone-received investments worth 5.5 billion USD (TCMB, 2013). In 2012 alone, Turkey invested 70% of its total OFDI in the Netherlands (TCMB, 2013). This is surprising since the Netherlands happens to be one of the smallest markets in terms of size in the European Union relative to some of its neighbors like Germany,

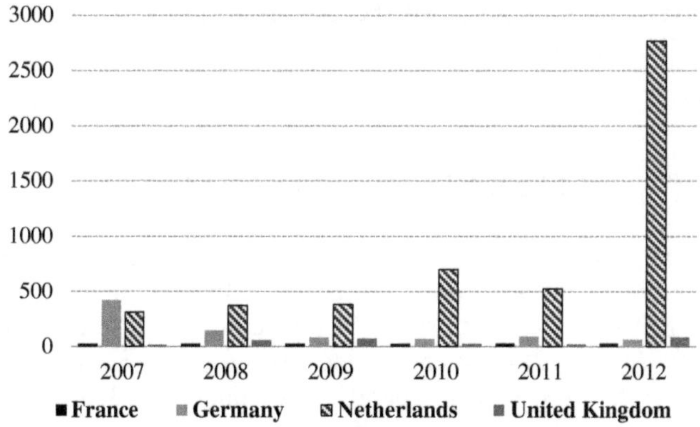

Fig. 1. Turkish Outward Foreign Direct Investment (million USD). *Source*: UNCTAD, 2012.

France, and the United Kingdom. Moreover, all these countries are similar in terms of level of development, quality of infrastructure, economic conditions, and the level of sophistication (see Tables 1 and 2). Surprisingly, this increasing investment by Turkish firms into the Netherlands comes against the backdrop of declining FDI flows in the Netherlands from other countries in the last five years (Agentschap, 2013). Thus, clearly, Turkish EMNEs seem to follow a different internationalization pattern than its contenders from China, India, and Brazil as well as their contenders from Anglo-American countries (Goldstein & Pusterla, 2010).

Given the above peculiarities related to OFDI by Turkish firms, we ask the question: Why do Turkish firms choose to invest in the geographically distant and more advanced countries of Western Europe? In particular, what makes the Netherlands particularly more attractive to these firms? We address these questions by specifically investigating the firm-level motivations of the extensive FDI activities of Turkish EMNEs in European developed countries. Our analysis of descriptive data at the level of each investment suggests that Turkish EMNEs invest in developed European countries for reasons beyond those explained by conventional FDI theories. The key finding of this paper is that Turkish EMNEs primarily prefer locations with hub-country characteristics for OFDI. Moreover, the presence of a high proportion of Turkish migrants seems to have a significant effect as well on the OFDI decision of Turkish firms.

The rest of this paper is structured in the following manner. First, a literature review on FDI theory will be outlined and integrated to develop hypotheses regarding Turkish EMNE motivations. Then we will describe the methodology and report the empirical findings. In the discussion, the contribution of our findings will be discussed and directions for future research will be provided.

LITERATURE AND THEORY

The classical FDI theory suggests that (1) firms internalize missing or imperfect external markets until the costs of further internalization outweigh the benefits (Hennart, 1982; Kindleberger, 1969; McManus, 1972; Rugman, 1981) and, (2) firms choose locations for their activities that minimize the overall costs of their operations (Williamson, 1975). A firm will internalize a transaction wherever the cost of using spot markets or contractual agreements is higher than that of organizing it within the firm.

Moreover, the costs of international operations can be kept low by investing in geographically proximal countries where knowledge, relationships, and experience have already been established through initial interactions (Johanson & Vahlne, 1977). The major FDI theories have progressively and interactively evolved over time, often build on one other and hence tend to differ incrementally from each other (Pitelis & Sugden, 1991).

Largely drawing arguments from transaction cost and resource-based theories, Dunning (1979) came up with the eclectic paradigm to integrate the existing theories in a more general model in which the pattern and motives would be explained. He proposed that a firm engages in FDI if three conditions are satisfied, namely, (1) the company possesses ownership advantages in respect of companies from other countries, (2) it is beneficial for a company to internalize those advantages rather than to use the market to pass them to foreign firms, and (3) there are location advantages in using the company's ownership advantages in a foreign country rather than at home. Dunning distinguishes between two sets of ownership advantages: (1) advantages that result from an exclusive access to intangible assets, inputs, or markets, and (2) the advantages that are associated with being multinational.

Above theories of FDI have been found to satisfactorily account for the investments made by the MNEs from developed countries like the United States and Europe. However, the last decade shows that FDI activities from developing countries are reshaping the international business literature (Liu, 2005). More so because EMNEs, mostly from Asian and South American countries, have engaged in OFDI for reasons beyond those explained by the dominant theories (Buckley et al., 2007). Although there is not yet consensus in the academic field concerning FDI motivations of EMNEs, first steps are already set in the literature by some scholars (Aulakh, 2007; Kalotay & Sulstarova, 2010; Li & Yao, 2010; Liu, 2005; Luo & Tung, 2007; Ramamurti, 2008; Zhao, Liu, & Zhao, 2010). Yet, a consistent and comprehensive theoretical framework that explains the FDI motivations of EMNEs is still lacking (Stucchi, 2012). According to Bonaglia et al. (2007, p. 371), "… the striking feature of internationalization by latecomer MNEs from emerging economies is that … they have to internationalize in order to capture the resources needed … to build their advantages cumulatively – a reversal of the traditional perspective."

Derived from the classical FDI theory, the motivations to engage in FDI are mainly grouped into the following broad categories (Dunning, 1979; Head, 2007): natural resource-seeking, market-seeking, efficiency-seeking, and strategic-assets-seeking motivations. Natural resource-seeking motivations in classical FDI theory imply spatial distribution of certain natural resources is lumpy and confined to specific geographic regions. Hence all OFDI aimed at acquiring certain natural resources are directed toward corresponding geographies. In this regard, Luo and Rui (2009) have reported that Chinese companies were urged by the government to gain natural resources from diverse locations in order to support the economic development of the home country. Luo and Rui (2009) called this motivation the government steward logic, which suggests that EMNEs can be subsidized or even compelled by the government to obtain natural resources. This government guidance can be expected among diverse OFDI motivations, as governments from developing countries have a mandate to shape the investments decisions of indigenous firms (Buckley et al., 2007).

The second motivation of market-seeking OFDI as per classical FDI theory may be a consequence of successful exports in which the firm wants a deeper involvement or the expansion of the firm to enter a whole new market. The main reasons behind market-seeking OFDI are to lower transportation costs (Head, 2007). However, in the context of developing countries it is found that EMNEs can follow both their competitors and the best performing MNEs to certain markets (Harrison, Dalkiran, & Elsey, 2000). Moreover, Deng (2012) reports that EMNEs attempt to derive higher profits by investing in markets with demand for high sophisticated products.

In classical FDI theory, efficiency-seeking OFDI corresponds with companies seeking a way to increase their cost efficiency by transferring production, especially to low labor cost countries. However, efficiency motivations are not one of the dominating motivations of why EMNEs internationalize (Wang, Hong, Kafouros, & Boateng, 2012). An important reason for this can be the already-possessed cost leadership position of these low cost countries with respect to developed countries. Finally, the motivation most closely identified with the emergence of EMNEs is strategic-asset-seeking motivation (Dunning & Lundan, 2008). EMNEs often lack technology and brands and face disadvantages like lack of international experience, late mover disadvantages and lack of resources. Since they operate in a dynamic and globalized international market they must quickly upgrade their competences to compete with MNEs from developed countries. Therefore, many EMNEs undertake upmarket acquisitions to gain these competences that they do not already possess (Luo & Tung, 2007). In the process of acquiring these critical resources and capabilities from global markets, the indigenous firms leapfrog to becoming multinational firms. We next examine the suitability of the current state of knowledge on FDI in the case of Turkey.

Macro-Level Features of Turkey

In order to account for the high levels of OFDI by Turkish firms into the advanced countries of Western Europe, we first compare a few macro-level features relevant to FDI. Here we draw parallels between Turkey, the Netherlands, the United Kingdom, France, and Germany since bulk of the foreign investment by Turkish firms concern these geographies.

Earlier, reasoning ruled out efficiency-seeking motivations as a likely driver for EMNEs to engage in OFDI given their own home country advantages as low cost location. The reasoning gets stronger when the OFDI relate to relatively developed and advanced economies like the Netherlands, the United Kingdom, France, and Germany. Also, given their geographic location and the availability of natural resources, none of the Western European countries compared support natural resource-seeking motivation as a likely driver for Turkish OFDI into these countries. Then, the only possibilities which remain based on classical theories of FDI are market- and strategic-asset-seeking motivations as the drivers of Turkish OFDI into the advanced countries of Western Europe.

According to the previously described market-seeking motivations for FDI, high levels of exports to a specific geography may be followed by greater OFDI, especially if the transportation costs are high. In this regard, as evident in Fig. 2, Turkey has the highest exports over the period 2007–2012 to Germany (averaging nearly 12 billion USD), followed by the United Kingdom and France (about 7 billion USD). The Netherlands accounted for just about 3 billion USD of Turkish exports. The high levels

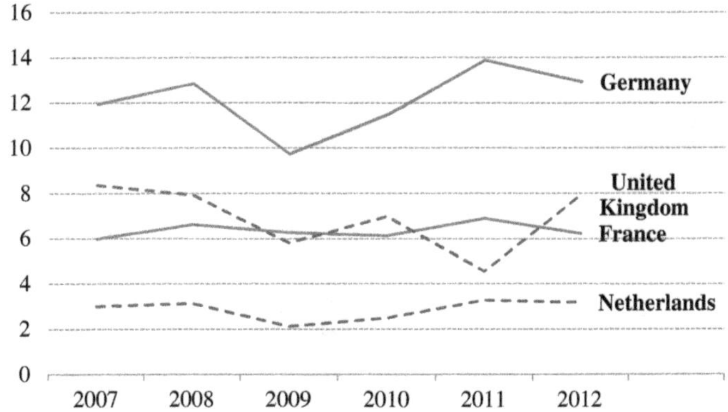

Fig. 2. Turkish Exports (billion USD). *Source*: TCMB, 2014.

of Turkish exports to these advanced countries of Western Europe are supportive of market-seeking motivations as one of the key drivers of Turkish OFDI into these markets.

Probing further, we compare these countries in terms of Gross Domestic Product (GDP) and the level of advancement of these destinations – a few broad indicators of market attractiveness for foreign investments. In Figs. 3(a) and (b) we have graphed the GDP both in terms of gross values and per capita. In terms of the overall market size (gross GDP), Germany is the largest followed by France and the United Kingdom. The

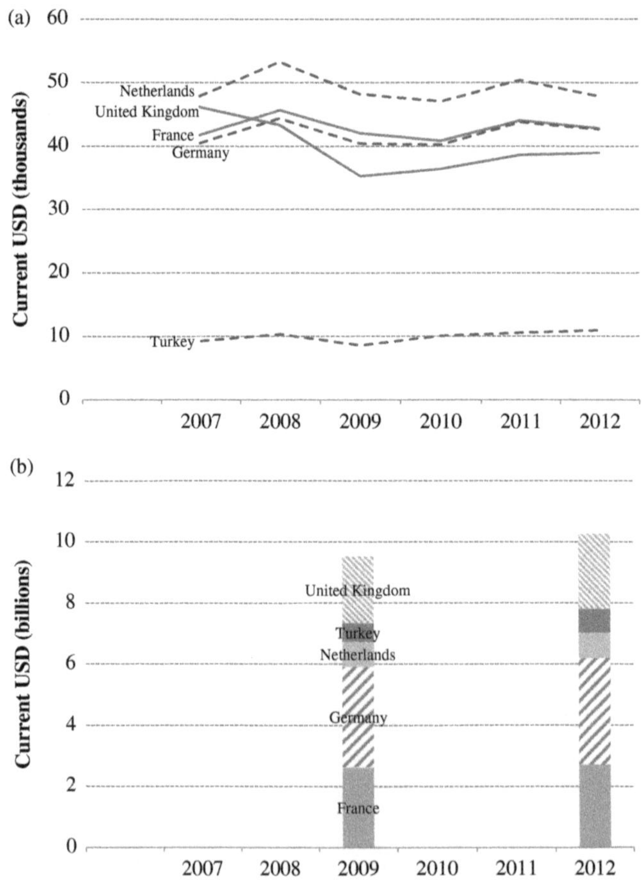

Fig. 3. (a) Gross Domestic Product per Capita. (b) Gross Domestic Product. *Source*: IMF, 2014.

Netherlands happens to be the smallest and has an economy that is comparable to that of Turkey. However, in terms of GDP per capita (capacity to consume), all the four Western European countries compared are similar and several times higher than the corresponding values for Turkey. Similarly, when compared in terms of quality of infrastructure (see Table 1) that is reflective of the level of advancement of a country, all the four destination countries were rated to be similar and found to be better than Turkey. Therefore, in terms of market attractiveness measured in terms of broad macro-level features, there is very little to differentiate between the countries of Western Europe. However, the bigger market size, capacity to consume goods and services, and the quality of infrastructure available compared to those of Turkey does support market-seeking motivations for Turkish firms to invest in these countries.

Next, in Table 2 we compare in terms of quality of resources and assets available. Quality of institutions reflects the level of advancement of a nation and hence signals the availability of high-quality resources and capabilities (Gubbi, Aulakh, Ray, Sarkar, & Chittoor, 2010). Here we look at quality of education, innovation, and sophistication factors and the global competitiveness index score for each of the countries compared. Given the big gap between Turkey and the rest in terms of these parameters, it is likely that strategic-asset-seeking motivations may also be the reason for high levels of Turkish OFDI into Western Europe. As discussed in the literature review, one of the highly recognized motivations of EMNEs is their strategic-assets-seeking motivation. According to Luo and Tung (2007) and others (Gammeltoft et al., 2010; Stucchi, 2012), EMNEs use OFDI as a springboard to acquire strategic-assets that they need to compete more

Table 1. Quality of Infrastructure.

Parameter	Country	2009	2010	2011	2012
Transport	France	6.47	6.40	6.30	6.25
	Germany	6.49	6.27	6.24	6.14
	Netherlands	5.88	6.00	6.14	6.11
	Turkey	4.40	4.58	4.83	4.91
	United Kingdom	5.54	5.74	5.84	5.66
Electricity and telephony	France	6.01	6.19	6.26	6.17
	Germany	6.37	6.43	6.48	6.34
	Netherlands	5.98	6.03	6.22	6.16
	Turkey	4.02	4.19	3.94	3.99
	United Kingdom	6.21	6.44	6.60	6.59

Source: WEF (2014).

Table 2. Quality of Resources and Assets.

Parameter	Country	2007	2008	2009	2010	2011	2012
Quality of education	France	5.39	5.38	5.28	5.15	4.98	4.76
	Germany	5.00	4.85	4.68	4.86	4.75	4.84
	Netherlands	5.51	5.45	5.47	5.50	5.59	5.63
	Turkey	3.96	3.76	3.76	3.63	3.61	3.76
	United Kingdom	5.12	5.02	5.02	5.12	5.35	5.35
Innovation and sophistication factors	France	5.08	5.08	4.90	4.83	4.93	4.96
	Germany	5.70	5.54	5.47	5.51	5.53	5.57
	Netherlands	5.21	5.20	5.17	5.16	5.30	5.47
	Turkey	3.90	3.70	3.70	3.63	3.62	3.79
	United Kingdom	5.10	4.93	4.92	4.98	5.17	5.32
Global competitiveness index score	France	5.22	5.13	5.13	5.14	5.11	5.05
	Germany	5.46	5.37	5.39	5.41	5.48	5.51
	Netherlands	5.41	5.32	5.33	5.41	5.50	5.42
	Turkey	4.25	4.15	4.16	4.25	4.28	4.45
	United Kingdom	5.30	5.19	5.25	5.39	5.45	5.37

Source: WEF, 2014.

effectively against global competitors and to avoid the weak institutional environment at home. Because of a late mover position, strong presence of global rivals in their home countries, quick-changing technologies and weak home institutional environments, EMNEs are pushed out of their home countries to internationalize (Luo & Tung, 2007). Gammeltoft et al. (2010) acknowledges that EMNEs perform OFDI to developed countries as these countries have a more sophisticated technological knowledge than EMNEs. Stucchi (2012) concludes in his study about EMNEs upmarket acquisitions, that they are guided by assets-seeking motivations because they lack traditional exploitable advantages.

Based on the broad macro-level features compared and the previous empirical evidence related to the internationalization of EMNEs, it is reasonable to believe that Turkish EMNEs invest in the advanced countries of Western Europe either due to market- or strategic-asset-seeking motivations or both. Therefore, we formulate the following hypothesis:

H1. Turkish OFDI is driven by search for new markets for growth and/or to acquire strategic-assets.

Although the macro-level features of Western European countries in terms of market size, capacity to consume goods and services, quality of infrastructure, and resources available tend to support both market-seeking and strategic-assets-seeking motivations for Turkish firms to invest, one clear anomaly is the Netherlands. Given its relatively small market size and the remarkably high flows of Turkish OFDI, neither market- nor strategic-assets-seeking motivations explain why the Netherlands should be preferred over its neighboring countries. Therefore, we need to move beyond the motivations provided by classical FDI literature. In the next set of hypotheses, we identify other factors likely to explain the high incidence of Turkish OFDI into the Netherlands.

Ethnic Connections

The decline in communication and transportation costs and the reduction in policy-induced barriers have led to a rapid increase in trade and people across borders. Javorcik, Ozden, Spatareanu, and Neagu (2010) report that little attention has been paid to the more subtle linkages and feedback mechanisms that have been shaping the global economy. One of these linkages is the influence of migration on FDI. There is a growing body of literature in support of a positive association between the presence of ethnic networks and international trade, however the relation between migration and FDI is relatively unexplored (Javorcik et al., 2010).

In the context of Taiwanese investments in China, a study by Filatotchev, Strange, Piesse, and Lien (2007) found that local networks underpinned by business, ethnic, and cultural links enable firms to reduce the risks associated with FDI in emerging markets by accessing vital information and complementary resources. This suggests that EMNEs are likely to invest in regions where they have established networks. China and Taiwan share a common culture and heritage and are both emerging markets in which 98% of the population of Taiwan is Chinese. Supporting this view, Rauch and Trindade (2002) and others (Combes, Miren, & Mayer, 2005) suggest that the presence of people with the same ethnic or national background on both sides of a border may alleviate information asymmetries. Their language and familiarity with the same culture can significantly lower costs and create opportunities for trade. Business and social networks that span national borders can help overcome many contractual and informational barriers to stimulate beneficial international transactions. Therefore, the presence of knowledge of a certain part of a foreign market can be used as an entry to the rest of the market or even only serving the migrant customer base can be profitable for companies. In the early 1960s the major immigration of Turkish citizens started to Western European countries to compensate for the labor force deficit faced in these countries. The main goal of these migrants was to collect capital in a few years and return to Turkey to start a small business (YTB, 2014). However, most of these migrants never returned and started a family or brought their families to these Western European countries to start a new life. Hence, currently 80% of the total of 5 million Turkish migrants live in Western Europe (see Fig. 4 for a countrywise breakup). In particular, the Netherlands ranks second next to Germany in terms of Turkish migrants as a percentage of total population. Therefore, the high presence of Turkish ethnicity is a likely motivation for Turkish OFDI into Western Europe and specifically to the Netherlands. Accordingly, we hypothesize:

H2. Turkish OFDI seeks foreign locations with a high Turkish ethnic presence.

Hub Countries

Since Turkey is located on the borders of the European Union (EU) and yet not an EU member, local presence in a host-country with positive reputation among other countries would make trade easier for Turkish EMNEs (Arikan, 2006). As this would mean that Turkish EMNEs can present themselves as an EU-based company within the borders of the European Union. Turkey desires to become an EU member, especially due to the boost in the economy that they expect after becoming an EU member

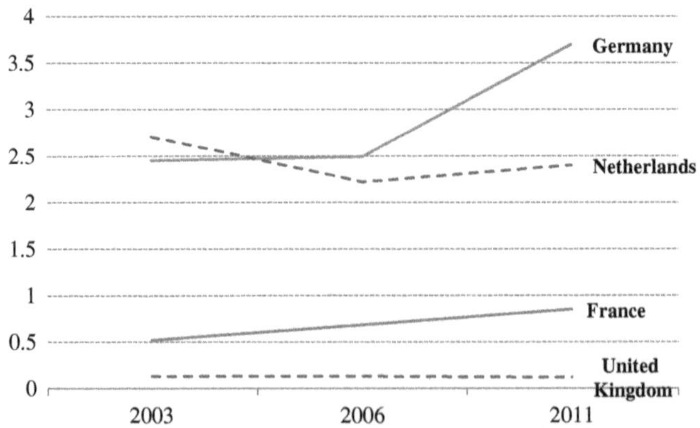

Fig. 4. Turkish Migrants (Percent Total Population). *Source*: YTB, 2014.

(Lejour, de Mooij, & Capel, 2004). However, it seems unlikely that Turkish accession will be achieved in the foreseeable future (Kentmen, 2008). To overcome the trade barriers of not being an EU member, Turkish EMNEs perform OFDI in certain European countries and use them as a hub to transact with other EU members. This is akin to hub and spokes model where the host-country acts like a hub and the spokes are the specialized networks/relationship linking that country with other regions (Guerrieri & Pietrobelli, 2004). For instance, Italy plays a central role in the textile and clothing industry, which makes it the cradle of the textile and clothing industry of Europe. Similarly, the Netherlands is for instance being recognized as the largest logistics hub of Europe with its port in Rotterdam (Shinohara, Roos, & Stam, 2002).

The country that received the greatest portion of Turkish OFDI in the last 10 years is the Netherlands with 5.5 billion USD. The Netherlands is also recognized as a hub-country by practitioners and researchers (Schueler, 2007). One of the hub characteristics of the Netherlands is its strategic position alongside a well-developed and established infrastructure. The macro-economic comparisons between the Western European countries show that the Netherlands has a very competitive position in comparison with the other strong economies of Europe. For instance in 2012, the Netherlands was ranked third in terms of quality of infrastructure (see Table 1), ranked first in terms of quality of education, ranked second in terms of innovation and sophistication, and ranked second in terms of global competitive index (Table 2). In support of the macro-economic numbers, in 1985 the transport of commodities via the Netherlands to other European countries was 62 billion ton km and rose sharply to 115 billion ton km in 2011 (CBS, 2013). Especially the port of Rotterdam is used as a hub to the mainland of Europe. Via the port of Rotterdam, commodities are being transported by railway, air, and highway to countries with high market sizes like Germany and France.

Moreover, as proposed by some scholars (de Mooij & Ederveen, 2003; Schueler, 2007) the Netherlands is an attractive investment destination because of its lenient tax treatment and especially its extensive network of tax treaties. Some call this the Dutch Sandwich, which stands for companies avoiding high tax rates by using the Netherlands as a hub for their capital transfer to other countries. From the Netherlands the capital is being sent to tax havens like Bermuda and others, as the Netherlands has tax treaties with a high number of countries. In Fig. 5 we have compared the corporate tax rates of some of the Western European countries with those in Turkey. Clearly, the Netherlands has not only kept the rate fixed

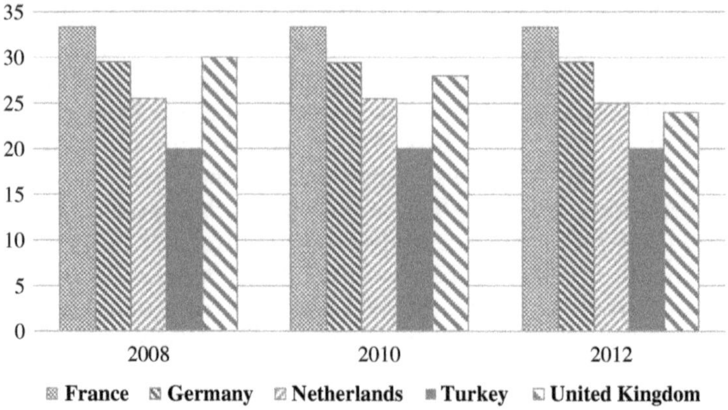

Fig. 5. Corporate Tax Rates (Percent). *Source*: KPMG, 2014.

across years, it is also the lowest next to Turkey. Amongst the countries compared, only the United Kingdom shows a declining trend in corporate tax rates over time. In de Mooij and Ederveen's (2003) opinion the Dutch government has integrated this tax policy on purpose to attract MNEs from all over the world. Because of its special treatments in their taxation policies for MNEs, the Netherlands is different from other European countries because it provides generic advantages for all sectors with its hub-country characteristics, strategic geographical position, infrastructure, and taxation policies. Therefore, considering these important hub-country dynamics with Turkey's ambition to present itself as an EU nation, the following hypothesis is formulated:

H3. Turkish OFDI seeks foreign locations with strategic position so as to serve as a hub for trade with regional neighbors.

METHODOLOGY

Sample and Data Collection

We tested our hypothesis using a sample of firms drawn from the companies that are listed on the Istanbul Stock Exchange (ISE) and appear in widely used database like Orbis. As the focus of our analysis was on those firms who invested in the advanced economies of Western Europe, we filtered out firms with subsidiaries located in this region. This resulted in 138 stock listed Turkish companies that performed OFDI in European developed countries. Amongst the non-listed Turkish companies, a close examination of news coverage by the four major Turkish newspapers, namely Hürriyet, Sabah, Habertürk, and Zaman, helped us identify further 111 firms who invested in the Western European countries. This resulted in a total sample of 249 Turkish firms that performed OFDI in European developed countries.

As the objective of this research is to reveal the motivations of Turkish EMNEs to perform OFDI and since there are no databases regarding the OFDI motivations of Turkish EMNEs, all EMNEs in the total sample are investigated by scanning and reading secondary sources in order to reveal their specific motivations. Namely, the LexisNexis database, company websites, company annual reports, online media, business reports, and the databases of especially the four major Turkish newspapers. As argued by Ciualla (1991), the use of media as a source of reality against which the conceptual description is to be checked is consistent with its use by researchers as a faithful mirror of reality. For some of the companies in our original sample, the main motivations for OFDI could not be found and hence these firms were omitted.

Our final sample comprised of 211 firms with 323 instance of OFDI into the advanced country markets of Western Europe. In the sample analyzed, only 13.3% of the OFDI was performed before 2000, indicating relative sluggishness of Turkish firms in terms of internationalization in the previous century. Also, 61% of the firms in the sample were listed on the stock exchange and accounted for 73% of the OFDI analyzed. In Tables 3 and 4, we provide details of the sample analyzed by country and by industry. According to the sample characteristics, the Netherlands accounted for the highest number of Turkish subsidiaries followed by Germany and the United Kingdom, respectively. Together, the Netherlands and Germany

Table 3. Sample Characteristics Turkish EMNES that Performed OFDI in Europe.

	N = Firms	%	N = OFDI	%
Stock listed on Istanbul Exchange	127	61	236	73
Non stock listed	84	39	87	27
Total	211	100	323	100

Table 4. Sample Characteristics (N = Firms (OFDI)).

	Belgium	France	Germany	Italy	Netherlands	Spain	United Kingdom	Total	% of Total
Auto and related equipment	1 (2)	1 (2)	3 (5)	– (–)	1 (2)	– (–)	– (–)	6 (11)	**2.8 (3.4)**
Banking and financial services	1 (1)	1 (1)	7 (10)	– (–)	12 (18)	– (–)	8 (12)	29 (42)	**13.7 (13)**
Chemicals	– (–)	– (–)	– (–)	– (–)	3 (6)	– (–)	– (–)	3 (6)	**1.4 (1.9)**
Electrical, electronics and durables	2 (3)	– (–)	10 (15)	1 (2)	8 (16)	2 (4)	2 (4)	25 (44)	**11.8 (13.6)**
Food and beverage	2 (4)	– (–)	3 (5)	– (–)	4 (7)	– (–)	1 (1)	10 (17)	**4.7 (5.3)**
Manufacturing and construction	– (–)	4 (6)	6 (7)	4 (8)	14 (18)	4 (5)	2 (3)	34 (47)	**16.2 (14.6)**
Products and goods	1 (2)	– (–)	16 (26)	2 (2)	11 (16)	– (–)	4 (4)	34 (50)	**16.2 (15.5)**
Services sector	– (–)	1 (2)	6 (7)	3 (4)	11 (19)	1 (2)	8 (13)	30 (47)	**14.3 (14.6)**
Textiles, apparel, and leather	– (–)	1 (2)	10 (11)	3 (2)	5 (6)	– (–)	8 (13)	26 (34)	**12.3 (10.5)**
Transport and logistics	1 (2)	1 (2)	8 (14)	(–)	4 (7)	– (–)	– (–)	14 (25)	**6.6 (7.6)**
Total	8 (14)	9 (15)	69 (100)	12 (18)	73 (115)	7 (11)	33 (50)	**211 (323)**	
% of Total	**3.8(4.3)**	**4.3 (4.6)**	**32.5 (31)**	**5.7 (5.6)**	**35 (35.6)**	**3.2 (3.4)**	**15.5 (15.5)**		**100**

account for over two-third of OFDI made by Turkish firms after 2000. It is important to note that neither country is geographically close to Turkey.

Our next objective was to identify and isolate the motivations for Turkish firms to invest abroad. A common procedure adopted previously in this regard is to design and administer a survey (Demirbag, Tatoglu, & Glaister, 2008). The survey method is a useful technique to identify and measure firm-level motivations, behavior, and perceptions regarding FDI decisions, especially when direct proxies are not available (Brouthers, Brouthers, & Werner, 2002; Harzing, 2002). However, the survey option may be highly influenced by the subject's view of what the researcher might want to hear (Harris, 2001) and there is possibility for respondent bias due to the heavy reliance placed on information obtained from questionnaires and interviews. Besides, response patterns of respondents can differ from those of non-respondents. Given these difficulties with primary data from surveys, Cowton (1998) has proposed that secondary data is highly attractive when compared to interview, questionnaire, and macro-economic data results.

Taking this view and the criticism of Harris (2001) and Cowton (1998) into account, for the purpose of our research we used the content analysis method (Cowton, 1998; Hsieh & Shannon, 2005; Morgan, 1993). Content analysis involves identification of texts to be examined, specification of the unit of analysis, determination of the categories, generation of the coding scheme, and the analysis of the collected data (Harris, 2001). In our case, the database was created by scanning and searching through the four major Turkish newspapers, the LexisNexis database, company websites, and company reports. Therefore, written text was examined and analyzed in order to gain deep insights on many aspects of Turkish OFDI. In Appendix A, we provide details of the various stated motivations for OFDI by Turkish firms. Typical samples of the content analyzed and the corresponding motivation coded is provided in Appendix B. As the different motivations of Turkish firms to invest in Europe are coded from secondary sources, a non-parametric approach was used for quantitative analysis (Neuendorf, 2002). This is the most appropriate approach as motivations are nominal variables manually coded from secondary sources. In such cases, a Pearson Chi-Square test and the Pearson crosstab comparison test has been recommended (Hsieh & Shannon, 2005). In order to validate the results of the Pearson Chi-Square crosstab comparison test, a Monte Carlo test was also used.

RESULTS

In Table 5, we have provided details of the various coded motivations for OFDI by Turkish firms in terms of frequencies and percentages. This reveals which motivations of Turkish EMNEs are the most important motivations to perform OFDI in European developed countries. We coded those motivations amounting to less than 1% as "other motivations." These mainly comprise of efficiency seeking, following the competitor into other markets, and geo-political considerations. As evident in Table 5, the most frequent motivation was hub-country characteristics motivation with 28.2% followed by presence of Turkish migrants motivation (25.1%), strategic-asset-seeking motivation (19.5%), and market-seeking motivation (16.1%), respectively. A one-sample Pearson Chi-Square test was conducted in order to find whether there are statistically significant differences in the observed frequencies and percentages of the motivation variables. In other words, we tested for the difference between expected and observed values. The one-sample Pearson Chi-Square test revealed that the observed frequencies differ from the expected frequencies at the 1% level ($X^2(6) = 152.935$). Thus the data analyzed supported all three hypotheses related to market- and strategic-asset-seeking motivations, ethnic connections, and strategic position of the destination country.

Going further beyond overall numbers, we segregated the coded information by country, as shown in Table 6. We find several additional features of OFDI by Turkish EMNEs into the advanced country markets of Western Europe. First, Germany accounted for the highest percentage of OFDI citing Turkish migrants as the main reason, closely followed by the Netherlands where the hub characteristics of the country appeared to be

Table 5. Motivations by Categories.

	Observed N	%	Expected N (14.29%)	Residual
Hub	91	28.2	46.1	44.9
Migrants	81	25.1	46.1	34.9
Strategic	63	19.5	46.1	16.9
Market	52	16.1	46.1	5.9
Tax	15	4.6	46.1	−31.1
Institutional	11	3.4	46.1	−35.1
Other	10	3.1	46.1	−36.1
Total	323	100		

the main motivation. Second, besides hub characteristics, the next highest percentage of OFDI was motivated by Turkish firms investing in the Netherlands driven by the presence of Turkish community. Third, after the Netherlands, Germany is the second most preferred destination for a number of reasons; prominent among those are the motivations of ethnic Turkish connections and strategic-assets. Furthermore, the top three motivations per country are hub-country characteristics, the presence of Turkish migrants, and strategic motivations.

Regarding the unique position of the Netherlands in Europe, a Pearson Chi-Square crosstab comparison test is conducted for motivation by country. Here, we evaluate for the difference from the expected values and determine the significance of the test. With this procedure, our analysis shows significance at the 1% level ($X^2(36)=81.968$). As argued by Dufour and Khalaf (1999), a Chi-Square crosstab comparison test is less conservative than a Monte Carlo test. Also, the Monte Carlo test is superior in cases where results are predicted without conducting hundreds of experiments or building thousands of samples to recreate different scenarios with nominal variables. Monte Carlo test for H3 provided significant result at the 1% level ($X^2=71.973$).

Although our data shows that Turkish OFDI assumed significant proportions after 2000, there have been investments made in the prior period also. In order to further strengthen our main findings, we carried out a Pearson Chi-Square crosstab comparison test for motivation by investment periods. We identified 1990 and 2000 as the two cut off years to split the data into three investment periods. We then compared the frequencies of motivation for OFDI across the three periods (see Table 7). The Pearson Chi-Square crosstab comparison test showed statistical significance at the 1% level ($X^2(12)=31.080$). The Monte Carlo test revealed a statistical

Table 6. Percent Motivations by Country ($N=323$).

	Motivation by Country						
	Hub	Institutional	Market	Migrants	Other	Strategic	Tax
Belgium	**1.5**	0.0	0.3	**1.5**	0.0	0.9	0.0
France	**1.9**	0.0	0.3	0.6	0.6	**1.2**	0.0
Germany	5.0	0.6	5.6	**12.4**	0.6	**6.8**	0.0
Italy	**2.2**	0.0	0.9	0.0	0.3	**2.2**	0.0
Netherlands	**12.1**	1.2	5.0	**7.5**	0.9	4.6	4.6
Spain	**1.5**	0.0	**0.9**	0.0	0.0	**0.9**	0.0
UK	**4.0**	1.5	3.1	**3.4**	0.6	2.8	0.0

significance at the level of 5% (X^2 =18.375). The results from Table 7 show that before 1990, the hub-country characteristic (1.2%) and the presence of Turkish migrants (1.5%) were the main reasons to perform OFDI. In the 1990s, strategic-asset consideration (2.2%) became the most important and 2000 onward the hub-country characteristics (25.1%), presence of Turkish migrants (21.8%), and strategic motivations (16.7%) were the main reasons for performing OFDI. Interestingly, tax advantages appear as a motivation for the first time after the year 2000. While institutional consideration as a motivation was prominent prior to 2000, post-2000 it was not the case. Regarding the presence of Turkish migrants motivation, Table 7 shows that as a percentage of all motivations recorded in the period there has been a steady decline: before 1990 it was 38% and post-2000 it went down to about 25%.

We next isolated the OFDI by economic activity and categorized the motivations based on the industry. Sectorwise details reveal that in the banking and financial services, food and beverage, products and goods sector, OFDI was mainly due to the Turkish migrant presence in the destination country. On the other hand, hub-country motivations dominated in

Table 7. Percent Motivations by Year (N=323).

	Hub	Institutional	Market	Migrants	Other	Strategic	Tax
1960–1989	**1.2**	0.0	0.6	**1.5**	0.0	0.6	0.0
1990–1999	**1.9**	**1.9**	1.5	**1.9**	0.3	**2.2**	0.0
>2000	**25.1**	1.5	13.9	**21.8**	2.8	16.7	**4.6**

Table 8. Motivations by Sector (N=323).

	Hub	Institutional	Market	Migrants	Other	Strategic	Tax
Auto and related equipment	**1.2**	0.0	0.3	0.0	0.3	**1.5**	0.0
Banking and financial services	**2.2**	1.2	0.9	**5.9**	0.3	1.5	0.9
Chemicals	**0.9**	0.0	0.0	0.0	0.0	**0.9**	0.0
Electrical electronics and durables	**3.4**	0.3	1.5	1.5	0.3	**5.9**	0.6
Food and beverage	**1.8**	0.0	0.9	**2.2**	0.0	0.3	0.3
Manufacturing and construction	**4.6**	0.3	**3.1**	0.6	0.6	**4.0**	1.2
Products and goods	2.8	0.3	**5.0**	**6.6**	0.3	0.6	0.3
Services sector	**5.0**	1.2	1.2	**2.8**	0.6	**2.8**	0.9
Textiles, apparel, and leather	**2.8**	0.0	**2.8**	**3.4**	0.3	1.2	0.0
Transport and logistics	**3.7**	0.0	0.3	**2.5**	0.3	0.6	0.3

the manufacturing sectors such as chemicals and auto and related equipment. The market-seeking motivation was found to be significantly high only for products and goods; manufacturing and construction; and textile, apparel, and leather sectors, respectively. Finally, the strategic motivation was significantly high in industries with high to medium-high technology involvement such as electrical and electronics, manufacturing and construction, and services sector. We also carried out a Pearson Chi-Square cross-tab comparison test for motivation by economic activity sector of the investing firm. Details of the sample distribution are available in Table 8. Pearson Chi-Square crosstab comparison test showed a statistical significance at the 1% level ($X^2(54)=112.172$) for the hub-country, strategic-asset, and Turkish ethnic connection motivations. The Monte Carlo test confirmed by showing significance at the 1% level ($X^2 = 105.375$). Motivations of tax advantages, institutional and others such as efficiency seeking were found not significant across sectors analyzed.

DISCUSSION AND CONCLUSION

Although there is a focus in research on OFDI motivations of emerging markets, there is almost no research on OFDI motivations of Turkish EMNEs. Even though Turkey has been widely discussed as the next big global economy after the BRIC countries, research till date has heavily focused on China and India. We advance the existing research on FDI by analyzing a sample of 211 Turkish EMNEs, both publicly listed and well recognized. Our systematic analysis of textual material related to nearly 323 foreign investments made by these firms over time reveals several interesting features of the motivations for Turkish EMNEs to invest in the advanced markets of Western Europe.

While EMNEs from India, China, and Brazil have been known to engage in OFDI, especially via the cross-border acquisition route to acquire strategic-assets (Gubbi et al., 2010; Luo & Tung, 2007; Ramamurti, 2008), our analysis of OFDI motivations by Turkish EMNEs to invest in Europe suggest other aspects. First, difference we note is that Turkish OFDI is often in the form of greenfield projects, while EMNEs from other emerging countries engage in mergers and acquisitions or equity joint ventures. A second point of departure from OFDI motivations recorded in the context of other emerging markets is that the Turkish EMNEs investments into Europe are largely driven by the hub-country characteristics of the destination country and by the presence of Turkish community in those countries. Previously, Luo and Tung (2007) report that EMNEs use internationalization as a springboard to acquire strategic-assets from diverse markets in order to overcome their disadvantages. In contrast, a high proportion of Turkish EMNEs appear to use European developed countries as a springboard to first present themselves as European company, derive benefits of the legitimacy and prestige in the marketplace (Shan & Hamilton, 1991), and to then conduct business with other countries.

In this regard, in spite of the small market size of the Netherlands as an investment destination, it happened to attract the highest amount of Turkish OFDI amongst the Western European countries entirely on account of its superior features as a hub-country. The high quality of infrastructure, education, and the Netherlands' strategic geographic position with the facilities to service several key European markets such as France, Germany, and the United Kingdom by road, rail, or waterways makes it highly attractive for the Turkish EMNEs as an investment destination. Coincidentally, the Netherlands also has the second highest concentration of Turkish immigrants in Western Europe after Germany.

In line with past research (Gammeltoft et al., 2010; Gubbi et al., 2010; Luo & Tung, 2007; Stucchi, 2012), our analyzed data of Turkish OFDI did support the rationale that EMNEs invest in advanced countries to obtain strategic-assets. Our analyzed data showed that Germany, followed by the Netherlands were the top two investment destinations for the Turkish EMNEs intending to augment the stock of resources and capabilities with those obtained from more advanced institutional contexts. On the technology intensity of a sector, our analysis of OFDI reveals that strategic-assets-seeking motivations was indeed the main reason for OFDI by Turkish firms operating in the high-technology sectors such as electrical and electronics goods (Table 6). Overall, our study reconfirms the reasoning proposed by Luo and Tung (2007) and other scholars. EMNEs from Turkey just as EMNEs from other parts of the world invest in industrially advanced countries to gain access to superior technology and other knowledge-based assets. Whether these EMNEs subsequently transfer the local knowledge gained back to their home country or whether they continue to develop these foreign locations as the centers for R&D and technology upgradation remains to be seen.

As regards motivations for OFDI driven by ethnic connections, almost 5 million Turkish migrants are known to reside in developed countries of Europe (TCMB, 2013). Our analyzed data shows that Turkish OFDI into Germany correlated highly with the Turkish ethnic community presence.

This is not surprising, as the presence of Turkish migrants in Germany is the highest with almost 3 million with respect to other European countries. Our research reinforces the finding by Filatotchev et al. (2007) who argued that EMNEs are likely to invest in regions where they have developed extensive networks by cultural, ethnic, and business activities. However, the research of the study by Filatotchev et al. (2007) is based on findings between Taiwan and China. Given the fact that both Taiwan and China are considered to be emerging markets and that 98% of Taiwanese have Chinese origins, it was not clear whether ethnic connections would facilitate OFDI, especially when the investment flows from a developing to a developed country. Our study contributes here by demonstrating that ethnic connections can play a key role to promote FDI between developing and developed countries.

Related to the previous, our analyzed data also reveals an interesting trend. In the period 1990–2000, strategic-asset-seeking motivations was the top cited reason for Turkish EMNEs to engage in OFDI (Table 5), however, in the current millennium it is ranked in the third place after hub characteristics and ethnic connection motivations. This suggests that with increasing globalization and the advances made in information and technology, communities spread across the globe are coming closer. Ethnic diaspora of a nation is increasingly becoming a key factor not only to promote trade between nations, they are also facilitating FDI by attracting investing firms to locate their investments in regions of high ethnic concentration. Turkey clearly seems to be benefitting from the presence of its community in the advanced markets of Western Europe.

This study does have certain limitations. First of all, this is an exploratory enquiry using content analysis of stated intent of the investing firms. There is a need for a follow on research, which builds on the existing and employs a large sample data for detailed quantitative analysis. A key drawback of content analysis approach is the possibility for multiple motivations driving the same investment. For instance, a Turkish firm may invest in the Netherlands for its strategic geographic location, high concentration of Turkish immigrants and for benefitting from the high quality of resources and assets available. In this case, unless explicitly stated by the top executives and recorded in the textual material analyzed, which one of the three motivations was the first priority is difficult to assess. Another drawback of content analysis is the fact that we cannot determine the extent to which a particular motivation for OFDI was fulfilled by a particular investment. In order to assess these outcomes, post-investment follow up on the field would be required. It would also make sense to administer specifically designed questionnaires where the informant can declare the extent to which a specific objective or motivation for OFDI was fulfilled. Second, as secondary sources are used to obtain possible motivations of Turkish firms, there is scope for suspicion. Often, the secondary sources carry information designed for a different purpose. Also, the informant of interest to us, the key decision maker in the investing firm, may proclaim something for public consumption while in private the objectives may be entirely different. For these reasons, there is a need to validate our findings with alternate approaches.

REFERENCES

Agentschap. (2013). *Balance of payments and international investment position.* Retrieved from http://www.statistics.dnb.nl/index.cgi?lang=nl&todo=Balans. Accessed on September 22, 2013.

Arikan, H. (2006). *Turkey and the EU: An awkward candidate for EU membership?* Aldershot: Ashgate.

Aulakh, P. S. (2007). Emerging multinationals from developing economies: Motivations, paths and performance. *Journal of International Management, 13*(3), 235–240.

Bonaglia, F., Goldstein, A., & Mathews, J. A. (2007). Accelerated internationalisation by emerging markets' multinationals: The case of the white goods sectors. *Journal of World Business, 42*(4), 369–383.

Brouthers, K. D., Brouthers, L. E., & Werner, S. (2002). Industrial sector, perceived environmental uncertainty and entry mode strategy. *Journal of Business Research, 55*(6), 495–507.

Buckley, P. J., Clegg, L. J., Cross, A. R., Xin, L., Voss, H., & Ping, Z. (2007). The determinants of Chinese outward foreign direct investment. *Journal of International Business Studies, 38*(4), 499–518.

Centraal bureau van de statistiek (CBS). (2013). *Ondernemingsklimaat.* Retrieved from http://www.cbs.nl/nl-NL/menu/themas/dossiers/ondernemingsklimaat/cijfers/default.htm. Accessed on October 24, 2013.

Ciualla, J. B. (1991). Business ethics as moral imagination. In R. E. Freeman (ed.), *Business ethics: The state of the art.* New York, NY: Oxford University Press.

Combes, P. P., Miren, L., & Mayer, T. (2005). The trade-creating effects of business and social networks: Evidence from France. *Journal of International Economics, 66*(1), 1–29.

Cowton, C. J. (1998). The use of secondary data in business ethics research. *Journal of Business Ethics, 17*(4), 423–434.

Culpan, R., & Akcaoglu, E. (2003). An examination of Turkish Direct Investments in Central and Eastern Europe and the commonwealth of independent states. In S. T. Marinova & M. A. Marinov (Eds.), *Foreign direct investment in central and eastern Europe.* London: Ashgate.

Demirbag, M., Tatoglu, E., & Glaister, K. W. (2008). Factors affecting perceptions of the Choice between acquisition and greenfield entry: The case of western FDI in an emerging market. *Management International Review, 48*(1), 5–38.

de Mooij, R. A., & Ederveen, S. (2003). Taxation and foreign direct investment: A synthesis of empirical research. *International Tax and Public Finance*, *10*, 673–693.

Deng, P. (2012). Accelerated internationalization by MNCs from emerging economies: Determinants and implications. *Organizational Dynamics*, *41*, 318–326.

Dufour, J., & Khalaf, L. (1999). *Monte Carlo test methods in econometrics. Companion to theoretical econometrics*. Oxford: Blackwell.

Dunning, J. H. (1979). Explaining changing patterns of international production: In defense of the Eclectic Theory. *Oxford Bulletin of Economics and Statistics*, *41*(4), 269–295.

Dunning, J. H., & Lundan, S. M. (2008). *Multinational enterprises and the global economy*. Cheltenham: Edward Elgar Publishing.

Erdilek, A. (2003). A comparative analysis of inward and outward FDI in Turkey. *Transnational Corporations*, *12*(3), 79–105.

Filatotchev, I., Strange, R., Piesse, J., & Lien, Y. (2007). FDI by firms from newly industrialised economies in emerging markets: Corporate governance, entry mode and location. *Journal of International Business Studies*, *38*(4), 556–572.

Gammeltoft, P., Pradhan, J. P., & Goldstein, A. (2010). Emerging multinationals, emerging theory: Macro- and micro-level perspectives. *Journal of International Management*, *16*, 95–101.

Goldstein, A., & Pusterla, F. (2010). Emerging economies' multinationals: General features and specificities of the Brazilian and Chinese cases. *International Journal of Emerging Markets*, *5*(3/4), 289–306.

Gubbi, S. R., Aulakh, P. S., Ray, S., Sarkar, M. B., & Chittoor, R. (2010). Do international acquisitions by emerging-economy firms create shareholder value? The case of Indian firms. *Journal of International Business Studies*, *41*, 397–418.

Guerrieri, P., & Pietrobelli, C. (2004). Industrial districts' evolution and technological regimes: Italy and Taiwan. *Technovation*, *24*, 899–914.

Guillén, M. F., & García-Canal, E. (2009). The American model of the multinational firm and the "new" multinationals from emerging economies. *Academy of Management Perspectives*, *23*(2), 23–35.

Harris, H. (2001). Content analysis of secondary data: A study of courage in managerial decision making. *Journal of Business Ethics*, *34*(3-4), 191–208.

Harrison, A. L., Dalkiran, E., & Elsey, E. (2000). *International business, global competition from a European perspective*. New York, NY: Oxford University Press Inc.

Harzing, A. W. (2002). Acquisitions versus greenfield investments: International strategy and management of entry modes. *Strategic Management Journal*, *23*(3), 211–227.

Head, K. (2007). *Elements of multinationals*. Berlin: Springer.

Hennart, J. F. (1982). *A theory of multinational enterprise*. Ann Arbor, MI: University of Michigan Press.

Hsieh, H., & Shannon, S. E. (2005). Three approaches to qualitative content analysis. *Qualitative Health Research*, *15*(9), 1277–1288.

IMF. (2014). International Monetary Fund, World Economic Outlook Database. Accessed on December 10, 2014.

Javorcik, B. S., Ozden, C., Spatareanu, M., & Neagu, C. (2010). Migrant networks and foreign direct investment. *Journal of Development Economics*, *94*(2), 231–241.

Johanson, J., & Vahlne, J. E. (1977). The internationalization process of the firm – A model of knowledge development and increasing foreign market commitments. *Journal of International Business Studies*, *8*(1), 23–32.

Kalotay, K., & Sulstarova, A. (2010). Modelling Russian outward FDI. *Journal of International Management, 16*(2), 131–142.

Kayam, S. S., & Hisarciklilar, M. (2009). *Determinants of Turkish FDI abroad.* Working Paper submitted to the 8th International Conference of the Middle East Economic Association.

Kentmen, C. (2008). Determinants of support for EU membership in Turkey. *European Union Politics, 9*(4), 487–510.

Kindleberger, C. P. (1969). *American business abroad: Six lectures on direct investment.* New Haven, CT: Yale University Press.

KPMG. (2014). *Corporate tax rates table.* Retrieved from http://www.kpmg.com/global/en/services/tax/tax-tools-and-resources/pages/corporate-tax-rates-table.aspx. Accessed on November 23, 2014.

Lejour, A. M., de Mooij, R. A., & Capel, C. H. (2004). *Assessing the economic implications of Turkish accession to the EU.* The Hague: CPB – Netherlands Bureau for Economic Policy Analysis.

Li, J., & Yao, F. K. (2010). The role of reference groups in international investment decisions by firms from emerging economies. *Journal of International Management, 16*(2), 143–153.

Liu, L. (2005). *China's industrial policies and the global business revolution: The case of the domestic appliance industry.* London: Routledge Curzon.

Luo, Y., & Rui, H. (2009). An ambidexterity perspective toward multinational enterprises from emerging economies. *Academy of Management Perspectives, 23*(4), 49–70.

Luo, Y., & Tung, R. (2007). International expansion of emerging market enterprises. *Journal of International Business Studies, 38*(4), 481–498.

McManus, J. (1972). The theory of the international firm. In G. Paquet (Ed.), *The multinational firm and the nation state.* Don Mills, ON: Collier-Macmillan.

Morgan, D. L. (1993). Qualitative content analysis: A guide to paths not taken. *Qualitative Health Research, 3,* 112–121.

Neuendorf, K. A. (2002). *The content analysis guidebook.* Thousand Oaks, CA: Sage.

Pitelis, C. N., & Sugden, R. (1991). *The nature of the transnational firm.* New York, NY: Routledge.

Ramamurti, R. (2008). What have we learned about emerging market MNEs? In R. Ramamurti & J. V. Singh (Eds.), *Emerging multinationals from emerging markets.* Cambridge: Cambridge University Press.

Rauch, J., & Trindade, V. (2002). Ethnic Chinese networks in international trade. *Review of Economics and Statistics, 84*(1), 116–130.

Rugman, A. M. (1981). *Inside the multinationals the economics of internal markets.* New York: Columbia University Press.

Sauvant, K. P., Maschek, W. A., & McAllister, G. (2009). *Foreign direct investment by emerging market multinational enterprises, the impact of the financial crisis and recession and challenges ahead.* Paris, France: OECD Global Forum.

Schueler, J. (2007). Hub Holland 2025. *Stichting Toekomstbeeld der Techniek.*

Shan, W., & Hamilton, W. (1991). Country-specific advantage and international cooperation. *Strategic Management Journal, 12*(6), 419–432.

Shinohara, M., Roos, H. B., & Stam, J. A. (2002). Japanese choice of a logistics hub in Europe. *International Association of Maritime Economics. Conference Proceedings,* 13–15 November, Panama.

Stucchi, T. (2012). Emerging market firms' acquisitions in advanced markets: Matching strategy with resource-, institution- and industry-based antecedents. *European Management Journal, 30*, 278–289.

TCMB. (2013). *Türkiye Cumhuriyet Merkez Bankası – Central Bank of the Republic of Turkey – Electronic data delivery system.* Retrieved from http://evds.tcmb.gov.tr/cbt.html. Accessed on October 14, 2013.

UNCTAD. (2010). *Global and regional FDI trends 2010.* New York, NY: United Nations.

UNCTAD. (2012). *World investment report: FDI from developing and transition economies: Implications for development.* New York, NY: United Nations.

UNCTAD. (2013). *World investment report 2013: Global value chains: Investment and trade for development.* New York, NY: United Nations.

Uray, N., Vardar, N., & Nacar, R. (2012). International marketing related outward FDI motives: Turkish MNC's experience in the EU. In R. Tulder, A. Erbeke, & L. Voina (Eds.), *New policy challenges for European multinationals.* Bingley, UK: Emerald Group Publishing Limited.

Wang, C., Hong, J., Kafouros, M., & Boateng, A. (2012). What drives outward FDI of Chinese firms? Testing the explanatory power of three theoretical frameworks. *International Business Review, 21*(3), 425–438.

WEF. (2014). *Global competitiveness reports.* Retrieved from http://www.weforum.org/reports. Accessed on December 10, 2014.

Williamson, O. E. (1975). *Markets and hierarchies: Analysis and antitrust implications.* New York, NY: Free Press.

Yurtdışı Türkler ve Akraba Topluluklar Başkanlığı (YTB). (2014). *Activities report.* Retrieved from http://www.ytb.gov.tr/tr/yayinlar/959-faaliyet-raporlari. Accessed on November 25, 2014.

Zaheer, S., & Mosakowski, E. (1997). The dynamics of the liability of foreignness. *Strategic Management Journal, 18*(6), 439–464.

Zhao, W., Liu, L., & Zhao, T. (2010). The contribution of outward direct investment to productivity changes within China, 1991–2007. *Journal of International Management, 28*(2), 121–130.

APPENDIX A

Table A1. Motivation Categories and Definition.

Motivations	Short Description
Hub	Presenting themselves as an EU company and/or making use of hub features of these countries in order to expand their businesses within and to other countries
Presence of Turkish migrants	Serving the Turkish migrant population
Strategic-asset seeking	Acquiring strategic-assets in order to become more competitive
Market	Widening the geographic footprint
Tax	Particularly making use of only the tax advantages of a country
Institutional	Pushed out of own country because of a weak institutional environment or pulled away to an European county because of a strong institutional environment
Other motivations	
Efficiency	Enhanced efficiency
Following competition	Following competition to certain countries
Geo-political	Mandated by the home government to perform FDI
Presence of other Turkish EMNEs	Following other Turkish EMNEs to aim an alliance with them

APPENDIX B

Table B1. Typical Examples for Motivation Coding.

Source	Content	Motivation
Newspaper: Hürriyet. 19-8-2011 Video: Bloomberg HT interview. May 2012	Cem Bozkurt. CEO of Alvimedica said that "Amsterdam is a well-positioned place in Europe to start the international expansion. because Netherlands has a high reputation in the expertise on medical devices ...." Bozkurt said further that: "Amsterdam will be used as a springboard to the rest of the world because of its ideal policies. Bozkurt states further: "the Netherlands is an ideal country to use it as a springboard ..." Bozkurt said further: "The Netherlands is the best country that matches the logistic deficiencies which Turkey faces in the international markets ..." Bozkurt said further: "The Netherlands Foreign Investment Agency worked like an internal department for us when we asked help of them ... Within 10 days we received information regarding possible offices which we could hire ... "We received in the same period an invitation of the Dutch tax department in which they informed us about the taxation policies and advantages in respect of other countries." "Within 2 months we had established an office in the Netherlands. while we are still busy with establishing an office in India which already takes 8 months and we are still waiting for approvals ...".	Hub motivation (the Netherlands)
Newspaper: Hürriyet Daily News 12-5-2012 Milliyet. 10-5-2012	Ziylan Group Chair Mehmet Ziylan told daily Hürriyet: "Italy is the heart of the global shoe sector. This is going to be the first step in carrying Ziylan Group into the global shoe league. Mehmet Ziylan said further: "The way we see it. this step we're taking today in Italy where the heart of the world shoe industry beats is the first in the Ziylan Group's march toward the major league of global brands ... the Lumberjack operation does not simply mean taking over the management of an Italian brand whose design and quality are acknowledged throughout the world. It also means we're getting a big-name brand that has strong foundations. enjoys widespread recognition coupled with a broad network. and offers new prospects."	Hub motivation (Italy)

Table B1. *(Continued)*

Source	Content	Motivation
Newspaper Hürriyet. 26-9-2010	CEO of Güllüoğlu. Nejat Güllü states that: "Amsterdam is a well-known location with a high presence of Turkish people which we can serve with our Turkish delights (Baklava's)."	Presence of Turkish migrants
Newspaper: Turkish Weekly. 31-10-2005	Vestel bought Cabot in 2001. The goal of the company, 90% of which is Vestel's and the remaining 10% is the employees', is to become the leader of the European market. Vice manager Alp Arslan Somyurek explains their success: "The company exchanges engineers for three or four months with the Cabot's branch at Izmir Urla and thereby communicates the know-how from Britain to Turkey." "Nowadays. we sell more advanced ones. but we earn more."	Strategic-asset motivation
Newspaper: Milliyet 10-8-2006	The chair group of Desa Deri Melih Çelet said: "It is time to show the world our leather designs and trends to the world. The first step set is that we opened a store in Debenhams in Oxford Street along with other famous brands."	Market motivation

FOREIGN ENTRY MODE CHOICES OF EMERGING MARKET MULTINATIONALS: THE ROLE OF INSTITUTIONAL VOIDS IN SHAPING STRATEGIC COGNITION

Michael Hilb

ABSTRACT

This paper introduces a conceptual framework to assess the foreign market entry behavior of emerging market multinationals (EMMs). By introducing strategic cognition as the underlying theoretical perspective, this paper postulates that different levels of institutional voids in home markets shape the strategic cognition of EMMs, influencing their market entry behavior due to the prevalence of organizational imprinting in the early stages of internationalization. The paper aims to contribute to the strategic cognition literature by introducing emerging markets as a relevant context in which to apply and extend current thinking. Additionally, it aims to contribute to the institutional

Emerging Economies and Multinational Enterprises
Advances in International Management, Volume 28, 471–502

ISSN: 1571-5027/doi:10.1108/S1571-502720150000028020

voids literature by providing a cognitive framework of behavioral patterns that is rationalized by institutional voids. Finally, the paper contributes to the entry mode literature by proposing strategic cognition as a relevant moderator for foreign entry mode choices, particularly those of EMMs.

Keywords: Foreign entry mode choice; market entry; strategic cognition; institutional voids; emerging market multinational

INTRODUCTION

Foreign market entries are key strategic decisions of any multinational company (Liang, Musteen, & Datta, 2009; Pehrsson, 2008). This is even more relevant in the case of emerging market multinationals (EMMs),[1] which are nearly on pace with multinationals from developed markets in establishing their global footprint (Guillén & García-Canal, 2009). There is an ongoing debate as to whether the current set of theoretical frameworks is sufficient to explain EMMs' internationalization behavior (Cuervo-Cazurra, 2012; Narula, 2012). While some (e.g., Rugman, 2010) argue that current theories can explain EMM behavior, others proclaim the need to develop new paradigms (e.g., Luo & Tung, 2007; Mathews, 2006) or propose that current thinking be extended and reconfigured (e.g., Cuervo-Cazurra, 2012; Ramamurti, 2009).

By subscribing to the latter view, I propose to integrate three complementary theoretical perspectives to better understand the entry mode choices of EMMs: strategic cognition as the underlying theoretical framework, institutional voids (IV) as antecedents, and foreign entry mode choice as the outcome. I will thereby build on existing studies linking strategic cognition and foreign entry mode research, though not for EMMs in particular (e.g., Liang et al., 2009), and connecting the home effects of EMMs and foreign entry mode choices without considering strategic cognition (e.g., Luo & Wang, 2012).

Strategic cognition is well suited to serve as the theoretical foundation for the propositional framework, given its extensive body of research as shown in multiple comprehensive reviews (e.g., Hodgkinson & Healey, 2008; Narayanan, Zane, & Kemmerer, 2011; Porac & Thomas, 2002; Walsh, 1995). There is, however, limited research on applying the concept in an emerging market context and specifically linking it to institutional voids, despite an established view on the importance of environmental factors (e.g., Rajagopalan, Rasheed, & Datta, 1993). This paper intends to fill this gap.

When it comes to the antecedent of the strategic cognition of EMMs, the concept of institutional voids offers promising perspectives. Although their existence (e.g., Khanna & Palepu, 1997; Meyer, 2001) and their impact on emerging market players' behavior in their home markets (e.g., Hoskisson, Kim, White, & Tihanyi, 2004; Khanna & Rivkin, 2006; Khanna & Yafeh, 2007; Kim, Kim, & Hoskisson, 2010) and host markets are widely acknowledged (e.g., Luo & Wang, 2012; Narula, 2012), Cuervo-Cazurra and Ramamurti (2014) call for further research to assess the home market effects on internationalization, as most studies thus far have focused on the impact of host market environmental conditions on entry mode decisions (e.g., Meyer, Estrin, Bhaumik, & Peng, 2009). Hence, this study aims to contribute to the emerging body of research on institutional voids by deepening the understanding of how institutional voids shape the behavior of EMMs at home and abroad.

Finally, this paper seeks to contribute to the mature body of foreign entry mode choice research (Shaver, 2013). The empirical richness of this stream offers the optimal foundation to derive baseline effects. As this paper views foreign entry mode choice as a strategic decision by EMMs, the integration of strategic cognition holds the potential to add granularity to the entry mode research as recommended (e.g., Hennart & Slangen, 2015). As such, the paper also attempts to contribute to the ongoing debate on EMM idiosyncrasies.

This paper unfolds as follows: It first provides a conceptual overview of the three bodies of literature in focus (i.e., strategic cognition, institutional voids, and foreign entry mode choices) by providing definitions, highlighting key findings, identifying research gaps, and defining the proposed contribution in greater detail. It then goes on to postulate the propositional framework in a three-step approach: First, I theorize the impact of the high and low level IV contexts on the strategic cognition of companies. Second, I postulate the baseline effect of the host country variables on the entry mode choices based on past research. Finally, I formulate how the strategic cognition of EMMs moderates the impact of the host country characteristics on market entry mode choices. I conclude by discussing the potential contributions and delineate limitations and directions for further research.

CONCEPTUAL OVERVIEW

Existing Research on Strategic Cognition

"Strategic cognition," first coined by Schwenk (1988) and by Porac, Thomas, and Baden-Fuller (1989), can be defined as the "linkages between cognitive structures and decision processes in strategic management with respect to strategy formulation and implementation" (Porac & Thomas, 2002, p. 165). These are based "on an actor's beliefs about the linkage between the choice of actions and the subsequent impact of those actions on outcomes" (Gavetti & Levinthal, 2000, p. 113), extending beyond individual cognition (Hodgkinson, 2005). Strategic cognition is rooted in the tradition of earlier views on cognition in strategy (e.g., Daft & Weick, 1984; Huff, 1990; Mintzberg, 1978).

With this understanding, Walsh (1995) advocates for the importance of distinguishing between the structure and the process of strategic cognition. While structure can be defined as "the relatively stable characteristics and repeated patterns of behavior," processes are "the (cognitive) activities taking place in organizations" (Narayanan et al., 2011, p. 309). For the sake of this paper, I will focus on the three structural dimensions as defined by Narayanan et al. (2011): organizational identity, strategy frames, and organizational routines, which are briefly introduced hereinafter.

Strategy frames are "the knowledge structure that informs strategic decisions, a cognitive template that individuals impose on the information environment to give it form and meaning" (Narayanan et al., 2011, p. 309). Kaplan (2011) suggests the interchangeable use of the terms "category," "cognitive frame," or "schema." They act as filters for management decisions (Huff, 1982) and cannot always be considered homogenous (Priem, Lyon, & Dess, 1999) or core (Nadkarni & Narayanan, 2007).

Organizational identity, as coined by Albert and Whetten (1985), "represents organization members' collective understanding of the features presumed to be central and relatively permanent" (Narayanan et al., 2011, p. 309). Organizational identity first defines the boundary of the firm, distinguishing an organization from the market (Kogut & Zander, 1996). It can be both a source of inertia (e.g., Abrahamson & Fombrun, 1994; Pratt & Foreman, 2000) as well as a driver of growth (e.g., Gioia, Schultz, & Corley, 2000). An organization may simultaneously assume various identities (Corley, 2004); however, organizational identity may not be stable over time (Gioia et al., 2000).

Organizational routines are "recurring patterns of behavior of multiple organizational members involved in performing organizational tasks" (Feldman & Rafaeli, 2002, p. 311). The term "routine" indicates that those activities are not deliberate.

Apart from distinguishing between the structure and the process of strategic cognition, various meta-studies (e.g., Hodgkinson & Healey, 2008; Narayanan et al., 2011; Porac & Thomas, 2002; Walsh, 1995) provide an overview of the many antecedents and outcomes assessed in the research on strategic cognition. In particular, the role of contextual factors, such as uncertainty, complexity, and munificence, is regarded as important antecedents to strategic cognition (Rajagopalan et al., 1993). In that sense, strategic cognition should not be seen as the opposite, but, rather, as a mechanism to translate contextual influences into action (Bogner & Barr, 2000; Nadkarni & Barr, 2008). Hence, of the three behavioral strategy frameworks identified by Powell, Lovallo, and Fox (2011, p. 1373) – the reductionist, pluralist, and contextualist – this paper subscribes to the latter, emphasizing "the primacy of context" in shaping strategic cognition.

While the rich literature on strategic cognition provides ample insights to build on, such as the three dimensions of strategic cognition introduced above, there are also gaps to be filled. On the one hand, despite a number of studies linking strategic cognition to various antecedents and outcomes, limited research has been conducted linking it to entry mode research (e.g., Liang et al., 2009) or employing institutional voids as an antecedent. By doing so, this paper intends to apply strategic cognition in the context of an important player that has not yet warranted much attention in the strategic cognition literature, the EMM, though the relevance of mental models in better understanding EMM behavior has been recognized (e.g., Contractor, 2014; Dhanaraj & Khanna, 2011; Nonaka & Zhu, 2012).

Existing Research on Institutional Voids

It is widely acknowledged that formal and informal institutions (Peng, 2000) matter in well-functioning markets, as they define the "rules of the game" (North, 1990) and the "terms of action" (Fligstein, 2001). Where such rules are incomplete or absent, "institutional voids"[2] occur (Khanna & Palepu, 1997; Meyer, 2001). Institutional voids, therefore, can be defined as "the absence of specialist intermediaries, regulatory systems, and contract-enforcing mechanisms" in an economy (Khanna & Palepu, 2006, p. 62). Building on new institutional economics and the transaction cost theory, Khanna and Palepu (1997) argue that institutional voids can help explain the existence of certain types of economic players, such as credibility enhancers, information analyzers, distributors, or transaction facilitators (Khanna & Palepu, 2013), among others, and diversified business groups[3] (e.g., Hoskisson et al., 2004; Khanna & Rivkin, 2006; Khanna & Yafeh, 2007; Kim et al., 2010), and can help to explain certain company behavior, such as the reliance on personal networks (Puffer, McCarthy, & Boisot, 2010), the emergence of rather weak governance standards (Khanna & Palepu, 2000), or the influence on family ownership patterns (Chakrabarty, 2009). Others have linked IV to the emergence of "institutional entrepreneurs," as proposed by DiMaggio (1988) (e.g., Mair & Martí, 2009; Mair, Martí, & Ventresca, 2012; Tracey & Phillips, 2011), or the role of nonmarket players such as NGOs (Boddewyn & Doh, 2011; Doh, Lawton, & Rajwani, 2012). The growing interest in institutional voids on the part of international business scholars must also be viewed in the context of the emergence of the institution-based view in international business strategy (e.g., Cantwell, Dunning, & Lundan, 2010; Marquis & Raynard, 2015; Peng, Wang, & Jiang, 2008).

When it comes to linking institutional voids to internationalization, two behavioral patterns are proposed: institutional escapism and institutional leverage (Luo & Wang, 2012). Whereas institutional escapism (e.g., Witt & Lewin, 2007; Yamakawa, Peng, & Deeds, 2008) proposes that firms internationalize in order to escape the poor institutional contexts in their home markets, institutional leverage (e.g., Boisot & Meyer, 2008; Cuervo-Cazurra & Genc, 2008) considers internationalization as a means of taking advantage of the experience gained in mastering complex institutional contexts. Cuervo-Cazurra and Ramamurti (2014) further stress that institutional voids equip EMMs with both advantages and disadvantages when they internationalize.

Although the literature has successfully linked the behavior of emerging market players to institutional voids in their home market and assumes an effect on their behavior abroad, the perspective still benefits from further conceptualization, integration, and application. This paper aims to provide one way to achieve all three by applying institutional voids in a clearly defined setting, integrating institutional voids with strategic cognition and, consequently proposing a cognitive conceptualization which shall help uncover the heterogeneity of the impact of institutional voids on EMMs' entry mode choices depending on their strategic cognition.

Existing Research on Foreign Entry Mode Choice

Ever since Brouthers' (2002) seminal article, the inquiry into the entry mode[4] choice of companies has become one of the most researched topics in international business (Brouthers & Hennart, 2007; Canabal & White, 2008; Shaver, 2013). Findings from foreign entry mode research, however, remain inconclusive, and ambiguity could even be declared the rule (Morschett, Schramm-Klein, & Swoboda, 2010). The reason is threefold: First, foreign entry mode choices have a high level of interdependency, which makes it impossible to address all factors in one single model (Shaver, 2013). Second, different internationalization theories tend to be complementary rather than exclusive in explaining the behavior of companies expanding abroad (Canabal & White, 2008). Finally, there is ongoing debate on how to define the entry modes (Hennart & Slangen, 2015). While some argue that the subsidiary's ownership mode (i.e., joint venture or wholly owned subsidiary) and establishment mode (i.e., acquisition or greenfield) should be viewed in sequence (e.g., Pan & Tse, 2000), others argue for a more simplified perspective. For the sake of this paper, I will subscribe to the latter and solely consider the ownership mode – that is, distinguish between cooperative operating modes, such as joint ventures, and wholly owned subsidiaries, ignoring other potential entry modes as outlined by Welch, Benito, and Petersen (2008), such as contractual modes (e.g., franchising, licensing, contracting, alliances) or exporting.

From the comprehensive body of entry mode research, three streams are of particular interest for the purpose of this paper: existing links to strategic cognition, existing links to institutional voids, and the state of empirical evidence regarding determinants of foreign entry mode choices. First, as internationalization and market entries are considered the central strategic decisions of any multinational company, Pehrsson (2008) argues for integrating the strategy perspective into the foreign operating mode discussion. Liang et al. (2009) demonstrate in their study that entry mode choices are linked to strategic types as defined by Miles, Snow, Meyer, and Coleman (1978), such as defenders, prospectors, analyzers, and reactors. However, they do not address the role of EMMs in particular. This paper intends to fill that gap.

Second, there is a rapidly growing body of research that links institutional voids to company behavior based on the understanding of ongoing interaction between companies and institutions (Banalieva & Sarathy, 2011). It is widely acknowledged that home country conditions influence EMMs' behavior (e.g., Luo & Wang, 2012; Narula, 2012; Ramamurti,

2012) and may result in firm-specific advantages, which are valuable in their own unique way (Cuervo-Cazurra & Ramamurti, 2014). At the same time, Cuervo-Cazurra (2012, p. 163) advocates for great specificity with regard to "which conditions of country of origin." This is one of the objectives of the propositional framework outlined in this paper.

Finally, the rich body of entry mode research has been assessed in a number of meta-studies (e.g., Andersen, 1997; Brouthers & Hennart, 2007; Canabal & White, 2008; Morschett et al., 2010; Sarkar & Cavusgil, 1996; Zhao, Luo, & Suh, 2004), and these provide an excellent starting point to establish the baseline effects. Furthermore, extant research is still undecided on the degree of idiosyncrasy of EMMs. This paper attempts to address this question as well.

THEORETICAL DEVELOPMENT

The integration of the three streams of literature described above shall be guided by three key questions: First, what is the impact of the different levels of institutional voids on the strategic cognition of EMMs (resulting in propositions 1a, 1b, and 1c)? Second, what is the baseline effect of host country institutional factors on foreign entry mode choices (as outlined in propositions 2a, 3a, and 4a)? And finally, to what extent does strategic cognition persist if these companies internationalize, and how does this impact the entry mode choices of these companies (described in propositions 2b, 3b, and 4b) (Fig. 1)?

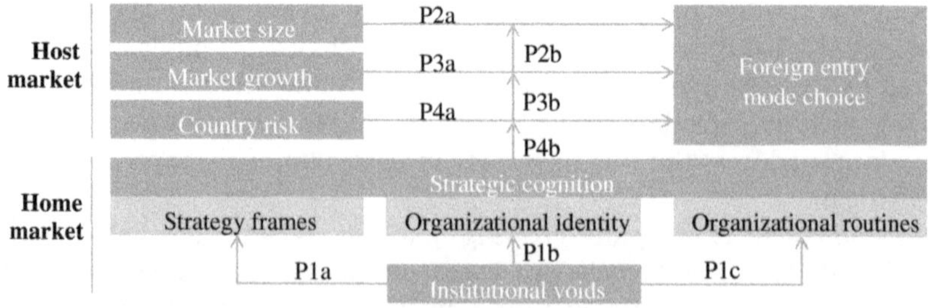

Fig. 1. Framework for Assessing Foreign Entry Mode Choices of Emerging Market Multinationals.

Home Country Institutional Voids as a Driver for Emerging Market Players' Strategic Cognition

The institutional setting is one of the many proposed antecedents to strategic cognition (e.g., Bogner & Barr, 2000; Rajagopalan et al., 1993). The concept of institutional voids can be considered a construct particularly well suited to serve as an antecedent in order to better understand the strategic cognition of emerging market players, given its acclaimed impact on the behavior of those firms, as outlined earlier. I shall distinguish between three ways in which institutional voids are expected to shape the strategic cognition of economic players in this particular environment: the perception of institutional voids as a source of value creation through opportunity spotting, rent seeking, as well as the perception of institutional voids as a source of uncertainty that is countered by interdependence securing.

Opportunity spotting is at the core of how institutional voids are conceptualized in terms of transaction cost economics: institutional voids are characterized by the absence of intermediaries and regulatory frameworks (Khanna & Palepu, 2006), which offers opportunities for "institutional entrepreneurs" (DiMaggio, 1988) to emerge and fill those gaps. This is particularly true in an emerging market context (e.g., Mair & Martí, 2009; Tracey & Phillips, 2011). Following this logic, institutional voids are likely to result in opportunity spotting as one of the key orientations of economic players in an emerging market context expected to influence strategic cognition.

A second behavioral pattern derived from institutional voids that is likely to shape strategic cognition is *rent seeking*. The concept, which originated with Tullock (1967) and was later coined by Krueger (1974), proposes that people strive to obtain benefits through manipulating the social and political environment without creating wealth for the larger public. In the case of markets with high IV levels, it is well established that the imperfect institutional arrangement invites ample opportunities for rent seeking, be it in the form of lax anti-trust enforcement or inadequate protective measures. This often contributes to the dominance of diversified business groups in many of those markets (e.g., Elango & Pattnaik, 2007; Fisman & Khanna, 2004; Khanna & Palepu, 1997, 2000) as they share a key advantage: one member can access resources, such as political decision power, for all other member firms, thereby establishing new opportunities not available to unaffiliated groups (Chittoor, Kale, & Puranam, 2014; Ramachandran, Manikandan, & Pant, 2013). This perceived logic is likely to make rent seeking a key strategic rationale forming strategic cognition, in contrast to contexts with low IV levels. There, conglomerates have been out of favor since the emergence of the core competence concept in the 1990s (Prahalad & Hamel, 1990). In other words, because capital markets have proven to be more efficient than conglomerates in allocating capital in developed market contexts, there is little incentive for an economic player to operate in a business group structure.

Finally, institutional voids are often associated with uncertainty, which companies try to overcome by either escaping (Witt & Lewin, 2007; Yamakawa et al., 2008) or by *interdependence securing* – that is, by establishing an alternative set of networks to compensate for the lack of trust in formal institutions (Puffer et al., 2010). This is in line with the well-established impact of risk perception on strategic cognition (e.g., Kaplan, 2011; Makhija & Stewart, 2002).

My own application of the three behavioral patterns rationalized by institutional voids shaping strategic cognition draws on the three dimensions of strategic cognition identified by Narayanan et al. (2011): strategy frames, organizational identity, and organizational routines. In this context, it should also be noted that institutional voids allow for an explanation of a variety of contexts with widely disparate levels of institutional development (Rodrik, 2008), and this must be understood as a continuum and not a binary concept (Tracey & Phillips, 2011). As a result, I will present the three dimensions of strategic cognition as a continuum, while focusing on the high level of IV contexts for theorizing. I present each of the three dimensions next, assessing the impact of the three behavioral patterns.

The Entrepreneurial (versus Managerial) Nature of Strategy Frames

Strategy frames provide a "cognitive template that individuals impose on the information environment to give it form and meaning" (Narayanan et al., 2011, p. 309) in guiding strategic decisions in a company. They constitute the underlying assumptions of value protection and creation. In accord with Stevenson (1983), who proposed the dichotomy of manager/administrator versus entrepreneur, Hilb and Casas (2015) further refine this logic by proposing three distinct frames – that is, the entrepreneurial, which is concerned with value creation beyond existing boundaries; the strategic, which addresses relative value protection (i.e., value creation within boundaries); and the administrative, which is oriented toward nominal value protection. For the sake of this paper, I shall highlight the managerial versus the entrepreneurial nature of the strategy frames. The former is concerned with nominal and relative value protection, while the latter is oriented toward value creation.

The three behavioral patterns rationalized by institutional voids strongly support the emergence of entrepreneurially driven strategy frames in high level IV contexts, which is also underscored by the entrepreneur-friendly traits of emerging market contexts (Tracey & Phillips, 2011) and the importance of growth in emerging markets, factors that extend beyond the fact that many emerging markets have experienced rapid growth (Guillén & García-Canal, 2013). While the links between the shaping of entrepreneurial strategy frames and opportunity spotting are obvious, such as how identifying and realizing new opportunities quickly and continuously is likely to shape the entrepreneurial mindset, the connection also becomes clear in the case of rent-seeking behavior. An entrepreneurial mindset is at the core of both identifying and capturing rents. First of all, identifying both rents at risk and new rent-seeking opportunities requires a strong entrepreneurial orientation, as it is all about navigating in unchartered and informal territory. Second, securing those opportunities requires influence, which is often associated with economic wealth accumulated through entrepreneurial growth-driven strategies, resulting in interdependencies between rent-seeking and rent-granting entities. That is, large, well-connected players tend to have more political capital, which they can invest to promote their interests. In an environment with perfect institutional settings, however, the market is more competitive, because the potential to influence the regulatory framework is limited. As a result, competition is driven more by economic than political means. This leads to the first proposition:

> **Proposition 1a.** Strategy frames dominant in companies based in high-level institutional void contexts are of more of an entrepreneurial than a managerial nature.

The Embedded (versus Independent) Nature of Organizational Identity

The organizational identity understood as the "collective understanding of the features presumed to be central and relatively permanent" in an organization (Narayanan et al., 2011, p. 309) answers the question "Who are we?" and drives the company's self-perception within its community. Behavioral patterns rationalized by institutional voids are likely to affect the interpretation of the relevant community and the role of the company within. In high-level IV contexts, companies are likely to see themselves as embedded in a wider fabric of economic, social, and political players closely contributing to and benefiting from each other. In low-level IV environments, on the other hand, companies perceive themselves as players within a given industry, influenced by national or global competitive forces that just happen to be based in a given social and political environment.

This is supported by assessing the impact of the three dominant behavioral patterns rationalized in high-level IV contexts. The identification of institutional opportunities requires a high level of embeddedness – that is, economic players view themselves as part of a clearly defined institutional framework. This mental understanding is critical in assessing the value of an institutional opportunity, as well as the most effective way to capture it. Rent-seeking behavior is also likely to promote the embedded nature of organizational identity. Because rent seeking is only legitimized if the economic players recognize their role in contributing to and benefiting from being part of a social and political community, it will foster the *raison d'être* as an embedded rather than an independent player. Finally, the behavioral trait of securing interdependencies between different players in high-level IV contexts clearly strengthens the organizational identity as a contributing player in a closely knitted community. Hence, I postulate the following proposition:

> **Proposition 1b.** The organizational identity dominant in companies based in high-level institutional void contexts is of more of an embedded than an independent nature.

The Relational (versus Transactional) Nature of Organizational Routines

Organizational routines, understood as "recurring patterns of behavior of multiple organizational members involved in performing organizational tasks" (Feldman & Rafaeli, 2002, p. 311), are the third dimension of strategic cognition. According to the definition of a market, economic players interact with other players to create or preserve value. Hence, one key routine of any firm is its approach to collaborating with other organizations, whether building relational capital and trust over time or engaging in more transactional relationships. The latter, however, requires well-functioning markets and legal systems, which are often absent in high-level IV contexts (Khanna & Palepu, 2013). Furthermore, the three behavioral patterns of players in emerging market contexts support the relational nature of organizational identity in high-level IV environments (Table 1).

The identification of institutional opportunities is unlikely to happen through transactional forms given the nature of the activity. A valuable opportunity is hard to formalize and price adequately, which would be

Table 1. Institutional Void Rationalized Behavioral Patterns Shaping Strategic Cognition of Emerging Market Players.

Behavioral Patterns Rationalized by the Existence of Institutional Voids		Dimensions of Strategic Cognition Shaped by Behavioral Patterns in Markets with High Levels of Institutional Voids		
		P1a: Entrepreneurial (vs. managerial) nature of strategy frames	*P1b*: Embedded (vs. independent) nature of organizational identity	*P1c*: Relational (vs. transactional) nature of organizational routines
		… are characterized by a strong orientation toward …		
Opportunity spotting	Lack of institutional solutions provide business opportunities	Identifying and realizing market opportunities quickly	Gaining access to opportunities through deep understanding of societal fabric	Ensuring information advantages through leveraging relationships
Rent seeking	Imperfect institutions allow for preferential rules and regulations	Realizing changes in power structures and dynamics instantly	Seeking legitimacy for rent seekers and rent grantors	Building on relational strength to create and safeguard rents
Interdependence securing	Informal networks compensate for lack of trust in formal institutions	Utilizing networks to identify and advance opportunities	Becoming trusted contributor to community	Strengthening and extending networks based on strong relational ties

required to facilitate an efficient transaction. Therefore, the relevance of opportunity spotting is likely to reinforce the relational nature of organizational routines. A similar logic applies when it comes to rent seeking. The informal nature of influencing political players to establish the conditions for rent seeking favors strong relational capabilities, as does securing interdependencies. This leads us to the following proposition:

> **Proposition 1c.** Organizational routines dominant in companies based in high-level institutional void contexts are of more of a relational than a transactional nature.

The Baseline Effects of Host Country Institutional Factors on the Foreign Market Entry Mode Choice

Andersson, Cuervo-Cazurra, and Nielsen (2014) stress the importance of being explicit regarding the baseline effect and underlying logic before elaborating on the moderation effect to ensure that the underlying theoretical explanations are consistent. The best way to test the validity of the strategic cognition of the EMM construct is to analyze it within the framework of a well-established body of knowledge, that is, foreign entry mode choices. This research stream includes a vast array of studies that determine how companies operate in foreign markets by examining such contextual factors as home and host country conditions, as well as industry- and firm-specific characteristics. For instance, in a meta-study focused exclusively on external variables, Morschett et al. (2010) found that only 5 of the 13 factors studied play a significant role in explaining the choice of mode: market size, market growth, country risks, legal restrictions, and the culture of the home country expressed by power distance acceptance.

I suggest that in the context of this paper, the power distance acceptance factor is not a key focus because the strategic cognition of the EMM construct is embedded in the institutional setting of the home country through the link to institutional voids. That is, the construct's organizational identity dimension fully encompasses the assumption that in high-level IV contexts, companies tend to favor control and hierarchy because of a lack of trust. In fact, the proposed construct may even offer an alternative approach to one of the most contentious issues in entry mode research: the impact of culture on foreign entry mode choices. That is, despite a common-sense view that culture matters, Harzing (2003,

p. 75), among others, argues that "an almost blind confidence in one specific measurement" (i.e., Hofstede's cultural dimensions) has led researchers to overestimate the role of cultural distance. Similarly, Tihanyi, Griffith, and Russell (2005, p. 270), in their extensive meta-study, caution against oversimplifying the role of culture and call for "substantial additional research" to fully understand this complex relationship. The legal restrictions are also not the focus here because the statutory limitations set by host countries define the firms' foreign entry mode choices, limit their options (Gomes-Casseres, 1990), and likely override any other considerations (Brouthers, 2002).

Therefore, I shall concentrate on the first three key factors identified by Morschett et al. (2010) explaining the choice of entry mode but from the perspective of the host country: host market size, host market growth, and host country risks. I define the host country as the foreign country of entry of the EMM. I define the home market as the domestic country of heritage of the EMM, ignoring special cases where cross-country listings or changes in ownership or management may distort the home country orientation.

The Relationship between Host Market Size and Foreign Entry Mode Choice

Host market size is often considered a key determinant of market attractiveness, given the profit potential that can be expected from such a market (e.g., Brouthers, 2002; Randøy & Dibrell, 2002). A key driver in terms of attractiveness stems from the expected economies of scale (Agarwal & Ramaswami, 1992), which also make it more efficient to internalize activities according to the transaction cost theory (Williamson, 1985). As a result, a larger host market is likely to be considered more strategic than smaller markets, which calls for more control to reap the full benefits and control the risks. Higher returns are expected to compensate for the higher associated risks (Agarwal, 1994), as failure in such a market also poses a higher potential for fallout (Gomes-Casseres, 1990). The expectation of higher future cash flows increases the inclination to make upfront investments, which is likely to be reflected in the establishment of a wholly owned subsidiary (e.g., Buckley & Casson, 1996; Ekeledo & Sivakumar, 1998). These arguments lead to the following proposition:

> **Proposition 2a.** Greater host market size is positively associated with the formation of wholly owned subsidiaries rather than cooperative operating modes.

The Relationship between Host Market Growth and Foreign Entry Mode Choice

Host market growth is usually considered to be the second key driver of market attractiveness. The underlying features, however, are different when compared to market size. Time is money, and any delay can result in missed opportunity (Hennart & Larimo, 1998) and may also result in opportunity costs (Chang & Rosenzweig, 2001). In particular, an acquisition or creation of a new entity is usually time consuming and also entails the risks that the local company will become less inclined to share knowledge (Hennart, 1991). As such, any entry mode choice that can be quickly realized is usually preferred, allowing companies to tap into critical capabilities faster than building them from scratch (Madhok, 1998), which usually favors cooperative operating modes, as reflected in the following proposition:

> **Proposition 3a.** Greater host market growth is positively associated with cooperative operating modes rather than the formation of wholly owned subsidiaries.

The Relationship between Host Country Risk and Foreign Entry Mode Choice

Host country risk, defined as the level of uncertainty resulting from the political and social conditions in a host country, is another important factor for companies preferring a specific entry mode. This definition complements the purely economic perspective applied to the two previous factors that comprise host market attractiveness: host market size and host market growth. The literature proposes two alternative corporate reactions to perceived country risk. Whereas some authors argue that high host country risks reduce companies' inclinations to make large investments entailed with acquisitions (e.g., Hildebrandt & Weiss, 1997), proponents of the transaction cost approach view an acquisition as a means to mitigate those risks through internalization (e.g., Contractor & Kundu, 1998). As Morschett et al. (2010) point out, the empirical evidence primarily supports the first argument, as high-risk environments call for additional flexibility to change modes if needed (Anderson & Gatignon, 1986; Erramilli & Rao, 1993). Furthermore, a smaller engagement at the beginning provides more options for future moves (Brouthers, Brouthers, & Werner, 2008). This leads to the following proposition:

Proposition 4a. Greater host country risk is positively associated with cooperative operating modes rather than the formation of wholly owned subsidiaries.

The Moderating Effect of Strategic Cognition of EMMs on the Aforementioned Baseline Relationships

In order to determine the impact of strategic cognition of EMMs on foreign entry mode choices, I must address both a theoretical issue, to what extent strategic cognition shaped in a home context persists in decisions related to a host market, and a methodological question, how to treat strategic cognition as a moderator for entry mode choices.

Let us start with the *theoretical* discussion. If I assume a distinct strategic cognition of EMMs, there are two competing dynamics that come into play in entry mode decisions: organizational imprinting and organizational learning. Broadly defined, organizational imprinting is "a process whereby, during a brief period of susceptibility, a focal entity develops characteristics that reflect prominent features of the environment, and these characteristics continue to persist despite significant environmental changes in subsequent periods" (Marquis & Tilcsik, 2013, p. 199). Applied to the strategic cognition of EMMs, organizational imprinting assumes that strategic cognition shaped by contextual factors in the home markets will persist, even when companies operate in foreign markets. Although he did not coin the term, the concept, when applied to the management literature, has its roots in Stinchcombe's (1965) seminal article, which describes how organizations are influenced by their founding environment and how this influence persists over time (the concept of imprinting originated in biology, for a detailed overview, see Marquis & Tilcsik, 2013). Since then, organizational imprinting has been applied to various contexts on various levels (see Marquis & Tilcsik, 2013 for examples).

The alternative explanations based on the learning school of thought (Argyris & Schön, 1978) postulate that companies would purposefully adjust their strategic cognition based on experience and learning. As a result, they will adopt the dominant strategic cognition in the host country context over time.

In line with other research (e.g., Cuervo-Cazurra & Ramamurti, 2014; Ramamurti, 2012), this paper subscribes to a time-dependent view in determining the relevance of the two dynamics at play. While the organizational imprinting hypothesis holds for the early phase of EMM behavior in foreign markets, learning will become dominant in later stages. Lessard and Lucea (2009), for instance, find that EMMs (i.e., Mexican firms) retain their imprint as they internationalize. Goldstein (2009), on the other hand, notes that the EMMs' home country affiliation wanes over time, in particular, if the owner is from another country or the company is listed on another stock market. Hence, it is fair to expect the imprinting effect to diminish over time (Ramamurti, 2012) given the need for foreign subsidiaries to adapt to the local conditions of the host markets under isomorphic pressure. In addition, the economic and institutional development of both the host and home countries may diminish contextual differences over time (Cuervo-Cazurra & Ramamurti, 2014).

I take these findings into account by treating the strategic cognition of EMMs as a moderator, with a particular focus on developing hypotheses on EMM behavior in emerging market contexts. From a *methodological* point of view, moderators must be treated with caution, particularly in an entry mode context. Andersson et al. (2014) highlight the importance of defining whether a moderator changes the nature (differential predictor) or the strength of the relationship (differential validity) a priori. In this case, I assume that strategic cognition moderates the strength and not the nature of the baseline relationship – that is, I assume differential validity. I will theorize about the expected moderating effect of the strategic cognition of EMMs on the aforementioned baseline relationships in the following section.

The Moderating Effect of Strategic Cognition on the Host Market Size-Foreign Entry Mode Choice Baseline Relationship

As stated in proposition 2a, greater host market size is generally positively associated with the formation of wholly owned subsidiaries rather than cooperative operating modes.

In the case of players from high-level IV markets, that is, EMMs, this effect is expected to be even stronger given the impact of strategic cognition. First of all, the entrepreneurial nature of strategy frames is likely to strengthen the need for rapid decisions and full control as the opportunity is considered attractive. There will be even less appetite for a sophisticated, formalized governance structure, which would be necessary in the case of collaborative operating modes. As a result, EMMs may also be inclined to preserve the identity of the companies they take over rather than fully integrate them (Kale, Singh, & Raman, 2009). A slightly smaller strengthening moderation is expected by the embedded nature of the companies' organizational identity, which compels the EMM to closely identify itself with the home market's political and social fabric and therefore offers little interest or confidence in splitting identity by aspiring to a similar assimilation in the host country's fabric. This may contrast an intuitive assumption that EMMs may try to emulate their embeddedness approach abroad. This view, however, neglects the time and efforts needed to do so, in particular in the case of a large market. Rather, these companies are more likely to rely on the relational nature of their organizational routines, which are more easily executed if the foreign operating entity is fully owned, as this provides a clear stake in those relationships to third parties. Within a company, a wholly owned subsidiary allows the firm to partly escape the legal constraints in the host country, which are a troubling element of many joint venture agreements. The proposition can thus be stated as follows:

> **Proposition 2b.** Strategic cognition of multinationals from high-level institutional void contexts further increases the likelihood of wholly owned subsidiary entry mode choice with greater host market size.

The Moderating Effect of Strategic Cognition on the Host Market Growth-Foreign Entry Mode Choice Baseline Relationship

In contrast to the first element of host market attractiveness (i.e., host market size), host market growth is expected to have a different impact on foreign entry mode choices. In general, greater host market growth is expected to be positively associated with cooperative operating modes rather than the formation of wholly owned subsidiaries, given the need for speed in learning more quickly (Madhok, 1997).

In the case of EMMs, the impact is expected to be less inclined to the cooperative operating mode given EMMs' strategic cognition. The entrepreneurial nature of their strategy frames renders EMMs very well suited for such a high-growth environment. Identifying new opportunities is at the heart of their strategic mindset. In many cases, EMMs may even be much better prepared to succeed in such high-growth environments than other, more sophisticated players. Given their organizational identity as embedded players in their home market's societal fabric also makes them less inclined to allow their identity to be influenced through collaboration with local partners, as elaborated above. However, they may realize that a local partner could offer access to relevant institutional insights, a key prerequisite in the successful identification of institutional opportunities in rapidly growing markets. Hence, the weakening moderating effect of the embedded nature of organizational identity is expected to be smaller than for the strategy frames. The same can be assumed for the relational nature of organizational routines. While the relational approach results in a strong need to control and, hence, favors strong control over local subsidiaries rather than loose partnerships, cooperative modes may be the only method of creating the relational bonds needed, as local players are likely to pursue similar opportunities in a rapidly growing market. This leads to the following proposition:

> **Proposition 3b.** Strategic cognition of multinationals from high-level institutional void contexts decreases the likelihood of cooperative operating modes with greater host market growth.

The Moderating Effect of Strategic Cognition on the Host Country Risk-Foreign Entry Mode Choice Baseline Relationship

When it comes to host country risk, baseline proposition 4a states that greater host country risk is positively associated with cooperative operating modes rather than the formation of wholly owned subsidiaries. This is mainly due to the limited inclination of companies to make large upfront investments and the future options cooperative operating modes offer.

In the case of EMMs, a weakening moderating effect can be expected as the strategic cognition is much more inclined to address political and social uncertainty, as elaborated above, which limits the need to gain experience through cooperation. First, addressing risks is at the core of the entrepreneurial nature of strategy frames. The entrepreneurial mindset is concerned with addressing uncertainty by betting on a certain outcome. Hence, addressing risk can be considered truly entrenched in strategic cognition. The same can be said for the embedded nature of organizational identity. As seen above, risk considerations are a key reason for organizations to identify themselves as truly embedded in the societal fabric to instantly identify changes in dynamics and structures. The desire to preserve this strong identity as a means of addressing risk is likely to considerably weaken the baseline effect. When it comes to the relational nature of organizational routines, the weakening effect is expected to be slightly diminished. While their well-established routine of engaging in relational activities will make the need for cooperation less relevant, organizations may still see some value in engaging in such cooperation as a means of building relationships. This points to the following proposition: (Table 2)

Table 2. Baseline Effects and Moderating Effects of Strategic Cognition on Foreign Entry Mode Choices of Emerging Market Multinationals.

Host Market Variables	Baseline Effects	Moderating Effects of Strategic Cognition of Emerging Market Multinationals			
		Overall moderating effects	Moderating effects by dimension of strategic cognition		
			Strategy frames: Entrepreneurial	Organizational Identity: embedded	Organizational routines: Relational
Market size (MS)	*P2a*: greater MS > WOS	*P2b*: +++	++++	+++	++
Market growth (MG)	*P3a*: greater MG > COM	*P3b*: −−	−−−	−	−−
Country risk (CR)	*P4a*: greater CR > COM	*P4b*: −−−−	−−−−	−−−−	−−−

WOS: wholly owned subsidiary; COM: cooperative operating modes; +: strengthening effect; −: weakening effect.

Proposition 4b. Strategic cognition of multinationals from high-level institutional void contexts decreases the likelihood of cooperative operating modes with greater host country risk.

DISCUSSION AND CONCLUSION

Theoretical Contributions

This paper developed a conceptual framework to assess the foreign market entry behavior of emerging market multinationals. By introducing strategic cognition, the paper postulates that different levels of institutional voids in home markets shape the strategic cognition of those players, which also become decisive in their foreign entry mode choices. It is proposed that this will help to explain different strengths in correlation with host country characteristics (i.e., market size, market growth, and country risk) and foreign entry mode choice (i.e., wholly owned subsidiary and collaborative operating modes) for multinationals originating in countries with a high level of institutional voids (i.e., emerging market multinationals). While the likelihood of EMMs choosing wholly owned subsidiaries as the foreign entry mode in the case of a sizable market is expected to be strengthened, the likelihood of choosing collaborating operating modes as the foreign entry mode in the case of high market growth and substantial country risk is expected to be weakened. This is driven by the entrepreneurial nature of EMMs' strategy frames, the embedded nature of their organizational identity, and the relational nature of their organizational routines, resulting from three behavioral patterns rationalized by a high level of institutional void contexts in their home markets (i.e., opportunity spotting, rent seeking, and interdependence securing).

As such, this paper provides a nuanced view of the impact of different levels of home country institutional conditions on company behavior abroad by reconfiguring three streams of literature: the strengths of strategic cognition in explaining mindset, the applicability of institutional voids in conceptualizing institutional factors that shape behavior in such contexts and, finally, the rich body of empirical evidence and conceptual sophistication of research into foreign entry mode choices. The paper also aims to contribute to the three streams of literature as follows.

Contributions to the Strategic Cognition Literature

Despite the lure of strategic cognition as a concept to better understand underlying strategic decision processes, further validation and development of this particular school of thought is said to benefit from additional application and detailing. This study attempted to contribute to this endeavor in three ways. First, by demonstrating how strategic cognition can serve as a theoretical foundation in a configuration approach to theory development, linking two distinct perspectives (i.e., institutional voids and foreign entry mode choices), this paper stressed the relevance of strategic cognition as an integrator of various theoretical perspectives, a key role in advancing the understanding of strategy. Second, this study intended to deepen the understanding of strategic cognition, which is understood as the combining of strategy frames, organizational identity, and organizational routines by applying this combination to a particular antecedent (i.e., the institutional environment) and a particular outcome (i.e., foreign entry mode choices). By applying strategic cognition to the emerging market contexts, this study focused on specific type of economic player that has recently gained significant relevance but has not received the same level of attention, particularly as it relates to strategic cognition research.

Contributions to the Institutional Voids Literature

Against the background of the growing relevance of emerging markets, research into institutional voids has recently attracted much attention. Given this subject's emerging stage of development, the perspective still benefits from further conceptualization, integration, and application, to which this paper intends to contribute. First, the paper provided a first step toward an integrated conceptualization of institutional voids by identifying three main behavioral patterns companies display in high-level IV contexts – that is, opportunity spotting, rent seeking, and interdependence securing, which shape the strategic cognition of those players. Second, despite calls to examine the persistence of home country effects in strategic decisions abroad, limited research has been conducted elaborating on the link. This paper attempted to answer this call by theorizing on the persistence of those traits when moving beyond the home markets through postulating the prevalence of imprinting over learning in the initial stage. Finally, the paper attempted to integrate institutional voids into a theoretical framework by defining institutional voids as an antecedent to the strategic cognition of EMMs, allowing to account for heterogeneity in company behavior beyond the impact of institutional voids.

Contributions to the Foreign Market Entry Mode Literature

Finally, this paper aimed to contribute to the extensive and mature literature on foreign entry mode choices in three ways. First, by assuming the entry mode choice as a key strategic decision and applying strategic cognition as the theoretical underpinning, this paper hopes to deepen the understanding of the underlying decisions behind entry mode choices, rather than merely linking the firm's external and internal characteristics with outcomes. Second, the paper provided an attempt to link one of the most established bodies of knowledge (i.e., foreign entry mode choices) with one of the emerging perspectives on international business (i.e., institutional voids), in hopes of enriching the debate by bridging generations of research. Finally, the paper contributed to the ongoing debate on EMM idiosyncrasies by providing a concrete contribution to and support of the configurational school of thought.

Limitations and Suggestions for Future Research

The analysis herein is subject to a few limitations that also offer the potential for future research. On the one hand, any configurational approach runs the risk of potentially ignoring competing axioms of the different *theories* applied. The particular framework proposed herein, for example, combines key concepts from different schools of thought: strategic cognition from the cognitive school, institutional voids from the institutional perspective, and organizational imprinting and learning from the behavioral view. Because it considers these concepts as complementary rather than competing, it is pivotal to be specific about the role they play in the configuration approach, that is, theoretical versus metaphoric (Morgan, 1980).

On the other hand, the focused approach proposed in this paper leads to inherent limitations in terms of *scope*. First, the propositional framework would benefit from the inclusion of further antecedents to strategic cognition of EMMs to better account for heterogeneity in EMM behavior. Second, while the theoretical framework focused on one of the two key components of strategic cognition – structure – future research could enhance this paper by further analyzing the other building block of strategic cognition, that is, process (Narayanan et al., 2011). Third, the focus on a single market entry, without considering previous experiences, does not account for path dependencies, as suggested by Hennart and Slangen (2015). Fourth, the emphasis on only one type of entry mode (i.e., investments in the form of joint ventures and wholly owned subsidiaries) may not fully account for the real-life heterogeneity of foreign entry mode choices (Welch et al., 2008). Fifth, the definition of the home market as the country in which the company's heritage can be traced may be misleading in some cases, such as cross-country ownership (Bonaglia, Goldstein, & Mathews, 2007). Sixth, the limitation on only three host country variables ignores a number of other relevant home and host country as well as industry-related and firm-specific variables that have been highlighted in previous research (e.g., Zhao et al., 2004). Finally, the framework could benefit from being more specific about the EMM, such as considering the five EMM types as proposed by Ramamurti (2009) (i.e., local optimizer, low-cost partner, global consolidator, global first-mover, and natural resource seeker), different purposes of internationalization (i.e., exploration versus exploitation) (Hoskisson et al., 2004), or different motives for international diversification (i.e., institutional escapism versus leverage) (Luo & Wang, 2012). The suggested extensions are likely to further improve the value of the propositional framework, which will offer ample opportunities for meaningful empirical testing.

NOTES

1. These companies are also referred to as "new multinationals," "third-world multinationals," "unconventional multinationals," "latecomer firms," "challengers," and "emerging multinationals" (Guillén & García-Canal, 2009).
2. Others refer to them as "underdeveloped institutions" (Cuervo-Cazurra & Ramamurti, 2014, p. 285) or "institutional hardship" (Luo & Wang, 2012, p. 249) which, however, includes both institutional voids as well as "institutional hazards" (Luo & Wang, 2012, p. 249), for example, corruption.
3. However, critics of the institutional void explanation of business groups (e.g., Manikandan & Ramachandran, 2015) point to the fact that business groups persists despite improvements in institutional environments.
4. Alternatively, the term "foreign operating mode" is suggested to better reflect the reality that companies usually pursue different modes for different business segments, value chain activities or customer segments, or change the mode over time through mode switching or stretching (Welch et al., 2008).

ACKNOWLEDGMENTS

The author would like to thank the participants at the AIM Emerging Markets and MNEs Conference in Boston on September 27–28, 2014, and especially Elitsa R. Banalieva, Laszlo Tihanyi, and Joseph A. Clougherty, as well as Dirk Morschett, for helpful comments on earlier versions of this paper. Any omissions and errors are, of course, my own.

REFERENCES

Abrahamson, E., & Fombrun, C. J. (1994). Macrocultures: Determinants and consequences. *Academy of Management Review*, *19*(4), 728–755.

Agarwal, S. (1994). Socio-cultural distance and the choice of joint ventures: A contingency perspective. *Journal of International Marketing*, *2*(2), 63–80.

Agarwal, S., & Ramaswami, S. (1992). Choice of foreign market entry mode: Impact of ownership, location and internalization factors. *Journal of International Business Studies*, *33*(1), 517–551.

Albert, S., & Whetten, D. A. (1985). Organizational identity. In B. Staw & L. L. Cummings (Eds.), *Research in organizational behavior* (Vol. 7, pp. 263–295). Thousand Oaks, CA: Sage.

Andersen, O. (1997). Internationalization and market entry mode: A review of theories and conceptual frameworks. *MIR: Management International Review*, *37*(2), 27–42.

Anderson, E., & Gatignon, H. (1986). Modes of entry: A transactions cost analysis and propositions. *Journal of International Business Studies*, *17*(3), 1–26.

Andersson, U., Cuervo-Cazurra, A., & Nielsen, B. B. (2014). From the editors: Explaining interaction effects within and across levels of analysis. *Journal of International Business Studies*, *45*(9), 1063–1071.

Argyris, C., & Schön, D. (1978). *Organizational learning: A theory of action perspective*. Reading, MA: Addison-Wesley.

Banalieva, E. R., & Sarathy, R. (2011). A contingency theory of internationalization-performance for emerging market multinational enterprises. *Management International Review*, *51*(5), 593–634.

Boddewyn, J., & Doh, J. (2011). Global strategy and the collaboration of MNEs, NGOs, and governments for the provisioning of collective goods in emerging markets. *Global Strategy Journal*, *1*(3–4), 345–361.

Bogner, W. C., & Barr, P. S. (2000). Making sense in hypercompetitive environments: A cognitive explanation for the persistence of high velocity competition. *Organization Science*, *11*(2), 212–226.

Boisot, M., & Meyer, M. W. (2008). Which way through the open door? Reflections on the internationalization of Chinese firms. *Management and Organization Review*, *4*(3), 349–365.

Bonaglia, F., Goldstein, A., & Mathews, J. A. (2007). Accelerated internationalization by emerging markets' multinationals: The case of the white goods sector. *Journal of World Business*, *42*(4), 369–383.

Brouthers, K. D. (2002). Institutional, cultural and transaction cost influences on entry mode choice and performance. *Journal of International Business Studies*, *33*(2), 203–221.

Brouthers, K. D., Brouthers, L., & Werner, S. (2008). Real options, international entry mode choice and performance. *Journal of Management Studies*, *45*(5), 936–960.

Brouthers, K. D., & Hennart, J. F. O. (2007). Boundaries of the firm: Insights from international entry mode research. *Journal of Management*, *33*(3), 395–425.

Buckley, P. J., & Casson, M. (1996). An economic model of international joint venture strategy. *Journal of International Business Studies*, *27*(5), 849–876.

Canabal, A., & White, G. O. (2008). Entry mode research: Past and future. *International Business Review*, *17*(3), 267–284.

Cantwell, J., Dunning, J. H., & Lundan, S. M. (2010). An evolutionary approach to understanding international business activity: The co-evolution of MNEs and the institutional environment. *Journal of International Business Studies*, *41*(4), 567–586.

Chakrabarty, S. (2009). The influence of national culture and institutional voids on family ownership of large firms: A country level empirical study. *Journal of International Management*, *15*(1), 32–45.

Chang, S. J., & Rosenzweig, P. M. (2001). The choice of entry mode in sequential foreign direct investment. *Strategic Management Journal*, *22*(8), 747–776.

Chittoor, R., Kale, P., & Puranam, P. (2014). Business groups in developing capital markets: Towards a complementary perspective. *Strategic Management Journal*. Retrieved from http://onlinelibrary.wiley.com/doi/10.1002/smj.2287/abstract

Contractor, F. J. (2014). Punching above their weight: The sources of competitive advantage for emerging market multinationals. *International Journal of Emerging Markets*, *8*(4), 304–328.

Contractor, F. J., & Kundu, S. (1998). Modal choice in a world of alliances: Analyzing organizational forms in the international hotel sector. *Journal of International Business Studies*, *29*(2), 325–357.

Corley, K. G. (2004). Defined by our strategy or our culture? Hierarchical differences in perceptions of organizational identity and change. *Human Relations*, *57*(9), 1145–1177.

Cuervo-Cazurra, A. (2012). Extending theory by analyzing developing country multinational companies: Solving the Goldilocks debate. *Global Strategy Journal*, *2*(3), 153–167.

Cuervo-Cazurra, A., & Genc, M. (2008). Transforming disadvantages into advantages: Developing-country MNEs in the least developed countries. *Journal of International Business Studies*, *39*(6), 957–979.

Cuervo-Cazurra, A., & Ramamurti, R. (2014). Conclusion: An agenda for EMNC research. In A. Cuervo-Cazurra & R. Ramamurti (Eds.), *Understanding multinationals from emerging markets* (pp. 271–299). Cambridge: Cambridge University Press.

Daft, R. L., & Weick, K. E. (1984). Toward a model of organizations as interpretation systems. *Academy of Management Review*, *9*(2), 284–295.

Dhanaraj, C., & Khanna, T. (2011). Transforming mental models on emerging markets. *Academy of Management Learning and Education*, *10*(4), 684–701.

DiMaggio, P. J. (1988). Interest and agency in institutional theory. In L. G. Zucker (Ed.), *Institutional patterns and organizations: Culture and environment* (pp. 3–22). Cambridge, MA: Ballinger.

Doh, J., Lawton, T., & Rajwani, T. (2012). Advancing nonmarket strategy research: Institutional perspectives in a changing world. *The Academy of Management Perspectives*, *26*(3), 22–39.

Ekeledo, I., & Sivakumar, K. (1998). Foreign market entry mode choice of service firms: A contingency perspective. *Journal of the Academy of Marketing Science*, *26*(4), 274–292.

Elango, B., & Pattnaik, C. (2007). Building capabilities for international operations through networks: A study of Indian firms. *Journal of International Business Studies*, *38*(4), 541–555.

Erramilli, K., & Rao, C. P. (1993). Service firms' international entry-mode choice: A modified transaction-cost analysis approach. *Journal of Marketing*, *57*(3), 19–38.

Feldman, M. S., & Rafaeli, A. (2002). Organizational routines as sources of connections and understandings. *Journal of Management Studies*, *39*(3), 309–331.

Fisman, R., & Khanna, T. (2004). Facilitating development: The role of business groups. *World Development*, *32*(4), 609–628.

Fligstein, N. (2001). *The architecture of markets: An economic sociology of twenty-first-century capitalist societies*. Princeton, NJ: Princeton University Press.

Gavetti, G., & Levinthal, D. (2000). Looking forward and looking backward: Cognitive and experiential search. *Administrative Science Quarterly*, *45*(1), 113–137.

Gioia, D. A., Schultz, M., & Corley, K. G. (2000). Organizational identity, image, and adaptive instability. *Academy of Management Review*, *25*(1), 63–81.

Goldstein, A. (2009). Multinational companies from emerging economies – Composition, conceptualization and direction in the global economy. *Indian Journal of Industrial Relations*, *45*(1), 137–147.

Gomes-Casseres, B. (1990). Firm ownership preferences and host government restrictions: An integrated approach. *Journal of International Business Studies*, *21*(1), 1–22.

Guillén, M. F., & García-Canal, E. (2009). The American model of the multinational firm and the "new" multinationals from emerging economies. *Academy of Management Perspectives*, *23*(2), 23–35.

Guillén, M. F., & García-Canal, E. (2013). Execution as strategy: How emerging-market multinationals thrive amid turbulence. *Harvard Business Review*, *90*(10), 103–107.

Harzing, A. W. (2003). The role of culture in entry-mode studies: From neglect to myopia? *Advances in International Management*, *15*, 75–127.

Hennart, J. F. (1991). The transaction costs theory of joint ventures: An empirical study of Japans subsidiaries in the Unites States. *Management Science*, *37*(4), 483–497.

Hennart, J. F., & Larimo, J. (1998). The impact of culture on the strategy of multinational enterprises: Does national origin affect ownership decisions? *Journal of International Business Studies*, *29*(3), 515–538.

Hennart, J. F., & Slangen, A. H. (2015). Yes, we really do need more entry mode studies! A commentary on Shaver. *Journal of International Business Studies*, *46*(1), 114–122.

Hilb, M., & Casas, T. (2015). Towards a construct of entrepreneurial strategising: The case of private equity. *International Journal of Entrepreneurial Venturing*, *7*(1), 84–101.

Hildebrandt, L., & Weiss, C. (1997). Internationale Markteintrittsstrategien und der transfer von marketing-know-how. *Zeitschrift für betriebswirtschaftliche Forschung*, *49*(1), 3–25.

Hodgkinson, G. P. (2005). *Images of competitive space: A study of managerial and organizational strategic cognition*. Basingstoke: Palgrave Macmillan.

Hodgkinson, G. P., & Healey, M. P. (2008). Cognition in organizations. *Annual Review of Psychology*, *59*, 387–417.

Hoskisson, R. E., Kim, H., White, R. E., & Tihanyi, L. (2004). A framework for understanding international diversification by business groups from emerging economies. *Advances in International Management*, *16*, 137–163.

Huff, A. S. (1982). Industry influences on strategy reformulation. *Strategic Management Journal*, *3*(2), 119–131.

Huff, A. S. (1990). *Mapping strategic thought*. London: Wiley.

Kale, P., Singh, H., & Raman, A. P. (2009). Don't integrate your acquisitions, partner with them. *Harvard Business Review*, *87*(12), 109–115.

Kaplan, S. (2011). Research in cognition and strategy: Reflections on two decades of progress and a look to the future. *Journal of Management Studies*, *48*(3), 665–695.

Khanna, T., & Palepu, K. (2006). Strategies that fit emerging markets. *Harvard Business Review*, *84*(10), 60–69.

Khanna, T., & Palepu, K. G. (1997). Why focused strategies may be wrong for emerging markets. *Harvard Business Review*, *75*(4), 41–51.

Khanna, T., & Palepu, K. G. (2000). Emerging market business groups, foreign intermediaries, and corporate governance. In R. K. Morck (Ed.), *Concentrated corporate ownership* (pp. 265–294). Chicago, IL: University of Chicago Press.

Khanna, T., & Palepu, K. G. (2013). *Winning in emerging markets: A road map for strategy and execution*. Cambridge, MA: Harvard Business Press.

Khanna, T., & Rivkin, J. W. (2006). Interorganizational ties and business group boundaries: Evidence from an emerging economy. *Organization Science*, *17*(3), 333–352.

Khanna, T., & Yafeh, Y. (2007). Business groups in emerging markets: Paragons or parasites? *Journal of Economic Literature*, *45*(2), 331–372.

Kim, H., Kim, H., & Hoskisson, R. E. (2010). Does market-oriented institutional change in an emerging economy make business-group-affiliated multinationals perform better? An institution-based view. *Journal of International Business Studies*, *41*(7), 1141–1160.

Kogut, B., & Zander, U. (1996). What firms do? Coordination, identity, and learning. *Organization Science*, *7*(5), 502–518.

Krueger, A. (1974). The political economy of the rent-seeking society. *American Economic Review*, *64*(3), 291–303.

Lessard, D., & Lucea, R. (2009). Mexican multinationals: insights from CEMEX. In R. Ramamurti & J. V. Singh (Eds.), *Emerging multinationals in emerging markets* (pp. 280–311). Cambridge: Cambridge University Press.

Liang, A. P. X., Musteen, A. P. M., & Datta, D. K. (2009). Strategic orientation and the choice of foreign market entry mode. *Management International Review*, *49*(3), 269–290.

Luo, Y., & Tung, R. L. (2007). International expansion of emerging market enterprises: A springboard perspective. *Journal of International Business Studies*, *38*(4), 481–498.

Luo, Y., & Wang, S. L. (2012). Foreign direct investment strategies by developing country multinationals: A diagnostic model for home country effects. *Global Strategy Journal*, *2*(3), 244–261.

Madhok, A. (1997). Cost, value and foreign market entry mode: The transaction and the firm. *Strategic Management Journal*, *18*(1), 39–61.

Madhok, A. (1998). The nature of multinational firm boundaries: Transaction costs, firm capabilities and foreign market entry mode. *International Business Review*, *7*(3), 259–290.

Mair, J., & Martí, I. (2009). Entrepreneurship in and around institutional voids: A case study from Bangladesh. *Journal of Business Venturing*, *24*(5), 419–435.

Mair, J., Martí, I., & Ventresca, M. (2012). Building inclusive markets in rural Bangladesh: How intermediaries work institutional voids. *Academy of Management Journal*, *55*(4), 819–850.

Makhija, M., & Stewart, A. (2002). The effect of the institutional environment on perceptions of risk: A comparison of planned versus free-market managers. *Journal of International Business Studies*, *33*(4), 737–757.

Manikandan, K. S., & Ramachandran, J. (2015). Beyond institutional voids: Business groups, incomplete markets, and organizational form. *Strategic Management Journal*, *36*(1), 598–617.

Marquis, C., & Raynard, M. (2015). Institutional strategies in emerging markets. *Academy of Management Annals*, *9*(1), 291–335.

Marquis, C., & Tilcsik, A. (2013). Imprinting: Toward a multilevel theory. *Academy of Management Annals*, *7*(1), 195–245.

Mathews, J. A. (2006). Dragon multinationals: New players in 21st century globalization. *Asia Pacific Journal of Management*, *23*(1), 5–27.

Meyer, K. E. (2001). Institutions, transaction costs, and entry mode choice in Eastern Europe. *Journal of International Business Studies*, *32*(2), 357–367.

Meyer, K. E., Estrin, S., Bhaumik, S. K., & Peng, M. W. (2009). Institutions, resources, and entry strategies in emerging economies. *Strategic Management Journal*, *30*(1), 61–80.

Miles, R. E., Snow, C. C., Meyer, A. D., & Coleman, H. J. (1978). Organizational strategy, structure, and process. *Academy of Management Review*, *3*(3), 546–562.

Mintzberg, H. (1978). Patterns in strategy formation. *Management Science*, *24*(9), 934–948.

Morgan, G. (1980). Paradigms, metaphors, and puzzle solving in organization theory. *Administrative Science Quarterly*, *25*(4), 605–622.

Morschett, D., Schramm-Klein, H., & Swoboda, B. (2010). Decades of research on market entry modes: What do we really know about external antecedents of entry mode choice? *Journal of International Management*, *16*(1), 60–77.

Nadkarni, S., & Barr, P. S. (2008). Environmental context, managerial cognition, and strategic action: An integrated view. *Strategic Management Journal*, *29*(13), 1395–1427.

Nadkarni, S., & Narayanan, V. K. (2007). Strategic schemas, strategic flexibility, and firm performance: The moderating role of industry clockspeed. *Strategic Management Journal*, *28*(3), 243–270.

Narayanan, V. K., Zane, L. J., & Kemmerer, B. (2011). The cognitive perspective in strategy: An integrative review. *Journal of Management*, *37*(1), 305–351.

Narula, R. (2012). Do we need different frameworks to explain infant MNEs from developing countries? *Global Strategy Journal*, *2*(3), 188–204.

Nonaka, I., & Zhu, Z. (2012). *Pragmatic strategy: Eastern wisdom, global success*. Cambridge: Cambridge University Press.

North, D. C. (1990). *Institutions, institutional change and economic performance*. Cambridge: Cambridge University Press.

Pan, Y., & Tse, D. K. (2000). The hierarchical model of market entry modes. *Journal of International Business Studies*, *31*(4), 535–554.

Pehrsson, A. (2008). Strategy antecedents of modes of entry into foreign markets. *Journal of Business Research*, *61*(2), 132–140.

Peng, M. W. (2000). *Business strategies in transition economies*. Thousand Oaks, CA: Sage.

Peng, M. W., Wang, D. Y., & Jiang, Y. (2008). An institution-based view of international business strategy: A focus on emerging economies. *Journal of International Business Studies*, *39*(5), 920–936.

Porac, J. F., & Thomas, H. (2002). Managing cognition and strategy: Issues, trends and future directions. In A. M. Pettigrew, H. Thomas, & R. Whittington (Eds.), *Handbook of strategy and management* (pp. 165–181). Thousand Oaks, CA: Sage.

Porac, J. F., Thomas, H., & Baden-Fuller, C. (1989). Competitive groups as cognitive communities: The case of Scottish knitwear manufacturers. *Journal of Management Studies*, *26*(4), 397–416.

Powell, T. C., Lovallo, D., & Fox, C. R. (2011). Behavioral strategy. *Strategic Management Journal*, *32*(13), 1369–1386.

Prahalad, C. K., & Hamel, G. (1990). The core competence of the corporation. *Harvard Business Review*, *68*(3), 79–90.

Pratt, M. G., & Foreman, P. O. (2000). Classifying managerial responses to multiple organizational identities. *Academy of Management Review*, *25*(1), 18–42.

Priem, R. L., Lyon, D. W., & Dess, G. G. (1999). Inherent limitations of demographic proxies in top management team heterogeneity research. *Journal of Management*, *25*(6), 935–953.

Puffer, S. M., McCarthy, D. J., & Boisot, M. (2010). Entrepreneurship in Russia and China: the impact of formal institutional voids. *Entrepreneurship Theory and Practice*, *34*(3), 441–467.

Rajagopalan, N., Rasheed, A., & Datta, D. K. (1993). Strategic decision processes: Critical review and future directions. *Journal of Management*, *19*(2), 349–384.

Ramachandran, J., Manikandan, K. S., & Pant, A. (2013). Why conglomerates thrive (outside the U.S.). *Harvard Business Review*, *91*(12), 110–119.

Ramamurti, R. (2009). What have we learned about emerging-market MNEs? In R. Ramamurti & J. V. Singh (Eds.), *Emerging multinationals in emerging markets* (pp. 399–426). Cambridge: Cambridge University Press.

Ramamurti, R. (2012). What is really different about emerging market multinationals? *Global Strategy Journal*, *2*(1), 41–47.

Randøy, T., & Dibrell, C. (2002). How and why Norwegian MNCs commit resources abroad: Beyond choice of entry mode. *Management International Review*, *42*(2), 119–140.

Rodrik, D. (2008). *One economics, many recipes: Globalization, institutions, and economic growth*. Princeton, NJ: Princeton University Press.

Rugman, A. M. (2010). The theory and regulation of emerging market multinationals. In K. P. Sauvant, G. A. McAllister, & W. A. Maschek (Eds.), *Foreign direct investment from emerging markets: The challenges ahead* (pp. 75–88). New York, NY: Macmillan.

Sarkar, M., & Cavusgil, T. (1996). Trends in international business thought and literature: A review of international marketing entry mode research: Integration and synthesis. *The International Executive*, *38*(6), 825–847.

Schwenk, C. R. (1988). The cognitive perspective on strategic decision making. *Journal of Management Studies*, *25*(1), 41–55.

Shaver, J. M. (2013). Do we really need more entry mode studies? *Journal of International Business Studies*, *44*(1), 23–27.

Stevenson, H. (1983). *A perspective on entrepreneurship*. Harvard Business School Working Paper. Boston, MA, USA.

Stinchcombe, A. L. (1965). Social structure and organizations. In J. G. March (Ed.), *Handbook of organizations* (pp. 142–193). Chicago, IL: Rand McNally.

Tihanyi, L., Griffith, D. A., & Russell, C. J. (2005). The effect of cultural distance on entry mode choice, international diversification, and MNE performance: A meta-analysis. *Journal of International Business Studies*, *36*(3), 270–283.

Tracey, P., & Phillips, N. (2011). Entrepreneurship in emerging markets: Strategies for new venture creation in uncertain institutional contexts. *Management International Review*, *51*(1), 23–39.

Tullock, G. (1967). The welfare costs of tariffs, monopolies and theft. *Western Economic Journal*, *5*(3), 224–232.

Walsh, J. P. (1995). Managerial and organizational cognition: Notes from a trip down memory lane. *Organization Science*, *6*(3), 280–321.

Welch, L. S., Benito, G. R. G., & Petersen, B. (2008). *Foreign operation methods: Theory, analysis, strategy*. Northampton, MA: Edward Elgar.

Williamson, O. (1985). *The economic institutions of capitalism*. New York, NY: The Free Press.

Witt, M. A., & Lewin, A. Y. (2007). Outward foreign direct investment as escape response to home country institutional constraints. *Journal of International Business Studies*, *38*(4), 579–594.

Yamakawa, Y., Peng, M. W., & Deeds, D. L. (2008). What drives new ventures to internationalize from emerging to developed economies? *Entrepreneurship Theory and Practice*, *32*(1), 59–82.

Zhao, H., Luo, Y., & Suh, S. (2004). Transaction cost determinants and ownership-based entry mode choice: A meta-analytical review. *Journal of International Business Studies*, *35*(6), 524–544.

IS SPRINGBOARD FDI STRATEGY EFFECTIVE? EVIDENCE FROM TURKISH ACQUISITIONS

Victor Z. Chen and Sedat Aybar

ABSTRACT

Emerging market MNEs often seek to advance their domestic competitive advantage through a springboard FDI strategy, which typically takes the form of an acquisition into a developed market (DM) for knowledge resources. We argue that if this strategy is effective and beneficial, then an emerging market parent firm would seek for higher ownership and control in its later domestic acquisitions. Such benefits would be higher if there are richer knowledge resources in a DM subsidiary or in a DM local network. Such benefits would also increase over time because of the accumulation of new knowledge back home. Using a sample of 1,303 complete domestic acquisitions made by 713 Turkish firms over the period of 1987–2013, including 196 deals involving a springboard FDI strategy, we have found highly supportive empirical evidence. It is found that holding a DM subsidiary by a Turkish parent firm is associated with

Emerging Economies and Multinational Enterprises
Advances in International Management, Volume 28, 503–528

ISSN: 1571-5027/doi:10.1108/S1571-502720150000028021

33.047% higher ownership in a later domestic acquisition. Both research and practical implications are discussed.

Keywords: Springboard strategy; foreign direct investment; emerging market; acquisitions

INTRODUCTION

There has been a rising literature focusing on the outward FDI strategies of emerging market MNEs (for reviews, see Gammeltoft, Barnard, & Madhok, 2010; Luo & Tung, 2007; Ramamurti, 2012). One notable emerging perspective, framed as "springboard" strategy, argues that emerging market MNEs make outward FDI into a developed market (DM) to address primarily their domestic market disadvantages and help increase their competitive advantages at home (Luo & Tung, 2007, p. 481). Built on a knowledge-seeking based view of outward FDI (e.g., Makino, Lau, & Yeh, 2002; Mathews, 2006), this set of literature examines the ways in which the parent firms of emerging market MNEs benefit from their external linkages abroad and generate reverse knowledge transfers (Chen, Li, & Shapiro, 2012; Gubbi, Aulakh, Ray, Sarkar, & Chittoor, 2010; Mathews, 2006; Rui & Yip, 2008). The springboard FDI strategy typically starts with an acquisition into DMs, where knowledge resources are relatively richer, followed by learning, transferring, and integrating these knowledge resources into home market activities (Mathews, 2006; Rui & Yip, 2008). It is argued that springboard strategy can strengthen an emerging market parent firm's capabilities and resources (Chen et al., 2012; Gubbi et al., 2010), ultimately enabling it to compete more effectively in the home marketplace (Luo & Tung, 2007).

However, is springboard really effective to achieve its goals for emerging market MNEs? The current literature has provided very thin empirical evidence. As a welcome exception, Chen et al. (2012) studied 493 MNEs from 53 EMs over the period 2000–2008 and found that MNEs with subsidiaries in DMs richer in technological resources (measured by industry-specific R&D investments and R&D employment) exhibited higher R&D spending at home. In a more indirect fashion, Gubbi et al. (2010) studied 315 cross-border acquisitions by Indian firms between 2000 and 2007 and found that an acquisition into an OECD country was associated with about 2.519% higher cumulative abnormal return over an 11-day window for the parent's shareholders compared to one into a non-OECD country.

Although these two studies have in part supported empirically the benefits of springboard FDI strategy, we offer alternative, more rigorous tests. First, R&D activities at home do not sufficiently capture all the effects on the competitive advantage of the headquarters in the context of emerging markets. Under relatively poor intellectual property rights (IPR) regimes at home, emerging market MNEs do not often try to apply foreign knowledge into tangible, technological development activities such as R&D, and also, and more often, infuse it internally into more tacit and intangible strategic assets such as goodwill, managerial skills, and operational efficiency (Chen & Puttitanun, 2005; Gubbi et al., 2010). Because of their very nature of tacitness and intangibility, such assets are, however, very difficult to be directly observed and empirically measured (Grant, 1996). Second, although overall firm performance is the ultimate goal of strengthening competitive advantages through reverse knowledge transfers, it is influenced by too many other alternative processes and factors, which may be unrelated to knowledge capabilities and resources (Ray, Barney, & Muhanna, 2004). Additionally, finding an appropriate measure of the firm performance in emerging markets is considerably challenging because long-term viability in emerging markets may not always be reasonably reflected in stock market price due to relatively illiquid stock markets and weak accounting disclosures (Lesmond, 2005).

For the above reasons, Ray et al. (2004) suggested that specific business processes should be the most appropriate level of analysis on competitive advantages. They serve as a direct mediation between capabilities and resources as the sources of competitive advantages and overall firm performance as the outcome of competitive advantages (Ray et al., 2004). From a knowledge-based view, business processes that exploit tacit and intangible resources are more likely to be the source of sustained competitive advantages because such resources are hard to be replicated, learned, codified, and traded (e.g., Barney, 1991; Ray et al., 2004). Therefore, studies on the effects of springboard FDI on home competitive advantages should focus on the heterogeneity in parent firms' business processes.

Following this suggestion, we propose to focus on ownership and control of domestic subsidiaries through acquisitions. It is a specific business process that emerges as a viable strategic choice for firm growth during the course of market transitions in emerging markets, enabled especially by the establishment and development of stock markets (Singh, 1997). Compared to the more traditional network-based growth in the absence of market-supporting institutions (Peng & Heath, 1996), acquisitions do not bear administrative costs of building and maintaining interpersonal trust and are encouraged by decreased transaction costs in capital markets because of stronger financial market institutions (Lesmond, 2005; Rossi & Volpin, 2004). For instance, in a sample of acquisitions between 1990 and 2002 in 49 countries, Rossi and Volpin (2004) found that acquisitions were more intensive in countries with such stronger financial market institutions as accounting standards and shareholder protection.

Theoretically, we propose that springboard FDI strategy leads to higher ownership and control in domestic acquisitions in emerging markets. Such effects are positively moderated by the richness of knowledge resources inside the DM subsidiaries as well as externally in the local networks in the host DMs. Because knowledge transfer and learning is accumulative, such effects would increase over time after a springboard FDI strategy. Empirically, significant evidence has been found in a sample of 1,303 completed domestic acquisitions made by 714 Turkish firms between January 1, 1987 and December 31, 2013, including 196 deals (or about 15% of the sample) that involved a springboard FDI strategy.

LITERATURE REVIEW

There has been a rising discussion in the international management literature on reverse knowledge transfer from foreign subsidiaries to headquarters. Studies have found ample evidence of such reverse knowledge transfer within MNEs. First, the knowledge stock at the subsidiary measured by size of employment (Gupta & Govindarajan, 2000) and years of operations (Rabbiosi & Santangelo, 2013) is positively related to the extent of such transfers. Second, the absorptive capacity of the headquarters is also a positive moderator (Ambos, Ambos, & Schlegelmilch, 2006; Mudambi, Piscitello, & Rabbiosi, 2014). Third, the extent of such transfer further depends on inter-unit collaborations such as joint R&D practice by researchers from different subsidiaries (Frost & Zhou, 2005), formal personnel exchange policies (Gupta & Govindarajan, 2000; Rabbiosi, 2011), as well as informal socialization among employees from different subsidiaries (Najafi-Tavani, Giroud, & Sinkovics, 2012; Rabbiosi & Santangelo, 2013). However, the extant empirical evidence is situated predominantly in the context of DM MNEs for their relatively high absorptive capacity to enable and enforce such transfers (Yang, Mudambi, & Meyer, 2008).

Recent years have seen some emerging efforts in the literature focusing on emerging market MNEs' reverse knowledge transfer practice (Borini, de Miranda Oliveira, Silveira, & de Oliveira Concer, 2012; Chen et al., 2012; Gubbi et al., 2010). From a springboard FDI perspective (Luo & Tung, 2007), emerging market MNEs are a unique setting in studying reverse knowledge transfer activities. First, facing fast transition to market competition and relatively low technological resources at home, emerging market MNEs see a relatively high urgency to acquire and reversely transfer foreign knowledge rather than develop their own knowledge proprietarily (e.g., Makino et al., 2002; Mathews & Zander, 2007). Second, as newcomers in global innovation management, emerging market MNEs tend to centralize their global knowledge resources back home rather than diffuse them globally (Wei, 2010). Third, home governments in emerging markets often have supportive policy measures such as fiscal incentives if emerging market MNEs do bring foreign technologies back home (e.g., Chaminade & Vang, 2008; Peng, 2010). These studies however, as discussed earlier, have provided very limited empirical evidence on the effectiveness of reverse knowledge transfer on the competitive advantage of emerging market parent firms at home.

HYPOTHESES

As explained previously, domestic acquisitions are an appropriate focal unit to examine the effectiveness of springboard FDI strategy on domestic competitive advantages (Ray et al., 2004). More specifically, ownership and control over a new domestic subsidiary through a domestic acquisition is an appropriate reflection of competitive advantages, directly enabled by capabilities and resources including tangible ones such as technology and new products and intangible ones such as managerial and operational skills. First, if a parent firm's capabilities and resources do increase after a springboard FDI, it would enjoy a higher bargaining power over its domestic target for ownership and control in an acquisition transaction. Holding a subsidiary in DMs would immediately enhance an emerging market firm's goodwill (an example of intangible capabilities and resources) in its home markets, since customers typically consider DM firms to represent higher standards, better product quality, and stronger management know-how (Peterson & Jolibert, 1995). Also, enabled by stronger managerial and operational capabilities, the parent firm tends to have a more positive expectation about future performance after restructuring the subsidiaries and replacing the management, and thus would be more willing to pay premiums for corporate control over the subsidiary (Slusky & Caves, 1991).

Second, with a greater knowledge intensity in its existing capabilities and resources, a parent firm has a higher incentive to internalize its relationship with the domestic subsidiaries through higher ownership and control in order to avoid unwanted knowledge leakages (Grant, 1996; Kogut & Zander, 1992; Zhao, Luo, & Suh, 2004). Grant (1996), for instance, suggests that production activities require the combination of a wide array of specialized knowledge that resides in different individuals. As a result, internal organization (as opposed to non-equity-based relationship) could largely reduce transaction costs of complex knowledge exchanges between these individuals (Eisenhardt & Santos, 2002). The poor quality of IPR regime in emerging markets increases the opportunism risks of knowledge spillovers from the parent firm to the domestic competitors, and thus amplifies the need for internalization through higher ownership and control (Zhao, 2006).

Therefore, we propose the first proposition below.

H1. If an emerging market firm owns a DM subsidiary, it tends to obtain a higher ownership of the subsidiary in its domestic acquisition.

There are two major mechanisms through which an emerging market firm can gain competitive advantage from its springboard FDI in a DM. The first mechanism is transfer and learning of existing knowledge resources available in the developed-market foreign subsidiary and integrating them into the parent capabilities and resources (Chen et al., 2012). Under an ownership relationship between the emerging market parent and its DM subsidiary, the parent firm has the authority to order different types of interactions with the subsidiary individuals for their knowledge (Grant, 1996). As one example, the parent can exchange personnel with the subsidiary on a regular basis, or relocate researchers from the subsidiary to the parent firm (Chen et al., 2012; Filatotchev, Liu, Buck, & Wright, 2009; Liu, Lu, Filatotchev, Buck, & Wright, 2010). For another example, parent firms could engage in internal transfer at a lower-than-market cost to purchase knowledge-embodied intermediate goods from DM subsidiaries and build them into final products in the home markets (Chen et al., 2012; Cheung & Lin, 2004; Javorcik, 2004). In addition, trying to learn and absorb new knowledge transferred reversely from the DM subsidiary, the parent firm will also be induced to make significant efforts to proprietary R&D activities to improve its knowledge absorptive capacity (Cohen & Levinthal, 1990). Therefore, a large extent of the benefits from springboard strategy comes from the existing knowledge resources embedded in the DM subsidiary, which can be reversely transferred. One would hence expect that the more such knowledge resources, the greater the effectiveness of springboard FDI strategy. More formally, we propose:

H2. The relationship in H1 is higher if an emerging market firm's DM subsidiary has richer knowledge resources.

More indirectly, as the second mechanism, the emerging market parent firm can leverage its DM subsidiary, regardless of its existing knowledge assets, to engage in many activities in the host-country networks to obtain external knowledge resources. First, the subsidiary is an integrative component in the local supply chains in the host DM. Compared to the efforts an emerging market firm has to devote to accessing knowledge suppliers in DMs through an international market, transaction costs for accessing local external knowledge suppliers are reduced with a physical component in the local network. For instance, the local subsidiary is relatively more familiar with potential knowledge suppliers in the local network and thus can reduce the emerging market parent firm's searching cost. The subsidiary is also more familiar with the quality and credibility of these suppliers and, with a physical and geographically closer location and cultural similarity, may bear lower costs for contract enforcement. Second, the local subsidiary in the DMs can raise the visibility and profile of the emerging market firm to local skilled workers and students who were looking for job opportunities in emerging markets, especially potential skilled returnees. For instance, with its active global subsidiaries, China-based Huawei hired about a quarter of foreign employees, including many into its Shenzhen headquarter (Osawa & Chu, 2013). Therefore, one would expect that the richer the local knowledge resources in the host DM, the greater the effectiveness of a springboard FDI strategy. Stated more formally:

H3. The relationship in H1 is higher if an emerging market firm's host DM has richer knowledge resources.

The positive effects of holding a DM subsidiary on an emerging market firm's competitive advantage at home are an accumulative process over time. In the immediate short term, after acquiring a DM subsidiary, there is a positive impact on an emerging market firm's goodwill in the home marketplace through public announcement and media reports (Peterson & Jolibert, 1995). If this is the only benefit that an emerging market parent can receive and there is no further knowledge transfer, we would expect to see a relatively flat relationship between the time of holding a DM subsidiary and the competitive advantage of an emerging market parent. However, as argued above, since the very motivation of springboard FDI strategy is to seek, learn, and obtain knowledge resources abroad, the impact of holding a DM subsidiary is likely increasing over time because of the reverse transfer and accumulation of new knowledge at the parent level.

In the medium term, the emerging market parent can explore and exploit codified, explicit, and tangible knowledge resources such as unpatented designs, new techniques, and inventions for internal use (Chen et al., 2012). Compared to tacit and implicit knowledge, these resources are relatively easier to understand, replicate, and imitate in the home country (Eisenhardt & Santos, 2002; Grant, 1996). In the long term, the emerging market parent can engage in interactive activities to obtain tacit and intangible knowledge that is embedded in the individuals in the subsidiary. Examples of such knowledge include managerial skills, innovative know-how, and mental models of innovation activities (Eisenhardt & Santos, 2002; Grant, 1996). The effectiveness of knowledge transfer in such activities takes a relatively long term because of the nature of tacitness and intangibility.

Not only is the transfer of knowledge resources an accumulative process, so is the integration of such resources into the home market context and appropriating them into competitive advantage. First, the home parent is induced to conduct trials and experiments to adapt DM knowledge into the home context (Chen et al., 2012). The contextual adaptation itself is a learning process over time. Second, to convert the adaptive knowledge into confidence of future profitability of the domestic acquisition target, and thus a higher ownership and control over it, the parent needs to make extra efforts to learning operations at a larger scale after an acquisition and developing new managerial skills to alleviate increased organizational and coordination costs (Hill & Hoskisson, 1987; Hoskisson, Johnson, Tihanyi, & White, 2005).

In summary, we expect that the benefits of a springboard strategy are correlated with time since the springboard FDI strategy.

H4. The relationship in H1 is higher if an emerging market firm has owned a DM subsidiary for a longer time.

METHOD

Empirical Setting

Our empirical setting of the emerging market home country is Turkey, which is a natural laboratory to study springboard strategies in the context of both domestic acquisitions activities and springboard FDI strategy. First, Turkey has a long-standing close relationship with the developed world. Indeed, Turkey is the only founding member of OECD that is not a DM (OECD, 2015). As of 2012, based on UNCTAD FDI statistics, 61.82% of Turkish OFDI stock located in DMs, leading all other top eight largest emerging markets except the Russian Federation (77%) (UNCTAD, 2015). Second, through the development of Istanbul Stock Exchange (ISE) in 1986, acquisitions had become more and more active in the turnover of ownership of Turkish firms. For instance, combining the *Turkish Capital Market Board Activity Reports* and SDC database, the total number of complete acquisitions on ISE increased from only one in 1989 to 179 in 2013.

More importantly, knowledge-seeking has been a major motivation behind outward FDI of Turkish MNEs. First, greater trade openness and increased foreign competition since Turkey's agreement with European Customs Union in 1995 challenged Turkish firms' competitive advantages at home and induced Turkish MNEs to initiate springboard FDI strategies. For instance, Yıldız Holdings' 2007 acquisitions of the U.S.-based Godiva for $1 billion and United Biscuits for $3.5 billion have provided its domestic subsidiary Ülker enhanced visibility and more efficient production technology. Second, the Turkish government has adopted a series of supportive policies for outward FDI activities, especially if the Turkish firms were to acquire strategic foreign assets. Seeking for positive spillovers of foreign acquisitions, the national government has been increasing EXIM bank's FDI credit tranches and developing an insurance scheme that facilitates such acquisitions, especially into developed countries. More importantly, a state-sponsored program known as "Turquality" was established to encourage the development of Turkish trademarks and other intellectual property rights by investing abroad.

Data and Sample

Our data came from multiple sources. In the first step, we retrieved M&A transactions data from two recognized M&A sources: Thomson Reuters

SDC Platinum™ M&A Database (SDC hereafter) and Bureau van Dijk (BvD) Zephyr (Zephyr hereafter). The search criteria include: the ultimate parent firm should be a Turkish national; the transaction should be completed; the entry ownership was reported; and the names and nationalities of both acquirers and targets should be disclosed for the purpose of finding and verifying information from other sources. We did not include any observations if data for any one of the above variables was unreported. As a result, there was no missing value for the dependent variable after this selection. Second, we filled missing values at the firm level from other secondary sources including BvD Orbis, Mergent Online, Mergent Reports, and local Turkish sources such as financial reports, firm online information, and direct surveys. Third, to keep as many observations as possible after the above efforts, for remaining missing values for independent and control variables, we used inter- and extrapolation technique as a function of year.[1] After removing further missing values, the final sample included 1,303 completed domestic acquisitions made by 714 Turkish firms between January 1, 1987 and December 31, 2013. After examining each firm's cross-border acquisition history in SDC and Zephyr based on official firm names (and any other names firms have used), we have identified 196 deals (or about 15% of the sample) in which the Turkish acquirers owned a DM subsidiary through cross-border acquisitions. The sample also suggests that acquisitions into DMs are relatively a recent phenomenon for Turkish firms, facilitated by Turkey's agreement with the European Customs Union in 1995 and especially negotiations for full membership of the EU since 2005. This has largely precluded the possibility that we might have missed springboard FDI before 1987, before when observations were not available in SDC or Zephyr. We have also downloaded country-level data from the World Bank database. We defined DMs following the IMF classification of advanced economies (IMF, 2014) and examined the sample and result consistency using the United Nations' classification (UN, 2014).[2] The majority of the deals took place after the financial crisis in 2007 (62%) and in the industries of manufacturing (37%), transportation, communications, electric, gas, and sanitary services (20%), and services (30%).

Variables and Measures

Dependent Variable

The dependent variable is measured as *Ownership after acquisition*, directly given by SDC and Zephyr.

Independent and Moderating Variables

To test H1, we have constructed a dummy variable, *Owning a DM subsidiary*, to measure whether a Turkish acquirer at the time of its domestic acquisition owned a DM subsidiary (1 for yes, 0 for no). This information is based on SDC and Zephyr. To test H2, we use *DM subsidiary R&D intensity*, measured as the ratio of R&D spending to net sales of the DM subsidiary at the time of domestic acquisition. If a Turkish acquirer held multiple DM subsidiaries, we took the average. Information for this is from SDC and Zephyr, complemented by other sources mentioned previously. To test H3, we constructed a composite index called *DM knowledge resources*. We first retrieved data for *number of patent applications in thousands*, *number of R&D researchers and technicians per thousand people*, and *R&D spending to GDP ratio* from the World Bank database. To reduce the number of highly consistent and correlated measures, this index was calculated as the Principal Component (PC) score (Jolliffe, 2005) of these three variables based on the full sample of the World Bank database. If a Turkish acquirer held foreign subsidiaries in multiple DMs, we took the arithmetic mean of these host countries' PC scores. Because original PC score contains negative values, we added each original PC score a positive constant in order to keep the non-negative characteristic of DM knowledge resources (Table 1). To test H4, we include *Time since owning a DM subsidiary*, measured as the natural logarithm of total days between the date when an emerging market acquirer had owned its first DM subsidiary and the date of a respective domestic acquisition. The value takes zero is the Turkish parent firm held no DM subsidiary. To maintain the non-negative feature of the original value, we added each original value by one before taking natural logarithm. Information for this measure is based on SDC and Zephyr.

Table 1. Correlation Matrix and Component Loadings of Components of DM Knowledge Resources (H3).

	(1)	(2)	(3)	Loadings
(1) DM number of patent applications (thousands)	1.000			0.388
(2) DM number of R&D researchers and technicians per thousand people	0.386*	1.000		0.639
(3) DM R&D spending to GDP ratio	0.846*	0.276*	1.000	0.664

Eigenvalue of the first principal component is 1.997. Proportion explained by the first principal component is 0.666. Number of effective observations in the full sample of World Bank database between 1989 and 2013 is 2,484.

*$p < 0.001$.

Control Variables

We included four groups of control variables. First, at the firm level, following prior studies focusing on acquisition ownership (e.g., Barkema & Vermeulen, 1998; Kogut & Singh, 1988) we controlled for *Acquirer firm assets* and *Target firm assets*, measured as the natural logarithms of total assets of the acquirer and domestic target firm of an acquisition respectively, *Acquirer firm size* and *Target firm size*, measured as the natural logarithms of total number of employees, *Acquirer firm profitability* and *Target firm profitability*, measured as net income to total assets ratio, and *Acquirer firm solvency* and *Target firm solvency*, measured as total liability to total assets ratio. All this information is from SDC and Zephyr, complemented by other sources mentioned previously. Second, at the transaction level, we followed Luo (2001) and controlled for *Deal value*, measured as the natural logarithm of the total transaction value (in millions of USD). This information is from SDC and Zephyr, complemented by other sources mentioned previously. Third, at the country level, following prior works on cross-border acquisitions (e.g., Barkema & Vermeulen, 1998), we controlled for *Home GDP*, *DM GDP*, *Home GDP per capita*, *DM GDP per capita*, *Home GDP growth*, and *DM GDP growth* in the year of acquisition, where "home" refers to Turkey and "DM" refers to the host country of the DM subsidiary. Next, we controlled for *Weighted distance* between Turkey and DM host countries, directly downloaded from CEPII. For each country pair, this measure is calculated as the geographic distance between two countries' major cities, weighted by each city's population density. If a Turkish acquirer held foreign subsidiaries in multiple DM host countries, the arithmetic mean of the *Weighted distance* measures was used. Lastly, we included dummies of years of acquisition, target industries based on one-digit SIC codes, and DM host countries to control for temporal, sectoral, and DM host-country effects. All DM-related variables took the value 0 if a focal domestic acquisition in Turkey did not involve any springboard FDI strategy. After pairwise correlations (threshold 0.60) (Kennedy, 1992) and VIF tests (threshold 5) (Hair, Black, Babin, Anderson, & Tatham, 2006), we removed control variables that cause multi-collinearity. Our final list of control variables included *Acquirer profitability, Acquirer size, Target profitability, Target size, Deal value, Turkey GDP growth, DM GDP growth, Weighted distance*, and *Year- Industry-, and DM host country dummies.*

Estimation Strategy

We use random-effects Tobit regressions (Greene, 2003) to run our main estimation because our dependent variable is bounded by 1% as the minimum (as the inclusion criterion) and 100% as the maximum. Fixed effects are technically not available in non-linear models such as Tobit due to incidental parameters problem (Greene, 2004). Specifically:

$$\textit{Ownership after acquisition}_i = \begin{cases} 1, \ \textit{if} \ \ \textit{Ownership after acquisition}_i^* = 1 \\ \textit{Ownership after acquisition}_i^*, \textit{if} \ \ 1 < \textit{Ownership after acquisition}_i^* < 100 \\ 100, \ \textit{if} \ \ \textit{Ownership after acquisition}_i^* = 100 \end{cases}$$

where $\textit{Ownership after acquisition}_i^*$ is a latent variable such that

$$\textit{Ownership after acquisition}_i^* = \beta{\cdot}X_i + u_i, u_i \sim N\left(0, \sigma^2\right)$$

where *Xi* include both independent and control variables.

Results and Analysis

Table 2 reports summary statistics and correlation matrix. Two emerging patterns are notable. First, domestic acquisitions by Turkish firms tended to take very high ownership, on average 72.67% in the sample. A further examination suggests that 605 observations out of 1,303 (or about 46% of the sample) took full ownership (100%). Second, because our independent measures are non-zero only if the parent firm held a DM subsidiary (15% of the sample), our independent variables are highly correlated and thus cannot be included simultaneously. For instance, *Holding a DM subsidiary* has a 0.76 correlation with *DM subsidiary R&D intensity*, 0.98 correlation with *Time of holding a DM subsidiary*, and 0.80 correlation with *DM knowledge resources*. Therefore, we include them step-by-step in order that we show all results without reporting biased estimations. We have also run a full model with all the independent variables to see if there are variable bias issues.

Table 3 reports the main regression results. With the exception of H3 (based on natural logarithm), all results are very straightforward, showing how much extra ownership a Turkish acquirer would acquire after a springboard FDI strategy compared to an acquirer that held no DM subsidiary. As the results have suggested, our hypotheses have been fully

Table 2. Summary Description and Correlation Matrix.

		(1)	(2)	(3)	(5)	(4)	(6)
(1)	Acquired ownership	1.00					
(2)	Holding a DM subsidiary (H1)	0.06**	1.00				
(3)	DM subsidiary R&D intensity (H2)	0.05*	**0.76*****	1.00			
(4)	Total days of holding a DM subsidiary, Log (H3)	0.06**	**0.98*****	**0.77*****	1.00		
(5)	DM knowledge resources (H4)	0.05*	**0.80*****	**0.76*****	**0.80*****	1.00	
(6)	Acquirer profitability	0.33***	−0.03	−0.04	−0.02	−0.04	1.00
(7)	Acquirer employment, Log	0.00	0.43***	0.20***	0.42***	0.41***	0.10***
(8)	Target profitability	−0.03	0.11***	0.05*	0.11***	0.10***	0.24***
(9)	Target employment, Log	0.01	0.42***	0.20***	0.40***	0.40***	−0.13***
(10)	Turkey GDP growth	0.01	0.12***	0.10***	0.13***	0.08***	0.02
(11)	Deal value	0.04	0.00	0.00	0.00	0.03	0.01
(12)	Weighted distance	0.05*	0.40***	0.32***	0.39***	0.36***	−0.02
(13)	DM GDP growth	0.00	0.52***	0.44***	0.54***	0.45***	0.01
	Mean	72.67	0.15	0.27	0.30	1.19	1.51
	Std. Dev.	32.42	0.36	0.84	0.89	2.81	0.73
	Number of observations	1,303	1,303	1,303	1,303	1,303	1,303

		(7)	(8)	(9)	(10)	(11)	(12)	(13)	VIF
(1)	Acquired ownership								
(2)	Holding a DM subsidiary (H1)								1.85
(3)	DM subsidiary R&D intensity (H2)								1.16
(4)	Total days of holding a DM subsidiary, Log (H3)								1.61
(5)	DM knowledge resources (H4)								1.88

(6)	Acquirer profitability								1.19
(7)	Acquirer employment, Log	1.00							1.98
(8)	Target profitability	0.16***	1.00						1.11
(9)	Target employment, Log	0.65***	0.11***	1.00					1.97
(10)	Turkey GDP growth	0.01	−0.03	0.01	1.00				1.07
(11)	Deal value	0.04	−0.09***	0.05*	0.00	1.00			1.02
(12)	Weighted distance	0.14***	0.04	0.14***	0.10***	−0.01	1.00		1.19
(13)	DM GDP growth	0.21***	0.05*	0.19***	0.21***	−0.05	0.21***	1.00	1.43
	Mean	2.56	2.20	2.51	0.67	0.10	1.10	0.21	
	Std. Dev.	1.31	0.91	1.28	0.77	0.10	0.50	0.98	
	Number of obs.	1303	1303	1303	1303	1303	1303	1303	

Note: Because we will include independent variables step-by-step, the VIF values for them are based on step-by-step regressions too. Bold numbers were above 0.6 threshold (Kennedy, 1992) and cannot be included in regressions simultaneously.
*$p < 0.1$, **$p < 0.05$, ***$p < 0.01$.

Table 3. Random-Effects Tobit Regression Results.

Dependent Variable is *Ownership in a Domestic Acquisition* (%)						
	(1)	(2)	(3)	(4)	(5)	(6)
Predictors						
Holding a DM subsidiary (H1)		33.047**				44.803
		(11.460)				(27.221)
DM subsidiary R&D intensity (H2)			5.411+			1.899
			(2.793)			(3.399)
Log of total days of holding a DM subsidiary (H3)				6.238*		0.815
				(2.950)		(4.054)
DM R&D resources (H4)					3.189*	−2.368
					(1.369)	(3.144)
Control variables						
Constant	104.285	63.367	101.873	154.365	−22.491	148.859
	(571.254)	(570.101)	(570.513)	(570.459)	(572.880)	(579.581)
Acquirer profitability	31.027***	31.361***	31.121***	31.357***	31.165***	31.454***
	(2.398)	(2.398)	(2.397)	(2.401)	(2.396)	(2.404)
Acquirer employment, Log	−5.960***	−6.367***	−5.795***	−6.305***	−6.328***	−6.224***
	(1.654)	(1.660)	(1.655)	(1.664)	(1.662)	(1.681)
Target profitability	−6.784***	−6.884***	−6.789***	−6.851***	−6.850***	−6.886***
	(1.779)	(1.776)	(1.778)	(1.778)	(1.777)	(1.776)
Target employment, Log	4.285*	3.675*	4.360*	3.713*	3.942*	3.665*
	(1.730)	(1.743)	(1.731)	(1.752)	(1.736)	(1.770)
Turkey GDP growth	−0.084	−0.179	−0.025	0.017	−0.142	−0.140
	(2.074)	(2.077)	(2.072)	(2.070)	(2.078)	(2.076)
Deal value	11.814	14.043	12.589	11.285	13.522	13.807
	(15.795)	(15.882)	(15.849)	(15.850)	(15.854)	(15.930)
Weighted distance	5.867+	1.760	4.325	3.744	2.774	1.773
	(3.331)	(3.626)	(3.428)	(3.480)	(3.589)	(3.630)

DM GDP growth	−0.852	−2.895	−1.865	−1.947	−2.685	−2.770
	(1.939)	(2.086)	(2.020)	(2.027)	(2.110)	(2.120)
Year dummies	Yes	Yes	Yes	Yes	Yes	Yes
Industry dummies (SIC1)	Yes	Yes	Yes	Yes	Yes	Yes
DM host country dummies	Yes	Yes	Yes	Yes	Yes	Yes
Sigma	48.881***	48.709***	48.814***	48.786***	48.762***	48.700***
	(1.483)	(1.477)	(1.480)	(1.480)	(1.479)	(1.477)
Statistics						
Number of observations	1,303	1,303	1,303	1,303	1,303	1,303
Number of left-censored observations (ownership = 1)	18	18	18	18	18	18
Number of right-censored observations (ownership = 100)	605	605	605	605	605	605
Chi-square	244.626	253.080	248.515	249.146	250.121	253.980
ΔChi-square (compared to model (1))		8.454	3.889	4.520	5.495	9.354
p-value	0.000	0.000	0.000	0.000	0.000	0.000

Standard errors in parentheses.
$^{+}p < 0.1$, $^{*}p < 0.05$, $^{**}p < 0.01$, $^{***}p < 0.001$.

supported. First, H1 is statistically significantly supported ($p < 0.01$), suggesting that a Turkish acquirer which held a DM subsidiary tended to acquire on average 33.047% higher ownership in its domestic acquisition, compared to a Turkish acquire which held no DM subsidiary. Considering that higher ownership is a business process mediating knowledge resources and improved domestic competitive advantages, it suggests that springboard FDI strategy by Turkish firms is significantly beneficial.

Second, H2 is statistically significantly supported ($p < 0.1$), suggesting that a 1% increase in a DM subsidiary's R&D intensity corresponded to 5.411% higher ownership in a Turkish firm's domestic acquisition. This can in part evidence that reverse knowledge transfer may take the form of learning DM subsidiary's R&D capabilities.

Third, H3 is statistically significantly supported ($p < 0.05$). If the DM knowledge resource index increased by 1%, a Turkish firm tended to acquire 6.238% higher ownership in its domestic acquisitions. Results also suggest that the effects of DM knowledge resources are more statistically significant than DM subsidiary R&D intensity. We speculate that there are two reasons. On one hand, a significant portion of capabilities and resources learned from the DM subsidiaries may not take the form of R&D activities but more tacit and implicit forms such as managerial and operational know-how. On the other hand, it may be relatively more important for the parent firm to leverage the DM subsidiary to learn capabilities and resources from a DM local network.

Lastly, H4 is statistically significantly supported ($p < 0.05$). The relationship is simulated in Fig. 1, based on real observations in the sample. As the figure illustrates, the Turkish firm that held a DM subsidiary for one year (365 days) tended to acquire approximately 13% more ownership in its domestic acquisitions than an acquirer that held no DM subsidiary. This provides evidence that benefits of springboard FDI strategy are accumulating over time. However, such accumulation has a diminishing margin. For instance, between 1 and 10 years (or about 3,285 days), the extra increase in domestic ownership was only about 5%, adding up to about 18% total extra ownership than an acquirer that held no DM subsidiary. To explain this diminishing pattern, we speculate that having benefitted from DM subsidiaries over time, the acquirer may seek to become more independent from DM resources and learn to rely on its own proprietary capabilities (Chen et al., 2012).

As explained above, our four independent variables are highly correlated (>0.6) and thus inclusion of all in one regression model may cause estimation biases (Greene, 2003). The results in Model (6), which has included all

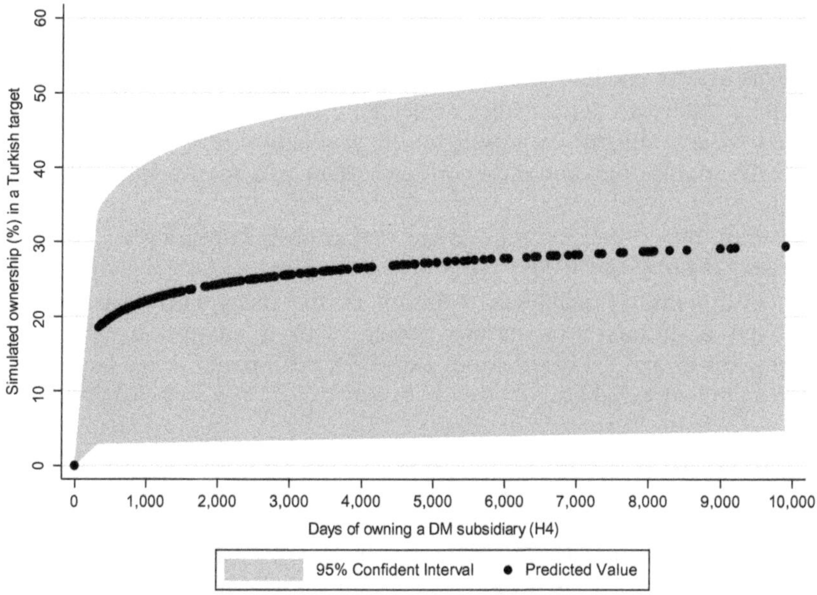

Fig. 1. Simulated Relationship between Extra Ownership in a Domestic Target and Total Time of Owning a DM Subsidiary.

independent variables, show potentially two of such estimation biases: first, coefficients have very high standard errors and low significant levels even though the overall significant of the model is relatively high (Chi-square is 253.980 or 9.345 increase from the base Model (1), with a p-value<0.001); second, coefficients may have the "wrong" sign (*DM R&D resources* turned out to have a negative impact, although it should be positive since the factor is highly positively correlated with the other three independent variables).

Some control variables exhibited statistically significant effects on the ownership in domestic acquisitions. Notably, acquirer's financial performance is a strong support in high ownership in domestic acquisitions. Statistically, a 1% increase in profitability of the acquirer would lead to averagely 31% extra ownership in domestic acquisition ($p < 0.001$). However, target profitability is a statistically significantly negative factor in ownership in domestic acquisitions, suggesting financially poor performers tended to give up more ownership and control to a new parent. A 1% increase in target profitability is statistically associated with approximately

7% lower ownership in a domestic acquisition ($p < 0.001$). The employment sizes of the acquirer and of the target exhibited statistically significant and opposite effects on domestic acquisition ownership. It suggests that larger acquirers tended to take smaller ownership ($p < 0.001$), and smaller targets tended to give up less ownership in an acquisition ($p < 0.001$). All other control variables did not show any consistent and statistically significant results.

Overall, our estimation models are very robust, exhibiting a Chi-square between 244.626 ($p < 0.001$) without independent variables and 253.080 ($p < 0.001$) with H1 included. Inclusion of the independent variables all exhibited additional explanatory power, with a change in Chi-square between 3.889 and 8.454 (or about 1.6–3.5%) compared to the base model of only control variables.

Robustness Checks

Although knowledge benefits from a springboard FDI strategy are important in all industries, one would expect that the requirement for a Turkish firm to learn and integrate foreign knowledge in a high-technology industries is considerably higher. If this is true, then the effectiveness of springboard FDI strategy might be less in high-technology industries and our results might be driven by only the non-high-technology sub-sample. For this reason, we conducted sub-sample replications based on the technology intensity of target industries. This offers a test if our main results were driven primarily by the results of certain industries and not the others. We followed the US National Science Foundation (NSF)'s list of high-technology industries (NSF, 2006) and divided our samples based on NAICS codes, which were reported by SDC and Zephyr. Following NSF (2006), 478 observations fall into high-technology industries and 825 into non-high-technology industries at the domestic target level. The results are reported in Table A1. As the table shows, results remain statistically significant in high-technology sub-sample for only H1 (coefficient 19.057; $p < 0.1$) and H3 (coefficient 6.650; $p < 0.1$) and statistically insignificant for H2 and H3 in the high-technology industries. In the non-high-technology industries, results remain strongly consistent and statistically significant for all independent variables: specifically, coefficient is 27.257 for H1 ($p < 0.001$), 7.593 for H2 ($p < 0.01$), 9.333 for H3 ($p < 0.001$), and 3.556 for H4 ($p < 0.001$). These findings suggest that our main results in the full sample are primarily driven by the Turkish domestic acquisitions into non-high-technology industries. This finding is consistent with our expectation that it is relatively more difficult to utilize springboard FDI strategy in high-technology industries, because it requires considerably more advanced absorptive capacity and integration skills at the parent level. Most Turkish firms may not possess such sophisticated capabilities at this stage.

CONCLUSION

The springboard FDI perspective has been a rising explanation in emerging market MNEs into DMs. The empirical evidence of the effectiveness of this strategy has been, however, relatively limited. Using a sample of 1,303 complete domestic acquisitions made by 713 Turkish firms over the period of 1987–2013, including 196 deals involving a springboard FDI strategy, we have found highly supportive empirical evidence for springboard strategy. On average, holding a DM subsidiary is associated with 33.047% higher ownership in a later domestic acquisition. Such relationship is positively moderated by the richness of knowledge resources both within the DM subsidiary and the local networks in the host DMs, as well as the time duration after its first acquisition into DMs. However, robustness checks suggest that such strategy is more effective when a later domestic acquisition takes place in non-high-technology industries.

These examinations can be replicated into most other emerging markets under three conditions. First, firms are constrained by limited knowledge resources at home such as a small pool of highly educated labor, low productivity, and lack of skilled managers. In such environments firms tend to be more motivated to take the form of springboard FDI strategy to acquire knowledge resources abroad. Second, domestic acquisitions are an efficient mode of achieving firm growth, enabled by decreased transaction costs, improved financial markets, and quality accounting standards and regulations. Third, firms are relatively familiar with DMs and thus could take advantage of their linkages there to access knowledge resources.

Our findings offer an empirical justification for springboard FDI strategy. There are a few practical implications for emerging market firms. First, springboard FDI strategy is a right thing to do. It can have a positive impact on an emerging market parent firm's capabilities and resources, which can be leveraged to expand in domestic markets through domestic acquisitions and control of local subsidiaries. Second, when considering springboard FDI strategy, an emerging market firm should focus not only on its target foreign subsidiary's existing knowledge resources (e.g., R&D intensity) but also, with stronger empirical support, on the knowledge resources available in the local networks that can be accessed through its local subsidiary. It is important to proactively leverage the advantage of a local presence and component in the supply chain and to access external knowledge resources. Lastly, the reverse knowledge transfer is an accumulative process. It is helpful to support the learning of foreign knowledge at headquarter and to facilitate the integration of it into home country capabilities and resources.

NOTES

1. We first downloaded the structured financial reports from all available secondary sources (e.g., BvD Orbis, Mergent Online, Mergent Reports, and local sources) for both acquirers and targets and kept all the original values for our focal variables. To fill the missing values in the year of a domestic acquisition, we used the *ipolate* code in Stata to create a new variable using a linear interpolation on year for missing values. The underlying assumption is that this focal variable is a linear function of the year and no radical, structure shifts happened. As an example, if BvD Orbis reported ROA ratios for a Turkish firm were 20% in 2006 and 40% in 2008 respectively, but missed the value of ROA in 2007, when the firm was recorded to have a domestic acquisition in SDC data. The filled value would be the arithmetic mean of the two, 30%. In addition, the Stata code *epolate* was specified since some of the missing values fall on either end of the year series. For example, if BvD Orbis reported a Turkish firm's ROA ratios for years 2004 and 2005 were 30% and 40% respectively, but missed the value for 2003, which was the year of acquisition in the SDC data. The filled value would be the linear extrapolation backward, which is 20%. However, for both interpolation (*ipolate*) and extrapolation (*epolate*), available data at two time points are required. Therefore, we had to drop observations which only had data for one year.

2. Using the IMF (2014) country classifications, we found that the DMs Turkish firms invested in include Austria (6 deals), Australia (3), Belgium (5), Canada (5), Finland (2), France (16), Germany (23), Hong Kong (1), Ireland (4), Israel (4), Italy (22), Japan (3), Norway (1), Netherlands (25), Portugal (3), Singapore (1), Spain (10), Sweden (3), Switzerland (7), the United Kingdom (28), and the United States (39). Because new EU members were classified as DMs after they joined EU, we removed deals in these countries that happened before their EU accession. The total number of deals into DMs is 216, which has exceeded 196 domestic acquisitions involving a springboard FDI strategy because some Turkish parent firms held subsidiaries in multiple DMs. To test for the consistency of our results, we also replicated the regression using the United Nations (UN) country classifications (UN, 2014). In this step, based on SDC and Zephyr samples, we removed Hong Kong (1), Israel (4), Singapore (1), but added Romania (2). Again, we did not include any deals into new EU members that happened before their EU accession. For instance, there

were 14 deals into Romania in SDC and Zephyr altogether, but only two occurred after 2007, when Romania joined EU. Largely because changes were minor, results remain very consistent and supportive.

REFERENCES

Ambos, T. C., Ambos, B., & Schlegelmilch, B. B. (2006). Learning from foreign subsidiaries: An empirical investigation of headquarters' benefits from reverse knowledge transfers. *International Business Review*, *15*(3), 294–312.

Barkema, H. G., & Vermeulen, F. (1998). International expansion through start-up or acquisition: A learning perspective. *Academy of Management Journal*, *41*(1), 7–26.

Barney, J. (1991). Firm resources and sustained competitive advantage. *Journal of Management*, *17*(1), 99–120.

Borini, F. M., de Miranda Oliveira, M., Silveira, F. F., & de Oliveira Concer, R. (2012). The reverse transfer of innovation of foreign subsidiaries of Brazilian multinationals. *European Management Journal*, *30*(3), 219–231.

Chaminade, C., & Vang, J. (2008). Globalisation of knowledge production and regional innovation policy: Supporting specialized hubs in the Bangalore software industry. *Research Policy*, *37*(10), 1684–1696.

Chen, V. Z., Li, J., & Shapiro, D. M. (2012). International reverse spillover effects on parent firms: Evidences from emerging-market MNEs in developed markets. *European Management Journal*, *30*(3), 204–218.

Chen, Y., & Puttitanun, T. (2005). Intellectual property rights and innovation in developing countries. *Journal of Development Economics*, *78*(2), 474–493.

Cheung, K. Y., & Lin, P. (2004). Spillover effects of FDI on innovation in China: Evidence from the provincial data. *China Economic Review*, *15*(1), 25–44.

Cohen, W. M., & Levinthal, D. A. (1990). Absorptive capacity: A new perspective on learning and innovation. *Administrative Science Quarterly*, *35*(1), 128–152.

Eisenhardt, K. M., & Santos, F. M. (2002). Knowledge-based view: A new theory of strategy. *Handbook of Strategy and Management*, *1*, 139–164.

Filatotchev, I., Liu, X., Buck, T., & Wright, M. (2009). The export orientation and export performance of high-technology SMEs in emerging markets: The effects of knowledge transfer by returnee entrepreneurs. *Journal of International Business Studies*, *40*(6), 1005–1021.

Frost, T. S., & Zhou, C. (2005). R&D co-practice and 'reverse' knowledge integration in multinational firms. *Journal of International Business Studies*,*36*(6), 676–687.

Gammeltoft, P., Barnard, H., & Madhok, A. (2010). Emerging multinationals, emerging theory: Macro-and micro-level perspectives. *Journal of International Management*, *16*(2), 95–101.

Grant, R. M. (1996). Toward a knowledge-based theory of the firm. *Strategic Management Journal*, *17*(S2), 109–122.

Greene, W. (2004). Fixed effects and bias due to the incidental parameters problem in the Tobit model. *Econometric Reviews*, *23*(2), 125–147.

Greene, W. H. (2003). *Econometric analysis*. Delhi: Pearson Education.

Gubbi, S. R., Aulakh, P. S., Ray, S., Sarkar, M. B., & Chittoor, R. (2010). Do international acquisitions by emerging-economy firms create shareholder: The case of Indian firms. *Journal of International Business Studies*, *41*(3), 397–418.

Gupta, A. K., & Govindarajan, V. (2000). Knowledge flows within multinational corporations. *Strategic Management Journal*, *21*(4), 473–496.

Hair, J. F., Black, W. C., Babin, B. J., Anderson, R. E., & Tatham, R. L. (2006). *Multivariate data analysis* (6th ed.). Upper Saddle River, NJ: Pearson Education.

Hill, C. W., & Hoskisson, R. E. (1987). Strategy and structure in the multiproduct firm. *Academy of Management Review*, *12*(2), 331–341.

Hoskisson, R. E., Johnson, R. A., Tihanyi, L., & White, R. E. (2005). Diversified business groups and corporate refocusing in emerging economies. *Journal of Management*, *31*(6), 941–965.

IMF. (2014). *World economic outlook, October 2014*. Washington, DC: Author. Retrieved from https://www.imf.org/external/pubs/ft/weo/2014/02/pdf/text.pdf

Javorcik, B. S. (2004). Does foreign direct investment increase the productivity of domestic firms? In search of spillovers through backward linkages. *American Economic Review*, *94*, 605–627.

Jolliffe, I. (2005). *Principal component analysis*. New York, NY: Wiley.

Kennedy, P. (1992). *A guide to econometric methods*. Cambridge, MA: MIT Press.

Kogut, B., & Singh, H. (1988). The effect of national culture on the choice of entry mode. *Journal of International Business Studies*, *19*(3), 411–432.

Kogut, B., & Zander, U. (1992). Knowledge of the firm, combinative capabilities, and the replication of technology. *Organization Science*, *3*(3), 383–397.

Lesmond, D. A. (2005). Liquidity of emerging markets. *Journal of Financial Economics*, *77*(2), 411–452.

Liu, X., Lu, J., Filatotchev, I., Buck, T., & Wright, M. (2010). Returnee entrepreneurs, knowledge spillovers and innovation in high-tech firms in emerging economies. *Journal of International Business Studies*, *41*(7), 1183–1197.

Luo, Y. (2001). Determinants of entry in an emerging economy: A multilevel approach. *Journal of Management Studies*, *38*(3), 443–472.

Luo, Y., & Tung, R. L. (2007). International expansion of emerging market enterprises: A springboard perspective. *Journal of International Business Studies*, *38*(4), 481–498.

Makino, S., Lau, C. M., & Yeh, R. S. (2002). Asset-exploitation versus asset-seeking: Implications for location choice of foreign direct investment from newly industrialized economies. *Journal of International Business Studies*, *33*, 403–421.

Mathews, J. A. (2006). Dragon multinationals: New players in 21st century globalization. *Asia Pacific Journal of Management*, *23*(1), 5–27.

Mathews, J. A., & Zander, I. (2007). The international entrepreneurial dynamics of accelerated internationalisation. *Journal of International Business Studies*, *38*(3), 387–403.

Mudambi, R., Piscitello, L., & Rabbiosi, L. (2014). Reverse knowledge transfer in MNEs: Subsidiary innovativeness and entry modes. *Long Range Planning*, *47*(1), 49–63.

Najafi-Tavani, L. D. Z., Giroud, S. L. D. A., & Sinkovics, R. R. (2012). Mediating effects in reverse knowledge transfer processes. *Management International Review*, *52*(3), 461–488.

NSF. (2006). *Technical note: Defining high-technology industries*. Arlington, VA: Author. Retrieved from http://www.nsf.gov/statistics/seind06/c8/c8.cfm?opt=9

OECD. (2015). *List of OECD member countries – Ratification of the convention on the OECD*. Paris: Author. Retrieved from http://www.oecd.org/about/membersandpartners/list-oecd-member-countries.htm. Accessed on February 12, 2015.

Osawa, J. & Chu, K. (2013). Huawei woos more foreign employees. *Wall Street Journal*, November 24. Retrieved from http://www.wsj.com/articles/SB30001424052702304465604579217402015955482. Accessed on January 11, 2015.

Peng, H. (2010). *China's indigenous innovation policy and its effect on foreign intellectual property rights holders*. King & Wood's IP Department China Law Insight Working Paper.

Peng, M. W., & Heath, P. S. (1996). The growth of the firm in planned economies in transition: Institutions, organizations, and strategic choice. *Academy of Management Review*, *21*(2), 492–528.

Peterson, R. A., & Jolibert, A. J. (1995). A meta-analysis of country-of-origin effects. *Journal of International Business Studies*, *26*(4), 883–900.

Rabbiosi, L. (2011). Subsidiary roles and reverse knowledge transfer: An investigation of the effects of coordination mechanisms. *Journal of International Management*, *17*(2), 97–113.

Rabbiosi, L., & Santangelo, G. D. (2013). Parent company benefits from reverse knowledge transfer: The role of the liability of newness in MNEs. *Journal of World Business*, *48*(1), 160–170.

Ramamurti, R. (2012). What is really different about emerging market multinationals? *Global Strategy Journal*, *2*(1), 41–47.

Ray, G., Barney, J. B., & Muhanna, W. A. (2004). Capabilities, business processes, and competitive advantage: Choosing the dependent variable in empirical tests of the resource-based view. *Strategic Management Journal*, *25*(1), 23–37.

Rossi, S., & Volpin, P. F. (2004). Cross-country determinants of mergers and acquisitions. *Journal of Financial Economics*, *74*(2), 277–304.

Rui, H., & Yip, G. S. (2008). Foreign acquisitions by Chinese firms: A strategic intent perspective. *Journal of World Business*, *43*(2), 213–226.

Singh, A. (1997). Financial liberalisation, stockmarkets and economic development. *Economic Journal*, *107*(442), 771–782.

Slusky, A. R., & Caves, R. E. (1991). Synergy, agency, and the determinants of premia paid in mergers. *The Journal of Industrial Economics*, *39*, 277–296.

UN. (2014). *Country classification*. New York, NY: Author. Retrieved from http://www.un.org/en/development/desa/policy/wesp/wesp_current/2014wesp_country_classification.pdf. Accessed on February 12, 2015.

UNCTAD. (2015). *Bilateral FDI statistics*. Geneva: Author. Retrieved from http://unctad.org/en/Pages/DIAE/FDI%20Statistics/FDI-Statistics-Bilateral.aspx. Accessed on February 12, 2015.

Wei, Z. (2010). The literature on Chinese outward FDI. *Multinational Business Review*, *18*(3), 73–112.

Yang, Q., Mudambi, R., & Meyer, K. E. (2008). Conventional and reverse knowledge flows in multinational corporations†. *Journal of Management*, *34*(5), 882–902.

Zhao, H., Luo, Y., & Suh, T. (2004). Transaction cost determinants and ownership-based entry mode choice: A meta-analytical review. *Journal of International Business Studies*, *35*(6), 524–544.

Zhao, M. (2006). Conducting R&D in countries with weak intellectual property rights protection. *Management Science*, *52*(8), 1185–1199.

APPENDIX

Table A1. Selected Results of Robustness Checks.

	High-Tech Sectors Only						Non-High-Tech Sectors Only					
	(7)	(8)	(9)	(10)	(11)	(12)	(13)	(14)	(15)	(16)	(17)	(18)
Predictors												
Holding a DM subsidiary (H1)		19.057^{+}				117.716*		27.257***				3.168
		(11.013)				(47.570)		(7.734)				(28.662)
DM subsidiary R&D intensity (H2)			4.458			0.300			7.593**			0.153
			(3.898)			(5.859)			(2.788)			(3.750)
Log of total days of holding a DM subsidiary (H3)				6.650^{+}		3.872				9.333**		4.372
				(3.765)		(5.411)				(2.921)		(4.178)
DM R&D resources (H4)					1.532	−13.752*					3.556***	2.201
					(1.363)	(5.844)					(0.996)	(3.688)
Statistics												
Number of observations	478	478	478	478	478	478	825	825	825	825	825	825
Number of left-censored observations	7	7	7	7	7	7	11	11	11	11	11	11
Number of right-censored observations	226	226	226	226	226	226	379	379	379	379	379	379
Chi-square	43.201	46.267	44.514	46.364	44.479	52.69	172.678	185.761	180.822	183.313	186.158	187.629
ΔChi-square (compared to base model)		3.066	1.313	3.163	1.278	9.489		13.083	8.144	10.635	13.480	14.951
p-value	0.000	0.000	0.000	0.000	0.000	0.000	0.000	0.000	0.000	0.000	0.000	0.000

Standard errors in parentheses.
$^{+}p < 0.1$, $^{*}p < 0.05$, $^{**}p < 0.01$, $^{***}p < 0.001$.

AUTHORS' BIOGRAPHIES

Africa Ariño is Professor of Strategic Management at IESE Business School, University of Navarra and a worldwide recognized scholar on strategic alliances. She has a B.A. in Economics from the University of Barcelona, an MBA from IESE, and a Ph.D. in Management from the University of California, Los Angeles. Currently, she is a member of the Board of Directors of the Strategic Management Society. She has also served in the Executive Committee of the Business Policy and Strategy Division of the Academy of Management. Professor Ariño is the Academic Director of the Research Centre on Globalization and Strategy at IESE Business School. She is Associate Editor of *Academy of Management Discoveries* and *Global Strategy Journal*. Her current research projects relate to internationalization to and from Africa.

Sedat Aybar is Professor of Economics and the Head of Department of Economics and Finance at Istanbul Aydin University. He received his Ph.D. in economics from University of London, UK. He is also a member of the Executive Board of the African Studies Centre. He taught, researched, and published on a variety of topics that includes, International Economics, Banking and Finance in Economic Development, Development Economics, Central Bank Independence, African economies, and Turkey. He has worked as a consultant to the Asian Development Bank (ADB), Overseas Development Agency (ODA), and the UNDP. He was the Director of joint Executive MBA Program of Kadir Has University with Fordham University of New York. He teaches distant study courses at graduate level at University of London's (SOAS), Centre for Finance and International Management (CeFiMS). He worked for the Economist Intelligence Unit (EIU), in London, England. He is currently the country team leader (Turkey) for a joint research project, Emerging Markets Global Players (EMGP) with the Vale Columbia Centre of the Columbia University in New York.

Sumon Kumar Bhaumik is a Professor of Finance at the University of Sheffield and a Research Fellow at IZA – Institute for the Study of Labor, Bonn. He received his undergraduate education at Presidency College,

Calcutta, and his masters and doctoral degrees in Economics from the University of Southern California. His research interests are wide ranging and include emerging market multinationals, corporate governance in family firms and business groups, and financial sector development. He has published in journals such as *Strategic Management Journal*, *Journal of International Business Studies*, *Journal of Corporate Finance*, *Journal of Banking and Finance*, and *Journal of Development Economics*. He has recently published a monograph entitled *How Family Firms Differ: Structure, Strategy, Governance and Performance*.

Murali D. R. Chari is an Associate Professor at the Lally School of Management at Rensselaer Polytechnic Institute. He is also the Academic Director of International Relations at the Lally School of Management. He received his Ph.D. in International Business Administration from Temple University. His research interests lie at the intersection of strategic management and international business. His recent and current research focuses on strategy in emerging economies and strategies of emerging economy firms. His research has appeared in leading journals including the *Strategic Management Journal*, *Journal of International Business Studies*, *Management Science*, and the *Journal of World Business*.

Victor Z. Chen is Assistant Professor of International Management at the Belk College of Business, University of North Carolina at Charlotte, USA. He is also a Fellow of Columbia Center on Sustainable Investment at Columbia University, where he acts as the EMGP Global Coordinator and Editor, managing a global research network on outward FDI and MNEs from large emerging markets. He is also a Cofounder and Associate Editor of Transnational Corporations Review. His research focuses on institutional diversity and dynamics, as well as corporate and global strategy under institutional diversity and dynamics. He received a Ph.D. in Strategy and International Business at the Beedie School of Business, Simon Fraser University, Canada.

Joseph A. Clougherty is Associate Professor of Business Administration at the University of Illinois at Urbana-Champaign, and a Fellow with the Centre for Economic Policy Research (CEPR) in London. He was previously Senior Research Fellow at the Wissenschaftszentrum Berlin (WZB), and faculty member at Tilburg University. He holds a Ph.D. from the University of Southern California, and completed dissertation research at the University of British Columbia. Among other journals, he has published in *Canadian Journal of Economics*, *International Journal of Industrial*

Organization, *Journal of International Business Studies*, *Journal of Law and Economics*, *Journal of Law, Economics & Organization*, *Journal of Management Studies*, and *Strategic Management Journal*. His research interests are interdisciplinary (combining management, industrial organization, and political economy) and international in both scope and nature. He employs an applied economics approach to research questions in both business and economics, and much of his research attempts to understand the antecedents and consequences of M&A activity.

David J. Collis is the Thomas Henry Carroll Ford Foundation Adjunct Professor of Business Administration within the Strategy Unit at HBS, having previously been an Associate Professor at the Harvard Business School, the Frederick Frank adjunct Professor of International Business Administration at the Yale School of Management and a professor at Columbia Business School. The winner of the 50th Anniversary McKinsey Award for the best article in the Harvard Business Review in 2008, and a Harvard Business Review best-selling author, he is an expert on corporate strategy and global competition, and is the author of the recent books *International Strategy*, *Corporate Strategy* (with Cynthia Montgomery), and *Corporate Headquarters* (with Michael Goold and David Young). As the author of over 25 articles and book chapters, his work has been frequently published in the *Harvard Business Review*, *Academy of Management Journal*, *Strategic Management Journal*, and in many books including *Managing the Multibusiness Company*, *International Competitiveness*, and *Beyond Free Trade*. The more than 50 cases he has authored have sold over 1 million copies worldwide and his articles over a quarter of a million copies, with nearly 7,000 citations. He received an M.A. (1976) with a Double First from Cambridge University where he was the Wrenbury Scholar of the University. He graduated as a Baker Scholar from Harvard Business School, MBA (1978), and received a Ph.D. (1986) in Business Economics at Harvard University where he was a Dean's Doctoral Fellow.

Jose Henrique Cordeiro is a doctoral candidate at the Department of Production Engineering of the University of São Paulo, the same department where he received his MSc degree with emphasis on Organizational Ambidexterity in Software Development Environments. Currently, his main research areas are International Operations Network Design and Strategic Ambidexterity in Internationalization, focusing in emerging country multinationals. He also teaches at Business and Technology Schools in the São Paulo region.

Sandra Corredor is a Ph.D. student at the College of Business, University of Illinois at Urbana-Champaign. Her research interest concerns the connections between innovation, corporate, and international strategies. Particularly, she studies the association between corporate and technology management, as well as the impact of firms' international engagement on their innovation approach. She has participated and presented her papers in several conferences, including the Academy of Management (AOM), Strategic Management Society (SMS), Academy of International Business (AIB), and Atlanta Competitive Advantage Conference (ACAC).

Alvaro Cuervo-Cazurra is a Professor of International Business and Strategy at Northeastern University. Before joining Northeastern he was a Faculty Member at the University of South Carolina and at the University of Minnesota, and a Visiting Professor at Cornell University. He was awarded a Ph.D. from the Massachusetts Institute of Technology and another from the University of Salamanca. Alvaro studies the internationalization of firms, with a special interest in emerging market multinationals. He also analyzes governance issues, with a special interest in corruption in international business. His research appears in leading academic journals, such as *Academy of Management Journal*, *Journal of International Business Studies*, *Strategic Management Journal*, and *Research Policy*, and in several edited books. He is the reviewing editor of *Journal of International Business Studies* and serves on the editorial boards of other leading journals, such as *Strategic Management Journal*, *Global Strategy Journal*, *Organization Studies*, and *Journal of World Business*. His geographical area of expertise is Latin America. He was elected to the Executive Committee of the International Management Division of the Academy of Management. Alvaro teaches courses on global strategy and sustainability at the undergraduate, masters, executive, and Ph.D. levels. For more information please visit www.cuervo-cazurra.com. He can be contacted at a.cuervocazurra@neu.edu.

Nigel Driffield is Professor of International Business ay Warwick Business School, and a former Dean of Aston Business School. He has a Ph.D. from Reading University, and has published some 70 academic papers across a range of disciplines including international business, regional science, finance, and economics. His main interests are around the impact of internationally mobile capital on both home and source countries, particularly in terms of competitiveness and labor markets. More generally, he has carried out research and consultancy projects for UNCTAD, World Bank,

European Commission, and in the United Kingdom several Government Departments and local Regional Development bodies.

Linda F. Edelman is Professor of Strategic Management at Bentley University. She received her MBA and DBA from Boston University. Before coming to Bentley she studied at London Business School and was a research fellow at the Warwick Business School and a member of the IKON research group. Her research examines small firms, women, and nascent entrepreneurs. Her work has appeared in *Journal of Business Venturing*, *Entrepreneurship Theory and Practice*, *Industrial and Corporate Change*, and *Organization Studies*. She serves on three editorial boards and as a reviewer for the Belgium FWO. She teaches strategic management to undergraduates, graduates, doctoral students, and executives.

Silas Ferreira Jr. is a doctoral candidate at the Department of Production Engineering – University of São Paulo, Brazil. With more than 15 years of work experience, he held managerial positions in foreign and Brazilian multinational companies in the areas of Supply Chain Management and Logistics. He holds a B.A. in Business Administration at the School of Economics, Business and Accounting as well as an MSc in Production Engineering at the Department of Production Engineering, both at the University of São Paulo. His research interests include Operations Management, Supply Chain Management, Internationalization, and Servitization.

Afonso Fleury is Professor in the area of Work, Technology and Organisation at the University of São Paulo and (former) head of the Production Engineering Department. His research work focused different industries such as Aeronautics, Automobile, Capital Goods, Computing and Information, Digital Games, Machine-tools, Shoes, Software, Telecommunications, and Textile/Apparel. He is currently engaged in research about International Operations and coordinates a large project about the internationalization of firms from emerging economies at the Centre for Technology Policy and Management at USP. His book *Brazilian Multinationals: Competences for Internationalization* was published by Cambridge University Press in 2011. He is Associate Editor of the *Journal of Manufacturing Technology Management* and Regional Editor of *Operations Management Research*.

Maria Tereza Leme Fleury teaches in the area of International Strategy. She is the Dean of the School of Business Administration of Fundacao Getulio Vargas, in São Paulo and former Dean of the School of

Economics, Business Administration and Accountancy of the University of São Paulo. She was Visiting Professor at ESSEC (France) as well as Research Fellow at the Institute of Development Studies (UK), Institute for Developing Economies (Tokyo), and Institute for Manufacturing, University of Cambridge. She has published several books and papers on strategy and competence management, internationalization of emerging countries firms, human resources management, management of organizational culture, and labor relations. She is member of Editorial Boards like the *International Journal of Human Resources Management* and other Brazilian and Latin American journals.

Clemente Forero is Full Professor at Universidad de los Andes School of Management in Bogota (Colombia), where he teaches Organization Theory, Public Management and a Seminar on Innovation in Emerging Economies. He holds a Ph.D. in Economics from Stanford University. He was Dean of the School of Economics and is Honorary and Emeritus Professor of Universidad Nacional de Colombia. He was General Director of Colombia's National Science Foundation, Colciencias. In the past decade he has followed two lines of research: innovation behavior and intellectual property institutions in emerging economies, and the relationship between violence and organizational forms of economic activity. He has published his research and serves as reviewer in various journals in the field of innovation and development.

Mauricio Garita is a Senior Researcher and Professor at the Universidad del Valle at Guatemala focusing on financial issues. He has a Doctorate in Political Science and Sociology from the Universidad Pontificia de Salamanca. He has served as Director at the Secretariat for Central American Economic Integration, Economist at the World Bank in Guatemala, and a Director in Business Intelligence for the private sector in Guatemala. Professor Garita currently serves as a Senior Researcher for the Institute of Central American Fiscal Studies.

Pankaj Ghemawat is the Anselmo Rubiralta Professor of Global Strategy at IESE Business School and Global Professor of Management and Strategy and Director of the Center for the Globalization of Education and Management at the Stern School of Business, NYU. Between 1983 and 2008, he was on the Faculty at the Harvard Business School where, in 1991, he became the youngest person in the school's history to be appointed a full professor. Ghemawat is also the youngest "guru" included in the guide to the greatest management thinkers of all time published in

2008 by *The Economist*. His latest book, *World 3.0*, should, according to *The Economist*, "Be read by anyone who wants to understand the most important economic development of our time"; it won the Thinkers 50 award for the best business book of 2010–2011. Other recent honors include the McKinsey Award for the best article published in the *Harvard Business Review*, the Educator of the Year Award from the Business Policy and Strategy division of the Academy of Management, and the Eminent Scholar Award from its International Management division.

José Godinez is an Assistant Professor of Management at Merrimack College. He has a BS in Business Administration from the Johns Hopkins University, an MS from the University of Manchester, and a PhD from the University of Edinburgh Business School. His research centers on the intersection of the international business, strategy, and entrepreneurship disciplines. Specifically, he focuses on strategies designed to minimize the detrimental effects of corruption on businesses; strategies to successfully operate in institutional voids; and value creation for all stakeholders of firms targeting the bottom of the pyramid. He has presented his research at the Academy of Management and the Academy of International Business annual meetings. José Godinez also advises policymakers in his native Guatemala and serves on the board of directors of a Massachusetts-based nonprofit focusing on financial literacy for traditionally nonbanked populations.

Sathyajit R. Gubbi is a Fulbright Scholar and currently Assistant Professor in International Business at the Faculty of Economics and Business, University of Groningen, the Netherlands. He obtained his Doctorate from the Indian Institute of Management, Calcutta, and a Bachelor's Degree in Chemical Engineering from the Indian Institute of Technology, Bombay. His research focuses on cross-border mergers and acquisitions and emerging economy multinationals. He has published papers in the *Journal of International Business Studies* and the *Long Range Planning*. Prior to his doctorate, he worked with several multinational companies around the globe offering technical, management, and consulting services.

Wenxin Guo is Visiting Assistant Professor of Strategic Management at the Scheller College of Business, Georgia Institute of Technology. She received her Ph.D. from University of Illinois at Urbana-Champaign. Her research focuses on the phenomenon of outward cross-border mergers and acquisitions by emerging market multinationals. She also studies firm's international patenting activities and knowledge transfer. She has published academic papers in *Management International Review* and *Enterprise and Society*. She is the finalist for the "Frontiers of International Management: Douglas Nigh Award" at Academy of Management Conference 2014 and the winner of Best Ph.D. Student Award at Academy of International Business Southeast USA Chapter 2014. She received a State Farm Fellowship and a Ph.D. Dissertation Award in the Department of Business Administration at the University of Illinois at Urbana-Champaign.

Michael Hilb is a Lecturer in Strategy and International Entrepreneurship at the Universities of Fribourg and St. Gallen, Switzerland, and Vice President Strategy of DKSH, a leading market expansion services provider with focus on Asia. He studied management at the University of Michigan's Ross School of Business, the Stockholm School of Economics and the University of St. Gallen, graduating from the latter with an MSc and a Ph.D. He was a Visiting Fellow at Harvard's Center for Business and Government and at INSEAD in France and Singapore, where he conducted research on entrepreneurial strategy in an international context.

Robert E. Hoskisson is the George R. Brown Chair of Strategic Management in the Jones School of Business at Rice University. His research topics focus on corporate strategy and governance and he teaches courses in corporate and international strategic management, among others. Professor Hoskisson has served on several editorial boards for such publications as the *Strategic Management Journal* (current Associate Editor), *Academy of Management Journal* (Consulting Editor), *Journal of International Business Studies* (Consulting Editor), *Journal of Management* (Associate Editor), and *Organization Science*. His research has appeared in over 100 publications including the *Strategic Management Journal, Academy of Management Journal, Academy of Management Review, Organization Science, Journal of Management, Journal of Management Studies, Journal of International Business Studies, Academy of Management Perspective, Journal of World Business*, among others. He has co-authored over 20 books including *Strategic Management: Globalization and Competitiveness* (11th edition), *Competing for Advantage* (3rd edition), and *Understanding Business Strategy* (3rd edition). He was recently ranked among the top scholars in business and economics by the Times Higher Education. He has served on the Board of Directors and is currently the Past President and a Fellow of the Strategic Management Society. He has served on the Board of Governors and is also a Fellow of the Academy of Management.

Heechun Kim is Assistant Professor of International Business in the J. Mack Robinson College of Business at Georgia State University. He received his Ph.D. in Strategic Management from the W. P. Carey School of Business at Arizona State University. His research interests include emerging market multinationals and family multinationals. His work has appeared in journals such as the *Strategic Management Journal*, *Organization Science*, and *Journal of International Business Studies*. He has served on the editorial review board of the *Journal of International Business Studies*.

Elko Klijn is an Associate Professor of International Business at Leeds University Business School. He holds an MBA (with Distinction) in International Business and a Ph.D. in Strategic Management, both from the University of Leeds, UK. His research interests revolve around the composition and roles of boards of directors in (international) joint ventures. His work has appeared in *Long Range Planning*, *Journal of Management Studies*, *British Journal of Management*, *Global Strategy Journal*, and *Strategic Management Journal*.

Cha Li is a Research Master student in the Organization and Strategy track at Tilburg University. Her research interests lie primarily in corporate political activities, organizational learning, and multinational corporations. Currently, her research focuses on understanding how political capital may influence the dynamics of cross-border collaborations, and the long-term performance of corporations.

Xingkun Liang is a Doctoral candidate at the University of Cambridge. He received his Bachelor of Management and Economics from Peking University. His research focuses on international R&D management of the multinationals and global intra-firm innovation networks. He has presented papers at the Academy of International Business and the Academy of Innovation and Entrepreneurship annual meetings as well as major Europe-based conferences on business and management.

Tatiana S. Manolova is an Associate Professor of Management at Bentley University, USA. She received her MBA from the University of Tampa, and her DBA from Boston University. Research interests include strategic management (competitive strategies for new and small companies), international entrepreneurship, and management in emerging economies. Tatiana is the author of over 50 scholarly articles and book chapters. She serves on the editorial boards of *Entrepreneurship Theory and Practice*, *Journal of Business Venturing*, and *Journal of Global Entrepreneurship Research*.

Xavier Martin (Ph.D., University of Michigan) is Professor of Strategy, International Business and Innovation, Deputy Head of the Department of Management, a Fellow of the Center for Research in Economics and Business, and Cofounder of the Center for Innovation Research at Tilburg University, the Netherlands. His research examines how (international) corporate strategies, interfirm relationships, and knowledge-based assets affect each other and jointly affect firm performance. His papers have appeared in *Administrative Science Quarterly*, the *Academy of Management Journal*, the *Strategic Management Journal*, *Organization Science*, *Management Science*, the *Journal of International Business Studies and Research Policy*, among others. He is a recipient of multiple research awards, including the Best International Paper Award (now Dexter Award) from the Academy of Management, both the Haynes Prize for Best Paper and the Richard N. Farmer Best Dissertation Award from the Academy of International Business, and several Best Paper/Best Student Paper Awards from the Strategic Management Society. He serves on the editorial boards of the Strategic Management Journal and other publications. He is a former Member of the Board of the Strategic Management Society and the former Chair of its Competitive Strategy Interest Group.

Ram Mudambi is Frank M. Speakman Professor of Strategy and Perelman Senior Research Fellow at the Fox School of Business, Temple University. Previously he served on the faculties of Case Western Reserve University, the University of Reading, UK, and the University of North Carolina – Chapel Hill. He is a Fellow of the Academy of International Business. His current research projects focus on the geography of innovation and the governance of knowledge-intensive processes. He has served as an Associate Editor of the *Global Strategy Journal* (2010–2013) and is an Area Editor at the *Journal of International Business Studies* (2013–2016). He has published over 80 peer-reviewed articles, including work in the *Journal of Political Economy*, the *Journal of Economic Geography*, the *Strategic Management Journal*, and the *Journal of International Business Studies*. He has been a Special Issue Editor for the *Journal of Economic Geography*, the *Journal of Management Studies*, and the *International Business Review*. He serves on the editorial boards of numerous journals.

Alessandra Perri is Assistant Professor of International Business at the Department of Management of Ca' Foscari University, Venice. She earned her Ph.D. at Luiss Guido Carli University, Rome and she worked as Post-Doc Fellow at the Department of Business Administration of Carlos III University, Madrid. Her research is focused on the impact of FDI on host-countries, knowledge and innovation management in multinational firms, and emerging countries' technological catch-up. Alessandra's research work has appeared in various journals, including *The Journal of World Business*, the *International Business Review*, and *The International Journal of Management Reviews*, among others.

Saptarshi Purkayastha is an Assistant Professor at the Indian Institute of Management, Calcutta. His main research interest is in the field of effective business groups' strategies in emerging markets, their performance indicators and how institutional transitions affect the impact of such strategies. He has published articles in academic journals such as *International Journal of Management Reviews*, *International Studies of Management and Organization*, and *Global Business Review*. He has also presented papers at several international conferences, such as the Academy of Management (AOM), Strategic Management Society (SMS), and Academy of International Business (AIB).

Jeffrey J. Reuer is the Guggenheim Endowed Chair and Professor of Strategy and Entrepreneurship at the University of Colorado. His research uses organizational economics to investigate firms' external corporate development activities and growth options (e.g., strategic alliances, acquisitions, and initial public offerings). Recent projects are on the governance and design of alliances, collaborative strategies, and applications of information economics to various corporate and international strategy problems. He is a Fellow of the Strategic Management Society and was the first recipient of the SMS' Emerging Scholar Award. He serves as an Associate Editor of the *Strategic Management Journal* and as a Consulting Editor for the *Journal of International Business Studies*.

Vittoria Giada Scalera is Ph.D. Candidate and Research Fellow at Politecnico di Milano, Italy. From October 2013 to September 2014 she was also visiting scholar at the Department of Strategic Management, Fox Business School, Temple University, USA. Vittoria's research focuses on internationalization strategies of MNEs, especially from emerging economies, knowledge-intensive acquisitions, innovation management, and globalization of R&D in global networks. Her studies appear or are forthcoming in *Multinational Business Review* and *The Routledge Companion to Mergers and Acquisitions*. She has presented her papers at the Academy of International Business, European Academy of International Business and Strategic Management Society annual meetings.

Yongjiang Shi is a Lecturer in the Institute for Manufacturing (IfM) of Cambridge University Engineering Department. He is teaching in a Masters Program called Industrial Systems, Manufacturing and Management (ISMM), and he is the Research Director of the Centre for International Manufacturing (CIM). Dr. Shi is a former lecturer in the school of Economics and Management at Tsinghua University, Beijing, before joining the IfM in 1994. He has undertaken extensive research into international manufacturing network configurations and has taken a leading role in the conceptualization and delivery of the Centre's research program. His research interests include global manufacturing networks, business ecosystem development, the strategies of multinational corporations in China, and sustainable industrial systems. He currently is also the Guangbiao Visiting Professor in Zhejinag University Management School where he is teaching Global Manufacturing and China Development for the EMBA Program.

Deepak Somaya is Associate Professor of Strategy and Entrepreneurship and the Steven and Christy King Faculty Fellow at the College of Business, University of Illinois at Urbana-Champaign. He also holds courtesy appointments in the College of Law and the Institute for Genomic Biology at the University of Illinois. In his research, he studies how companies strategize about and derive competitive advantage from their intangible assets, particularly their human capital, relational assets, and intellectual property. His research has been published in over 25 journal articles, book chapters, and conference proceedings, and has received numerous awards including a best dissertation award, several conference best paper awards, and the 2012 California Management Review Best Article Award. He currently serves on the editorial boards of the *Journal of Management*, *Organization Science*, *Strategic Entrepreneurship Journal*, and *Strategic Management Journal*, and is Program Chair for the Strategic Human Capital interest group of the Strategic Management Society.

Sinan A. Sular is a Digital Strategy Analyst at one of the top consulting firms in the world. He holds an MSc in International Business and Management from the University of Groningen in the Netherlands. In addition to his career as an analyst, he has a strong interest in FDI theory. His research focuses in particular on the internationalization process of multinational enterprises from emerging economies. He has presented his research on annual meetings of the Academy of International Business.

Xuanli Xie is an Assistant Professor of Strategic Management at Peking University. She received her Ph.D. in Strategic Management from the University of North Carolina at Chapel Hill, and her M.A. and B.A. from Peking University. Her research interests include corporate governance, international business, and entrepreneurship. Her studies have appeared in various journals including *Strategic Management Journal*, *Organizational Dynamics*, and *Journal of Business Strategies*.

Ying Zhou is currently a Lecturer in Economics at the University of Birmingham. Prior to her current post she worked in Aston Business School. She is specialized in applied economics, in particular on emerging economy, firm performance, investment, and resource allocation. She has published in a numbers of top international journals in her field. Ying obtained her BSc in Economics in 2004 with First Class Honour and Ph.D. in Economics in 2008 from the University of Birmingham. She was awarded the Department of Economics Prize in 2002 and 2003, Hargreaves Beare Prize and Kirkcaldy Scholarship in 2004, and Overseas Scholar Award in 2005 and 2006.